CW01072567

SPORT, BUSINESS AND
THE LAW

Maurice

Pleasant Neams!

17th June 1999

SPORT, BUSINESS AND THE LAW

Richard Verow, Solicitor,
Collyer-Bristow

Clive Lawrence, Partner, McCormicks

Peter McCormick, Senior Partner,
McCormicks

JORDANS

1999

Published by
Jordan Publishing Limited
21 St Thomas Street
Bristol BS1 6JS

British Library Cataloguing-in-Publication Data
A catalogue record for this book is available from the British Library.

ISBN 0 85308 481 5

Typeset by Mendip Communications Ltd, Frome, Somerset
Printed in Great Britain by MPG Books Ltd, Bodmin, Cornwall

DEDICATIONS

To my Grandmother – RV
To my Mother – CSL
To Kathryn, Guy and Charlotte for all their patience and support – PDGM

PREFACE

This practitioner text is aimed at lawyers and business people who are working in or wish to become involved in the business of sport. The work grew out of a short series of lectures given by Richard and Peter for The College of Law in early 1997. The aim was to provide a book that covered the subject in a practical way and gave guidance on the drafting of 'typical' agreements. This work is by no means definitive, nor could it ever be, but it is hoped that it is a useful introduction to a dynamic and interesting area of legal practice and an important growing business.

In selecting topics, we have aimed to cover those which relate to the core commercial transactions which take place on a daily basis in the business of sport by considering the relevant areas of background law and following that with precedents for those core types of transaction. In that context, it did not seem appropriate to deal with those less commercial matters which arise in the sporting context, such as disciplinary matters and personal injury litigation, which are, no doubt, worthy of separate treatment on their own.

Sport, like any other business, has to be looked at in a business context and against the appropriate legal background. The law is not standing still and the effects of the Competition Act 1998 will surely be felt over the coming months and years as all businesses, not only that of sport, come to grips with its effect. Additional developments in intellectual property, the Internet and database protection, driven by Europe, will also bite keenly on this truly multi-disciplinary topic.

We would like to thank our friends, family and colleagues, as well as the staff at Jordans and, in particular, Stephen Honey, for their patience and help in seeing this project through. Particular thanks must go from Peter and Clive to Jillian Slaughter for all her hard work wrestling with unwieldy and messy typescripts and to Julian Harris and Glenn Skivington for their general assistance. Peter and Clive would also like to thank, for permission to use and adopt certain materials, Adam Pearson and his team at Leeds United Football Club, Holly Roper-Curzon of The Football Association Premier League Limited and Graham King of Televideo Limited, together with a multitude of colleagues in the profession who have perhaps unwittingly helped in the refinement of certain of the advice and documentation in this book even if it did not always feel like they were helping at the time.

The law stated is at 1 April 1999.

Richard Verow
Collyer-Bristow
4 Bedford Row
LONDON

Peter McCormick and Clive Lawrence
McCormicks Solicitors
Britannia Chambers
4 Oxford Place
LEEDS LS1 3AX

CONTENTS

Chapter 4 INTELLECTUAL PROPERTY RIGHTS AND SPORT   75

Richard Verow, Clive Lawrence and Peter McCormick

COPYRIGHT

Chapter 5   EMPLOYMENT AGREEMENTS   137
Clive Lawrence, Peter McCormick and Richard Verow

SPORTS PERSONALITY MANAGEMENT

COMMERCIAL RIGHTS AGENTS

TABLE OF CASES

References are to paragraph numbers.

TABLE OF STATUTES

References are to paragraph numbers.

TABLE OF STATUTORY INSTRUMENTS

References are to paragraph numbers.

TABLE OF INTERNATIONAL LEGISLATION

References are to paragraph numbers.

TABLE OF CODES OF PRACTICE

References are to paragraph numbers.

TABLE OF ABBREVIATIONS

ACAS	Arbitration Conciliation and Advisory Service
ADR	Alternative Dispute Resolution
CDPA 1988	Copyright Designs and Patents Act 1988
EEA	European Economic Area
ERA 1996	Employment Rights Act 1996
FA	Football Association
FASDA	Association of First and Second Division Clubs
FIFA	Fédération Internationale de Football Association
IAAF	International Amateur Athletics Association
IPR	intellectual property rights
ITC	Independent Television Commission
MCPS	Mechanical Copyright Protection Society
PGA	Professional Golfers Association
PPL	Phonographic Performance Limited
PRS	Performing Rights Society
RFU	Rugby Football Union
TMA 1994	Trade Marks Act 1994
UCC	Universal Copyright Convention
UEFA	Union des Associations Européennes de Football
WRU	Welsh Rugby Union

CHAPTER 1

INTRODUCTION

1.1 Is there such a thing as sports law? – 1.2 The business of sport – 1.3 The commercial structure of sport – 1.4 Corporate finance – the new frontier? – 1.5 New proposals

1.1 IS THERE SUCH A THING AS SPORTS LAW?

It has become fashionable for reasons that will be considered below for a number of practitioners of law to designate themselves 'sports lawyers'. The main guides to the legal profession now include sports law as a separate category of work in which firms and practitioners are rated. The sceptics, perhaps with a little justification, question whether there is such a thing as sports law at all. It may be considered a fad, a typical example of professionals attempting to jump on a bandwagon and create a demand for services which they have got themselves into a position to supply.

Traditionally, the law has been divided into areas of specialism along juristic lines. The demarcation line between tort, contract, criminal law, company law and so forth is not always clearly defined but grows clearer for having a literature based upon the assumption that such a demarcation exists. What has resulted is a broad consensus of categories of law under which textbooks are written, student courses taught and legal practices divided.

It is becoming more common, however, to look instead down industry lines as an alternative means of demarcation of the categories of law. Quite respectable academic categories such as shipping law, construction law and insurance law would have been considered at their inception as being no more than specific adaptations of principles derived from the categories of law divided on juristic lines as outlined above. Those industries, by long practice and the gradual adaptation of the courts to their specific conditions and requirements, have built up bodies of law which have, to some extent, set them apart from other industries and resulted in a characteristic legal environment.

What we are now witnessing is the business of sport finally joining those industries which require their own specialised legal practitioners and the likelihood that over coming years it will evolve its own distinctive body of law. There have been a number of authorities in a sporting context which suggest that a distinctive approach to the industry may be in the course of evolution by the courts but these authorities have been a trickle rather than a flood. By the repeated practice of the industry, sports law, without having acquired a body of case-law, has evolved already into a specialised area. The purpose of this book is to set out a coherent survey of how the business of sport has come to use the law commercially to achieve its ends.

1.2 THE BUSINESS OF SPORT

Sport is one of the later arrivals amongst the world's great industries. Only in the 20th century could it really be described as an industry at all. Now that it has arrived at that status, it is here to stay and, in terms of spending, the business of sport is now larger than the chemical, agricultural or motor industries in the UK.

The primary economic unit in sport is the professional: the professional footballer, tennis player or golfer. They will be employed by a sports club or engaged in tournaments organised by a club. The club will also employ managers, administrators, clerical staff, maintenance staff, catering staff, marketing staff and so forth. It will have property interests, retailing interests and promotional and advertising interests quite apart from its fundamental role of admitting spectators to watch professional sport. It will be involved in broadcasting and sponsorship on potentially massive scales. Sport, in this way, reaches out into many industries: for instance, chocolate bars may not have much to do with sport but their manufacturers sponsor World Cups. It can work both ways, though, as the Nestlé FA Premier League authorised chocolate bar proves! A whole host of businesses, from any sector of industry, have identified sport as the ideal vehicle for advertising and promotional endorsement, often combined with corporate entertaining opportunities which are simply not available elsewhere.

The result of this is that almost two-thirds of the total marketing spend of UK companies is on sport-related marketing. The sport industry, as long ago as 1996, created 376,000 full-time jobs with the total expenditure on sport-related activities in the UK totalling £4.4 billion, including £750 million on clothes and shoes, £690 million on sports goods, and £530 million on participation in sport. These statistics look set to increase for the foreseeable future.

Sport is really a vital component of the culture we inhabit. It acts as a focus for many of the dominant aspirations of our time: health, excellence, the achievement of individual and collective goals and the sense of belonging. It falls to a sociologist rather than to the authors of this book to muse on the role of sport in society but it is safe to say that most people would find it as difficult to imagine a nation without organised sport as it is to imagine a nation without the internal combustion engine.

1.2.1 The 'traditionalist' argument

This view of sport, however, as an emerging world industry, constantly spreading further and further into the developing economies and bringing more nations into the global market place, is not always popular. There remains a well-publicised body of opinion which deplores the commercialisation of sport and essentially wishes for a return to the days of the amateur. It may be as fair as it ever is to generalise to say that this opinion largely originated and remains strongest amongst those individuals in society who need not look to sport for their economic survival. The persistence of this opinion may appear to have declined along with an apparent decline of the establishments which fostered it, but it remains a cogent argument which cannot be written off.

The argument is, effectively, that sport should not be valued in terms of mere success and, indeed, success is only a by-product of the true value of sport. That value lies in the character-building quality of sport which tests the physical and mental reserves of individuals and their sense of honour and fair competition, and through sport, all the nations of the world can strive against each other without enmity or deception in shared pursuit of human excellence.

These ideals are enshrined in the rhetoric of the Olympic Movement and often in the general attitude of many governing bodies in sport. It is the traditional, conservative (with a small 'c') view of the purpose of sport and, as such, it is largely inimical to the development of a viable commercial structure for sport. The same view, when represented in the judiciary, is also a hindrance to the evolution of a distinctive jurisprudence for sport. The power of the 'old guard' can be seen in the ructions that have shaken rugby union almost from the very beginning of its relaunch as an openly professional sport.

Opponents of this view claim to regard sport with a greater extent of realism. Perhaps the most famous demolition of the ideal was by George Orwell in his essay written back in 1945, 'The Sporting Spirit':

> 'Then, chiefly in England and the United States, games were built up into a heavily financed activity, capable of attracting vast crowds and rousing savage passions, and the infection spread from country to country . . . there cannot be much doubt that the whole thing is bound up with the rise of nationalism – that is, with the lunatic modern habit of identifying oneself with large power units and seeing everything in terms of competitive prestige.'

Orwell's essay was intended to raise hackles and controversy in its suggestion that we would all be better off without sport. Its cynicism must, therefore, be seen from that angle and in the context of a world weary of international conflict in 1945. There is, however, an element of truth in what he says and, in recent years the Olympic Movement, for all its high ideals, has been rocked by scandal after scandal over drug doping, and amateur rugby union was notorious both for its rigid hatred for the professional code of rugby league and for its ability to bend its own regulations when it suited.

Today, amateurism has almost totally departed from the highest level of sport. The high standards of international sporting competition mean that competitors cannot pursue other careers and retain the ability to compete at that level, and the number of competitors with private incomes has diminished since the earlier years of the century when the amateur idea was formulated. Top-level competitive sport cannot be compared with recreational sport. It is not a leisure pursuit for those involved but rather their livelihood, and as the rewards are potentially massive for those who succeed, the consequences of success and failure are, likewise, immense. But sport has not simply wished itself into this new professionalism; it has been half carried, half driven there by growing public demand for sport as entertainment and brought with it a corresponding interest from commercial organisations. It is suggested that the ideals of the amateur are a valuable ethos for all participants in sport but those ideals will not regulate a 21st century industry. The ethos of the commercial endeavour which sport now incontestably has become is not the cynical ethos of 'win at all costs' caricatured by the opponents of commercialism as a Hobbesian nightmare of brutality and deceit, but rather a commercial ethos based on principles of law. The bottom line of commercial ethics is legality and the entrance of legality into sport is an inevitable consequence of sport's commercialisation. As those from the Realist school of jurisprudence would point out, modern man has sacrificed his ideals of freedom and equality for the practical virtues of freedom under the law and equality before it, and sport is confronting exactly the same compromise.

Therefore, we have a business of sport and a law of sport. Both are opposed by those who find their very existence 'unsporting'. There is also something of a resistance from other quarters who have seen sport traditionally as an industry largely unregulated by the law. Deals have been done on the handshake and problems resolved informally for many years, as well as certain other commercial practices which have attracted the attentions of the Inland Revenue and the tabloid newspapers. Many sports clubs and even governing bodies are not yet equipped to respond to the more rigorous working practices necessarily introduced by increased commercialisation and legalisation. The process is developing and emerging at an alarming rate. In sport, perhaps more than any other industry, the emergence of new commercial and legal principles is accelerating all the time. For administrators, business people and professional advisers connected with the business of sport, these are revolutionary times.

1.3   THE COMMERCIAL STRUCTURE OF SPORT

This book gives an overview of the central commercial relationships involved in sport and begins with a discussion of the rules and regulations and the position of the governing bodies which are fundamental to the discussion in the rest of the book and to anyone advising on the business of sport. Rules and regulations govern the competitions in which the participants engage, the commercial agreements they are able to make; the manner in which they can exploit their reputation by sponsorship; merchandising, broadcasting and advertising; the employment of players and managers; their relationships with other commercial organisations both in terms of ownership and individual transactions; the internal market for services within the sport and the control they must exert over their venues.

Chapters 3, 4 and 5 deal with the essential areas of law with which sports lawyers need to be familiar. A sports lawyer is, properly speaking, something of a generalist. The modern habit of lawyers specialising within fairly narrow fields is not necessarily conducive to the development of sports lawyers. For that reason, it was considered useful to provide some fairly elementary background law before dealing with the specific application of that law to the sporting context.

The remaining chapters deal with specific topics from the point of view of the practitioner and are to a certain extent 'how to do it' guides. They deal with the principal terms of the main agreements into which a sports organisation or professional will enter and seek to provide guidance for negotiation together with specimen precedents.

1.3.1   A case study

Many references are made to professional football in this book. This is not a reflection necessarily of the interests of the authors so much as a recognition that football is the most popular sport in the world, the wealthiest sport and the most commercialised. In some ways, it offers a blueprint and in other ways perhaps even a warning to other sports as they rapidly develop their commercial structure. It may be useful to consider the manner in which football is organised and exploited as a model for the organisation and exploitation of other sports.

Structure of organisation

Football has a world governing body, FIFA, which is effectively an autonomous body whose members are the national governing bodies of football. It legislates on a world-wide basis for certain aspects of football such as the rules of the game and is responsible for the overall organisation of international football and the World Cup competition which is open to all nations whose football associations are members of FIFA. International teams are organised by the national governing body which has membership of FIFA.

For the European governing bodies, there is a similar body, UEFA, which organises the European club competitions, regulates matters such as broadcasting and commercialisation of the sport in many material respects throughout Europe and promotes the European Championship between international teams.

On a domestic front, there are in effect three governing bodies. The first of these is the Football Association, which is the central governing body of the sport and which controls all football throughout the country, including non-professional and recreational football. Alongside the Football Association, there is the Football League which governs the professional football leagues known as Divisions 1, 2 and 3. Finally, there is the Football Association Premier League which governs the top division known, obviously, as the Premier League. The inter-relationship of these three governing bodies is complex. When a club plays in the Premier League, obviously it is subject to its rules which extend throughout the whole gamut of that club's activities. The Premier League regulates, for instance, the dimensions of the playing area, the conduct of matches, the advertising and use of video replay at grounds, the ability of the clubs to broadcast footage of or commentary on their matches on radio and television, the employment of players and of young players, the application of funds generated by the League throughout its participant members – the list is almost endless. If that club is relegated to the Football League, it then passes into the jurisdiction of the Football League which has the same extent of regulation on its own terms. In both cases the club remains under the jurisdiction of the Football Association as to other matters and its players are subject to the call of the Football Association for international matches. Entry into the FA Cup is under the rules of the Football Association which controls that competition.

Broadcasting rights

In each case, the governing body is affected in turn by the rules of UEFA and FIFA in the classical pyramid structure of organisation. Each governing body both gives and takes: it takes from clubs certain rights which it then has the power (subject to challenge under UK and European competition law) to grant to third parties. A crucial example is broadcasting which will be dealt with further in Chapter 9. Briefly, any broadcaster wanting to offer its subscribing public a programme during a season of competitive and interesting football will choose to contract with a governing body, which can potentially grant rights over all matches played under its jurisdiction, rather than choosing to contract solely with one club, risking a dull programme should that club's season became dull. When it contracts with a league it can choose week-to-week the most interesting matches, regardless of the identity of the participants within that league. It also has the comfort that all participants in all matches are obliged to provide their cooperation in the process. Where that process shows signs of breaking down, as currently where the Office of Fair Trading is investigating the collective grant of broadcasting rights over football, and the launch of Digital TV offers clubs the chance to operate their own TV channels, the major broadcasters will look to 'hedge their bets'; hence the current interest of leading broadcasters in owning Premier League football clubs.

Subject to that, and in the case of practically all sports (Premier League football still having the potential to be an experiment to the contrary), from the broadcaster's point of view, the deal with the governing body is far more attractive and cost effective than deals with individual clubs. For all but the very biggest clubs there is the legitimate consideration that they will generate far greater revenue from participation in an overall scheme of broadcasting than from exploitation of broadcasting agreements on their own. In return for the grant of exclusive rights in relation to broadcasting from, and the sole power to conclude broadcasting agreements on behalf of, the clubs, the League shares out the revenues thus generated amongst them according to agreed formulae, which often include an element of ranking according to league position and the number of times that club's matches are broadcast. Similar deals may be done on a collective level in respect of advertising, main competition sponsors (who are therefore granted rights at all Premier League grounds) and even for endorsement of specific products by all of the Premier League clubs either collectively, or on an individual basis.

Commercial regulation

As a result the regulation of the conduct of those clubs in a commercial context is justified on the basis that it permits the governing body to ensure both the maximisation and the equitable division of the spoils by the governing body amongst the participants in their competitions.

Within the governing bodies, the clubs occupy the status of members either by virtue of shareholding in a company or otherwise. Governing bodies take either a corporate form or the form of unincorporated associations. These are dealt with in greater detail in Chapter 2.

Commercial activities of clubs

The sports club sits at the very centre of commercial relationships. Subject only to regulation by the governing body, a football club will exploit its business in a multitude of ways. The first and most obvious way is the sale of tickets to the public. A football club will offer a vast range of packages to spectators of all types starting with executive packages involving season tickets and catering for all matches in specific exclusive areas, through season tickets offering like catering packages, family season tickets, individual season tickets and finally tickets for individual matches. The club will provide catering services itself or let out areas within the stadium for concessionaires to provide those catering services. It will operate retail outlets selling huge ranges of sport merchandise both produced for the club and produced by third parties and sold to the club and into the market in general, and it will let out other spaces to other retailers. It will produce a range of magazines, programmes, souvenir products, promotions, entertainments, competitions, in-stadium radio stations etc for match days. It will offer a huge range of sponsorship options including:

- sponsorship of stadium name;
- sponsorship of kit by kit manufacturer;
- 'shirt' and main club sponsorship;
- sponsorship of executive areas;
- sponsorship of individual stands;
- sponsorship of individual players;
- sponsorship of players' cars;
- sponsorship of ball boys, match balls, scoreboards, display screens, man of the match awards;
- ground perimeter boards;
- signage in and around the ground.

The club will also usually have an arrangement with a local radio station granting the right to broadcast commentary on all the club's home and away matches either exclusively or non-exclusively. This is less regulated than the market for television broadcasting.

Sponsorship is not, however, solely confined to the playing activities of the club. A huge range of goods badged with the club's logos is usually available. These goods may have no direct relevance to the game. As part of that process, the clubs will usually have applied both in the UK and often throughout the European Community under the Community Trade Mark Scheme for registration of central club trade marks. These would include the following:

(1) the club's official name as a word only mark;
(2) any specific representation of the club's official name such as in the form of stylised writing as a word and logo mark, possibly one of a series of two with (1) above;
(3) the club's official logo;
(4) unofficial logos;
(5) representations of the club's mascots as a 'character mark' often in a series of poses;
(6) the name of the club's mascot as a word only mark;
(7) players' nicknames as word only marks;
(8) players names in the form of signatures;
(9) brand names adopted by the club for merchandising lines;
(10) contractions of the club's name.

The above list is not exhaustive.

Classes in which registrations may be effected for such trade marks, taking into account the range of merchandise commonly available from sports clubs, are set out in full in Chapter 4.

In addition, the club should consider concluding with both its players and major staff members employment agreements involving 'personality rights'. This is dealt with in further detail in Chapter 5 (employment agreements) but, briefly, the club should have the right to exploit the name, fame, image and representations of its players and coaching staff as far as is possible as part of its marketing strategy. It should also ensure that its historical archives of old kit, old photographs, old video footage etc is its own intellectual property and readily available, which can be exploited as a very useful 'back catalogue'.

Using these intellectual property rights, the club will enter into a number of agreements. Mention has already been made of official club programmes and official club publications such as magazines. The club will also produce books, videos showing footage of the club's games (subject to the regulations of the governing body) together with interviews with players and staff, and will usually have an official website. The club must ensure that it has undiluted rights to the main website addresses using the club's names and should be vigilant to ensure that the club's website is not compromised by 'counterfeit' official websites. It should be vigilant to protect its domain name as far as possible.

It is impossible to list exhaustively all the merchandise which a club might offer to the public branded under its own trade mark. The following is a list of those things which are practically universal:

- magazines;
- soft drinks;
- CD-ROMs, computer games, tapes, cassettes, compact discs and videos;
- replica figures of players;
- clothing;
- sports goods;
- ceramics;
- fabrics and wall coverings;
- soft toys;
- clocks and watches;
- pens;
- confectionery and cake decorations;
- souvenir pictures and novelties;
- alcoholic beverages;
- phone cards;
- rugs and carpets;
- towels;
- air fresheners;
- razors;
- replica kit.

All of these products to a greater or lesser extent are the constant target of counterfeiters. The club must be vigilant to ensure that these counterfeiters are opposed at every turn both by restricting the flow of official merchandise to the authorised channels, attempting to prevent counterfeit goods of any nature entering the market and also keeping away unwanted traders from the club's stadium. These issues are dealt with in further detail in Chapters 4 and 8 on intellectual property and venue.

Many clubs are now diversifying their commercial branding into yet other areas, particularly service industries. Just as supermarkets have opened banks, clubs are now looking to open financial services wings, travel arrangement companies, ticketing agencies and a whole range of other services. The power of the brand in the hands of a successful sports club extends beyond the confines of sport.

Employment contracts

The club will employ a large number of individuals as players, managers, trainers, medical staff, administrative staff, catering staff, groundsmen, stewards, ticketing staff etc. In particular, the contracts of employment of playing staff and team managerial staff have become a specialised area in themselves, owing to the unique nature of careers available in professional sport. These are dealt with in further detail in Chapter 5.

A major issue for all clubs is the ability to attract and retain players and senior team management personnel. Increasingly, sports agents are involved and dealings with them are particularly sensitive both from the point of view of regulation by the governing body and the commercial point of view of the club. Sports agents are not necessarily the most popular individuals involved in sport, but are here to stay, as they offer invaluable expertise to their clients. If a club feels aggrieved at the amount of money negotiated by its player's agent, it can look to the advice given to it by its own sponsorship agent as to exploitation of its sponsorship rights and recoup the balance over the course of a season.

One of the major factors for the future is the effect of the *Bosman*[1] ruling on players' contracts, considered in detail in Chapter 5. Briefly, the massive inflation in players' earnings over recent years is directly linked to this ruling, which establishes that once a player's contract has expired he is a free agent and the Club cannot demand a transfer fee. Players are therefore encouraged to sign longer, more lucrative, contracts, as a consequence of the club having to offer substantial inducements for a player to forgo what would otherwise be a big pay day on the expiry of a shorter term contract.

There is no doubt that the *Bosman* ruling has brought about a shift in the power base in football and the effect will be felt in any other professional sport where players are transferred. The power has shifted to the players. Money which would have circulated within the game by being used for transfer fees from club to club is now going to the player for signing on fees and salary because players are waiting until their contracts expire before moving to other clubs. When that happens, the acquiring club no longer has to pay a transfer fee and so the player demands (and gets) a larger slice of the cake. Money that goes to the players is money that goes out of the game. Quite simply, therefore, to attract and retain players and remain competitive in a sporting sense, clubs need to commercialise in order to generate income in any way they can.

Ground sharing

Many clubs will have considerable interest in the exploitation of their grounds. It may be possible for the club to share its ground with other sports clubs and the promoters of other events such as rock concerts. These issues are dealt with in further detail in Chapter 8.

The above is only a very brief and necessarily limited overview of the commercial structure of professional football. The same details would apply in a similar fashion to any commercially advanced sport. Each of the relationships discussed will give rise to commercial agreements dealing adequately with the club's rights and obligations in a manner which allows the entire business of the club, the governing body and the sport as a whole to regulate itself cohesively.

1 *Union Royale Belge des Sociétés de Football Association ASBL v Bosman* (C415/93) [1996] All ER (EC) 97.

1.4   CORPORATE FINANCE – THE NEW FRONTIER?

With the increasing commercialisation of sport, it is only logical that it takes an additional step into the region of corporate finance. As all businesses grow, they reach a threshold where they require sources of finance which cannot be generated solely by their existing operations in order to break through to a higher level. If a second division rugby club, for instance, had £5m to purchase players and set up commercial structures enabling it to enter the first division and be financially viable in that new environment, the initial investment could be repaid over a short period. Where money dictates the level at which a club can play, it will be prudent for any club with financial constraints to look for additional finance. The traditional form of finance for many sports clubs has been the local millionaire who loves the game and most of the major football clubs have at some time had the support of wealthy individuals who have effectively 'bankrolled' the club's advance. There are few of those individuals left in football. First, to make a significant difference, often the millionaire has to be a very wealthy man indeed and prepared to commit in the region of £60–80m to the club if he is looking to propel it into the Premiership. Secondly, the increasing commercialisation of the sport has led to a growing perception in the community of commercial lenders that sports clubs may justify their attention, and not just be a way for wealthy men to subsidise their local community. In a sport such as rugby union, where the jury is still out on the question of commercial viability, the local tycoon still has a place, but perhaps those who are in place have more mercenary ambitions than their predecessors.

1.4.1   Traditional financing

The purpose of corporate finance is to go beyond the familiar bank debt funding available to businesses, which effectively provides against security of fixed assets and the undertaking as a whole an increased financial facility by way of overdraft or loan, and to look to introduce funds into the business in return for the right to participate in that business's future success. It is classically used by businesses which are looking to break through a 'glass ceiling' where their self-generated income cannot provide the expansion they need to increase returns. As such, the proposition for a potential funder is inherently riskier. It cannot rely simply on enforcing its security and selling assets to recover its investment if things go wrong, but in the event of the failure of the company must look at the likelihood of participating in that failure and loss. Consequently, the rewards to the institutional funder must be attractive in order to justify the risk.

1.4.2   Venture capital

If venture capital is to be introduced by a venture capital house, the club must realise the demands the venture capital house will place upon it. They will require a genuine stake in the shares of the company. They will require an ongoing income return from year-to-year and an 'exit route' from the company which will, at least, discharge the full amount of their initial investment within a comparatively brief period of time, such as five years. Finally, once all their funding has been returned to them, they will expect to retain a share in the club in order to participate in its ongoing success, capital value and possible 'windfalls' in the event of an admission to listing on a recognised stock exchange or a take-over by another company.

Classically, therefore, an institutional funder would look for a wholesale restructuring of the club. It would look for either the formation of a new company which would then acquire the assets of the old or would at least expect a wholesale corporate reorganisation of the old company. It would require usually redeemable preference shares paying a percentage of the total value of those shares such as 8% or 9% each year by way of dividend. Those shares would often then have to be redeemed by the company in annual tranches over a period of perhaps five years. This gives a commercial return on funds and a form of repayment of the capital investment. On top of that, it would expect to hold ordinary shares comprising a healthy proportion of the overall equity value of the company even after redemption of its preference shares. To back these shareholdings up and provide the venture capitalist with comfort as to the future conduct of the business, the company's articles of association would be prepared in such a way as to guarantee the venture capitalist's rights. Often a shareholders' agreement would be required with the club's other shareholders to regulate the future conduct of the company's business. In the event of a crisis, the venture capitalist would have a residual power of management guaranteed in those articles of association.

The use of shares as suggested above gives the venture capitalist its income, its exit route and the right to participate in the future success of the company by holding a genuine percentage of the company's value. It also leaves the way clear to other lenders such as banks to provide debt finance by way of usual overdraft and other banking facilities which are secured over the company's assets. That is a lower risk, lower reward form of investment and its presence means that the company then has further working capital facilities.

Before entering into any such arrangement with a club the venture capitalist would require a very strict audit of all financial matters within the club and a business plan to which the club must strictly adhere. The purpose of a venture capital business is to make money and the club will be judged by different standards to those to which it is accustomed. Put bluntly, a venture capitalist will not care about the club's league position in a season if the club cannot pay dividends or redeem preference shares. The structure outlined above effectively requires the club to trade in profit year-by-year and, therefore, clubs looking to raise venture capital will need to be very clear as to their requirements and their future prospects, and the deal proposed to a venture capitalist must be on that realistic basis. Nebulous plans, plans which require too many imponderables to come to pass in order to succeed, or which predict success at too long a distance into the future will simply be rejected. The club must go into any such proposals with its eyes open and knowing that it will require management of a nature which few clubs have received historically.

The type of venture capital indicated here will probably be quite rare in the sporting context for those very reasons. The business of sport is not like that of retailing, for instance, where a certain element of the business will be closely predictable and certain economic givens can be assumed. Sport is a turbulent and unpredictable business by its very nature. Success in the enterprise of sport does not always equate with straightforward business success in terms of profits. It is, however, safe to say that one rule inevitably holds good. If the club's team succeeds, the club will stand a chance of being commercially successful. If the team does not succeed, it will not. Retailing of goods by sports clubs follows certain retailing norms such as an increase around Christmas time but often retail sales can show an almost identical pattern to the club's sporting success. If the club is top of the league, children want replica kit. If it is not, they want another team's replica kit. It is as simple as that. Other services and commercial ventures rely on an association with success and a 'feel-good factor'. The potential for conflict between institutional finance and the business of sport lies where the conventional wisdoms of business, such as the desirability of cutting overheads, conflict with the idiosyncrasies of sport. An accountant looking at a sports club will often feel that the task is comparatively simple: just cut the overheads and costs (which look unjustifiable) and tighten up budgets within the club and the savings will go straight to the bottom line as profit. In sport, as in a number of industries relying on an emotional response, however, that is not necessarily correct.

For instance, a new star player for a team may cost a large amount of money and the transfer fee is effectively money out of the club. Following the *Bosman* ruling, football clubs are best advised not to reflect predicted transfer values for players on their balance sheets. However, the signing of a new player may have an impact upon season ticket sales, merchandising and corporate sponsorship, and also upon the club's league position, with considerable financial effects in each case. None of these will be straightforwardly predictable. They may not follow the market laws on the basis of which venture capital decisions are made.

A venture capitalist may also seek to operate a degree of control over the company which is not conducive to good relations in that there may often be a conflict between the views of those managing the sporting activities of the club and those managing its financial affairs. Whilst this form of finance has genuine potential to assist sports clubs, some creativity is required in structuring the deal and in identifying from the outset the club's unbreakable parameters. Venture capitalists may be uncomfortable with these but the club should be firm in its negotiations. Too often there is pressure to take the money at any price. The result of doing so in sport would simply be to postpone the time and exaggerate the extent of the crash.

For that reason, such venture capital deals have, to date, been rare in sport. Often rescue packages have been put together for ailing sports clubs where the participants are those who are are likely to put money in largely for sentimental reasons rather than strictly commercial reasons. Often – practically always – those transactions have ended in heartache for all concerned. The harsh truth is this: if people are putting money into sport they should either treat it as a gift or be very careful indeed with what will always be a difficult investment to judge properly.

1.4.3   Stock exchange listing

There has also been a growing number of sports bodies, particularly football clubs, which have looked to raise capital by obtaining listings on the stock exchange. For a while this appeared to be something of a 'holy grail' for many football clubs, who saw it as an ideal way to raise finance. Although the preparatory work is extensive and rigorous, there are not the same preconditions of investment as exist when institutions invest in private companies as discussed above. At the same time, many of the institutional investors such as insurance companies, pension funds and the like saw football as being a growth industry offering attractive investments. It is likely that the first flush of enthusiasm on both parts has passed. Few of the football clubs admitted to listing or owned by listed companies have enjoyed consistently high share values or good sporting fortunes after listing. Once again, there is something of a conflict between the business of finance and the business of sport. The shares sought by the major institutional investors (who to a large extent lead the market) are those which offer high returns and the prospect of long term growth. For high returns one needs to generate high profit. For the shares to be attractive those high returns must be something the investor can expect with some confidence. A football club's share price again often tracks to a certain extent the success of its season and, therefore, the times when the club is most in need of investment are the times when it is least likely to raise that investment through the City.

There are many reasons why companies seek flotation. Some may be purely competitive reasons – because other companies have done so and they need to follow in order to maintain profile and to keep track of the opposition. However, classically, where a company is in urgent need of funding at a level which cannot be achieved by other corporate finance routes, it will look to listing if its business is strong enough to justify that step. Shareholders in private companies use flotation as a way of realising personal wealth from their holdings. Often listing is the second phase of capitalisation, in that the sort of venture capital structures outlined above might be used as a first phase, with flotation seen as the 'exit route' for those who have funded the company during that interim period.

The process of obtaining an admission to listing is very far from easy. It should only be undertaken upon the best and most realistic professional advice. It is a process which must be prepared for over a considerable period of time, possibly even two to three years. In that period the club must effectively rationalise its operations from top to bottom and eliminate to the fullest possible extent any historical factors which would make the club unattractive to institutional investors. For instance, many sports clubs have long been hotbeds of personal rivalry and rival shareholders will frequently build up factions within the club leading to dissension at board level. That must be eliminated as far as possible for there to be a realistic likelihood that the club will be admitted to listing. The structure of the board must reflect the expectations of those who invest in listed companies: they will be more impressed by having a chartered accountant as finance director than by having a former player responsible for marketing, for instance. The informal and sometimes emotional management methods which sports clubs have often experienced will be unpopular (although any observer of a number of football clubs currently quoted on the stock market will note that a listing does not exile these factors altogether!).

Clubs should also be very much aware before entering into the process of obtaining a listing, that as and when they are successful, the management and financial structures must reflect the various codes which are incumbent upon listed companies such as the Cadbury and Greenbury Codes and the 'Supercode' resulting from the Hampel report. The system of regulation of public companies is effectively a new system of company law superimposed upon that incumbent upon all companies and is specifically designed to protect the interest of shareholders and to avoid wherever possible the accumulation of powerful factions at board level. A fair summary of the fundamental principle may be that the company belongs to the shareholders and the directors and managers of the companies are stewards of the shareholders' property. It is not the case that the company continues to belong to large shareholders and existing directors, with the shareholding public along for the ride. This can be something of a culture shock for strong personalities at boardroom level who thrive on exerting control.

In listed companies, the role of non-executive directors is crucial and the new 'Supercode' and the codes of best practice to which companies must conform place a heavy burden of responsibility on non-executive directors, who are largely seen as the independent arbiters of the shareholders' interest. These non-executive directors must be appointed before flotation and chosen with extreme care. They should be able to bring some distinctive expertise to the board, preferably in a form which is not already available from the executive directors. There are lists available of those who are available to act as non-executive directors and the choice of these is a difficult one to make which should be accorded great care: those advising the company on its way to flotation will probably advise with particular care on the identity of the non-executive directors to ensure that they will promote confidence amongst potential investors. Companies should look to have at least one-third of the total membership of the board as non-executive directors.

It is a good idea for the company to gear itself up effectively to the regime that is incumbent upon a listed company under the various codes of practice before it is admitted to listing. A principal feature of this is the remuneration committee of the company, which decides on the remuneration of executives according to certain fairly stringent criteria. This is to ensure that salaries given to executives are not excessive and remain in all the circumstances a fair reflection of the value of those executives to the company on a formula which reflects performance.

The company will need to have systems in place which ensure that all internal reporting and control systems are in place and are rigorous and frequent. Management information must be reliable leading up to flotation. The financial systems and controls must be tight. The company must not have any questionable relationships with third parties and its contracts should be placed on the proper formal footing of written contracts. Ideally, prior to listing, the company should also have a period of sustained growth and profitability and there should not be any great risks awaiting round the corner. For instance, if the company is involved in major litigation, the settlement of that litigation may be necessary before the company can think seriously of admission to listing.

For all the culture shock admission to listing brings, it is likely to remain an attractive option for sports clubs. Many of the club's fans will be interested in buying shares not solely as an investment, but to feel that they have some ownership of their club to accompany their emotional commitment. A club which has properly prepared for listing may well offer an attractive prospect to institutional investors. The initial release of funds from the sale of the company's shares could pave the way to a new prosperity for the club, and, provided that the club is prepared to undergo the growing pains and the very genuine influence from external bodies such as institutional investors and the shareholders as a whole (which may often be considered as an intrusion into current cultures), there can be genuine benefits.

Those who live by the sword, however, must die by it. Public companies cannot stagnate and must maintain share prices. To do so there may be pressure upon them to diversify operations and to seek out ever greater levels of earnings. It is partly the pressure exerted upon the listed clubs by their shareholders of that nature which has caused some of the commercial turbulence within Premier League football and some of the new proposals which have come to the fore.

1.5 NEW PROPOSALS

Many sports are seen currently to be in a state of turmoil. The rapid commercialisation of many sports has led to new pressures upon clubs, particularly financial. Those financial pressures have often then transmitted themselves to the public through intense controversy between different factions in the sport. For instance, rugby union has been in turmoil for a considerable period of time. The demarcation line between the two main factions is largely between those clubs who need desperately to play a game where top players are demanding payments which cannot be funded from orthodox income streams, and who are looking to emulate professional football clubs in their commercial activities, and those clubs which remain largely the preserve of amateurs who see themselves as custodians of the game's soul. The result has been a long and sustained fight for control of the game's governing body and the repeated threat of breakaway alternative unions.

These breakaways are often the brainchild of broadcasters. The rugby league 'Superleague' was really the creation of BSkyB. The power of BSkyB within Premier League football is immediately obvious to all observers. Proposals for a European Superleague will be largely organised and bankrolled by broadcasters.

When a competition is the creation of a broadcaster one has to be very careful indeed. Broadcasters are interested in selling advertising and satellite dishes or have other objects which have nothing to do with the sport. They will pay for a competition to take place if they feel that that is 'flavour of the month'. If it ceases to be so, it will be dropped without compunction. There is a quest for novelty and when novelties pass their sell-by dates there is nothing left in many cases but the disintegration of those who have based their business upon them. The experience of rugby league in Superleague has been instructive in this regard.

BSkyB came together with the Rugby Football League to create the Superleague, but the project has not been a success. The move to playing the game in the summer seemed at first potentially innovative. The result was a short playing season with games often very sparsely attended. The culture of rugby league was more in sympathy with watching a game on winter Sundays rather than weekday evenings in the summer, which were selected because that was when the gap in the broadcasters' schedules existed. The longer closed season meant that the clubs were left for a very long period without their source of income from ticketing and if they wished to retain their players under contract they had to pay money hand-over-fist with no corresponding income stream. The TV audiences were disappointing and it is very unlikely that the same value for the broadcasting rights would be achieved again. The result has been a huge rift in the game of rugby league, an agonising period for many of the participants (both those within the Superleague and those kept out of it) and the prospect of a game that cannot go back to its roots and yet has no clear future mapped out for it.

A European Superleague for football may suffer from the same problems. First and most crucially, one has to look at the paying public. Not only are they crucially important to the club as its historical raison d'être but also they are the best guide to the activities of the broadcast public. For all the glamour of European football, it is often not so well attended as domestic football. Fans think in terms of traditional rivalries. If Arsenal Football Club enter a European Superleague, it is likely that for a long period of time its supporters will not feel the same about a clash with Bayern Munich as they do about a clash with Tottenham Hotspur. It is questionable in fact whether the broadcast public for such a league would be as great as many are currently predicting.

There is also the crucial question of the competitive nature of the league. If those clubs leave their domestic leagues, they will need a guarantee of income over the foreseeable future for that to be a justifiable step. If the Superleague does not come into existence with the blessing of home authorities, they may ban those clubs which enter. That, in the opinion of many, would be the conclusive death knell of the proposal, as the question arises, if a club then leaves the Superleague, where is it to go? Even the biggest club in the world cannot survive on a diet of non-competitive friendly games. There is even the prospect that the League itself may become exactly that circus of non-competitive friendly games. Whilst the cash rewards for winners may make the chase meaningful, leagues need to have bottoms as well as tops to retain the interest of the public. There is, therefore, the tension between the desire of a club to have a guaranteed tenure in the league in the light of its ban from the league it has left and the need for the league to have relegation from and promotion to it in order to keep new blood and competition. Relegation from and promotion to the league are dependent upon the relationship with domestic leagues and governing bodies and those domestic leagues and governing bodies may not want to see their best teams play elsewhere.

The principles will no doubt be worked out but whilst eyes may light up at the prospect of immense broadcasting and sponsorship deals for those clubs which participate, those eyes need to be kept on to the long term future and a very close and cold inspection needs to be made of the basis on which the league is organised. The worst case scenario is of a largely disregarded circus of uncompetitive games on pay-per-view television which would set the immense commercial progress made in the game of football back a considerable number of years. However, one has to be realistic and recognise that the broadcaster is interested in buying the product for the years of its intended duration and little more.

The potential for sport and new proposals for sport are immense but optimism must be tempered by realism. It should never be forgotten for one minute that the business of sport is sport. The commercial spin-offs are exactly that – sports clubs and professionals ignore or neglect the pursuit of excellence in their sporting performance at their peril.

CHAPTER 2

RULES AND REGULATIONS

2.1 The role of the governing body – 2.2 The example of football – 2.3 Conflict with the governing body

2.1 THE ROLE OF THE GOVERNING BODY

2.1.1 Introduction

It is essential to look at governing bodies and the rules and regulations that they put in place to govern sport because this gives a grounding on issues which have a direct bearing on subsequent commercial arrangements.

A governing body does not consist simply of a group of men in suits, described on one occasion by the former England rugby union captain, Will Carling, in a more derogatory fashion, setting out rules and regulations in order to preserve the Corinthian principles of sport. A revolution has been required in the way in which governing bodies and leagues manage themselves. They have had to respond to the pressures created by broadcasters, sponsors, clubs, sportsmen and the public.

Money may well be said to be the root of all evil, but it is certainly at the heart of the causes that have required a rethink in the way in which sport is managed. Sport must be run in a business-like way to ensure that it is adequately funded and that the wealth which is created is spent in a careful and prudent way. Some sports are handling the situation better than others.

Leagues and governing bodies have a vital part to play in a number of areas which have direct financial consequences for the sport.

The governing body of any sport is in a unique position to push the sport forward and even to create new competitions or refine old ones. In the USA, the way in which David Stern, the lawyer-turned-Commissioner of the NBA, has revitalised basketball and made it into the most profitable sport in the world, illustrates what sound management can achieve.

In the UK, the FA, by creating the Premier League, has again revitalised a sport and the popularity of football rose rapidly after a period of decline. The Premier League is a classic example of a governing body that has woken up to commercial reality by replacing dilatory decision-making processes in committee with well paid, commercial management that is pushing the interests of the League forward at all times.

Most of the great controversies of modern sport turn upon the role of existing government bodies and the pressure placed upon them by the new commercial realities of sport and the conflicting interests they engender. Just a few examples from the time of writing will suffice: the collapse of the British Athletics

Federation; the formation of the Rugby League Superleague and the consequent fallout between the Superleague Clubs and the Association of First and Second Division Clubs (FASDA); the conflict between the Rugby Football Union (RFU) and English Professional Rugby and just about any other Rugby Union Club, its players and its internal officers; the formation of a new Scottish Premier Football League; the proposals for a two-tier County Championship in county cricket; the list could go on. Each of those matters raised crucial issues, the first of which is the constitution, organisation and accountability (internally and through the courts) of the relevant governing body.

2.1.2   Functions of the governing body

If one is seeking a definition for the difference between genuine bona fide sport and a mere pastime, one would perhaps fall back on the fundamental question of whether there is a governing body in respect of that sport which operates the functions that are set out below. Most modern sports date their true beginnings from the foundation of their governing bodies and, indeed, some sports are quite simply the creatures of specific governing bodies such as rugby league, a code of rugby which arose effectively from an argument over professionalism within the sport under the auspices of the old governing body, the Rugby Union.

In considering the governing body in sport, regard should always be had to the evolutionary history of that body. This is not so much a matter of academic interest, but rather because such knowledge may give a clue toward the somewhat archaic rituals of a governing body, and an identification of those rules and procedures of the governing body which are historical hangovers rather than constructive contributions to the future. The ever increasing pace of modernisation in all sports means that almost every governing body, to a certain extent, has been left behind and is suffering growing pains. From the resolution of those issues which currently engage the vast majority of the world's professional sports will come the sports of the future. In the context of such radical growth, bodies which are essentially Victorian members' clubs find their constitutions often wanting and, rather than wholesale constructive modernisation, find their time, energy and money being expended in undignified turf wars between interest groups.

The role of a governing body is effectively parallel within a sport to that of a government within a nation. It has control over the system of law and the economy of sport and any sports lawyer must ensure, before considering any agreement of whatever nature in any sport, that he is familiar with the rules of the governing body of that sport. Any absence of attention to detail in this regard could be disastrous.

We will now deal with the separate heads of control the governing body will or ought to exert over the sport.

Legislation for sport

A governing body can take several legal forms such as a limited company, an unincorporated association, a partnership or other creature of statute such as The Jockey Club (which is a body corporate incorporated by Royal Charter). It is crucial, however, that whatever the legal form used, it has the necessary powers deriving from its legal status, members and/or shareholders (which, where the body is a company, are usually the member clubs) to legislate and to bind its member clubs contractually, both between each other in relation to internal legislation and with the outside world in relation to sponsorship and the exploitation of other rights.

Internal legislation takes the following main forms.

(a) Rules of the game

The governing body should codify and promulgate the rules of the game. In so doing, it should have regard to the rules of the game internationally and, indeed, this part of the governing body's function may be curtailed by its international contacts effectively to the mere ratification into the domestic governing body of decisions made by the international governing body. However, sport relies upon rules and regulations which are common, identifiable and as simple as possible.

The rules of the game go deeper, however, than questions of the dimensions of the pitch, the number of players and what constitutes an off-side rule. Other rules become more and more contentious. Included within this heading would be rules in relation to the use of drugs and the penalties to be imposed on those who fall foul of those regulations. This is an area which has exposed governing bodies to some of the most bitterly fought and expensive legal challenges and, indeed, the Diane Modahl case was no doubt instrumental in the demise of the British Athletics Federation.

(b) Rules of procedure and the relationship between participants

The governing body must legislate to provide rules for leagues, the playing of fixtures between member clubs and the relationships which may exist between the member clubs. For instance, the governing body will in almost all cases regulate in some way the transfer market for players. The governing bodies of most sports in most countries operate 'transfer deadlines' to avoid the use of market forces unfairly to distort the personnel within teams at crucial points in the season. They will also regulate when approaches may be made to players or managers by other clubs and even look to regulate in certain cases how many clubs any individual or company may be concerned in. This last area is one which may become liberalised in the future as institutional shareholders looking for passive investment only look to diversify their interest in sports teams which are floated on the Stock Market. However, the world governing bodies of football have tightened up the international dimensions of these regulations, concerned at the possibility of clubs in common ownership playing each other for major trophies leading to very serious conflicts of interest.

This legislative function of the governing bodies is crucial to ensure that, as far as is consistent with proper competition (in the commercial sense), an equal playing field (in the sporting sense) between the participant clubs and organisations or individuals exists and to ensure the integrity of the sport as a competition offering the public the 'uncertainty of outcome' which the sociologists, psychologists and Desmond Lynam assure us is crucial to the enjoyment of the game by the public.

(c) Rules of commercial exploitation of the game

This topic is perhaps the area where some of the most fertile ground for dissension arises. The governing body must legislate for what can and cannot be done in terms of commercial exploitation of the game. In so doing, it must recognise the importance of commercial income to sports – and indeed, a sport without extraneous commercial income relying solely upon selling tickets to the general public in the current conditions of professional sport probably cannot survive – and the interest of spectators who wish to see the integrity of the sport preserved. In other words, the governing body must ensure that commercial sponsorship is secondary to the fundamental competition presented by the sport, rather than see the sport dwindling to a mere pretext for the competition of advertising messages. For instance, the sport may permit a certain number of endorsement messages to appear on a player's clothing or on a car, a boat, or a cycle; it may have certain rules about the naming of the team or a team stadium so that, for instance, the Mars Bar Warriors do not take on the Kelloggs Sunshine Boys at the Bells Whisky Bowl (without disrespect to those fine products!). It may also seek to set limits to the commercial exploitation of its sporting endeavour by any member club in favour of the greater good. For instance, we will deal below with centralisation of certain rights for exploitation purposes within the governing body. Part of the rationale behind this is convenience and certainty; another crucial issue is that of redistribution and fairness between the individual participants within the sport. As such, the governing body becomes enmeshed in the ancient battle between free marketeers and protectionists and in 'competition law', both domestic and European. Competition law issues are crucial in considering the role of governing bodies.

This final balancing act is the single most important issue confronting governing bodies at this stage in their development. Some governing bodies are ready to meet the challenge, such as the FA Premier League. Some are patently not ready, and the dialectic between the interests of the powerful few who see no finite limit to their potential save that imposed by the legislative power of the governing body, as against the lack of economic power and reliance on the trickle down of the general prosperity of the game on the part of the many smaller participants, is the defining language of sport at the present time.

A case study

To put some of the above generalities into context, let us take a hypothetical set of facts about a hypothetical sport. Imagine that owing to a decline of viable war footage available on satellite news services, team paint balling has become a major spectator sport. Thirty clubs join to form a governing body, The British Paint Balling Association. After a period of consultation the teams are settled into three divisions of ten teams each. Each year, one team is relegated to the division below and the champion team of the league below is promoted into the division above. Free market transfers of professional paint ballers can take place between the clubs. The Association itself is a private limited company limited by shares. Each club by virtue of its membership of the League owns one share in the company, with class rights in the shares weighted in favour of the top division.

Paint balling is a sport with a national appeal but its particular hotbed is in the south east of England and in particular Essex. Local entrepreneurs see a great future in the sport and develop great new arenas for the sport to be played in and invest money in assembling teams which are as successful as possible and creating a multitude of commercial spin-offs.

After a few years, it is quite clear that the three Essex teams are the strongest, most successful and richest teams in the league. They have dominated all competitions and have started negotiations with their counterparts in other countries looking towards creating a European Super League. However, the Essex teams feel aggrieved that the money they feel they are attracting to the sport through broadcasting is being shared in a manner they consider unfair to their interests. Only 20% of it is available to the most successful clubs by virtue of league position and the number of appearances on television and the remainder is simply divided amongst the other clubs. Likewise, the arrangement and negotiation of many other sponsorship opportunities are arrogated to itself by the governing body in its rules so that it can contract on behalf of all its member teams. The resulting funds are diluted by distribution across the sport as a whole rather than targeted solely at the successful teams, and are shared out amongst the successful and unsuccessful alike with, again, the same small success bonus for the clubs which, in the main, attract those funds to the sport. The Essex teams feel not only could they conclude their own broadcasting deals with local television companies, but they could also in the new era of digital television promote their own television stations and accept advertising for those stations. On top of this, they have an ever-lengthening queue of arms manufacturers wanting to sponsor them in a tasteful and appropriate manner. The governing body would veto such an arrangement under its powers in relation to the sport's profile. There are opportunities for them to join to form a composite team which would then enter the even more lucrative European League in what is the British League's close season and the only major obstacle to that is the governing body's insistence that they participate in no other leagues and respond in all cases to the call of the national team on their players.

Meanwhile, the onset of broadcasting and the runaway successes of the Essex teams have brought many of the smaller teams located around the West Midlands to a sorry pass. Their share of broadcasting money is the only thing that keeps them afloat as professional undertakings. Their better players are immediately snapped up for much bigger wages by the larger clubs, attendances at their stadia are low and sponsorship is almost non-existent save for that arranged by the governing body on behalf of all the clubs. However, whenever these teams play in Essex capacity crowds attend.

The challenge for the British Paint Balling Association is to reconcile the seemingly insoluble differences between the competing interests of the two parties. If it were merely to give the larger more successful club its head the result would be effectively monopoly of the sport by a small band of wealthy teams. This would lead to the smaller clubs going out of business or becoming effectively amateur or semi-professional teams. The pool of players for international development would be greatly reduced, development at grass roots and youth level would be severely restricted and the prospect would be of a new form of the game played for a television audience by international select teams with no real connection to their immediate locality, in competitions which are effectively 'round robins' without promotion or relegation, and for which the uncertainty of outcome is severely restricted. The governing body sees the sport degenerating into a 'flavour of the month' for satellite television which, when the immediate fashion for it is past, will be left without any basis for independent development.

Talks are currently ongoing between the Essex clubs and their allies in Europe and the UK for the formation of a breakaway governing body, which will arrange its own broadcasting and sponsorship on behalf of a smaller pool of clubs thus greatly increasing each participant's possible stake. Broadcasting of this league would be the death of broadcasting for the British Paint Balling Association Leagues.

The above example is set out as an illustration of the issues at stake for the governing body. Later in this chapter we will look at a fairly familiar line of cases where the decisions of governing bodies have been challenged in the court (2.3.3). What should also be considered actively by any sports lawyer is that the governing body itself may be the forum of major and bitter disputes and the internal constitution of the governing body and the manner in which it derives its legislative powers from its constituent members is a crucial area for attention. Battles are likely to be fought in most sports in the near future not only between a club and the governing body but between clubs for control of the governing body and even in relation to the ongoing survival of the governing body.

Promotion of the sport itself

Development of the image of the sport

The governing body has a crucial role to play in developing the image of the sport. For instance, many sports are still marred by hooliganism, racism and allegations of financial wrongdoings. The governing body, partly through the legislative function outlined above and partly through an active public relations role involving its relationship with government and higher international governing bodies, must promote the best interests of the sport in general. It should provide structures for recruitment of juniors and apprentices into the lowest levels of the sport and seek links with educational establishments, youth organisations and charitable trusts.

The issue of lottery funding is likewise crucial and the governing body should look to maximise lottery funding for the sport. It should look as far as possible to attract international tournaments, such as World Cups, European Cups and so forth to the nation over which it has jurisdiction for the sport. It should organise, promote and use what powers it has to enhance the potential of international teams and the participation of its member teams and participants in international tournaments by association with the wider governing bodies of the sport at European or World level. Most importantly, however, it should organise and regulate the running of domestic tournaments.

Each of these activities leads to detailed regulations which will then move on to impact upon all of the commercial issues raised in this book.

Centralised exploitation of rights

In the constitution of almost all governing bodies, no matter what form they take, there will be a provision whereby all the participating member clubs or participants will assign to the governing body certain rights relating to commercial exploitation of the sport. Parallel to this assignment of rights, the governing body must use its legislative function to restrict categorically the independent exploitation of those rights by the member clubs or participants as dealt with above.

For instance, in the context of broadcasting, the governing body must have the right to make, on behalf of all its member clubs or participants, broadcasting arrangements, the proceeds of which are then divided amongst the participant members according to the governing body's regulations. Any broadcasting company will wish to deal with the sport's governing body rather than suffer the chaos of trying to deal with the clubs individually and will wish to see that the governing body has the power to contract on behalf of all of its members. Broadcasters want to televise or report on radio leagues and tournaments rather than specific clubs. No matter how successful a club is, its participation in any given tournament can either end or become fundamentally uninteresting comparatively quickly. The tournament or the competition will always, however, have a winner and losers and that is the interest to a broadcaster. The broadcaster does not want to be dealing with twenty, thirty or more conflicting interests but with one body only. There will always be a role for the governing body in these arrangements and whilst moves are afoot in a number of sports to try to by-pass them, many would say that no matter how successful clubs are at present, they do so at their peril. The governing body, however, does need to provide exclusive rights where appropriate and that is the reason for the parallel prohibition on competition by individual participant members against the governing body.

Similarly, many governing bodies will look to provide centralised rights packages to potential sponsors. Sponsors of the tournament as a whole are far more likely to pay larger amounts in total than they would pay to any individual club and those proceeds are then available to the body of clubs as a whole. The championship or tournament itself may be sponsored, or such peripheral sponsorship rights as ground level advertising hoardings may be sponsored most lucratively on a tournament wide basis. Here again, the governing body requires the authorisation to make such agreements from its participant members and the power to prevent those participant members from going behind that authorisation and contracting separately. Modern technologies such as EPSIS (virtual advertising superimposed on television pictures) also permit such packages to be combined with the broadcasting rights package and maximise revenue. Out of such revenue the governing body's expenses can be paid and the proceeds distributed to the participant members.

Without such centralisation, it is questionable whether the immense amounts of money being poured into sport would be available. Any sponsor has one clear objective and that is the maximisation of the exposure of its product in the most favourable light. It is far more likely to see that product best promoted by its association with a top flight tournament and therefore all the participants in that tournament rather than simply one of the participants whose fate may be uncertain. The huge amounts of money washing around in football derive largely from the immense success of its broadcasting packages, and whilst one or two clubs may be able to do better than their share of the overall broadcasting pay day for a season or two, on the whole it is undoubtedly the case that the centralisation of such packages is inextricably linked to the value of the package to any broadcaster. The only real alternative is for the governing body to become the broadcaster itself and, as we write, the FA Premier League is a prime example of a body that may do just that.

Such centralisation of rights also gets around certain technical problems. If a broadcaster was to come to an arrangement simply with one club, there would always be potential arguments in relation to the participation of the visiting team. If both visitor and host are participating members in the governing body which has granted the rights and both are deemed to have given their consent to the broadcaster, the broadcaster can relax and treat itself as fully authorised to broadcast. The alternative to centralisation of broadcasting is therefore of comparative administrative chaos and impoverishment of the sport in general. However, this is not an argument which is necessarily won. The Restrictive Trade Practices Court is at the time of writing investigating the FA Premier League broadcasting arrangements. Centralisation of this nature is always likely to come across potential problems in relation to European Community and domestic competition law, and in particular Article 81 of the Treaty of Rome (formerly Article 85, now renumbered by the Treaty of Amsterdam)[1] which deals with the general prohibition of arrangements which tend to prevent, restrict or distort competition within the European Community.

For instance, in 1980 the Office of Fair Trading indicated that it would be unlikely to recommend against the referral of certain categories of agreement in a sporting context. These included agreements which required pooling the revenue from commercial sources and curtailed the ability of clubs to exercise their individual rights.

This is not the place for a thorough review of the provisions of European and domestic competition laws. The tendency in this context would be to drastic over-simplification. However, it is crucial that whenever a governing body is seen to be active in a way which effectively forms a cartel of its participant members regard should be had to all appropriate competition laws. Most of the restrictive practices of sport do still remain but the challenge of competition law is a severe threat to the customary structure of sport throughout the world.

2.1.3   International governing bodies

This chapter is concerned with the British governing bodies of sport but regard should always be had to the relationship between any British governing body in sport and its corresponding international governing body. In many cases, the domestic governing body is required at all times to act in accordance with directives that are made on an international level. The domestic governing body may be part of the electorate for the international governing body and subject to its rules and therefore some knowledge of the international governing body's regulations is essential. However, there can be fault lines in the relationship between the domestic and the international governing body.

For instance, English law has on occasion (such as *Grieg v Insole*[2] and *Gasser v Stinson*[3]) taken the view that notwithstanding the existence of regulations of an international governing body, if such regulations or their effect infringe the rules of English Law particularly in relation to restraint of trade they will be struck down as regards their applicability within the jurisdiction. Indeed, the IAAF has had problems in relation to the ban stipulated in its regulations for doping when

---

1   Henceforth in the text the renumbered Treaty of Rome Articles will be used, with their former numbers in brackets.
2   [1978] 1 WLR 302.
3   (1988) (unreported).

that has been challenged in domestic courts. The four year ban imposed upon Paul Edwards (see **2.3.3**), the British shotputter expelled from the 1994 Commonwealth Games, was effectively made the subject of a double standard when German courts overruled a similar ban in relation to German athletes, cutting the ban to two years. The result has been the IAAF recommending a reduction of its general ban to two years as being a period it feels is enforceable in the domestic jurisdictions of the athletes to which it may apply. However, the potential embarrassment for a domestic governing body which as a result of its domestic law cannot 'toe the line' with the directives of the international governing body is a potentially fruitful area of future conflict.

2.2   THE EXAMPLE OF FOOTBALL

Much of the above is general. It may be useful to illustrate by way of an example. In the UK, football provides the best example of clubs participating in leagues working together for the common good and accepting the imposition of rules which govern their commercial activities. Both the FA Premier League and the Football League rules delegate power to the organisations to enter into commercial contracts in respect of broadcasting or sponsorship. For example no league matches shall be televised or recorded or transmitted by satellite or cable or any similar method, except with the written consent of the Board in each case (Rule C 7.1 and 7.3 of the Premier League and Rule 23 of the Football League).

In the case of the Premier League a formula for allocating the broadcasting contract money is specified in the rules. Rule 8.1 confirms that broadcasting fees will be split into three parts as follows:

(a)   50% to be divided equally amongst each of the clubs;
(b)   25% to be divided amongst each of the clubs on merit based on positions in the League table at the end of the relevant season;
(c)   25% to be divided as facility fees between the clubs whose matches are broadcast (on the basis of an equal share being allocated to the Home Club and the Visiting Club for each match broadcast).

Rule 9.1 provides that further television money from the sale of the overseas broadcasting rights is divided equally between the clubs.

Rule 10 of the Premier League goes on to confirm that the League shall enter into sponsorship and other commercial contracts and that those contracts are binding on each club for so long as the club is a member of the League. The rule provides for equal distribution of the proceeds between the clubs.

The creation and operation of these Rules have enabled the League and, in turn, the participating clubs, to ensure that substantial funds generated by the sale of broadcast and sponsorship rights are received by every club in the League, whilst still maintaining the ability to reward the most successful clubs by the merit awards and by acknowledging that those clubs who appear on television more frequently will receive additional revenue.

There has been considerable debate on the subject of whether or not the clubs should be allowed to negotiate their rights individually and indeed this is exactly what the Director General of Fair Trading is arguing in the forthcoming case.

The League argues that the prospect of 20 individual club Chairmen or Chief Executives negotiating with different television companies would create chaos rather than order and the additional problem is that a club selling its own rights has to have some kind of agreement with the visiting club because no matter how attractive the home club would be for the televiser, two teams are needed on the pitch!

Interestingly, the rules which we have used as examples do not contain provisions which request an undertaking from each club that it will not enter into any sponsorship contracts which clash with those of the League. Clearly, Bass Brewers (Carling) would not attempt to sponsor an individual Premier League club when it already was the sponsor of the League. Carlsberg were delighted, however, to sponsor Liverpool FC and this led to a considerable degree of ill-feeling which was resolved by the classic British compromise of a dignified silence! It is likely that provisions will be introduced in due course to avoid clashes and for example rugby union contracts for players do contain provisions which seek to prevent players from obtaining sponsorship and endorsement contracts which clash with those of the club for whom they play. These provisions should, and no doubt will, be extended to standard forms of contract for players in all sports.

Sponsorship has become the driving force of much of what happens in sport and its importance can be seen, for example, in the Football League rules which contain a provision (Rule 42(ii)) that each club, if required by the relevant sponsor of the League, shall make available services and facilities at matches including perimeter advertising boards; advertising or editorial material in the match day programme; acknowledgement of the sponsor on the cover of the match day programme; acknowledgement of the sponsor in public address announcements; complimentary tickets and assistance with hospitality.

Most rules also impose guidelines and limitations on advertising material such as the emblems that can be displayed on kit and even the size of those emblems.

2.3   CONFLICT WITH THE GOVERNING BODY

As can be seen from the issues raised above, the potential for conflict between the governing body of a sport on the one hand and the players, clubs and organisations whose interests the governing body is forced to attempt to reconcile is wide indeed. These conflicts come under various categories and arise in various contexts. What needs to be considered is the extent to which those conflicts are regulated by law.

Most sports have rules and regulations designed to allow the governing body to control the sport and to try to exclude interference from third parties and in particular the judiciary. In many ways, the justification for this is correct – sports do not want to resolve their internal disputes in public and so prefer the courts to be excluded. Provided the governing body is acting in good faith and in accordance with its rules and regulations, the courts have, on most occasions, tended to keep out. To achieve this the majority of sporting organisations seek to regulate their sports by providing in their rules for arbitration rather than litigation.

For example, the Football Association rules state that the FA governs all football in this country and all clubs and players have to adopt and abide by the rules. Even spectators are made to abide by the same rules as each club is regarded as being responsible for the behaviour of its supporters. If, therefore, there is a riot in the stadium or within the confines of the stadium gates, it will be the club that is punished, even if none of the offenders are arrested. However, if there is a riot five miles away in the city centre two hours after a game has finished, then the club will not be held responsible.

Rule 38(a) states that any affiliated association, member club or member of the FA (which includes players) shall submit and refer all differences and questions between itself and any other such association, club, member or person concerning the laws of the game or any rule or decision of the association to the Council of the FA. The Council may either determine the difference or question itself, delegate the determination to a committee or require a reference to arbitration and there is no obligation to grant an oral hearing!

Rule 39(a) provides that if anyone is aggrieved at an FA Council decision then arbitration is the remedy.

Rule 41(a) states that the fact of membership of or affiliation to the FA shall constitute an agreement to refer all differences and questions to arbitration.

2.3.1 Internal disciplinary processes

Almost all governing bodies will have internal disciplinary rules which affect certain specified classes of people. For instance, in horse racing, those who are deemed to be governed by the Rules of Racing include jockeys, trainers and owners of horses. Sanctions available to The Jockey Club under its own regulations include the exclusion of a given individual for life from racecourses during the course of race meetings. In the regulations of the FA Premier League and the Football Association, the parties concerned include clubs, managers, coaches and players. The list again could be multiplied. In each case a certain pattern emerges about the nature of the disciplinary rules. Certain disciplinary rules will be, as outlined above, those which relate to the proper conduct of the sport. For instance, if a player is considered to have overstepped the mark in the manner of playing the game, or to be guilty of some form of drug or doping infringement, that will place him in difficulties with the governing body. These are offences which take place in the course of the sport. However, there will also be another category of offences which might be broadly described as 'bringing the game into disrepute'. These offences can spread out beyond the conduct of the individual in direct relation to participation of the sport and might even encompass aspects of the players', managers' or coaches' (or clubs') personal, social or commercial conduct generally.

In any case where such disciplinary rules are invoked, the first question to be asked is by what authority the subject of the disciplinary proceedings (called for the sake of brevity the defendant) is made subject to the sanction of the governing body's tribunals. Governing bodies can pass regulations bearing upon their sport, but the shorthand term 'legislation' used above should not be mistaken for the reality. The governing bodies do not have general legislative powers to affect the general law and they must rely on the concept of consent and thus of contract.

In other words, they must prove that there is some contractual link between themselves and the defendant which incorporates the disciplinary rules on which the proceedings are based and the mechanism for punishment which is the ultimate sanction. In most cases, proving this contractual relationship will be comparatively straightforward.

A jockey cannot ride in competitive racing in this country without a licence to ride from The Jockey Club. In applying for such a licence, the jockey voluntarily submits himself to The Jockey Club and the Rules of Racing it promulgates, and this has been held to be a contract.[1]

A sports club will, in most cases, be a member of the governing body, whatever form that governing body takes – see **2.3.2**. In any event, it should be assumed in most cases (but not go unquestioned) that there is a contractual submission on the part of that club to the rules of the governing body either by virtue of its membership of the unincorporated association constituting the governing body or by virtue of its membership of the company constituting the governing body pursuant to s 14 of the Companies Act 1985. This provides that the terms of the Memorandum and Articles of Association of the company are enforceable in contract between the member on the one hand and the company on the other.

For players in team sports, however, the submission to the rules of the governing body will usually be a mandatory provision in the employment contract stipulated by the governing body for use by its member clubs and participating organisations. However, the governing body will not usually be a party to that contract and the legal analysis of the matter could create some interesting difficulties. Practically, the governing body will hold the cards in that unless the player submits to its jurisdiction he will simply be banned from participation by a direct route, namely an edict from the governing body to the player's club to that effect. Effectively, governing bodies can control their sports in practice even where the legal framework is, in strict analysis, not wholly binding. Where the legal framework is not complete, however, there is the possibility for challenge to the governing body's jurisdiction, even though the benefits of such a challenge may be limited in practice.

Particular attention should be given, therefore, to the status of those connected with professional sports whose role is not necessarily circumscribed by active participation in the sport, such as agents. The general climate is to attempt to create a 'closed shop' of approved agents whereby agents enter into contractual relations with the governing body by payment of a bond and signature of a protocol thus bringing themselves under the control of that body; the governing body looks to exclude agents who do not submit by making it an offence for a club or a player to deal with them. In all cases where such disciplinary procedures are considered, the precise structure of the relationship between the defendant and the governing body should be carefully analysed.

Usually the disciplinary rules constitute a 'domestic tribunal' to deal with disciplinary disputes; in other words, a body within the governing body which operates quasi judicial procedures and hands out quasi judicial penalties such as fines, suspensions, bans and so forth. Usually rules of procedure will be laid

---

1   *Wright v The Jockey Club* (1995) *The Times*, 16 June.

down and these again need to be carefully analysed. Some governing bodies have evolved rules of considerable sophistication which effectively provide for a tribunal which in many ways resembles an official tribunal similar to those established by statute such as employment tribunals. The sophistication of these tribunals is often a direct response to the interventions which have taken place on the part of the courts. Where there is any vagueness or confusion as to the procedure, advisers should attempt to secure the following privileges for anyone they represent:

(1) The opportunity to know before attending the tribunal each and every charge laid against the defendant and the evidence on which it is based.

(2) Legal representation at the tribunal or in default of legal representation the opportunity to bring as representative or adviser either a representative of the appropriate body such as the Players' Association or a colleague such as a club manager.

(3) The opportunity to cross-examine and question any witnesses of fact whose evidence is to be relied upon by the tribunal.

(4) The opportunity to be heard in detail in rebuttal of the charges together with the opportunity to call witnesses on behalf of the defendant.

A demand to that effect is best placed in writing at the outset of the proceedings in such cases. Not all governing bodies afford all of these privileges and, indeed, in the past certain governing body's tribunals have resembled rather more the format of a headmaster dressing down a naughty schoolboy than a legal tribunal. The general standard of 'justice' available at these tribunals is generally improving but there is still some way to go in many sports and an adviser should be vigilant in attempting to secure as many of the above facilities for the defendant as possible. Where they are denied, the adviser should consider carefully the line of cases dealt with below at **2.3.3**.

Attention should also be paid to whether there is any internal appeal procedure. In the absence of such a procedure or following the exhaustion of such a procedure, consideration again should be given to reference to the external law in accordance with the cases at **2.3.3**.

2.3.2 Commercial and structural conflicts

In the example given earlier of the British Paint Balling Association (**2.2.2**), the crisis point has been reached between the apparently irreconcilable interests of different members. A decision may be taken by the governing body to accede to the demands of the most powerful in order to prevent a breakaway. In those circumstances, an aggrieved party should consider what its internal rights are within the governing body.

In that regard, the first question is what form the constitution of the governing body takes. Usually a governing body is in effect the creature of its member organisations. The FA Premier League, for instance, is a limited company of which the members from year to year of the FA Premier League are the shareholders. The Rugby Football League is an unincorporated association whose members are the clubs which formed the association and those admitted in accordance with its rules since formation, minus those who have left in accordance with those rules.

Dealing first with the structure of a company governing body, company law recognises that a company is a democracy governed by the majority of the members. The company is obliged in law to act in accordance with its powers vis-à-vis the outside world (the Memorandum of Association) and its internal constitution (the Articles of Association). As indicated above, these core documents of the company are enforceable as contracts taking effect between all the members and the company (and in some cases between the members inter se) pursuant to s 14 of the Companies Act 1985. The Companies Acts provide that certain acts of the company can only be performed with the consent of a majority of the shareholders of the company entitled to vote on a given resolution. In most cases, the votes of any more than 50% of the shareholders entitled to vote will carry the day. In more drastic circumstances, 75% of the shareholders entitled to vote must vote in favour for a motion to be carried and these motions deal with most of the crucial or drastic changes a company may seek to make such as alteration of the Memorandum and Articles. It is not the place here to set out a lengthy discussion on the control of a corporate body by its shareholders but the point does need to be made that general company law does not stop on the boundary of a sports ground. Corporate power is vested in the members and is there to be used.

In many cases of conflict, however, majority control is not the issue. Often the aggrieved party is a minority. The law will intervene to protect an aggrieved minority from unfair prejudice caused to it by the actions of the majority in certain specific cases.

Where the governing body is a company – personal and derivative actions

Actions by shareholders

Where directors of a company are perceived to have taken the company off in a direction which is not in its interests, the shareholders do have a right to enforce the company's rights against a director who has managed to control the board and maintain sufficient influence over the decisions of the general meeting of the company to ensure that litigation is not commenced against him in the company's name. This situation might arise when a particular individual abuses executive power which has become vested in him and is supported by, for instance, strong interest groups. Here, an individual shareholder can enforce rights belonging to the company either by suing in the name of the company or on its behalf in what is known as a derivative action. In most cases the action by the individual shareholder in the name of the company will be halted by an application to strike out on behalf of the company which the judge will usually adjourn pending the meeting of the shareholders of the company. If the shareholders of the company do not support the proceedings then the case will be struck out on punitive cost conditions. This therefore does not appear to be a very useful way of proceeding.

However, an individual shareholder does have the right to take action against the alleged wrongdoers within the company with the company itself joined in as a nominal defendant so that it can be bound by the terms of the judgment in the event that the shareholder is successful. The company must be the beneficiary of any damages or recompense sought in the action and indeed as a corollary to this a shareholder can make an application to the court at the outset of the action for the court to order that the company should indemnify him against the costs of the action whether it succeeds or not.[1] At such a hearing, detailed instructions for the onward conduct of the case will be given alongside a review of the right of that shareholder to bring the case at all. An indemnity should be granted when the legal action constitutes a reasonable and prudent course to take in the interests of the company.

In taking proceedings in the company's name, the plaintiff shareholder effectively puts himself in the position of a fiduciary owing duties to the company in relation to his conduct of the action. He must, as in all equitable actions, beware that his own hands are clean in coming to a court of equity and particularly where he has acquiesced in the conduct which he later complains of he will find his position compromised, possibly to the extent that the court will deny relief. He must be acting in the company's best interests and not in the furtherance of some ulterior purpose of his own.

The remedy under a derivative action is a remedy of last resort. If an alternative is open to the shareholder, he should take it (see below). The range of actions which are potentially the subject of such proceedings are limited.

This area of law is often known as 'the exception to the rule in *Foss v Harbottle*'. In essence the reasoning goes as follows. The proper plaintiff, where a wrong is done to the company, is the company itself. The individual shareholder should therefore ask the board or the general meeting (which has power to authorise proceedings by ordinary resolution, ie simple majority of the shareholders entitled to vote on the resolution) to commence litigation in the company's name. However, if the wrongdoers are in control of the company and the wrong is not a wrong which is capable of ratification by the general meeting of the company under the company's Articles of Association and the general law then the derivative action will lie. There are effectively three recognised exceptions to the general rule (and thus three sets of circumstances where such a derivative action will lie), set out below.

First, if there are any irregularities in the passing of a resolution which requires more than 75% of the company's shareholders entitled to vote to support it (which would include a resolution approving an act which is outside the company's powers according to the Memorandum) the shareholder can launch a personal action which would not in fact be an action in the company's name.

Secondly, an action which infringes the personal rights of an individual shareholder will also give the individual shareholder a right to sue the company under the contract provided by the Articles of Association and Memorandum of the company which, by virtue of s 14 of the Companies Act 1985, constitute a contract between the company and its members.

Finally, there is a category of case known under the general heading of 'fraud on a minority'. The definition of fraud in this case is difficult precisely to tie down. Perhaps the most famous formulation is *Burland v Earle*[2] where Lord Davies

---

1   *Wallersteiner v Moir (No 2)* [1975] 1 QB 373.
2   [1902] AC 83.

stated that fraud in this definition would include cases where the wrongdoers in control of the company are endeavouring, directly or indirectly, to appropriate to themselves money, property or advantages which belong to the company or in which the shareholders are entitled to participate. The action under this heading therefore has been used in the case of misappropriation of company assets and the diversion of business from the company in question to another in which the wrongdoers in control of the company were interested.

This action, therefore, may be of assistance in certain circumstances to a minority within a governing body: on the facts outlined of the British Paint Balling Association, this may be an action to be considered by the minority in the event that, for instance, sponsorship business is directed away by the controlling majority into their alternative vehicle. It might be relevant in the case of any diversion, for instance, of broadcasting and sponsorship opportunities from the governing body to a new body representing only a proportion of the governing body's total membership, such as a breakaway 'Premier League'.

Section 459 of the Companies Act 1985
Section 459 of the Companies Act 1985 as amended by the Companies Act 1989 reads as follows:

> 'A member of a company may apply to the court by petition for an order under this Part on the ground that the company's affairs are being or have been conducted in a manner which is unfairly prejudicial to the interests of its members generally or of some parts of its members (including at least himself) or that any actual or proposed act or omission of the company (including an act or omission on its behalf) is or would be so prejudicial.'

The range of powers available to the court on petitions of this nature is very extensive. Persons other than the company can be added as respondents to a petition and by s 461 of the Companies Act 1985 the court, if it is satisfied that a petition under s 459 is well founded, may make such order as it thinks fit for giving relief in respect of the matters complained of, including s 461(2) orders regulating the company's affairs in the future, requiring the company to refrain from doing or to do an act, authorising proceedings being brought in the company's name on such terms as the court may direct and providing for the purchase of shares of any members of the company by other members or by the company itself.

Effectively, therefore, the court's power is extremely broad. The power can be invoked to complain of a past act or to restrain the company from committing a planned act.

The essence of the action, however, is that there has been unfair prejudice to the interests of the member taking out the petition. A general definition of unfair prejudice is provided by *Re Bovey Hotel Ventures Limited*.[1] Slade J stated the test for unfairness should be an objective and not a subjective one. The petition need not necessarily show that the persons in effective control of the company have acted as they did in conscious knowledge that this was unfair or even that they were acting in bad faith. The test is whether a reasonable bystander observing the consequences of their conduct would regard it as having unfairly

---

1   [1983] BCLC 290.

prejudiced the petitioner's interest. Mere prejudice, however, is not necessarily unfair of itself.

The question then arises as to what is sufficient unfair prejudice to the shareholder to ground the action. A fall in the value of the petitioner's shareholding is neither necessary to ground the action nor in itself sufficient to do so without more. Indeed, where the loss of value of the petitioner's shareholding is not distinct from the loss caused to the company through the diminution of its assets caused by the alleged wrongdoing the proper plaintiff is the company itself.[1]

The essence of the action, of course, is damage to the shareholder's interest in the sense of his legal interest and entitlement under the Memorandum and Articles of Association. However, the wrong which can be complained of under this section goes further than that and extends even to the legitimate expectations over and above mere constitutional rights. For instance, in many small companies a member who has ventured his capital in the company's business may have a legitimate expectation that he will continue to be employed as a director and his dismissal from his office as director and exclusion from the management of the company in those circumstances may ground an action under s 459.[2] There does not need to be any act which of itself would be illegal on the part of the company for the action to be grounded and it is likewise no bar to relief under this section that the act complained of may have affected all the members equally.

The range of a shareholder's legitimate expectations is in each case a matter of fact involving a close inspection of the company in question. Section 459 petitions can be grounded in an informal understanding between the shareholders that the affairs of the company would be regulated in a specific way. However, these 'legitimate expectation' cases are more likely to succeed in a company which has some of the aspects of a 'quasi' partnership company. In each case the existence of the informal arrangement must be proved and the court will not give effect to mere wishful thinking on behalf of the petitioner. It will not enforce an undertaking which is merely a good idea, but only those which have factually existed.

Hoffman LJ stated in *Re Saul D Harrison:*[3]

> '. . . the personal relationship between a shareholder and those who control a company may entitle him to say that it would in certain circumstances be unfair for them to exercise a power conferred by the Articles upon the board or the company in general meeting. I have in the past ventured to borrow from public law the term "legitimate expectation" to describe the co-relative "right" in the shareholder, to which such a relationship may give rise. It often arises out of a fundamental understanding between the shareholders which forms the basis of their association but was not put into contractual form, such as an assumption that each of the parties who has ventured his capital will also participate in the management of the company and receive the return on his investment in the form of salary rather than dividend.'

The range of legitimate expectations that may exist within a sport's governing body is potentially quite wide. In each case, it will have to be grounded on solid

---

1   *Stein v Blake* [1998] 1 All ER 724.
2   *Re A Company* [1986] BCLC 376.
3   [1995] 1 BCLC 14.

facts rather than mere wishful thinking. However, there may be identifiable issues of principle which were behind the formation of the governing body or which have become the policy of the governing body by the common understanding of the members which, when breached, may be reasserted through use of the s 459 petition. The categories of unfair prejudice are not closed and the remedies available to the court are extremely flexible.

In the example of the British Paint Balling Association, therefore, if there is a move by the majority to divide up broadcasting funds only amongst those teams which have been televised in more than five games per season, that could be the basis of a s 459 petition, particularly where it can be proven that the association was formed on the explicit although informal understanding that funds from the broadcasting and sponsorship income available to the association should be shared by all the members.

Winding up on the just and equitable ground

It is usual for consideration of the court's powers pursuant to s 122(1)(g) of the Insolvency Act 1986 to be considered alongside s 459 of the Companies Act 1985. The right under s 122(1)(g) provides that a company may be wound up by the court on the ground that the court is of the opinion that it is just and equitable to do so. Once again, the words are broad and can admit a number of meanings. However, this is most frequently used in the case of a 'quasi partnership' company relying on the leading case of *Ebrahimi v Westbourne Galleries Limited*.[1]

A shareholder who has held shares for at least 6 months during the 18 months prior to the commencement of the winding up can petition the court for the company to be wound up, particularly where there is lack of probity in the management of the company or where the company was an association formed and continued on the basis of a personal relationship involving mutual confidence, often where a pre-existing partnership has been converted into a limited company; an agreement or understanding exists that all or some of the members shall participate in the conduct of the business; and where there is a restriction upon transfer of shares.

It is doubtful that this is a remedy that is likely to be seen as having any real relevance to the context of a sports governing body. It is far more likely that it will be appropriate for unfairly prejudicial conduct to be restrained under s 459 of the Companies Act 1985 and the wide powers granted to the court under s 461 to be invoked as opposed to requesting that the governing body be wound up. In the context of a governing body, it is unlikely that in all the circumstances it will be just and equitable for that to happen and certainly few governing bodies will fit readily within the parameters of the 'quasi partnership' example set out in *Ebrahimi*. Whilst there might be some facts which appear to 'fit' the example, such as a pre-existing relationship, possibly as an incorporated association which is founded to a certain extent on trust, and an agreement that all shareholders shall have some say in the management and restrictions on transfer of shares, the overall profile of a sports governing body and the relationship of its constituent members borrows little from a concept such as partnership: the 'feel' of a partnership or quasi partnership simply does not exist in this context. In any

---

1   [1973] AC 360.

event, if another remedy is appropriate the court can refuse to wind up a company even where the grounds of that winding up are present under s 125(2) of the Insolvency Act 1986. Most s 122(1)(g) petitions are coupled with s 459 petitions in any event and in the circumstances it is unlikely that s 122(1)(g) would be appropriate in this context where relief lay under s 459.

In the past, it might have been said with some force that the commercial democracy model of company law sat perhaps uneasily with the objects of a sports governing body. Now that cannot be said with the same conviction. Sports governing bodies are very much in the business of making money for the sport through sponsorship and all the other income streams dealt with in this chapter. The law does not sit so uneasily in this context alongside the considerations of sport as it does in other areas, such as that of judicial intervention into specific acts or decisions of the governing body which involve those who often do not have the status of being members of the governing body itself but are subject to its rules. Those cases are dealt with below at **2.3.3**.

Where the governing body is an unincorporated association – a legal vacuum?

Where a governing body is an unincorporated association, the position is less clearly regulated by the law. This is largely because the law has traditionally seen itself as the custodian of commercial interests and the unincorporated association has in its traditional form been the preserve of members clubs, non-profit organisations, political parties and so forth whose primary function is not commercial. In many ways, those governing bodies which retain the unincorporated association form are hangovers from the days when a governing body of a sport was really there simply to organise a league and to ensure that the trophies were polished between presentations. Those days are now long gone and if there is to be any new law generated in relation to unincorporated associations that new law is likely to emerge from the sporting context. It may even be a shrewd move to maintain unincorporated association status for a governing body wary of intervention by the courts.

Certain things are, however, clear. First, an unincorporated association, unlike a company, does not have any legal personality separate and distinct from that of its members. It is simply treated as being all of its members acting in concert. This does give potential problems in that the 'target' for any action taken on behalf of one of the members effectively in law includes itself. It is not practicable, for instance, where there are 30 members of an unincorporated association constituting a governing body for one member to take action against all 29 others. The Rules of the Supreme Court (Ord 15, r 12) allow representative actions to be brought against a small number of members where all members have a common interest in the outcome of the proceedings. Whether that is the answer to all the problems posed by this absence of legal personality is very much open to doubt. Whether the new 'Brown Book' contains a similar provision is not known at the date of writing.

The court will recognise, however, on the paradigm of *Clarke v Earl of Dunraven*[1] that the constitution or rules of an association form a contract between the members which may be legally enforced. That case, however, dealt

---

1   [1897] AC 59.

with an action between one member and another and does not necessarily assist in the context of one member against all the remaining members or against the majority of the members on the analogy of the company law actions dealt with above.

Most unincorporated association governing bodies, however, do have rules and regulations which closely resemble those of a company governing body. These rules will usually provide for a broad democracy within the governing body where changes to rules and certain actions can only take place following the vote of the majority of members. Votes may be weighted in favour of certain more powerful members (as indeed they can be in a company governing body) but there is not the same body of law to offer protection to members of an unincorporated association as the protection afforded to company members where that majority acts oppressively.

Again, like the company governing body, the unincorporated association governing body will often confide certain powers and responsibilities in a committee which might even be termed a 'Board of Directors'. The status of such a committee or board is somewhat dubious. They do not, for instance, owe to the members of the unincorporated association generally the clearly defined fiduciary duties owed by directors of limited companies. It may be that on the specific facts of an individual case, or on the interpretation of the rules of a specific governing body, such a fiduciary relationship or duty of care may be established, but it is not automatic as it is in the context of a limited company. Certain actions taken by officers of the unincorporated association may place them in a position of owing a duty of care, such as when a specific danger is known to such an officer as in *Jones v Northampton Borough Council*.[1] Relationships between the governing body and the outside world will usually be mediated through such a committee or 'Board of Directors'. However, those individuals do not necessarily have the power to bind the unincorporated association in the same way as directors would have the power to bind a limited company. The rules of agency apply in the context of an unincorporated association and therefore whilst the rules will usually confide to those individuals specific agency powers in their role as 'directors' the test of whether agency exists either on an express or ostensible basis is still one which might exercise the mind not only of third parties dealing with the governing body, but also members disgruntled at the results of such dealings.

Control of the unincorporated association by its members, therefore, is a much vaguer topic than that of control of companies by their members. There is no great body of law on the topic and it is suggested that the law is there to be made. The commercial powers of a modern governing body of sport surely must be seen by the law in a different light from the traditional unincorporated association governing body which is effectively treated by the law as a group of friends on an outing. The survival of the rule of the professional amateur is still strong in many contexts, as will be seen from the attitude of the law to the decisions of domestic tribunals in sport (see **2.3.3**). There may be, however, the start of a change in attitude.

---

1   (1990) *The Times*, 21 May.

Where a governing body acts to the detriment of a member the rules and regulations of a governing body must in any re-evaluation of the law be seen as enforceable against the other members to restrain that detrimental action where it is unfair; and given that the governing body is effectively the creature of contract by virtue of the contractual relationship between members, it is submitted that contractual terms could be implied into such a contract on the ground of business efficacy, or 'making the contract work'. Custom might also provide further implied terms, such as implied duties not to act unfairly and to the detriment of individual members or to take a course of conduct which would lead inevitably to the demise of the governing body itself in the interests of certain only of the members.

2.3.3 Conflicts arising out of specific decisions

There is a line of cases which might be (and are) generally grouped together in a discussion of intervention by the courts into the actions of sports governing bodies. These arise usually when a club or individual is unhappy at a specific decision made in relation to themselves and seeks the intervention of the courts but often with only limited success. The cases themselves rely on a broad spread of principles and it is difficult to be very systematic about them. However, the following heads may assist:

– cases concerning exclusion from entry to schemes of licensing or authorisation;
– cases of wrongful exclusion following entry into such a scheme;
– cases where rules have been struck down contrary to public policy;
– cases where decisions of domestic tribunals within sporting bodies are amenable to review.

The first type of case is one where there is no real legal footing for the aggrieved individual to apply to the courts save a general 'stand alone' right of action permitting application to the court to prohibit action by a sports governing body which is deemed to be restraint of trade. It is established that the power of the general restraint of trade doctrine recognised in English law is not limited in its application solely to contractual arrangements.[1] The most famous example of this is *Nagle v Fielden*.[2] This case concerns the refusal by the Jockey Club to grant a trainer's licence to the plaintiff, Mrs Nagle, simply because she was a woman. She issued a writ for a declaration and an injunction ordering the grant of the licence. The Jockey Club applied to strike out the statement of claim for failure to disclose a cause of action.

At first instance, Mrs Nagle's answer to the application was firmly based on an alleged contract between herself and the Jockey Club and once the judge had rejected that argument he had no difficulty striking out the claim.

The Court of Appeal in turn rejected the contractual argument but found a different basis on which to preserve the claim – not as a decided judgment in the plaintiff's favour but as a claim which had at least some prospect of success at a full trial (the trial never took place because the matter was resolved without it).

---

1 *Pharmaceutical Society of Great Britain v Dickson* [1970] AC 403.
2 [1966] 2 QB 633.

The Court of Appeal took the view that a monopolistic body which was not merely a social club but had complete control over a nationwide industry was able, by refusing a trainer's licence, to prevent a person from earning a living in that industry; if that refusal was arbitrary or capricious the court might intervene and declare the refusal to be contrary to public policy.

Similar principles from European Community law can have potential bearing in cases of 'restraint of trade'. In *Edwards v The British Athletics Federation (BAF) and The International Amateur Athletics Federation (IAAF)*[1] such a challenge failed, although no doubt the same principles will be invoked in future. This case concerned an athlete (Paul Edwards) who had been banned for four years having tested positive for, inter alia, anabolic steroids.

Rule 60 of the IAAF anti-doping rules imposes various sanctions and for anabolic steroids, in the case of a first offence, the relevant sanction is a ban of four years, rendering the athlete ineligible for competition.

It was argued that an anti-doping ban imposed by a governing body is unlawful as it fetters the sportsman's ability to offer his services within the European Community and, as such, is in breach of Community Law. Articles 49(59) to 55(66) of the Treaty of Rome prevent discrimination on the basis of nationality which interferes with the freedom to provide services.

Lightman J took as his starting point the *Bosman* decision which had confirmed that Community Law had no application to rules of an exclusively sporting nature such as rules determining the length of a match or the points to be awarded for a victory. Community Law only affects sport in so far as it constitutes an economic activity.

The judge decided that the rules which had been applied merely regulate the sporting conduct of participants in athletics. They are designed to ban cheating by taking drugs. A rule designed to regulate the sporting conduct of participants does not cease to be such a rule because it does not allow those who break it to earn remuneration by participating in the sport for an appropriate period. He ruled against Mr Edwards.

A similar case to *Nagle v Fielden*, dealing once again with the refusal of a licence by a governing body is *McInnes v Onslow-Fane*.[2] The plaintiff had been refused a boxing manager's licence without any reason being given. He asked for an oral hearing which was refused. His writ asked for a declaration that the Board had acted in breach of natural justice and unfairly in failing to inform him of the reasons for refusal and to give an oral hearing.

The application was refused and the particular decision is not relevant for present purposes. What is valuable is the analysis by the judge (Megarry V-C) of the non-contractual rights of a person in relation to applications for membership of private bodies or licences granted by such bodies.

The starting point, following the approach of *Nagle v Fielden*, was that in the case before him, where the licence was required for the plaintiff to pursue his livelihood and was in the hands of what was an effectively monopoly licensing

---

1   [1997] TLR 348.
2   [1978] 1 WLR 1520.

authority, the court was entitled to intervene to enforce the appropriate requirements of natural justice and fairness.

From that starting point, the Vice-Chancellor set out a classification of three different types of case while making it expressly clear that it was not intended as an exhaustive scheme:

(a) Forfeiture cases in which an existing right or position was taken away, such as expulsion from membership or revocation of licence.

(b) Application cases such as where membership or a licence is refused in the first place rather than taken away.

Then, in between those categories:

(c) Expectation cases, where a new applicant has some legitimate expectation from what has already happened that his application will be granted.

The requirements of natural justice and fairness vary according to the particular case.

In forfeiture cases, they generally require notice of the reasons for expulsion or forfeiture and an opportunity to answer them. On mere application cases the requirements will usually be very slight. A simple refusal with no reasons and no opportunity of being heard will generally not be regarded by the courts as unfair.

The Vice-Chancellor regarded the expectation cases as in some respects more like forfeiture cases:

> 'Although in form there is no forfeiture but merely an attempt at acquisition that fails, the legitimate expectation of a renewal of the licence or confirmation of the membership is one which raises the question of what it is that has happened to make the applicant unsuitable for the membership or licence for which he was previously thought suitable'.

The *McInnes* case, on its facts, was held to be a mere application case so the judge did not need to consider what would have been required to meet the duty of fairness if it had been an expectation case.

This case is therefore crucial for the second category in the classification of cases at the head of this section, which are effectively forfeiture cases. Here, it is suggested that although the three categories set out by the Vice-Chancellor in *McInnes v Onslow-Fane* are treated as three types of the same beast, a forfeiture case is different in that it is generally a case in which there is an existing contractual relationship, which accounts for the greater level of duty incumbent upon the licensing body.

Cases where rules have been struck down on the grounds of public policy again derive their principles primarily from the doctrine of restraint of trade and the rules of natural justice. An example of a restraint of trade case is *Stevenage Borough FC Limited v The Football League Limited*.[1] In May 1996, Stevenage finished top of the GM Vauxhall Football Conference, the league of semi-professional football clubs immediately below the three divisions forming the Football League. In principle, that result would entitle them to be promoted to the Third Division of the Football League.

---

1   [1996] TLR 470.

Under the League's rules, promotion depended upon Stevenage satisfying certain admission criteria, including requirements relating to ground capacity which had to be satisfied at the end of December in the previous year and financial criteria which had to be satisfied in respect of accounts for the current and previous years. Stevenage did not satisfy those criteria at the relevant dates, although following completion of works currently underway, they expected to be able to satisfy them before the beginning of the new season in August. If Stevenage were promoted, the bottom club in the Third Division, Torquay United, would be relegated. Stevenage challenged the criteria on the ground that they were in restraint of trade and unreasonable.

Effectively, therefore, Stevenage sought a court order for admission to membership of a private body with the necessary corollary of expulsion of an existing member. This basic principle alone troubled the judge, Carnwath J, who pointed out that no case had been cited in which the court had forced a private organisation to admit a member against its will. It also concerned the Court of Appeal, though their emphasis was rather more on the other side of the same coin – the protection of Torquay from expulsion as a member.

The judge decided that where the restraints (the admission criteria) were part of a system of control imposed by a body exercising regulatory powers in the public interest, the onus lay on those seeking to challenge particular rules to establish that those rules were unreasonable in the narrow sense – in other words 'arbitrary and capricious'.

Two elements of the criteria were found to be open to objection on the ground of restraint of trade:

(a) the requirement to carry out ground improvements to achieve a capacity of 6,000 before it was known whether the club was going to be able to qualify for promotion; and

(b) the imposition of financial criteria on entrance to the Third Division without any corresponding criteria imposed upon existing clubs.

The judge doubted whether those objections were so serious as to justify the terms 'arbitrary or capricious'. The question of discretion was critical, however, and the judge was concerned by the issues of delay and prejudice to third parties.

It was said that it would be unreasonable to expect Stevenage to commence expensive legal proceedings until they knew they had won the competition. That might seem fair from their point of view, but it was not in the judge's view fair to all the others involved. The advantage of earlier proceedings would have been that the validity of the criteria could have been tested well before the end of the season and the League and the Conference would have had an opportunity to make alternative arrangements. The judge felt it was unfair to Torquay that they should be left in uncertainty until very shortly before the new season. Accordingly, Stevenage lost on the basis that they had delayed in bringing proceedings until after the end of the season, which was viewed to be too late. This might seem a convenient way for the judge to reach his decision but the basic point of the case is that the judge was loth to interfere unless and until the rules of the League and/or the exercise of them by the governing body had been proved to be arbitrary and capricious.

An example where the courts showed a willingness to strike down the rules of a governing body on the ground that they were unreasonable is provided by *Wilander and Novacek v Tobin and Jude*.[1] Here, in the second application in proceedings dealing with the suspension of two internationally famous tennis players following their failure of random drug tests, Lightman J permitted a statement of claim to proceed toward trial which was based upon the premise that the rules of the International Tennis Federation were unreasonable in failing to provide for an appeal against suspension. The Court of Appeal struck out the statement of claim on the basis that it considered that an appeal was provided by the rules but made the interesting point in addition that the players had an inalienable right to challenge their suspension by court proceedings in any event.

The final category of cases comprises those where it is alleged that sporting bodies have 'got it wrong' in an adjudication by an internal or domestic tribunal. Classically, in this sort of case the aggrieved party effectively seeks to use the court as an external appeal from the internal processes of the governing body. There has been in the past some considerable confusion as to what form proceedings of this nature should take. For some considerable period of time, it was considered appropriate to take proceedings seeking judicial review. However, judicial review is a cause of action controlling abuse of power by a body operating powers which are governmental or quasi governmental conferred by statute or by Royal prerogative. This approach has been found to be acceptable in other jurisdictions as close as Scotland in, for instance, *Ferguson v Scottish Football Association*[2] and, indeed, some encouraging dicta such as those by Roche J in *R v Disciplinary Committee of The Jockey Club, ex parte Massingberd-Munday*.[3] However, in *R v Disciplinary Committee of The Jockey Club ex parte Aga Khan*,[4] it was established that The Jockey Club was not susceptible to judicial review on the ground that The Jockey Club is not a public body in origin, history, constitution or membership and plays no part in any system of governmental control of horse racing. Whilst certain of its powers may be described as public they are not governmental and therefore any action against such a governing body must be grounded either on a contractual basis or on some other basis recognised by law outside judicial review.

The same case effectively pointed out the way forward for those who wished to challenge the decisions of governing bodies on grounds similar to judicial review. Hoffman LJ in giving a concurring judgment in the Court of Appeal stated as follows:

> '[The Aga Khan] has a contract with The Jockey Club, both as registered owner and by virtue of having entered his horse in the Oaks. The Club has an implied obligation under the contract to conduct its disciplinary proceedings fairly. If it has not done so, the Aga Khan can obtain a declaration that the decision was ineffective'.

This brings the sporting cases in line with *Lee v Showman's Guild of Great Britain*[5] where Lord Denning stated that even where a tribunal was constituted on the grounds of a contractual relationships, that tribunal must observe the

---

1   [1997] 1 Lloyd's Rep 195.
2   1 February 1996, unreported.
3   [1993] 2 All ER 207.
4   [1993] 1 WLR 909.
5   [1952] 2 QB 329.

principles of natural justice. A party appearing before that tribunal must be given notice of the charge he has to take and reasonable opportunity of meeting it and stipulations to the contrary are and would be invalid.

Although the Jockey Club is fairly unique in its constitution (a body corporate incorporated by Royal Charter) this is authority for saying that in the case of almost any conceivable sporting body the route to be followed in such cases is one based on contractual relationships rather than administrative law. The summary of reasons for the inapplicability of judicial review to the Jockey Club given by the judge would apply equally to any governing body of sport.

Another instance where the courts have provided an external appeal mechanism is *The Notts Incorporated Football Club Limited v (1) The Football League Limited and (2) Southend United Football Club Limited*.[1] In June 1995, Southend United complained to the Football League that their manager had been the subject of an illegal approach from Notts County. The Football League appointed a commission which determined the case in favour of Notts County. The costs of the hearing and the proper and reasonable costs of Notts County were ordered to be paid by Southend United. Southend United had a right of appeal under rule 16 of the Football League rules.

The rule sets out that any club or person on which a penalty has been imposed may appeal. Southend duly sought to appeal but Notts County argued that on the construction of the rules, despite what the Commission had indicated, there was no right of appeal. It was argued that no penalty had been imposed because an order for costs alone could not be said to be a penalty.

Notts County issued proceedings in the High Court for a determination of whether Southend had the right to appeal and in turn the Football League applied for a stay of Notts County's application because all differences and questions arising between members were to be referred to arbitration in accordance with Rule 41(a) of the Football Association referred to at **2.2**.

In what he described as the exceptional circumstances of this case, Neuberger J decided that it would not be appropriate to grant a stay. He was concerned that if the matter was referred to arbitration there was a likelihood that in a case where costs awarded had been in a sum less than £20,000 and where both Notts County and Southend were before the court ready to argue the point, to refer the matter to arbitration would only increase the costs already expended. The judge was also influenced by the fact that the point he was being asked to determine was a point of construction where there were no facts in issue. The Court of Appeal case of *S L Sethia Liners Limited v State Trading Corporation of India Limited*[2] was authority for the proposition that if summary judgment of the point in issue was applied for and the court was able to grant it, then it should grant judgment rather than referring the matter to arbitration. The judge emphasised that the particular facts which justified him refusing a stay were exceptional and even the factors against a stay only just outweighed those in favour. In the end the judge decided that costs would be regarded as a penalty and so Southend did have the right of appeal.

---

1   28 November 1996, unreported.
2   [1986] 2 All ER 395.

This is an example of the court becoming involved and making a decision, but when one looks at the particular facts and the purpose of the hearing, it supports the view that if an organisation has rules which are properly and clearly drafted and which provide for resolution of disputes by internal procedures or arbitration, then the courts will only interfere in very exceptional cases. Sporting associations should consider their rules and have them properly drafted.

These potentially encouraging dicta to plaintiffs must, however, be seen in the context of the law's traditional attitude to cases where it is asked to intervene in the internal management of the sport on grounds such as those in the above categories of case. It has been quite quick to intervene where restraint of trade is at stake. Where, however, the allegation is that governing bodies have 'got it wrong' there has been on the part of judges an instinctive dislike of the concept of sports being intruded upon by the courts on the assumption that sports administrators know their own sports best. Megarry V-C in *McInnes v Onslow-Fane*[1] made clear his view which has tended to be the view which has been expressed until comparatively recent times (such as in *Wright v The Jockey Club*).[2] Megarry V-C said:

> 'I think that the courts must be slow to allow any implied obligation to be fair to be used as a means of bringing before the courts for review honest decisions of bodies exercising jurisdiction over sporting and other activities which those bodies are far better fitted to judge than the courts. This is so even where those bodies are concerned with the means of livelihood of those who take part in those activities. The concepts of natural justice and the duty to be fair must not be allowed to discredit themselves by making unreasonable requirements and imposing undue burdens. Bodies such as the Board which promote a public interest by seeking to maintain high standards in a field of activity which otherwise might easily become degraded and corrupt ought not to be hampered in their work without good cause. Such bodies should not be tempted or coerced into granting licences that otherwise they would refuse by reason of the courts having imposed on them a procedure for refusal which facilitates litigation against them.'

It may be, however, that in the context of the greater commercialisation of sport and the rapid progression of sport to the status of a leading edge industry rather than a game for the professional amateur and those they choose to employ, the policy of the law may undergo some change. The law is there and is ready to be used and the judges must decide whether or not they choose to use it. Where judicial policy is treated as a matter of importance this is only ever because the judges themselves have raised the issue by appealing to policy in cases they find difficult.

There have been some dicta which have attracted perhaps more publicity than in themselves they may necessarily have merited, on account of their rarity in this context. In *Jones v Welsh Rugby Union*,[3] Mark Jones, the Ebbw Vale No 8 forward, was sent off for fighting during a game against Swansea. As a result, the Welsh Rugby Union Disciplinary Committee held a disciplinary hearing and he was suspended for four weeks. Despite lodging an appeal against the decision and

---

1   [1978] 1 WLR 1520.
2   (1995) *The Times*, 16 June.
3   (1997) *The Times*, 6 March.

the suspension, it was decided that the suspension would still have to be served even though an appeal was pending.

Jones went to the High Court and Ebsworth J granted an injunction allowing Jones to play again until an appeal over the Disciplinary Committee's decision was heard.

Apparent defects in the Disciplinary Committee's hearing formed the basis of the appeal. Jones argued that the disciplinary hearing was unfair because there was no proper enquiry into the facts, he had no legal representation and the video of the incident was viewed in private. In simple terms, therefore, he argued that he did not have a sufficient chance to argue his case. The real basis of the matter is the amenability to challenge of an 'arbitrary and capricious' rule as stated above aided by the refusal to lift the ban pending appeal.

What is interesting is the justification for the court's interference given by Ebsworth J. She said that sporting decisions had for years been made from 'wet and windy touchlines'. The new professional game meant, however, that those decisions now affected 'many people who earn a living'. The judge said that it was 'naive to contend' that the decisions of disciplinary committees could not be challenged because the sanctions imposed now had 'economic results' on those affected. She held that the disciplinary proceedings gave the player no real rights and that the committee exercised powers and gave decisions which affected the livelihood of players and for those reasons, the court was prepared to interfere.

At the end of the day, the decision may not be as earth-shattering as the newspapers and media reported at the time. If the committee behaved in a high-handed capricious way and gave the player very little opportunity to make representations, then that would be a lack of good faith on their part and the courts would interfere on the usual grounds accepted in the earlier cases.

Certainly, the Court of Appeal decision on the injunction illustrates the different approach that the courts will take if the procedures provide for fairness. In her original decision, Ebsworth J suggested that if the WRU changed their disciplinary procedures and made them fairer, then the courts were not likely to intervene. This is exactly what the WRU did and they reconvened the disciplinary hearing with new procedures and making allowance for legal representation. Mr Jones and his representative failed to attend, presumably relying upon the injunction and the dicta of Ebsworth J and the Disciplinary Committee imposed the suspension for 28 days.

The Court of Appeal took the view that in the light of the changed procedures which made them much fairer, it was entirely Mr Jones's decision and that of his advisers not to attend and they could not now complain that the proceedings were unfair and so the injunction would be lifted.

At the time of writing the full trial of the case is still pending and it will be interesting to see what judgment is reached or whether the matter even proceeds to trial.

This case and others like it are likely to cause sporting bodies (if they have any sense) to do everything possible to show that fair play has operated during any disciplinary matter and we are likely to see lawyers given access to the proceedings far more than in the past. For example the FA rules say that anyone involved in a disciplinary hearing may only be legally represented with the written consent of the FA. It is likely in the future that consent will be given in any case where it is requested, because to do otherwise might expose the Association to an allegation of breach of natural justice.

The fundamental point remains however, that provided governing bodies behave fairly and reasonably and give the parties every opportunity to argue their cases fully, then the courts will not intervene.

CHAPTER 3

COMMERCIAL AGREEMENTS

COMMON TERMS

3.1 INTRODUCTION

The sports industry covers a diverse mixture of business activities ranging from the broadcasting of events to the endorsement of products by leading sports personalities. But despite these widely differing businesses, there are common legal and contractual considerations which form the basis of commercial practice in this growing business.

3.2 THE CONTRACT

Most contracts in the sports industry follow a familiar pattern. The basic structure of a commercial contract should include a statement of the parties, any recitals and the operative part of the document.

The operative part should contain a list of defined terms, any conditions precedent, the agreed rights and obligations of the parties, a list of representations and warranties, as well as the usual standard or 'boiler-plate' terms.

The basic terms of the contract should deal with the following points:

– who grants the rights;
– what rights are being granted;
– when, or for how long, can the rights by exercised;
– where can the rights be exercised;
– how exclusive are the rights;
– how much will the rights cost.

These points are considered in more detail below.

In addition, the contract must be properly formed.[1] Even a properly formed contract may still be susceptible to challenge on a variety of grounds.[2] If an

---

1   See **3.3**.
2   See **3.5**.

agreement is breached or an action is anticipated, the common remedies and damages available in the contract must also be considered.[1] Similarly, the effect of UK and EC competition law and the EC free movement of goods legislation should be considered.[2]

3.2.1 Parties

The parties to an agreement must be correctly identified at an early stage. In particular, both parties to a contract must have the capacity and authority to enter into a binding agreement.

The legal status of the parties may involve one or more of the following either granting or acquiring rights and/or obligations under the contract. The possible parties are as follows:

- an individual;
- a partnership;
- a company;
- a company limited by guarantee;
- an unincorporated association;
- a charity;
- an agent.

A number of issues may arise when dealing with any of these legal entities and as the following is a brief guide only to legal status, reference should be made to specialist texts for fuller details on particular problems or situations that arise.

Individuals generally have capacity to contract unless they are minors in which case particular problems may arise[3] or if they are under some other form of disability.

Partnerships may also be involved in the acquisition and/or exploitation of rights and the usual rules concerning authority should be followed.

A company is governed by its memorandum and articles and must act within its powers; any acts outside its powers are *ultra vires* and do not generally bind the company unless the other party was acting in 'good faith'.[4] Companies may also be limited by guarantee, in which case the members liability is not called upon until after commencement of any winding up. This format is increasingly used by sports governing bodies.

Sports governing bodies also commonly use the unincorporated associations as their method of trading. Unincorporated associations do not have the benefit of a distinct legal personality and as such the association itself cannot be used. However, its members can[5] and this leaves its individual members open to sue or be sued. Such associations have a constitution which governs the members relationships between themselves[6] as well as their capacity and ability to contract

---

1   See 3.10.
2   See 3.9.
3   See 3.6.
4   Companies Act 1985, s 35.
5   See for example *Brown v Lamb* (1896) 12 TLR 455 and *Reel v Holder* [1981] 1 WLR 1226.
6   *Clark v Earl of Dunraven* [1897] AC 59.

with third parties. This latter ability depends on the authority delegated to the association by its members (for example, to appoint sponsors) but it is also important that individual officers within the association and within the rules and powers delegated to them by the member as (usually) defined within the constitution. These are matters generally dealt with by the rules of agency.

A partnership is governed by the terms of the Partnership Act 1890 and the terms of a partnership deed. A partnership has no legal personality other than that of its individual partners who are jointly and severally liable for the acts and defaults of the partners. Each partner is liable, under s 5 of the Partnership Act 1890, for the partnership's breaches of contract. A partnership is not a common form of business organisation for sports bodies although it is not uncommon for other commercial entities involved in the business of sport.

Charities are subject to strict regulation of their own regarding their formation as well as the way they go about their own 'business'. A charity must qualify for charitable status (ie relief of poverty, advancement of education or religion or other purposes beneficial to the community) although achieving charitable status for sport is not without its problems and available in only limited cases[1] particularly for youth development schemes in a sporting context. Generally though, charities are able to contract and operate with some care and regard to relevant legislation[2] particularly if a charity is fund raising or trading in any way.

Agents are dealt with elsewhere[3] but generally will be governed by the common law of agency as well as the terms of any relevant legislation[4] and any contract with their principal.

3.2.2 Rights

In the sports industry, the rights clause in the contract is fundamental to the purpose of the agreement. The rights clause may relate to a grant of intellectual property rights, such as a trade mark, between the parties, or may relate to the services provided by an individual, such as a sportsman.

The agreement must specify what rights are being granted; it may also (but does not have to) specifically reserve rights that are not granted. A specific reservation of rights is very common where a category of rights has already been granted to a third party in another agreement and the rights owner wants to make this clear in the new agreement.

The grant of rights varies from one sports contract to another, and, when drafting a contract, regard has to be had to the prevailing practice within the specific part of the industry.

It is important also to consider, as far as possible, that the rights clause is sufficiently well thought out that it will not cause future problems for the rights owner. If too much is granted in the way of rights, this could limit the possibilities for exploiting future opportunities as new developments come along. Recent examples are electronic publishing and multi-media which create

---

1   *IRC v McMullen* (1981) AC 1.
2   Charities Act 1992, Charitable Institutions (Fund Raising) Regulations 1994. See **6.6**.
3   Chapter 7.
4   The Agency Regulations may apply to certain agency relationships.

opportunities even within sport where web sites and advanced video games are all part of the exploitation mix.

3.2.3   Term

When, or for how long, rights can be exercised is known as the 'term' of the agreement. This is clearly an important aspect of the agreement.

The term of an agreement is usually a specified period of time, although an indefinite period may be used with a notice period exercisable by either party to the agreement to end the contract. The term may also be until so many days after the end of a specified event. The term of a contract is one of the factors considered in restraint of trade disputes and in Article 81(85) problems.

Dealings with intellectual property rights are often tied to the length of protection given by law. An assignment or licence of copyright may be limited in a number of ways.[1]

If a contract deals with the personal services of a sportsman, the term could be one day or several years.

The term of an agreement may be extended in a number of ways.

Options

An option clause allows one party to give notice to the other extending the agreement on agreed terms. In this context, an option is a contractual term allowing a party to acquire a right to extend the term of an agreement. Options are frequently found in sponsorship and broadcasting agreements where an initial fixed period is followed by a number of consecutive contractual 'option' periods allowing an extension of the original term.

All option clauses in agreements should set out the method by which, and the time-limit within which, they should be exercised. An option should also contain its own separate consideration upon exercise. Options when exercised should constitute valid binding contracts themselves. An option which is contingent upon terms of the subsequent contract being agreed or negotiated in good faith may not constitute a binding contract at all, but may simply be an agreement to agree or an agreement to negotiate, both of which are unenforceable.

If an option is included in a contract, the person with the benefit of the option must usually call for its performance by notice in accordance with the terms of the agreement. There is only a right, not an obligation, to demand performance.

First refusal

A right of first refusal, or a pre-emption right, gives a party the ability to make an offer or to negotiate for a certain number of days on such terms as it sees fit. The other party may choose to accept these terms (or not) as it sees fit. These clauses are sometimes also known as a 'right of first negotiation'. All such clauses must be carefully considered as they are not, in the main, binding contractual terms. A court would not enforce them.[2] Because of this, such clauses are often coupled with a 'matching right' clause.

---

1   See **4.12**.
2   See **3.3.2**.

Matching rights

A grant of 'matching' rights to a party is, when properly drafted, a binding contractual commitment. Upon termination, and possibly after the period of time for the right of first negotiation has ended the party with the matching rights is entitled to match any offer the other party has obtained for the contract. The rights owner may choose to go to the open market to obtain the best offer or term it can for the rights in question. The party with the benefit of the matching right is then given the opportunity to match those terms. Such clauses are popular upon termination of many agreements or where new opportunities exist for the exploitation of rights which parties will deal with later.

3.2.4 Territory

Most sports contracts contain a clause which defines and limits the territories where the rights granted can be exercised. The clause should set out the territories which are included in the grant of rights and may set out those which are excluded. The rights owner can maximise his income this way with deals in a number of territories.

Territorial restrictions may be by language, country or territory. It is common for rights to services or intellectual property to be restricted in this way. However, the EC rules on freedom to provide goods and services, and competition law can give rise to certain legal problems on such restrictions.[1]

3.2.5 Exclusivity

The next point to consider is how exclusive the rights are.

An agreement may contain:

– exclusive rights, whereby only the party granted the rights and no other party, including the rights owner, can exercise the rights; or
– sole rights, whereby the party granted the rights and the rights owner can exercise the rights; or
– non-exclusive rights, whereby the party granting the right, may grant any other party the rights.

The issue of exclusivity is an important one for both parties to any agreement to consider as it can bring both advantages and disadvantages depending on the circumstances.

For example, exclusivity usually carries with it a premium in terms of price for the party receiving its benefit. It may also mean that the party granting it may be required to protect the exclusivity by taking steps against third parties infringing these rights.

There are also potential legal problems with such arrangements. Exclusivity can lead to restraint of trade. It can also lead to breach of the freedom of goods and services provisions of the EC. Exclusivity may also mean that the agreement is anti-competitive – which is possible, particularly where the distribution of goods or the exploitation of rights is concerned.

---

1   See, further, **3.9**.

3.2.6   Payment terms

The cost of the sale of rights is the next point to consider. The payment terms in contracts may vary enormously.

A fee
The contract may provide for a fee, normally a lump sum payment, which will cover all rights granted in the agreement. This may be payable in a lump sum or in several instalments.

A royalty
Another method of payment is the royalty payment. This is a payment method preferred in the music, publishing and merchandising businesses. The royalty is a set percentage of income and/or of the sale price of the product in question. Royalty rates can be altered and recalculated in numerous ways. This has been elevated to an art form in the music business.[1] If there is a royalty, there may also be an advance against royalties, which represents a payment on account of future earnings. Such an advance is always recoupable from future royalties although it is rarely returnable. This means that until enough royalties are earned to recover the amount of the advance from sales, no royalty is paid.

A share of profits
The contract may pay a share or profits. This may be a share of net profits which means that, once all the expenses are covered, profits are shared in an agreed way. In such cases, the way 'net profits' are defined and the actual deductions that can be made from gross income by the paying party must be carefully considered.

Other financial terms
Where royalty and profit share arrangements are used there may be other important financial terms attached to them. The contract may guarantee a certain minimum level of income for a rights owner whatever the actual income. If the guarantee is exceeded, the greater sum is paid. If the actual income is less than the guarantee, there is an effective income and/or sales floor to the agreement.

Future advances and guarantees in the contract may be based on income levels earned during the earlier part of the contract. These advances may be subject to a minimum and a maximum amount based on the income under the contract. Some agreements also provide that royalties or profit shares increase. This increase may occur as the contract is extended or because certain levels of income and/or sales have been exceeded, triggering the higher rate.

3.3   PROBLEMS IN FORMATION

3.3.1   General considerations

It is important to establish the status of agreement the parties expect to reach. If the agreement is to be legally binding, there must be: an intention to create legal relations; an offer that is accepted; and some consideration. The terms of a

---

1   See Carey and Verow, *Media and Entertainment: The Law and Business* (Jordans, 1998) Chapter 16.

binding agreement should normally be negotiated and recorded in a written contract.

Occasionally the parties agree 'heads of terms' before a comprehensive document is drawn up and negotiated. Such heads of terms often relate only to the matters dealt with in **3.2**. The terms are then reflected in a short document that sets out the basic aspects of the agreement. Later the parties negotiate and draw up a full document that supersedes the heads and sets out the full terms of the agreement including the common terms as outlined in **3.4**.

3.3.2 Lock-in agreements

Occasionally, situations arise where parties suggest that an 'agreement to agree' is entered, or that they will 'negotiate in good faith', or that one party will not negotiate with anyone else. Such agreements must be carefully drafted to be enforceable.

An agreement to agree or a duty to negotiate in good faith is contractually uncertain and therefore not binding on the parties. An agreement between the parties that one of them will not negotiate with anyone else for an agreed period of time is enforceable, provided consideration is given. This is a lock-out agreement. In such a case, the party agreeing to the restriction is not obliged to negotiate, they are simply saying that they will not go elsewhere. An agreement which requires them to negotiate with the other party, a lock-in agreement, is unenforceable being void for uncertainty.[1]

3.3.3 Renegotiation

Rights holders frequently wish to renegotiate the terms of their contracts. The terms of a valid existing contract should be adhered to, as failure to do so by either party may result in a claim for breach of contract. There may be different reasons for a renegotiation. The rights holder may simply feel that it deserves more money, or it may have been advised that the existing contract is unenforceable on a legal ground such as restraint of trade. All renegotiations are normally conducted 'without prejudice' and 'subject to contract' to reserve a position in case of litigation, or to make sure that an agreement is not inadvertently reached and a binding contract entered.

If one party threatens proceedings for breach of contract and then subsequently settles the dispute, that party may not be able to reopen that dispute at a later date before the courts. Public policy prohibits the settlement of a previous dispute being reopened at a later date.[2]

If a contract is successfully renegotiated, the new agreement should be recorded in writing to reflect its terms. A novation agreement or a variation should also be executed to alter or replace the previous agreement.

3.3.4 Letters of intent

One party may not be willing to commit itself to a full agreement. This may be for a number of reasons, for example because it wants to take more time to review

---

1   See *Walford v Miles* [1992] 1 All ER 453.
2   See *Colchester Borough Council v Smith* [1992] Ch 421.

the prospects of a sportsman or the viability of an event. A letter of intent may be a binding contract if all the necessary elements for a contract are present. A letter of intent written 'subject to contract' may not be binding. It has been said that 'there can be no hard and fast answer to the question of whether a letter of intention is a binding agreement: everything must depend upon the circumstances of the particular case'.[1]

A person who signs a letter of intent must consider whether he is entering a binding contract, what obligations he is being committed to and whether he will be called upon to perform those obligations. Payment for work undertaken on the basis of a letter of intent may, if no binding contract is reached, be recovered on the basis of a quantum meruit.

3.3.5   Independent advice

Although all the factors necessary to constitute a binding contract may be present, there may be other matters to consider before signing an agreement. Particular problems arise whenever artists enter any form of contract. Advice should always be taken on the terms of the contract.

The quality and availability of professional advice may be an important factor in any subsequent attempt to challenge a contract. Many agreements with individual sportsmen contain a specific declaration that the sportsman has been given independent professional advice.

An independent adviser should explain the contract and the reasonableness of the obligations imposed. If necessary, terms should be varied by negotiation. All advice should be recorded in writing. If a client refuses to accept advice, that fact should also be recorded in writing.

If there is a later challenge to an agreement and one party can point to the fact that independent advice was taken, it is harder to establish that the sportsman did not understand the extent of his commitment. Independent advice is of particular value in cases where undue influence is alleged.

3.4   COMMON TERMS IN COMMERCIAL AGREEMENTS

The structure of commercial agreements is relatively standard. The structure of a typical commercial agreement is outlined below.

3.4.1   Commencement, date and parties

Most commercial documents contain a title or heading describing the type of agreement. In longer agreements, this title page may be followed by an index to the clauses in the agreement.

The date of the document should be inserted when the agreement is finalised and signed by the parties.

The parties to the agreement should be stated along with their addresses. It is usual for the registered office and number of a company to be inserted.

---

1   *British Steel Corporation v Cleveland Bridge* [1984] 1 All ER 504.

The capacity of the parties to the contract should be established at a very early stage in negotiations.[1] Where dealing with a company or partnership, the capacity or authority of the representative of that party to bind it may also need to be confirmed. In many cases, a company or partnership is bound by the acts of its representatives.

3.4.2 Recitals

The recitals to an agreement simply set out the background to the contract. Recitals are not essential to an agreement and not always used. Where a particular agreement has an unusual or complicated background, recitals can be useful to clarify the context of the agreement. There is a risk that overlong or complex recitals introduce ambiguity into an agreement which may otherwise be clear. Where recitals are included in a deed, they are binding on the parties.

3.4.3 Operative part

The operative part of the agreement creates the legal rights and obligations of the parties. This part of the agreement contains clauses setting out the 'deal points' discussed above. The operative part also sets out the 'standard' terms of the agreement, many of which may be anything but standard because of the way they are drafted. These standard terms are often known as the 'boiler-plate' clauses.

3.4.4 Definitions

Most agreements contain a list of defined terms. There are a number of ways of using a definition. A definition is generally a shortform to avoid repetition of a particular word or phrase.

The first defined term in an agreement usually relates to the parties to the agreement. Each party is defined and that term is then used throughout the agreement when referring to that party, a typical example being 'Buyer' and 'Seller'. Wherever possible, terms which appear similar should be avoided, thus 'Licensor' and 'Licensee' could be replaced by 'Owner' and 'Company'. Definitions such as these for the parties are sometimes referred to as nicknames or shorthand definitions. These defined terms are given a capital letter when they are being used in their defined sense.

Defined terms are also used to specify exactly what a particular term means. This sets out the exact parameters of a term. This can be particularly important where the rights clause of an agreement is concerned. For example, a video distribution contract may provide that:

'Rights' means the right to manufacture, distribute, exploit and sell videos in any audio-visual configuration, and in any medium now known or subsequently created

In such a case the reference to audio-visual configuration and to any medium may be considered too wide. The purpose of the definition is to set the

---

1   See **3.2.1**.

parameters of the particular word's meaning, but the definition may none the less be open to negotiation.

Other definitions expand or reduce a word's meaning. A defined term may specifically 'include' other items or matters within the definition of a word. Equally, a definition may state that it 'does not include' certain other items or matters. For example:

'Drink'   means non-alcoholic drinks including milk drinks but does not include carbonated drinks

3.4.5   Obligations

A contract should set out the rights and obligations of both parties. Paragraph **3.2** considers the main points that create some of the rights and obligations of the parties. The obligation that is central to most contracts is the promise for payment by one party in return for the grant of rights from the other party. The agreement may then go on to set out a number of other issues such as when payment is due and how it should be paid. The agreement will also contain clauses dealing with a number of other obligations and rights that have been agreed.

Where an obligation is not absolute part of the negotiation of the terms of the agreement may centre around how certain obligations can be qualified. Once an obligation is qualified, it is easier for the party subject to the qualification to argue that it has done its bit to achieve the derived result. Clearly, where a party feels there is no prospect of it ever fulfilling an obligation, however it is qualified, it should not undertake the obligation. None the less, there are a number of terms commonly used to mitigate the effect of absolute obligations. Instead of creating an absolute obligation to do something, varying degrees of obligation can be created. This usually involves a 'best' or 'reasonable' endeavours obligation.

The term 'best endeavours' means that the persons concerned are:

> 'bound to take all those steps in their power which are capable of producing the desired result . . . being steps which a prudent, determined and reasonable owner acting in his own interests and desiring to achieve that result would take.'[1]

Where the obligation is to use 'reasonable' endeavours the obligation is a lower one. In such a case, the balance is between the obligation on the one hand and other commercial considerations on the other. This is a lesser duty and, where it proves difficult to perform, is assumed to involve a lower degree of expenditure in the attempt to perform the obligations.

The stringent effects of compliance with an absolute obligation may be mitigated by including provisions in an agreement which provide that any breach of obligation must be a 'material' breach. A material breach in the context of the agreement may be defined; it may be left to the parties to determine if the eventuality arises and it may even be that one party to the agreement is left to decide if the breach is material if it occurs. Breach or non-compliance with an obligation or of other terms in an agreement can also be dealt with in the termination provisions of the agreement.[2]

---

1   *IBM UK Limited v Rockware Glass Limited* [1980] FSR 335.
2   See **3.4.13**.

3.4.6 Conditions

A condition is a term of the agreement which must be satisfied before the agreement as a whole or part of the agreement comes into effect. A condition precedent in an agreement imposes a specific requirement on a party which must be fulfilled before part or all of the agreement comes into effect. This is despite the fact that the parties have signed the agreement. Conditions precedent may be used where, for example, a sportsman is joining a new club but has to receive a satisfactory medical examination or immigration matters need to be completed before he starts his employment. Usually, there will be some obligation upon the party who has to meet the condition to use their best or reasonable endeavours to do so. There may also be a time-limit within which the condition has to be met.

At common law, a breach of condition in an agreement allows the injured party to terminate the agreement. The common law position is usually reflected in the termination provisions.

3.4.7 Representations and warranties

A representation is a pre-contractual statement made by one party and relied upon by the other party which induces that party to enter the agreement. These representations are often incorporated into the contract as express terms of the contract by way of warranties given by the parties to the agreement. A false representation is only actionable under the Misrepresentation Act 1967 if the representation was of a material fact, which was intended to induce the other party to enter into the contract and did induce them to enter the contract. The party claiming the misrepresentation must show some reliance on the representation.

Misrepresentation actions fall into the categories of fraudulent, negligent and innocent misrepresentation. There is also a common law action for negligent misstatement.[1]

A warranty in a contract is a statement which has been incorporated in a contract as one of its terms. If the warranty is breached the claim is easier to establish than a normal breach of contract claim. A warranty claim is often supported by an indemnity provision.[2] Most agreements describe certain terms of the agreement as warranties and representations. The difference between representations and warranties, and the reason they are described as such in the contract, is in the remedies available to the injured party for a breach of warranty as opposed to a misrepresentation.

A misrepresentation may permit the injured party to rescind the agreement or, if rescission is no longer available, a claim for damages for the misrepresentation. Damages for a misrepresentation are those which are needed to put the plaintiff in the position he would have been in had he not entered the contract. The plaintiff is not, in a misrepresentation case, able to recover damages based on the position he would have been in if the misrepresentation were in fact true. Thus damages for misrepresentation do not cover the plaintiff for loss of profit or

---

1   This is based on the case of *Hedley Byrne & Co Ltd v Heller and Partners Ltd* [1967] AC 465.
2   See **3.4.8**.

bargain. A breach of warranty gives a right to contractual damages but no right to rescind the agreement, the measure of damages being the amount of money required to put the plaintiff in the position he would have been in if the warranty were correct.

Many contracts allow the injured party to terminate the agreement if any of the representations and warranties turn out to be incorrect. This means the injured party does not actually have to establish that he relied upon the representation. The contract may also provide a method of calculating the damages for a breach of such a term.

3.4.8   Indemnities

An indemnity is a term of a contract that can, if enforced, enable the 'injured' party to claim payment of any expenses it incurs if there is a breach of warranty by the other party. The indemnity applies whether or not the injured party is subsequently able to establish the basis of its claim and prove the amount of its loss. An indemnity provision is a strong additional safeguard to the warranties in an agreement providing as it does for full repayment of costs and losses.

A breach of warranty claim only entitles the injured party to claim its losses for breach of contract and those losses claimed must be mitigated. Indemnities are common in commercial agreements and provide a useful means for a party to the contract to recover the full amount of loss and expenses suffered. There is no duty to mitigate. The indemnity provisions are, however, only as good as the finances of the party giving the indemnity. Very often liability under an indemnity or for breach of warranty is capped in the agreement.

Although an indemnity between two commercial enterprises is common, a company must carefully consider the imposition of an indemnity provision in a contract with an individual. The individual may not have the means to pay, in which case the indemnity is effectively worthless. Alternatively, the clause may not be enforceable on grounds of restraint of trade or undue influence.

3.4.9   Common warranties

There are a number of warranties commonly encountered in commercial agreements. Some warranties relate to specific intellectual property matters, other warranties are more general in nature and not concerned with the intellectual property aspects of the agreement. Some typical contractual warranties are as follows:

- neither party has entered into any conflicting agreements;
- the parties have full authority to enter the agreement;
- neither party will do anything to derogate from the rights granted in the agreement;
- neither party will incur any liability on the other's behalf;
- each party will comply with all applicable national and international rules and regulations;
- each party will indemnify the other against any claims for breach of warranty.

3.4.10 Limiting liability

As part of the drafting and negotiation process, many contracts will attempt to exclude and limit the parties' liability to each other in the event of a breach of contract. Part of this process centres on the scope of the representations and warranties contained in the agreement and may involve the deletion or the amendment of those terms. There may be a specific minimum and maximum limit placed on claims arising from the agreement. The maximum liability may operate to limit the amount recoverable for a breach of contract under the common law measure of contractual damages. The minimum limit may set a de minimis level under which a claim cannot be brought but once the minimum is reached the whole amount may be recoverable. The agreement may also specify time limits within which a claim must be brought. The statutory limitation period for claims may be reduced from the six-year period for breach of contract claims to a shorter period. Any liability is thus effectively extinguished once the agreed term ends.

In addition to the contractual limitation, one or both parties may have to insure against specified risks.

3.4.11 Accounting provisions

Many agreements contain ongoing payment terms and obligations. Such commitments often arise where the agreement contains royalty provisions but may equally apply in ongoing agency and distribution contracts. Whilst it is important to establish precise payment terms and the basis upon which payments are made, the time and manner of accounting for monies due should also be set out in the agreement. This usually involves setting a specific date during the course of a year when accounts have to be drawn up to establish any payments due. The payments usually then have to be made a specified number of days after the accounts have been drawn up.

A typical term may state that accounts are drawn up twice yearly, on 30 June and 31 December. Accounts may be drawn up four times a year, in which case the additional quarter days are usually 31 March and 30 September. The accounts, along with any payment due, are then sent not later than 90 or 60 days after the accounts are drawn up. This second period should not be unduly long. Modern computer-based accounting systems should be able to draw accounts up quickly once the accounting period is over, thus allowing payments to be made quickly. The person to whom the account and payment should be sent must also be set out in the agreement.

There is then often a limited time and right to challenge the account. There may also be a specific contractual right to audit the paying party, although this right may be limited to no more than once in a given year. Where there are deficiencies in the accounts which exceed a specified percentage of the amount due, the party at fault should pay for the cost of conducting the audit as well as paying the deficit.

The accounting provisions in the agreement may be affected by matters such as the payment and recoupment of advances under the other financial terms of the agreement. The agreement may have a stipulated minimum guaranteed income which may also affect the amount of payment due with the accounts. The accounting provisions may also allow the retention of a reserve against future liabilities, such as for returned goods or future expenditure. Where monies are due from overseas exploitation, the agreement may also contain currency conversion terms so that the foreign currency is converted into the accounting currency.

The accounting provisions must be as carefully scrutinised as the method of calculating payments due under the agreement. Royalty and profit share provisions in agreements can be particularly sophisticated and must be carefully scrutinised.[1]

3.4.12 Intellectual property aspects

An agreement may need to deal with the assignment or licensing of various intellectual property rights ('IPR'),[2] typically registered and unregistered trade marks and copyrights.[3] Although the essential terms of ownership or right to use the IPR must be included,[4] there will also be important provisions regarding the protection of the IPR. Exactly who should take action to protect the IPR should be clearly set out to ensure that, where practicable, the IPR are protected. Accordingly, there may be an obligation to notify the other party of any infringements which come to its attention; to assist in prosecuting any action; and (in the case of the IPR's owner) an obligation to take action to protect the IPR. The contract may go on to deal with the division of income from successful actions as well as how expenses should be recouped. In the case of licenses, the IPR owner may wish to exclude any rights the licensee may have to take action for infringements if the licensed IPR.[5]

3.4.13 Termination provisions

When and why a contract ends are important matters to deal with in the agreement. There are a number of aspects to this.

(a) Expiry of term

The agreement may end simply because the agreed 'term' has ended or, in accordance with the terms of the contract a notice has been served bringing the agreement to a close. Such termination does not usually arise because of any breach of contract. The agreement should, even where the agreement ends naturally, deal with the final accounts and any other matters such as the return of materials which formed the basis of the agreement. There may need to be a defined sell-off period for goods that have already been manufactured.

Some agreements, even though certain rights have ended, create rights that can continue to be dealt with and exploited. A typical example is the filmed recording of an event. When the agreement ends, the rights in the film may remain with the broadcaster or production company who, if it continues to sell and exploit the product of the contract, may be obliged to continue to account to the event

1   Payment terms are discussed further at **3.2.6** above.
2   See **4.12, 4.13** and **4.25.9**.
3   See generally Chapter 4.
4   See **4.12.4**.
5   Trade Marks Act 1994, s 30.

organiser or rights holder. However, in this situation, once the contract has terminated, the event organiser or rights holder is able to grant the rights to another broadcaster or production company for the next event.

Agreements that have simply licensed rights for the period of the agreement may specifically deal with the return of those rights (along with any improvements) and materials at the end of the agreement. This is common in agreements where the rights granted may be the right to manufacture or distribute a product. In such agreements, there is often a sell-off period during which products can continue to be sold for a short period on a non-exclusive basis.

(b) Terminating events

Where there is a breach of contract by one party the agreement will usually contain express provisions allowing termination of the agreement. In such a case, there may be a notice requirement before the agreement can end. Some typical examples of events which can trigger termination or the right to terminate an agreement include:

–   failure by a party to pay an amount due under the agreement within a specified period of time from the amount becoming due;
–   any of the representations or warranties in the agreement turning out to be incorrect or untrue;
–   a failure by a party to perform its obligations under the agreement;
–   a party becomes unable to pay its debts as they fall due, is declared insolvent or makes arrangements with its creditors;
–   a party ceases to carry on the business which is the subject matter of the agreement;
–   a change of control of the company.

If such an event occurs, the innocent or non-defaulting party may be given a number of options. These usually include the right to serve a notice that:

–   terminates the agreement with immediate effect; or
–   gives the other party time to remedy the breach, failing which the agreement ends.

3.4.14   Effect of termination

Once the agreement is terminated then as far as the future is concerned all but certain specified rights and obligations will cease to have effect. Rights and obligations before termination may be specifically preserved and continue to have effect. Any rights that the parties have to damages or breach of contract will also be specifically reserved.

3.4.15   Post-termination restrictions

Where the agreement ends either prematurely or in the normal course of events there may be some specific restrictive covenants. These are frequently found in employment contracts and concern matters such as competitive activities and the use of confidential information. Whether or not any restrictions are enforceable under UK or European law depends on the particular circumstances.

3.4.16   Boiler-plate

Boiler-plate clauses are those clauses which are often considered to be the standard clauses in a contract. Boiler-plate provides the finishing touches to the main terms of the contract. Boiler-plate essentially either restates the common law or else attempts to impose more precise obligations than the common law itself provides in various circumstances. Some important boiler-plate clauses are considered below.

Force majeure

A term in the contract dealing with force majeure is intended to deal with circumstances where contractual performance is no longer possible because of events outside the control of the parties to the contract. The expression covers diverse matters outside the parties' control such as acts of God, war, strikes and embargoes. The occurrence of such an event may operate to frustrate the contract. The common law application of the frustration doctrine creates uncertainties because it is not always clear what events frustrate the contract or indeed when an event becomes a frustrating one. If there is no specific clause, the Law Reform (Frustrated Contracts) Act 1943 may apply.

In *Gamerco SA v Fair Warning Ltd*,[1] a contract for Guns'n'Roses to perform at a rock concert was frustrated because the stadium in which they were to perform was unsafe. The plaintiffs in this case recovered advances paid to the defendants on account of ticket sales. A similar situation could occur in relation to a sports event where the stadium was not fit for use. It is possible to insure against such occurrences. Ill health or death of an individual may frustrate a contract (*Condor v Barron Knights*).[2]

A well-drafted force majeure clause should:

–   set out in general terms what the parties understand by the term force majeure;
–   oblige the affected party to inform the other party to the contract of the event of force majeure, in particular the nature, extent, effect and likely duration of the event. It may also oblige the affected party to take reasonable steps to mitigate any loss;
–   state that if force majeure applies the affected party is not in breach of contract and that the contract is suspended until the event ends; and
–   either resume performance once the event has ended; or
–   set out a continuous period of time after which the event permits the parties to give notice ending the contract.

On termination in this manner the agreement should set out the effects of termination.[3] If the contract is a standard term agreement, or one party deals as a consumer, a force majeure clause as an attempt by the party relying on the clause not to perform the contract is subject to the reasonableness test set out in the Unfair Contract Terms Act 1977, s 3.

---

1   [1995] EMLR 263.
2   [1966] 1 WLR 87.
3   See **3.4.13** above.

Notices

An agreement usually contains a clause making express provisions for service of documents and notices under the contract. Certain clauses, particularly the options, force majeure and termination provisions, require one party to serve notice on the other to acquire or reserve specified rights. For absolute contractual certainty a term that states where to serve, how to serve and when a notice is deemed served on each of the parties to the agreement is useful.

Severance

It is possible for a court to sever an offending clause from a contract. A clause that allows a court to strike out any clauses it considers invalid is often inserted by the parties to alleviate the risk that the court will declare the whole agreement unenforceable or void. Severance clauses have only limited value as a court will not rewrite an agreement to give it commercial efficacy, particularly where the offending clause is fundamental to the agreement as a whole.

Assignment

It is possible to transfer the rights created under an agreement. Section 136 of the Law of Property Act 1925 permits the assignment of all debts and choses in action as long as the assignment is in writing, is signed by the assignor, is absolute, and written notice is given to anyone against whom the assignor could enforce the assigned rights.

The obligations of the assignor cannot, with any real degree of certainty, be assigned unless the other party to the contract agrees or the contract is novated. A novation involves a new contract being substituted for an existing contract. Typically this involves the rights and obligations under an existing contract being assumed by a new third party. The rights and obligations under the existing agreement are cancelled by the novation in favour of the new agreement, the consideration being the discharge of the old contract and the undertaking of the rights and obligations under the new contract by the new party.

Because of the general freedom to transfer the rights under an agreement a term is often included restricting this right. There may be complete freedom to assign, but it is more likely that a party with any bargaining power will seek to restrict the other party's ability to assign their rights. Thus assignment may be: prohibited; prohibited without prior written consent; or prohibited without prior written consent, such consent not to be unreasonably withheld. Despite any such prohibitions, there may be a term that none the less permits assignment to associated companies within a group. There may also be provisions which deal with a change of control of the company, avoiding assignment by the back door. In such circumstances, there may be a specific right to terminate the agreement.

Choice of law and jurisdiction

Choice of law and jurisdiction clauses govern which court and law govern any dispute that arises between the parties. The parties have a wide discretion to choose the court and law to govern the contract.

Arbitration and ADR

Arbitration is a useful method of resolving disputes quickly, cost effectively and confidentially. An arbitration clause in an agreement is binding and ensures that disputes covered by the arbitration clause are referred to arbitration. Alternative Dispute Resolution (ADR) involves the parties attempting to achieve a compromise through the services of a mediator. ADR is not generally binding on the parties and either party may, having agreed to ADR, withdraw from it at any time.

COMMON PROBLEMS AND REMEDIES

3.5 INTRODUCTION

Commercial agreements can raise various issues that lead to problems of enforceability and may leave contracts open to challenge. In the business of sport, common problems arise from the restraint of trade doctrine. EC law poses unique problems which may affect the drafting and the enforceability of a wide variety of contracts. This section considers some common problems as well as various issues arising out of breaches of contract.

3.6 CONTRACTS WITH MINORS

The sports industry attracts young aspirants. Whilst all inexperienced sportsmen need to be carefully and independently advised, minors need special consideration. A minor is a person under 18 years of age. Any agreement with a minor is voidable at the instance of the minor on attaining the age of majority.

However, it is less likely that the contract will be avoided at that time if the sportsman has either positively affirmed the contract (for example, by continuing to fulfil his contractual obligations) or done nothing to dispute the contract within a reasonable time ('reasonable time' will vary according to the circumstances). The same will apply if the contract is manifestly advantageous to the sportsman, or if the sportsman had taken independent legal and financial advice prior to signing and thus can be said to have understood fully the terms of the agreement. In general, the court will consider all relevant circumstances, and it is by no means the case that a contract can be avoided solely because the minor has reached his eighteenth birthday.

To reduce the risk of the contract being terminated, the terms of the contract should be reasonable and allow a reasonable financial return for the minor. The contract should be for the minor's benefit so that it provides in some way for adequate training and other aids to a successful career. In addition, the terms of the contract should be properly explained to the minor, and preferably also to his parents or guardians, so that there can be no scope for future misunderstanding.

Where the contract provides for a guarantor of the performance of the minor's obligations, and the contract is held to be unenforceable against the minor, the guarantor is not obliged to fulfil the contract but may find himself liable to compensate the other party for loss caused by the non-performance of obligations by the sportsman. A guarantor should take independent advice on his obligations before committing himself and should ensure that those obligations cease when the minor attains the age of majority. As a rule, no one should guarantee the performance of a third party if he can reasonably avoid doing so.

3.7 UNDUE INFLUENCE

A court will not hold someone to a bargain if undue influence can be established. This is an equitable doctrine. If a person enters an agreement where undue influence is presumed, the inference is that no free and deliberate judgement has been exercised upon entering the agreement and the agreement will be set aside.

A presumption of undue influence often arises with the existence of a fiduciary duty. The influence involved will be of a psychological or mental nature and will be an undue influence when the individual involved believes he does not have a free choice. As a result of the undue influence, the person feels obliged to sign the agreement. There are two types of undue influence. First, there are those cases of actual or express undue influence, and secondly, cases where undue influence is presumed. In a number of cases dealing with the entertainment industry involving undue influence, it is this latter category of cases, ie those where undue influence is presumed, which have troubled the courts. Similar situations may arise in sport, where young athletes sign oppressive contracts.

In order for the presumption to arise, the party seeking to avoid the contract must prove that the other party involved acquired an influence over his mind which precluded his free consent. In cases where there is a fiduciary relationship, undue influence is presumed. A fiduciary relationship exists where one party relies on the guidance or advice of the other. There are certain categories of relationships which are by their very nature fiduciary. For example, the relationships between solicitor and client, doctor and patient, and trustee and beneficiary are all fiduciary relationships. In the sports and entertainment businesses, this category may include the relationship between a manager and an individual sportsman.

Recent cases concerning undue influence have been concerned particularly with the relationship between husbands and wives and lenders.[1] Where undue influence is presumed, rather than proved, the party seeking to avoid the contract must prove that the contract is manifestly disadvantageous to that party.

It is possible to rebut the presumption most easily by showing that the weaker party took independent advice. In the context of a sportsman's contract, this should involve the terms of the agreement being explained to the sportsman by a truly independent third party adviser. One solicitor should not act for both parties in a negotiation (to avoid any conflict of interest) even if there appears to be complete accord between the parties. A separate solicitor from a different firm should be instructed. If the presumption of undue influence is to be rebutted successfully, it will also help if the independent adviser is experienced in the appropriate area of law. The 'weaker' party should also understand the terms of the agreement.

The relationship between sportsman and manager is one that may give rise to a presumption of undue influence. It may also be possible for the relationship

---

1   See, for example, *Barclays Bank v O'Brien* [1994] 1 AC 150.

between a sportsman and his trainer/coach or club and employer to give rise to such a presumption.

3.8 RESTRAINT OF TRADE

Restraint of trade is usually understood to mean or to involve a restriction on a person and his future ability to carry on a trade or profession. Such restrictions were originally regarded as unacceptable because of the monopolies they created in providing services or skills in industry. Restraint of trade makes all contracts or covenants which restrict trade unenforceable unless they are reasonable as between the parties and not injurious to the public interest. A distinction must be drawn between those contracts which are in restraint of trade and those which regulate the normal commercial relations between the parties to a contract.

In the context of sport, the doctrine may apply in a number of different contexts such as disciplinary procedures, employment contracts, endorsement and sponsorship agreements.

The present law is based on the speeches of the House of Lords in *Esso Petroleum v Harper's Garage*.[1] This case set out some of the main principles of the doctrine of restraint of trade.

(1) Is the contract in restraint of trade?

The House of Lords refrained from laying down a rigid approach as to what constitutes a restraint of trade and stated that 'the doctrine of restraint of trade is one to be applied to factual situations with a broad and flexible rule of reason'.

At one end of the scale, there are contracts which 'merely regulate the normal commercial relations between parties' and, at the other end of the scale, there are contracts where the doctrine undoubtedly does apply. Examples of the latter include contracts where an employee restricts his ability to compete against his employer after he has left his employment, and contracts where the seller of a business agrees not to compete against the buyer of that business. The contracts with which this work is concerned, such as governing bodies' rules and employment contracts, may also fall within this category. When considering a contract, all of the terms are important. If 'contractual restrictions appear unnecessary or to be reasonably capable of enforcement in an oppressive manner, then they must be justified before they can be enforced'.[2]

One way of looking at this is to consider whether the agreement is aimed at the absorption or the sterilisation of a sportsman's services. A certain amount of protection is permissible, but it must be limited to the amount necessary for the protection of a commercial interest.

(2) Does it protect a legitimate interest?

The term which is in restraint of trade must protect a legitimate interest. What amounts to a legitimate interest for a sports business in imposing restrictions in a

---

1   [1968] AC 269.
2   *Schroeder Music Publishing Co Ltd v Macaulay (formerly Instone)* [1974] 1 WLR 1308, [1974] 3 All ER 616, HL.

contract varies. However, it seems that the commercial needs of the company in its desire to sell as much product as possible will be paramount. Such commercial considerations relate to the need to make a profit and a high quality product, and the ability to make informed and reliable business decisions based on the availability of products, as well as the ability to recover its investment in the contracted individuals.

A sports company, like any other business, needs to be able to plan ahead for marketing, manufacturing and distribution purposes. Similar considerations will apply to companies involved in the entertainment business where exclusively signed performers seek to challenge those agreements. These considerations may all amount to a legitimate business interest.

(3) Is it reasonable between the parties and is it in the public interest?

The term must also be reasonable between the parties and in the public interest.[1] In *Nordenfelt*, it was also stated that the plaintiff's motives in challenging the contract are not material.

If a term is to be reasonable between the parties, the restraint must be no more than is necessary for the adequate protection of the person in whose favour it is created. The balance is between protecting an investment and achieving a good return, and allowing the sportsman to pursue his career.

A number of terms should be scrutinised, for example the duration of the agreement, particularly with regard to any options to extend the term; provisions for assignment of the obligations and the ownership of rights created under the agreement; the consideration involved; provisions for terminating the agreement; and any obligations to promote and manufacture the product of the agreement. The fact that certain terms are not included in the agreement may be important, as is the relative bargaining position of the parties, their age and the availability of professional advice. The test laid down in *Schroeder* was 'is the agreement taken as a whole fair?'.

Not only must an agreement be reasonable as between the parties, but it should also satisfy the public policy test. The guiding principle is that 'everyone should be able to earn a living and give to the public the fruits of his particular abilities'. As long as the agreement does not conflict with this aim, it will satisfy the public policy requirement.

When considering an agreement it is necessary, first, to decide whether the contract is one that attracts the doctrine of restraint of trade at all. Secondly, if it is established that the contract is in restraint of trade it must then be determined whether it protects a legitimate interest and whether it is reasonable.

(4) Effect of an agreement being in restraint of trade

If a contract is found to be in restraint of trade, it appears that the contract is voidable or unenforceable.[2] A voidable or unenforceable contract ceases to exist for future purposes at the date of judgment.

---

1   *Nordenfelt v Maxim Nordenfelt Guns and Ammunition Co Ltd* [1894] AC 535.
2   *Schroeder Music Publishing Co Ltd v Macaulay (formerly Instone)* [1974] 1 WLR 1308, [1974] 3 All ER 616, HL.

It is possible that an offending clause could be severed from the contract. Severance involves separating the void part of the contract from the valid part. In principle, the courts will only apply the 'blue pencil test' and sever an illegal promise if this can be done by cutting words out of the contract so that the meaning of the remaining part of the contract is not affected. The court will not rewrite the contract, although it will delete offending terms provided that the other terms of the contract can remain sensibly intact. In principle, with exclusive entertainment contracts, the terms on which the parties will seek a declaration will be central to the contract and, accordingly, if the court is unwilling to rewrite the contract, the severance of those terms will leave no contract at all.

In claims involving restraint of trade and undue influence, it is common for the defendants to allege laches and/or acquiescence in the action.

Laches involves a delay in coming to court to seek a remedy for the alleged wrongdoing. The delay must not be one that takes the plaintiff outside the limitation period. However, even within a limitation period, action should be taken as promptly as possible. It is important to consider the length of the delay and the nature of acts done during the interval before action is taken which might cause a balance of injustice to one party or the other in the remedy sought.

In principle, a person should not be deprived of his legal rights unless he has acted in a way which would make it fraudulent for him to assert his rights.

The restraint of trade doctrine has been invoked in a number of cases involving performers and writers and in cases involving sportsmen as well as in frequent cases involving employees.

The application of the doctrine in sport is discussed further elsewhere.[1]

3.9   EC LAW AND COMMERCIAL CONTRACTS

3.9.1   Introduction

This part briefly considers some other issues that affect the negotiation, drafting and implementation of agreements within the EC and the EEA. The relevant issues relate to:

–   Articles 28(30)–30(36), which prohibit restrictions imposed by import and export controls and measures having equivalent effect on the free movement of goods. These articles are particularly important where IP rights are concerned;
–   Article 81(85), which prohibits agreements, decisions and concerted practices between undertakings which may affect trade between member states and which have as their object or effect the prevention, restriction or distortion of trade within the common market; and
–   Article 82(86) of the EC Treaty, which prohibits the abuse of a dominant position within the common market or a substantial part of it.

---

1   See **5.9**.

In addition to these articles the effect of Art 39(48) of the EC Treaty may be felt where contracts for the provision of personal services are at issue. This article prohibits restrictions on the free movement of workers between member states within the EC. Its effect has recently been felt in the *Bosman* decision[1] where restrictions on the movement of footballers between member states were held to be unlawful.

The effect of Arts 28–30(30–36), 81(85) and 82(86) can create a conflict between, for example, the desire of a rights owner to control the exploitation of its rights and the circulation of products manufactured using the protection those rights give. This control may be asserted by the rights owner contractually, for example by placing restrictions on the territory of the agreement, or by relying on national legislation to control imports of goods. This section looks at the underlying principles and subsequent chapters deal with their application to specific sports agreements.[2]

3.9.2 Free movement of goods

It is possible for national intellectual property rights to restrict the flow of goods around member states of the EC. For example, a company in the UK may try to rely on UK trade mark law to prevent a German company from importing goods from Germany into the UK by claiming the imported goods infringe its UK trade mark on the goods. In such a case, Art 81(85) would not apply because there is no relevant agreement open to challenge.

Article 28(30) prohibits such restrictions on imports between member states as being incompatible with the free movement of goods. Some derogations from this principle are permitted under Art 30(36), which permits the 'protection of industrial or commercial property rights' as long as they do not amount to 'arbitrary discrimination' or 'a disguised restriction on trade'.

The European Court of Justice has developed a doctrine that allows an intellectual property rights owner to rely only on national laws to control the exploitation of rights in limited circumstances. The rights owner must establish that the action he is taking is necessary to control the 'specific subject matter' of the right in question. This concept is allied to the doctrine of 'exhaustion of rights'. These two concepts attempt to balance the aims of the treaty in ensuring the free movement of goods with the interests of the rights owners.

3.9.3 Intellectual property: specific subject matter

The idea that intellectual property rights have a specific subject matter has been applied to trade marks as follows:

> '[the specific subject matter] is the guarantee that the owner of the trade mark has the exclusive right to use that trade mark for the purpose of putting goods into circulation for the first time and is, therefore, intended to protect him against

---

1 Discussed at **5.9.3**.
2 Broadcasting (Chapter 9); sponsorship (**6.2**); merchandising (**6.4**); ticketing (**8.4**); agency (Chapter 7).

competitors wishing to take advantage of the status and reputation of the trade mark by selling products illegally bearing that trade mark.'[1]

The specific subject matter as far as copyright is concerned is slightly different because of the diverse nature of the right. Holyoak and Torremans in *Intellectual Property Law* (Butterworths) suggest the specific subject matter of copyright is split into non-performance copyrights and performance copyrights. The ability of a rights owner to control subsequent use of a performance copyright is much greater than their ability to control the use of non-performance copyrights. For example, a copyright owner cannot stop the importation of videos from France to Germany where the videos have been lawfully marketed in France.[2]

However, it appears that with a right such as the right to authorise the broadcasting of a film on national television, the rights owner can rely on copyright to prevent the film being shown. This is so even though a film has already been shown with the rights owner's permission on national television in another member state. The specific subject matter with the performing right in a film is the right to restrict each performance of the film.[3] The specific subject matter with non-performing rights is the protection of an author's moral rights and the reward of the author for his creative effort.

3.9.4   Intellectual property and the exhaustion of rights

Once goods have been first lawfully marketed in a member state the rights owner cannot rely on his intellectual property rights to control what happens next to those goods. His rights are 'exhausted'. This means non-infringing goods can travel freely around member states. The position noted above in relation to the performance copyright is different, as the rights owner can control subsequent exploitation of his rights.

3.9.5   Competition law

Competition law may affect an agreement. The position with the free movement of goods provisions leads some rights owners and manufacturers to try to control the circulation of goods by other means. Article 81(85)(1) gives some examples of agreements, decisions and concerted practices which 'have as their object or effect the prevention, restriction or distortion of competition within the common market . . .', in particular those which:

(a) directly or indirectly fix purchase or selling prices or any other trading conditions;
(b) limit or control production, markets, technical development or investment;
(c) share markets or sources of supply;
(d) apply dissimilar conditions to equivalent transactions with other trading parties, thereby placing them at a competitive disadvantage;
(e) make the conclusion of contracts subject to acceptance by the other parties of supplementary obligations which by their nature or according to commercial usage have no connection with the subject matter of such contracts.

---

1   *Centrafarm BV v Winthrop BV* [1974] ECR 1183.
2   *Deutsche Grammophon v Metro* [1971] ECR 487.
3   *Coditel S A v Cine Vog Films S A (No 1)* [1980] ECR 881.

These may be specific contractual restrictions imposed on distributors and licensees or less formal agreements or practices with similar aims. The nature of intellectual property rights may also cause a conflict with the fundamental aims of the Treaty. The owner of intellectual property rights enjoys certain exclusive rights which can be used to prevent others exploiting the rights in question. Patents, with their extensive monopoly protection, can cause competition law problems. It is possible that a rights owner licenses or exploits his rights on such onerous or restrictive terms that trade between member states is inhibited. EC Law recognises that a balance must be struck between the rights owner's interests and the interests of the common market.

For competition law purposes the EC competition authorities distinguish between the existence and the exploitation (or exercise) of intellectual property rights. It is the exploitation of rights that is likely to cause the competition law problems. Problems may arise in a number of circumstances, for example: where a licence agreement contains terms which prohibit competition once the agreement ends; export bans during the course of the agreement; and extensive exclusivity provisions.

An agreement that offends Art 81(85) is void. The agreement may be saved if:

– it is between a parent and a subsidiary, as they are taken as one undertaking for the purposes of Art 81(85);
– it is an agency agreement covered by the Notice of 24 December 1962 on Exclusive Dealing Contracts with Commercial Agents;
– it is 'de minimis' and thus covered by the Notice on Agreements of Minor Importance;[1]
– negative clearance is given by the commission stating that Art 81(85) does not apply;
– the commission grants an individual exemption under Art 81(85);
– it is covered by and drafted to comply with a relevant block exemption.

There are block exemptions covering a number of matters such as franchising,[2] exclusive purchasing agreements[3] and exclusive distribution agreements.[4] Relevant agreements must be drafted to comply with the block exemption. For example, under the distribution block exemption an agreement may be drafted that prohibits active but not passive unsolicited sales outside the territory of the agreement.

3.9.6 Particular examples

Cases referred to and investigated by the Commission have involved sponsorship and merchandising;[5] tickets;[6] broadcasting[7] and even disciplinary procedures, rules and regulations.[8]

---

1   OJ 1986 C231/2.
2   Regulation 4087/88.
3   Regulation 1984/83.
4   Regulation 1983/83.
5   *Dunlop Slazenger v EC Commission*, T–43/92: [1994] ECR II–441; Danish Tennis Federation, 1996 OJ C138/7.
6   *Panwels Travel v FIFA Local Organising Committee Italia* 1990 [1994] 5 CMLR 253.
7   *Metropole Television SD v EC Commission* [1996] ECR II–649.
8   *Bosman* (discussed at **5.9.3**) and *Wilander and Novacek v Tobin and Jude* [1997] 1 Lloyd's Rep 195.

3.9.7   Competition Act 1998

The provisions of the Competition Act 1998 mirror the provisions of Arts 81(85) and 82(86) enacting similar prohibitions on anti-competitive behaviour within the UK.[1] This legislation is likely to affect all types of commercial agreements within the UK.

3.10   REMEDIES

3.10.1   Damages

General damages

Damages recovered for breach of contract are those which arise 'fairly and naturally ... from such breach of contract or such as may reasonably be supposed to be in the contemplation of the parties at the time of the contract'.[2] The general principle is that, where a contract has been breached and the damage is not too remote under the rule in *Hadley v Baxendale*, the innocent party should be awarded damages to place it in the same position as if the contract had been performed.

Loss of profits and wasted expenditure

A claim may be made for loss of profits or for wasted expenditure. Both heads cannot be claimed and an election must be made. In certain circumstances, a claim for wasted expenditure may be better than one for loss of profits, which, particularly in the entertainment and sports business, may be very difficult to prove.[3]

Loss of publicity

There is an exception to the normal rule that a breach of contract gives rise only to a claim for damages for the loss arising from the breach. An artist engaged to perform is promised both a salary and the opportunity to enhance his reputation.[4]

Accordingly, damages for breach of contract may be awarded to reflect both loss of earnings and loss of publicity. The damages in such cases are awarded on the basis of *Hadley v Baxendale*, so they must be in the contemplation of the parties at the time of the agreement. A court may consider the stage of the artist's career, as well as the prominence and popularity of the venue. The publicity right appears to extend to performers as well as to writers and directors. In addition, professional sportsmen may be able to claim for loss of publicity if they lose the chance to compete in particular competitions or on specific occasions.

---

1   Competition Act 1998. See further Tim Frazer and Stephen Hornsby *The Competition Act 1998: A Practical Guide* (Jordans, 1999).
2   *Hadley v Baxendale* (1854) 9 Exch 341.
3   See further *Anglia TV v Reed* [1972] 1 QB 60, and *CCC Films v Impact Quadrant Films Ltd* [1985] 1 QB 1461.
4   *Withers v General Theatre Corpn Ltd* [1933] 2 KB 536.

Inducement to breach contract

A typical claim for inducement to breach a contract arises where a third party attempts to entice someone away from his contract, perhaps by offering better terms. Alternatively, a claim may occur where a party cancels a contract with the result that a third party is no longer required to perform a service ancillary to the first contract.

It is an actionable wrong to induce a party to a contract to breach the contract. There are four elements to the tort:

(1) a third party knows that a contract exists;
(2) he persuades or induces or in some way acts so as to cause a breach of contract by one party to the detriment of the other party;
(3) a breach of contract directly attributable to that interference results; and
(4) damage is caused to the other party.

3.10.2 Enforcement of negative covenants

A contract which contains express negative terms or covenants may be enforced by injunction. However, an injunction to enforce a negative covenant will not be granted where it indirectly requires specific performance of a contract for personal services (such as a recording contract or a footballer's contract) because, effectively, an individual then has no choice but to go back to work for the 'employer'.

A sportsman may be restrained from performing for an event organiser if he has already agreed to perform for another and nobody else.[1] The court cannot compel the sportsman to perform under the original contract, but it can stop him performing elsewhere.

Where the terms of a contract are in restraint of trade, no injunction will be granted requiring performance of the contract. However, where the contract is a reasonable one, the court will grant an injunction unless in so doing it would amount to an order to perform the positive obligations in the contract (to work, record or play), as long as the employee or artist is left with some means of earning a living. This involves a careful evaluation of whether the employee or artist can actually work elsewhere or has to remain idle. In *Warren v Mendy*,[2] a case involving the sport of boxing, the court set out the appropriate principles:

(1) a court ought not to enforce the performance of negative obligations if that will compel performance of the contract;
(2) the longer the term of the injunction, the more readily that compulsion will be inferred;
(3) compulsion may be inferred where an injunction is sought against a particular third party or may be sought against any third party who attempts to replace the employer; and
(4) an injunction will be less readily granted where there are obligations of mutual trust and confidence between the parties which have dissolved.

None the less, in appropriate cases, the court will grant an injunction enforcing negative terms even where the injunction lasts for a long time as happened in the

---

1   See *Lumley v Wagner* [1852] 1 De GM & G 604.
2   [1989] 1 WLR 853.

George Michael case.[1] It is also important that a party seeking to rely on a negative covenant must not itself have acted in breach of contract.

1   See **3.8.**

CHAPTER 4

INTELLECTUAL PROPERTY RIGHTS AND SPORT

COPYRIGHT

4.1 INTRODUCTION

Copyright is a property right. It is a right to stop others from copying works without permission. The various categories of copyright work protect materials as diverse as architecture, dress design and computer software.

This work generally describes categories of copyright work and concentrates on aspects of copyright law that apply to the business of sport. Although there is no particular 'sports right' in copyright or other intellectual property rights, such rights may arise in appropriate contexts.

4.2 SOURCES OF COPYRIGHT LAW

The Copyright Designs and Patents Act 1988 (CDPA 1988) is the principal statute governing UK copyright law. This statute has recently been amended by the Copyright Regulations 1995. This legislation applies not only to UK citizens but to many other nationals by virtue of the reciprocal protection granted in various international conventions. The CDPA 1988 is supplemented by case-law which has developed and interpreted the statute. The CDPA 1988 is the most recent copyright statute. The previous Copyright Acts of 1911 and 1956 are of considerable practical relevance.

Copyright protection extends internationally through a network of reciprocal agreements governed by membership of one or other or both of the international copyright conventions.

Two international copyright conventions lay down minimum standards of protection for copyright owners between those countries which have ratified the conventions. These are the Berne Convention and the Universal Copyright Convention (UCC). Both have many members, and some countries, such as the UK, have ratified both treaties. Whilst both conventions lay down general rules for copyright protection, there are some important differences for the formalities of protection. Under the UCC, the copyright work must contain the copyright symbol © along with the name of the copyright proprietor and the year of first publication. There is no requirement for such a mark under UK Law, although it is essential for wide international protection. International aspects of copyright infringement are beyond the scope of this book. The UK courts will not hear disputes where no infringement has taken place within the UK,[1] although contracts may require claims to be settled in accordance with UK Law and in the courts of England and Wales.

4.3   THE SUBJECT MATTER OF COPYRIGHT

There are detailed rules that often need to be considered to determine whether copyright subsists in a given work which are generally beyond the scope of this work.

Copyright may subsist in:

   '(a) original literary, dramatic, musical or artistic works;
   (b) sound recordings, films, broadcasts or cable programmes; and
   (c) the typographical arrangement of published editions.'[2]

There is no registration requirement for copyright to subsist in a work. The position is different in other countries, such as the USA, where rights should be registered for full protection. There are various qualifying provisions which must be met for copyright protection under UK Law.[3]

Ownership of copyright is quite distinct from ownership of the material which records that copyright work. Although a consumer buys a book, the rights in the actual copyright work are those granted by the author and publisher over the work.

---

1   *Tyburn Productions v Conan Doyle* (1990) *The Times*, 17 February.
2   CDPA 1988, s 1(1).
3   Discussed in **4.8**.

4.4   ORIGINAL LITERARY, DRAMATIC, MUSICAL AND ARTISTIC WORKS

Literary, dramatic, musical and artistic works are the corner-stone of subsequent exploitation in any publishing, music or film business. They must be recorded in writing or otherwise.[1] Writing is defined as any form of notation or code.[2] It does not matter if the work is recorded by or with the permission of the author (s 3(3)); copyright subsists immediately. There is no notice requirement under UK Law, although international law has different requirements. A prudent author dates and names a work and puts it in safe keeping. Section 3 of the CDPA 1988[3] elaborates on the meaning of literary, dramatic and musical works, and s 4[4] on that of artistic works. The courts have considered the requirement for 'originality' as it relates to literary, dramatic, musical and artistic works.

4.4.1   Originality

Literary, dramatic, musical and artistic works must be 'original' to acquire protection. The question therefore arises as to what is original. In *University of London Press v University Tutorial Press*,[5] it was held that 'original' does not mean that the work must be the expression of original or inventive thought. Copyright is not concerned with the originality of ideas but with the expression of thought. In *Ladbroke (Football) Ltd v William Hill (Football) Ltd*,[6] the court held that the word 'original' requires only that 'the work should not be copied but should originate from the author'. An author needs to show he has expended his own skill and effort in order to justify protection. This requirement should be of little concern for most categories of work as they will obviously have the necessary originality. Skill and effort may lie in the selection and the obtaining of information, or the generation of information and ideas in the first place. This means an author may use the same source of information as another to create his own work, but he must not copy from another, he must use his own skill and effort.

Whilst original works require skill and effort to justify protection, that protection extends only to the language or composition or the chosen form of expression. It is often said that copyright does not protect ideas but only the expression of ideas.[7] It may be a question of degree or extent as to whether copyright in a work has been infringed. Questions of infringement apart, copyright is mainly concerned with the expression of ideas and not the ideas themselves.

4.4.2   Literary works

Section 3(1) provides that 'literary work' means any work, other than a dramatic or musical work, which is written, spoken or sung, and includes a table or compilation and a computer program.

---

1   CDPA 1988, s 3(2).
2   Ibid, s 178.
3   See **4.4.2–4.4.4**.
4   See **4.4.5–4.4.6**.
5   [1916] 2 Ch 601.
6   [1964] 1 WLR 273 at 291.
7   See, for example, *Football League v Littlewoods Pools Ltd* [1959] Ch 637.

A common example of a literary work is a book – it may be a work of fiction or a scholarly tome. Articles in a newspaper or magazine benefit from protection as literary works. A literary work does not need to have any particular literary merit. Accordingly, copyright protection is not limited to novels, poems, articles or the lyrics of a song. Case-law has established categories of information which may be protectable such as examination papers;[1] pools coupons;[2] television programme listings;[3] and letters and business letters;[4] directories;[5] lists of Stock Exchange prices;[6] and trade catalogues[7] have been similarly protected as compilations.

Names and slogans

Various categories of works have been refused protection as literary works on a de minimis principle. In *Exxon Corporation v Exxon Insurance Consultants International Ltd*,[8] the plaintiff invested considerable time and money in finding a suitable name for its oil business only to find the defendant insurance business using the same name. In a subsequent copyright infringement action by the plaintiff, the court held that the word 'Exxon', even though it was original, did not qualify as a literary work. The name was simply an artificial combination of letters that provided no information, no instruction and gave no pleasure.

The titles of books, magazines, the names of events and individuals will not usually qualify for protection as literary works.

In such circumstances, a plaintiff may have recourse under the law of passing off or it may be appropriate to register a trade mark.[9] In *Ladbroke (Football) Ltd v William Hill (Football) Ltd* (above), it was said that, whilst as a general rule titles will not be protected, in a proper case a title would qualify for copyright protection. Similarly, there will rarely be copyright in an advertisement slogan such as 'youthful appearances are social necessities, not luxuries'.[10] Advertisements may be capable of copyright protection as literary or artistic works[11] and, where appropriate, on films, sound recordings and broadcasts.

News and sports results

Whilst information itself is not subject to copyright, the actual expressions used to report the information are protected as literary or other copyright works. Accordingly, the actual results of an event or a series of games in a league are unlikely to qualify for copyright protection to the extent that they are not directly copies from another newspaper column or broadcast by simple photocopy or recording. Results will be in the public domain and as such not capable of protection.

---

1   *University of London Press v University Tutorial Press* [1916] 2 Ch 601.
2   *Ladbroke (Football) Ltd v William Hill (Football) Ltd* [1964] 1 WLR 273.
3   *Independent Television Publications v Time Out Ltd* [1984] FSR 64.
4   *Donoghue v Allied Newspapers Ltd* [1938] Ch 106.
5   *Kelly v Morris* (1866) LR 1 Eq 697.
6   *Exchange Telegraph Co Ltd v Gregory & Co* [1896] 1 QB 147.
7   *Davis v Benjamin* [1906] 2 Ch 491.
8   [1982] RPC 69.
9   See **4.24**.
10 *Sinanide v La Maison Kosmeo* (1928) 139 LT 365.
11 *Newsgroup Newspapers Ltd v Mirror Group Newspapers* (1988) *The Times*, 27 July.

In *Walter v Steinkopff*,[1] one news service copied verbatim the material from another news service. This was found to be an infringement of copyright. Where it is simply the same information which is used but not the wording, there is no copyright infringement. Provided the actual wording is not copied from someone else's reporting, no problems should arise.

In the case of news items, there will usually be other sources available. If the information is publicly available (and there is no question of breach of confidence or contract), then there is no reason why the news item cannot simply be re-cast in another form (which will in itself attract copyright protection) and be conveyed in that new form. It is common industry practice to give an acknowledgement of the source of a story or news item.

Some news agencies provide a constant information service to subscribers who are then permitted to use the information received for news bulletins or in articles. In this situation, the recipient pays for the right to use the information and stories for certain permitted uses. The uses to which information can be put are defined in an agreement which governs the parties' relationship and may limit the rights they would otherwise have.

4.4.3 Dramatic works

Section 3(1) of the CDPA 1988 defines a 'dramatic work' as including a work of dance or mime. A work cannot qualify as both a literary work and a dramatic work, although a dramatic work which contains musical elements may be protected under both dramatic and musical categories. A dramatic work is one which is capable of being performed, for example, by acting or dancing. A dramatic work is distinct from the literary elements of the work.

Once again, a de minimis principle applies. In *Green v Broadcasting Corporation of New Zealand*,[2] the Privy Council held that the features which constituted the 'format' of a television show, which were simply accessories used in the presentation of, and additional to, other dramatic or musical performances, did not attract protection. A dramatic work must be one which is capable of being performed. In this case the features of the show for which protection was sought did not form a cohesive whole capable of performance. The format of *Opportunity Knocks* consisted of the use of a 'clapometer' and various catchphrases, which the court held did not amount to a dramatic work for the purposes of copyright protection. It seems unlikely that a game or a 'move' within a game will qualify as a dramatic work. Although the point has not been tested, despite the amount of work that coaches and players put into set piece moves in sport, and however 'dramatic' the effect may be, the lack of any certainty in the outcome of such a move may prohibit such protection.

4.4.4 Musical works

The CDPA defines a 'musical work' as a work consisting of music, exclusive of any words or action intended to be sung, spoken or performed with the music.[3] The copyright for the music of a song is distinct from the literary copyright in the

---

1   [1892] 2 Ch 489.
2   [1989] 2 All ER 1056.
3   CDPA, s 3(1).

lyric and, indeed, any dramatic copyright if the music is accompanied by a dance or other type of performance. Copyright in musical works is in the composition itself. Quite separate rights arise in respect of any sound recording or broadcast of a musical work. There are separate copyrights, perhaps in separate ownership, for music, lyrics and recording.

4.4.5   Artistic works

Section 4(1) of the CDPA 1988 defines an 'artistic work' as:

'(a)   a graphic work, photograph, sculpture or collage, irrespective of artistic quality;
(b)   a work of architecture, being a building or a model for a building; or
(c)   a work of artistic craftsmanship.'

Most artistic works are protected, irrespective of artistic quality. The result of this is that as long as some effort has been expended in making the artistic work original it is protected – personal taste will not matter. Section 4(2) of the CDPA 1988 defines a 'graphic work' as including a painting, drawing, diagram, map, chart or plan, and any engraving, etching, lithograph, woodcut or similar work.

A similar de minimis principle applies with artistic works as with other categories of copyright.

Protection also extends to sketches and patterns for dress design[1] and so by implication items of sports kit. There are significant areas of overlap between copyright and design right in this area, which are beyond the scope of this book. It is important to appreciate that copyright protects only three-dimensional works if they are sculptures or works of artistic craftsmanship. Under various decided cases,[2] the latter category requires a significant degree of aesthetic merit to warrant copyright protection. Accordingly, industrial designs and purely functional articles must usually rely upon design law for protection. The protection afforded to the designers of costumes and sets for film, television and theatre productions relies on these areas of law. If copyright law cannot be relied on, then protection must be sought from the registered or unregistered design regimes.

Works of architecture (such as sports stadia) are protected under copyright laws. Section 17(3) of the CDPA 1988 provides that copying an artistic work includes the making of a copy in three dimensions of a two-dimensional work and the making of a copy in two dimensions of a three-dimensional work. Copyright in works of architecture may be infringed in this fashion.

4.4.6   Photographs

A significant artistic work in the context of sport is the photograph. A photograph is defined as 'a recording of light or other radiation on any medium on which an image is produced or from which an image may by any means be produced, and which is not part of a film'.[3] Single frames of a film are capable of

---

1   *J. Bernstein Ltd v Sidney Murray Ltd* [1981] RPC 305; *Merlet v Mothercare plc* [1984] FSR 358.

2   See, for example, *George Hensher v Restawhile* [1976] AC 64.

3   CDPA 1988, s 4(2).

protection as part of a film. The definition is wide enough to cover holograms. No artistic merit is required for copyright protection. Although photographs may not be copied, the scenes they represent can be independently photographed. A photograph may be exploited in many different sporting contexts. Indeed, it is quite unusual for photographic agencies, or an official photographer to be appointed to a particular event.

4.5 SOUND RECORDINGS, FILMS, BROADCASTS AND CABLE PROGRAMMES

Sound recordings and films are, in most cases, 'derivative works', ie they are based on other copyright works. Broadcasts and cable transmissions are often derivative works, as they either consist entirely of previously recorded films or sound recordings, or they are live transmissions of copyright works. Broadcasts and films may also be of subject matter which is unprotectable under copyright law or the performers' rights legislation such as sporting events.

The sale of broadcast rights to sporting events is based on contract law and a simple licence to enter property and is discussed elsewhere.[1]

4.5.1 Sound recordings

A 'sound recording' is defined as:

'(a) a recording of sounds, from which he sounds may be reproduced; or
(b) a recording of the whole or of any part of a literary, dramatic or musical work, from which sounds reproducing the work or part may be produced',[2]

and this is regardless of the media on which the recording is made or the method by which the sounds are reproduced or produced.

4.5.2 Films

A 'film' is defined as a recording on any medium from which a moving image may by any means be produced.[3]

This clearly covers video recordings and is wide enough to embrace new technology such as CD-ROM, interactive media and the visual aspects of computer games.

Copyright will not subsist in a sound recording or film which is a copy of a previous sound recording or film.[4] A filmed recording of an event is often the first actual copyright that applies to the event itself.

4.5.3 Broadcasts

A broadcast is defined[5] as a transmission by wireless telegraphy of visual images, sounds or other information which:

---

1   See Chapter 9.
2   CDPA, s 5(1).
3   Ibid, s 5(1).
4   Ibid, s 5(2).
5   Ibid, s 6(1).

(a)   is capable of being lawfully received by members of the public; or

(b)   is transmitted for presentation to members of the public.

Copyright will not subsist in a broadcast which infringes the copyright in another broadcast or cable programme. 'Broadcast rights', as they are often described, do not arise (at least in terms of copyright law) until the broadcast of a live event is made. A broadcast of a previously recorded/filmed event is similar to a copyright licence.

4.5.4   Cable programmes

A cable programme is defined as any item included in a cable programme service.[1] 'Cable programme service' is defined as a service consisting wholly or mainly in sending visual images, sounds or other information by means of a telecommunications system, ie by electronic means.

There is no copyright in a cable programme which infringes copyright in a broadcast or other cable programme.

4.6   PUBLISHED EDITIONS

Copyright also subsists in the typographical arrangement of published editions. A published edition is defined as: 'the whole or any part of one or more literary, dramatic or musical works'. These provisions are aimed at giving a publisher of a work (whether in or out of copyright) some protection in the typesetting and arrangement of the published work.

4.7   CONDITIONS FOR PROTECTION

Copyright does not subsist in a work unless the qualifying requirements are met.[2] The relevant requirements as to qualifying conditions for all works are contained in CDPA 1988, s 153. Copyright does not subsist unless qualifications are met as to:

(a)   the author; or

(b)   the country of first publication; or

(c)   in the case of broadcasts, the country from which the broadcast was sent.[3]

A work qualifying under any such category is protected.

4.7.1   Qualifying authors

A work qualifies for copyright protection if the author was at the 'material time' a 'qualifying person'.[4] A 'qualifying person' is defined as a British citizen, a British dependent territories citizen, a British national (overseas), a British overseas citizen, a British subject or a British protected person within the

---

1   CDPA 1988, s 7.

2   Ibid, s 1(3).

3   Ibid, s 153(1).

4   Ibid, s 154(1).

meaning of the British Nationality Act 1981, or an individual domiciled or resident in the UK or another country to which the relevant provisions of the Act extend, or a body incorporated under the law of a part of the UK or of another country to which the relevant provisions of the Act extend.[1]

4.7.2   Material time

The 'material time' in relation to a literary, dramatic, musical or artistic work is defined as:

'(a)   in the case of an unpublished work, when the work was made or, if the making of the work extended over a period, a substantial part of that period;

(b)   in the case of a published work, when the work was first published or, if the author had died before that time, immediately before his death.'[2]

The material time in relation to other descriptions of work is defined as:

'(a)   in the case of a sound recording or film, when it was made;

(b)   in the case of a broadcast, when the broadcast was made;

(c)   in the case of a cable programme, when the programme was included in a cable programme service;

(d)   in the case of the typographical arrangement of a published edition, when the edition was first published.'[3]

4.7.3   The place of first publication

All types of works, except broadcasts and cable programmes, qualify for copyright protection under CDPA 1988, s 155(1) if they were first published in:

(1)   the UK; or

(2)   another country to which the relevant provisions of the CDPA 1988 have been extended.

It is also possible for works to qualify for protection where they were first published in a country to which an order has been made under s 159 of the CDPA 1988.

To qualify under this heading a work must be published. 'Publication' is defined as the issue of copies to the public.[4] Publication is also defined to include making copies available to the public by means of an electronic retrieval system.

4.8   DURATION OF COPYRIGHT

There are various rules for the duration of copyright which depends on the type of work under consideration. These periods have been amended by the Duration of Copyright and Rights in Performances Regulations 1995, which came into force on 1 January 1996, and which generally increase protection to 70 years.[5]

---

1   CDPA 1988, s 154.
2   Ibid, s 154(4).
3   Ibid, s 154(5).
4   Ibid, s 175(1).
5   See **4.8.2**.

4.8.1 Literary, dramatic or musical works

Copyright lasts for 70 years from the end of the calendar year in which the author dies.[1]

Copyright in a work of unknown authorship expires 70 years from the end of the year in which it was written, or 70 years from the end of the year in which it was made available to the public.[2] A number of presumptions operate to counter this potentially perpetual copyright. Copyright is not infringed if it is not possible to ascertain by reasonable enquiry the identity of the author, and it is reasonable to assume that the copyright has expired or the author died 70 years or more before the beginning of the calendar year in which the act in relation to the work was done.[3] There is also a presumption that where a work is anonymous, the publisher of the work as first published is presumed to be the owner of the copyright at that time.[4]

4.8.2 Sound recordings

Copyright lasts for 50 years from the end of the year in which a sound recording was made and, if not released immediately, the copyright will expire at the end of the period of 50 years from the end of the calendar year in which it was released. A sound recording is 'released' when it is first published, played in public, broadcast, or included in a cable programme service.[5] Unauthorised acts are ignored. Publication is defined as being the issue of copies to the public.[6]

4.8.3 Films

The term of copyright in films is increased to 70 years from the death of the last to survive of: the principal director, the author of the film screenplay; the author of the film dialogue; and the composer of music specifically created for and used in the film.[7]

The meaning of 'author' is extended beyond the definition in CDPA 1988, s 9(2) to include the principal director of the film. This does not apply to films made on or before 30 June 1994. In the case of sports programming the duration of the copyright is most likely to be based on the life of the principal director who is likely to be an employee of a production company.

4.8.4 Broadcasts and cable programmes

For broadcasts and cable programmes, copyright expires 50 years from the end of the calendar year in which the broadcast was made or the programme included in a cable programme service.[8]

Section 14(5) of the CDPA 1988 ensures that the copyright in repeats of broadcasts or cable programmes expires at the same time as the copyright in the

1 CDPA 1988, s 12.
2 Ibid, s 12(2).
3 Ibid, s 57(1).
4 Ibid, s 104(4).
5 Ibid, s 13A(3).
6 Ibid, s 175.
7 Ibid, s 13B.
8 Ibid, s 14(2).

original. Accordingly, no copyright arises in respect of a repeat broadcast or cable programme where such is included in a service after the expiry of copyright in the original broadcast or programme.

4.8.5 Typographical arrangement

The copyright in the typographical arrangement of a published edition expires at the end of the period of 25 years from the end of the calendar year in which the edition was first published.[1]

4.8.6 Revived copyright

Since the regulations extend the term of copyright for various categories of work the possibility of extended and revived copyright exists. Copyright in works which had expired before 1 July 1995 subsists as if the regulations had been in effect at the date the work was made. This will affect the works of authors who died between 1925 and 1945. The provisions for ownership of the extended or revived copyright are set out in the regulations and are beyond the scope of this work.

EXPLOITATION OF COPYRIGHT

4.9 AUTHORSHIP

Authorship and ownership are distinct concepts in copyright. The author of a work is the person who creates it.[2] The author of a work is the first owner of any copyright in it.[3] The author of certain works (as distinct from the owner) is entitled to the moral rights[4] in the work, the benefits of which remain with the author despite the fact that someone else may initially or subsequently own the work. Correctly identifying the author of a work and the first owner are essential if a work is to be successfully exploited.

4.9.1 Literary, dramatic, musical and artistic works

The author of a work is the person who creates it. Accordingly, it should usually be obvious who is the author of a given work. For example, the author of a novel is the person who wrote it, and the author of a piece of music is the person who composed it. For the purposes of copyright, the author of a photograph is the photographer.

The position of 'ghost writers' will usually be governed by a contract between the person who provides the material for the work and the actual writer of the work. In the absence of any such agreement, the position is that the author of the work is the person that fixes it and gives it form. However, where a work is simply dictated to a secretary or shorthand writer, the author is the person dictating the work and not the person transcribing it.[5]

---

1   CDPA 1988, s 15.
2   Ibid, s 9.
3   Ibid, s 11.
4   Ibid, s 77.
5   See *Donoghue v Allien Newspapers Ltd* [1938] Ch 106.

4.9.2   Sound recordings and films

The author of a sound recording is the producer.[1] The authors of a film are the producer and the principal director.[2] Accordingly, a film is treated as a work of joint authorship unless the producer and the principal director are the same person.[3] The producer is defined[4] as the person who makes the arrangements necessary for the creation of the work.

4.9.3   Broadcasts and cable programmes

The person making a broadcast, invariably a company, is the author of the broadcast. In the case of a broadcast which is received and re-transmitted from another broadcast, the person who made the first broadcast is the author. The person making a broadcast is the person who transmits it if he has responsibility to any extent for its content and any person who makes the arrangements necessary for the programme's transmission.[5] Broadcasts will often involve more than one party and, strictly speaking, there may be two makers of a broadcast for the purposes of the legislation. In such a case, the work will be treated as a work of joint authorship.[6]

In the case of a cable programme, the person providing the cable programme service in which the programme is included is the author.[7]

4.9.4   Published editions

In the context of copyright in the typographical arrangement of a published edition of whole or part of a work, the publisher is the author.[8]

4.10   JOINT AUTHORSHIP

Many works will be the result of more than one person's endeavours. A work of 'joint authorship' is defined as a work produced by the collaboration of two or more authors in which the contribution of each author is not distinct from that of the other author or authors.[9]

The duration of the copyright in a work of joint authorship expires at the end of the period of 70 years from the end of the calendar year in which the last author dies.[10]

Copyright distinguishes between joint authorship and joint ownership. As far as ownership is concerned, the parties can reach any agreement they like. The question of authorship relates to the contribution to the work. In joint

---

1   CDPA 1988, s 9(2)(aa).
2   Ibid, s 9(2)(ab).
3   Ibid, s 10(1A).
4   Ibid, s 178.
5   Ibid, s 6(3).
6   Ibid, s 10(2).
7   Ibid, s 9(2)(c).
8   Ibid, s 9(2)(d).
9   Ibid, s 10.
10   Ibid, s 12(3).

authorship, each individual author must be an 'author' for the purposes of CDPA 1988, s 9(1). Each author must have been responsible to some degree for reducing the work to a material form.

It is clear from CDPA 1988, s 173 that if copyright in a work is owned by more than one person jointly then the agreement of all the owners is required for any exclusive dealing with the work. The author of a work is the first owner of any copyright in it.[1] Quite how ownership is divided will vary. Joint authors may be either tenants in common or joint tenants. The law usually presumes they are tenants in common.

4.11 OWNERSHIP OF COPYRIGHT

4.11.1 Author as first owner

The author of a work is the first owner of the copyright in the work. Subject to the discussion at **4.10**, the person who creates the work owns the copyright in that work. It is that person who can deal with the copyright in the work. Authors frequently sign contracts granting rights to individuals and companies. These agreements may entitle others to some or all of the rights in a work.

4.11.2 Employees

There is an exception to this general rule. Where a literary, dramatic, musical or artistic work is made by an employee in the course of his employment, the employer is the first owner of any copyright in the work, subject to any agreement to the contrary.[2] It is not enough that a literary, dramatic, musical or artistic work is made by an employee; it must also be made in the course of employment.

Whether or not an employee acts 'in the course of his employment' is a question of fact. In most instances, it should be obvious whether or not the work is carried out in the course of employment by considering, for instance, what the employee is employed to do and whether the work produced falls within the employee's job description. Ownership of copyright may be dealt with expressly in a contract of employment, or by way of future assignment. Ownership of copyright will also be dealt with by implication under CDPA 1988, s 11(2). It may also be important to determine whether the person in question was in fact an employee. A distinction is drawn between contracts for services (independent of the employer) and contracts of service (employees). The practical significance of the distinction in the creative industries is that an employer may find that rights in a piece of music or advertising copy or other copyright work are not owned and only a limited licence to use the work exists. Whilst there are potential theoretical difficulties with the distinction between a contract for services and a contract of service, the best advice is to make specific contractual arrangements for copyright ownership. In most cases, it should be made clear that copyright is owned by the employer whatever type of employment contract exists. Failure to make proper provision can result in enormous problems and even litigation.[3]

---

1 CDPA 1988, s 11(1).
2 Ibid, s 11(2).
3 *Ray v Classic FM* (1998) unreported.

4.11.3 Commissioned works

Where a work is commissioned from an independent third party, ownership of copyright should be dealt with at the time the work is commissioned. In the absence of an employer/employee relationship, CDPA 1988, s 11(2) does not apply. Express contractual provision should be made dealing with the copyright. The CDPA 1988 makes no express provision for commissioned works. A written agreement evidencing any dealing with copyright is preferable, although not always essential.

A court may decide that the commissioning party has a beneficial interest, as in *Warner v Gestetner Ltd*,[1] where the court held that there had been a beneficial assignment of copyright in a number of drawings.

Alternatively, there may be an implied licence of copyright. A licence will not be *implied* between parties simply because it is reasonable to do so; it must be the *intention* of the parties. In one case,[2] an architect was commissioned to draw building plans for the purpose of obtaining planning permission for some houses. The site was subsequently sold with the benefit of planning permission, and the plans transferred to the purchaser.

The original commissioner and the purchaser both had an implied licence to use the plans for the purpose of building the houses. The court restricted the implied licence to use the plans for building houses on the site in question. If the purchasers had attempted to use the plans to build houses to those specifications on another site, they would have been prevented from so doing. A licence of copyright should be obtained in writing on terms agreed between the parties.

4.11.4 Ownership of other works

The author of sound recordings, films, broadcasts, cable programmes or typographical arrangements will be the first owner for copyright purposes. Where a film is made in the course of employment, the employer is the first owner of copyright.[3] However, it is common for the companies financing sound recordings and films to insist on full assignment of copyrights from all personnel to avoid any subsequent problems.

4.11.5 Ownership of copyright and sports events

The CDPA 1988 lays down rules for establishing authorship and thus ownership of copyright works. It is extremely unlikely that a sports rights owner or events organiser will be the author and accordingly the first owner of copyright in a work. It is more likely that this will be the broadcaster, or production company involved in a broadcast, or the photographer at an event. As has already been seen authorship may subsequently be quite distinct from ownership of copyright in a work. It is important therefore that a sports rights owner or event organiser at the very least considers whether or not it should own the copyright in works which are created with its permission, such as films and broadcasts. The mechanics of such an arrangement are dealt with below.[4]

---

1 [1988] EIPRD 89.
2 *Blair v Osborne & Tompkins* [1971] 2 WLR 503.
3 CDPA 1988, s 11(2).
4 See **4.12**.

4.12 EXPLOITATION OF COPYRIGHT

Most copyright owners want to exploit their rights. This may be done on a 'bulk' basis by collection agencies like the Performing Rights Society or Phonographic Performance Limited. On the other hand, copyright owners often have individual needs and will exploit works individually. The methods of exploitation of their copyright vary: for example, a copyright owner could choose to exploit all rights himself. Copyright is a form of personal property and may be dealt with by assignment, by testamentary disposition or by operation of law.[1] Copyright is exploited by way of assignment or licence, and the terms of these agreements should be recorded in writing.

The first and subsequent owners of copyright works have a number of options as to the manner of exploitation of the copyrights. For example, they may decide:

–   to keep their rights and not to exploit them in any way; or
–   to exploit the copyright material themselves (although this inevitably involves a third party's cooperation at some stage to print, distribute or sell the work); or
–   to assign rights to a third party; or
–   to license third parties to do otherwise prohibited acts in relation to the work.

Copyright may be divided in a number of ways. The method of exploitation is more dependent on the medium than the choice of the individual owner. The division of rights is extremely important in considering the most effective way of exploiting particular works Assuming the sports rights owner or organiser owns the copyright in a work a number of opportunities arise. A sports rights owner or organiser may be advised to appoint a UK broadcaster to broadcast the event within the UK, but that broadcaster may not be the best placed to exploit the event in the USA. Likewise, the UK broadcaster may not be the best placed to exploit the video of the event. As technological advances take place, the rights owner may have to decide who should exploit the CD-ROM and other electronic rights. Great care must be taken in defining the rights, territory and duration of all these agreements.

4.12.1 Assignments and licences

An assignment is usually a sale of rights, whereas a licence is a contractual permission to use rights subject to ongoing obligations. An assignment may also be by way of gift or testamentary disposition. An assignment of copyright is not effective unless it is in writing and signed by, or on behalf of, the assignor.[2] The assignor will usually sign the document himself although, in the case of a company, CDPA 1988, s 176(1) requires the company seal to be affixed to satisfy this requirement. Whoever signs a document must have authority to do so, and this authority should be checked where an agent is dealing with copyrights.

Assignments and licences may be limited in a number of ways. The dealing may be limited to:

---

1   CDPA 1988, s 90.
2   Ibid, s 90(3).

–   one or more, but not all, of the things which the owner has the exclusive right to do; and/or
–   part, but not the whole, of the period of copyright protection.[1]

An assignment or licence may thus be absolute or partial. Examples of the stratification of rights are given below but exploitation of copyright is based on the owner giving someone permission to perform one of the 'restricted acts' in a copyright work.[2] Under CDPA 1988, s 90, the stratification of rights is not limited to categories of exploitation but can extend to the length of time for which a right is to be assigned or licensed. The assignor may also attempt to control where the rights will be enjoyed by the assignee, for example, only in the UK and not in Canada or the USA. However, such territorial divisions are not contemplated by the CDPA 1988 assignments of copyright.[3] Accordingly, an assignment of copyright that limits exploitation on a territory by territory basis would be construed as a licence by the court.

An assignment may be of future as well as existing copyright,[4] and in such a case, clarity is all-important. An agreement which deals with future copyright should be carefully considered to ensure that it is not unduly onerous or restrictive.

Example
The author of a book may sign an agreement which assigns all the rights in his novel to one publisher. Alternatively, he may enter a number of separate agreements dealing with hardback, softback and serialisation rights for the novel. In addition, he may then deal with stage and film rights, which will involve the adaptation and performance of his novel. Most authors will rely on an agent and publisher to do this for them. As technology develops, the author may be given the opportunity to exploit the work on CD-ROM as an interactive book or game. The author may also decide that he would like to write a sequel to his book, and before the book is written, may assign the sequel rights to a publisher.

4.12.2   Form of assignment

Although CDPA 1988, s 90(3) requires an assignment to be in writing to transfer the legal and beneficial title, the content of the document which forms the assignment is not specified by the statute. An assignment may be in very simple words or it may be a more complicated document containing a number of obligations. There are various problems that can arise with both assignments and licences, even though the s 90 requirements may have been followed. An assignment by the original owner is often referred to as a 'grant of copyright'.

The question of whether copyright has been assigned, and what form of words will suffice to do this, is sometimes problematic. A receipt stating that a sum of money was received 'inclusive of all copyrights' was deemed sufficient to assign the copyright in a number of card designs.[5]

It is usual commercial practice to include a more comprehensive assignment which also deals with various obligations, warranties and indemnities, together

1   CDPA 1988, s 90.
2   See CDPA 1988, s 16 and Chapter 5 below.
3   CDPA 1988, s 90.
4   Ibid, s 91.
5   See *Savory Ltd v The World of Golf Ltd* [1914] 2 Ch 566.

with the extent and duration of the rights granted and the consideration. An assignment from the author of certain categories of work may also contain an assertion of the author's moral rights.[1]

An effective assignment removes the copyright or part of the copyright from the control of the assignor. The assignor can, if necessary, be restrained from subsequently doing anything which infringes the rights of the assignee. If the rights to publish a novel are assigned by an author, that author cannot then grant the same rights to someone else without being in breach of contract and the subsequent publication being an infringement of copyright.

4.12.3 Licences

A licence of copyright is a contractual right or permission from the owner of the copyright to do certain acts. A licence does not pass title in the copyright. Licences are frequently used to permit publishers and distributors to exploit copyright. For example, an author or publisher may license the serial rights in a new novel for publication in a newspaper or magazine. A sound recording may be licensed by the owner for a film soundtrack or compilation album.

There are various types of licence. A licence may be exclusive or non-exclusive. An exclusive licence is one which authorises the licensee, to the exclusion of all other persons, including the licensor, to exercise a right that would otherwise be exercisable by the licensor.[2] Such a licence must be in writing. The holder of a valid exclusive licence has the same rights as if the licence were an assignment. Rights are also concurrent with the copyright owner.

A bare licence requires no formalities – it need not be in writing – yet will bind the copyright owner who granted it and any assignees except a bona fide purchaser for valuable consideration without actual or constructive notice.[3] A licence can even be implied from circumstances: for example, where an advertising agency designs a company logo, the company has an implied licence to use the logo. A licensee cannot usually restrict any other exploitation of the work by the licence owner unless the licence is an exclusive licence. A licensee has no direct right to assert the copyright against third parties; it must act through the licensor.

A licence may be distinguished from an assignment in a number of ways:

(1) Ownership of rights is not transferred: an assignment gives a property right, a licence a contractual right.
(2) An assignee has the right to sue to protect his copyright. A licensee does not usually have this right.
(3) After assignment, the owner will usually have no more rights in the work.
(4) A licence may be exclusive or non-exclusive.
(5) Because a licence is a contractual right it is conditional on the performance of obligations by the licensee which, if breached, will lead to the termination of the contract.

---

1   See CDPA 1988, ss 77–85.
2   Ibid, s 90(1).
3   Ibid, s 90.

(6) On a licensee's insolvency, rights usually revert to the owner, whereas an assignee retains rights. In such a case the assigner can only sue to recover money owed on a debt and may rank as an unsecured creditor. The property in the copyright remains with the assignee.

(7) Assignments must be in writing (although an agreement to assign may be oral).

(8) An assignee has the right to alter the work by way of correction and additions. A licensee does not automatically have such a right.

There are occasions when the distinction is particularly important. A licensee who wishes to sue is precluded from doing so as he has no title; only an assignee can sue, although an exclusive licensee does have such rights. Where there are continuing obligations on the assignee, such as an obligation to make royalty payments, there may be a presumption of a licence rather than an assignment.

Both assignments and licences may provide for the payment of a royalty to the copyright owner. The payment of a royalty may in fact point to the document being a licence. This point has been considered in a number of cases. A presumption against assignment may arise wherever there are continuing obligations between the parties. The case of *Jonathan Cape v Consolidated Press*[1] concerned the grant to a publisher of the exclusive right to publish a work in volume form. This was held to constitute an assignment. Conversely, in *Re Jude's Musical Compositions*,[2] an agreement to publish in 'volume form', subject to payment of a royalty, constituted a licence. An agreement to publish a work subject to the performance of conditions is likely to constitute a licence.

When drafting the documents, the extent of the rights granted, the exclusivity of the rights and the obligations imposed by the copyright owner are important to clarify the arrangement. An express provision stating that the agreement is 'by way of assignment/licence' only assists in the construction of the document. Modern precedents usually deal clearly with such matters.

There are two further problems which may arise where there are continuing obligations – such as royalty payments – contained in an agreement. If copyright is assigned in return for a royalty, the assignee should be prohibited from assigning the copyright to a third party. As there is no privity of contract between the original copyright owner and the third party, the royalty terms cannot be enforced against the third party, only against the original assignee. A restriction on assignment may be included or, alternatively, an express require-ment may be made in the original agreement that, on any subsequent assignment to a third party, the assignee will enter into a direct written covenant with the original owner.

Barker v Stickney[3] considered the rights of an unpaid author whose copyrights had been assigned to a third party. The court concluded that the author had no right of action for royalties against a third party assignee. Appropriate contractual terms (as suggested above) must be included which limit such assignments. The best protection is to ensure that the agreement is not assignable and that the agreement is conditional on the payment of royalties.

---

1   [1954] 1 WLR 1313.
2   [1907] 1 Ch 651.
3   [1919] 1 KB 121.

Because of the difficulties which have arisen in distinguishing between the two, great care should be taken in drafting the necessary contracts between the parties. Where any continuing obligations are envisaged, appropriate restrictions such as limitations on the right to assign the benefit of the contract and termination provisions should be included in the contract. This ensures that, even though property has been transferred, there may still be a re-assignment of rights in certain circumstances. This has become the norm for assignments and licences.

4.12.4   Drafting the documents

Although the form of an assignment or a licence is prescribed, its contents are not. The most important consideration for an assignor or licensor is to transfer that which is intended and no more. This means that care must be taken with the rights definition in the agreement. A useful rule is for the assignee to give away as little in terms of rights as can accord with the parties' intentions and give the contract business efficacy. Except in the case of an outright assignment, the owner may retain control over other rights and exploit them as it sees fit.

All parties to an agreement will be concerned about precisely what rights are granted, in what territories, and for how long. A licensee must also ensure that the person granting rights has the ability to do so. Good title must be established, and account may have to be taken of the contractual matters discussed elsewhere in this book, such as duress and restraint of trade.

Most agreements deal with the exact rights granted, the territory and duration of the agreement. There should also be terms dealing with the exclusivity of the agreement. Basic warranties as to ownership and the 'basic' copyright warranties should be considered. Terms for payment should be included unless the dealing is by way of gift. Various boiler-plate and termination provisions should always be included.

Basic warranties
There are three basic warranties in a licence or assignment of copyright. These are that:

(1)   the work is written by a qualifying person;
(2)   it is original; and
(3)   it is not defamatory (or in breach of any third party rights).

Additionally, assignments and licences should be made with full or limited title guarantee. Implied covenants apply as much to dealings with copyright as they do to dealings with land. It is common for specific warranties to title to be included whether a specific title guarantee is mentioned or not. Stamp Duty also applies on the assignment of copyright.

4.12.5   Construction of contracts: assignments and licences

As technology has developed, so have the ways in which copyright is exploited. This has had an important effect on the assignment and licensing of rights. Early cases involved the granting of film rights in novels and plays where, at the time of drafting the licence or assignment, innovations such as sound had not been envisaged. A recent dispute involved the exploitation of a film by means of video where such rights did not exist at the time of the original assignment of performers' rights.[1]

The starting-point in the construction of any contract is the document itself. If the words used in the contract are clear and precise, then in the absence of fraud, mistake or other contractual circumstance, the contract stands. Despite what appears to be a perfectly clear document, disputes may arise where a novel form of exploitation is developed which did not exist at the time of the agreement. A current example is the development of multi-media products which incorporate various copyright works. It is often unclear whether an original assignment or licence was intended to include the right to exploit copyright in this way. This is a matter of interpretation.

The interpretation centres upon the form of words used by the parties in their agreement. If the words are wide enough to cover the new rights (for instance, CD-ROM exploitation) and those rights were at the least in the contemplation of the parties at the time of the agreement, then clearly those rights pass. A plaintiff may seek to open up the document to wider consideration. Whilst a court looks to the document as a whole for its meaning, it is possible to use extrinsic evidence as an aid to construction of the contract by looking at what was properly in the consideration of the parties at the time of the agreement. In *Hospital for Sick Children v Walt Disney Productions*,[2] the court had to consider the grant in 1919 by Sir James Barrie of a licence in all his literary and dramatic works to the defendants for the duration of the copyright term 'in cinematograph or moving picture films'. The court held that the proper construction of these words rested upon the view of the parties at the time of the agreement. The wording of the document itself provided no assistance (the words used being so wide) so the court looked at matters in the contemplation of the parties at the time of the agreement. Since silent films were the only means of commercial exploitation in the cinema at the time of the licence, a narrow view was taken and the talking rights were excluded from the licence.

Similar disputes may arise over licences granted to put films in video formats as new formats are constantly being developed. Widely drawn definitions clauses in agreements cause problems for licensors, who now give more careful thought to the definitions in licences.

It appears that contracts will be construed in one of the following ways.

(1) The assignment will be interpreted by what was in the minds of the parties at the time it was drafted, as evidenced by the words used in the agreement and facts that were then relevant.[3]

(2) The agreement must be looked at in the light of circumstances and conditions surrounding the agreement, as long as the parties have knowledge of the relevant circumstances and conditions. This may involve looking at the state of the art at the time of the agreement.[4]

There are further important considerations when there are insolvency issues. In such circumstances, the distinction between assignments and licences is import-

---

1   See *Bourne v Walt Disney Co* (1995) US App Lexis.
2   [1966] 1 WLR 1055.
3   This reflects the majority view in *Hospital for Sick Children v Walt Disney Productions* (above).
4   See *J. C. Williamson v MGM Theatres Ltd* [1937] WLR 140.

ant as this may determine the right of the copyright owner to the return of the property as opposed to merely ranking as an unsecured creditor.

4.12.6   Assignment, licences and sports rights owners

As has already been seen[1] the position in sport may be very different. A sports rights owner or organiser it unlikely to be the author of a work so must rely on a contract to first acquire and secondly authorise the exploitation of rights in a copyright work created out of its event. Although the precise terms of broadcast agreements are dealt with elsewhere[2] the principle of acquiring copyright where the sports rights owner or organiser are not the author and thus the first owners are as follows:

(1)   identify the rights in question;
(2)   consider whether to acquire the rights outright or partially;
(3)   draw up an appropriate assignment or licence of the rights;[3]
(4)   consider what rights the author/first owner of the work requires if he is to exploit any rights in the work;
(5)   either draft the document in (3) so as to leave sufficient rights with the author/first owner and reserve rights to the sports rights owner or grant back rights to the author/first owner; and finally
(6)   consider how else to exploit the work and grant rights that can be granted to a third party to do so.

---

1   See **4.11.5**.
2   See Chapter 9.
3   This may be part of another document.

PRECEDENT

4.13 COPYRIGHT ASSIGNMENT

THIS ASSIGNMENT is made the   day of   [   ].

BETWEEN

(1) ('Author') and

(2) ('Company')

IT IS AGREED as follows:

1   DEFINITIONS

The following definitions apply in this Agreement:

'Act'	means the Copyright Designs and Patents Act 1988 as amended from time to time
'Fee'	means £[ ]
'Right'	means all vested, contingent and future copyrights, all accrued rights of action and all other rights of whatever nature in the Work whether now known or created in the future to which the Author is entitled by virtue of any of the laws in force in any part of the Territory [excluding the Reserved Rights]
[alternatively]	means the [non] exclusive licence to [insert details of rights licensed]
'Reserved Rights'	means the rights granted to [inserts details of reserved rights]
'Term'	means the full period of copyright in the Work including all renewals, reversions and extensions of copyright in the Work arising under the laws in force in each part of the Territory
'Territory'	means [the world]
'Work'	means the [literary] work written by the Author entitled [insert title] a copy of which is annexed as Exhibit 1.

2   ASSIGNMENT

2.1   In consideration of the Fee the Author assigns the Rights to the Company with [full/limited title guarantee] in the Territory for the Term;

2.2   the Company shall pay the Author the Fee on signing this Agreement;

[2.3   the Author reserves the Reserved Rights.]

2.4   at any time after the date of this Agreement each of the parties shall, at the request and cost of the party, execute or procure the execution of any document and do or procure the doing of any act as the party requires so that the party receives the full benefit of all the provisions of this agreement.

3 WARRANTIES

The Author represents and warrants to the Company that:

3.1 the Author is sole author of the Work and was throughout the writing of the Work a 'qualifying person' within the meaning of the Act;

3.2 the Author is the absolute and unencumbered legal and beneficial owner of the Rights throughout the Territory and has not assigned or licensed the Rights in the Work to any person;

3.3 there is no present or prospective claim in respect of any rights in the Work which may infringe any of the Rights;

3.4 the Work is original to the Author and does not infringe any right of copyright, moral right or right of privacy or right of publicity or personality or any other third party right;

3.5 the Company may use the name, likeness and biography of the Author in connection with the exploitation by the Company of the Rights;

3.6 copyright in the Work is valid and subsisting pursuant to the laws of the United Kingdom and the United States of America and the provisions of the Berne Convention and Universal Copyright Convention;

[3.7 all published copies of the Work have borne a copyright notice in such form as shall secure protection for the work pursuant to the provisions of the Universal Copyright Convention.]

3.8 the Work contains nothing which is obscene, blasphemous, libellous or otherwise unlawful and the exploitation of the Work will not infringe the rights of any third party.

4 INDEMNITY

The Author indemnifies the Company from all proceedings (including without prejudice to the generality of this provision the Company's legal costs on a solicitor and own client basis) arising directly or indirectly as a result of any breach or non-performance by the Author of any of the Author's obligations or warranties in this Agreement.

5A MORAL RIGHTS

5A.1 The Author asserts to the Company its assigns, licensees and successors in title his moral right to be identified as the author of the Work in accordance with ss 77 and 78 of the Act.

5A.2 Company must ensure that every copy of the Work published by or under licence from it in the Territory bears the following notice on the reverse title page:

'The right of [name of author] to be identified as the author of this work has been asserted in accordance with the Copyright Design and Patents Act 1988'.

[for an alternative clause to 5A consider clause 5B below]

5B AUTHOR'S CREDIT

5B.1 Company must include the name of Author prominently on all versions of the Work published by or under license from Company. In this context 'version' includes any method of exploitation of the Work.

5B.2   The Author irrevocably and unconditionally waives all rights in respect of the Work to which he is now or may be entitled under the Copyright Design and Patents Act 1988 ss 77 and 78 and any similar rights in force during the Term in any part of the Territory.

6   ALTERATIONS TO THE WORK

6.1   The Author irrevocably and unconditionally waives all moral rights in the Work to which he is entitled under section 80 of the Act and any similar rights to which he is entitled in any part of the Territory.

6.2   The Company reserves the right to alter the Work as in its discretion it sees fit and Author consents to any alterations.

7   MISCELLANEOUS

7.1   Nothing contained in this Agreement constitutes a partnership or contract of employment between the parties.

7.2   Nothing contained in this Agreement constitutes an undertaking on the part of the Company to exploit the Work. If the Company decides not to exploit the Work the Author may not make any claim for loss of opportunity to enhance the Author's reputation or loss of publicity.

7.3   This Agreement and all obligations and warranties contained in it endures for the benefit of the successors and assignees of the parties.

7.4   This Agreement, together with any documents referred to in it, contains the whole agreement between the parties relating to its subject matter and supersedes any prior drafts, undertakings, representations and warranties whether written or oral relating to the subject matter of this Agreement.

7.5   No variation of this Agreement is effective unless made in writing signed by all the parties to this Agreement.

7.6   This Agreement is governed by the laws of England and Wales whose courts have exclusive jurisdiction.

[7.7   It is certified that this transaction does not form part of a transaction or a series of transactions worth more than [£60,000]].

SIGNED BY
[Company]
acting by [a director and its secretary] [two Directors]

Director
Director/Secretary

SIGNED BY
[Author]
in the presence of:

Witness's signature
Name
Address
Occupation

COPYRIGHT INFRINGEMENT

4.14 RESTRICTED ACTS

Copyright is infringed if a person does an act within the exclusive rights[1] without the permission of the copyright owner. There are two categories of civil copyright infringement, known as primary and secondary infringements. There are also various criminal offences which can arise where rights are infringed.

The categories of primary infringement relate to infringement of the exclusive rights to acts which only the owner of copyright can do or authorise, known as the acts restricted by copyright. These rights are dealt with in ss 16–21 of the CDPA 1988. Acts of secondary infringement involve dealing with or making commercial use of infringing copies of a copyright work. Secondary infringement is dealt with in CDPA 1988, ss 22–27.

There are various permitted acts dealt with in CDPA 1988, ss 28–76 which provide defences to infringement.

4.14.1 Exclusive rights

The exclusive rights set out in CDPA 1988, s 16 are the basis of protection for copyright owners. They are:

- the right to copy the work;[2]
- the right to issue copies to the public;[3]
- the right to perform the work in public;[4]
- the right to broadcast or send a cable transmission;[5] and
- the right to make adaptations of the work.[6]

Copyright will be infringed where any of these acts are done without the consent of the copyright owner.[7] An act restricted by copyright may be done in relation to the work as a whole or any substantial part of it.[8] An infringement of copyright may take place not only where the whole of a work has been copied, but also where something less than the whole but none the less 'substantial' has been copied. The question of what amounts to a 'substantial part' of a copyright work is discussed at **4.14.2**. Section 16(4) provides that the restricted acts are subject to permitted acts[9] and the copyright licensing provisions of the CDPA 1988.[10] The latter provisions are beyond the scope of this work.

Matters may be complicated where, in an action for copyright infringement, it is alleged that the defendant has copied a work or a substantial part of it but the

---

1   See CDPA 1988, s 16 and **4.14.1** below.
2   CDPA 1988, s 17.
3   Ibid, s 18.
4   Ibid, s 19.
5   Ibid, s 20.
6   Ibid, s 21.
7   Ibid, s 16(2).
8   Ibid, s 16(3).
9   Permitted acts are listed in CDPA 1988, ss 28–76.
10   See CDPA 1988, ss 116–144.

defendant denies that in fact copying has taken place. Where an allegation of infringement is disputed, the courts have then to decide two elements that must be present:

(1) there must be sufficient objective similarity between the infringing work and the copyright work, or a substantial part of it, for the former to be properly described, not necessarily as identical with, but as a reproduction or adaptation of the latter;

(2) the copyright work must be the source from which the infringing work is derived.[1] This case made the possibility of subconscious copying a possibility. If, in substance, there is a similarity, it must be proved that the defendant had access to the plaintiff's work, in which case, a presumption will be raised that the defendant had copied the other work. In such a case, the defendant must rebut that presumption. If one author arrives by independent work at the same result as another author, there will be no infringement.

A number of factors will be relevant: the degree of familiarity between the works; the characteristics of the plaintiff's works; the objective similarity between the works; the inherent possibility that any similarity is due to coincidence; other factors which may have influenced the defendant; and, finally, evidence with respect to the defendant's state of mind.[2]

4.14.2   Substantial part

The copyright in a work is infringed where someone other than the copyright owner does any of the restricted acts in relation to the whole or a substantial part of a work. Whilst it is usually obvious what constitutes the whole of a work, the question of what constitutes a substantial part of a work can be problematic. The approach the court has adopted is that the question of what constitutes a 'substantial part' is a qualitative rather than a quantitative question. *Hawkes v Paramount Films*[3] concerned a newsreel that contained 20 seconds of a four-minute piece of music. The newsreel was held to infringe the copyright in the music. However, the inclusion of such a piece of background music in a piece of film would now be permitted as incidental inclusion. In *Ladbroke (Football) Ltd v William Hill (Football) Ltd*,[4] Lord Pearce said that the question as to what is substantial must be decided by quality rather than quantity. Additionally, the parts of a work copied will not amount to a substantial part if the parts copied were not in themselves original.[5]

Guide-lines

The following guide-lines may be useful in determining whether infringement has taken place.

---

1   Per Diplock LJ in *Francis Day & Hunter Ltd v Bron* [1963] Ch 587.
2   *L. B. Plastics Ltd v Swish Products Ltd* [1979] RPC 551.
3   [1934] Ch 593.
4   [1964] 1 WLR 273.
5   See for example *Warwick Film Productions Ltd v Eisinger* [1967] 3 All ER 367, *Ravenscroft v Herbert* [1980] RPC 193, *EMI Music v Evangelou Papathanassiou* [1987] 8 EPR 244.

(1) Even short extracts of works may, when assessed qualitatively, be vital parts of a work and thus substantial. Even though there may be only a fleeting resemblance between two works, such as a melody line, or the selective use of scenes, incidents and language from another work, this does not preclude infringement of copyright.

(2) The courts adopt a de minimis approach to some uses for copyright purposes, such as the use of a name or title, and will not hold that infringement of copyright has taken place. Alternative remedies such as passing off, defamation or trade mark infringement may be pursued.

(3) The fact that the work in question is short does not preclude a conclusion of copying or substantial taking.

(4) Some very simple ideas may only be represented in a limited number of ways – such as a photo of a view or a commonplace instruction. In such cases, a court will be reluctant to hold that infringement has taken place.

(5) A similar theme or plot for a literary work may be unprotectable as an idea – although care must be taken to avoid copying any text or dialogue. The similarities must be of the unprotectable elements of the work: broadly speaking, the idea rather than the expression of the work.

In spite of all this, a good general guide-line is that set out in *University of London Press v University Tutorial Press*:[1] 'what is worth copying is worth protecting'.

4.15 COPYING

4.15.1 Literary, dramatic, musical or artistic works

CDPA 1988, s 17(2) provides that copying in relation to any literary, dramatic, musical or artistic work means reproducing the work in any material form. This includes storing the work in any medium by electronic means.

At its simplest, copying will be very easy to prove: for example, where a compact disc is recorded onto a cassette, or the pages of a book are copied using a photocopier. In the case of artistic works, copying also occurs if a two-dimensional copy is made of a three-dimensional work, or a three-dimensional copy of a two-dimensional work.

4.15.2 Films, television broadcasts and cable programmes

In addition to the copying of the work as a whole or any substantial part of it, CDPA 1988, s 17(4) establishes that copyright in a film, television broadcast or cable programme is infringed if a photograph of the whole or any substantial part of any image forming part of the film, broadcast or cable programme is made. The producers of 'Starsky and Hutch' were able to prevent the defendants from publishing a single frame from an episode infringing their copyright.[2]

---

1   [1916] 2 Ch 601.
2   *Spelling-Goldberg Productions Inc v BPC Publishing Ltd* [1981] RPC 280.

4.15.3   Typographical arrangements

CDPA 1988, s 17(5) states that the copying of a typographical arrangement of a published edition means making a facsimile copy of it.

4.16   ISSUING COPIES TO THE PUBLIC

In the case of this restricted act, the issuing to the public of copies of a work means the act of putting into circulation copies not previously put into circulation in the UK or elsewhere.[1] This restricted act does not apply to the subsequent distribution, sale, hiring or loaning of copies nor to any subsequent importation of such copies into the UK. However, the rental of copies of sound recordings, films and computer programs to the public is prohibited.

4.16.1   Rental or lending of copies to the public

The rental or lending of works to the public is a restricted act which applies to literary, dramatic, musical and artistic works as well as films and sound recordings.[2] 'Rental' means making a copy available for use on terms that it will be returned for direct or indirect commercial advantage.[3] This covers video rental shops. 'Lending' means making a copy of the work available through an establishment accessible to the public for use on terms that it will be returned but otherwise than for direct or indirect commercial advantage.[4] This covers public libraries.

There are other provisions affecting authors' rental rights. An agreement for film production between an author and film producer is presumed to transfer any rental right the author has to the film producer.[5] This is the case unless the agreement provides otherwise. The rental right may arise because the author's work is included in the film.

The author of a literary, dramatic, musical or artistic work and the principal director of a film have a right to equitable remuneration for the rental of their work.[6] An agreement cannot exclude or restrict the right to equitable remuneration under the section. There are no guide-lines as to what constitutes an equitable amount. Either party may apply to the Copyright Tribunal to determine the amount payable. It is also possible to vary any agreement as to the amount payable or vary a previous decision of the tribunal.[7]

In principle, these provisions will apply as much to films and recordings of sports events as they do to films and recordings in the mainstream entertainment business.

---

1   CDPA 1988, s 18(2).
2   Ibid, s 18A(1).
3   Ibid, s 18A(2)(a).
4   Ibid, s 18A(2)(b).
5   Ibid, s 93A.
6   Ibid, s 93B.
7   Ibid, s 93C.

4.17 PUBLIC PERFORMANCE

The performance of a literary, dramatic or musical work in public is an act restricted by copyright.[1] 'Performance' of a work includes delivery of lectures, addresses, speeches and sermons, and, in general, includes any mode of visual or acoustic presentation, including presentation by means of a sound recording, film, broadcast or cable programme of the works.

The playing or showing of a sound recording, film, broadcast or cable programme in public is a restricted act, although CDPA 1988, s 72 provides some limited exceptions to this right.

When will a performance not be in public? It appears that a monetary limitation is not sufficient to ensure that the performance is private. If payment is made to see a performance, the economic rights of the copyright owner are being affected, since an opportunity to exploit the work is being lost and, accordingly, the performance will be in public. For a performance not to be a public performance, it appears that the performance must be limited to a domestic situation. Playing records or having friends round to watch a film at home will not be a public performance of the work. If the film or music is played in a hall of residence at a university, however, it constitutes a public performance. If there is a degree of recurrence or regularity about such performances, a licence would also be required from the relevant licensing authority or copyright owner.[2]

Music played in shops, over telephones, in waiting rooms and in reception areas constitutes a public performance for which a licence is required. The playing of videos to guests in hotels or the transmission of cable or satellite programme services to guests will also constitute a public performance, and a licence will be required. The administration of the performance right in music is usually assigned by composers and publishers to the Performing Rights Society (PRS), which deals with the incensing of public performance and broadcast rights on behalf of its members. In practice, the right to perform a copyright work is of tremendous value.

These provisions are important to the owners of sporting venues as well as to pubs and cafes where music is played.

4.18 BROADCASTING

The broadcasting of a work or the inclusion of a work in a cable programme service is an act restricted by copyright.[3] The owner of the copyright in a literary, dramatic, musical or artistic work, sound recording or film, or a broadcast or cable programme may prohibit others from broadcasting the work or including it in a cable programme service. This section does not apply to copyright in the typographical arrangements of published editions.

'Broadcast' is defined in s 6 of the CDPA 1988, and 'cable programme service' in s 7.

---

1   CDPA 1988, s 19.
2   See, further, *Jennings v Stephens* [1936] Ch 469, *PRS v Harlequin Records* [1979] FSR 233, *Ernest Turner Electrical v PRS* [1945] Ch 167.
3   CDPA 1988, s 20.

4.19 ADAPTATIONS

Making an adaptation of a literary, dramatic or musical work is restricted by copyright. CDPA 1988, s 21(3) defines an 'adaptation' in relation to a literary or dramatic work as: a translation of the work; a version of a dramatic work in which it is converted into a non-dramatic work or, as the case may be, of a non-dramatic work in which it is converted into a dramatic work; or a version of the work in which the story or action is conveyed wholly or mainly by means of pictures in a form suitable for reproduction in a book, newspaper, magazine or similar periodical. In relation to a musical work, 'adaptation' means an arrangement or transcription of the work.

An adaptation is 'made' when it is recorded in writing or otherwise. CDPA 1988, s 21(2) states that the doing of any of the acts specified in ss 17–20 or s 21(1) in relation to an adaptation of the work is also an act restricted by copyright in a literary, dramatic or musical work. For the purposes of s 21(2), it is immaterial whether the adaptation has been recorded in writing or otherwise at the time the act is done.

'Writing' is defined as including any form of notational code, whether by hand or otherwise, regardless of the method by which, or medium in or on which, it is recorded.[1]

Where an adaptation of a work has been made, subsequent dealing with it will infringe the other exclusive rights of the copyright owner.[2]

4.20 SECONDARY INFRINGEMENT OF COPYRIGHT

As well as the infringing acts restricted by the copyright in the work under CDPA 1988, ss 16–21, there is another category of infringing act known as 'secondary infringement'. The category of secondary infringement generally relates to commercial use of infringing copies of a copyright work. Secondary infringers are often also prosecuted in the criminal court.

In contrast to the position under CDPA 1988, ss 16–21, secondary infringement under ss 22–26 requires a mental element on the part of the infringer: the infringers must know or have reason to believe that they are dealing with infringing copies of a work.

In *LA Gear Inc v Hi-Tec Sports plc*,[3] it was stated that the test as to what a defendant 'has reason to believe' is an objective one. It requires a consideration of whether the reasonable man, with knowledge of the facts that the defendant had knowledge of, would have formed the belief that the item was an infringing copy. This is important because, under CDPA 1988, s 97, if it can be shown in an action for infringement of copyright that at the time of the infringement the defendant did not know, and had no reason to believe, that copyright subsisted in the work to which the action relates, the plaintiff is not entitled to damages.

---

1   CDPA 1988, s 178.
2   Ibid, s 21(2).
3   [1992] FSR 121.

There is provision in s 97(2) for the court to award damages notwithstanding the defendant's lack of knowledge if the infringement is flagrant and the defendant has benefited from the infringing activity. In such a case, the court may award 'such additional damages as the justice of the case may require'.

Sections 22–26 of the CDPA 1988 set out the acts that constitute secondary infringement of a work.

4.20.1 Importing infringing copies

Importing an infringing copy of a work without the permission of the copyright owner, other than for private or domestic use, constitutes secondary infringement.[1]

4.20.2 Possessing or dealing with infringing copies

Copyright in a work is infringed where, without the permission of the copyright owner, a person possesses, sells or lets for hire, or offers or exposes for sale or hire, exhibits or distributes, or distributes otherwise than in the course of a business to such an extent as to affect prejudicially the owner of the copyright, an infringing copy of the work.[2]

4.20.3 Providing the means for making infringing copies

Anyone who provides the means to make infringing copies is liable.[3] However, in *Amstrad Consumer Electronics v BPI*,[4] similar provisions were not construed so as to hold the manufacturer of a twin deck tape recorder liable for subsequent breaches of copyright.

Copyright is also infringed where a person without permission transmits a work by means of a telecommunication system (this does not include broadcasting or inclusion in a cable programme service) if an infringing copy will be made at the point where the transmission is received.

4.20.4 Permitting the use of premises for infringing performance

If copyright in a literary, dramatic or musical work is infringed by a performance at a place of public entertainment, any person who gave permission for that place to be used for the performance is also liable for the infringement.

CDPA 1988, s 25(2) explains that 'places of public entertainment' includes premises which are occupied mainly for other purposes, but are from time to time made available for hire for the purposes of public entertainment. This might include a room in a pub which is occasionally used for performing plays or for live bands to perform.

---

1   CDPA 1988, s 22.
2   Ibid, s 23.
3   Ibid, s 24.
4   [1986] FSR 159.

4.20.5   Provision of apparatus for infringing performance

Supplying the apparatus to infringe the copyright in a sound recording or film or to receive visual images or sounds conveyed by electronic means will result in liability for the person who supplied the apparatus or any substantial part of it. An occupier of the premises who gave permission for the apparatus to be brought on to the premises may also be liable, as may any person who supplied the copy of the sound recording or film used to infringe the copyright.[1]

4.20.6   Infringing copies

An article is an infringing copy if its making constitutes an infringement of the copyright in the work in question. An article is also an infringing copy if it has been imported into the UK, and making it in the UK would have constituted an infringement of the copyright in the work.[2] It must be shown that the article is a copy of a work and that copyright subsists in the work, in which case it is presumed until the contrary is proved that the article was made at a time when copyright subsisted in the work.

These provisions do not apply if the copyright work may be lawfully imported into the UK under any of the provisions of the European Communities Act 1972. This applies particularly to the doctrine of 'exhaustion of rights'. Effectively, once a copyright work has been put on the market within the EC with the owner's permission, the owner cannot restrict the subsequent sale of those goods The exhaustion of rights principle does not apply where the articles in question infringe the copyright in a work.

Apart from secondary infringement involving public performance of the work, the CDPA 1988 requires that the person 'knows or has reason to believe' that the work in question is an infringing copy or will be used to infringe copyright. The requirement for 'public performance' is that the person who gave permission 'believed on reasonable grounds that the performance would not infringe copyright'.

CDPA 1988, ss 104–105 contain various presumptions relating to the proof of authorship and other matters in proceedings. In relation to literary, dramatic, musical and artistic works, where an author is named on the published work, he is presumed, until the contrary is proved, to be the author of the work.[3] Similar presumptions are made for sound recordings which bear the name of the copyright owner and year of first publication[4] and for films which bear the name of the author or director, the name of the copyright owner at the date of issue and year of first publication.[5] These presumptions can help to avoid the cost of proving title to copyright works.

---

1   CDPA 1988, s 26.
2   Ibid, s 27.
3   Ibid, s 104.
4   Ibid, s 105(1).
5   Ibid, s 105(2).

4.21 DEFENCES AND PERMITTED ACTS

4.21.1 Introduction

The provisions of CDPA 1988, s 16 take effect subject to the 'permitted acts' contained in ss 28–76. If a person can establish that what has been done in relation to the copyright work in fact falls within these provisions, there will be no infringement of the copyright in the work.

There are various categories of permitted acts grouped together under a number of headings.

4.21.2 Fair dealing

The first of these categories deals with the concept of fair dealing. This applies in a number of contexts, namely fair dealing for the purposes of research and private study, and fair dealing for criticism, review and news reporting.

The permitted acts centre around the concept of 'fair dealing'. This is a concept that has troubled the courts on numerous occasions.[1] The copying of the work in question must be of the whole or a substantial part of the work to be an infringing act in the first place. The question of what amounts to a substantial part of a work and the application of the fair dealing defence are different issues.

The defence is only available as set out below.

Fair dealing for research and private study

The provisions of CDPA 1988, s 29 permit fair dealing with a literary, dramatic, musical or artistic work for the purposes of research and private study. Copying in these circumstances does not infringe any copyright in the work.

The application of the provisions is not without difficulty. There is no rule or indication as to the amount of work which may constitute fair use of the work.

The application of the rules clearly relates to the quality as well as the quantity of the material used. It is clear that, in certain circumstances, a work may be copied.

The making of multiple copies or habitual copying of a work (because, for example, it is part of a syllabus) amounts to infringement. In the latter case, different rules apply and the copying should be licensed.

It is also clear that copying may be done by another person on behalf of the researcher as long as that copying does not result in copies of substantially the same material being made for more than one person at substantially the same time.[2] The making of copies for research or study is thus limited to single and not multiple copies.

There are extensive provisions in CDPA 1988, ss 37–44 setting out the conditions upon which librarians (who may not be protected by s 29) may make copies of works for others. There are also provisions in CDPA 1988, ss 32–36 dealing with copyright works, and use and reproduction by educational establishments.

---

1   See, further, the discussion of *Time Warner v Channel Four* [1994] EMLR 1, below.
2   CDPA 1988, s 29(3).

Fair dealing for the purposes of criticism, review and news reporting

CDPA 1988, s 30(1) provides that fair dealing with a work for the purpose of criticism or review, of that or of another work or of a performance of a work, does not infringe any copyright in the work. A copyright acknowledgement must be given. Section 30(2) states that fair dealing with a work (other than a photograph) for the purposes of reporting current events does not infringe copyright in the work. No acknowledgement is required if reporting takes place by means of a sound recording, film, broadcast or cable programme. If no particular category of work is mentioned, the act does not infringe copyright in any category of work.[1]

Fair dealing in this context is also problematical. The basis is that copyright will not be infringed if *either* the use does not amount to a substantial part *or* the fair dealing provisions apply. The question of what amounts to a substantial part is a vexed one. The fair dealing defence adds a significant weapon in cases of alleged infringement.

In *BBC v British Satellite Broadcasting Ltd*,[2] the defendants used excerpts from the plaintiffs' World Cup football coverage in their news broadcasts. BSB gave an acknowledgement – which the legislation does not require – to the BBC for use of the excerpts. The court held that the use of the excerpts, even though it was of the interesting parts, mainly goals, amounted to fair use within the meaning of the CDPA 1988. The limitation on the use suggested by the court related to the timing of the showing of the excerpts. As long as an item is current, its use will be covered by fair dealing.

This case resulted in an agreement between major broadcasters known as the 'Sports News Access Code of Practice' governing the use of excerpts from sports broadcasts.

The court will look at a number of factors in considering fair use. Lord Denning, in *Hubbard v Vosper*,[3] described fair dealing as 'a matter of impression'. The factors to be considered include the following.

–   The amount of the work used will clearly be important. Fair dealing is not a carte blanche to reproduce copyright works.
–   The status of the work reproduced may also be important. If the material in question is confidential in nature, a plaintiff may have other remedies, but the availability of a defence of fair dealing may also be limited. In *Beloff v Pressdram*,[4] the reproduction of the contents of a 'leaked' memo could not be fair dealing. In contrast, the criticism of a work that is already in the public domain (even though not readily available to the public in this country) can, in principle, amount to fair dealing.[5]
–   The purpose of or the motive behind the copying may also be relevant. The fact that the publication is for commercial gain may not be relevant – a reviewer may be keen to help sell copies of his paper – but if the use of the

---

1   CDPA 1988, s 28(2).
2   [1991] 3 WLR 174.
3   [1972] 2 QB 84.
4   [1973] 1 All ER 241.
5   See *Time Warner v Channel Four* [1994] EMLR 1, which sets out further useful guidelines.

work will compete with the copied work, then that may be unfair. This applies whether the copying is for research or for criticism and review.

A recent case concerned fair dealing and the provisions of s 30(1) and s 30(2). A photographer successfully sued a newspaper for infringement of copyright in a photograph. The newspaper was unsuccessful in its defence of fair dealing under this section.[1]

4.21.3 Incidental inclusion

Section 31 permits the showing, playing, broadcasting or inclusion in a cable programme service of anything which was incidentally included in the making of an artistic work, sound recording, film, broadcast or cable programme.

Section 31(3) 'helpfully' states that a musical work, words spoken or sung without music, or so much of a sound recording, broadcast or cable programme that includes a musical work or such words, shall not be regarded as incidentally included if it is deliberately included.

This exception exists to permit programme makers and news broadcasters to show works that might otherwise be protected by copyright.

A typical example might involve a film crew doing interviews or filming footage in the street. A number of works which are protected by the laws of copyright may be included in the film, such as buildings, advertising hoardings, music from cars or shops, and even other television broadcasts.

The exception to this is the use of musical works – most usually, records played over the radio – where the inclusion is deliberate. Thus, a film maker is presumed to have control over his set to the extent that any musical work playing in the background would then have to have clearance. Even a live broadcaster could find itself in breach of copyright. It will be a question of fact as to what constitutes deliberate inclusion. However, the existence of the PRS and PPL and the block licensing regimes should mean most broadcasters' are granted permission under the terms of the block licence. The inclusion of any copyright work should, nevertheless, be carefully considered.

4.21.4 Other provisions

There are various other permitted acts listed in ss 57–63 which apply to certain categories of works, for instance, literary, dramatic and artistic works, as follows.

(1) Section 57 covers acts done in relation to anonymous or pseudonymous works where it is not possible to trace the author and it is reasonable to assume that copyright no longer exists.
(2) Section 58 is important for journalists using a recording of spoken words. As long as the recording is a direct record which is not prohibited by the speaker or copyright owner, and the owner of the recording allows the use, then the words may be used. This is most likely to be relevant where an interview has taken place. The interviewee has copyright in his spoken words, and permission is required for their use. As long as the conditions are satisfied, the interview may be used.

---

1   *Banier v NewsGroup Newspapers* [1997] FRS 812.

4.21.5   Public interest defence

The public interest defence is not a statutory defence. This defence has been developed by the courts in a number of cases involving the publication of material which has been obtained illicitly.

The defence applies in both the law of confidence and the law of copyright. In essence, a defendant argues that disclosure of the information in question is necessary.

The reasons vary, but the defence has applied where the publication relates to an iniquity (although a wrongdoing is not essential), to religious matters and to persons in the public eye. The courts have also stated that there is a difference between what is interesting to the public and what is in the public interest.

The commercial interests of publishers and broadcasters must be distinguished from the public interest, which might be best served by giving the information to the police or some other responsible body.[1]

4.22   CIVIL REMEDIES

The remedies available for primary and secondary infringement of copyright include damages, an account of profits, injunctive relief, as well as delivery-up and destruction of infringing copyright materials.

4.23   CRIMINAL REMEDIES

In addition to the various civil remedies available for primary and secondary infringement of copyright, there are criminal remedies contained in the CDPA 1988.[2]

There are provisions for delivery-up,[3] search warrants,[4] as well as corporate liability.[5] There may also be offences under s 1 of the Trades Descriptions Act 1968. A person who applies a false trade description to any goods or supplies, or offers to supply goods to which a false trade description has been applied, may be liable. They must also be acting in the course of a business. There are various criminal remedies available under the Trade Marks Act 1994 for the unauthorised use of a trade mark in relation to goods. The Criminal Justice and Public Order Act 1994, s 165 introduced ss 107A and 198A into the CDPA 1988. These sections require the local weights and measures authorities to enforce the provisions of ss 107 and 198 within the areas. The local authorities have the power to make test purchases and seize offending items in their areas under the copyright and trade marks legislation.

---

1   For a further discussion see *Lion Laboratories Ltd v Evans* [1984] 2 All ER 417.
2   CDPA 1988, s 107.
3   Ibid, s 108.
4   Ibid, s 109.
5   Ibid, s 110.

TRADE MARKS AND PASSING OFF

4.24   INTRODUCTION

This section is designed to be an introduction to the field of trade marks and passing off. Practitioners are referred to standard texts where further detail is required. The final section of this chapter considers the application of the law in the business of sport.

4.25   TRADE MARKS

4.25.1   General

The law is mainly governed by the Trade Marks Act 1994 (TMA 1994), which was passed to give effect to Directive 89/104 on the harmonisation of national trade mark laws. This Act applies to infringements which occur after the commencement of the 1994 Act (31 October 1994).

4.25.2   What is a trade mark?

A trade mark is defined as:

> 'any sign capable of being represented graphically which is capable of distinguishing goods or services of one undertaking from those of other undertakings'.[1]

This includes, but is not limited to:[2]

– words, including personal names;
– designs;
– letters;
– numerals;
– the shape of goods or their packaging, except those which consist exclusively of the shape which results from the nature of the goods themselves or which is necessary to obtain a technical result or which gives substantial value to the goods.[3]

The definition is wide enough to cover distinctive colours and/or colour combinations, sounds and smells although the extent to which these will be relevant in sport varies.

4.25.3   Registration

A mark falling within the s 1(1) definition should be registered unless there is a specific reason to the contrary. A mark may be refused an application for registration on the basis of the absolute and the relative grounds for refusal.

---

1   TMA 1994, s 1(1).
2   Ibid, s 1(2).
3   Ibid, s 3(2).

(1) Absolute grounds for refusal of registration
If the mark:

- is devoid of any distinctive character;[1] or
- consists of signs or indications which may serve, in the relevant trade, to designate the kind, quality, intended purpose, value, geographical origin, time of production or of rendering, or other characteristics of the relevant goods or services;[2] or
- consists exclusively of signs or indications which are customary in the current language or the bona fide and established practices of the trade;[3] or
- is contrary to public policy or accepted principles of morality;[4] or
- is likely to mislead the public, for example as to the nature, quality or geographical origin of the relevant goods or services;[5] or
- is prohibited from registration by UK statute or EC law;[6] or
- is a specially protected emblem, for example royal emblems or insignia, or national flags (subject to certain exceptions as described in s 4); or
- consists exclusively of the shape which results from the nature of the goods themselves, or the shape which is necessary to obtain a technical result, or the shape which gives substantial value to the goods;[7] or
- is the subject of an application in bad faith, for example an application filed to block the application of another;

then it will be refused registration.

The first three of these grounds can be displaced if the applicant can prove 'a distinctive character' through use of the mark prior to the application.

(2) Relative grounds for refusal of registration
Registration will be refused on the relative grounds if a mark:

- is identical to an earlier mark and the application is in respect of identical goods or services;
- is identical to an earlier mark and the application is in respect of similar goods or services, or is similar to an earlier trade mark and the application is in respect of similar goods or services, or is similar to an earlier trade mark and the application is in respect of identical goods or services, provided (in each case) there is a likelihood of confusion between the marks in the public mind;
- is identical or similar to an earlier trade mark in respect of non-similar goods or services where the earlier mark has established a reputation and the later mark would take unfair advantage of or be detrimental to that reputation; or
- would be liable to be unusable because of any rule of law or some earlier intellectual property right.

---

1   TMA 1994, s 3(1)(b).
2   Ibid, s 3(1)(c).
3   Ibid, s 3(1)(d).
4   Ibid, s 3(3)(a).
5   TMA 1994, s 3(3)(b).
6   Ibid, s 3(4).
7   Ibid, s 3(2).

4.25.4 Procedure

The Act contains detailed rules governing the procedure for trade mark applications[1] which are beyond the scope of this work. The applicants must, however, choose a category of goods or services to register the mark against. There are 42 classes and a mark may be registered in more than one category. The classes of registration into which sporting merchandise will most commonly fall include the following:

Class	Specification/Goods
03	Soap; toothpaste; perfumery; toiletries; gift and presentation sets comprising personal toiletries; cosmetics and cosmetic kits; essential oils; bath foam and bath salts; shower gel; shampoo and hair conditioner; fragranced air-freshener articles and preparations; boot polish and boot cream; deodorants for personal use; shaving and aftershave preparation; talcum powder
06	Badges (for vehicles) and bars for use therewith; keys, key blanks, key rings and key chains; locks and ornaments, all included in class 6; all made of common metal and their alloys
08	Cutlery, razors, razor blades
09	Audio and video cassettes, digital audio tape, compact discs, computer disks and software including computer games
11	Lampshades and lighting; torches; gas lighters
14	Jewellery and imitation jewellery; clocks and watches, cases, bands, straps and parts therefor; key rings and key fobs; cuff links and tie pins; containers (none being smoker's articles); badges of precious metals; statuettes; cruet sets
16	Stationery; books; book markers; printed matter and printed publications; magazines; brochures; pens; pencils and writing implements; transfers (decalcomanias); rulers; pencil sharpeners; cases and containers, all for stationery and for writing implements; playing cards; writing pads; instructional and teaching material; photographs and photograph albums; posters; post cards; wall charts; calendars; diaries; cards; labels; coasters; car stickers; car tax disc holders; car window blinds
18	Articles made of leather or imitation leather; travelling bags; handbags; backpacks, duffel bags, boot bags, holdalls; bags; belts; straps; wallets, purses, credit card holders and cheque book holders; key cases; umbrellas
20	Furniture, mirrors, picture frames; goods (not included in other classes) made of wood, cork, reed, cane, wicker, horn, bone, ivory, whalebone, shell, amber, mother of pearl, meerschaum and substitutes for all these materials, or of plastics

---

1   TMA 1994, s 37–39.

21	Domestic utensils and containers (not of precious metal or coated therewith); china, glassware, porcelain and earthenware; combs and sponges; drinking glasses; tankards and tumblers; brushes; money boxes; toothbrushes
24	Textile articles; curtain and upholstery fabrics; pillow cases; bed sheets; bedspreads; bed and duvet covers; towels and bath linen; table linen; handkerchiefs; banners, flags, pennants and textile wall hangings
25	Articles of sports clothing; foot wear; leisure wear; underwear for men, women and children; slippers; socks; ties; headgear; gloves; scarves; sweatshirts; T-shirts; sweaters; articles of clothing for babies; bibs; dungarees; pyjamas; tracksuits
26	Badges; patches and rosettes; lapel pins; buttons; belt clasps and buckles; hair ornaments; ribbon; braids, appliques, tapes, trimmings and tassels, all being textile smallwares; textile fancy goods
27	Floor coverings; wall hangings and wall coverings; wallpaper and borders
28	Toys; games; playthings; footballs; darts and flights therefor; bags adapted for carrying sporting articles
30	Preparations made from cereals, bread and pastry; confectionery
32	Beers, minerals and aerated waters and other non-alcoholic drinks; fruit drinks; fruit juices; syrups and other preparations for making beverages
33	Alcoholic beverages (except beers)
34	Tobacco; smokers' articles; matches
35	Advertising; business management; business administration; office functions
36	Insurance; financial affairs; monetary affairs; real estate affairs
39	Transport; packaging and storage of goods; travel arrangements
41	Education; providing of training; entertainment; sporting and cultural activities
42	Providing of food and drink; temporary accommodation; services that cannot be placed in other classes

Registration is initially for 10 years, and is then renewable for further periods of 10 years.[1]

4.25.5 Infringement

A trade mark is an exclusive property right which is infringed by use of the mark, in the course of trade, without the proprietor's consent. The infringing acts

1   TMA 1994, ss 42 and 43.

reflect the relative grounds for refusal of registration[1] dealt with above. The infringing acts are:

- using a mark which is identical to a registered mark in relation to identical goods or services; or
- using a mark which is identical to a registered mark in relation to similar goods or services provided there is a likelihood of confusion on the part of the public, which includes the likelihood of association with the trade mark; or
- using a mark which is similar to a registered mark in relation to similar goods or services or to identical goods or services provided (in each case) there is a likelihood of confusion on the part of the public, which includes the likelihood of association with the trade mark; or
- using a mark which is identical or similar to a registered mark in respect of non-similar goods or services where the proprietor of the registered mark has established a reputation and the later mark, being without due cause would take unfair advantage of or be detrimental to that reputation.

The meaning of 'likelihood of association' has been considered in a number of cases.[2]

A trade mark must be used; 'use' of a mark includes:

- putting it on goods or packaging; or
- offering, marketing or stocking goods, or offering or supplying goods under the mark; or
- importing or exporting goods under the mark; or
- putting it on business papers or advertising material.[3]

The requirement of 'use' means that not every instance where a trade mark is seen or applied will constitute an infringement. For example, does the appearance of a trade mark in a photograph used in a newspaper infringe the trade mark? Likewise, will the incidental appearance of a trade mark on an item of clothing or a piece of merchandise used in a film or an advertisement necessarily infringe the trade mark owner's rights? The answer appears to be 'not necessarily': where the mark is not being used in the course of trade to sell the product in the category in which it is registered there may be no infringement.

The authority for this is *Trebor Bassett v FA*[4] where Trebor Bassett successfully sought a declaration that the appearance of the FA's 'Three Lions' logo on pictures of players on their shirts given away with sweets was not trade mark use. There will be a line here that cannot be crossed which will relate to the prominence and specific 'use' to which the registered mark is put. The result here is a common sense one and a different decision could have required newspapers and broadcasters to require a specific consent whenever a trade mark appears rather than when used in the way the legislation appears to require.

---

1   TMA 1994, s 5.
2   *Wagamama Limited v City Centre Restaurants plc and City Centre Restaurants (UK) Ltd* [1995] FSR 713, ChD.
3   TMA 1994, s 10(4).
4   [1997] FSR 211.

Anyone who applies a registered mark to labelling, packaging or advertising material or business papers is liable if, at the time of application, he knew or had reason to believe that such application was not duly authorised.[1] A trade mark can be used in comparative advertising in certain circumstances.[2]

There are also various criminal offences under the TMA where identical and/or similar marks are applied to goods or used in advertising materials for goods.[3]

4.25.6 Remedies

The right to bring proceedings vest in the proprietor from the date of filing of the application. However, no proceedings may be brought before the mark is actually registered.[4]

An infringement is actionable by the registered proprietor who has the right to such relief as would be appropriate in relation to infringement of any other property right, including damages, injunctions and accounts.[5]

Specific remedies include:

- an order for erasure of the mark or destruction of the infringing goods, materials or articles;[6] or
- an order for the delivery up of infringing goods, materials or articles,[7] but subject to a six-year limitation period.[8]

The owner of a 'well-known' (but unregistered) trade mark may apply for injunctive relief (but not damages) preventing use in the UK of a mark which is similar or identical to his mark in relation to similar or identical goods or services.[9] Well-known marks are those protected as such under the Paris Convention for the protection of intellectual property. The owner of the well-known mark must be based in a country which is a signatory to the Paris Convention (which covers most of the industrialised nations). The owner is barred from relief if he has acquiesced for a continuous period of five years or more, ie if, with knowledge, he has allowed the action about which he now complains.

4.25.7 Comparative advertising

Comparative advertising is permitted by s 10(6), ie a trade mark may be used to identify goods or services as being those of the proprietor so long as the use:

- is in accordance with honest practices in industrial or commercial matters; and
- is not such as to take unfair advantage of or cause damage to the distinctive character or reputation of the trade mark.

1   TMA 1994, s 10(5).
2   Ibid, s 10(6).
3   Ibid, s 92.
4   Ibid, s 9(3).
5   Ibid, s 14.
6   Ibid, s 15(1).
7   Ibid, s 16(1).
8   Ibid, s 18.
9   Ibid, s 56.

Possible trade mark infringement is only one element of a claim in comparative advertising. The possibility of a trade libel, defamation or copyright claim exists as does a passing off claim or a complaint for breach of the British Code of Advertising and Sales Promotion.[1]

There is also a proposed EC Directive on comparative advertising.

A trade mark is not infringed by use in accordance with honest practices where the use is:

–   by a person of his own name or address; or
–   to indicate the kind, quality, quantity, intended purpose, value, geographical origin, time of production of goods or of rendering of services, or other characteristics of goods or services; or
–   necessary to indicate the intended purpose of goods and services, provided there is compliance with honest practices, for example, in the sale of spare parts or accessories for third party products.[2]

Under s 11, there is no infringement by use in a particular locality of an earlier right applying only in that locality which would have enough goodwill to protect it by any rule of law, for example a passing off action.

There will be no infringement by use of a mark in relation to goods put on the market in the European Community under the mark by the owner or with his consent, because by doing so the rights are exhausted.[3] There is an exception if there are legitimate reasons for the proprietor to oppose further dealings with the marked goods, for example if the condition of them has been changed or impaired after they were put on the market.

4.25.8   Groundless threats

If an owner of a mark (or indeed its representatives) makes unjustified threats of infringement, it may be subject to:

–   a declaration that the threats are unjustifiable; and
–   injunctive relief; and/or
–   damages,

unless the owner shows that the acts (or proposed acts) in response to which the threats were made infringed (or would infringe) the mark.[4] Even if the owner establishes such actual or intended infringement, the other party can still get relief by showing that the registration of the mark is invalid or liable to be revoked.

4.25.9   Assignments and licences

A registered mark is a property right[5] which can be transferred or charged by assignment, will or operation of law,[6] so long as the disposition is in writing and

---

1   See further Carey and Verow, *Media and Entertainment: The Law and Business* (Jordans, 1998).
2   TMA 1994, s 11.
3   Ibid, s 12.
4   Ibid, s 21.
5   Ibid, ss 2(1) and 22.
6   Ibid, s 24(1), (4) and (5).

signed by or on behalf of the assignor or (if appropriate) a personal representative.[1]

Any disposition may be entire or partial. It may be limited so as to apply to some, but not all, the goods or services to which its registration applies, or in relation to use in a particular manner or locality.[2]

Licences may be entire or partial, and must be in writing and signed by or on behalf of the person granting the rights.[3]

A licensee may require the proprietor of the registered mark to take infringement proceedings.[4] If the proprietor refuses or delays for two months in doing so, then the licensee can bring proceedings in his own name as if he were the proprietor. Unless the court orders otherwise and in relation to interlocutory relief, the proprietor must be joined as a plaintiff or defendant to the proceedings.

By s 31, exclusive licensees[5] can (if the licence so provides) sue for infringement of the mark instead of or alongside the proprietor. Non-exclusive licensees do not have such a right. It is quite common for both these sections to be varied in the term of the trade mark licence limiting the rights of the licencee to take such steps.

Details of transactions (including charges, assignments, assents, disposition by court order and licences) have to be noted on the register.[6] If they are not, then they are not effective against a person who acquires a conflicting interest in ignorance of the transaction.[7]

Until a licence is noted, any right the licensee may have to the s 30 or s 31 rights or remedies in relation to infringement is ineffective.[8] If a new proprietor or licensee does not register his interest within six months of assignment or licence, the effect is that he loses the right to claim damages or an account of profits for the period between date of transaction and registration.[9]

Contrary to the previous situation, there is no requirement that the Registrar of Trade Marks examine assignments and licences before agreeing to register them.

No notice of any trust is to be entered on the register.[10]

Applications to register trade marks can also be treated (mutatis mutandis) as property for the purposes of ss 22–26.[11]

---

1   TMA 1994, s 24(3).
2   Ibid, s 24(2).
3   Ibid, s 28.
4   Ibid, s 30.
5   As defined in TMA 1994, s 29.
6   TMA 1994, s 25(2).
7   Ibid, s 25(3)(a).
8   Ibid, s 25(3)(b).
9   Ibid, s 25(4)(b).
10   Ibid, s 26(1).
11   Ibid, s 27(1).

4.25.10   Revocation and invalidity

A trade mark can be revoked on various grounds[1] or may be declared invalid.[2] Trade mark owners should take care that these rights are not lost in this way.

4.26   THE OLYMPIC RINGS

The Olympic Symbol (Protection) Act 1995 creates exclusive rights in relation to the use of the five-ring symbol, the Olympic motto and certain words, such as 'Olympic(s)', 'Olympiad(s)' and 'Olympians'. These rights are infringed if any of the marks are used without the consent of the British Olympic Association. The rights are similar to normal trade marks in that there are civil and criminal remedies for infringement.

4.27   PASSING OFF

4.27.1   General

The passing off action pre-dates the trade mark legislation and is unaffected by it. The tort of passing off can be seen to complement the statutory action for infringement of a registered trade mark. It is both wider than its statutory counterpart and less hampered by precise legal definition. The Trade Marks Act 1994 has resulted in many more marks being registerable and thus protected under the Act although the flexibility of an action in passing off is still useful and may be essential where no rights have been or are capable of registration. Although registered trade marks are easier to enforce (the plaintiff does not have to establish he has goodwill or, in the main a misrepresentation) the passing off action is a useful weapon.

4.27.2   The passing off action

The passing off action is based on the premise that 'nobody has any right to represent his goods as the goods of somebody else'.[3]

In *Warnink v Townend*,[4] Lord Diplock set out five characteristics necessary to launch a valid passing off action:

(1)   a misrepresentation;
(2)   made by a trader in the course of trade;
(3)   to prospective customers of his or ultimate customers of goods or services supplied by him;
(4)   which is calculated to injure the business or goodwill of another trader (in the sense that this is a reasonably foreseeable consequence); and
(5)   which causes actual damage to the business or goodwill of the trader by whom the action is brought or (in a quia timet action) will probably do so.

---

1   TMA 1994, s 46.
2   Ibid, s 47.
3   Per Halsbury LC in *Reddaway v Banham* [1896] AC 199.
4   [1979] AC 731.

In *Consorzio del Prosciutto di Parma v Marks & Spencer plc and others,*[1] Nourse LJ reduced these characteristics to:

> 'the classical trinity of:
> (1)   a reputation (or goodwill) acquired by the plaintiff in his goods, name, mark etc;
> (2)   a misrepresentation by the defendant leading to confusion (or deception); causing
> (3)   damage to the plaintiff.'

The three characteristics will now be examined in turn.

(1)   Reputation or goodwill acquired by the plaintiff in his goods, name, mark etc

In order to acquire and maintain the type of goodwill which can be protected by a passing off action, the owner must:

–   establish a reputation in a mark by using it in business (some kind of commercial activity is required);
–   ensure the mark is associated with particular goods or services of the owner, or with the owner personally; and
–   protect that reputation against misuse.

A mark is, very broadly, something which is used to try to give an identity to a supplier and/or its goods and services which is distinguishable from other, otherwise similar, suppliers and/or their goods and services.

The mark could be the:

–   style of packaging;
–   colour;
–   'get-up'. It should be noted that this relates to the container, not the shape of the goods themselves.

Unlike the registrable trade mark, there are no restrictions for protection by a passing off action save that the mark must distinguish the owner and/or his goods and/or his services.

Where the plaintiff's business is locally based in one part of the country he may nevertheless get protection (and obtain an injunction) against persons using a similar name in other parts of the country. This will be more certain where the plaintiff can show some possibility of geographical expansion of his business at some future time.[2] Where the plaintiff is outside the UK, he is not likely to succeed in a passing off action against a UK defendant unless he can show some business activity here. Such activity might be in the form of doing business through an agent in the UK or having customers here. However, goodwill may be established very quickly through advertising and/or actual sales and, indeed, it may be quite localised.[3]

The following are examples of particular applications of the law.

---

1   [1991] RPC 351.
2   See *Brestian v Fry* [1958] RPC 161.
3   *Stannard v Reay* [1967] RPC 589.

- **Initials**
  Initials of themselves are hard to establish as a mark. There must be a distinctive presentation of them.

- **Place names**
  Place names are hard to protect unless they are associated in the public mind with goods or services – like Champagne – when a protectable mark may well arise. Such cases also show that it is possible, although not usual, for goodwill to be shared jointly (eg by those in the Champagne region).

- **Generic names**
  As with place names, if goods are marketed under a generic name and associated with standards of quality and production, then goodwill can be generated.

  In *Warnink*,[1] the manufacturers of Advocaat (a high quality product with a substantial reputation and which sold in large quantities) were able to stop sales of an allegedly inferior and cheaper liqueur called 'Keelings Old English Advocaat'.

  The risk, however, is that extreme success of the genre may cause loss of distinctiveness. If the mark is not distinctive, it cannot be protected. 'Hoover' swept the market when first sold by Mr Hoover, but now even an Electrolux vacuum cleaner is commonly described as a Hoover.

- **Descriptive names**
  It will be difficult to show a protectable interest in a name which is merely descriptive (eg corona applied to a cigar) until the name has been exclusively used for long enough to create a secondary meaning which relates only to the owner and not to any competitor.

  Even when the secondary meaning is established, the courts will construe the name strictly unless fraud or misrepresentative intent is shown. So even a slightly different name used by the competitor may escape liability.[2]

- **Character merchandising**
  Usually the name of a fictitious character (like Sherlock Holmes) cannot be protected as goodwill. But if it can be shown that a competitor intends to exploit the character's reputation and goodwill, and that a substantial number of people would believe the plaintiff was associated with the competitor then protection may be given.[3]

  Even then, it is normally necessary to show that the parties are in the same or similar fields of activity. If not, then the claim may fail, as in *Wombles Ltd v Wombles Skip Hire Ltd*.[4] In that case, the plaintiff was the holder of copyright in books and drawings featuring the Wombles. These were characters known for collecting rubbish. The defendant was a skip hire company which had adopted the Wombles name. The plaintiff could not

---

1   *Warnink v Townend* [1979] AC 731.
2   *Office Cleaning Services Ltd v Westminster Office Cleaning Association* [1946] 1 All ER 320.
3   *IPC Magazines Ltd v Black and White Music Corporation* [1983] FSR 348.
4   [1977] RPC 99.

prove that there was confusion sufficient to lead to damage to his goodwill.

The courts have recognised and protected 'character merchandising'. The *Ninja Turtles* case[1] involved use of drawings (rather than the names) of turtle-like characters. Such use was restrained by interlocutory injunction. More recently though there has been a move away from granting such protection[2] leaving most cases to turn on their own facts and plaintiffs finding it increasingly difficult to stamp out 'unauthorised' merchandise.[3]

– **Area of sale or operations**
Cases about the geographical limits of goodwill are difficult to reconcile. On the one hand, the product must be available on the open market rather than amongst a small, defined and limited class. For example, the drinking of beers by UK-based American servicemen in private bars will not qualify.[4] However, it is not necessary for the owner to set up a business in the UK, merely that the product is freely available here.

In 1967, the Crazy Horse Saloon of Paris (which had no UK base but was known in the UK) was unable to stop the opening of a similarly named, but otherwise unconnected club in the UK. In contrast, in 1964, the Sheraton hotel group (which again had no UK base but was known and took bookings for its overseas hotels from the UK) was able to stop the opening of a similarly named hotel in the UK. Finally, in 1977, Maxim's restaurant of Paris (owned by a UK company) was able to stop the opening of Maxim's restaurant of Norwich.

However, there can be no action for passing off if the allegedly infringing acts take place entirely outside the UK.[5] There may, of course, be a local action.

(2)   A misrepresentation by the defendant leading to confusion or deception

The representation may be express or implied. It does not matter that it is true if the overall effect is to mislead. A comparison with other goods is not a representation in this sense even if the comparative statements are false. There is no need for the misrepresentation to be a duplicate of the plaintiff's name and/or mark.

The misrepresentation must be made by a trader in the course of trade. Trade in this context (and in the context of those who may claim goodwill) includes business generally, the professions, service providers, charities and clubs. The misrepresentation must be made to prospective customers of his or ultimate customers of goods or services supplied by him.

A finding of fraud on the part of the person making the misrepresentation will put the evidential burden on the defendant but there is no need for the misrepresentation to be fraudulent. The essential pre-condition is the confusion

---

1   *Mirage Studios v Counter-Feat Clothing* [1991] FSR 145.
2   See *Panini* case (1996) unreported.
3   See Chapter 8 for more details.
4   See *Anheuser-Bush Inc v Budejovicky Budvar Narodni Podnik* [1984] FSR 413 ('the *Budweiser* case').
5   *Intercontex v Schmidt* [1988] FSR 575.

of the customer by the representation. There is no need for the representation to be made by the defendant with the intention (or even the knowledge) that confusion would result. Innocence is no defence.[1]

Normally it will be necessary for the plaintiff to show that he and the defendant are engaged in the same field of activity[2] but this is not an absolute requirement. In *Stringfellow v McCain Foods*,[3] there was held to be confusion between the plaintiff's night club (called Stringfellows) and the defendant's chips of the same name! The evidence of confusion was, no doubt, bolstered by the defendant's television advertising campaign which included a disco sequence. The claim was, however, unsuccessful as the plaintiff could not prove damage.

The real issue is the effect of the misrepresentation on customers. Will they believe that there is an association between the defendant's goods or services and the reputation of the plaintiff? That is a question of fact and may vary from case to case. In *Lego Systems A/S and another v Lego M. Lemelstrich*,[4] the toy brick manufacturers were able to stop the defendant's use of the 'Lego' name in connection with plastic irrigation and gardening equipment. This was largely because Lego is a household name associated with plastic.

Where the plaintiff is not yet involved in a particular field, it may be able to prevent use of its name if it has plans to go into the new field as soon as possible.[5]

It must be likely that customers will be deceived by the representation. This is another question of fact. Expert evidence can be adduced. So, too, can evidence of market research, but this is likely to be criticised by the court, for not being helpful,[6] in which case the court may want to see all the individuals who took part in the survey as witnesses in court.

It need not be all or even the majority of customers who are confused, but it must be more than the 'moron in a hurry'. In *J. Bollinger v Costa Brava Wine Co Ltd (No 2)*,[7] the defendants claimed that only the ignorant would be confused by the sale of Spanish Champagne. The court said that a substantial part of the public, who did not know about wine, might be confused and that was enough for an injunction to be granted.

It does not matter that the confusion is transitory. In a retail case, first impressions count. The 'confusion' element will be satisfied if people 'conclude that the defendants are connected with the plaintiffs, or are a branch of the plaintiffs or in some way mixed up with them'.[8]

Confusion alone is not enough to found an action for passing off. All the other characteristics must also be present. In particular, there must be a misrepresentation and loss. If confusion results simply from the 'collision of two

---

1   *Baume & Co Ltd v A.H. Moore Ltd* [1958] RPC 226.
2   See *Granada Group Ltd v Ford Motor Company Ltd* [1973] RPC 49 discussed above.
3   [1984] FSR 175.
4   [1983] FSR 155.
5   *Nationwide Building Society v Nationwide Estate Agents Ltd* [1987] FSR 579.
6   For example, see *Mothercare UK Ltd v Penguin Books Ltd* [1988] RPC 113, which arose from the defendant's publication of a book entitled 'Mothercare/Othercare'.
7   [1961] 1 All ER 561.
8   *Ewing v Buttercup Margarine Co Ltd* [1917] 2 Ch 1.

independent rights' then neither party can complain. It is one of the misfortunes of life.[1]

Examples of misrepresentation include the following:

– a misdescription, provided there is a class of products or services to which the description can validly be applied (Champagne, for example, in relation to sparkling wine produced in the Champagne region of France) and provided the association of that description and the reputation of the plaintiff (Bollinger, for example) is established so that the customer expects such products and services to meet certain standards;

– claiming without reason a connection with some well-established business;

– using the plaintiff's advertising to give the impression that the defendant's goods or services are those advertised by the plaintiff or even that low quality goods of the plaintiff are the plaintiff's normal quality goods (eg where the defendant collects used razor blades manufactured by the plaintiff and resells them as new, having repackaged them in the plaintiff's distinctive containers);

– use of a mark similar to the plaintiff's mark;

– use of a name or trading name similar to that of the plaintiff. Distinctions here can be especially fine. Normally, no one can be stopped from using his own name (or one which has by association become his own: for example, in the way that Harry Webb has become known as Cliff Richard), but they must do so 'honestly' and 'not go beyond that'.[2] However, it seems that if a person uses his natural or assumed name with the intention of taking business from another, then there can be a misrepresentation and such action may be restrained. Where the defendant's name is his own, the burden of proof on the plaintiff is usually heavy, but when it is an assumed name, the burden is lighter. Use by a company of its registered name may still amount to a misrepresentation. It should be remembered that all this assumes some misrepresentation on the defendant's part. If there is no such intent, then use of one's own name, or one to which a right has been established independent of the plaintiff, is usually not actionable – it is a normal commercial hazard;

– alteration of or addition to the plaintiff's product;

– imputing the authority or consent of the holder of the goodwill. This has a variety of guises, for example claiming membership of The Law Society or the British Medical Association. An interesting and novel example is *Associated Newspapers Group plc Insert Media Ltd and others*.[3] The plaintiff published various magazines and wished to prevent retailers and distributors inserting advertising material between the pages of the magazines, which the publisher had not authorised or arranging with third parties to make such insertions. It was held that insertion of advertising leaflets into newspapers would be a misrepresentation that the inserts were made or

---

1   See *Marengo v Daily Sketch and Daily Graphic Limited* [1992] 19 FSR 1.
2   See *Wright, Layman & Umney Ltd v Wright* [1949] 66 RPC 149.
3   [1991] FSR 380.

authorised by the publishers if there was also evidence that a substantial number of readers would believe the inserts were so made or authorised;

– substitution of rival goods.

4.27.3 Trade marks, passing off and sport

Capturing the goodwill associated with sport and exploiting (as well as protecting) the commercial benefits that arise from that goodwill is the purpose of the trade mark. The sport business attempts to achieve in its commercial programmes and relationships the packaging and exploitation of the goodwill in a form which can be readily exploited and easily protected.

Sport and its associated goodwill is exploited by means of advertising, merchandising, sponsorship and television deals which all capitalise – whether officially or otherwise – on the business and goodwill of sport.

Trade mark protection provides a ready means of packaging various elements of a sport into a readily exploitable and profitable form. The goodwill is captured in the names, logos and various insignia which are created around various sports.

The protection is available at every level of sport, from rights holders and governing bodies (such as the FA with the 'Three Lions' logo), participating teams (Manchester United own various trade marks), the individual sportsmen (the 'Gazza' trade mark being one of the better known trade marks) as well as the name of certain events (France '98 and its logo being an example of an unregistered mark which is also protected as a copyright artistic work, in football, or the Prutour and its associated logo owned by Prudential Assurance for cycling in the UK.)

When a sport sets out about protecting its assets the first steps will involve an agreement of what rights it can protect using the registered and/or unregistered trade mark system. This will usually involve the registration of the name and logo of the organisation or individual concerned.

Once the mark is in place it may be licensed to third parties for use in merchandise and by sponsors. Broadcasters will also use the mark to promote the broadcast coverage of the competition in question.

The best example of a well protected event name and logo is the Olympic symbol and name[1] which has effective statutory protection. Other sports and events are not so fortunate as they must first register and then protect their marks. The registration has been effected for the IOC and, locally, the British Olympic Association, which is left to exploit and police its rights. Elsewhere the individual sport or event will have to ensure that it registers the rights itself and that enterprising third parties do not do so themselves. Whilst a sport trading and exploiting its goodwill (even though it has not registered its marks) may be able to recapture its rights, challenge the registration or even co-exist peacefully, it is not unknown for an unconnected third party to establish rights in a name or mark to the detriment of the 'official' but indolent or ill-advised rights owner. An organised and thorough approach to registration and protection in all relevant territories is essential.

---

1   See **4.26**.

Sport may then roll out its 'brand' in any number of ways, as follows:

(i)   merchandising;
(ii)   licensing (eg on credit cards and financial products);
(iii)   sponsorship;
(iv)   advertising;
(v)   broadcasting, television and video;
(vi)   video games;
(vii)   internet rights and other new technology;
(viii) publishing and official journals;

some of which are dealt with in this work.

PATENTS

4.28   APPLICABILITY TO SPORT

In some ways, a patent could be seen as the most powerful form of intellectual property recognised by English Law. Like a trade mark, it confers by a system of registration what is effectively a statutory monopoly upon the holder of the right. A patent does not come into being as a by-product of the creative process, in the same way as copyright does. The process of applying for a patent is long, complex and frequently very expensive, but the resultant right can be of immense commercial value. Patents, however, are only of limited application in the business of sport. Patents protect inventions which are capable of industrial application. Effectively, a patent can be granted for a new type of article (a product patent) or for a new way of making an old or new type of article (a process patent). Many businesses, therefore, in the sporting arena would have little or no use for this area of law given that they are not in the process of industrial manufacture or industrial process, but rather are a service industry, and s 1(2) of the Patents Act 1977 specifically excludes from those things which are capable of patent registration most if not all of the original conceptions that might form the output of a sports club or governing body. For instance, aesthetic and purely intellectual creations of any nature, be they literary, dramatic, musical or artistic works, or schemes, rules or methods of performing any mental act, playing any game or doing business, or any form of presentation of information will not be eligible for protection by the law of patents. Broadcasts, logos, strip designs and so forth, which are the intellectual property 'stock in trade' of sports clubs, are not therefore the subject of patent protection.

However, this does not mean that patents are irrelevant to sport. They are, however, confined to the manufacturing side of sport: in other words, those businesses which produce sporting equipment and so forth. A new design of golf club should be considered for patent protection, as should a new design for a football boot. A new way of manufacturing golf balls should be considered in the same way. One famous example is the development by the former Liverpool footballer, Craig Johnston, of the 'Predator' football boot. Protection was sought for this invention by way of a patent to recognise the novelty of the article, which effectively turned upon the design of the portion of the boot which has contact with the ball, allowing the player greater grip on the ball and therefore a greater ability to impart, swerve or spin to the ball.

4.28.1 The law of patents

The law of patents is effectively a compromise between two conflicting interests. Inventors will only undergo the privations of working in research and development and the long, lonely road of the inventive process if they have the ability, when their invention comes to fruition, to exploit it on an exclusive basis. However, it is of paramount public importance that new inventions are not solely confined to one concern for all time or to a concern which may not exploit them in the proper manner. New advances in technology should be available to all. The system of patent protection therefore seeks to steer a middle line through these potential conflicts by providing a patentee with a statutory monopoly for a period of 20 years (which can be extended to 25 years in relation to pharmaceuticals) and providing that, at the end of those 20 years, the patent is available for anybody to work without any charge. A common experience of this is where certain medicines become 'generic'. The public is used to a brand name drug and, upon the patent expiring, it suddenly finds that now the drug has a different generic name and everybody is making it.

In order to be granted a patent, the inventor must publish full details of the invention and details of what makes it unique in such a way as allows others to 'see the workings'. Others are held back from reproducing that invention by the ability of the patent holder to prevent infringement for at least 16 years. In the last four years of the patent's life, compulsory licences will be granted in certain circumstances to those who wish to have them. There is, therefore, a brief period of potentially huge profit for a patentee in return for disclosure of his ideas and a general free-for-all at the end of the designated period.

4.28.2 The territoriality of patents

A word needs to be said here in relation to the territoriality of patents. A UK resident will first think of a UK patent application. He may decide that a European application should be filed with the European Patent Office (provided the UK Patent Office consents, which it will do if the patent does not compromise national security). However, the international nature of commerce means that, for real protection, a patent should be applied for in all the major jurisdictions in which it is believed that the invention could be exploited by the proposed patentee or copied by other persons. A UK patent does not bind the world. The adding of one territory to another can lead to a huge increase in the expense and difficulty of obtaining patent protection. The expense is twofold: not only must the applicant for the patent pay extensive fees through the process of application, but also any applicant who is not very highly skilled in the area should employ a specialist patent agent. This does not come cheap, as it is a highly specialised and skilled job. It is, however, utterly crucial that the patent application is considered by experts, as not only will this have a direct effect on whether it is granted or not, it will also be crucial that the claims made for the patent (see below) are correctly set out so as to prevent infringement by others.

4.29 'PATENTABILITY'

The law of patents is regulated by the Patents Act 1977. This sets down a comprehensive scheme governing everything from what may be patented, through what will infringe a patent, and beyond. In logical order, s 1 deals with those things which are requirements before a patent will be granted. To be made the subject of the patent, therefore, an invention must be new; it must involve an inventive step; it must be capable of industrial application; and, finally, it must not be an invention of a nature where patent grant is excluded, such as in the instances given above relating to schemes, rules or methods for playing games and so forth.

Each of the components of this provision is the subject of very extensive case-law. Patents law is a very specialised area and also a very litigious area. Put bluntly, where patents are concerned, it is often worth the money of litigation. The present outline, therefore, can only be a rough guide to the area.

4.29.1 'New invention'

Section 2(1) of the Patents Act 1977 provides that an invention is new if it does not form part of what is called 'the state of the art'. This is defined further in s 2(2), which states effectively that 'state of the art' is all material, of whatever nature, bearing upon the subject matter and techniques of the invention in question, which has been made available to the public in any way, whether by written or oral description or by use before the date known as the 'priority date' in the course of filing the patent application. Usually, this date is simply the date on which the application is received by the Patent Office.

This not only means that the patent must not be effectively the same thing as somebody else has manufactured or written about. It also means that the inventor himself must be very careful not to make his own invention available to the public before applying for his patent, because that makes it part of the 'state of the art' and therefore invalidates his claim to the patent. His own use can defeat his own application. In other words, if details of the invention have already been published, if it has been used in public or even is the subject matter of another application for a patent with an earlier priority date, then the invention in question is not new and therefore will not be patentable.

There are, of course, as in all matters relating to patents, large numbers of cases debating what precisely may constitute prior use of an article. The position is not as straightforward as stated above: for instance, merely experimental use will not make the invention part of the prior art but the precise nature of that experimental use needs to be very clearly defined. Fundamentally, if the public as a whole have had the opportunity of seeing how the thing works, then the invention is not new. Commonly, inventors wish to discuss their invention with others before proceeding to lodge patent applications. There are two crucial precautions. First, any discussion of the invention with anybody must be under strict terms of confidentiality. Any demonstration must be strictly private and not open to the public. Secondly, the precise details of the invention must be retained by the inventor. He should not go into any detail.

Fundamentally, the inventor must take advice as soon as he feels he has a viable invention and follow it; he must file his patent application at the earliest opportunity and keep disclosures to an absolute minimum and ensure they take place only under strictly controlled circumstances.

4.29.2 'Involving an inventive step'

Following the logical order of the Patents Act 1977, this concept is defined in s 3. Effectively, what this requires is that the new invention is not an entirely obvious extension to the state of the art. The test for what is obvious involves an interesting intellectual fiction by the Patents Office or the courts. First, they put themselves in a position of a very technically knowledgeable person with a complete knowledge of the state of the art, and then they divest that person's mind of any inventive flair whatsoever. If that notional person would immediately happen across the new step in the invention for which patent protection is sought then that will not be an inventive step and patent protection will not be granted. The problem, of course, is actually deciding what is or is not obvious. The simplicity of the solution is not an issue: many of the most brilliant solutions to long-standing problems involve a fundamental simplicity. The question is one of obviousness and that is a difficult concept to grasp. However, a fairly useful formulation in this context was given by Millet LJ in *PLG Research Limited v Ardon International Limited.*[1] Here, an inventive step was defined as something which was not 'merely an obvious extension or workshop variation of what was already known at the priority date'.

4.29.3 Capability of 'industrial application'

Section 4 of the Patents Act 1977 states effectively that if the invention can be manufactured or used in any kind of industry, including agriculture, it is capable of industrial application. This requirement overlaps somewhat with the exception made to the specific exclusions from patentability dealt with above, such as new mathematical methods and so forth. A new mathematical method is not patentable; however, the use of a new mathematical method to produce a technical effect by virtue of that being incorporated in an item which is capable of being worked industrially will be patentable. The crucial test both for the capability of industrial application and the 'technical effect' test in relation to exclusion from patentability is that something is produced as a result of the invention which is capable of being manufactured or of forming part of a manufacturing process and is not simply an intellectual construct.

It should be noted in addition that, as a general rule, computer programs are not protected by patents. This is a position which is capable of erosion for reasons which have no real relevance here, but, as a rule of thumb, computer programs are protected by copyright.

4.30 APPLICATIONS FOR PATENTS

As mentioned above, the process of applying for a patent is long and arduous. The applicant must file his application and then file his claims within 12 months, together with various other documents and fees. These claims effectively form a

---

1   [1995] RPC 287.

specification of the process or product for which protection is sought, explaining how and why the product or process is susceptible to protection as a patent. The patent is then investigated on a preliminary basis by an examiner of the Patent Office who will search through a vast amount of material, mainly set out in existing specifications of patents. He then reports to the applicant, showing the applicant those inventions he feels could be effectively the same and thus could obstruct the patentability of this invention. The result of that report may lead the applicant to abandon the application or more frequently leads to amendments of the claims by the applicant.

Generally, within 18 months of the date on which the application was made there will be an initial publication (known as 'A' publication) of the application. This blows the lid off any confidentiality or secrecy surrounding the invention and there is no guarantee that it will ultimately be accorded patent protection. This is one of the crucial areas of risk for anyone planning to apply for a patent.

The patent examiner then does his substantive examination. This is the most rigorous period, when each of the claims made for the invention and relating to whether or not it is patentable is examined. All the criteria of patentability are used to test the patent and all aspects of the application are rigorously considered. Objections will be raised by the examiner to various aspects of the patent, which will often lead to amendments, culminating sometimes in rejection of the application, and, on other occasions, to the grant of the patent in a form which reflects the responses of the applicant to the objections raised. Once the patent has been granted, it is published in a form known as 'B' publication.

Once the patent has finally been granted, it is an item of personal property. Usually, the grant will be made to the inventor or to any person with a better claim to it than the inventor, such as the inventor's employer. Patents can be owned jointly and are subject to assignment and licence in the same way as other intellectual property rights. There are also certain compulsory schemes for the licensing of patents. For instance, in the last four years of the life of any patent, any person may take a licence of the patent on terms considered to be fair both to the patentee and the licensee. The patentee will usually be compensated by way of royalty. In addition, there are certain circumstances where one can apply to the Patent Office for a compulsory licence of that patent. These licences are available effectively when an invention is being in some way suppressed by means of the patent system rather than worked to the fullest extent reasonably practicable and where there is a refusal by the proprietor to grant licences on commercial terms. The Crown may also claim a licence in certain circumstances where such a licence is required for the services of the Crown or any government department. In each case, these automatic licences will usually give rise to an obligation on the part of the licensee to pay a royalty to the owner of the patent.

The patent obviously has a twofold value. First, there is a positive value, in that the patent is property which can be turned to account: it can be sold, mortgaged or licensed like other forms of property. This can obviously give rise either to direct profit or an income stream from royalties from licensees. However, it also gives the negative right to prevent others from copying. This is the most powerful form of intellectual property protection, in that it is the only form of intellectual property protection that be said in any significant way to give monopoly over an idea.

4.31 INFRINGEMENT AND DEFENCES

4.31.1 Infringement

Patent infringement is governed primarily by s 60 of the Patents Act 1977. This sets out that a patent of an invention which is a product is infringed if any person without the proprietor's consent makes, disposes of offers to dispose of uses or imports the product or keeps it whether for disposal or otherwise (Patents Act 1977, s 60(1)(a)). A patent of an invention which is a process can be infringed in two main ways, as follows. Under s 60(1)(b) it is infringed if the process is used or offered for use in the UK, when the person so doing knows that use would be without the consent of the proprietor and would be an infringement of the patent, or in circumstances where it would be obvious to a reasonable man that that was the case. Under s 60(1)(c), a person infringes this type of patent if he disposes, or offers to dispose of, uses or imports or keeps, whether for disposal or otherwise, any product obtained directly by means of the process.

Any patent is infringed, under s 60(2), if a person supplies, or offers to supply, in the UK, a person who is not a licensee of the patent, or entitled to work with the invention, with any of the means relating to an essential element of the invention for putting the invention into effect. The infringer must know that the means are suitable for so doing or circumstances must be such that it is obvious to a reasonable man that that is the case.

Variants

The question, of course, turns then on wheher the product or process allegedly infringed is the product or process protected by the patent. It is quite rare for exact copies to be made in this area, and a lot of ingenuity and skill is expended in trying to make such subtle alterations to patented products and processes that the patent is not infringed. The question of whether the patent is infringed by these 'variants' therefore turns very closely on the precise interpretation of the claims made for the patent at the time of its grant, and this is one of the main reasons why it was stated above that the nature of the claims drafted is utterly crucial. When dealing with variants, therefore, to patented products or processes a structured approach has been evolved as set out classically in *Catnic Components Limited v Hill & Smith Limited*.[1] Fundamentally, the test is threefold. The court identifies the areas of variation between the product or process allegedly infringing the patent and the patent itself. If that variation has a material effect upon the way the invention works, then the offending article does not infringe the patent. If there is no material effect, then the question is asked whether, at the time the patent was published, a skilled reader of the claims for the patent would have seen it as obvious that the variation has no material effect. If it would not have been obvious, then the offending article does not infringe the patent. If it would have been obvious that the variation had no material effect, a third question is asked. This question is whether the skilled reader at that time would understand that a particular descriptive word or phrase used in the claims for the patent could not have been intended to exclude from the ambit of the patent minor variants which would have no material effect on the way the invention worked. If the skilled reader would have understood this, the

---

1   [1982] RPC 183.

offending product does infringe. If he would not, then the offending article does not infringe the patent.

4.31.2   Defences

There are, of course, various defences to a claim of patent infringement. These are also set out in s 60 of the Patents Act 1977. Private and non-commercial acts will not infringe, and neither will acts done for experimental purposes only. Perhaps the most powerful offensive weapon in the alleged infringer's armoury, however, is to deny the validity of the patent, by effectively arguing that the patent should never have been granted in the first place. Most of the case-law on patentability, for instance, comes where this is raised in infringement proceedings. Also, acts done in good faith before the priority date of the patent will not infringe under s 64.

A patent owner cannot be too bullish in his defence of the patent. If he makes groundless threats of infringement proceedings, he is liable for damage he causes to the person receiving those threats.

4.32   RIGHTS IN DESIGNS

The law of rights in designs is complex. It is particularly complex when dealing with rights in designs which were created before the Copyright, Designs and Patents Act 1988 came into force, that is, before 1 August 1989. Designs created before that date are protected by an amalgam of copyright and registered design law, which gives rise to some fairly unusual anomalies, and some convoluted case-law. The effect of this old regime is now of less importance, as the transitional arrangements for the 1988 Act include a provision that copyrights existing from the period prior to the 1988 Act coming into force, and which would have had the effect of design rights following the coming into force of the Act, will expire 10 years from the Act coming into force, namely in August 1999.

The simplistic distinction between design rights and registered design is that registered designs protect decorative articles or the decorative component of articles. Design right protects functional articles and the functional component of articles.

4.32.1   Registered designs

Registered design provides a system of registration for articles which are new (largely in the same way as patents are new by not having been published to the public – see **4.29.1** above). The protection is given in relation to the shape or configuration of an article and also to any surface pattern or ornament on an article applied by an industrial process. When the design has been registered, the owner therefore has the exclusive right to that design for a period of five years, which can be renewed for up to 25 years in total.

Registration criteria are set out at s 1 of the Registered Designs Act 1949, as amended by the Copyright, Designs and Patents Act 1988 (CDPA 1988). To qualify for registration, the features being registered must have what is called 'eye appeal'. In other words, the considerations in purchasing or using it must include that of the way the article looks. The appearance of the article must be material, namely the usual considerations used by people acquiring or using articles of that description include aesthetic considerations. If those aesthetic considerations do not apply to the article, but do apply to the design which is attached to it, then the appearance of that design is material and the design attached to it will be registerable.

Registration will not be granted for designs which are methods or principles of construction or for features, shapes or configuration of articles which are dictated solely by the function of the article, or for those which are wholly dependent upon the appearance of another article for which the article in question is intended to form an integral part.

Other items are also excluded from registerability by the Registered Designs Rules 1995.[1] These include articles which are effectively artistic and literary works which would be protected in any event by copyright.

By s 7 of the Registered Designs Act 1949, registration of a design confers the exclusive right upon the registered proprietor to make, import for sale or hire or for use for the purposes of trade or business, or to sell, hire or offer or expose for sale or hire the article registered. Any person attempting to perform these operations without the consent of the proprietor of the registered design would infringe the registered design. As with patents, the most potent form of defence to infringement proceedings will be to claim that the registration was invalid because the criteria for registration were not properly made out.

Registered designs are primarily used, therefore, for decorative items. Fashion designs are clearly appropriate for this form of protection and therefore registration under this system has a considerable area of potential applicability to sport from the point of view of the sports kit and other clothing commonly sold by sports clubs as a major component of their merchandising activities. Mascots, cuddly toys and other similar items could well be protected in the same manner. The requirements of novelty and aesthetic interest required for registration of registered designs are not so onerous as to make it particularly difficult or expensive to obtain registration. However, there does need to be a question mark over how much variation from the design is required by a potential infringer in order to avoid liability for an infringement. As a result, the number of applications for registered designs is small compared to the number of trade mark applications or patent applications. Consideration should however be given to the use of this form of protection for merchandising lines which would fit the criteria outlined above.

4.32.2 Design right

Design right is a right quite separate from that conferred by the registration of a design. There is necessarily an area of overlap between the two rights because the criteria for the two separate regimes of protection cannot be identified with such distinctness as to categorise every single design into one area or the other. One may hold design right in an article, or in a component of an article, which is the subject of a registered design or of which decorative components are the subject

---

1   SI 1995/2912.

of a registered design. However, as a rough rule of thumb, design right is invoked to protect functional rather than aesthetic designs. The inadequacy of this distinction will be seen, of course, by anyone familiar with the theory that what is functional is in itself aesthetically beautiful.

Design right is the new creation of the CDPA 1988. Brief mention has been made above of the previous applicability of copyright in this context. It was felt, by experience of the previous regime of protection by copyright, that to extend copyright protection into three-dimensional functional articles of an industrial nature was an artificial hindrance to fair competition in industrial products, given the length of time for which copyright gives protection. The unregistered design right, therefore, was introduced, together with certain amendments to the scope of copyright from previous legislation, in order to rationalise the system as far as possible.

Design right comes into being as a by-product of the creative process in the same manner as copyright. It subsists in original designs which must be fixed in some tangible form, be it a drawing, a computer disk or whatever. Section 213(2) of the CDPA 1988 defines 'the design' as meaning the design of any aspect of the shape or configuration of the whole or part of an article. The overall functional appearance or form is therefore protected rather than in the case of registered designs particular features having eye appeal of the article are protected.

By s 213(3) of the CDPA 1988, design right specifically does not extend to underlying principles or ideas behind the design. These principles or ideas are only protectable by way of patent. Where an item has its form solely because it must fit together with another item or within another structure in order to perform its function, design right will not subsist in those parts of that article which are solely dictated by that requirement. The same applies where the form of an article is dictated by the need to match another article of which it is intended to be an integral part. Further, a method or principle of construction will not be the subject of a design right nor will surface decoration.

A design, to be the subject of design right, must be a new design in that it is not a copy of another design; further, it must also be 'original'. This is an additional requirement to that which arises under the often similar law relating to copyright. Section 213(4) of the CDPA 1988 states that a design is not original if it is common place in the design field at the time of creation.

A design right lasts for a period of 15 years from the end of the year in which the design was first placed in tangible form. However, if articles are made to the design and made available for sale anywhere in the world within a period of five years from the end of the creation year, then the design right will expire 10 years from the end of the calendar year during which the design was first exploited. This is a significantly shorter period of protection than that provided by copyright. The policy behind this is mentioned above.

Section 226(1) of the CDPA 1988 provides that the owner of the design right has the exclusive right to reproduce the design for commercial purposes by making articles to the design, or by making design documents recording the design, for the purpose of enabling such articles to be made. Any person performing these acts without the licence of the right owner infringes that design right. A form of secondary infringement occurs where a person imports into the UK, or has in his possession for commercial purposes, or sells, hires, or offers or exposes for sale or hire in the course of a business, any item which infringes the design right.

The overlap between copyright and design right is problematical. Often the two subsist co-extensively. In other words, an industrial designer making a sketch of a new design which would qualify for design right will also have copyright in that sketch. Two provisions are therefore relevant. These are s 51(1) and s 236 of the CDPA 1988. Section 236 provides that, where design right and copyright co-exist under the rules provided in s 51, then copyright overrides design right and that item is protected by copyright alone. For instance, in a straightforward design drawing, if a copy were made of the design drawing, that would be a copyright infringement, even though there would simultaneously be a design right in that drawing for other purposes. The only infringement proceedings the designer could take would be in respect of infringement of the copyright.

However, the effect of s 51, put simplistically, is to prevent copyright, in this context of functional industrial articles, from extending into three dimensions. If that same design drawing from the example given above were used to manufacture the product set out in it, or if the product set out in it were 'reverse engineered' from the product itself and a copy made by that means, s 51 provides that there is no copyright infringement. There is, however, a design right infringement.

From what is stated above, it is unlikely that design right would be of immense relevance to the business of sport. Where it is possibly relevant is in the same context as where a patent may be relevant, namely in those engineering businesses impacting upon sport. In that context, it is a right coming into operation by law rather than registration and offering a lesser form of protection in the same context where, were the criteria of registration fulfilled, an application might have been made for a patent.

CHAPTER 5

EMPLOYMENT AGREEMENTS

5.1 Introduction – 5.2 Employment v self-employment – 5.3 Formalities – 5.4 Terms of contract of employment – 5.5 Statutory rights in respect of termination of employment – 5.6 Discrimination – 5.7 Maternity rights – 5.8 Wrongful dismissal – 5.9 Restraint of trade and the Bosman *ruling – 5.10 Player transfers – 5.11 Regulatory issues – 5.12 Checklist: employment contract*

5.1 INTRODUCTION

5.1.1 'Player power'

The business of sport, like every other business, is built upon the employment relationship. Whilst it has become a platitude of modern management newspeak that the people employed by a business are its most valuable asset, in sport perhaps more than any other area of business the old chestnut is emphatically true in the practical – and possibly the economic – sense. Football has led the way to the rapid commercialisation which is now sweeping many sports, and its experience in this regard is instructive.

Only comparatively recently, the Football Association sought to control the movement of players from one club to another, and to impose a maximum wage for the players at all the clubs in the football league. As the doctrines of restraint of trade, formed by English law in its traditional role as champion of free markets, were brought to bear on these restrictions, most notably in *Eastham v Newcastle United Football Club Limited*,[1] a rapid escalation has taken place in the amounts paid both for players to other clubs, and to players for their services. Not only the great players of the day, but also a substantial number of more or less mediocre journeymen, command multi-million pound transfer fees (where such fees are still payable following the *Bosman* decision), and per annum salaries parallel to those of the most successful entertainers. The Premier League football clubs themselves stagger beneath the burden of wage bills running into many millions of pounds per year. The revenue provided from the most direct and traditional source, tickets and season tickets sold to the fans, in most if not all cases, comes nowhere near satisfying the wage bill, never mind the other running costs of the club. The clubs are almost entirely reliant upon the new levels of income available from broadcasting and merchandising to offer the financial packages demanded by the players in the new post-*Bosman* era of player power. As the Premier League becomes more and more like an arms race, with each team trying to recruit more and more of the world's finest players at costs which have the potential to cripple the team financially after only one poor season, the potential dangers to the other sports newly fledging themselves as professional games, and perhaps particularly Rugby Union, are clear.

---

1   [1964] Ch 413.

At the same time, having paid many millions of pounds for the services of a star player, the Club cannot in prudence reflect any value for that expenditure on its balance sheet. The 'stock' of players does not appear amongst the Club's assets for most clubs. This new era of player power, largely the effect of the *Bosman* case and its categorical statement of the freedom of the players to ply their trade in a free market, combined with the move away from the traditional source of funding of football clubs by a local tycoon for whom money is no object and towards the less starry eyed paymasters of the City of London and their institutional shareholders, makes the considerations raised in this chapter perhaps the most immediately and universally pressing for the proper adminis-tration of all team sports.

Employment law is, of course, an entire field of the law in its own right, both academically and for practitioners. A book of this nature can never seek to replace, or obviate the need for the practitioner to consult, the many excellent standard works on this topic. The purpose of the present chapter is to point out both to sports lawyers dealing with employment law issues, and to employment lawyers dealing in the particular area of sport, the major issues of employment law which impact directly upon professional sport. The staple fare, therefore, of most works on employment law, such as the law relating to redundancy, unfair dismissal, maternity rights and the law of discrimination in employment will not be dealt with in the detail available elsewhere. This work can only seek to highlight these issues, leaving detailed analysis of the underlying law to those specialised texts. The focus will be rather to point towards a unified and workable employment policy for the professional sport employer.

5.2   EMPLOYMENT v SELF-EMPLOYMENT

Employment law is the name given to the law of contract as it relates to the daily work of individual men and women, and the surrounding structures and regulations introduced by statute. The relationship of employer and employee is one strictly circumscribed by law, which comes into being according to law rather than solely according to the labels attached to the relationship by the parties themselves. The difference between two parties dealing with each other as independent contractors (the contract for services) and those dealing as employer and employee (the contract of service) may be so minimal in practice as to lead to very considerable complexity in the tests applied by the law to decide the issue, but the outcome and effect of that procedure of testing is crucial. The result, from the employee's point of view, decides the difference between on the one hand working on one's own account in a harsh world of free market economics, accounting for one's own taxes and reliant entirely on the contractual arrangements one makes, and on the other hand working at the risk of the employer, with one's taxes deducted at source and even partially subsidised by the employer, in a legislative framework controlled (at least in theory) by the paternalistic ideals of social policy.

The tests applied by the courts to the question of whether a given worker is an employee or an independent contractor are complex, and have to adapt to the changing forces of the labour market.

The test applied traditionally by the courts to the question was a blunt instrument largely based on the question of whether the employer was in control not only of what the employee did, but how he did it (*Mersey Docks and Harbour Board v Coggins and Griffiths (Liverpool) Limited.*[1]). Whilst this still remains a powerful influencing factor in the overall decision as to whether or not the employer/employee relationship exists, it is not the sole criterion, as indeed it could not be in the modern world where highly skilled specialists are frequently the employees of those without the technical knowledge to offer even a sensible opinion on how the job should be done. The courts have found, for instance, as in *Cassidy v Ministry of Health*[2] where the case related to a surgeon in employment, that the old 'control' test no longer reflected the realities of the situation. A series of proposed alternative tests has been advanced but the ultimate decision reached has been for the courts to take a 'pragmatic' view of the situation that exists between the parties, applying a number of alternative tests and balancing those tests before coming to an ultimate view. This means therefore that the tests are not a hard science, but at least there is sufficient flexibility to avoid manifest injustice.

The courts and industrial tribunals therefore ask a number of questions designed to identify whether the individual about whom the question is asked is in his business on his own account or not. Classically, the questions which a court may ask would be along the following lines:

(1) Is remuneration paid to the 'employee' direct on a regular basis, or against invoices? (If the former, this suggests the worker is an employee.)

(2) Are PAYE tax and National Insurance contributions deducted at source from payments made to the 'employee' in question? (If yes, this suggests the worker is an employee.)

(3) Does the 'employer' have the power to select the worker and/or dismiss them? (If yes, this suggests the worker is an employee.)

(4) Does the 'employee' supply his or her own tools and materials for the performance of the work, or does he or she use those supplied by the 'employer'? (If the latter, this suggests the worker is an employee.)

(5) Does the 'employer' dictate the manner in which the work place at which the 'employee' provides his or her services is organised? (If yes, this suggests the worker is an employee.)

(6) Does the 'employee' in reality bear the financial and/or business risk of the undertaking or is that risk solely reposed in the 'employer'? (If the latter, this suggests the worker is an employee.)

(7) Is there real 'mutuality of obligation'; in other words, is there an understanding, tacit or otherwise, that the parties are bound together and under reciprocal obligations as opposed to a looser, more 'commercial' relationship?[3] (If the former, this suggests the worker is an employee.)

The answers to these questions together become the criteria on which the court or tribunal makes its decision as to the status of the 'employee'.

In sport, the vast majority of players and managers themselves will want to be, and will be required by their clubs to be, employees. The relationship of

---

1   [1947] AC 1.
2   [1951] 1 All ER 574.
3   See *Market Investigations Limited v Minister of Social Security* [1968] 3 All ER 732.

employer and employee allows the employer to require that the employee's services be supplied on an exclusive basis to that employer for a fixed period, and permits the employer, within reason, to dictate to the employee what services are to be supplied, when and where they are to be supplied, using what equipment, methods and techniques the employer directs. From the player's point of view, the existance of an employment agreement guarantees (usually) a steady income even at times when a player, for instance, may not be playing. In effect, even if the 'employer' in a sporting context wished to engage a player or manager as an independent contractor, by the time he had stipulated in the contractual relationship all his requirements of that relationship, as will be seen from the tests outlined above, he will have arrived at the position where the court would, in all probability, construe the relationship to be that of employer and employee, regardless of his intended categorisation. In any event, for players, most governing bodies will stipulate engagement upon employment contracts and often upon standard forms of such contract.

However, players are not the entire story. There are more and more opportunities for sports clubs to engage the services of individuals outside the usual employment relationship. For instance, specialist technical coaches, such as a kicking coach to a rugby union team, may provide services both to individuals and to teams but not necessarily exclusive services to those teams. Clubs may wish to expand the range of individuals with whom they contract, particularly for provision of the more technical or 'consultancy' type services (as opposed to those provided in a straightforward manner by players) and should therefore be careful to ensure as far as possible that, according to the above tests, there is some clear distinction between the relationship they come to with the intended independent contractor and that they have with an employee. There has been conflicting authority over the extent to which the parties are able to choose their label for the arrangement and to have that label ultimately borne out in the courts: the label placed on the relationship by the parties is a significant factor which could be taken into consideration and may indeed be of considerable importance in the case of true ambiguity, or in the case where one party has changed from one regime to another.

With that caveat, however, and with the passing comment that it is likely that the range of providers of services to sports organisations operating as independent contractors will increase, we will turn to an examination of some of the major issues relating to sport in the general law of employment.

5.3 FORMALITIES

The relationship of employer and employee comes into being not necessarily by signature of a written document but by the law deeming a given relationship to have that quality, as set out above. Contracts of employment can arise between an employer and a minor (defined as being someone under the age of 18) but caution should be exercised in these circumstances as the fundamental principle of contracts involving minors applies also to the employment relationship: the contract will bind the minor only if the contract can be said on the whole to be for the minor's benefit at the time of its formation. This does not mean that each and every clause in the contract must be for the minor's benefit but rather that that contract taken as whole should be. Therefore a contract term which makes the entire contract unfair will invalidate the contract, whereas one which is just an isolated incident of unfairness may be severable from it. However, in relation to the employment of young players in most sports, there will be standard guidelines and forms of contract laid down by the sport's governing bodies. These ensure that the benefit of the minor is properly considered and have the accompanying effect of reassuring the employer that the contract would stand investigation by the courts and effectively be accepted in most cases as an industry standard.

The employer is under no obligation to provide a written contract of employment but must under s 1 of the Employment Rights Act 1996 (ERA 1996) provide notice to the employee of the terms of his or her employment. The status of this written statement is that it is not in itself a contract of employment but rather evidence of what the terms of the contract of employment are. The written statement must include various information as to the terms of the employment contract. A full list of the points which must be covered is set out in the Employment Rights Act 1996. If the employer fails to give such a written statement, or if there is a dispute as to the correctness of the particulars which ought to be included or referred to, either party may refer the matter to an employment tribunal which will then have wide powers to determine what should have been included or whether any particulars which were included should be altered or confirmed. In doing so it does not have the ability to rewrite the terms wholesale: its role is effectively declaratory of what the situation is, not what it should be.

An employment contract is naturally a bilateral relationship and therefore the employer may not vary the terms of the contract unilaterally unless specific power has been reserved in the contract to do so. Even if such a power were reserved in the contract, there is a question of whether or not it would be enforceable. However, if any terms are to be altered in the contract by a bilateral arrangement requiring the employee's consent, the employer must notify the employee within one month of instituting the change in writing.[1]

An employment contract must not include illegal provisions. This may seem obvious, in that the employer cannot employ the employee to commit crime, for instance. However, there are other provisions which are considered contrary to statute or common law which would be considered void. For instance, a contract which provides for some form of income which should be taxed to be paid without taxation may be void. This could have an impact upon some 'image contracts' where the marketing and promotional services supplied by a player purport to be supplied by a company which is entitled to contract out the player's services in this regard. Such a company is often an offshore vehicle requiring payment without deduction of tax. Great caution is required therefore in this regard when the player – or his agent – suggest such an arrangement.

---

1   ERA 1996, s 4.

5.4 TERMS OF CONTRACT OF EMPLOYMENT

Before dealing later in this chapter with the express terms suggested for an inclusion in a contract of employment relating to a sports professional, this section will deal with the means by which the law may imply terms into or impose terms upon a contract of employment. These terms may be of considerable importance and should be borne in mind in formulating express terms. This is for two reasons. Firstly, there is authority now for the proposition that the law may impose terms upon contracts of employment which have the power to override and/or to amend the effect of express terms. These are known in some circles as 'overriding terms' and are dealt in **5.4.1**. Secondly, terms may be implied into the contract of employment where the contract is otherwise silent from a number of sources. These are dealt with in **5.4.2** and should be considered on the basis that where the law may imply a term it is a matter of good practice to stipulate an express term to avoid the uncertainty of what the law may otherwise imply.

5.4.1 Overriding terms

As indicated above, these are a comparatively recent development in the law and remain perhaps controversial. They deal with two main issues, both of which may be relevant in the context of sport.

The first such overriding term for which there is judicial authority is a term to the effect that the employer should treat the employee with trust and respect. That formulation appears unproblematic in itself. Where the law may bite is where that overriding term is used effectively to contradict or circumscribe a clear express term of the contract. This problem has arisen in the context of relocation clauses where the employee has a term in his contract permitting the employer to stipulate that he relocate to any place the employer chooses. In *United Bank Limited v Akhtar*,[1] it was held that, even where an employee had such a clause in his contract, it was a breach of contract by the employer to stipulate unreasonably that he relocate over a long distance without giving proper notice and without sensitivity to the employee's personal circumstances. This was treated as conduct which was calculated or likely to destroy or seriously damage the relationship of trust and respect between employer and employee and therefore could not be justified even by the express term of the contract.

The potential for such an overriding term to be invoked by an employee in various ways and in relation to various grievances is clear. Relocation in itself as the explicit example may not be relevant, although there is the prospect of football teams for instance relocating their entire operations to other cities. There are, however, any number of potential areas where the player may complain that he has been treated in such a way as to breach this overriding term; for instance, where a contractual term stipulating that the player shall play according to the instructions of the team manager is used to place the employee in a position he finds humiliating. One example might be of an England forward being asked to play in defence, or perhaps a motor racing driver obliged to follow team instructions perpetually being asked, notwithstanding his greater driving ability, to finish in a position behind that of the lead driver.

---

1   [1989] IRLR 507.

The second potentially overriding term arose in a celebrated case relating to the hours of a hospital junior doctor, *Johnstone v Bloomsbury Health Authority*.[1] This case may be authority for the proposition that similar overriding status would be accorded to a term that the employer must act in such a way as to have regard for the employee's health and safety. This is parallel to the general duty on all employers under the Health & Safety at Work etc Act 1974, s 2(1): 'It should be the duty of every employer to ensure, so far as is reasonably practicable, the health and safety and welfare of all his employees'.

The application of this duty to the sporting context is immediately apparent and it is no doubt unnecessary to multiply examples. However, one pressing issue of modern sport which perhaps deserves mention at this point is the tendency for sport to become a year round intensive occupation requiring the participation of players in an ever increasing number of matches, with the corresponding possibility of injury leading to the shortening of the working life of the player. The time may come where this concept of the law is tested out in that forum.

5.4.2   Implied terms

There are various traditional sources from which terms may be implied into contracts, such as collective bargains and the usages and customs of the trade and business in which the contract falls. Neither of these, it is suggested, is likely to have a great deal of direct relevance to sport. The players' 'unions', such as the PFA in professional football, do negotiate regularly with the governing body of the game, but rather than forming collective bargains with the employers, their influence is usually transmitted into the formulation by those governing bodies of standard terms of employment for all players in the game, or standard advice to all employers. The more traditional legal routes by which these deliberations and the customs and usages of the game become law are by-passed by the more direct form of 'legislation' by the governing body. For instance, in the FA Premier League Limited Handbook for the 1998/99 Football Season it is laid down that all contracts of service between clubs and players must be on the official form approved by the FA Premier League. The same section contains a number of regulations relating to the club's treatment of players, trainees and associated schoolboys. It deals with a number of other matters, including matters relating to transfers and even provides that disputes or differences not otherwise expressly provided for in the rules, between a club or clubs and any player, must be referred in writing to the Board of the Premier League for consideration and adjudication, before which the club or the player may request a personal hearing. This is one, perhaps extreme, example of how all matters of employment law in sport must be seen in the context of the regulatory issues dealt with earlier in this book. However, for sports less commercially developed and regulated, those customs of the sport which are certain, general and reasonable may be implied into a contract of employment, and regard should be had so far as possible to that likelihood. However, it is suggested that the rules of the regulatory body would be the primary source for anyone considering these issues.

The law will also have the effect of introducing into the contract of employment where the contract is otherwise silent various provisions which arise effectively as a result of what the law considers to be the standard characteristics of the

---

1   [1991] IRLR 118.

employment relationship. These terms can be seen under several general headings and will be split between those held to be incumbent upon the employee and those held to be incumbent upon the employer.

Duties of the employee

Duty of co-operation with lawful orders
It is generally a matter of trite law that the employee is obliged to co-operate in a reasonable fashion with a lawful order which requests that he or she perform a task which is reasonably within the ambit of the job they are employed to do. 'Lawful' does not necessarily mean anything that is not a criminal offence: it also means something which is not a civil wrong or a breach of contract. Self-evidently, also, it is not something which an employer is not entitled by virtue of the contract of employment to ask.

Duty to work with care and skill
Since as long ago as the 1850s[1] it has been clear law that an employee must perform the tasks allotted to him or her by the employer to a reasonable level of care and skill. There is a corollary to this duty which is that the employer must at the same time provide sufficient training or supervision to allow the employee to perform his tasks to this standard or not to assign tasks to an employee which are beyond the capacity that is reasonably to be expected of him.

The practical importance of this duty often arises in cases where the employer is sued as being vicariously liable for an act of the employee. One example from a sporting context may be where the employee has acted negligently on the field of play resulting in serious injury to an opponent, who then takes proceedings against the employer. Often in practice, those proceedings will be against both the employer and the employee in any event but in that case the same principles would stand, in that it is open to the employer to seek a remedy against the employee for failure in this duty or to seek contribution or indemnity under the Civil Liability (Contribution) Act 1978. In such circumstances the court would award a contribution which it considered just and equitable having regard to the extent of the employee's responsibility for the damage.

Duty to act in good faith in the employer's interest
An employee must look to serve the employer faithfully and act in the interests of the employer. For instance, even where a decision is within the ambit of discretion allowed to the employee, that decision should be taken in the best interests of the employer and consulting the employer's interests as opposed to the employee's potentially conflicting interests.[2] The employee must not act in such a way as to put himself in direct conflict with the employer, such as by working in his spare time for a competitor in a way which would injure the employer's business.

The duty should not be taken too far – the employee is not under a duty to disclose absolutely everything that he or she may know to the employer, but, essentially, the dividing line is that where the employer's interest is in danger of

---

1   *Harmer v Cornelius* (1858) 5 CBNS 236.
2   *Boston Deep Sea Fishing and Ice Co v Ansell* (1888) 39 Ch D 339.

prejudice the employee should act in such a way as to benefit the employer's interest. The relationship is not a fiduciary relationship such as that between a director and a company but whilst it is at a slightly lower level it is in some ways analogous.

One example of this duty coming into play in a sporting contract may be where a player in a team is aware of the possibility of a potentially lucrative transfer to another team. That player may fail to exert himself fully in such a way as to depress the transfer price, thus potentially increasing the player's own share of the proceeds of the transfer. This has become particularly important in the light of the *Bosman* ruling where players whose contracts have expired are able to transfer from one club to another without the payment of a transfer fee. It has been suspected in certain instances that players have deliberately acted in such a way as to discourage transfers until such time as the transfer can take place without a fee, with a view to obtaining the equivalent to the 'fee' themselves. This is perhaps one instance where the player would be in breach of this implied term.

Another facet of this implied term relates to confidential information concerning the employer's business and the use of it by the employee. This area of the law would be perhaps more appropriate to the managerial level of staff as opposed to players. The employee must not misuse confidential information, or trade secrets of the employer, (which might extend to simply confidential information coming to the employee in his capacity as an employee, such as information about the customers of the employer or potential deals the employer may have in the offing) in such a way as to compete with or harm the interests of the employer. For this obligation to bite, however, there needs to be a distinction made between the duty which subsists during the contract of employment's currency and that which survives the termination of the contract of employment as set out in *Faccenda Chicken Limited v Fowler*.[1] During the currency of the employment relationship the duty may extend much more broadly and effectively be subsumed within the duties set out above; after employment, the protection of the law is only extended to those things which are effectively genuine secrets and not the ordinary skill in or knowledge of the business obtained by the employee during the course of his or her employment. There is therefore something of a difficulty in the dividing line between the skill and knowledge that the employee has generated whilst working for the employer and those matters which might be considered protectable trade secrets. This duty will not arise either in such a way as to prevent proper lawful competition.

One area where this may arise in the context of an ongoing employment relationship in sport may be in its application toward comments concerning the business of the employer to the press and media. It is generally held that disclosure in the public interest of information relating to the employer which would otherwise be confidential is not a breach of duty, although regard must be had to the distinction generally forgotten by the tabloid press between what is in the public interest and what the public is interested in.

In practice, however, these are matters which would be covered by explicit clauses in any contract and the question of restraint of trade is important enough to merit a section to itself at **5.9**.

---

1   [1986] IRLR 69.

The duty to adapt to new developments

Where new methods or techniques are adopted by the employer, and where the employee needs to acquire new methods or skills in order to adapt to that changing situation, there is authority in *Cresswell v Board of Inland Revenue*[1] for the proposition that where the employer provides the necessary training or retraining and where the retraining does not involve the acquisition of such esoteric skills that it would be unreasonable to expect the employee to acquire them, that the employee would be expected to adapt himself or herself to those new methods and techniques.

For most sports, this matter may be irrelevant; however, in sports where technology plays a major role, such as motor sports, it would no doubt be incumbent upon both technical and racing staff to move with the times.

Duties of the employer

The duty to pay wages

There is no general rule of law that the employer must pay a salary to an employee. There are various ways in which an employee can be recompensed for his services, for instance by way of commission only, by way of opportunity to earn a salary only, or even by way of tips received from customers of the employer. There may even be support for the proposition that in certain unusual cases there is no obligation to pay wages at all. However, where there is any possible reference to remuneration, or any appearance of consent between the parties that remuneration is payable, then it is incumbent upon the employer to pay that remuneration and even if no level is set then there may be a claim on the basis of how much the employee has deserved (quantum meruit). However, the important principle remains that if the employee declines to perform his or her duties, the employer may withhold pay: *Cresswell v Board of Inland Revenue*.[2] Indeed, even if the employee has not withdrawn all his or her services, where the employer has specifically stated that it will not accept the reduced performance of the contract, the employer may still withhold all wages notwithstanding that some of the contract has been performed: *British Telecommunications plc v Ticehurst*.[3] This power to withhold wages rather than take dismissal action can be a very powerful weapon in the business of sport for the employer against the uncooperative employee.

The obligation to pay wages may often continue as an implied term of the contract of employment even when the employee is off work sick, but this is not an inevitable rule: *Mears v Safecar Security Limited*.[4] However, this, together with the whole question of wages in general, will usually be laid out in black and white in the employment contract and, indeed, is a matter of which the employer is bound to give written details to the employee in the written statement of terms provided for by ERA 1996, s 1.

On top of this there is the regime of statutory sick pay which is payable under the Social Security Contributions and Benefits Act 1992. The employer now has an obligation by law to pay an amount to the sick employee equivalent to that which

1   [1984] IRLR 190.
2   [1984] IRLR 190.
3   [1992] IRLR 219.
4   [1982] IRLR 183.

the employee would have received by way of benefit from the state. The employer must therefore pay for a maximum of 28 weeks a statutory minimum amount to the employee largely by way of substitution for benefit which it can only recoup in certain tightly circumscribed circumstances. The employer is not able to contract out of this obligation.

In practice, most employment contracts will have a provision whereby the employer pays a full contractual wage during periods of sickness as an express term of the contract. The contract may provide for instance that the full pay usually payable to the employee will be paid for a given period of time. Thereafter, only statutory sick pay will be paid; finally, incapacity to work on account of sickness for a specific period may give rise to a right on the part of the employer to terminate the employment.

In most sports employment contracts, statutory sick pay is unlikely to be of any real importance particularly in view of the sports professional's likely incapacity being related to injuries sustained in the service of the employer. This is eminently an area where the contract should provide expressly what is to take place and, indeed, may be circumscribed by directions and regulations of the sports' governing body.

Before leaving the question of wages, the issue of deductions from wages should be considered. Many sportsmen's contracts deal with the specific power of the employer to fine the employee in given circumstances of breach of contract. This is usually a more effective and less self-defeating method than those routes taken elsewhere in other industries, such as written warnings leading to potential dismissal, suspension or dismissal itself. Under ERA 1996, Part II, it is provided at s 13 that an employer must not make any deduction from wages of employees unless the deduction is required by statute, required or authorised by a provision of the contract of employment which has been given to the employee or notified to him in writing prior to the deduction being made, or agreed to by the employee in writing prior to the deduction being made. The regime of fines therefore should be made explicit on the employment contract.

The duty to treat the employee with respect
This has been dealt with largely above in terms of an overriding term to that effect. The point is made again here as even if the concept of an overriding term is not ultimately followed it is certainly decided law that this is a standard implied term.

The duty to care for the employee's health and safety
This again has been dealt with in the context of overriding terms (5.4.1) and again the point is made that even if it is not an overriding term it is certainly settled law that this is an implied term of all contracts of employment. It may have some unforeseeable consequences; for instance, it may lead to a dismissal of an employee being fair because that employee posed a danger to other employees, as the general duty has been interpreted by the courts to mean that the employer is obliged to provide an employee with fellow employees who do not pose a danger to him.[1] The employer should also ensure that it takes account where appropriate of issues raised as to the safety of the working conditions provided.

---

1   *Hudson v Ridge Manufacturing Co Limited* [1957] 2 QB 348.

Consideration should also be given to the effects of the European Working Time Directive (No 93/104), the enactment of which into domestic law is affected by the Working Time Regulations 1998, SI 1998/1833. This provides, amongst other things, that unless the employee contracts out of his rights (which is a revocable step in any event), he is entitled to a maximum working week of 48 hours, compulsory rest periods after six hours' consecutive work, a minimum daily rest period of 11 consecutive hours, at least one full day off per week and a minimum of four weeks' paid holiday per year. It would be foolish to assume that these new developments would have no applicability to sport; the training, travelling and playing commitments of many sportsmen could well lead to the necessity for contracting out and the revocability of that step could be a management problem of the future.

The duty to deal with the employee's grievances

Most properly drawn employment contracts have terms dealing with disciplinary and grievance procedures. This again is an item which the employer must identify in the statement of written terms under ERA 1996, s 1. However, in addition to that, in *W A Goold (Pearmak) Limited v McConnell*,[1] the employment appeal tribunal held that as an implied term in the contract of employment, employers must reasonably and promptly provide to their employees the opportunity to raise their grievances and have those grievances fairly dealt with.

The duty to provide work

This is an area of employment law which has specific reference to sport and where sport may constitute even a specific case. It is generally the law that there is no obligation to provide work for the employee to perform but rather only to provide the wages that would be payable in respect of the employee performing that work if it was provided: *Collier v Sunday Referee Publishing Co Ltd*.[2] By the same token, the employee's obligation is not strictly speaking to work but to be ready, able and willing to work when requested by the employer.

That general position is, however, moderated by special considerations which doubtless have an impact upon sportsmen. The cases where it has been decided that there would or may be an obligation to provide work fall under several headings. Some deal with piece workers or those paid on a commission only basis. Here it would be unfair to deprive the employee of any ability to earn. However, there are decisions such as *Herbert Clayton and Jack Waller Limited v Oliver*[3] where it was recognised that certain occupations such as that of an actor or singer are such that there is an obligation incumbent upon the employer to provide work for that actor or singer. In those cases the justification is that the actor or singer needs the public recognition involved in performing in order to maintain the career they have chosen either at a given level or at all. Indeed, the obligation may extend beyond the mere obligation to provide work to an obligation to provide work of a given standard, in the case quoted, for instance, where the standard was of work for an actor in a leading part as opposed to a supporting part.

---

1   [1995] IRLR 516.
2   [1940] 2 KB 647.
3   [1930] AC 209.

The potential for this concept to extend to sport is clear. A sportsman has the same considerations in many cases as an actor in that his career is largely dependent upon public exposure. A player who is not playing in the first team for his club is unlikely to be considered for international teams, and some sportsmen such as boxers are entirely reliant on a ranking system for career advancement and, indeed, this point has been taken to the courts by the boxer Nigel Benn. The potential, therefore, for sports professionals to attempt to invoke this term is clear and so it is essential that some explicit reference is made in the employment contract of this issue; for a team sportsman there must be a clear reference to the prerogative of the team's manager or coach to pick the team in accordance with his own discretion. Caution should be had, however, in drafting any clause which grants too great a discretion to the employer as such a clause may be found to be in restraint of trade and therefore void: see below **5.9.2**.

Duty of confidentiality

There is no developed law on this topic, but there is the intriguing possibility that parallel to the employee's well-recognised duty of confidentiality to the employer there may be a duty of confidence imposed upon the employer in relation to information which is confidential and held by the employer solely by virtue of the employer/employee relationship.[1] This is an authority of the Court of Session in Scotland and it relates to an interdict which was granted against the employer providing the authorities with the addresses of Poll Tax defaulters.

Too much weight should not be placed upon this authority, but the question may arise in the sports context in relation to such things as the medical records of the employee. A contract with a sportsman should include reference to the sportsman's medical fitness and the right of the employer to require medical examination by a doctor of the employer's choice; the results of that examination, however, could be the subject of such a duty of confidentiality on the part of the employer and caution should therefore always be operated in that regard. Likewise, matters relating solely to a player's private circumstances may similarly fall subject to this implied term.

5.5 STATUTORY RIGHTS IN RESPECT OF TERMINATION OF EMPLOYMENT

5.5.1 Introduction

The contract of employment is clearly a contract which in many ways is like any other and can be breached like any other. The remedies available to the parties are the standard contractual remedies, but, over and above the straightforward contractual position, a huge body of legislation has grown up treating the employment relationship as a specific relationship protected by the law. As such, the employee has rights which go beyond the orthodox contractual rights arising under the Employment Rights Act 1996 and other legislation. The detailed law surrounding and created by that legislation is a matter for specialist works upon employment law but it is necessary to provide an overview of that legislation for

---

1   *Dalgleish v Lothian Borders Police Board* [1991] IRLR 422.

the present purposes. It is also necessary to mention that a further major piece of legislation, which at the time of writing is the Employment Relations Bill, will shortly come into effect and will make radical changes to English Law to bring it closer into line with European Union developments in this area. Only brief mention will be made of this legislation, as, at the time of writing, all that can be said is that these are proposals. When considering the law of unfair dismissal and redundancy, it should be recognised that the statutory framework is largely aimed at protecting the rights of workers earning benefits in the lower and middle income bracket and the relevance of this law to the higher wage earners in sport is likely to be comparatively, but by no means entirely, limited. However, it must be remembered that all professional sportsmen are not Premier League Footballers, First Division Rugby Players or Grand Prix Drivers: the expansion of professionalism throughout all levels of sport is an ongoing process and a large number of professional sportsmen are in a position where it cannot blithely be assumed that their contractual rights are so lucrative as to make the statutory position irrelevant. Indeed, one of the provisions of the Employment Relations Bill will have the effect, if it becomes law, of raising the compensation limit for unfair dismissal to £50,000. This is a major increase from the maximum available under the law at the time of writing and will bring more high earners squarely within the ambit of the statutory scheme, in that their interests may be best protected on that basis rather than under common law contractual provisions, as is the case when the compensation limit is artificially low.

5.5.2   Overview of unfair dismissal and redundancy rights

The law of unfair dismissal and redundancy is set out in the Employment Rights Act 1996, which is effectively a consolidation of a large number of earlier statutes. Jurisdiction over unfair dismissal cases is vested in employment tribunals, which consist of a legally qualified chairman and two lay members, one representing an employer's association and the other representing an employee's association. The purpose of the constitution of the employment tribunal is to seek a more pragmatic solution than might be available by virtue of the more strictly legalistic approach taken by a court of law. The lay members of the employment tribunal in particular are intended to bring their practical experience of industrial relations to bear upon the issues before them.

As such, decisions of employment tribunals are not binding upon subsequent tribunals. Appeal from a decision of an employment tribunal lies to the Employment Appeal Tribunal which consists of a High Court judge and two or four lay members constituted similarly to the lay members of the employment tribunal. The appeal, however, exists only on a point of law, not on a point of fact. The point of law must be that either the tribunal has made an error in the law or has come to a decision which is perverse. From there an appeal lies to the Court of Appeal and thereafter to the House of Lords.

The application to the employment tribunal must be made within a period of three months and the exceptions to this time period are very narrow, based on the tribunal considering it reasonable to extend the period in a case where it was satisfied that it was not reasonably practicable for the complaint to be presented before the end of that three-month period. There are set forms for an employment tribunal application and once those have been submitted to the tribunal a process of conciliation then takes place under the auspices of ACAS. In the event that that resolution procedure fails, the matter proceeds to a hearing at which either side has the right to call witnesses, give evidence, cross-examine witnesses called by the other side and make submissions to the tribunal at the close of the case.

The starting point of most employment tribunal applications will be the statement of reasons for dismissal issued by the employer. Under ERA 1996, s 92 an employee who has been employed continuously by that employer for a period of two years or more who has been dismissed has the right to receive within 14 days of his request a written statement of the reasons for his dismissal. Usually the unfair dismissal case will be grounded on the basis of these reasons.

The first component of any claim for unfair dismissal is to establish that the employee has been dismissed. Usually this will be clear, but the employer may suggest that the employee resigned, or that the contract was terminated by the mutual consent of the parties, or that the contract was frustrated.

Dismissal

Definition
A dismissal is defined in ERA 1996 s 95. An employee is dismissed if:

(a) the contract under which he is employed is terminated by the employer (whether with or without notice),
(b) he is employed under a contract for a fixed term and that term expires without being renewed under the same contract, or
(c) the employee terminates the contract under which he is employed (with or without notice) in circumstances under which he is entitled to terminate without notice by reason of the employer's conduct.

Case (a) is the usual manner in which employment contracts are terminated. Resignation from his post by the employee or other consensual termination is not dismissal. However, if a resignation is effectively procured from the employee either by pressure or some other wrongful means, that will be dismissal notwithstanding initial appearances, such as for instance, where a manager tells an employee that if he does not hand in his resignation he will be dismissed. If, however, an employee knows that he is likely to be dismissed or that he would be dismissed and negotiates for himself an acceptable means of terminating the employment by way of resignation, that would be a true resignation.

If an employee is dismissed on notice and, during the notice period, serves notice effectively resigning with effect from a date earlier than the expiry of the notice of dismissal, he would still be treated as dismissed by the employer for the reason for which the notice was given to him.

Category (b) is effectively self-explanatory. Category (c), however, covers the case of what is known as 'constructive dismissal'. One key conceptual issue that must be grasped is that a constructive dismissal may be a fair dismissal. It is often assumed that if constructive dismissal can be shown then that dismissal will be unfair but this is not the case: having proven he was constructively dismissed, an employee must then be able to show that that dismissal was unfair in the same way as any other dismissal.

Constructive dismissal

A constructive dismissal takes place where the employee walks out on his job in circumstances where the employer has breached the employment contract in a manner so grave that it constitutes what is known as a repudiatory breach: *Western Excavations (ECC) Limited v Sharp*.[1] The employer must act in a way which constitutes a significant breach of the employment contract going to the root of that contract, or which shows that the employer no longer intends to be bound by one or more of the essential terms of the employment contract. Examples of this would be an unjustified demotion of the employee in status, failure to pay wages or similar action. One particularly fertile area in this region is the so-called 'overriding term' implied by the law into all contracts of employment that the employer should treat the employee with trust and respect (see **5.4.1**). Breach of that clause will constitute constructive dismissal. This may even be the case where there might be express authority within the contract of employment for the employer's actions.

Frustration

Not all contracts of employment terminate by the wish of either party. Where circumstances change such that the contract becomes impossible to perform or, if performed, would yield a radically different result from that anticipated by the parties, a contract may be frustrated. Employment contracts are no exception. Where that change of circumstances strikes at the very root of the contract the employment contract may be frustrated and therefore would terminate without there being a dismissal. As there would be no dismissal there would be no question of a case being taken in unfair dismissal (which requires dismissal as the first pre-condition), nor would there be any entitlement to compensation to the employee. The employee may, however, receive compensation for wages owing up to the date of the frustration under the Law Reform (Frustrated Contracts) Act 1943. Where the event affects the employer rather than the employee then the employee may still have the right to a redundancy payment which is specifically reserved by ERA 1996, s 136(5).

Frustration has most often occurred in two specific circumstances: the illness of the employee, or the employee's imprisonment. Other matters such as the calling up of the employee for war service have also been held to be frustrating events but these are not dealt with here.

The case which is obviously of relevance to the context of sport is where a career threatening injury occurs. This is slightly different from most 'sickness' cases which deal more with the question of the employee's being unable to attend for work, whereas a serious injury might mean that the employee might continue to be able to attend nominally for work but would be incapable of performing the work to any reasonable standard. Frustration has frequently been found to have occurred in cases where specific engagements have taken place for a limited number of appearances, for instance in the entertainment context, and these are

---

1   [1978] IRLR 27.

probably not directly relevant to longer term contracts, although they may be relevant in sport for instance where a player is loaned to another club.

In considering whether frustration has taken place, the court should have regard to the following factors laid down in *Marshall v Harland & Wolff Limited*:[1]

(1) the terms of the contract and any provisions of the contract relating to sick pay;

(2) the anticipated length of the employment but for the potentially frustrating event: where the employment is anticipated to be a long standing engagement it is less likely to be frustrated by transitory sickness or injury than a shorter term agreement;

(3) the nature of the post held by the employee and particularly whether it could be held open indefinitely or whether a replacement was urgently required – in the case of a sportsman it is likely that the indefinite holding open of the role performed by that player would not be expected;

(4) the nature of the illness or injury and the likely prognosis – if it is likely that a recovery will be made within a reasonable time the contract is less likely to have been frustrated;

(5) of how long standing the employment relationship has been in the past.

Where a player's career is ended by an injury, it is almost certain that that would have a frustrating effect on the contract of employment. Where the injury is one which might not necessarily end the player's career but might greatly reduce the player's effectiveness, that is a matter which needs to be weighed in the light of the criteria set out above. This is clearly an area where express terms in the contract of employment are desirable.

In the case of imprisonment, this is also capable of constituting a frustrating event: *FC Shepherd & Co Limited v Jerrom*.[2] Once again, a short spell of imprisonment may not be such a frustrating event, but a longer spell may be, particularly by reference to the anticipated length of the contract but for the term of imprisonment. This is perhaps of less practical significance, given that dismissal of the employee on the grounds that he has been convicted of a criminal offence justifying a term of imprisonment may well be fair, but once again this is something best dealt with in the express terms of the contract of employment.

The effective date of termination

The next task in an unfair dismissal action is to identify the date on which the employment contract terminated. The rules surrounding this determination are set out in ERA 1996, s 97.

Where a contract is terminated by notice on either side, whether or not that notice was of the correct length, the contract will terminate on the date of the expiry of that notice. Where a fixed term contract expires without being renewed the date of expiry will be the effective date of termination. Where no notice is given for the termination of the contract, the effective date of termination will be the date on which the termination takes effect – a nicely circular definition dealt with below. Finally, under the example where the employee effectively gives a counter-notice terminating the employment before the end of the employer's

1   [1972] 2 All ER 715.
2   [1986] IRLR 358.

notice to terminate already served on him, the effective date of termination will be the date of expiry of the counter-notice by the employee.

The most troublesome of these definitions is the circular definition of when a contract is terminated without notice. Sometimes the matter will be straightforward: the employee may commit an enormity so great that the employer simply orders him off the premises and tells him that he is dismissed. Often it will simply mean the date when the employee was sacked or walked out. More common, however, is payment of wages in lieu of notice where again the employee leaves straight away, but is paid a sum equivalent to the wages he would have earned during the notice period if he had been required to work during that period. The question arises then whether the contract's effective date of termination is the end of the notice period that would have been served but for the employer's dispensing with that obligation, or whether it is simply the date on which the employee is asked to leave. The answer to the dilemma once again does not lead to great clarity: the date depends upon the true construction which should be placed on the dismissal. In other words, if the employment is terminated as an instant dismissal and the money in lieu of notice is paid by way of damages for wrongful dismissal (see **5.8**), the date of the dismissal would be the date on which the employee leaves. If, however, the more usual course is taken and the payment should be construed as payment for the work during the notice period for which the employee would be entitled to be paid but from which the employer has released the employee, then the date of termination will be the date of expiry of the proper notice which would have been given: *Adams v GKN Sankey Limited*.[1]

If the employee is given less than the notice to which he is entitled by virtue of statute (see **5.8.2**), the termination date is deemed, for the period of qualification for claiming unfair dismissal (see below) and for certain other statutory purposes, as being the date on which the dismissal should have taken effect had the statutory minimum notice been given.

In the case of constructive dismissal, this will usually take place on the day the employee walks out. However, this is not a hard and fast rule and the employee may jeopardise his right to walk out and claim that he was constructively dismissed by attempting to use this argument to prolong the employment, possibly in order to reach the qualification period for unfair dismissal claims.

Qualification for unfair dismissal and redundancy claims
In order to take an action in unfair dismissal or to qualify for a redundancy payment, an employee must qualify to do so by virtue of continuous employment by the employer for a period of two years. This qualification is unnecessary in the event of a dismissal connected with sexual, racial or disability discrimination, with maternity (see **5.7**), a dismissal relating to a complaint made about health and safety procedures, dismissal for reason of membership or non-membership of any trade union, or dismissal by virtue of the employee insisting upon his statutory rights or acting as an employee trustee of a pension scheme or as an elected employee representative. There has been some controversy, however, about the legality under European Law (Art 141(119) of the Treaty of Rome and the Equal Treatment Directive) of the two-year qualifying period on the basis that it was sexually discriminatory. This was stated

---

1   [1980] IRLR 416.

to be because the result of the two-year qualification period was an adverse impact upon women which could not be justified objectively. The matter is complicated and is not one for detailed discussion here: the ultimate position is that in general the two-year qualification period applies – for the time being. However, the uncertainty of the position on this point only serves to underline the importance of proper disciplinary and grievance procedures which are fairly followed for all employees regardless of their status or length of service.

It used to be the case that the two-year qualifying period related to an employee who had worked a minimum average of 16 hours per week for those two years, but now there is no such qualification: this was an instance where European Community Law was held to overrule the previous British legislation on the grounds that it was discriminatory to women.

Provided, therefore, that the employee has the required period of two years qualification (where necessary) and unless the employee is someone who is ordinarily engaged in work at or from a base being outside Great Britain, or is over the standard retirement age either for an employee holding the position held by that employee in the undertaking where the employee was employed or 65 years of age, the employee will have a right to take unfair dismissal proceedings. The only other remaining exception of relevance to sport is that of fixed term contracts which will be dealt with below.

One of the proposals mooted for the Employment Relations Bill was that the qualification period be reduced to one year. That proposal was, at the time of writing, not guaranteed to reach the final legislation.

Definition of continuous employment
There are detailed provisions in ERA 1996, ss 210–219 dealing with the concept of continuous employment. Continuity of employment means an unbroken period of employment with that employer, which will of course be unaffected by various moves by the employee around the organisation and even the issue of new contracts of employment, provided that the employment was effectively continuous in that there was no intervening period when the employee was not employed by that employer.

Weeks are used as the sub-unit in calculating the two-years continuous employment. If a week counts, it counts towards continuity; if there is a week which does not count in the middle of the employment period it will break continuity and the first week following that week which does count will be week one in a new period of qualification. A week which counts is any week during the whole or part of which the employee's relationship with the employer is governed by a contract of employment.[1] There are certain statutory exceptions so that absence from work for up to 26 weeks on account of sickness or illness will not break continuity, nor will a temporary cessation of work. In *Ford v Warwickshire County Council*,[2] it was held that where a school teacher was employed annually September to July for academic years on consecutive fixed term contracts, continuity was made out. The relevance of this to contracts applying to specific sports seasons is clear. However, there is some room for

---

1   See **5.2.**
2   [1983] IRLR 126.

debate as to how long the interval between the contracts may be without breaking continuity. To a certain extent the question is always one of degree for the tribunal which may take a fairly simple arithmetical view as to whether the intervals exceed the periods of employment. Therefore, it may be the case that hirings for the comparatively short cricket season would not even if successive in this way be able to take advantage of this exception in that the 'closed' season is longer than the season itself, whereas a similar series of hirings for the longer football or rugby union seasons may give rise to continuity of employment. The point is not certain and would be for the discretion of the tribunal in each case.

Where the issue of temporary cessation of work arises in circumstances where by arrangement or custom the employee is considered to continue in the employment of the employer there will be no break of continuity.

Absences on account of pregnancy will not break continuity even if the case is one of the 'right to return' as opposed to maternity leave (see **5.7**).

Definition of unfair dismissal
Where an employee has established that he has been dismissed the employer must, in order to show that the dismissal was not unfair, then prove two things: he must prove what the reason or the principal reason for the dismissal was and that that reason fell within one of the categories of potentially fair dismissals set out at ERA 1996, s 98(2), being a dismissal which:

(a) relates to the capability or qualifications of the employee for performing work of the kind which he was employed by the employer to do, or
(b) relates to the conduct of the employee, or
(c) is for the reason that the employee was redundant, or
(d) is for the reason that the employee could not continue to work in that position without contravention (either on his part or on that of his employer) of a duty or restriction imposed by or under an enactment.

Further, the employer could show as an alternative to (a) to (d) above that the dismissal took place for 'some other substantial reason of a kind such as to justify the dismissal of an employee holding the position which the employee held'.

The tribunal must then decide whether in the circumstances (including the size of administrative resources of the employer's undertaking) the employer acted reasonably or unreasonably in treating the reason for dismissal as a sufficient reason for dismissing the employee according to equity and the substantial merits of the case.

As will be anticipated, each of the above components of the determination of whether a dismissal is unfair is surrounded by a forest of case-law. That case-law should be treated with caution, as it does not follow the rules of stare decisis but is to be taken into account in considering new cases. However, there is no point threading through that case-law in detail here. The purpose of the present discussion is to point out where certain of the above issues may relate specifically to sport.

Capabilities or qualifications
The relevant capabilities of an employee in this context are defined as capabilities assessed by reference to the skill, aptitude, health or any other physical or mental

quality of that employee. Qualifications relate to academic, technical or professional qualifications, and these are unlikely to be appropriate in the sports context, although they may justify dismissal where the governing body stipulates certain qualifications for employees in the position occupied by the employee in question, and he does not have them; for instance, a given coaching qualification. The lack of capability should be such that the employee is incapable of satisfactory work. Where the employee is capable but declines to exert himself, that is a case more of misconduct.

Incapability owing to prolonged illness or injury may not even come under this heading; it is more likely to lead to a frustration of the contract, thus leading to termination without dismissal. However, in the event that an employer is seeking to rely upon illness or injury as a reason for terminating the employment then fairness procedurally will be of great importance. Procedural fairness at all stages of any dismissal is of considerable but not paramount importance to the question of substantive fairness: the two types of fairness are not identical but they are closely related. The employer should therefore look to discuss the matter with the employee and to seek reliable medical evidence. He must then take a fair decision according to the criteria of fairness set out below.

Misconduct

Misconduct has so many possible instances that examples are unnecessary. Once the conduct leading to the dismissal – which is not defined in any way by reference to the contract but which in practice would be conduct which effectively is in breach of the express or implied terms of the employment contract – has been established, the fundamental question is whether it was fair to treat that as being a reason justifying dismissal of the employee.

Once again in any dismissal for misconduct the importance of proper disciplinary procedures cannot be over-stressed. Detailed disciplinary provisions need to be set out in the written statement of terms to be provided to the employee under ERA 1996, s 1, and the fairness of the procedure used is hugely important to the questions of fairness of any resulting dismissal. These disciplinary procedures often include provisions for investigations by employers; suspensions from work of employees with or without pay; the administration of oral warnings, written warnings and final written warnings; disciplinary hearings followed by dismissal; and appeal mechanisms from that dismissal. If a procedure has been completely by-passed, the employer is in practice something of a sitting duck to an unfair dismissal claim.

Redundancy

Redundancy is a statutory concept and will unfortunately be of some relevance to sports organisations. Indeed, it has happened on several occasions in certain sports that employers who have been unable to meet their ongoing commitments have found it necessary to make redundancies.

Once again, the conceptual issue should be clear. Redundancy is a potentially fair reason to dismiss. However, that dismissal must then be fair and, even though it is a fair dismissal, there is the obligation, in cases which qualify, for the employer to pay a redundancy payment to the employee.

Redundancy is defined at ERA 1996, s 139. An employee is taken to be dismissed by reason of redundancy if the dismissal is wholly or mainly attributable to:

(a) the fact that his employer has ceased or intends to cease
    (i)   to carry on the business for the purposes of which the employee was employed by him, or
    (ii) to carry on that business in the place where the employee was so employed, or
(b) the fact that the requirements of that business
    (i)   for employees to carry out work of a particular kind, or
    (ii) for employees to carry out work of a particular kind in the place where the employee was employed by the employer,
    have ceased or diminished or are expected to cease or diminish.

Where this takes place, the employee may present a claim for a redundancy payment to an employment tribunal within six months of the relevant date of dismissal which is the same as the effective date of dismissal as outlined above. The employer may choose to rely on another reason for the termination of the employee's employment, but there is a presumption of redundancy in an application for a redundancy payment against the employer. In practice, the employee may make two applications, one for unfair dismissal and the other for a redundancy payment. Whilst the employee cannot be compensated twice, this does prevent his being caught between the two separate regimes. The employer may defend the claim for unfair dismissal on the ground that the dismissal was for reasons of redundancy and that the dismissal was fair. The employee would then be entitled to a redundancy payment.

A dismissal which is for reasons of redundancy will be deemed to be unfair if the employee shows that he was unfairly selected for redundancy, on the basis that the circumstances of redundancy applied equally to other employees who were not selected, and the selection of the complaining employee was made for a reason relating either to union membership or non-membership, or because he had made health and safety complaints, acted as an employee representative or employee trustee of a pension fund, or asserted statutory rights.

The employee may also show that his redundancy was unfair generally. He may prove that his selection for redundancy was capricious, or that the employer made no reasonable effort to look for alternative employment for him within the undertaking, or failed to give reasonable warning and consult with the employee in advance of the redundancy. Once again, therefore, the procedure followed by the employer is crucial. There must be proper consultation with the employee and a genuine effort to find alternative work within the undertaking if such is possible. As in all cases of perceived procedural unfairness, a finding that the employer has failed to operate a fair procedure is not fatal to the employer's case, as there are always circumstances in which it may be fair to dispense with the procedure. However, failure by the employer to use a reasonable procedure and to use it reasonably will leave the employer at a substantial disadvantage.

Where redundancies have occurred in sport, this has almost always been on the collapse of the employer's undertaking or upon the perception of there being an urgent need to cut the wages bill. Care is needed, however, in relation to the statutory definitions: if a player is a goalkeeper, for instance, the need for goalkeepers has not come to an end; it may not even have diminished. It is not enough to show that the employer simply cannot afford to pay.

'Some other substantial reason'

This is obviously an open category included within the legislation to permit a wide range of circumstances, not all of which may be identifiable in general terms, to justify a dismissal. However, one particular and recurring circumstance which has been found to constitute a substantial reason for the purposes of the Act is a 'genuine business reorganisation' where the employer may need to make specific alterations to the manner in which work is performed within the undertaking. The problem here is that the contract of employment with the employee remains the same and, therefore, in contract the employer is clearly unable to impose a unilateral variation of its terms. In some ways, however, this ties into the need for the employee to adapt to changing circumstances, which is an implied term of all contracts of employment (see **5.4.2**). In any event, in the strict contractual analysis, the employee may find himself in a position where he is able to walk out and then claim he has been constructively dismissed. Alternatively, the employer may find that certain employees refuse to adapt to the changes. It may therefore fairly dismiss those employees for that reason. In the context of a genuine business reorganisation the dismissal, either constructive or otherwise, may, however, be fair (subject to the usual test of fairness) or may even be a redundancy (if the statutory definition is made out).

Fairness

Each of the above heads of potentially fair dismissal are subject to a test of actual fairness. The test here is of the employer's conduct and not of the perceived injustice caused to the employee by the dismissal. The employer's reasonableness is assessed by reference to the facts and assumptions in the employer's possession at the time of the dismissal (and not matters which may have come to light following dismissal). Procedural fairness is important, as outlined above, in that even though a lapse in procedure would not automatically make the dismissal unfair, the employer must show that the decision to dismiss was, when made, taken fairly in view of all the circumstances at the time. In dealing with the question it is clearly important to know that reference may be made to the lack of adherence to, or unfairness within, the employer's own procedures at that time.[1]

In determining the fairness of the dismissal, however, the tribunal is not invited simply to place itself in the shoes of the employer and to make its own decision. The test is to a certain extent subjective: what is considered is what the employer reasonably believed at the time of the dismissal. There is a discretion in management when making decisions whether or not to dismiss: if one employer dismisses in certain circumstances and another does not, it does not necessarily follow that one is fair and the other is not. It is established within the decided cases that in most given circumstances there is a range of reasonable responses which a reasonable employer might make acting reasonably. Provided the dismissal falls within this range of reasonable responses it will be fair.[2]

---

1   *Polkey v A E Dayton Services Limited* [1988] AC 344, [1987] IRLR 503.
2   *Iceland Frozen Foods Limited v Jones* [1982] IRLR 439.

Remedies of the employee

Redundancy payments to employees are calculated by reference to the employee's age, length of service and pay at the time of his dismissal. The payment is subject to a statutory maximum which at the time of going to press is £6,300.

For unfair dismissal, it is possible technically for the employment tribunal to order the reinstatement of the employee, but this remedy is to most intents and purposes a dead letter. The relationship between the employer and the employee has usually broken down to such an extent that this remedy is neither sought nor appropriate and damages are the only appropriate remedy.

Damages for unfair dismissal are split into two. The basic award is the first head of damages and is calculated similarly to the redundancy payment. It is automatically reduced by the amount of any redundancy payment received by that employee in respect of that dismissal, and where the tribunal finds that there was compensatory fault on the part of the employee in the dismissal, or where the employer has made an ex gratia payment meant to off-set or extinguish legal rights, this award will be reduced either to reflect the element of fault or to reflect the payment made. On top of this, a compensatory award will be payable, dealing with various heads such as the loss to the employee caused by his dismissal; future loss in terms of how long it might take the employee to return to a position such as that from which he was dismissed; loss of other statutory rights than the rights in respect of unfair dismissal; loss caused by the manner of the dismissal, such as the dismissal making it more unlikely that the employee would find employment immediately; and loss of pension rights. However, the employment tribunal will review the extent to which it feels that the employee was at fault and reduce the compensatory award as well as the basic award to reflect the extent of the employee's fault. The employee is under a duty to mitigate his loss in respect of the compensatory award. Any ex gratia sums paid by the employer prior to the finding of unfair dismissal must be deducted from the amount of the compensatory award. Once again, there is a limit fixed upon the compensatory award which at the time of going to press is £11,300. However, this maximum does not arise in the case of sexual or racial discrimination or dismissal for those reasons for which no two-year qualification period is required to base a claim for unfair dismissal (see above). Further, the maximum is not the starting point for calculations related to contributory fault and subtraction of monies paid by the employer already: effectively the calculation takes place on 'real' figures and the maximum only comes in potentially to affect the bottom line result of that calculation.

Avoidance of the statutory framework by employers

As can be seen, the statutory framework of employment rights granted to employees in respect of unfair dismissal and redundancy superimposes upon the orthodox contractual position a large number of further considerations. It is necessary, therefore, for the sports employer to consider taking such steps as it can to exclude the statutory employment rights. The extent to which this is possible is limited, but it is suggested that even so, advantage should be taken of the facility that exists, namely by the issue to employees of fixed term contracts of employment. An employee, under a fixed term contract by virtue of ERA 1996, s 197, may agree in writing to exclude any claim in respect of his rights under unfair dismissal if the contract is for a period of one year or more and to a redundancy payment if the contract is for two years or more. The fixed term contract of employment may even contain a provision that the contract is terminable upon notice and still count as a fixed term contract for the purposes of the section. However, before anyone becomes too excited about this possibility of excluding the statutory rights, the rights are only excluded in respect of a dismissal which arises by virtue only of the expiry of the term without it being renewed, or a redundancy payment in respect of the expiry of that term without it being renewed. Therefore, if an employee with the requisite continuity is dismissed summarily after six months of a two-year fixed term contract, he can still, notwithstanding the exclusion of the statutory rights, take an action in unfair dismissal against his employer, as the dismissal does not arise by expiry of the term of the contract.

However, the protection extended is none the less important in the context of engagement for specific seasons. It would be prudent for sports employers in sports where there are specific seasons to ensure that their employment contracts run for fixed terms of years terminating at appropriate times so that the club may determine whether or not the employee is required before the outset of the fresh season.

However, the Employment Relations Bill was, at the time of writing, set to prohibit waivers of statutory rights relating to unfair dismissal in fixed term contracts. The legislation should therefore be monitored carefully.

Relevance of the statutory rights in sports

The law of redundancy and unfair dismissal has had only limited effect in the sporting context to date. Usually where a player falls out with his club, or similar circumstances arise, the player is placed on a transfer list and in due course is transferred to another club with the employment contract thus being effectively discharged by mutual consent. In the case of managers, who tend to be sacked rather than transferred in the event of conflict with their employers, the employment contract between the manager and the club will generally provide for such periods of notice for termination on either side as to make the potential award in wrongful dismissal (see **5.8**), and thus the pay-off negotiated at the time of the manager's departure, such that the law of unfair dismissal can effectively be ignored at the time of writing. The proposals to lift the statutory maximum of compensation to £50,000.00 in the Employment Relations Bill may, if they become law, change that. In addition, as indicated above, now that the range of professional sport is growing and the range of playing and managing employees extends further, the statutory remedies will come more strongly into play.

There is an inherent problem in the application of the statutory remedies to sport. If one were looking to sack a football manager, the usual grounds which would be invoked would be those of competency or qualification. How is that to be determined? These issues are frequently debated in the media and in the pubs of Britain but given the test that the employee must be found to be factually unable to find the services required, the problems are immediately apparent. The idea of proving that circumstance to the satisfaction of an employment tribunal would send shivers down the spine of any right-thinking club director. Indeed, one could say that in sport the reason for termination of the relationship between the sports professional and other sports employer is not something that can be compartmentalised within the statutory regime. The parties simply lose confidence in one another, or find one another surplus to their requirements. The question of procedural fairness in these contexts is likewise fraught with difficulties. Does one administer a written warning to a goal kicker who is persistently slicing the ball, or to a cricketer who keeps bowling half volleys at crucial times? The prudent scheme one would follow with most other employees of holding hearings to review situations, setting time scales for measurable improvement within the context of the disciplinary procedure and so forth are inherently unreasonable in this context. The statutory remedies and the requirements they import into the employment relationship should be considered closely in relation to matters of employment discipline, but the non-disciplinary 'performance' aspect of the employment should be recognised as a different, and potentially problematic issue in the light of the law as it stands. In relation to the sports employer's desire to maintain success and the optimum standard of playing and coaching staff, the employer must look to express contractual provisions with the employees concerned, but be aware that all such contractual tests are subject to the statutory provisions and be prepared where employees who fulfil the qualification criteria for the statutory remedies are dismissed, to make ex gratia payments rather than fight causes in the employment tribunals. They should also use what power they have to exclude by contract the statutory rights and gear their personnel policy accordingly in line with renewal dates for fixed term contracts for so long as that facility exists.

5.6 DISCRIMINATION

5.6.1 Introduction

It is unlawful for any employer to discriminate on the grounds of sex, race or disability. However, complicated issues of law surround that straightforward statement of principle. Once again the issue of discrimination within and related to employment is in its detailed form a matter for a more general work on employment law. From the point of view of sports employers, however, discrimination issues remain important. Naturally, sports employers do not only employ playing and coaching staff, but the present work is concerned with that group of the employees and the discussion following will relate to that group only.

5.6.2 Sexual discrimination

Sources of law
Sexual discrimination is prohibited both by the UK's own sexual discrimination legislation such as the Sex Discrimination Act 1975 and the Equal Pay Act 1970 and also by European Community Law, in particular the Equal Treatment Directive and Article 141(119) of the Treaty of Rome, which is concerned with the provision by employers of equal pay and conditions to employees of both sexes. There is academic controversy which occasionally also enters the courts as to whether or not there is a separate cause of action in the hands of the mistreated employee under EC Law in addition to their rights under domestic laws: in all likelihood these are separate actions.

The sex discrimination legislation deals with discrimination in relation to employment and is equally applicable to men as to women. It prohibits discrimination at all stages of employment, including the employer's policy of selection of employees, the benefits offered to employees such as promotion and advancement, and even dismissal. Once employment has commenced complaints as to inequality of treatment should be taken under the Equal Pay Act rather than under the Sexual Discrimination Act.

Direct discrimination

The fundamental rule is that an employer cannot on the ground of a woman's sex treat her less favourably than he treats or would treat a man. To fall foul of the prohibition, the unlawful motive need not be the sole motive or even the most important.[1] The fundamental question at stake is whether or not the complaining employee would have received the same treatment but for his or her sex. If the answer to that is no, and the result is that that employee has been treated less favourably on the grounds of his or her sex, then direct sex discrimination will be made out. Differentiation will not always be discrimination but the line is obviously a thin one. The question of whether the treatment is less favourable is a matter for the employment tribunal which has jurisdiction over such complaints. Direct discrimination can never be justified: it is a straightforward matter.

Indirect discrimination

Indirect discrimination takes place where a person applies to a woman a requirement or condition which applies or would apply equally to a man but:

(1) which is such that the proportion of women who can comply with it is considerably smaller than the proportion of men who can comply with it,
(2) which he cannot show to be justifiable irrespective of the sex of the person to whom it is applied, and
(3) which is to her detriment because she cannot comply with it.[2]

The practical effect of this multiple definition is that if the complainant can show that the requirement or condition has been imposed and that the proportion of women who can comply is considerably smaller than the proportion of men who can comply and that it is to her detriment, the burden will shift to the employer to show that the requirement or condition is justifiable, irrespective of the sex of the person to whom it is applied. The precise definition of what the requirement or condition is is not entirely clear: perhaps the safest common sense definition is any aspect of the employment or of the application for employment or selection criteria of employment which is made compulsory at the behest of the employer.

Whether a considerably smaller proportion of women than men are able to comply with the condition, a requirement may be a matter of fact for the tribunal. Regard should be had to ensure proper statistical methods, however, in ascertaining the proportions of women to men who can comply for the purpose of this judgement. The question of compliance, however, is pragmatic: the test is whether it is pragmatically impossible for women to comply with the condition not whether it might technically be possible.

---

1   *Owen & Briggs v James* [1982] IRLR 502.
2   Sex Discrimination Act 1975, s 1(1)(b).

The defence of justification lies in employers' hands and of course is central to the concept of indirect discrimination. Note always that it has no relevance to direct discrimination. There must be an objective balance struck between the discriminatory effect of the condition and the needs on the part of the employer which led to its imposition in determining whether it could be a justifiable condition.[1]

The exception of sport

In practice, the question of sexual discrimination may be irrelevant to most areas of sport. Interestingly, however, the professional sport employer cannot call in aid any assistance from the general statutory exemption from liability for unlawful discrimination laid down by the Sex Discrimination Act 1975, s 7. In particular, s 7(2) is relevant: it is not unlawful to stipulate that a man be employed in a job where being a man is a genuine occupational qualification, which includes a job where the essential nature of the job calls for a man for reasons of physiology (*excluding physical strength or stamina*).[2] It can be seen, therefore, that exclusion of physical strength and stamina effectively excludes the main difference between the majority of men and the majority of women in relation to sport from the protection of the exception. This leads, however, to a specific term in relation to sport at s 44 of the Sex Discrimination Act 1975 as follows:

> 'Nothing in Parts II-IV [of the Act – the main anti-discrimination provisions] shall, in relation to any sport, game or other activity of a competitive nature where the physical strength, stamina or physique of the average woman puts her to a disadvantage to the average man, render unlawful any act related to the participation of the person as a competitor in events involving that activity which are confined to competitors of one sex.'

It is to be noted that this rule only relates to competitors and does not relate, for instance, to referees.[3] It is also to be noted that the question hangs on whether the strength, stamina or physique of the average woman puts her at a disadvantage to the average man in relation to the sport. There are therefore sports, perhaps those involving motor racing, equestrianism or the less physical sports such as snooker, where this saving from the general rule may not apply and the stipulation that a man be employed, or detrimental treatment of women, will be unlawful. In the main the headline professional sports will come under this exemption but barriers will continue to be pushed, as will perhaps the general perception of the relative physical abilities of the average woman and the average man.

Complaints in relation to sexual discrimination are made to employment tribunals. Two specific issues should be noted. Firstly, in relation to complaints of sexual discrimination no qualifying period of two years applies. Secondly, in relation to such a complaint where it relates to dismissal, there is no statutory maximum award.

---

1   *Hampson v Department of Education and Science* [1991] 1 AC 171, [1989] IRLR 69.
2   Sex Discrimination Act 1975, s 7(2)(a).
3   *British Judo Association v Petty* [1981] IRLR 484.

5.6.3   Equal pay and conditions

Introduction

Most questions in relation to discrimination between male and female employees doing jobs of equivalent nature or work of equal value are dealt with under the Equal Pay Act 1970 as amended by the Sex Discrimination Act 1975. Indeed, disputes in relation to discrimination in terms and conditions of employment whilst the complainant is employed should be taken under the Equal Pay Act 1970 on the basis of the equality clause rather than under the Sex Discrimination Act. That claim should be made to an employment tribunal which may declare the existence of the equality clause and may award arrears of pay or damages for breach of that equality clause going back in terms of compensation up to two years from the date of the institution of the claim.

The equality clause

The Equal Pay Act 1970 implies into every woman's contract of employment what is known as 'the Equality Clause'. Section 1(2) of the Act provides that the clause has the effect that where the woman is employed on like work with a man in the same employment and if any term of her contract is or becomes less favourable to the woman than a term of a similar kind in the contract under which the man is employed, that term of the woman's contract should be treated as so modified as not to be less favourable. If at any time the woman's contract does not include a term corresponding to a term benefiting a man included in the contract under which he is employed, the woman's contract should be treated as including such a term.

Where a woman is employed on work which is rated as equivalent (as opposed to 'like work') to that of a man in the same employment the same implied terms must stand. The third category of comparable work to which these implied terms apply is where a woman is employed on work which is in terms of the demands made on her (for instance under such headings as effort, skill and decision) of equal value to that of a man in the same employment.

These provisions are subject to the qualification that the 'Equality Clause' shall not operate in relation to a difference between the woman's contract and the man's contract if the employer proves that that difference is genuinely owing to a material factor which is not the difference of sex and which (in relation to the 'like work' comparison and the 'work rated as equivalent' comparison) *must* be a material difference between the woman's case and the man's, and in the case of the 'work of equal value' comparison *may* be of such a material difference.

'Like' work is defined as work of the same or of a broadly similar nature and therefore insignificant or unimportant differences are not taken into account in the comparisons. Further, the real practical difference – if any – between the woman's job and the man's is of more importance than theoretical differences. In order to establish that the jobs done by the woman and the man are different, therefore, the employer should be able to point to genuine differences in the nature of the employment or the responsibility involved in the employment. Work is rated as equivalent where a job evaluation scheme covering that employment has taken place and the two employments are rated in that scheme as equivalent. This does not necessarily mean that if such a scheme is based on a false premise it should be accepted by the tribunal.

A question of whether work is of equal value is one which has genuine problems in practical proof. A claim under this head, once it is made to the tribunal and ACAS conciliation has failed, is considered on a preliminary basis as to whether there is a reasonable prospect of success. At that early stage the employer can raise his defence that there is a genuine material factor explaining the differential between the woman's conditions and the man's conditions. The tribunal can then commission a report by an independent expert as to whether or not the work is genuinely of equal value. This is a time consuming process and the results are not necessarily entirely scientific.

The comparator against which the woman is entitled to measure her terms and conditions for the purpose of the equality clause must be in the same employment as the applicant, namely employed by the same employer or an associated employer at the same establishment or at another establishment at which 'common terms and conditions of employment' are observed. The phrase 'common terms and conditions' has been a matter for some judicial debate. Effectively, what it means is that the terms and conditions are sufficiently similar to the terms and conditions which would apply to a male employee at the complainant's own establishment for a comparison to be made.[1] The requirement of common terms and conditions relates to terms and conditions of the establishment at which the woman is employed and the establishment at which the chosen comparator is employed – it is a comparison between the respective establishments rather than a comparator between the two employees.[2]

Provided that the comparator fulfils the criteria outlined above the woman can then choose the man to whom she should be compared and she does not need to choose somebody who is necessarily a fair representative of that group of workers except where the comparator is at a separate establishment. It is no defence for the employer to be able to point to a token man employed on the same disadvantageous terms as the women – he would be treated simply as one disadvantaged man rather than as a fair comparator.

All the above is subject to the employer's defence that the difference is due to a material factor other than the difference of sex.

Naturally there are some fairly straightforward matters which are shown to be material factors, such as the qualifications of employees, geographical location, efficiency and ability within the job. However, where the employer's argument rests on the existence of market forces which justify the differential there has been some controversy. There is authority for the proposition that economic factors which affect the efficient carrying on of the employer's business can constitute material factors.[3] However, market conditions which merely serve to perpetuate sex discrimination do not provide justification under s 1(3) of the Equal Pay Act 1970.[4]

In relation to sport, it is unlikely in the near future that the equal pay legislation will be of substantial moment, but the principle is clear and in those sports where men and woman compete on an equal basis it will remain an important issue for

1   British Coal Corporation v Smith [1996] IRLR 399.
2   Leverton v Clwyd County Council [1989] IRLR 28.
3   Rainey v Greater Glasgow Health Board Eastern District [1987] IRLR 26.
4   Ratcliffe v North Yorkshire County Council [1995] IRLR 439.

consideration. There is also the possibility, for instance, that where the same employer may have a men's team and a women's team playing the same sport, that a claim on the basis of 'work of equal value' or even 'like work' may be instituted. In those circumstances the legislation would surely apply: the anticipated defence on the part of an employer for a differential which were to exist between women employed by that organisation and men employed by the organisation could well be one relating to economic factors: if it were proven that the men's team generated higher attendances at the stadium, higher payments in relation to broadcasting and higher prize money, and that the labour market for players was genuinely such that the rates paid to the men were necessary in order to secure their services, it is submitted that that would be a material factor sufficient to ground a defence. It should, however, be noted that there are no foregone conclusions: as the numbers of women participating professionally in sport increase (as they doubtless will) the significance to sport and its traditional male monopolies will grow more marked.

5.6.4 Racial discrimination

Introduction
Discrimination on the ground of race in employment is dealt with in the Race Relations Act 1976. The operative parts in relation to employment are practically identical in terms of their formulation to the provisions relating to discrimination on the ground of sex. Indeed, the race discrimination legislation was in many ways modelled upon the sex discrimination legislation.

Definition
By s 1 of the Race Relations 1976:

'(1) A person discriminates against another in any circumstances relevant for the purpose of any provision of this Act if:
(a) on racial grounds he treats that other less favourably than he treats or would treat other persons; or
(b) he applies to that other a requirement or condition which he applies or would apply equally to persons not of the same racial group as that other but
   (i)   which is such that the proportions of persons of the same racial group as that other who can comply with it is considerably smaller than the proportion of persons not of that racial group who can comply with it; and
   (ii) which he cannot show to be justifiable irrespective of the colour, race, nationality or ethnic or national origins of the person to whom it is applied; and
   (iii) which is to the detriment of that other because he cannot comply with it.'

As with sex discrimination, the definition at (a) is referred to as 'direct discrimination', and that at (b) is referred to as 'indirect discrimination'.

Certain things should be identified clearly. First, it is not unlawful to discriminate on religious grounds under the Race Relations Act 1976. However, it is recognised that the followers of certain religions are also members of specific ethnic groups. In *Mandla v Dowell Lee*,[1] it was held that Sikhs constitute an ethnic group for the purposes of the Act.

---

1 [1983] IRLR 209.

Meanings

The meaning of 'racial ground' and 'racial group' is set out at s 3 of the Act:

> 'racial grounds means any of the following grounds, namely colour, race, nationality or ethnic or national origins;
>
> racial group means a group of persons defined by reference to colour, race, nationality or ethnic or national origins, and references to a person's racial group refer to any racial group into which he falls.'

Regard should be had to each of the issues raised in these definitions: they should not be treated as an accumulation of synonyms. There is a difference between a race and an ethnic group just as there is between a race and a nationality.

Perhaps the most difficult concept here is that of the ethnic group: in *Mandla v Dowell Lee*, it was held that an ethnic group is a group which regards itself and is regarded by others as a distinct community with a long shared history and cultural tradition of its own. This will not always be the case in relation to religion. In addition to those as the essential characteristics, other relevant factors include common geographical origin between the members of the group, or descent from a small number of common ancestors; a common language; a common literature; a common religion; or even being in a minority or a recognisable group within other communities. Members of that group can belong to it either by birth or adherence of choice.

As with sex discrimination, inherent in the definition of indirect discrimination (but not direct discrimination) is the defence open to the employer where an allegation is made against him of racial discrimination that he can seek to show that the requirement or condition applied to the workforce is justifiable irrespective of race. Matters of proper commercial hygiene therefore which have the effect of indirectly discriminating against, for instance, the Sikh community can be justifiable: *Singh v Rowntree Mackintosh*.[1]

The exception of sport

By s 39 of the Race Relations Act 1976:

> 'Nothing in Parts II-IV [the effective provisions of the Act] shall render unlawful any act whereby a person discriminates against another on the basis of that other's nationality or place of birth or the length of time for which he has been resident in a particular area or place, if the act is done
>
> (a) in selecting one or more persons to represent a country, place or area, or related association, in any sport or game; or
> (b) in pursuance of the rules of any competition so far as they relate to eligibility to compete in any sport or game.'

This therefore prevents the obvious nonsense of, for instance, a Frenchman insisting that his failure to be picked for the England team is racial discrimination. However, attention should be paid to the wording of this exception. It is not unlawful to discriminate in relation to such matters on the basis of nationality, place of birth or length of residence. It is unlawful, however to discriminate on the remaining 'racial grounds', namely colour, race, or ethnic or national origins (in so far as national origins differ from nationality). It is,

---

1   [1979] IRLR 199.

therefore, permissible to govern sport by adherence to regional boundaries in the traditional way. This really applies now only to national teams, now that even traditionalists such as Yorkshire Cricket Club have removed the bar on players born outside the representative boundary representing the team. In theory, a Premier League Football Club represents the town in which it plays but the composition of the team would give very little clue in most cases as to what that town is. It would be interesting, perhaps, if the test ever came as to whether a modern football rugby union, rugby league or other major team sports team was truly representing a place or area for the purposes of this section. It is also clearly the case that no matter what the nature of the team or the competition in relation to which selection criteria are applied, selection on the ground of race, ethnic origin or national origin remains discriminatory.

Outside this statutory exception, it is difficult to see where there could be justification within the terms laid out in the Act for the application of any indirectly discriminatory requirement or condition to the employment of a sports person. One possibility, however, might be where the employment contract requires work on a given day, such as a Saturday which is the Jewish Sabbath. Here it is clear that the number of Jews who could comply with that would be smaller than the proportion who were not Jewish and there may be indirect discrimination. However, the fact that all fixtures for the entire country were predominantly arranged on that day and that the economy of that sport was specifically designed around the use of that day for events would surely be held to be sufficient reason. In any event, there is authority from an unreported case[1] where the employment tribunal found that between 5% and 10% of Jews observed the Sabbath and held that this was not enough of a proportion for the 'substantially smaller' criterion in the definition of indirect discrimination to apply in relation to other facts: this, however, was effectively a decision on the basis of what that definition in s 1(1)(b)(i) means, and other tribunals may find otherwise.

5.6.5   Disability discrimination

There is further legislation relating to discrimination against the disabled in relation to employment pursuant to the Disability Discrimination Act 1995. The discrimination outlawed under this Act, however, is only direct discrimination, namely that discrimination is made out if an employer 'for a reason related to the disabled person's disability treats him less favourably than he treats or would treat others to whom that reason does not or would not apply'. There is, in contrast with race discrimination and sex discrimination, a defence to a complaint of direct discrimination if the employer can show that the treatment less favourable to the disabled person is justifiable on the ground that the reason is 'both material to the circumstances of the particular case and substantial'. There is no prohibition on indirect discrimination but rather positive duties on an employer to make reasonable adjustments to his arrangements or physical features of his premises to ensure that the disabled are not unduly disadvantaged.

The applicability of the disability discrimination legislation to sport may be thought likely to be limited for obvious reasons, namely that sport is

---

1   *Wetstein v Misprestige Management Services Limited.*

predominantly an area of endeavour where physical capacity is of the essence of the employment. However, if the disabled employee or prospective employee is the subject of direct discrimination within the meaning of the Act and the reason is not material to the circumstances of the particular case and substantial, a complaint would lie. For instance, if the disability was simply not material to the sport in question, discrimination on the ground of that disability would be unlawful.

Consideration should also be given to the definition of what disability is for the purposes of the Act. That definition is complex: suffice it to say here that it includes not only permanent physical impairment but also recognises mental illness, sporadic impairments such as epilepsy or long-term and degenerative diseases such as AIDS.

5.7   MATERNITY RIGHTS

5.7.1   Introduction

It may be questioned how far maternity rights are relevant to the employment of sports professionals. The answer to this is largely the same as that to the question of the relevance of sex discrimination: women as well as men are sports professionals and the likelihood is in future years that the number of women employed as sports professionals, both as opposed to the number who are simply self-employed professionals, and in general, is likely to increase. It would be short-sighted indeed to suggest that employment in the sports industry is a male preserve and in any way likely to remain so.

5.7.2   Unfair dismissal for maternity reasons

The statutory maternity rights effectively split into four. First, it is automatically unfair if the reason for a dismissal of a woman is on the ground that she is pregnant or any reason connected with her pregnancy or that she has given birth to a child or any connected reason where the dismissal occurred during the maternity leave period (see 5.7.3); that the woman in question took advantage of the maternity leave provisions (see 5.7.3); where within four weeks of the end of the maternity leave period the employment is ended where the employee gives the employer a medical certificate stating that she would be incapable of work after the end of the maternity leave period, and the dismissal is on the ground that the woman has given birth to a child or for any reason connected with that birth; or where the woman is suspended from work on maternity grounds or that she is made redundant during the maternity leave period without being offered suitable alternative employment.

The statutory provisions relating to this area of the law are complicated and the present discussion can only be a brief overview. Reference should be made to the appropriate provisions of ERA 1996, Part VIII, ss 71–85 and 99.

There is no general defence, as there was prior to 1993, giving the employer the opportunity to prove that the employee was not capable of doing her job because of her pregnancy or could not carry on working without falling foul of statutory prohibitions on her working. Regardless of these issues the termination of her employment would now be unfair and these situations are now covered by a right to paid suspension from work on maternity grounds.

Any selection for redundancy on the above grounds will also be unfair. These provisions are set out in ERA 1996, ss 99–105.

A complaint of unfair dismissal on the grounds of maternity does not require that the employee has served the two-year qualification period which usually applies. If a woman is dismissed while pregnant, she is entitled to a written statement of the reasons of her dismissal, again without the need to have served any qualification period, pursuant to ERA 1996, s 92(4). However, if the woman does not have two-year qualification, she will have to prove first to a tribunal that the reason for her dismissal was one of the prohibited reasons under s 99 (as set out above) before the tribunal will entertain the complaint.

It is also the case that a dismissal for a reason of pregnancy is likely to be found directly discriminatory on the ground of sex for the obvious reason that pregnancy is wholly gender related. It should be considered the general rule that a dismissal for a pregnancy reason will necessarily be direct discrimination although there is support for the proposition that this may not be the case in certain very restricted circumstances, such as where the contract of employment is to take effect only for a short, finite term.[1] Where such a dismissal is found to be directly discriminatory, there is no justification available. It may be that a dismissal not directly on the grounds of pregnancy but related to a consequence of pregnancy, such as long absences from work on grounds of sickness, may be found to be indirectly discriminatory and, therefore, potentially justifiable on the part of the employer within the scheme of the Sex Discrimination Act 1975. All issues relating to pregnancy should be considered in the light of the sex discrimination legislation dealt with above, particularly bearing in mind that in relation to dismissal which is unfair as a result of sex discrimination, there is no upper limit for the potential award of the employment tribunal.

5.7.3 Maternity leave

There are two distinct regimes which need to be distinguished in the context of a woman's absence from work on the ground of her pregnancy. The first is an automatic right of 14 weeks leave (which the Employment Relations Bill at the time of writing proposes to increase to 18 weeks) for all employees irrespective of the length of their service or the hours of their work. The woman during the period of her absence is still employed by the employer. The right to the 14 weeks absence commences no earlier than the beginning of the 11th week before the expected week of childbirth and the leave period is automatically triggered by any day on which she is absent from work wholly or partly because of the pregnancy or childbirth after the beginning of the 6th week before the expected week of childbirth. If childbirth occurs for any reason prematurely, the maternity leave period begins with the date of the birth. If the birth is delayed for any reason, the maternity leave extends to provide for two weeks compulsory leave beginning with the date of childbirth.

There are complex provisions relating to the notice the employee must give in relation to this absence. First, the employer must be given at least three weeks

---

1   *Webb v EMO Air Cargo (UK) Limited (No 2)* [1995] IRLR 645.

notice of the intended date on which the leave is to commence where that is reasonably practicable.

For the 14 weeks of the employee's absence, provided that the employee has been employed by this employer for a continuous period of 26 weeks ending with the 15th week before the expected week of confinement and she has given the employer the required medical evidence and notice of her intention to be absent, and provided that the woman has been earning more than the lower limit for making national insurance contributions, she will be entitled to statutory maternity pay at the higher rate (nine-tenths of her normal weekly earnings) for six weeks and thereafter at the lower rate which effectively is equivalent to the rate of statutory sick pay for the remainder of the maternity pay period subject to an overall maximum of 18 weeks.

5.7.4   The right to return to work

Over and above the 14 weeks absence and statutory maternity pay provisions, there is also the right to return to work. Where an employee has been continuously employed for at least two years by the beginning of the 11th week before the expected week of childbirth, and can satisfy the correct procedure by giving proper notice as if going on maternity leave, and has notified the employer that she intends to exercise her right to return to work, the woman will be entitled to return to work within 29 weeks of the date of childbirth. When taken together with the maternity leave period, the total period of absence is potentially 40 weeks, being the 11 weeks before the expected date of childbirth and the 29 weeks following. The woman must then give her employer at least 21 days written notice of the date on which she intends to return to work.

The job to which the woman returns should be on terms and conditions not less favourable than those which would have been applicable to her had she not been absent. There are provisions, where the employer can prove that she is redundant, for the return to work to be transformed effectively into a right to a redundancy payment: further, where the old job is no longer available, the employer may offer alternative work on terms not substantially less favourable which is suitable and appropriate to the employee. In the event that she is not given her job back, or is taken back on terms less advantageous than those which she enjoyed prior to her absence, there is no separate remedy, but where the employer refuses to permit her to return to work she is treated as being unfairly dismissed on the date she notified as being the intended date of return; if the employment is disadvantageous in comparison with her previous employment she would be treated as having been constructively dismissed if she refuses to accept the new position, and that constructive dismissal in all likelihood would be unfair if the employer cannot prove that it is for reasons of redundancy.

The position as regards pay for the woman in question is that set out above, namely statutory maternity pay: there is no preferential treatment in relation to pay arising as a result of a woman's enjoying her statutory rights to return to work as opposed to the 14 weeks of statutory maternity leave.

5.7.5   Parental leave proposals

The Employment Relations Bill proposes, at the time of writing, that a new right to up to three months' unpaid leave be created for 'domestic emergencies'. This right would apply equally to a man as to a woman. At the end of the three-month period, a similar right to return to work to that discussed in **5.7.4** would exist.

The potential for disruption in the context of professional sportsmen is immediately apparent. Upon the birth or adoption of a child, or other domestic emergency, a professional team sportsman or sportswoman could insist on taking unpaid leave for a period of three months. This could cause disruption to a sports team of a nature similar to that which would occur were that player to be seriously injured. In addition, the possible use of these rights for manipulative purposes, such as by disgruntled players coming to the end of their contracts and not wanting to risk injury lest it impairs their chance of a big move under the *Bosman* ruling (see **5.9.3**), should not be ignored. These new provisions, if they do become law and apply to sport rather than being made the subject of an exception, have the potential to cause major cultural change within sport.

5.7.6   Suspension on maternity grounds

As set out above, there used to be certain situations where the dismissal of the employee on the grounds of pregnancy could be justified by the employer, where the employee could not properly perform her job on account of her pregnancy, or could not carry on working without falling foul of a statutory provision. That is no longer the case and now there is an obligation on the employer to suspend an employee from work on maternity grounds in circumstances set out in the Suspension from Work (on Maternity Grounds) Order 1994.[1] Where a woman of child bearing age who is engaged on work which poses a health risk to a new or expectant mother or her baby from any processes, conditions or agents, and it is not reasonable to alter working conditions or hours of work, or where alteration will not avoid such risk, that woman should be suspended on maternity grounds. A woman should also be suspended if she is a new or expectant mother who works at night and there is a certificate from a medical practitioner or midwife showing that it is necessary that she should not do so for the sake of her health and safety.

The woman has the right to be offered suitable alternative work before her suspension provided a vacancy for such work exists. Alternative work is suitable if it is of a kind which is suitable in relation to her and appropriate for her to do in the circumstances and on terms and conditions which are not substantially less favourable for her. Provided that the woman does not refuse to undertake such reasonable alternative work where it has been offered the woman is entitled to be paid for the period of her suspension by her employer. Failure on the part of the employer to provide these rights may ground a complaint by the employee to the employment tribunal.

The applicability of the right to suspension to sport is clear. Dependent naturally upon the sport, it may be that the pregnant sports professional is entitled to a period of suspension on the ground that continued participation by the woman

---

1   SI 1994/2930.

poses a risk to her or her baby, and thereafter she will be entitled to leave from the 11th week preceding the date of confinement combined with statutory maternity pay for a maximum of 18 weeks and possibly the right to return 29 weeks following the date of confinement.

Over and above this complicated statutory regime there is naturally also the right to make specific contractual provision for these circumstances. It is submitted that that is a sensible course for the employer to take.

5.8   WRONGFUL DISMISSAL

5.8.1   Introduction

It should be recognised that, in the main, the employment protection legislation is primarily directed at those employees in the low to middle income brackets who have not independently negotiated the terms and conditions of their employment with their employer but, rather, have received from their employer a contract of employment on standard terms. This is a pragmatic distinction rather than any qualification for those rights – the rights are available to all but those who have excluded them by contract as permitted (see **5.5.2**): in practice the higher earners and those who have individually negotiated their contract of employment with their employer provide within that contract for contractual entitlements which exceed the 'bare minimum', statutory entitlement. As such, in the event of termination of the employment relationship for any reason, their remedy is more likely to take place under the contract than on the basis of a statutory scheme.

5.8.2   Dismissal on notice

At common law, as opposed to under the statutory regime of unfair dismissal and redundancy, there is no right not to be unfairly dismissed nor any recourse to questions of substantive fairness. The matter is judged entirely on a contractual basis. A wrongful dismissal is one which is wrongful under the contract: in other words a dismissal where the employee has been given no or insufficient notice of the termination of his employment. His compensation is dealt with below at **5.8.3** but is generally limited to the wages he would have earned but for the abbreviation of his notice period. Most contracts will have specific clauses as to the notice on which they can be terminated. In default of such clauses, contracts will be construed as being terminable on reasonable notice if they are not for a fixed term. There are also statutory minimum notice periods laid down under ERA 1996, s 86. The minimum notice period is for an employee with under two years' continuous employment and is of one week. Where more than two years' continuous employment has been served the employee is entitled to one week's notice for each year up to a maximum of 12 weeks notice. These statutory minima will not, however, always be the reasonable notice the court may stipulate if the question were raised.

In the case of a dismissal on notice, there are several possible effects on the question of the employee's entitlement to pay for the notice period and the effective date of termination (see **5.5.2**). First, where the employee works the notice period, that is comparatively straightforward. His effective date of termination is the day he leaves and he has all the pay he is entitled to. Where the employer indicates to the employee that the employee need not present himself for work during the period of notice, advance payment of wages takes place and there is no wrongful dismissal. This might include 'garden leave' cases where the employer reserves the right to stipulate that for his notice period the employee remains at home and does not work for any competing employer in return for receiving the wages payable under the remainder of his contract. Secondly, a contract may provide for termination by notice or by the payment of wages in lieu of such notice as alternatives. Here, where wages in lieu are paid, the effective date of termination would be the date the wages were given rather than the end of the period of notice that would have otherwise applied, and there would be no wrongful dismissal as dismissal has taken a form provided for in the contract. The question of whether wrongful dismissal has taken place is at least partly irrelevant where wages have been paid, as that would be effectively the same amount in most cases as would be payable in damages for wrongful dismissal: but where an employee is wrongfully dismissed a post-termination restraint of trade clause would not apply and therefore that is potentially important: see **5.9.2**.

Thirdly, the employer and employee may simply agree on a variation to the ordinary notice period. That is obviously something that is open to them and in those circumstances they can come to whatever arrangements they wish without breaching the contract.

Fourthly, if the employer simply orders the employee from the premises, summarily terminating the employment, but giving wages in lieu of notice, the employer is probably in breach of contract with the corresponding knock-on effect on any post-termination covenant, but he has paid effectively the quantum of damages he would have to pay for that breach of contract.

5.8.3 Summary dismissal

Wrongful dismissal takes place where the employee is neither given the notice period to which he or she is entitled, nor compensated for the loss of that notice period. Effectively, the contract is terminated wrongfully because it does not follow the terms of the contract rather than by virtue of an appeal to any external concept of justice. It is clear, however, that in certain cases an employer is entitled to 'dismiss summarily', in other words, simply treat the contract as being repudiated by the employee's breach of contract, and dismiss the employee without any requirement to give notice or wages in lieu of notice or by way of damages. It has been said that the true test for whether the employer is so entitled is whether the acts and conduct of the employee evince an intention no longer to be bound by the contract.[1] The employee has committed repudiatory breach of contract and the employer has simply accepted that breach in terminating the contract.

Care should be had, however, with exercising any purported right of summary dismissal. First, any business properly run would have a proper disciplinary and grievance procedure which should be followed in all cases and it is rare in the context of such a procedure that summary dismissal would take place for a

---

1   *Freeth v Burr* (1874) LR 9 CP 208.

one-off offence save in most serious cases. Secondly, what constitutes repudiatory breach of the employment contract should be seen in the context of current thinking in terms of labour relations. Sometimes, old decided cases show an attitude to the level of deference required within the employment relationship which would not find general acceptance under today's conditions.

All that said, the right to dismiss on the basis that the employee has notified an intention not to be bound by the employment contract remains of crucial importance particularly perhaps when dealing with the higher profile players. In Premier League football, there have been instances of high profile players effectively absenting themselves without leave for long periods of time and in such circumstances the employer should be mindful of the ability to terminate the agreement on such grounds. The employer may wish to terminate the contract of a rogue player or manager: however, the player may be wanting to provoke exactly that so that he is 'out of contract' and thus free under the *Bosman* ruling: see **5.9**. Under the *Bosman* ruling, the employer would then not be entitled to demand a transfer fee: great care is therefore required in the tactics of such a situation. For the right to refuse wages, see **5.4.2**.

The question of whether damages are payable is reliant on the parties' contractual entitlement, as opposed to general concepts of fairness in termination of the employment, and becomes of great importance when the amount the employer might have to pay out for wrongful dismissal greatly exceeds the potential loss in unfair dismissal, as will commonly be the case where fixed term contracts of several years may be involved. It is important, therefore, that detailed consideration be given when formulating the employment contract to the specific instances in which termination is contractually authorised rather than simply to rely on the common law right to dismiss summarily. For instance, if the contract states that upon the occurrence of a given event the employer would be entitled to terminate the contract, in common law the occurrence of that event in fact will permit dismissal in accordance with the contract and will thus permit the employer the comfort of knowing that he will not be obliged to pay for the entire unexpired portion of a fixed term contract. Great care should be taken therefore when drafting those sections of the contract as a great deal of money may be at stake. There may still be a claim that, notwithstanding the employer's contractual entitlement, he acted unfairly, but that claim could only lead to the statutory claim of unfair dismissal and its limited scale of recompense as set out at **5.5.2**. In this regard, however, care should be taken in relation to the so-called 'overriding terms' of contract which could have the overriding the express terms of the contract: see **5.4.1**.

Where dismissal has taken place in breach of the employment contract, the remedy in the hands of the complaining employee is effectively damages alone. There is long-standing and detailed case-law where notwithstanding many detailed academic debates the fundamental situation is that the courts will not specifically enforce the employment agreement by imposing any injunction upon the employer to take the employee back, as in *De Francesco v Barnum*.[1]

There are exceptions and once again, there is a complicated case-law. For the present purposes, however, it can safely be assumed that the remedy available to

---

1   (1890) 45 Ch D 430.

the employee in these circumstances is damages and not any order of the court to reinstate the employee. The damages payable would reflect the anticipated earnings available to the employee during the period for which the employee should have been employed by the employer, but for the wrongful dismissal. If, therefore, the contract is for a fixed term without the right to terminate earlier, that would be effectively the anticipated earnings, whether by way of wages and/or business and/or commission or a combination of all of those things, up to the proper expiry date of that contract. Where the contract was terminable upon three months notice it would be those figures for those three months regardless of when the dismissal took place. There is also, in cases involving entertainers, the prospect that there may be an additional head of damage relating to loss of the reputation of the performer caused by the wrongful termination of the contract. In certain cases, such as the duty to provide work, the principles that relate to a theatrical performer may be seen to be analogous to that which may be applied to certain categories of sports persons. The analogy may hold once again in this area: *C Marbé v George Edwardes (Daly's Theatres) Limited*.[1]

For such a case to succeed, it would arguably not be enough to show simply that as a result of the dismissal the sportsman's career may have suffered. It is submitted that the wrongful dismissal must have deprived that sports person of a specific opportunity that would have enhanced his or her career: for instance, a world title fight for a boxer. The actual damage to the reputation of the sports person caused by the breach which has taken place – usually the failure to give adequate or full notice – must be made out.

The employee is under a duty to mitigate his loss. If the employee goes from the dismissal to another fairly lucrative employment, then there will be a high level of mitigation. The employee cannot rely simply on receiving damages, sit back and not make any attempt to find alternative employment. This does not mean that the employee must take any job that offers itself: he is entitled to require a reasonable standard of employment and to wait for a certain time for that to turn up. The nature of mitigation may also go beyond simply the obtaining of a further job and may extend to other benefits that accrue as a result of the dismissal, such as the removal of some prohibition upon the employee during the course of the employment which can then be exploited to the employee's benefit. The gains made by the employee would be set against the damages payable by the employer. Where payment in lieu of wages has been made, the employee has no need to mitigate his loss: it is cash in the bank from his point of view. In contentious and potentially expensive cases, therefore, it is good policy for an employer to wait a while and withstand some pressure before making any payment to see what the extent of mitigation of loss is that takes place. In the case, for instance, of a sports manager, the actual loss – which is the test ultimately to be applied – may be minimal.

---

1   [1928] 1 KB 269.

5.9 RESTRAINT OF TRADE AND THE *BOSMAN* RULING

5.9.1 Post-termination non-competition covenants

In most employment contexts, an important consideration for the employer is that of securing covenants on the part of the employee designed to protect the employer's business, whereby the employee may not be employed by a competing employer, often for a specific period and within a specific geographical radius and/or in a specific industry sector. For instance, a solicitor may have in his employment contract a provision that within six months of termination of his employment he may not work as a solicitor within a given geographical radius of the practice employing him. These clauses are always subject to stringent construction on the part of the courts against the employer who seeks to rely upon them based on the fundamental principle that subject only to legitimate interests properly protectable by the law, there should be freedom of employment for employees and free competition between employers. For the employer to succeed in enforcing such a term he must prove that it is reasonable as between the parties and in the public interest.[1] The applicability of these covenants in sports is severely limited. This is not because sport is any special case or that there are no circumstances at all in which they may be enforceable in the sports industry. However, the courts have been vigilant to uphold the rights of individuals to ply their trade freely, often on the part of sportsmen, and the exceptions to the general hostility of the law to such covenants do not bite on the employment of most sports professionals.

The general rule is that post-termination covenants prohibiting competition or employment by competitors can only be used to uphold the employer's protectable interests which are usually defined either as trade secrets and/or customer connections.[2] Both concepts are comparatively difficult to define but it is clear that it is not likely that either of these categories of protectable interests are likely to arise in the sport context. If a player leaves a given team, it may well cause that team some difficulty: if the player is a good player, it is better to have him on your side than against you. However, his change of employment is very unlikely to prejudice any secret processes or designs, and thus effectively come under the trade secrets banner; nor indeed is it likely that the player would have such access to the customer connection of the employer that his departure would affect that. The player is unlikely to have personal contact with customers, nor is he likely to take those customers with him to his new employment. The main customer of any sports employer is the paying spectator, either corporate or individual, and their custom is attracted by the team as a whole. If season ticket applications drop on the departure of a star player that is not something which the employer can justifiably complain of so as to enforce any restrictive covenant, as it is not a case in which the employee is likely to misuse his knowledge of the customer connections of the club either to his own benefit or that of another employer. The player probably does not know any of the customers' names and addresses and is certainly unlikely to attempt to contact them in order to bring them to his new team.

---

1   *Nordenfelt v Maxim Nordenfelt Guns and Ammunition Co* [1894] AC 535.
2   *Herbert Morris Limited v Saxelby* [1916] 1 AC 688.

Such restraint of trade covenants need not therefore concern us further in the context of players and managers. Anyone employed primarily with a view to obtaining or servicing marketing and sponsorship aspects of the club should, however, be under such covenants. To attempt to import any such covenant into a player's contract in any sport would, it is submitted, be clear nonsense. Likewise, the so-called 'garden leave' clause where the employee, on notice of termination of his employment, is kept out of the labour market for the notice period preceeding the termination of his employment is for the same reasons likely to be inappropriate – such a clause can only be justified on the same basis as any other similar post-termination covenant.

5.9.2 Restraint of trade

The doctrine that clauses in contracts which tend toward the restraint of trade are generally void, combined with European developments along the same lines, has for some time operated a powerful influence in the context of the employment of sports professionals and continues to do so. Indeed, sport has in some areas led the way in the development of certain principles in this regard, such as in *Eastham v Newcastle United Football Club Limited*,[1] where it was established that the individual who is powerfully affected by any arrangement which tends towards restraint of trade has the right to challenge an agreement of this nature, even though he may not be a party to it. In that case, George Eastham, the Newcastle United Footballer (and *Bosman* of his time) successfully challenged 'the retain and transfer' system which greatly impeded the free movement of players from club to club. He did not, however, overturn the right to the transfer fee for the club even where the player was out of contract: that further victory was left for *Bosman*.

Fundamentally, any rule which tends to restrict the freedom of employees to ply their trade, especially across European boundaries, should be looked on with some suspicion. For instance, in *Greig v Insole*[2] it was held that the Test and County Cricket Board disqualification of players who had joined the Kerry Packer 'World Series Cricket' circus, both from participating in official test matches and English county cricket, was in both cases unreasonable restraint of trade and therefore void. Notwithstanding that the cricket authorities were acting in what they perceived to be the best interests of the game, that did not justify the restraint of trade. This doctrine might even apply to clauses taking effect during the currency of the employment contract, for instance where the effect of the term of the contract of employment is effectively to neutralise the ability of the employee to contract freely for his services. For instance, in *Watson v Prager*[3] the boxer Michael Watson took action against his manager Mickey Duff on the ground that the agreement with Duff constituted an unreasonable restraint of trade, as Duff not only was his manager, but also the promoter of the majority of the fights Watson had entered. There was a stipulation in the agreement between Watson and Duff that Watson was not to enter into arrangements with other persons without Duff's consent. It was held that the essential conflict of interest arising where a manager whose job is effectively to

---

1   [1964] Ch 413.
2   [1978] 1 WLR 302.
3   [1991] 1 WLR 726.

maximise the potential earnings of the boxer is also the promoter with whom the manager theoretically should be negotiating the best deal on behalf of the boxer led to the agreement being unenforceable as a result of its being in restraint of trade.

5.9.3   EC Law and the *Bosman* case

The detailed rules of European law relating to the promotion of a single market through the European Union are of course a matter for specialist works on European Community law. However, of particular relevance in the context of the present discussion, are Art 39(48) (dealing with restriction on the free movement of persons in the EU), Art 81(85) (dealing with anti-competitive behaviour affecting trade between member states) and Art 82(86) (the abuse of a dominant market position) of the Treaty of Rome. These Articles apply to sport as to other businesses, as the activities of sportsmen, whether professional or even semi-professional, are governed by EU law where the practice of sport where payment is made in respect of the sportsman's performance qualifies as an 'economic activity' as defined by Art 2 of the Treaty of Rome. The *Bosman* case[1] is the most famous and important decision in relation to restraint of trade and sport and the effects of that decision are still being worked out. The decision relates to football but should be considered as one affecting professional sport of all kinds.

The context in which the case falls is that, at the time of the events complained of, for the player (Bosman) to be transferred from one club in Belgium to another in France such transfer was conditional on the issue of an international clearance certificate, for which the transferring club needed to give its consent. Bosman was offered a new contract with his club, RFC Liège, the terms of which were less favourable to him than the contract which had expired. A transfer was negotiated to a French club, US Dunkerque, on the basis that this was to be a temporary transfer for one year with an option thereafter for a full transfer to take place. The transfer fee was agreed but the deal collapsed, owing to doubts on the part of RFC Liège as to the solvency of Dunkerque. Following the collapse of the deal, Bosman was suspended from playing anywhere. He therefore took action in the Belgian courts seeking a declaration that both transfer fees and clauses prohibiting more than three foreign players per team and two 'assimilated players' per team were unlawful restrictions upon competition and upon the free movement of workers. The Belgian Court referred the case to the European Court of Justice on the basis of Articles 39(48), 81(85) and 82(86) of the Treaty of Rome. The European Court declared that the requirement that a transfer fee be paid to the transferring club for players who were out of contract, and the regulations adapted by European Football authorities governing maximum numbers of foreign or assimilated players were unlawful, because they were incompatible with Art 48 of the Treaty of Rome. Articles 85 and 86 were not considered in this context but of course are potentially relevant.

The consequences of the case have been immense. First, the freedom from restriction on numbers of overseas players has led to a vast increase in the number of foreign players in the FA Premier League. There has also been a shift

---

1   *Union Royale Belge Des Sociétés de Football Association ASBL v Bosman* C415/93 [1996] All ER (EC) 97.

of power, both financial and otherwise, to players from clubs. High transfer fees are likely to be less frequent, given that the player when out of contract will have the ability to move without transfer fee to another club within the European Union and even possibly within the country in which he played, up to the expiry of his contract. On the expiry of his contract, therefore, the player may seek to go himself to the highest bidder, taking himself what formerly might have been the transferring club's share of the money payable in respect of his transfer, either by way of a signing on fee or by way of higher wages through the period of the contract. The wage bill for clubs will, on this model, increase as the transfer bill decreases. The value of a player to a club is thus much reduced and should not be shown on the club's balance sheet.

Clubs also, therefore, need to protect their investments. The tendency will be to award longer contracts, in order to keep a player under contract, so that if he wishes to move a transfer fee is payable for a longer period. To induce a player of value to sign for such a long-term agreement, however, the wages payable to that player will have to reflect his loss of opportunity in selling his services in a free market on the expiry of a shorter contract. As a result, the wages bill for many clubs has taken huge leaps, as players are effectively bribed to stay in circumstances where the old rules used to allow the clubs to be paid handsomely if the player left. However, the player may look to moderate the potential effect of the long term contract he is now asked to sign by seeking 'a get-out clause' in the event that the club is relegated from the Premier League, or in other circumstances which the player considers disadvantageous to his career progression.

Great care also needs to be taken by the club to avoid the termination of a player's contract if there is the likelihood that a transfer fee can be obtained for the player.

It would be wholly wrong to confine the discussion of the *Bosman* case solely to professional football. It has an equal ability to bite on other sports which have a genuine market of players with a European dimension. This would include, for instance, rugby union, where highly evolved club games exist throughout Britain, France and Italy and are growing elsewhere. The ramifications of the *Bosman* ruling lead to a certain redistribution of bargaining power between the club and the player which must be reflected in the terms of the contract of employment. There are also dangers raised by the *Bosman* case which must be addressed, such as those of players seeking to manipulate their commercial status under the *Bosman* ruling. One instance might be where a player adamantly declines to agree terms for transfer whilst under contract with a view to arranging such a transfer at the expiry of contract. This is of course difficult to address. In other cases, players may even cease to exert themselves at a club where they feel they have no future, continue to enjoy their high salaries and look to a transfer at the expiry of their contract to redress their fortune. The worst situation the employer can be in is to have a high cost employee offering little or no value to the club and just 'playing out time' until he can leave in circumstances where his departure provides no benefit to the club.

The specimen contract that follows (see **5.12.1**), therefore, should be seen in the light of this new situation. Before moving to that specimen contract regard should be had to the power and influence of the sport's governing bodies upon the employment relationship involving sports professionals.

5.10   PLAYER TRANSFERS

The transfer market for employed players in all professional sports was radically altered by the *Bosman* ruling,[1] enabling out-of-contract players to transfer free of any claims by their previous employer. None the less, players employed under existing fixed term contracts who wish to find a new employer or who are required to find a new employer need to be released from their existing contract. The risk to a new employer is that, in enticing the player from his current employer, they risk penalty under the governing bodies' rules (usually a fine) and a legal action for inducement to breach contract[2] by the current employer. A player transfer is usually affected as follows:

– the current employer gives consent to the potential employer to speak to the player or his representative;
– the player seeks to agree personal terms with the new employer;
– the existing employer agrees transfer terms (usually in the form of a fee) with the new employer in return for which the existing employer releases the player's registration and consents to termination of the player's contract;
– the player's contract is finalised;
– the transfer agreement is finalised;
– the player's registration is transferred to his new employer.

5.11   REGULATORY ISSUES

The relationship of employer and employee in sport does not exist by any means in a vacuum. All commercial dealings by employers involved in any sport will be closely circumscribed by the regulations laid down by the sports governing bodies, and those bodies will particularly lay down detailed rules governing the status and conduct of players and the manner in which clubs must deal with players. Sometimes these will have been issued simply as edicts from the governing body, designed to ensure the proper conduct of the sport. Obvious examples would relate to the prohibition upon being concerned in betting on the outcome of matches and the disciplinary structures affecting players. These provisions can only be treated as givens, unless they are open to challenge, for instance on grounds of restraint of trade, and if they are reflected at all in the contract between player and club that will be only by way of straightforward reference, or the specifying of certain consequences of non-compliance between player and club over and above the consequences laid down by the governing body.

However, in addition, there will frequently be general directives of the governing body concerning the contents of the player's employment contract itself, and even a stipulated standard form of employment contract. The reasons for such directives and standard forms are various: sometimes they will reflect a wish to maintain a 'level playing field' for all players and/or for all clubs, and may be in danger of being exposed to the courts on the ground that they are in restraint of

1   *Union Royale Belge Des Sociétés de Football Association ASBL v Bosman* C415/93 [1996] All ER (EC) 97.
2   *Warren v Mendy* [1989] 1 WLR 853.

trade or necessarily involve anti-competitive practices; sometimes, to put the matter bluntly, they may be reactions to particular problems, such as a visit by the Inland Revenue's Special Compliance Office to a number of clubs (the tax authorities having a traditional view of sports clubs as dens of fiscal iniquity); most commonly, however, these directives represent the outcome of negotiations over a number of years with players' representatives, and might be considered analogous to collective agreements.

It is obvious good sense that anyone concerned with advising in connection with employment terms in this context should be thoroughly familiar with all the applicable regulations and standard forms, and most importantly should know, first, to what extent divergence from and addition to these standard forms is tolerated. In some cases, the standard form will be advisory only. If it is in any way mandatory, the form will usually lay down only a bare skeleton of standard terms, leaving still a very wide discretion to the clubs and players to negotiate around the mandatory framework. Secondly, however, the adviser or negotiator should also make sure he or she is aware of what the penalty of non-compliance may be. The importance of ensuring detailed knowledge of the regulatory framework cannot be over-stressed, particularly given the increasing complexity of the arrangements proposed by players and their agents.

There is little purpose here in attempting any sort of authoritative summary of the regulatory framework that exists in specific sports under their different governing bodies, but the following is proposed as a brief checklist of some of the most important matters of which the adviser or negotiator must be aware before concluding any employment agreement with any manager or player.

5.12 CHECKLIST: EMPLOYMENT CONTRACT

– Is the player of an age where specific rules relating to the terms on which they may be employed are relevant; eg, junior players, affiliated schoolboys, apprentices etc where regulations as to pay, hours and education may be relevant.
– Is the player of a non-EC nationality making it necessary for a work permit to be issued before he/she can play for the club; in such cases, agreements should be made subject to the obtaining of such a work permit and contain obligations upon both parties to use reasonable endeavours to obtain such a permit (some knowledge of the process of obtaining such work permits is useful in such cases).
– Does the player have any characteristic leading to or breaching any mandatory restrictions in respect of playing staff; eg, limitation on numbers of overseas players in county cricket.
– If the player is represented by an agent or other representative, is that agent or representative properly accredited according to all applicable criteria; in this regard, the FIFA mandatory system for accreditation of football players' agents is a case in point.
– Are there any applicable regulations of governing bodies in this or in other jurisdictions in relation to timing to consider; for instance, must the deal be concluded by any specific time to fit around transfer deadlines for the purposes of any competition or generally.

- Will the proposed length of the contract have any effect upon applicable regulations; eg, the provision in football's Premier League rules that players over 33 years of age with five years' continuous service at one club shall be entitled to a free transfer.
- Is there a standard form of contract applicable; to what extent is that form mandatory; see above.
- If any payment is required by way of signing-on fee, benefit (such as paying for travel expenses) or bonus to the player or to any third party, is that payment permitted. In particular, payments to agents whether they are accredited or not or whether they are called 'agents' within the confines of the deal or not, are important matters of principle.
- What prohibitions, if any, might there be on any of the terms of the deal required by either side; eg, there may be a prohibition on the use of intermediate companies to supply certain components of the player's services by purporting to employ the player for marketing work and contracting with the club to provide the player's marketing services. Some players may seek this type of arrangement for what they believe to be the opportunity to capitalise upon beneficial taxation treatments.
- What notifications and/or registrations need to be supplied to any given governing body before, during or after the negotiations.
- What clearances or permissions, if any, are required from any governing body before the transfer can take place; eg, international clearance certificates.
- Are any mandatory medical checks on the player to be made.
- Does the governing body lay down any mandatory insurance schemes for players for which the player must be registered.

5.12.1   Employment contract

THIS AGREEMENT is made the   **day of**

BETWEEN:

(1)   [Name] whose registered office is situate at and known as [address] ('the Employer') of the one part and

(2)   [Name] of [address] a [specify role of employee] ('the Player') of the other part

COMMENTARY *See section 5.3 for contracts of minors. Often there will be specific forms of contract for players at the outset of their careers (such as apprentices and so forth) laid down by the Governing Body.*

In some sports the Governing Body will require that an individual is nominated on behalf of the Employer rather than the sports club contracting direct with the Player.

RECITALS

A   The Employer is a professional ([club] participating in the [league])

B   The Employer wishes to engage the services of the Player to participate in its matches and to provide other services as specified in this Agreement and the Player wishes to accept such engagement

C   The Employer and the Player have entered into this Agreement in order to establish the terms of the Player's engagement by the Employer

OPERATIVE PROVISIONS:

In consideration of the matters set out in this Agreement the Employer and the Player agree as follows:

I   **DEFINITIONS AND INTERPRETATION**

    1.1   **Definitions**

In this Agreement the following words shall have the meanings set out in this clause 1.1:

'Authorised Official'	means a director of the Employer, the Team Manager employed by the Employer from time to time [add in others as necessary];
'the Club's Colours'	means ;
'Employer's Logo'	means the Employer's official logo attached to this Agreement as annex number;
'Employer's Playing Context'	means any occasion where the Player is engaged on any of the services provided for in this Agreement and/or is within the Employer's premises and/or is depicted in or wearing the Employer's Official Kit and/or Training Kit and/or other clothing displaying the Employer's colours and/or logo;
'the Employer's Premises'	means the Employer's home ground situate at and known as ;
'Governing Body'	means [define the domestic Governing Body under whose auspices the Player will be playing for the Employer];

'Kit'	means any and all of [set out standard kit requirements for Player engaged in the sport in question which are branded with the Employer's colours and/or logo excluding those items left to player's discretion such as boots in football or rugby, bats etc in cricket];
'Laws of the Game'	means [define the main statement of the laws for participants in the sport in question ie those rules governing the conduct of Matches or competitions as opposed to the Rules of the Governing Body by reference where possible to specific documents as amended from time to time];
'Match/Event'	means [Define the Matches or Events for which the Player is engaged. This should be done inclusively, for instance: 'Any and all matches whether competitive or otherwise of whatever nature undertaken by any team representing the Employer in any competition and/or howsoever arising'];
'Rules of the Employer'	means [set out the in-house rules of the Employer such as a staff handbook and/or Player's instructions and training rules. If such do not exist – draft them – they are crucial.];
'Rules of the Governing Body'	means [define the rules promulgated by the Governing Body relating to the conduct of the sport on a commercial and regulatory basis by reference where possible to specific documents as amended from time to time];
'Sponsor'	means any person, company or organisation with which the Employer may contract to provide promotional, marketing or other services from time to time as the Employer may advise the Player from time to time;
'Term'	means the period for which this Agreement shall take effect in accordance with the terms of clause 6 hereof save where this Agreement is previously terminated by substitution of a further or revised agreement or by the consent of the parties;
'Training Kit'	means [set out standard training kit provided by the Employer for Player engaged in the sport in question].

1.2   **Interpretation**

Unless otherwise stated, any reference in this Agreement to a clause should be a reference to a clause of this Agreement, and any reference to a sub-clause should be a reference to a sub-clause of the clause in which such reference appears.

2   OBLIGATIONS OF THE PLAYER

COMMENTARY *In relation to playing services, please see generally* **5.4** *and in particular,* **5.4.2**. *In relation to the use of the employer's rights granted under this section to give instructions, please see* **5.4.2** *in particular.*

In relation to the provision set out at Clause 2.2 of this agreement, please see Chapter 6 which deals with sponsorship and endorsement issues.

It is of considerable importance to the employer to obtain the player's co-operation with its sponsorship activities and to ensure that the player is not used as a focus for ambush marketing. For instance, the Club might have given its official endorsement to a given soft drink manufacturer. A major rival of that soft drink manufacturer may approach one of the Club's star players and then use in its promotional activities a picture of that star player wearing the Club's kit thus effectively hijacking the official endorsement. Usually, the contract with the Club's Sponsor will include provisions to avoid this in the Sponsorship Contract if the Sponsor has been correctly advised and it is therefore crucial that these clauses are included.

Likewise it is important that the player does not set off on commercial frolics of his own which might militate against the proper performance of his duties under the contract. For instance, forecasting results for spread betting rings whilst expressly prohibited usually by Governing Bodies is only one example of the manner in which players could become serious liabilities.

The licence of image at Clause 2.2.5 should be seen in the light of the contents of Chapter 6 dealing with endorsements.

*Generally, this section should be dealt with by the Employer in a manner consistent with its duty to act in good faith and to treat the employee with respect – see **5.4** in particular.*

2.1	**Playing Services**

At all times during the Term of this Agreement:

2.1.1 as and when so instructed by an Authorised Official the Player shall attend any Match/Event in which the Employer is engaged anywhere in the world and/or at any place such Authorised Official may require for the purposes of training and/or Match preparation;

2.1.2 the Player shall use all reasonable endeavours to play to the best of the Player's ability and potential at all times whether in training and/or match preparation and in any and all Matches in which the Player is selected to play on behalf of the Employer;

2.1.3 the Player shall at all times observe the Laws of the Game and/or the Rules of the Governing Body when engaged in Matches on behalf of the Employer and/or in the performance of any duties hereunder;

2.1.4 the Player shall play [the game] only for the Employer and/or as authorised by the Employer and/or as required by the Rules of the Governing Body;

2.1.5 the Player shall ensure that he/she is aware of and observes all Rules of the Employer always provided that in the event of conflict the provisions of this Agreement shall have precedence over the Rules of the Employer;

2.1.6 the Player shall observe at all times the Rules of the Governing Body which in the event of conflict shall take precedence over the Terms of this Agreement;

2.1.7 the Player shall submit promptly to such medical and dental examinations as the Employer may reasonably require and provided that the same is at no expense to the Player shall undergo all reasonable treatment which may be prescribed by the medical and/or dental advisors of the Employer;

2.1.8 the Player shall comply with all lawful and reasonable instructions which may be issued to the Player by an Authorised Official. The Player hereby acknowledges that such lawful instructions may on occasions include instructions to the Player to play in a manner representing the interest of the Employer's team as a whole rather than the Player's own interests;

2.1.9   the Player shall be ordinarily resident in close proximity to the Employer's premises.

2.2   **Community Public Relations and Marketing Services of the Player**

At all times during the Term of this Agreement:

2.2.1   for the purposes of the sponsorship, promotional, community and public relations activities of the Employer and/or of any Sponsor the Player shall attend at and participate in such events as may reasonably be directed by the Employer. The Employer shall give as much notice as it is reasonably able and in any event reasonable notice to the Player of the Employer's requirements in this regard always provided that nothing in this clause shall oblige the Player to provide the services set out in this sub-clause 2.2.1 for an average of more than [   ] hours per week;

2.2.2   the Player shall at all times whilst the Player is providing the services set out in this Agreement wear only such Kit and/or Training Kit as the Player may be instructed to wear by any Authorised Official and the Player shall not display any badge, mark, logo or trading name on any Kit and/or Training Kit or other clothing worn during the provision of the services set out in this Agreement other than the badges marks logos and trading names of the Employer and/or any Sponsor as the Employer may direct without the express written consent of an Authorised Official [always provided that nothing in this clause shall prevent the Player wearing and/or promoting the [fill in excluded items from the definition of 'Kit'] of the Player's choice];

2.2.3   the Player shall not become involved or connected with any activity whether or not of a commercial nature or any publication likely to bring [the game] into disrepute or to damage the reputation of the Player the Employer any Sponsor or any officer or employee of the Employer and/or of any Sponsor;

2.2.4   the Player shall not do anything which may reasonably be considered as promoting or endorsing any product or service or providing promotional marketing or advertising services of whatever nature for or on behalf of any company or person where such product or service or such company or person's interests may reasonably be considered by the Employer to conflict with the interests of the Employer and/or any Sponsor and/or any products and/or services of the Employer and/or of any Sponsor and in any event shall not undertake any services of a promotional or endorsement nature in the Employer's Playing Context save upon the express instructions of the Employer;

2.2.5   nothing in this Agreement shall have the effect of preventing the Player from undertaking promotional activities on behalf of persons other than the Employer and/or Club Sponsors always provided:

2.2.5.1   the said promotional activities do not infringe the terms of sub-clause 2.2.4; and

2.2.5.2   the Player shall not in the course of any such promotional activities be presented or depicted in the Employer's Playing Context; and

2.2.5.3   the Player shall advise the Employer of any promotional activities he/she intends to undertake not less than 14 days prior to undertaking the same and shall not undertake such activities until the Employer approves the same in writing such approval not to be unreasonably withheld or delayed;

2.2.6   the Player hereby grants to the Employer the right to use the Player's name, fame, image, signature, voice, filmic and visual portrayal and reputation in the Employer's Playing Context for the purposes of promoting the Employer and the Employer's products in such reasonable manner as the Employer may see fit and the Employer shall further be entitled to sub-licence the rights granted in this clause to any and all Sponsors for use by them in a like reasonable manner ALWAYS PROVIDED THAT no such use of the rights granted in this clause shall take place following the termination of this Agreement for any reason.

2.3 **Dealings with the Media**

At all times during the Term of this Agreement:

2.3.1 the Player shall whenever the Player is reasonably able to do so seek approval from the Employer for any contribution to the public media in order to provide the Club with the opportunity to make representations to the Player if it so desires and in any event the Player shall not make any comment or statement to the public media which is derogatory to the Employer and/or any officer or employee of the Employer or any Sponsor or which is likely to bring the Player and/or the Employer and/or any Sponsor and/or any officer or employee of the Employer and/or [the game] into disrepute;

2.3.2 the Player shall use his reasonable endeavours in all dealings with the public media to enhance the reputations of himself, the Employer and any and all Sponsors.

2.4 **Restrictions upon the Player**

At all times during the Term of this Agreement:

2.4.1 the Player shall use all reasonable endeavours to keep himself physically fit so as to be able to play [the game] to his full ability and potential and shall not engage in any sport or activity which may reasonably be considered by the Employer as likely to be of a dangerous nature and/or make any policies of insurance maintained by or for the benefit of the Employer in relation to the Player's life or physical well-being voidable and/or which is in the Employer's reasonable opinion likely to impair or place in jeopardy the ability of the Player properly to carry out the services set out in this Agreement. In particular the Player shall refrain from any form of motor sport, parachuting or parascending, hang-gliding, rock climbing and/or snow water or dry skiing;

2.4.2 the Player shall not undertake any other employment in any trade business or occupation without the prior written consent of the Employer. Nothing in this clause shall have the effect of preventing the Player making investments in any business which do not in the Employer's reasonable opinion interfere with his obligations under this Agreement;

2.4.3 the Player shall not knowingly commit any act or omission which may cause the Player and/or the Employer to be in breach of the Laws of the Game and/or the Rules of the Governing Body.

3 REMUNERATION

COMMENTARY *The question of remuneration is only touched on in basic outline here. It may be that remuneration is staggered allowing for increases year by year. Bonuses are usually dealt with in the Rules of the Employer which will provide specific scales of bonus for wins, qualification for European competition and other bonuses payable on the reaching of certain stages or positions in different competitions.*

In addition Players may negotiate other clauses appropriate to the work that they have to provide. For instance, a Rugby Player might want to be paid an additional bonus per try, a Cricketer additional bonuses for reaching 1000 runs or 50 wickets in a season, and the examples can be multiplied. However, there are other issues which can be addressed at this point such as:

1.   *Signing on fees. In particular, a player who has been out of contract under the* Bosman *Ruling may stipulate a specific signing-on fee the payment of which may be staggered over a period of two or three years.*

2.   *Insurance. This is touched upon in the schedule but one idea is for the Player to have insurance paid for by the Club under which he is paid out the entire value of his contract in the event of being permanently incapacitated whilst in the Club's service.*

Anyone advising a Player should be very careful to ensure that the Player's insurance is given top priority – the working life of a professional sportsman is short but lucrative if he is successful and a catastrophic injury, as in the case of the Coventry City player, David Busst, can leave a Player not only in physical suffering but in financial hardship.

3.   *Share of Future Sale. Some players may want to negotiate a share for themselves of any profit made by the Club when the Player is sold on.*

4.   *Relocation costs. Particularly for overseas players, finding new accommodation is not entirely straightforward and they may stipulate the supply of a house on a rental basis for a period of time followed by some assistance with relocation expenses.*

5.   *Loyalty bonus. Some players would want to receive a bonus upon having played for a Club for five years or so. It is suggested that the Employer does not grant any loyalty bonus which falls to be payable during the course of the contract term given that it is a strained definition of loyalty simply to fulfil a contractual obligation!*

6.   *Issues in relation to wage structure within the Club. Some Players may want the provision that nobody at the Club is paid more than they are and if someone comes in who is paid more than they are the salary they are paid is lifted to reach that level.*

*Please see in general in relation to this heading **5.4.2**.*

Players may also wish to negotiate the clauses concerning pensions, cars and other benefits that are familiar from other employment relationships.

3.1   Throughout the term of this Agreement the Employer shall pay to the Player remuneration as set out at Schedule 1.

3.2   The Employer will be responsible for the costs of all travel, accommodation and incidental expenses in connection with the Player's services as set out in this Agreement and shall reimburse to the Player all reasonable expenses wholly and exclusively incurred by the Player in relation to the services provided by the Player pursuant to this Agreement provided that such expenses are incurred with the prior authorisation of an Authorised Official and evidenced by such vouchers receipts or other evidence as the Employer may reasonably require.

3.3   The Employer is hereby authorised to deduct from any remuneration payable by the Employer to the Player any amounts owing by the Player to the Employer of whatever nature including but not limited to any amounts payable by the Player pursuant to the Rules of the Employer.

4   OBLIGATIONS OF THE EMPLOYER

At all times during the Term of this Agreement:

4.1   The Employer will observe all Rules of the Governing Body affecting the Employer and shall provide the Player with copies of all Rules of the Governing Body which affect the Player.

4.2   The Employer shall maintain in force any insurance arrangements set out in Schedule 1 for the benefit of the Player and in the event that any material term of such arrangement is changed the Employer shall forthwith notify the Player in writing of such change.

4.3 The Employer shall arrange at the Employer's expense for such appropriate medical and dental examinations and treatment for the Player as the Employer may see fit in the event of any illness or injury befalling the Player in the course of his employment which is likely to impair the Player's performance of the services provided for in this Agreement. The Employer shall continue to be responsible for all costs of such treatment whether or not this Agreement terminates for any reason during the course of such treatment.

4.4 For the avoidance of doubt the parties hereto agree that the Employer shall not be under any obligation to provide work of any particular nature or at all to the Player.

5 ILLNESS AND INJURY

COMMENTARY *Once again please see* **5.4.2**. *See also* **5.5.2**.

The clause which appears here as clause 5.4 is a basic skeleton of a clause which should be negotiated and customised. It may be reasonable to make the yardstick of the employer's ability to terminate more flexible than the concept of 'permanent incapacity'; for instance, incapacity lasting a given period of time in line with the length and nature of the contract.

5.1 In the event that at any time the Player shall be suffering from any illness or injury the Player will report the same to the Club immediately.

5.2 In the event that the illness or injury suffered by the Player has arisen other than in the course of the Player's employment as set out in this Agreement the Employer shall pay to the Player for the duration of his incapacity his basic remuneration as set out in Schedule I for the period of [   ] days and thereafter may make such payments in addition to statutory sick pay as the Employer in its absolute discretion sees fit.

5.3 In the event that the illness or injury has arisen in the course of the Player's employment as set out in this Agreement and the Employer shall throughout the period of the Player's incapacity pay to the Player the Player's basic remuneration as set out in Schedule I.

5.4 In the event that as a result of any illness or injury the Player shall be permanently incapacitated from providing the services set out in this Agreement to an acceptable standard in the Employer's reasonable opinion the Employer shall be entitled to terminate this Agreement by not less than 6 months written notice save where such illness or injury has arisen other than in the course of the Player's employment as set out in this Agreement in which case the Employer shall be entitled to terminate this Agreement by service of 3 months written notice ALWAYS PROVIDED THAT no such notice may be served until such time as the said permanent incapacity is confirmed by independent medical examination of the Player [*or pursuant to certification in accordance with the rules of an appropriate insurance scheme*].

5.5 All payments of the Player's remuneration provided for in this Clause 5 shall be deemed to include any and all entitlement the Player may have to statutory sick pay.

5.6 Where the Employer has made payment to the Player during any period of incapacity owing to illness or injury and the Player's absence is due to the action of a third party giving the Player a right of recovery against that third party the Player must where reasonably able to do so recover from the third party and upon such successful recovery repay to the Employer the total of the remuneration paid by the Employer to the Player during the period of incapacity over and above Statutory Sick Pay. All sums paid to the Player in the circumstances set out in this Clause 5.6 shall be deemed to be loans made to the Player and it is a term of the employment that the Player incorporates this claim into his claim against the third party and repays sums recovered accordingly.

6   TERMINATION

COMMENTARY *Please see generally* **5.5** *and* **5.6**.

6.1   This Agreement shall commence upon the date hereof and shall take effect for a fixed term of [   ] years to terminate upon the [   ] anniversary of the date hereof save in the event of earlier termination in accordance with the terms of this Clause 6.

6.2   This Agreement may be terminated forthwith by the Employer without prior notice if the Player shall at any time:

6.2.1   refuse to accept any reasonable change in his responsibilities duties or status from time to time determined by the Employer;

6.2.2   commit any serious or persistent breach of any of the provisions contained in this Agreement;

6.2.3   be guilty of any gross misconduct or willful neglect in the discharge of his duties hereunder;

6.2.4   become bankrupt or make any composition or arrangement with his creditors;

6.2.5   become of unsound mind or if while he is a patient pursuant to the Mental Health Act 1983 or any statutory re-enactment or modification thereof replacing the same an order should be made in respect of his property under that Act or any statutory modification or re-enactment of that Act;

6.2.6   be convicted of any criminal offence which results in a sentence of imprisonment and which in the opinion of the Employer affects his position as a Player of the Employer.

7   DISCIPLINARY AND GRIEVANCE PROCEDURES

COMMENTARY *The Clause here is less detailed than that which appears in many employment contracts as it simply refers to an external document. This is because no model disciplinary and grievance procedure will necessarily fit all sports. Often, these procedures are laid down by the sport's Governing Body and attention should be directed as to whether that is the case in relation to all agreements. Reference should be made in the absence of such regulatory framework to the recommendations of ACAS. ACAS Guidelines are effectively that disciplinary procedures should be fair, should comply with rules of natural justice, at all times give opportunity for calm reflection by the Employer and clear and thorough investigation of all matters before disciplinary action is taken, and for that disciplinary action then to be commensurate with the offence the employee has allegedly committed.*

Before any disciplinary action is taken there should be investigation by the Employer and the chance for the Player to put his side of the case. At disciplinary hearings, there should be some outline of procedure. The Player may be entitled to representation by the Team Captain, a representative of the players' association, or whatever is fair in the circumstances. Some idea of whether witnesses can be called and what manner of evidence will be received at the disciplinary hearing and how the disciplinary body set up within the employer is to be constituted should be laid down. Often, a system of warnings will be appropriate. For comparatively minor misdemeanours and first offences an oral warning of which a note is made by the Employer and retained on the personnel file may be appropriate. For more serious or second offences a written warning may be appropriate. That written warning should ideally identify the issue of complaint and the manner in which the complaint is to be avoided in future or the subject matter of the complaint is to be eradicated, giving proper reasonable steps to be taken by the Player and an anticipated time scale so that the Player and the Employer can review together the progress that has been made at the end of that time scale.

There may then be a further written warning which again is to be implemented as outlined above.

The final sanction prior to dismissal may be a final written warning. This is effectively the 'yellow card'. Once again, it should follow clear and fair investigations by the Employer and, if appropriate, disciplinary hearings with the Player. It should be a clear document indicating the items of which complaint is made and the ultimatum which effectively that final written warning constitutes.

At all points in the disciplinary process there should be the opportunity for the Player to appeal above the first disciplinary tribunal which effectively decides the matter to a higher internal authority, often the board of directors of the Employer. This, however, may again be unnecessary as an appeal may be available under the Rules of the Governing Body to a specifically constituted tribunal operated under the auspices of that Governing Body.

In relation to grievance procedures, there should be a provision that the Player raises any grievances with a specified individual who must then fairly investigate the player's grievance and then give a response, preferably in writing. The Player should then have an appeal against the determination made by that person if he is dissatisfied with the determination he has received. Once again, there should be fairness in the investigation and resolution of such a grievance.

The disciplinary procedure should also give a right to the Employer to suspend the player with or without pay depending upon the circumstances and during that period of suspension to prohibit the Player from attending the Employer's premises or any Match or Event in which the Employer is engaged.

The scale of fines available for the Employer by way of sanction should be clearly set out and there should be uniformity of approach in this regard: a tariff of fines to offences may be appropriate.

The above is only an outline and reference should be made to the appropriate rules of Governing Bodies and/or the appropriate ACAS Publications. In this regard, please see particularly **5.5.2**.

7.1   Any disciplinary action by the Employer or any grievance that the Player may have relating to his employment shall be dealt with in accordance with the Employer's disciplinary and grievance procedures set out in the Rules of the Employer which shall be deemed to form part of this Agreement.

8   HOLIDAYS

8.1   The Player shall be entitled to 20 working days paid holiday in each year (for which purpose the leave year shall be a calendar year from 1st January to 31st December) to be taken at such times as the Employer shall consider most convenient having regard to the business of the Employer. The Player shall not have the right to carry holidays over from one calendar year to another. For the avoidance of doubt the Player shall not be entitled to leave from work at the normal Bank and Public Holidays. At no time during any holiday period shall the Player participate in professional sport of any nature.

9   MISCELLANEOUS

9.1   Any and all contracts of employment taking effect between the Employer and the Player and/or any transfers of the Player's registration to any other employer shall be negotiated between the Employer and the Player and no payment shall be made to any other person or agent in respect of any such dealing other than appropriate legal and accountancy fees save that either the Employer or the Player may engage the services of a duly accredited or licensed agent pursuant to the Rules of the Governing Body but in the event of either party engaging such an agent such agent may only represent one party and full particulars of such agent must be disclosed by that party to the other.

9.2   The Player's period of continuous employment with the Employer commenced on [   ]. No period of employment with any previous employer nor any earlier period of employment with the Employer counts towards the Player's period of continuous employment.

9.3   The Player's normal hours of work shall be such as from time to time the Employer may reasonably require in order that the Player may properly perform the services set out in this Agreement and the Player shall not be entitled to any additional remuneration for any additional hours of work which take place outside normal working hours if so far as such normal working hours exist.

9.4   The Player will be employed mainly at the Employer's Premises and the Employer's training ground at [address] but the Employer shall be entitled to require the Player to play and to perform the services provided in this Agreement at any other place in the world.

9.5   No contracting out Certificate is in force in relation to the Player's employment for the purposes of the Pension Schemes Act 1993.

10 PREVIOUS AGREEMENTS

10.1   This Agreement takes effect in substitution of all previous agreements or arrangements whether written or implied between the Employer and the Player relating to the services of the Player all which agreements and arrangements shall be deemed to have been terminated by mutual consent as from the date on which this Agreement is deemed to have commenced.

11 JURISDICTION

11.1   This Agreement is made pursuant to and governed by English Law and in relation to any dispute in connection with this Agreement not resolved pursuant to the Rules of the Governing Body the Courts of England and Wales shall have exclusive jurisdiction.

12 EXCLUSION OF UNFAIR DISMISSAL/REDUNDANCY CLAIMS

COMMENTARY Please see **5.5.2**.

12.1   The Player agrees that in the event that this Agreement expires by effluxion of time and is not renewed the Player hereby agrees to exclude in accordance with section 197 of the Employment Rights Act 1996 any claim he may have either for unfair dismissal pursuant to Part X of the Employment Rights Act 1996 and/or for a redundancy payment under Part XI of the said Act.

SCHEDULE I

REMUNERATION

I   The Player's basic wages shall be as follows:

£   **Per Week from**   **To**

Together with such bonuses and incentives as the Player shall be entitled to receive under the terms of the Club's bonus and incentive scheme from time to time in force to this Agreement which shall be deemed to form part of this Agreement.

2   Insurances in favour of the Player whose Premiums shall be paid by the Employer:

Insurer   **Risks**   **Premiums**

5.12.2   Note on managers and coaches

The specimen Employment Contract presented here is one for a player, as of course the majority of employees in sport are players. A specific word may be appropriate, however, for coaches and managers and the manner in which their contracts may differ from those of players.

First, the coach or the manager may have very similar demands in relation to pay and conditions as those set out in the terms and commentary on the specimen agreement. There is no reason why he should not enter into an agreement largely in the same terms as this, only modulated to take account of his different function. The coach or manager is not exempt from the marketing obligations of the employer and may even be expected in order to reflect his greater importance on the whole to the employer's enterprise to give up more of his time than his players for marketing and promotion purposes. There are many players, and the burden can be shared out amongst them, but there is only one manager. The employer should likewise be under the same restrictions as to other commercial interests and the media as the players, although regard should be had to the fact that he may have more experience with the media, long-standing business interests and in general expect to be treated as a mature individual who can make his own decisions in this regard.

Obviously, the section relating to illness and injury is less important for the coach or manager, in that the coach or manager would not be forced to retire on account of injury: however, illness affecting a coach or manager can also have an immense effect on the employer's fortunes and his point needs careful consideration.

Codes of conduct for managers will often be promulgated by the Governing Body but those will be set out in the Rules of the Governing Body and the clauses relating to adherence of those rules should in most cases still fit the case of a coach or manager.

The coach or manager's bonus structure will no doubt best be dealt with specifically in the contract. The rules of the employer will set out the bonus payments that will be made to players as a whole but the manager or coach would no doubt wish to negotiate those aspects himself.

The coach or manager's duties will be different from the player's and some mention should be made of that. He should have it specifically identified in his contract that he shall undertake such duties as the board shall assign to him and in particular he shall make the appropriate appointments both to playing and supporting staff required for the furtherance of the employer's business. It may well be best to state that the manager shall not make any appointment without prior written consent of the board both as to the nature of the appointment and the remuneration to be paid to the appointee. He should be responsible to the board for the proper conduct of the team's affairs and fitness of the players and transfer to or by the employer of the players. There should be some provision dealing with a chain of command such as, for instance, a formal report to the Employer's Board Meeting each month.

The manager or coach may wish it to be explicitly set out in his agreement that his team selection is a matter for his own exclusive discretion.

The employer may wish to include a termination clause permitting termination on short notice. This obviously may be difficult to negotiate.

The coach or manager is obviously closer to the administrative and financial functions of the employer than the players are. As such, a full confidentiality clause, very much of the standard 'boiler-plate' type available in most employment precedents for senior executives, would be appropriate.

Another standard 'boiler-plate' clause which might be relevant to a coach's or manager's appointment is the standard declaration of the position under the Copyrights Designs and Patents Act 1988 that as he is an employee of the company, his inventions and copyright works created in the course of his employment shall vest in the employer. Many set moves and planned routines used in football or rugby, for instance, are very extensively documented and may therefore constitute copyright works and if the club can retain rights to these this is no bad thing.

Managers may wish to have certain other rights. There will always be the usual provisions familiar from many executive appointments as to cars, insurances, death in services benefits and so forth and the manager may well have a pension to which contributions are to be made. Further, where a club is publicly owned he may wish to acquire share options or if it is not publicly owned he may wish to have certain entitlement to shares in the event of any admission of the club to listing. He may also wish to have the right to be appointed a director of the club on termination of the contract through effluxion of time; the classic example might be if a manager stays for five years and thereafter becomes 'director of football' or some similar post.

Finally, in view of recent scandals, there should be a full provision dealing with financial affairs of the manager in the course of his employment. It should be clearly set out that the manager must not accept any payment from any third party in respect of any transfer of any player's registration and must give a full account to the Board of Directors of the employer of all financial dealings in which he is involved on behalf of the employer. The manager should be prohibited from arranging the business affairs and representation by agents of any player.

CHAPTER 6

SPORTS MARKETING

*6.1 General – 6.2 The sponsorship agreement – 6.3 Endorsement agreements –
6.4 Merchandising – 6.5 Commercial conflicts and ambush marketing – 6.6 Charitable
fund raising*

6.1 GENERAL

Before looking at the terms of the various contracts associated with sports marketing in detail it is useful to consider what is actually meant by sports marketing. It commonly takes the form of an association with a particular sport or sports event. This association may be in an 'official' capacity or in a general or perhaps 'unofficial' capacity. Where business and sport meet in an official capacity it is usually by means of a sponsorship, endorsement, merchandising or a broadcasting agreement. Sports marketing may also take the form of corporate hospitality which may, or may not, involve a sponsorship or other arrangement. These arrangements all tend to be official in the sense that there is a contractual commitment between the sport (or its participants) and the commercial organisation.

It is, of course, also possible to use sport as a marketing tool in a more general or unofficial manner. This may at one extreme simply involve the use of a sporting 'theme' in advertising and marketing. This may simply mean that football or rugby are used in a very general sense to promote a company, its name, image and products. The extreme of unofficial sports marketing is commonly known as 'ambush marketing'[1] and this is felt to be a great bug bear of sports marketing. It involves an unauthorised attempt to take advantage of the goodwill and name of a particular sports event or participant without a formal arrangement with that person. There are a number of ways of achieving such ambushes and the categories of ambushing opportunism are by their very nature unpredictable and difficult to control. Nevertheless, sports marketing in its official sense remains a popular and effective marketing tool. It is used to drive the value not only of the sport itself by ensuring its wide promotion but also to drive the value of the businesses investing in sport through increased exposure for companies and increased sales of their products.

6.1.1 Types of sports marketing agreements

The methods by which businesses invest in sport are generally categorised as sponsorship, (which includes endorsement arrangements with individuals), merchandising and broadcasting agreements. These agreements all rely upon a sports body having and controlling some rights which it is able to grant to the business investor. In any agreement between sport and business, both parties will

---

1   See **6.5**.

need to satisfy themselves that they actually have some rights which they can grant. As has been seen[1] there is no specific property right (intellectual or otherwise) which exists to protect sport. Any protection that does exist must be found from pre-existing property rights such as intellectual property rights,[2] the right to provide services perhaps by an individual or from an organisation or, even, rights of access to a piece of property (commonly the arena where an event is being held).

It is not uncommon for a number of persons to lay claim to various rights. Governing bodies in sports, participating clubs and players as well as the venue owners may all have a legitimate claim to some category of right which it may feel it can grant to an investor, or to 'commercial parties', as they are sometimes known, in sport. An obvious example is a competitive league (whether it be rugby, football or any other team sport) where there are a number of potential business partners for the sport. Sponsors and broadcasters may look to the governing body to grant rights of sponsorship and the right to film and broadcast the league. Very often the league will have an agreement with its participating clubs and players which delegates these commercial rights to itself on behalf of its members. The members will also commonly wish to and be able to pursue their own commercial interests and may appoint their own sponsors and even (for certain events or matches not covered by their agreement with the League) their own broadcasters. The extent to which such rights can be limited and regulated by any agreement between the clubs and the league may be subject to the scrutiny of the competition authorities[3] and so may be subject to external regulation. Whilst the member clubs have their own interests, it is also quite common for participating players (especially the higher profile ones) to pursue their own commercial interests. Obviously their interests will be limited by their contract of employment with the club[4] as well as the rules of the governing body but they will almost always retain certain commercial rights for themselves. In football and rugby these commercial rights may be limited to their own 'boot deals' although it is quite common for well known individuals to pursue commercial programmes which rival those of their clubs in terms of sophistication and income. These factors are all issues which a well advised and sophisticated business partner for sport will be aware of and will seek to regulate. There are also issues which increasingly sophisticated sports governing bodies, leagues, teams and players are aware of and will exploit to maximum effect. The following chapter examine the ways in which these rights are exploited contractually. This work does not cover the marketing theory behind such contracts but rather contains practical contractual tips and considers aspects of regulating the relationship between sport and business. In very general terms, it is in the interests of both the sports rights holder and the business partner to identify exactly what rights they are dealing with, to consider how those rights will be protected and exploited and how, if at all, they can control the unauthorised use of the rights in any given case.

1   See Chapter 4.
2   See Chapter 4.
3   See Chapter 3.
4   See Chapter 5.

6.1.2 Rights owners

Most active commercially viable competitive sports contain a number of tiers of organisation all of which may, in appropriate circumstances, be able to control and grant various commercial rights in their sport in certain events and other competitions to investing businesses. At the top level, most sports are governed by an international federation or governing body. This organisation will take ultimate control of the rules and regulations governing participation in sport and will also, usually, control and even hold a number of events in its own right. These will often be the 'big ticket' events such as the football and rugby world cups, the world championships in athletics and similar events in other sports.

Below the international federations there will be continental federations and organising committees, for example, UEFA and the Five (soon to be six) Nations organising committee. These will be responsible for the running of the sport in their own region and will often organise their own events which, although perhaps not as prestigious as the international events, are none the less high profile and important in both a competitive and commercial sense. Very often the continental governing body will take responsibility for implementing the international federation rules in its own locality. The precise relationship between a continental governing body and the international federation is almost always a contractual one and relies upon the continental governing bodies continued membership and acceptance of the international federation. It is possible that the international federation could withdraw the status and ability of the continental governing body to govern its sports in its area and to organise its own events.

In certain sports, there will be no continental association beneath the international federation. In such circumstances, the international federation usually recognises one national federation or governing body in any particular country. There will usually only be one national body which is eligible for membership of the international federation. National federations implement the rules of the international federation locally and they also organise their own events.

It is also quite common in certain sports for one or more national league structures to operate. These leagues may operate quite independently of the national governing body. They are often organised as separate companies (usually limited by guarantee) which operate with the sanction of the national federation. The relationship between the League and a national federation is not always an easy one. Indeed, even the relationship between the leagues and its own members is not always an easy one.[1]

The League will run its own competitions and will be delegated or assigned certain commercial rights of its own; although leagues are usually sanctioned by the national federation they retain a commercial independence of their own which is usually regulated by the agreement of their members. There is often a battle for supremacy between the League itself and the national federation where the two claim the right not only to organise and govern the sport but also to exercise the commercial rights associated with the exploitation of that sport. A

---

1   For instance, the Premier League and its relationship with the Football League and Football Association involved a difficult legal action; see *R v The Football Association ex parte The Football League Limited* [1993] 2 All ER 833.

classic example was the break away from the football league of the top English football clubs to form the FA Premier League. More recently the ongoing dispute between the top rugby clubs in England and the RFU demonstrates that although on one view the rights to regulate and promote the game are granted by international federations in a very real sense the rights also stem up from the ground of the sport from the individual member clubs and players who take part in the sport.

The current trend seems to be for the regulation of sport to be left in the hands of the international federations and national governing bodies. It is these bodies then that organise the international events. However, the day-to-day business of the sports (as distinct from the international world cup events) is run as a business where the participants claim their right to control their own commercial destinies within the reasonable parameters set by the rules of the governing body. This is a trend arguably encouraged by the European and UK competition rules. As increasing amounts of money are invested in clubs and participants this trend will surely continue. It is also the case that the supremacy of the international and national governing bodies is subject to increased scrutiny not only from the participants in sport but also from national and international competition authorities. This is particularly true in the European context where the ramifications of competition law and the free movement of goods, services and individuals increasingly affects the way that sport is able to regulate its own business.[1]

In a team sport the next tier in sport tends to be the club. The club may simply be an organisation run by a number of individuals or it may be a commercial organisation which is a substantial limited or public limited company. Such a club will certainly be involved in professional rather than amateur sport and as such will be keen to maximise its commercial revenue. An amateur club is likely to be run as an unincorporated association or as a company limited by guarantee. Clubs are almost invariably members of or sanctioned by national federations. Almost all their activities will be regulated in some way by the rules of the national and international governing bodies and it is within these bounds that the professional clubs seek to make their money and achieve success on the field of play.

Ironically the lowest placed of the hierarchical tier in sport are the individual players themselves. In professional team sport the individuals are usually employees of a club and where appropriate they will be released by their clubs from their employment contracts for international duties. Indeed, it is very often a condition of a club's membership of a national federation that their employed players are released for international duties. This in itself can be a battle ground between clubs and the national federations who vie for primacy of contract with the players. The battle ground has been particular fierce in English rugby where players contracted directly to the new owner backed clubs have occasionally found themselves caught up in the middle of disputes between the clubs and national federations with the threat that they will not be released for international duties. Obviously it is very much a matter for players to negotiate with clubs to ensure that their clubs are obliged to release them for appropriate international training and playing commitments.

---

1   See Chapter 3.

Where a sport is not a team sport the individual players will usually find that they are masters of their own playing and commercial destinies. Although they will be governed by the rules of their national and international federations they will not be bound by employment contracts with particular clubs.

In almost all sports, there are also associations which represent the interest of the participants. In the case of individuals, these are often effectively (and sometimes specifically) trade unions which represent the interests of their player members. This is the case in professional football where the Professional Footballers Association represents its members and in golf where the Professional Golfers Association (PGA) represents the interests of its members, organises events and exploits commercial rights.

The role of the organising committee in sport is also important. Many of the larger events (such as the Football World Cup, the Olympic Games and the Rugby World Cup) are run by local organising committees. These committees will very often be a combination of national federations and their members who will bid for and be granted the rights by the international federation to run events which are staged in their country. These are effectively extremely complicated event management agreements. The bidding process is very often a hotly contested and extremely contentious process resulting as it does in the opportunity to run an event which is significant not only in international reputation but also in commercial terms.

6.1.3 Commercial agents and entrepreneurs

Whilst the on-field competitions are invariably regulated by sports governing bodies, the business side of sport is populated with various entrepreneurs and representatives who pursue their own commercial interests. These characters fall into a number of broad categories. The club owners in many sports, particularly football and rugby, wield tremendous financial influence. Increasingly, such owners insist on controlling and exploiting the commercial rights in sport. The breakaway of the FA Premier League was to some extent a ramification of this trend and resulted, ultimately, in the flotation of a number of the clubs competing in the newly formed league as the commercial rights were freed up and various other factors, such as satellite television and the full impact of European legislation, drove the potential value of these rights up. A similar situation is taking place in professional rugby union as the governing bodies and the club owners feel their way in a new era. There are also various agents involved in sport. These include the agents or 'managers' that represent individual players.[1] These individuals will represent the players in negotiations to do with their commercial activities and employment. Typically this will involve deals with clubs, sponsors and broadcasters as well as any number of other organisations such as publishers, the media and the press generally.

There are also a large number of marketing agencies that specialise in sports marketing who represent either one or other or both of the governing bodies and the commercial partners in sport itself. These agencies tend to be organised very much along the lines of traditional advertising and marketing agencies. The role of such agencies varies enormously from on the one hand the simple finding and

---

1   See Chapter 7.

negotiation of a sponsorship for an event through to the consultancy and involvement in actual delivery of the rights to a sponsor or rights holder. Many agencies are also actively involved in the setting up and running of sports events and they are obviously paid significant fees for doing so.[1]

There are various other bodies which are involved in the business of sport. These include broadcasters who will negotiate and pay substantial rights fees for the right to broadcast and exploit live footage and highlights of sport events. The broadcasting arena is probably the fastest developing and most sophisticated area of sport business as the onset of pay-per-view and digital television provide the means to supply an almost infinite amount of sport footage.

The role of the media generally in highlighting and promoting sport and its commercial partners cannot be underestimated. Although sport's commercial partners gain a certain amount of exposure and coverage from the actual sport itself it is the role of the media which often adds real value to the sponsorship of the sport. Much of this coverage will be measured in column inches devoted to reporting sport and events as well as to the amount of coverage and the number of mentions that a sponsor receives in the coverage of an event by a broadcaster.

There are also a number of other bodies involved in the governance of sport. In the UK these include the Institute of Sports Sponsorship, the Central Council of Physical Recreation, the Sports Council and the European Sponsorship Consultants Association to name but a few. The role of government in sport on an international and national level cannot be underestimated. Although, on the one hand sport has increasingly come under the legislative eye of the government (look at, eg, tobacco sponsorship and advertising), it is also seen as an area where government policy can be influenced to help finance and develop sport.

6.2   THE SPONSORSHIP AGREEMENT

6.2.1   The aim of sponsorship

A sponsorship agreement is a marketing tool for the sponsor and an important method of raising finance for sport. The aim of the sponsor is to take advantage of the goodwill associated with the particular sporting property that is being sponsored. The sponsorship agreement will set out the manner in which the sponsor is able to take advantage of its association with the sport and to combine the goodwill of the sport with its own name and products to the advantage of both the sport and itself. A well-structured and properly delivered sponsorship provides both the sport and the sponsor with a significant opportunity to develop and enhance their goodwill and profile. Sponsorship is now viewed by many companies as an important marketing tool which provides access to distinct sectors of the public. The sport becomes part of the sponsor's brand image and much of its marketing will be directed towards enhancing that brand image.

This chapter does not aim to provide any sort of marketing analysis of the benefits of sponsorship; rather it sets out to outline the important terms in a

---

1   The role of players and agents and marketing agencies are dealt with in Chapter 7.

sponsorship agreement and the types of sponsorship that are commonly entered into.

6.2.2   A typical sponsorship agreement

A typical sponsorship agreement will be entered into by one person, usually a company, who will be known as the sponsor, and another person who will be the sponsored subject. Typically, this latter party will be a rights owner of some sort. For ease of reference, the sponsored party will be referred to as a 'rights holder' throughout the rest of this chapter. A sponsor may seek to contract with any number of different rights holders. Each of the bodies and individuals outlined in **6.1.2** may be the subject of the sponsorship agreement. An agreement with an individual is typically known as an endorsement agreement. Sponsors also frequently contract with clubs and governing bodies both of whom may be able to grant significant commercial opportunities to a willing sponsor. In the case of global events, a sponsor will usually seek to contract with an international federation or the agent or event organiser that represents the international federation. It is also quite common for sponsors to enter into agreements with stadium owners where they will be granted the rights to name the stadium or a stand in the stadium itself.

It is also possible to sponsor broadcasts and such contracts are usually agreed with the broadcaster rather than the sports rights holder itself.

Although there is no such thing as a 'standard' sponsorship agreement the clauses considered under various headings in this chapter as well as the precedent[1] are a useful starting point. A further 'model' agreement prepared by the CCPR/ISS is also available.[2]

6.2.3   Parties to the agreement

The first consideration for both the sponsor and the rights holder is that they both have the power to enter into the agreement. A particular problem may arise with rights holders of representative federations and governing bodies. The sponsor should always ensure that in these circumstances the rights holder can grant the rights it is purporting to grant. For example, it is important to establish that a rights holder that is a federation or governing body can bind its members (who may be clubs or individuals) so that the agreed sponsorship package is binding upon those members.

Usually, the rights holders' powers are delegated by its members who may if appropriate go on to ratify the deal. In such a case, the power to enter the contract may be found in the rules of the relevant rights holder or in appropriate cases a vote of the membership may grant the commercial rights to it. It is often the case that the sponsorship agreement will contain a clause or a recital stating in what capacity the rights holder is contracting and this may very often be on its own behalf and on its members' behalf as well. If there are any doubts or concerns about the ability of the rights holder to bind its members then it is not unusual for the sponsor to ask the members to ratify the agreement or to sign a 'side' or

---

1   See **6.2.5**.
2   For a copy, write to the Institute of Sports Sponsorship.

'inducement' letter acknowledging the sponsorship agreement and the rights granted to the sponsor.

The rights holder will be concerned to ensure that its members are bound to it and will take part in or at least not inhibit the delivery of the sponsors' rights. The possibilities for conflict in sponsorship and commercial arrangements generally are enormous[1] and it is up to the sponsor and the rights holder (whether it is an international or national federation, club or an individual player) to ensure that it is able to deliver the rights to the sponsor. Although this is a question of the granting rights holder's capacity to enter into the agreement it is also a matter that will be reflected elsewhere in the contract in the various warranties and obligations that the rights holder undertakes. It is also important that the rights holder acts within the scope of the rules of its own association as well as those imposed on it by any continental and international federations.

The doctrine of privity of contract will prohibit the sponsors from taking contractual action against anyone other than the rights holder unless another party is also a party to the contract. It is unlikely and ultimately unworkable for all the members or individuals involved in the sport to bind themselves directly to a sponsor other than in a representative manner. The rights holder will need to ensure that its rules of membership grant the sponsor any control it is seeking as to the ability of the rights holder to grant the rights contained in the sponsorship agreement. The ability of the rights holder to grant an unencumbered package of rights to sponsors must be carefully considered by the rights holder who may, ultimately, find that despite having entered into a binding contract to that effect it is unable to deliver the package of rights that it has promised.

It is not only the rights holder who should consider its ability to contract; the sponsor must also ensure that it has appropriate authority to commit itself to the sponsorship agreement. It is not unknown for large national and international sponsorships to fall at the final hurdle because the commercial or marketing director of a company is unable to gain Board approval for the proposed sponsorship. Whilst, at best, this may simply be embarrassing for the marketing or commercial director and the company, at worst, the rights holder may have turned down other potential sponsors during the negotiation process and find it difficult to reopen negotiations in such circumstances. Although negotiations are usually conducted 'subject to contract' it is possible that some liability (perhaps on the basis of a quantum meruit) has arisen because the rights holder has started to put the procedures in place to enable it to deliver the rights to the potential sponsor.

6.2.4   The grant of rights

The agreement should set out the sponsor's rights in some detail. The rights represent the sponsor's return on its investment and its ability to exploit its association with the rights holder and its sport. There will be important defined terms in the contract which will relate to a number of matters. Typically these matters are as follows.

---

1   See **6.5**.

(a) Sponsor's title rights

At the top end of its 'shopping list' of rights a sponsor will wish to obtain title rights or naming rights to use in association with the rights holder. The title sponsorship right allows the sponsor to have the event re-named to reflect its involvement. The Worthingtons Cup (formerly the Coca Cola Cup) and the Carling Premiership are good examples of such arrangements. The agreement will usually contain a term obliging the rights holder to name and always refer to the event which is being sponsored by reference to the new title granted to the sponsor under the agreement.

(b) Designations

Sponsors typically additionally ask the rights holder to grant them a right to use a 'designation' or 'official status' in a specified way. In cases where the sponsor is not able to obtain title rights to an event these designations are of fundamental importance to the sponsor as they identify its association with the rights holder. The agreement will contain the right for the sponsor to describe itself as 'official sponsor of' a stated product or service or 'official supplier to' the rights holder and the sports rights which are the subject of the agreement. Occasionally these rights relate to a product or service completely unrelated to the sponsor business. This may mean a sponsor also becomes the 'official statistics' supplier to the rights holder or takes another right, such as travel or ticketing and sub-contracts the service but supplies it under its own banner.

These designations may usually only be used in relation to specific products manufactured by the sponsor. The categories of product over which the sponsor is granted rights will be set out and defined in the agreement. A sponsor may wish to promote its involvement with the rights holder by using one particular brand, a range of products or services or it may use the companies umbrella brand as a whole. A sponsor will very often wish to reserve to itself the right to use other brands in its product category in association with the rights holder. Where the sponsor requires such flexibility over the use of the designations against different products then the rights holder may well wish to retain some right of approval over the sponsor's ability to change product group.

(c) The event logo and sponsor's marks and the sponsored title

The rights holder will have a name or logo of its own which will be the symbol used to promote its rights. This may simply be the 'name' of the event or other sports rights which are the subject of the agreement (eg the 'premier' league) or the name of the competition or club concerned. The agreement may grant the sponsor the right to combine the rights holder's name or event logo with the sponsor's own name or logo. This combination of the rights holder's logo and the sponsor's logo (the 'sponsored title') may often be designed by one of the parties but will be subject to the approval of the other party. The combined logo may also be the subject of separate trade mark protection[1] and the agreement may contain various obligations obliging both the sponsor and the rights holder to protect such rights and to notify each other of any infringements of such rights which come to their attention.

---

1   See **6.2.4**(o).

It is also quite common, and probably essential, for the combination logo to be used in most marketing and merchandising relating to the event and in any situation to which the sponsorship and the sponsor are referred. Indeed, this combined logo is one of the most effective ways of promoting the sponsor, the rights holder and the property.

(d)   Rights delivery

The sponsor will expect the rights holder not only to grant it the various rights contained in the agreement (whether title rights and/or designations or otherwise) but also to do its best to assist the sponsor's exploitation of the rights and to ensure that those rights are actually delivered to the sponsor. This means that the rights holder will have to do its best to ensure that its members, any broadcasters or relevant third parties that refer to the property which is being sponsored do so using the new sponsored title or where appropriate by referring to the designations granted to the sponsor.

This means that any official publications and other printed matter (including press releases and stationery used by the rights holder) refer to the sponsorship. It also means that competitors or members of a team wear clothing incorporating the sponsor's name or logo. In such cases, the size and placing of the sponsor's name and logo should be set out in the agreement. Match programmes, tickets, back drops during press conferences and any material relating to the sports property which is being sponsored should all refer to the sponsor's rights, the sponsored title, or the designations. Wherever possible, the sponsor will expect these obligations to be passed on to third parties.

Some of these third parties may have a contractual relationship with the rights holder (where for example they are its members) or if they have no contractual relationship at all may 'choose' to refer to the sponsor's rights. This will often be for the purposes of broadcasting and news reporting.

The flip side of the above is that as part of the rights delivery under the agreement the sponsor will be able to use and to authorise the use of the rights holder's name and/or logo as well as the combined logo which is created for the purposes of the agreement. These logos may be used on the packaging for company products as well as in all promotional and publicity material created by the sponsor to exploit its rights and its association with the rights holder. This will usually involve exploitation in the media of the sponsor's choice and will certainly include all printed and broadcast media.

(e)   Ancillary or secondary rights

Sponsors of an event, whatever their title or other status, will also obtain a further raft of rights. These rights are often known as the 'secondary' or 'ancillary' rights and will be granted to the sponsor by the rights holder and often set out in a schedule to the main operative part of the agreement. They may include some or all of the following rights:

- rights to use the designations on any advertising, promotional or publicity material produced by the sponsor in connection with the event in any media of the sponsor's choice (including 'new' media such as investment rights);
- the exclusive right to manufacture and sell company products using the designations for the period of the agreement;

- the non-exclusive right to reproduce the rights holder's name and/or logo on all promotional materials and in any promotional activities run by the sponsor and associated with the sponsored rights;
- the non-exclusive right to occupy and use hospitality facilities and events and venues run or organised under the auspices of the rights holder. Such facilities may or may not be at the expense of the sponsor. An organiser may not be able to contract on behalf of a site caterer which may mean that hospitality is at the expense of the sponsor and subject to the usual terms of the caterer or, indeed, the management and owner of the venue where the corporate hospitality is being granted. A separate agreement (usually in a standard form) for these facilities is often necessary. In such cases the sponsor may be concerned to ensure that it is not bound to use such corporate hospitality facilities if, in its view, they are too expensive. In such a case although the sponsor may not be obliged to actually use these facilities it may find that its only choice is not to use them and not to hold any hospitality at all. The sponsor may wish to ensure hospitality facilities are not available for use by its competitors, or at the very least that they cannot promote the fact that they use such facilities;
- the rights holder will also grant the sponsor a specified number of tickets at specified prices and locations. There may be a certain number of free seats which the sponsor can use as it wishes and there may be various other seats which the sponsor will have the right to purchase if it so wishes. Although it is usual to forbid the re-sale of these tickets, their use in promotions – such as for prizes in competitions – should be permitted. Any additional rights such as tickets for post-event celebrations, refreshments or additional facilities as required should also be dealt with in this way;
- a sponsor will certainly require a specified number of advertising hoardings at any venues owned by or under the control of the rights holder. These advertising hoardings may be of a static variety or they may be rotational boards. This obviously depends on the venue in question. It is frequently (but not always) the case that such advertising boards will be non-adjoining: that is to say they will be interspersed with other advertisers' boards. The sponsor should also take care to ensure that its boards receive appropriate prominence at the event and very often this will mean that they should be placed in view of any television cameras in cases where the sponsored sport is being broadcast;
- the sponsor may agree that the event logo and the sponsors' designation will appear in the programme which is sold to the public. This may be on the cover of the programme, on the title page and on various pages within the programme. The sponsor may additionally require some editorial referring to its involvement with the rights holder as well as a number of pages of free advertising within the programme. Such advertising may be used as the sponsor sees fit for any of its products;
- the sponsor's involvement with the rights holder and its designation should be agreed and referred to in all press releases and other promotional or advertising material released by the rights holder;
- the sponsor may be granted the right to exploit its association with the rights holder by way of merchandising. This right may be limited depending on what usage the sponsor has in mind and what merchandising rights the rights holder has already granted. In particular, the rights holder may not

wish the sponsor to manufacture and sell merchandise relating to its events and may limit such merchandising rights to give away any promotional items;

– the sponsor may wish to undertake joint promotions with other companies. These may be other sponsors who have contracts with the rights holder or companies which are entirely unrelated to and have no formal agreement with the rights holder. Any such joint promotional initiatives will usually be restricted by the rights holder to ensure that the sponsor does not dilute the cachet and goodwill of the event by promotional initiatives that the rights holder does not approve of by companies it has not appointed;

– the sponsor may wish to exploit its rights on an appropriate Internet web site; where appropriate the rights holder will wish to ensure that this does not conflict with any web site which it sets up itself;

– the sponsor may be granted the non-exclusive right to use extracts and broadcast footage of any events run by the rights holder. Such footage may in appropriate circumstances be incorporated on an Internet site run by the sponsor or in its advertising run to promote its sponsorship;

– the rights holder may be obliged to re-name the trophy associated with its events and the sponsor may be granted the right for one of its board members to jointly present any relevant trophy to the winners of an event along with runners up medals to the runners up;

– the sponsor will wish to have its association with the rights holder and its events referred to on all tickets sold for the event;

– the sponsor may also require certain rights on the field of play and during play in any competitions run by the rights holder. This may include branding of pitch corner flags and scoreboards as well as on-pitch and in-field-of-play markings; such rights are likely to be limited by the international federation rules governing the sport;

– the sponsor may also wish the rights holder to provide access to the individuals taking part in the rights holders events and this is something that the rights holder must carefully consider as it may not be able to compel the third parties concerned to cooperate with the sponsor;

– the sponsor may also wish to make various awards to competitors and this may include man of the match and other similar awards.

Sophisticated rights holders are now offering rights packages that combine elements like these for the sponsor's package of rights. It is common for rights holders to offer such ancillary or secondary rights as virtually standard packages to sponsors. In the case of larger international and national events, the rights holders will often set out in a sponsorship proposal defined packages of rights which vary very little.

(f) Exclusivity

A successful sponsorship is dependent upon the rights holder granting and the sponsor receiving a certain degree of exclusivity. It is possible for rights holders to grant sponsorship rights to a number of different companies each of whom provide different products or services. Many rights holders will offer sponsorship opportunities in various packages which may involve title sponsorship rights along with various designations and a package of secondary or ancillary rights. It is in the sponsor's best interests to ensure that rights holders do not offer such packages with impunity and that they are given some comfort on the degree of exclusivity which they are granted in their agreement. Obviously the considerations here will vary enormously depending on the rights holder and the sport in question. A sponsor may be able to obtain complete exclusivity and ensure that no other sponsors are appointed for any number of reasons including the amount of money committed to the sponsorship, the popularity of the sport or the event involved and the availability of broadcast coverage. The fact is that most rights holders will be unable or unwilling to grant complete exclusivity to any sponsors or event title sponsors. Although it is unlikely that the agreement will give the rights holder complete freedom to appoint other sponsors they will usually be able to do so if they agree a well-structured package of rights and sensible exclusivity provisions with their sponsors. A sensible, well-advised sponsor will be unwilling to accept the possibility that the rights holder can grant rights to its major competitors with impunity.

The issue of exclusivity in an agreement usually starts with the type of sponsorship that is anticipated. A major title sponsor of an event will not only obtain the right to re-name the event but will also be granted a number of designations.[1] The agreement will then typically state that the rights holder will not grant any third party the same rights or the right to use the same designations to any other sponsor or third party. This prohibition needs to be tempered by the fact that the rights holder may grant third parties the right to use the name of the event and the designations in ways anticipated by the sponsorship agreement, ie to promote the event itself.

If the rights holder is only selling a single package of sponsorship rights then there will usually also be a prohibition on appointing anyone else to be a sponsor. If the rights holder anticipates selling a number of other sponsorship packages then the agreement will usually deal with this in two ways. First, the sponsor will seek to state its general exclusivity over its rights granted in the agreement. Secondly, the agreement will contain important definitions of who the sponsor's main competitors are, a careful definition of the products that the sponsor may use to promote its rights, a definition of who its competitors are and prohibition on the grant of rights to manufacturers of competitive products. The relationship between the definitions used in the agreement then sets the tone for the remaining exclusivity provisions contained in the agreement.

The rights holder may agree not to grant any rights to a competitor or a manufacturer of competitive products. The result of this drafting is that the sponsor obtains exclusivity not only in its category of products but also as against its major competitors. The difficulty with this approach from the rights holder's point of view is that some of the sponsor's main competitors may manufacture more than just competitive products. Indeed, competitor's prod-ucts may just be one small range of the products which they manufacture. The drafting here may require some further fine tuning depending on the commercial principle agreed between the sponsor and the rights holder. In certain circumstances the sponsor may be able to say quite legitimately that some of its competitors who manufacture not only competitor products but many other lines of products as well are a complete 'no go' because any association between the rights holder and such a company will devalue the exclusivity of the rights

---

1   See **6.2.4**(b).

granted to the sponsor. Particular sensitive areas tend to arise with soft drinks/sports drinks categories of sponsorship as well as companies who manufacture photocopying/printing/computing/photography ranges of products. In such cases if the sponsor concedes anything then it must ensure that the rights holder can only appoint such competitors in respect of non-competitive products and in such a way that the competitor is only allowed to exploit any rights it is granted in connection with such non-competitive products. For example, if the sponsor is a drinks manufacturer whose competitors manufacture a range of so-called sports drinks as well as soft drinks and other beverages then, assuming such a company can be appointed at all, it could only be appointed in respect of a particular brand of products and should not be allowed any joint promotional opportunities between its non-competitive and its competitive products. In practice, such provisions should not be difficult to negotiate if the rights holder and the sponsor both appreciate that there may be a potential for conflict and deal with the problem in the contract.

Although sponsor's exclusivity may be particularly strong with title rights and designations it is unlikely that the sponsor will be able to achieve any significant exclusivity with certain categories of the secondary or ancillary rights that it is granted. Although the sponsor should be able to obtain complete exclusivity in its product category for the secondary promotional rights (such as advertising hoardings and the use of footage from the event) it is unlikely that the sponsor will be able to obtain exclusivity over the availability of tickets or corporate hospitality. Indeed, such exclusivity would be undesirable as it may pose greater problems if the agreement is ever scrutinised by the competition authorities, as such restrictions would arguably be unrelated to the main purpose of the sponsorship agreement.[1]

Certain sponsors may also wish to require exclusive rights over the sale of their products within the grounds and venues of the rights holder's events. Where food and drink are concerned these are often known as 'pourage rights' but simply tacking such obligations on to a sponsorship as a matter of course may make it susceptible to attack on the grounds that it restricts competition. Such rights should be the subject of a completely separate and unrelated negotiation.

Part of the sponsor's due diligence should also relate to whether the rights holder has any existing arrangements which may breach the carefully negotiated exclusivity provisions of the agreement. It is possible that the exclusivity provisions will only relate to future appointments and will not cover existing sponsorships. It is quite possible that the rights holder (in the case of its individual members if the rights holder is a governing body) has appointed a number of sponsors some or all of whom may be competitors or manufacturers of competitive products. If the sponsor is acquiring rights and the rights holder's members are participants in the event then it may be unrealistic or even impossible to prohibit those members from exercising their own commercial rights. If this is the case, then the agreement may have to contain some acknowledgements that there are existing contracts which breach the provisions of the sponsorship agreement and that their existence does not constitute a breach of the terms of the agreement. If such existing contracts also contain

---

1   See Chapter 3.

renewal provisions (such as an option or matching rights clause)[1] the drafting may need to make it clear that renewal pursuant to such provisions does not in itself constitute a breach of the agreement.

This level of detail is only likely to be a concern where the sponsor is sponsoring an event and is not able to obtain any rights over the participants in that event. If the sponsor is concerned about its competitors or competitive products being promoted by participants in an event then it may have to ask the rights holder it is dealing with whether such competitors can be required to compete 'clean'. This means such competitors will be required to compete without any visible sponsorships whilst they are actually on the field of play. Their commercial activities off the field of play could not easily be restricted by the rights holder because this may be viewed as a restraint of trade or as being anti-competitive.[2]

A sponsor with sufficient commercial clout may be able to go one step further even than all the steps outlined above and require that competitors and manufacturers of competitive products cannot be appointed at all. If this is not possible, it may be that all other sponsors can only be appointed with its prior approval, although the rights holder will doubtless argue that such approval must not be reasonably withheld or indeed that any approvals process over the appointment of other sponsors itself is completely unreasonable.

The sponsor and the rights holder must also not forget that a major sporting event will attract not only sponsors but also any number of other commercial partners who will be interested in merchandising rights, official photography rights, broadcasting, videos, video games, Internet sites and any other number of commercial opportunities. The sponsor and the rights holder may wish to go further when considering the exclusivity provision of the agreement and state that all such commercial partners must not be competitors or manufacturers of competitive products and that they must not seek to detract from any of the rights granted to the sponsor. Where such commercial partners will be using any of the sponsor's intellectual property rights the sponsor may wish to impose conditions on their usage of such rights.[3]

(g) Duration of the agreement

The duration of a sponsorship agreement can be fixed in a number of ways. It is quite common for a sponsorship agreement to cover a fixed period of time such as a club season or an annual event or competition.

A fixed term sponsorship arrangement will expire on an agreed date subject to any options to renew or any other extensions to the agreement. Although the precise length of a sponsorship arrangement will be subject to a number of commercial factors, the actual provisions of the agreement relating to the term tend to be reasonably straightforward. The sponsor should ensure that it obtains the rights for a sufficient length of time to exploit its association with the rights holder and its event and to build up a certain amount of goodwill to successfully exploit its sponsorship. The termination date of the sponsorship agreement

---

1   As to such clauses, see **3.2.3**.
2   See **3.8** and **3.9**.
3   Generally, these depend on the types of IPR but the sponsor must retain control over IPR to ensure it controls their use and exploitation.

should take account of all the opportunities the sponsor wants to exploit from the relationship. If the sponsor wishes to advertise before and after the event and not just on the day of the event, or to sell off merchandise and promotional products after the event has ended then it may be simplest for the rights to expire on a set number of days (eg 90 days) after the event has ended. If merchandise is involved then the seasonal nature of many sports and shopping habits should also be taken into account and sell-off rights provided for in the agreement.[1]

If a contract relates directly to the holding of a number of events scheduled to take place during a given period of time then the agreement should carefully define precisely what is meant by the event in question but also provide that the rights expire so many days after the final matches (including play-offs or replays) of the event.

The agreement should deal with cancellation or postponement of the event and its effects on the term of the agreement as well as the rights granted. These matters are commonly dealt with in the termination provisions of the agreement[2] but it is also common for the term of the agreement to be extended until the event does actually take place. In such a case, the rights holder may insist that there is a long-stop to such extensions so that the agreement is not extended indefinitely. In practice it is much more likely that the force majeure provisions[3] would come into play giving either party a right to terminate the agreement if the event was not held or was postponed for an undue length of time.

(h)   Renewal of the agreement

There are a number of drafting and commercial options open to the parties upon the expiry of the term of the agreement. The first is that all rights of both parties come to an end and they move on to pastures new, free from their present contracts.

The next possibility is that the parties agree a valid and binding option to extend the duration of the agreement[4] in which case, if the party with the benefit of the option exercises it then the agreement will be extended upon the new agreed terms.

Another alternative is that the contract states that the parties have a certain amount of time to attempt to agree new terms for the sponsorship. This may be a complete renegotiation of the agreement or else it may just be an agreement that certain parts (usually the fee and the duration of the agreement) are renegotiated. Both the rights holder and the sponsor must take great care to ensure that if they intend such a clause to be enforceable it is actually enforceable. It is well established that an agreement to agree[5] is not binding under UK law as it is not sufficiently certain to be a binding contractual term. Many agreements effectively acknowledge this fact by providing that during this period the rights holder cannot negotiate with any third party and that if, at the end of this period, nothing is agreed then the rights holder may attempt to find a new sponsor. The

---

1   See Chapter 6.
2   See **6.2.4**(p).
3   See **3.4.16**.
4   See **6.2.4**(g).
5   See **3.3.2**.

previous sponsor will then have a right to be notified of the terms of the proposed sponsorship by the rights holder and then has a right to match those terms. The sponsor should ensure that it only has to match the main financial terms of the new sponsorship as there may be terms of the proposed arrangement which it is unable to match; for example, it may not be able to provide particular personnel or particular services which a new sponsor proposes to provide.

Obviously the rights holder may not find it is in its best interest to agree anything other than the right of first negotiation. An option or a matching rights clause can tie it into an existing sponsor for an undue length of time and effectively restrict it from going to the open market to get the best deal possible. If the agreement does contain a right of first negotiation and then a matching rights clause, any potential sponsor should always ask a rights holder whether there are any binding terms with a previous sponsor which would mean that it may not be able to sponsor the event. The rights holder may find that it is not allowed to disclose the terms of a matching rights clause to any third party as the confidentiality provisions of its agreement with the existing sponsor will prohibit this. In such a case, if the proposed sponsor asks a question and receives no reply or receives a reply from the rights holder that it is not allowed to disclose the terms of its existing agreement, then it may decide it is not worth wasting its time negotiating an agreement only to find that a matching rights clause kicks in and is then subsequently exercised, meaning that the proposed sponsor has wasted its time negotiating with the rights holder. In many situations, the rights holder will be best advised to fight tooth and nail against the grant of anything other than a valid option or a right of first negotiation with no matching right attached. Such clauses may also come to be considered in the context of competition law especially if they operate to exclude competitors and competitive products from the sponsorship market.

(i) Fee

The agreement will contain a clause specifying what amount is payable for the rights granted along with the method and timing of any payments. There will usually also be VAT payable upon sponsorship monies and the sponsor should be invoiced by the rights holder for such payment.

A sponsor may also agree to provide certain in-kind benefits which may assist the rights holder and its competitors and provide extra promotional value for the sponsor. The value of such in-kind benefits may also need to be identified for VAT purposes. This is often the case with tickets and hospitality facilities.

If the payments are staged over the term of the sponsorship, the rights holder will need to plan carefully for its cash flow needs and the sponsor will need to ensure that it has the budget at the required time to actually pay the rights holder. The agreement may contain provisions stating that interest will be payable on overdue payments. Although the sponsor can avoid such provisions by paying on time it may nevertheless wish to delete such provisions from the agreement.

The sponsor may also wish to consider whether the agreement will contain any bonus or incentive payments. These payments may be tied to performance by the rights holder such as obtaining a minimum attendance at the event, a minimum number of hours of live or as live broadcast coverage or the appearance of a certain number of top participants. It is quite common for the termination provisions of a sponsorship agreement to anticipate repayment of some sponsorship monies if the agreement terminates early but the sponsor may choose or prefer to structure the payment terms of the agreement so that rather than having to get money back from the rights holder it pays bonuses if certain events occur. This has the added advantage of giving the rights holder an incentive to perform its obligations under the agreement. Such terms are a matter for negotiation and depend upon the commercial bargaining power of the parties.

(j) Territory
This does not tend to be an aspect of the agreement which is particularly heavily negotiated. A sponsor and the rights holder will usually require world-wide rights, although the extent to which the rights granted are exploited throughout the world will depend upon the brand coverage of the sponsor and the popularity and coverage of the event and of the sport involved.

A sponsor will wish to ensure that the rights holder does not carve the sponsorship rights up territory by territory selling more sponsorship packages in the process. For many sponsorship agreements, territory will be quite simply stated as 'the world' and there will be few further concerns. The advent of certain technology as well as restrictions on certain types of sponsorship in certain parts of the world may mean there is scope for the sponsor and the rights holder to exploit some of the rights granted in the sponsorship package in different ways throughout the world. The common example is that certain types of advertising may be prohibited in certain territories. If an international event is being held in a country that prohibits tobacco advertising at its venues then a tobacco sponsor of the event may not be able to use its advertising boards at the venue. This may mean the rights holder sells those boards to another advertiser or that the sponsor does that itself.

There are other issues which have the potential to effect the territory of the rights granted. The advent of post-production technology which has the ability to superimpose different advertisements on existing venue advertising and broadcast to different parts of the world presents a potential lucrative opportunity for rights holders and broadcasters alike. It also presents an opportunity for sponsors who may wish to promote different brands in different parts of the world. Although at the time of writing these technologies are very much in their infancy and are not proven in commercial broadcasting they will doubtless improve to the extent that they are commercially viable for rights holders, broadcasters and sponsors alike.

A sponsor should also ensure that merchandise sales and promotion of the event throughout the world takes place using its title and designations. This may be particularly important where the rights holder grants branding opportunities on the associated merchandise which will be sold world-wide. Such merchandise may be manufactured for sale in different territories and the sponsor should ensure that apart from the usual quality control and approval obligations that the merchandise bears their appropriate sponsor's titles and designations.

(k) Broadcasting
The sponsor will have a number of main concerns. The first will be whether there is any broadcast coverage which will relate to the rights they are acquiring;

secondly, the sponsor will wish to know how much broadcast coverage is anticipated; and thirdly, it will wish to know what restrictions there are on the ability of the sponsor to exploit its rights through the broadcast media.

Broadcast rights will usually be the subject of a separate agreement between the rights holder and a broadcaster. It is not uncommon for less popular sports to find a production company to produce an event feed which they will then give or sell to a broadcaster.[1] If there is existing broadcast coverage in place then this could add greatly to the media and promotional value to the sponsor of the rights it is obtaining. The sponsor may enquire as to the precise level of broadcast coverage. This may be assessed in any number of ways but it is quite common to enquire as to how many hours of broadcast coverage the rights holder obtained and what type of coverage. The broadcasts may be in any number of different mediums. For example, it may be terrestrial or satellite/cable transmissions and in turn these transmissions may be live (ie simultaneous with the event) or 'as live' (ie the full event but not simultaneously with the event) or in recorded highlights form. Obviously broadcast coverage may be a combination of any of these and may be shared between terrestrial and satellite broadcasters.

A sponsor may also wish to know whether broadcast coverage is restricted to any particular territory or whether it is available world-wide. This consideration may only be important to sponsors with international brands or with an international presence.

The answers to these questions should enable the sponsor and the rights holder to deal with the issue of broadcasting in the sponsorship agreement. They may choose to ignore the matter altogether or, which is more likely, they are likely to seek minimum warranties as to the amount of and the quality of broadcast coverage. The warranties may specify a minimum number of hours of live or highlights broadcasts and they may further specify that such broadcasts have to be by way of terrestrial and/or satellite transmissions. The broadcast coverage may be dealt with in a different way and assessed simply by means of media value to the sponsor. Media value can be calculated in any number of ways but the value to the sponsor will be on the number of clear shots of its branding and the mentions of its relationship with the event in broadcast and in other media. This figure tends to represent the value to the sponsor of its rights and its association with the rights holder. If media value is to be used as a factor in determining the level of broadcast coverage then it should be calculated carefully using an agreed formula.

The effect in contractual terms of the level of broadcast coverage, however it is valued or assessed, may be either that the sponsor has a right to terminate if a certain level of broadcast coverage is not attained or conversely, if a certain minimum level is met, then bonus payments may click in. Equally some sponsors may be completely unconcerned about broadcast coverage as the main purpose of the sponsorship may simply be in any packaging promotions and in free or promotional opportunities at any event.

The other aspect of broadcasting which should concern the sponsor will be the sale of broadcast sponsorship and broadcast advertising as well as the existence of

---

1   See Chapter 9.

any restrictions on the broadcaster in mentioning the sponsor's rights. The title sponsor will wish to ensure that the broadcaster mentions the event using the sponsored title of the event. If the broadcaster is unable to do so because of legislative or other restrictions on it the sponsor may need to reconsider whether it obtains any value from its sponsorship rights.

The sale of broadcast sponsorship and broadcast advertising time to its competitors is another matter which will concern the sponsor. Although it may not be possible to obtain anything more than a right to negotiate for broadcast sponsorship the sponsor should ensure that no competitors or manufacturers of competitive products are able to sponsor the broadcasts and thus devalue their rights. Broadcast sponsorship is a particular concern for many sponsors as a successful broadcast sponsor may obtain a much higher level of recognition with its sponsorship than the sponsor of a particular rights holder's event (for ambush marketing).

(l) Sponsors obligations

The sponsor's primary obligations will be set out at various points in the sponsorship agreement. These obligations will include the obligation to pay the agreed sponsorship fee as well as the provision of any other services and products to the rights holder. The sponsor often agrees to provide a supply of its own products as well as prizes or trophies for the event. There will also be various other obligations on the sponsor which may include some or all of the following:

–   to comply with all applicable national and international media and domestic rules and regulations. Since the sponsor has been given the right to advertise and promote its rights it is important that this assurance is given. Failure to do so by the sponsor may give rise to third party claims and/or complaints against the sponsor and the rights owner. At one end of the scale these may be legal consequences whilst at the other the sponsor may find that it is in breach of relevant and generally accepted codes of practice which apply to the rights owners and the sport in general. It is not uncommon for the rights owner to require an indemnity from the sponsor if it breaches this obligation;

–   as well as external regulations, the sport and/or the rights owner may have its own rules and regulations that the sponsor should agree to comply with. These will usually be set out by a governing body and these may be rules which are set both nationally and internationally. If these rules apply to a particular sporting event or its competitors and the rights owner then the sponsor should be aware of them and obey them;

–   there will also often be a general prohibition on the sponsor against it acting in any manner or way which would prejudice the image or the running of the sport in question as well as the rights owner;

–   there may also be restrictions on the way in which the sponsor can exercise its rights. In particular this may mean that it cannot indulge in any joint promotions of the rights granted to it under the agreement. This means that, for example, the sponsor could not team up with a newspaper to promote the event without the rights owner's say so. It would also mean it could not cooperate with manufacturers of other products and/or services who had not been granted rights by the rights owner;

– the sponsor may also be required to provide samples of any materials that it produces to exploit its rights under the agreement. There will obviously be some cross-over here between the intellectual property obligations contained in the agreement. Generally, rights owners require sponsors to pass most material by them for their prior approval before it is used by the sponsor to exploit its association with the rights owner.

(m) Rights holders obligations

The rights holder's primary obligation should be to make the rights properly available to the sponsor. Very often this will mean that it should organise the event or field the team which is the subject of the sponsorship agreement. Coupled with this, the sponsor might want any number of other assurances from the rights holder. In the case of an event the sponsor might require specific organisational targets to be met by the rights holder by certain dates. This may mean that tickets are on sale by a given date, or that advertising and promotional campaigns for the event are instituted both locally and nationally by the rights holder. This may also be coordinated with the sponsor's campaign.

Additional obligations may require the rights holder to:

(1) maintain all necessary insurances and other cover. This may include insurance covering the cancellation or postponement of the event as well as any liability that it may have to the members of the public who attend the events in question;

(2) comply with all relevant rules and regulations in the organisation, running and promotion of the event. This should include any internal and relevant external regulations;

(3) the sponsor will also be concerned that the organiser does nothing to prejudice the sponsor's own image or reputation and there will be an obligation in the agreement reflecting this;

(4) there will be a general obligation to run the event in a business-like manner and to ensure the sponsor obtains maximum media exposure from its grant of right;

(5) procure that the sponsor is granted all the rights under the agreement which the rights holder purports to grant it;

(6) (in the case of an event) ensure that the rights holder does nothing to change the way in which an event or team is structured so that the sponsor does not get the full benefit of the rights it has been granted. This may mean that in the case of a league cup competition the rights holder does not reorganise the event in such a way as to mean the sponsor gets no value from the rights. In the case of a team or individual competitor it may mean that it takes part in the event in question and does not willingly withdraw from it.

(n) Mutual warranties and undertakings

These would be the usual warranties contained in most agreements of this type[1] and will include the following:

(1) that both parties are free and entitled to enter into the agreement and to perform their obligations;

(2) that neither of them have entered into any conflicting agreements;

---

1   See **3.4.7.**

(3) that they will keep the terms of the agreement confidential and will not disclose them to anyone other than their professional advisers or as is generally required by law;

(4) there may also be a general indemnity from one party to the other in the case of breach of any terms of the agreement. This may be coupled with a limitation of liability to ensure that the parties are only liable for any direct losses attributable to any breaches of contract by either of them.

These mutual warranties and indemnities will be the subject of some negotiation between the parties, particularly where liability is concerned, as neither party will want some open-ended liability for breaches of contract.

(o) Intellectual property

A sponsorship agreement will typically contain a number of provisions dealing with intellectual property rights. Both the sponsor and the rights holder will have intellectual property rights (typically rights in trade marks (whether unregistered or registered) as well as copyrights) which they will want to protect. The agreement must deal clearly with pre-existing rights of both the sponsor and the rights holder as well as the rights that come into existence during the term of the sponsorship agreement.

The sponsor will want to be able to use the rights holder's intellectual property. This may be the name and/or logo of the event as well as other intellectual property rights (such as copyrights in film footage of an event) to help it exploit its rights under the agreement. Any rights to use the rights holder's name and/or logo will generally be non-exclusive, as it is quite common for any number of other third parties to use the rights owner's name and/or logo.

The sponsor's right to use the rights owner's intellectual property will normally be quite extensive and will relate to usage in promotional publicity material relating to the exploitation of the rights and will very often extend to usage in any and all media. This would cover advertising and promotional campaigns on television and radio, as well as above and below the line advertising and marketing exploitation.

If the sponsor is also obtaining the right to use copyright film footage (typically of the event itself) then the sponsor will want an appropriate warranty that the rights owner has those rights to grant. The rights owner will want to ensure that the sponsor's use of such copyright material does not go beyond the usage permitted in the agreement and that it does not compete with the commercial rights granted to any broadcaster or video distributor the rights owner appoints.

The rights owner may also wish to ensure that the rights granted to the sponsor are not so extensive as to cover the rights which would more usually be granted in the terms of a merchandising agreement or granted to another commercial partner. Merchandising agreements are dealt with elsewhere[1] and they are usually the object of a separate agreement.

The sponsor will very often grant the rights owner limited rights to use its name and/or logo and again this usage will be in a strictly defined and anticipated way for the purposes of the agreement.

---

1   See **6.4.**

The question of ownership of rights that are created as a result of the sponsorship may also arise. The obvious example relates to a new sponsored logo which is designed and created by the sponsor (or on its behalf) and which both the sponsor and the rights holder will use to exploit and promote the rights associated with the event. Whilst first ownership of such intellectual property rights will require an examination of the underlying principles of the law involved[1] the question of subsequent ownership is a matter that may be dealt with in the agreement by way of an assignment or a licence of the rights involved. It is a matter for agreement between the parties and will reflect their bargaining powers.

It is in both parties' interests to incorporate terms dealing with the protection and exploitation of all their respective intellectual property rights. These terms will cover some or all of the following:

–   the notification by either party of any suspected or actual infringement of the intellectual property rights of the other party which they become aware of. There may also be terms requiring the relevant party to assist the other party in protecting their rights;
–   there may be limitations on the extent to which either party can authorise unconnected third parties to use any of their intellectual property rights. In circumstances where a third party does require use of the intellectual property then it will be up to the owner of that right to specifically licence it or authorise its use;
–   there may also be provisions relating to the registration, protection and enforcement of registerable intellectual property rights. In particular this may relate to any newly designed logos or marks relating to the sponsor's sponsorship of the event;
–   where either party is licensing registered rights to the other then it is worthwhile considering whether the transaction should be registered.[2]

There may also be extensive provisions governing the manner in which both parties' intellectual property rights and in particular their trade marks may be used. These terms will often state that any use of either party's marks should be accompanied by an appropriate marking and/or attribution as to the ownership of the rights. There may also be a form of style bible which will state exactly how the marks may be represented. There may be other restrictions on incorporating one party's marks with other marks as well as terms which will be aimed at ensuring that neither party's registered trade marks may be revoked or liable to attack in some other way as a result of the other's action or inaction.

(p)   Termination provisions

Ideally, the sponsorship will run its course and terminate (or be renewed) once its term expires. The agreement is likely to contain a number of provisions which will be regarded as usual which relate to termination,[3] but these may also be supplemented by a number of other terms which will relate specifically to the sponsorship in question.

---

1   See Chapter 4.
2   See Chapter 4.
3   See **3.4.13**.

Such terms may cover a change in the law which governs sponsorship, for example, the introduction of legislation which prohibits certain types of marketing or introduces further restrictions on the manner in which certain products may be promoted. The most obvious examples are the current restrictions and outright prohibitions on the promotion and marketing of tobacco and tobacco related products as well as possible future restrictions on the promotion and marketing of alcohol and alcohol related products. Such safeguards are essential for certain sponsors.

A sponsor may insist on additional rights to terminate if, for example, the rights owner does not deliver a certain agreed level of broadcast coverage for its sport or event. There may also be termination provisions which will vary depending on the precise type of sponsorship. In the case of a league or cup competition, there may be provisions which allow the sponsor to terminate the agreement if the constitution undergoes a change in format or certain clubs or individuals do not compete. There may also be termination provisions if the rights holder fails to deliver on some of its contractual promises, especially those promises which relate to rights granted to the sponsor.

Where a sponsor is particularly concerned about the level of media value which it receives under the sponsorship then a formula may be inserted in the agreement which is used to set the base level of such media value. If the sponsor finds that its exposure or media value calculated under this formula drops below a certain level then there may be a specific right to terminate or renegotiate certain terms of the agreement.

The relative importance of these terms will depend upon the type of sponsorship in question. The sponsor is usually well advised to negotiate wide protection for itself, particularly if it finds itself in a situation where, despite having paid for certain rights and the expectation of a certain minimum level of exposure, none of it is forthcoming. This situation may defeat the whole purpose of the agreement.

The effect of termination will usually be that both parties' rights cease from that point onwards. This means that the sponsor may not incur any future liability to pay sponsorship fees and, indeed, it may seek a refund if it has paid substantial fees for a long term arrangement.

If either party has any contractual or other rights on termination then these will usually survive the termination of the agreement. For example, a breach of contract, although giving the right to terminate the agreement, may also give rise to other liability for the defaulting party.

Once the agreement is over, the parties' rights to use their respective intellectual property rights will almost certainly end. There may need to be a period of time during which merchandise and promotion materials manufactured bearing the marks are sold off. This may be as long as six months. Such a right is particularly important for the sponsor, especially where it is using a manufactured product to help promote the sponsorship.

(q) Competition law

The relevant provisions of competition law as it may affect sponsorship agreements have been considered elsewhere.[1] The agreement may seek to deal with the possible effects of European and UK legislation by ensuring that the parties to the agreement cooperate in the preparation and submission of any necessary application or notification to the relevant competition authority.

(r) Other terms

The agreement will contain numerous 'standard' or 'boiler-plate' terms.[2]

---

1   See **3.9.5.**
2   See **3.4.16.**

6.2.5   Event sponsorship agreement

THIS AGREEMENT is made the   day of   [   ]

BETWEEN:

(1)   ('the Association'); and

(2)   ('the Company').

The Association is the proprietor and organiser of the Event and the Company has agreed to sponsor the Event.

IT IS AGREED as follows:

I   **DEFINITIONS**

    1.1   In this Agreement the following terms have the following meanings:

'Company Marks	means the [*registered trade marks*] owned by the Company set out in Schedule Four;
'Company Products'	means [*insert*];
'Company Rights'	means the rights granted in clause 2 and further set out in Schedule One;
'Competing Product'	means any product (other than the Company Products) which is a Drink;
'Designation'	means (i) 'official [*sport drink*] supplier to [*the Association*]';
	(ii) 'official [*sport drink*] to [*the Association*]';
'Drink'	means any alcoholic or non-alcoholic drink whether carbonated or non-carbonated and whether intended to be drunk alone, diluted or as a mixer with other drinks and including mineral water, milk and all so called isotonic, hypotonic, energy and fluid replacing drinks;
'The Event'	means the event comprising the matches details of which are set out in Schedule Three;
'Event Logo'	means the device in Schedule Two;
'Premium'	means any article which is used to promote the Company, the Company Products or the Company Rights which are distributed free which bears or is distributed in association with the Event Logo;
'Rights'	means the Company Rights, the Designations and all rights granted under this Agreement (without limitation);
'Sponsorship Fee'	means [*insert amount*];
'The Existing Sponsor'	means the contracts entered into before the Agreement with persons who currently sponsor the Association a list of which is set out in Schedule [ ];
'The Sponsored Logo'	means the official logo used by the Association and the Company in connection with the ....;

'Match'	means any [......... *sport*] match forming part of the Event;
'The Sponsored Title'	means the title by which the Event will be known for the term as designated by the Company from time to time;
'Term'	means the period in *Clause 6*; and
'Territory'	means the world.

1.2   In this Agreement:

1.2.1   references to statutory provisions shall be construed as references to those provisions as amended or re-enacted or as their application is modified by other provisions from time to time and shall include references to any provisions of which they are re-enactments (whether with or without modification);

1.2.2   references to 'this Agreement' or to any other agreement or document referred to in this Agreement mean this Agreement and includes the schedules, each of which shall have effect as if set out in this Agreement;

1.2.3   references to clause(s) and schedule(s) are references to clause(s) and schedule(s) of and to this Agreement and references to sub-clause(s) or paragraph(s) are unless otherwise stated references to sub-clause(s) of the clause or paragraph(s) of the schedule in which the reference appears;

1.2.4   references to a '*person*' include any individual company body corporate corporation state or agency of a state firm partnership joint venture association organisation or trust (in each case whether or not having separate legal personality and irrespective of the jurisdiction in or under the law of which it was incorporated or exists) and a reference to any of them shall include a reference to the others.

1.3   The headings and sub-headings are inserted for convenience only and shall not affect the construction of this Agreement.

2   GRANT OF RIGHTS

2.1   Subject to the terms and conditions of this Agreement and in consideration of the Sponsorship Fee the Association grants the Company in the Territory for the Term:

2.1.1   the exclusive right to be described as the official title sponsor of the Event using the Sponsored Title;

2.1.2   the Company Rights;

2.1.3   the non-exclusive right to describe itself as an official sponsor of the Event and the Association;

2.1.4   the exclusive right to describe itself as the official supplier of [*sports drinks*] to the Event and to use the Designations in describing itself as such.

2.2   The Company shall only use the Rights in relation to Company Products and the Rights shall not be used in connection with any other goods or services of the Company.

2.3   The Company shall not use any designations other than the Designations without the prior written consent of the Association.

2.4   The Company may exercise the rights granted under this clause on the Company Products, their packaging, promotional, advertising and marketing material in any and all media.

3   EXCLUSIVITY

3.1   The Association shall not during the Term:

3.1.1   grant the Company Rights (or any rights similar to the Company Rights) to any third party that manufactures, distributes or sells Competing Products;

3.1.2   grant to any third party the right to describe itself as the title sponsor of the Event;

3.1.3   grant to any third party the right to use the Designations;

3.1.4   appoint any third party that manufactures Competing Products to be a sponsor or official supplier of the Event.

3.2   The Association may during the Term appoint up to [specify number] secondary sponsors on terms substantially the same (except as to the right to be described on the official title sponsor of the Event) as those granted in this Agreement in relation to the Event.

3.3   Notwithstanding the provisions of this clause the Company acknowledges that the Association has entered into agreements with the Existing Sponsor the terms of which may conflict with the provision of this Agreement and the grant of the Rights to the Company and that the existence or renewal of such agreement with the Existing Sponsors does not constitute a breach by the Association of the term of this Agreement.

4   FEES

In consideration of the rights granted and on the terms of this Agreement the Company shall:

4.1   pay the Association the Sponsorship Fee as follows:

4.1.1   [insert amount] on signature of this Agreement; and

4.1.2   [insert amount] on [specify date].

4.2   the Sponsorship Fee is exclusive of any VAT that may be or become payable and the Association shall invoice the Company separately for any such VAT.

5   COMPANY OBLIGATIONS

The Company shall:

5.1   not exercise the Company Rights in any way which, in the reasonable opinion of the Association, is prejudicial to the image and reputation of the Association, or [the sport];

5.2   not without the prior written consent of the Association engage in any joint exploitation of the Company Rights with any third party or with any products of the Company other than the Company Products;

5.3   supply to the Association samples of any proposed use by the Company of the Event Logo whether on Company Products or otherwise, for the prior approval of the Association, such approval not to be unreasonably withheld or delayed;

5.4   in consultation with the Association, publicise and promote the Event in such manner as the Company thinks fit in the course of exercising the Rights;

5.5   cooperate with the Association in the media and other promotion possibilities for the marketing exposure of the Event;

5.6   provide the Association with sufficient agreed amounts of Company Products free of charge at the Event and the press conferences organised by the Association to promote the Event and at such other promotional opportunities organised by the Association as may arise from time to time during the Term;

5.7   shall provide samples of packaging for Premiums which are to be associated with or bear the Event Logo and shall not use Premiums in connection with the Company Rights without the prior written consent of the Association; and

5.8   shall inform the Association in writing of any suspected infringements of the Event Logo which comes to its attention.

6   ASSOCIATION'S OBLIGATIONS

The Association shall:

6.1   use its reasonable endeavours to hold the Event at the places and on the dates set out in Schedule Three;

6.2   organise the Event to the best of its ability and in accordance with good business practice;

6.3   ensure that the Event is properly and reasonably promoted, advertised and marketed and that wide media coverage of the Event is obtained;

6.4   not grant or purport to grant any third party any rights in relation to the Company Marks or any rights over Company Products without the prior written approval of the Company;

6.5   advise the Company of any further promotional or marketing opportunities that arise out of or in connection with the Event;

6.6   not during the Term do anything which may undermine the value of the Rights;

6.7   ensure that all third parties (including without limitation any broadcaster of the Event) refer to the Event using the Sponsored Title and the Sponsored Logo;

6.8   ensure that the Sponsored Title and the Sponsored Logo appear on all tickets, promotional materials and publications relating to or promoting the Event produced by or on behalf of the Association;

6.9   not knowingly do any act during the Term which, in the opinion of the Company, is prejudicial to the image of the Company, the Company Marks or the Company Products; and

6.10   immediately notify the Company of any suspected infringements of the Company Marks which come to its attention.

7   TERM OF AGREEMENT

7.1   This Agreement shall commence on the date of its signature and shall last until [ninety] days after the Event unless terminated earlier in accordance with the terms of this Agreement.

7.2   The Company may extend the Term for a further one (1) year by giving notice in writing to the Association at least one month before the date on which the Term would otherwise expire. If the Company gives such notice this Agreement shall continue in force on the terms of this Agreement except as to this Clause 7.2 and this Agreement shall continue in force until [90] days after the subsequent Event.

8   WARRANTIES

Each party warrants to the other that:

8.1   it has the full right title and authority to enter into this Agreement;

8.2   it is free and able to grant the rights and perform the obligations undertaken by it in this Agreement;

8.3   it has not entered into any agreement with any third party that conflicts with the terms of this Agreement;

8.4   its trade marks, name, logos and intellectual property rights, do not infringe the trade marks, names, logos or intellectual property rights of any person;

8.5   it shall indemnify the other against any claims, proceedings, losses, expenses and liabilities (including without limitation legal fees) arising out of or in connection with any breach of the terms of this Agreement;

8.6   it will not disclose to any third party other than its professional advisers or as required by law or as agreed between the parties any information relating to the business or affairs of the other or the contents of this Agreement

9   BROADCAST COVERAGE

9.1   During the Term the Association shall procure at least [   ] matches (including semi-final and final matches) are broadcast on television live and/or as live.

9.2   The Association shall further procure that any broadcaster broadcasting any match forming part of the Event:

9.2.1   refers to the Event using the Sponsored Title;

9.2.2   does not exclude or restrict any of the Company Marks or any coverage of the advertising boards bearing the Company Marks or any reference to the Company Products;

9.2.3   does not enter into any broadcast sponsorship arrangements with any manufacture of a Competing Product;

9.2.4   shall not alter, delete or add to any of the Company Rights by use of any electronic imaging system.

10   TERMINATION

10.1   Rights of Termination

Either party may terminate its obligations under this Agreement forthwith by giving written notice to the other party if:

10.1.1 such other party commits any breach of any of the other terms and conditions of this Agreement;

10.1.2 any warranty or undertaking given by such other party in this Agreement is found to be untrue or misleading; or

10.1.3 such other party goes into liquidation (except for the purposes of amalgamation or reconstruction) or receivership (including administrative receivership) or has an administrator appointed, stops or suspends payment of all or a material part of its debts or makes any arrangement or composition with its creditors.

10.2   The Company may terminate this Agreement if:

10.2.1   the broadcast coverage of the Event falls below the minimum level set out in
          clause 9.1;

10.2.2   the Association breaches its obligation in clause 6.

10.3   Notification of Termination Events

Either party shall notify the other party promptly upon the occurrence of an event or
circumstance which may give rise to the occurrence of an event in Clause 7.1.

10.4   Consequences of termination

Upon termination:

10.4.1   the rights and obligations of the parties under this Agreement shall terminate
          and be of no future effect except that clauses [   ] shall remain in full force and
          effect;

10.4.2   any rights or obligations to which any of the parties to this Agreement may be
          entitled or be subject before such termination shall remain in full force and
          effect;

10.4.3   termination shall not affect or prejudice any right to damages or other remedy
          which the terminating party may have in respect of the event which gave rise to
          the termination or any other right to damages or other remedy which any party
          may have in respect of any breach of this Agreement which existed at or before
          the date of termination;

10.5   on termination of this agreement for whatever reason both parties shall cease
          forthwith to use the other party's logo and intellectual property rights and any
          other print and promotional material prepared under this Agreement and each
          party's property shall be returned to it.

11   FORCE MAJEURE

11.1   Effect of force majeure

Neither party to this Agreement shall be deemed to be in breach of this Agreement or
otherwise liable to the other as a result of any delay or failure in the performance of its
obligations under this Agreement if and to the extent that such delay or failure is caused by
force majeure (as defined in clause 11.2) and the time for performance of the relevant
obligation(s) shall be extended accordingly.

11.2   Definition of force majeure

For the purpose of this clause 'force majeure' means any circumstances not foreseeable at the
date of this Agreement and not within the reasonable control of the party in question including
without limitation:

11.2.1   any strike lockout or other industrial action nor any shortage of or difficulty in
          obtaining labour or raw materials;

11.2.2   any destruction temporary or permanent breakdown malfunction or damage of
          or to any premises plant equipment (including computer systems) or material;

11.2.3   any breach of contract default or insolvency by or of any third party (including
          an agent or sub-contractor) other than a company in the same group as the
          party affected by the force majeure or an employee or officer of that party or
          company;

11.2.4   any action taken by a governmental or public authority of any kind including not
          granting a consent exemption approval or clearance;

11.2.5   any civil commotion or disorder riot invasion war threat of or preparation for war;

11.2.6   any fire explosion storm flood earthquake subsidence epidemic or other natural physical disaster.

11.3   Obligations of affected party

A party whose performance of its obligations under this Agreement is delayed or prevented by force majeure:

11.3.1   shall immediately notify the other party of the nature extent effect and likely duration of the circumstances constituting the force majeure;

11.3.2   shall use all reasonable endeavours to minimise the effect of the force majeure on its performance of its obligations under this Agreement; and

11.3.3   shall (subject to clause 11.4) immediately after the force majeure event has ended notify the other party and resume full performance of its obligations under this Agreement.

11.4   Termination for force majeure

If any force majeure delays or prevents the performance of the obligations of either party for a continuous period in excess of one month the party not so affected shall then be entitled to give notice to the affected party to terminate this Agreement specifying the date (which shall not be less than seven days after the date on which the notice is given) on which termination will take effect. Such a termination notice shall be irrevocable except with the consent of both parties and upon termination the provisions of clause 10.4 apply.

12   PROVISIONS RELATING TO THIS AGREEMENT

12.1   This Agreement constitutes the whole Agreement between the parties relating to its subject matter and supersedes and extinguishes any prior drafts, agreements, undertakings, representations, warranties and arrangements whether written or oral relating to its subject matter.

12.2   The warranties, obligations and terms contained in this agreement shall continue in force after the date of signature of this Agreement and continue in full force and effect for the duration of the terms of this Agreement.

12.3   At any time after the date of this Agreement each of the parties shall at the request and cost of the other party acknowledge, execute and deliver such documents and do all acts as the other party may request for the purpose of giving to the other party the full benefit of the terms of this Agreement.

12.4   If any provision of this Agreement is held to be illegal, void, invalid or unenforceable the legality, validity and enforceability of the remaining terms of this Agreement shall not be affected.

12.5   Any notice required to be given under this Agreement shall be in writing and may be:

12.5.1   personally delivered or sent by facsimile in which case it shall be deemed to have been given on delivery at the relevant address or in the case of facsimile on transmission subject to confirmation of uninterrupted transmission by a transmission report, if it is delivered not later than 16.30 hours on any business day, or, if it is delivered later than 16.30 hours on a business day or at any time on a day which is not a business day at 09.00 hours on the next business day; or

12.5.2   sent by first class pre-paid post, in which case it is deemed given two business days after posting;

12.5.3   in this clause 'business day' means a day other than Saturday or Sunday or a bank holiday and all notices shall be addressed to the respective addresses of the parties set out at the head of this Agreement.

12.6   Nothing in this Agreement constitutes a partnership between the parties.

12.7   This Agreement shall be governed by and construed in accordance with English law.

12.8   In relation to any legal action arising out of this Agreement both parties submit to the exclusive jurisdiction of the English courts and waives any objection to legal action in such court.

SCHEDULE I

1.   The exclusive right to advertise on sixteen adjoining perimeter boards at the Event.

2.   The exclusive right to use the Event Logo and the designation on Company Products and other advertising promoting and marketing materials and in promotional and advertising campaigns related to the Event.

3.   The exclusive right to one full page of colour advertising in the official souvenir brochure of the Event and which will be positioned on the inside front cover of the brochure facing editorial text the artwork for which the Company agrees to provide at its cost within applicable previously notified production deadlines.

4.1   The right to receive fifty (50) tickets free of charge to the Event

4.2   In addition the Company will have the right to purchase an additional two hundred (200) tickets to the Event at face value, provided the Company notifies the Association of its desire to purchase such tickets not less than one (1) month prior to the commencement of the Event. Any tickets which are so supplied shall not be resold by the Company

4.3   In addition, the Company will be entitled to VIP access for 10 people to each of the opening and closing dinners.

4.4   All costs incurred by the Company, its directors, employees, clients or customers in attending such functions, facilities or matches including travelling expenses and the costs of food and drink consumed, shall, except where otherwise advised or agreed, be borne by the Company.

5.   The exclusive right to create the Sponsored Logo to a design approved by the Association (such approval not to be unreasonably withheld or delayed) in connection with Company Products and related advertising and promotional materials.

6.   The right to receive a copy of the media analysis commissioned by the Association as soon as practicable after the Event which will relate to the ratings, quantity and audience composition of the television coverage of the Event.

7.   The non-exclusive right (without further Agreements) during the term to use film footage of the Event for promotional and advertising purposes only subject to the following conditions:

7.1   such footage shall be supplied through the Association's appointed broadcaster;

7.2   the Company shall pay the technical costs connected with such usage;

7.3   the conditions of use of such footage shall be agreed with the Association in writing in advance.

The Company shall not use any such film footage in such a way that implies an endorsement of the Company or any of its products or services by any competition or official of the Event and the Company shall indemnify the Association with respect to all claims of, and liability to, any third party for loss or damages of any type arising out of the Company's breach of such restrictions.

8.   The exclusive right to distribute Premiums in connection with the Event. The Company shall ensure that the Premiums are used only in connection with Company Products, and that if Premiums are sold, they shall only be sold in direct conjunction with sales of Company Products.

9.   The exclusive right to display the Company Marks on the back-drop during player interviews and press conferences.

10.   The right to sell or provide samples of Company Products at Matches forming part of the Event.

6.3 ENDORSEMENT AGREEMENTS

6.3.1 Introduction

An endorsement is a promotional and marketing tool that takes advantage of a personality's reputation. In the context of sport the endorsement usually makes an obvious association between the sportsman and the tools of their trade. This may be a rugby player's boots, the golfer's clubs or the tennis player's racquet. However, deals may relate to items other than kit or equipment and extend to the endorsement and promotion of any number of other products such as pizzas, crisps and soft drinks. There may be no-go areas of endorsement such as alcohol and cigarettes. Endorsements are not just limited to sports personalities, they are popular marketing methods for all personalities.

An endorsement is the personal recommendation by a personality of a product or service. It is a specialised form of advertising and marketing which, when used well, can be a unique and distinctive method of marketing a product or service. The form of the endorsement varies. On the one hand, there is usually an obligation of some sort for the personality to wear and use the product or service being endorsed. On the other hand, the sponsoring company will advertise their relationship with the personality. This may be done with an advertisement showing a simple still photograph of a personality featured with the product. For a sportsman this may be a still from a competition or game or from a studio session. There may be a quotation or characteristic catchphrase from the personality chosen and used with the advertisement.

If there is a broadcast advertisement the personality may do a voice-over. If footage of the personality is used, it may be footage from competition or specially shot material. The methods and manner of advertising are already so diverse that a well-advised personality must ensure he knows exactly which media are going to be used in the endorsement. The sponsoring company may also use the personality on product packaging, competitions and for general promotional work.

6.3.2 Personality rights

A common problem for personalities is what they can and cannot stop other people from doing with their name and likeness. For example, can a newspaper print a picture of the players in a five nations rugby squad in its sports pages? Can that newspaper go further and print that same picture in an advertisement for the newspaper's new improved Sunday Magazine sports section?

A question that often arises is on what, if any, legal basis individuals can control the use of their name and reputation. One method of control is by means of a contract. This will usually be a contract between the personality and various sponsors, perhaps an employer and even the rules of the sport governing body of which he is a member. An agreement can set out the specific limits on the use of the personality's endorsement and the precise circumstances in which its rights end.

Whether there is an agreement or not, the question is frequently raised as to exactly what proprietary basis there is for individuals who are in the habit of exploiting their likeness and personality to protect themselves from unauthorised 'endorsements'. There are various legal considerations and they relate mainly to intellectual property rights.

There is no specific law of privacy or right of personality in the UK. Where there is no contract between an individual and a person using his name or likeness there are a number of possible rights which can be used to protect an individual from unauthorised use of their name or likeness.

(a) Trade marks

Trade mark protection may be available for an individual's name or likeness. The broad definition of the term trade mark means that as long as the mark is distinctive it should be registered. This may apply to an individual's name, their nickname and even to their likeness. The fact that it is now possible to register a mark even though the proprietor may not be trading in products under which the mark has been registered but licensing others to use the mark is no longer prohibited. The extensive protection provided by registration means the unauthorised use of an individual's registered name or likeness in an advertisement or on a particular product may lead to actionable trade mark infringement taking place.

A number of sports personalities have registered trade marks, such as the 'Gazza' trade mark (registered to Paul Gascoigne Promotions). The registrations extend beyond the name and include registration of, for example, the image of Damon Hill looking through the visor of his helmet. As long as the image is distinctive, the wide definition of trade mark[1] makes it possible for a personality to register much more than their name. If possible all professional sportsmen should register their name and likeness.[2] This is the best protection available for an individual to prevent the unauthorised exploitation or appropriation of his name and likeness. Although there are limits to trade mark protection (such as for comparative advertising), unauthorised commercial use can be prohibited and an ordered scheme of licensing and exploitation maintained.

(b) Passing off

The difficulty with passing off protection is that an individual has to establish each element of the tort before an action lies. A trade mark registration is public and unauthorised use of the mark is often actionable. An individual relying on the tort of passing off must establish he has a trading reputation that results in goodwill. This may be difficult if no trade in the product in question is actively carried on. The next hurdle is to establish a misrepresentation that leads to consumer confusion resulting in damage to the personality. The traditional difficulty for individuals trying to establish a right to stop people using their name or likeness is that they do not trade in the same area as their tormentors. A DJ trying to stop a cereal manufacturer from using his name on their 'Uncle Mac' cereal was unable to do so because there was no common activity between him and the cereal manufacturer. The DJ worked in radio, the cereal manufacturer in cereal manufacturing. Accordingly, the court held, there was no risk of

1   Trade Marks Act 1994, s 1.
2   The Trade Marks Registry Handbook contains guidelines on the registration of names.

confusion to consumers as there was no common field of activity.[1] Likewise an actor could not prevent an advertiser using a sound-alike voice over on an advertisement because he was in the business of acting and not of selling beans and soups.[2]

The situation changed for the better after the Ninja Turtles case[3] where the court recognised that the defendant's actions could lead to the damage to the plaintiff's business. Since that case, the courts have not granted protection in similar situations and the situation (such as it is) provided by passing off is limited.[4] Personalities that actively exploit their reputation now stand a much better chance of success in a passing off claim as they may be able to prove they have the necessary goodwill to found an action, that the defendant's misrepresentation in appropriating their name or image would lead to an association between themselves and the defendant's products resulting in damage to their licensing rights. This may be so even though the defendant's activities are in an otherwise unrelated commercial areas to the personality's day-to-day business as a sportsman. The action is still not without its difficulties as confusion must be established. Commonwealth jurisdictions are a lot more relaxed about passing off claims by personalities. In the Australian case of *Hogan v Pacific Dunlop*,[5] a claim for passing off was upheld. An advertisment using the idea of the 'knife scene' from the film *Crocodile Dundee* was used by the defendants in an advertisement. In this case the misrepresentation occurred because the Dundee character in the advertisement was seen to be sponsoring the defendant's shoes. Unfortunately for individuals, this authority has not been followed in the UK.

(c) Copyright

Copyright law does not provide any direct protection of personality rights. The categories of protected copyright work may be used to control certain matters. Names cannot be protected using copyright law as they are not a 'work' for copyright purposes.[6] An individual cannot stop a person from painting him (even if it is not a posed protrait) or reproducing that painting unless he owns the copyright in the painting or another actionable wrong occurs, such as passing off or trade mark infringement. Similarly, taking and reproducing photographs of an individual are not an infringement of the individual's copyright unless he actually owns or acquires that copyright. The exploitation of copyright works are based on authorship and ownership of the works. Unless specific contractual provision is made for ownership of copyright the personality that is the subject of a photograph or indeed any other copyright work will not own the copyright in the resulting work.

Other categories of copyright works such as films, sound recordings and broadcasts do not infringe any individual's copyright because the individuals do not generally own the copyright in those works. Authorship and ownership of those works vests initially in the producer or director production responsible for

---

1   *McCulloch v Lewis A May Ltd* (1948) 65 RPC 58.
2   *Sim v Heinz Ltd* [1959] 1 All ER 547.
3   *Mirage Studios v Counter-feat Clothing Ltd* (1991) FSR 145.
4   See *Panini* case (1996) unreported.
5   (1989) 12 IPR 225 (F. Ct. Australia).
6   *Exxon v Exxon* [1982] Ch 119.

them. The only rights an individual may have are performance rights and these do not generally apply to sports performers.[1]

Ownership of copyright may change hands and that is a matter an individual may be able to control or influence. For example, a sportsman could only permit photos to be taken of him or give interviews on the condition that ownership of the copyright is assigned to him or his representatives. A sportsman may also try to control all photo opportunities although this can be very difficult to achieve, particularly where the individual concerned is a public and newsworthy figure. These conditions may not be practicable for anything but commercial photo shoots. Stopping the press taking and publishing photos is next to impossible.

In the case of films, sound recordings and broadcasts, individuals may seek to impose terms as to their appearance in the way actors or musicians do. This tends to be more akin to performers' rights protection and is discussed below.

(d)   Rights in performances
An individual sportsmen taking part in his chosen, or indeed any, sport does not fall within the definition of 'performance' in CDPA 1988, s 180(2). However hard the sportsmen try, it is not a dramatic performance within the meaning of the CDPA 1988, nor is it a musical performance, it is very unlikely to be a reading or recitation of a literary work and is not a variety act.

If, however, an individual sportsman takes part in a pantomime, a quiz show, a documentary or something that does fall within one of the above categories then their consent is required for the recording and exploitation of their performance.

Although a sportsman taking part in his chosen sport does not qualify for performers' rights protection under CDPA 1988, s 180(2), an event organiser or broadcaster will usually obtain a formal written consent or release to the inclusion of their sporting performance in the broadcast. This consent permits the appearance of the sportsman to be filmed and broadcast and exploited however the person with the benefit of the release wishes. Such a form is useful because other jurisdictions provide greater protection for personality rights than the UK. A personality and his advisers must consider the terms of any release very carefully so that no more rights than necessary are granted to the organiser or broadcaster. Of course, a particularly popular or successful sportsman may try to impose quite specific requirements particularly as to remuneration for exploitation. It is not regular practice in most sports for personalities to enter full performer's agreements covering their activities as competitors in broadcast and filmed events. Such agreements are commonplace in boxing and are creeping into other sports, particularly in athletics where broadcasters are very keen to secure the participation of named individuals. This topic, along with a form of release, is considered further in Chapter 9.

(e)   Defamation and malicious falsehood
Where an individual is depicted in a derogatory manner the law of defamation may protect that person. Particular instances may occur in press reporting of an individual's on-and-off the field activities. Defamation may also occur where an individual is depicted in an advertisement in a derogatory way. The classic

---

1   See **6.3.2**(d).

example of this is the case of *Tolley v Fry*[1] where Mr Tolley, an amateur golfer, was depicted in an advertisement for Fry's chocolate with a bar of chocolate sticking out of his pocket. The sting of the libel in this case was that, as an amateur golfer, Mr Tolley had compromised his amateur status. In the current era of professionalism in sport, such a case may be harder to sustain.

An action for malicious falsehood may lie where an untrue statement is made, the words were published maliciously and caused financial loss. The statement must be false. It must also be made maliciously. Malicious in this sense means spitefully, dishonestly or recklessly. This may apply to a false endorsement, especially if the individual can show that he would normally charge for such an endorsement. Proof of special damage is not necessary if the statement was calculated to cause pecuniary damage to the plaintiff, and:

(a)   was published in writing or some other permanent form; or,

(b)   was made in respect of any office, profession, calling, trade or business held or carried on by him at the time of publication.[2]

The actor Gordon Kaye was successful in a claim for malicious falsehood when a newspaper took photographs and conducted an interview after he had been in a serious accident. The court granted a limited injunction preventing the newspaper from pretending that the actor had consented to the interview. The malicious falsehood occurred because of the false representation that he had given up a valuable property right, the right to give an exclusive interview concerning his accident, for which he could charge.[3]

(f)   Advertising standards

The British Code of Advertising and Sales Promotion provides some limited protection for the personality against unauthorised use of name and image in an advertisment. Rule 13 states that advertisers are 'urged to obtain written permission in advance' if they propose to use a personality in an advertisement. It also provides that people with a high public profile must not be portrayed in 'an offensive or adverse way. Advertisments should not imply an endorsement where none exists.' The Code also helpfully points out that 'individuals who do not wish to be associated with a product may have a legal claim'.

(g)   Trade descriptions

It is an offence to apply a false trade description to goods or to supply or expose for sale goods with such a description. For the personality's purposes a trade description is most likely to mean:

'an indication, direct or indirect ...... of ...... approval by any person or confirmity with a type approved by any person'.[4]

For example, a statement that a pair of rugby boots are 'as used by' a named player may amount to a false trade description. A trade description is false if it is 'false to a material degree'.[5] The use of false trade descriptions in advertising is

---

1   [1931] AC 333.
2   Defamation Act 1952, s 3.
3   *Kaye v Robertson* [1991] FSR 62.
4   Trade Descriptions Act 1968, s 2(1)(g).
5   Ibid, s 3.

also an offence.[1] There are various defences to the offences set out in ss 24 and 25 of the act. The summary offence has a maximum fine of £5,000 whereas on indictment there may be an unlimited fine and up to two years in jail.

6.3.3   Endorsement agreements: an overview

(a)   Introduction

An endorsement agreement is an agreement for the right of a sponsoring company to use a personality's services and the right to use their name and likeness in an agreed manner. This latter provision may involve the licensing of proprietary rights such as trade marks. The purpose of the agreement is to carefully regulate the rights and, to some extent, the expectations of both parties. This helps ensure that, for example, the sponsor does not assume that the personality is at its beck and call. Likewise, if the agreement is to be mutually beneficial, the personality must accept some reasonable restrictions on the way he spends some of his time and exercises his commercial freedom.

(b)   Rights

An endorsement agreement should carefully set out the various rights and obligations of both parties. There are usually two aspects to the rights granted in an endorsement agreement. There is a right to use the personality's services and a limited contractual licence of rights in the personality's name and likeness.

The personality must carefully consider and manage the use that is to be made of his services. These services must be carefully controlled, they may be defined as the 'promotional services' of the personality and often include the right to require the personality to make a certain number of appearances to promote or facilitate the promotion of the goods or services which are the subject matter of the agreement. The maximum number of such appearances should be set in the agreement. It is important that the personality is able to fulfil all his other training and playing commitments as well as any other sponsor commitments he may have under other personal or club agreements. It is quite common for a personality to be involved in the promotion of a number of products or services. In extreme cases, this may mean their performance suffers and, eventually, their marketing value declines.

The scope of the definition of these promotional services may be for some or all of the following:

–   attending and participating in promotional events (this may include all sorts of marketing and PR work, including in-store promotions for products, autograph sessions, celebrity events, sponsor's functions, etc);
–   photo or recording sessions for the purpose of producing advertisments and marketing material endorsing products (it may be sensible to limit these sessions to particular media such as broadcast, non-broadcast, print media only, billboard posters, bonus pay structures can be built in to the agreement to reflect the differing profile given to different types of marketing);
–   appearing at sponsor's press conferences;

---

1   Ibid s 5.

- training sessions;
- charity work; and
- sports or media clinics, where the public are given the opportunity to question the personality.

Whenever the sponsor calls on the personality to provide his services the sponsor should pay the personality's expenses. The sponsor should give reasonable notice of their requirement and the time of the appearance should be limited to a defined working day. The notice requirement should help ensure there are no conflicts with the personality's training or playing commitments.

A point that sometimes arises in personality employment contracts may have a knock on effect with endorsement agreements. A player in a team sport may find that his promotional services are acquired by his club or governing body. Such agreements often make a distinction in the capacity of the endorsement rights granted by the personality to the club or governing body. For example, the employment contract may state that the promotional services granted under the employment contract are in the personality's capacity as a player for the club. This may mean that the player is not free to conclude an endorsement agreement in his capacity as a sportsman but only as a 'person'. Effectively this may mean that no sports kit or goods can be endorsed.

The player and his representatives should carefully consider any such terms in employment contracts as they may be overly restrictive of a personality's individual commercial activities. Although it is possible to promote some personalities in their capacity as team member, individual and national player the practical opportunities open to a personality in such a position may be limited. It may only be practically open to a personality to conclude an individual deal with a sponsor that is already involved in some capacity with a particular sport or one not already directly involved in and not competing with an existing sponsor involved in that sport.

In addition to the personality's promotional services the sponsor may also be granted various 'licensing rights'. These rights may include the right of the sponsor to exploit the personality's:

- name, likeness, nickname, image, voice, autograph, biographical details, and performances;
- to use, reproduce and publish photos, films, videos, sound recordings, and images in any media of the personality (this may be wider than product of the promotional services but should be limited);

and may even extend to branding for products (although such provisions should be resisted unless there are separate merchandising provisions in the deal which raise separate legal and financial issues).

Where the licence relates to the use of a trade mark then a specific trade mark licence must be included and the class and number of the mark set out in the agreement. These promotional services and licensing rights will be in connection with specified 'products' or 'services'. Traditionally this means a 'boots deal' or such like. Products may be defined very widely to mean 'all leisurewear and footwear'. Such a definition does not leave much else in such a category for the personality.

The wider the definition the greater the implications for the player and it is essential to check that the sponsor does actually produce all these products. Otherwise, the player may not be able to use other products even where the sponsor does not produce them.

There may be an additional requirement on the player to wear the products at all possible times. This will usually be extended to the promotion of other (non-competing) products. If the player has to wear the products, it is also necessary to make sure that the sponsor has to supply them.

(c) Exclusivity
The issue of exclusivity must be addressed at this stage as it impacts on other opportunities available to the personality.

–   There will be exclusivity within the product category. There may also be a prohibition on any work for a competitor whether or not it is in the same product category.
–   There should, however, be a specific contractual saving for any higher rights, for example entry requirements to competitions, player contracts with clubs and national teams. The player may not be able to wear the products at all times. If he has to wear the products for other promotions check what that covers.
–   For some players, they may also want to place other (non-competing) sponsors' names on their shirt or boots etc when they compete. If this is anticipated it must be catered for in the contract in which case the exact place and size of the both this sponsor's name and any others must also be specified. A limit must be placed on the number of other names on the shirt.
–   The effect on the player's long-term career must also be considered. An unduly restrictive sponsor deal could impact on future club signings.

(d) Duration
The length or term of the deal is important. Deals are usually 1–3 years long with an option or matching rights clause at the end of the term. Age is also a factor in this as younger players with it all before them may want a shorter agreement. An older player may want a longer agreement for the opposite reason. Older players may also look for different activities as they branch out in their career.

At the end of the deal the sponsor will be allowed a run-off period, after which it must not use the licensing rights any more. There should be as few ways as possible of extending the term. If the term has to be extended, there should be a long-stop to prevent it being overlong.

(e) Payment terms
The financial terms of the deal are important. Deals may start with the simple provision of free goods for the personality and go up to substantial financial deals.

As with any deal, the longer it is, the more likely it is that the player will be paid in instalments. In such situations, the personality may consider:

–   trying to get escalations for each year of the agreement and the exercise of any option;

– if the agreement covers a number of territories, the personality may ask for
  more money for use of the Licensing Rights in each part of the territory;
– try to get further fees for different types of advertisements. Thus billboards
  should be worth more and not included in the basic fee and broadcast
  advertisements should command a separate fee along with repeat fees every
  time they are used.

A contractual right to renegotiate the term or the money available is unenforceable as an agreement to agree although frequently such a term may be inserted as
a good faith term.

(f) Territory
The territory of the agreement must be specified; 'the world' is usual.

This may be limited if, for example the sponsor does not trade in a particular
country or the personality already has an agreement in a particular country. If the
deal is restricted to a specific territory it may be possible to do separate
advertisements in different territories for goods other than the main product
category. Despite a seemingly small territory, it is important to remember that
television broadcasts make most deals world-wide in nature. Thus different
territories may not be practicable for sports and leisurewear but they may be for
other products such as crisps or other snack foods.

(g) Miscellaneous terms
Other miscellaneous matters to deal with in the agreement include:

– Product development: the player may have to help the sponsor develop new
  products, and what rights the player has in any designs etc he develops
  should be considered. Copyright and design rights should be reserved and
  agreement reached at the time.
– Merchandising is another issue and should not be included with all other
  rights.

The agreement is also likely to include termination provisions which in addition
to the 'usual' termination and boiler-plate provisions may include specific rights
to terminate if the personality acts immorally or dishonestly, or commits a
criminal offence. There may also be a termination right if the personality wears
competing products other than as permitted under the agreement.

6.3.4 Endorsement checklist
– SPONSOR SHOULD TAKE AUDIT OF THE PERSONALITY'S
  OTHER AGREEMENTS AND OBLIGATIONS
– PARTIES
  personality's capacity
  management or service company
  personality side letter
  see copies of employment contracts
  sponsors budget authority
– RIGHTS AND EXCLUSIVITY
  what rights
  product/service category exclusivity

define product categories
'secondary rights' including:
personal appearances
filming/recording and photographic appearances for:
posters and advertising hoardings
broadcast advertising
product launches
general corporate appearances
ticket allocation
corporate hospitality
press conferences
post event interviews and branding
occasions for use of products, eg:
playing/competing/training
other advertising and promotion

– DURATION
term of years
fixed term referable to minimum time and/or minimum number of events
postponement and extension of the term
rights of renewal:
options
first negotiation
matching rights

– PAYMENT
cash fee
supply of products and in kind consideration
performance related payments, eg:
scoring goals
winning certain games
international selection
royalties and accounting terms
VAT

– SPONSORS OBLIGATIONS
payment
use of rights on terms of the agreement
not to exercise the rights in a derogatory manner
comply with rules and regulations of the sport
supply samples of materials using event name or logo for prior approval

– PERSONALITY'S OBLIGATIONS
to train and perform
to turn up for promotional work
assign rights and consent to exploitation of products of promotional work
limitations on other sponsorship packages, eg agreed number of sponsors
and no competitors
authority to grant the rights
not grant the rights to a third party
no conflicting contracts
to deliver the rights
morality provisions, eg:
no anti-social, dishonest or illegal behaviour

- TERRITORY
  specify territory
  separate deals
  separate financial provisions for different territories
- MERCHANDISING
  grant of rights
  fees
  royalties
  guarantees/minimum levels of income
- MUTUAL WARRANTIES
  authority to enter the agreement and perform its terms
  no conflicting agreements
  confidentiality of terms
  mutual indemnity for breaches of contract
- INTELLECTUAL PROPERTY
  ownership of any IPR
  registration of trade mark
  use of IPR
  sub-licensing of IPR
  protecting IPR
  notification of infringements
  action for infringements
- TERMINATION
  list breaches
  effect of breaches
  particular breaches, eg morality clause

6.3.5 Sports promotion and endorsement contract

Dated: [   ]

Parties:

1.   of   ('Personality')
2.   of   ('Company' [which expression includes its successors in title, licensees and assigns]).

1   DEFINITIONS

In this Agreement the following terms have the following meanings:

'Company Marks'	means the [registered] [unregistered] trade marks [insert details];
'Company Products'	means those Products which are manufactured by the Company and marketed under or in connection with the Company Marks;
'Company Products'	means any Product other than a Company Product;
'Fee'	means all amounts payable by the Company to the Personality under clause [3];
'Governing Body'	means [insert details];
'Licensing Rights'	means the right of the Company to use, reproduce and publish:

         (a)   the Personality's name, likeness, voice, signature and biographical details;
         (b)   agreed quotations;
         (c)   photographs, films, videos, sound recordings and electronic images of the Personality in any medium

endorsing the Company Products, or in promotional, sponsorship, advertising or marketing material relating to the Company Products;

'Promotional Services' means attending and participating on up to [six (6)] occasions during each year of the Term:

         (a)   promotional events and public relations exercises organised by or involving the Company, including but not limited to marketing, press conferences, product promotions, signing sessions, celebrity events, Company functions;
         (b)   photographic sessions to shoot advertising and marketing material endorsing Company Products including but not limited to posters, brochures, in store displays, billboards and wall boards;
         (c)   photographic, filming, recording or broadcasting sessions for the purpose of producing advertisements and marketing material endorsing Company Products;
         (d)   training sessions;
         (e)   benevolent or charity work; and
         (f)   sports or media clinics;

'Products'	means [insert details, for example: all leisurewear and footwear];
'Term'	means the period in clause [4];
'Territory'	means [the world].

2   RIGHTS

2.1   In consideration of the Fee the Personality grants to the Company the exclusive right in the Territory during the Term to use and exploit the Licensing Rights.

2.2   The Personality:

2.2.1   grants to the Company the entire copyright and neighbouring rights for [*the full period of copyright (including any extensions and renewals)*] [*the Term*] in all products of the Promotional Services;

2.2.2   waives all so called moral rights under the Copyright Designs and Patents Act 1988, sections 77–80;

2.2.3   consents to the use of his performer's non-property rights and assigns his performer's property rights (as such terms are defined in Part II of the Copyright Designs and Patents Act 1988 (as amended)) to the Company for the use of the product of the Promotional Services.

2.3   If requested to do so by the Company the Personality must perform the Promotional Services.

3   PAYMENTS

3.1   Subject to the Personality performing his obligations in this Agreement and in consideration of the grant of rights made to it the Company shall pay the Personality the following sums during the Term:

3.1.1   [£   ] for the first contract year;

3.1.2   [£   ] for the second contract year, and

3.1.3   [£   ] for the third contract year.

3.2   The amount due in each contract year is payable in two equal instalments on 31st March and 30th September of the contract year.

3.3   If during any contract year the Personality:

[3.3.1   *is appointed captain of his full representative national side; or*

3.3.2   *is selected to represent his full representative national side, or*

3.3.3   *plays in a cup or league winning team, or*

3.3.4   *scores more than [state number of goals]*]]

then in addition to the amounts payable under clause 3.1 the Company shall pay the Personality a one off bonus payment of [£   ] for that contract year.

4   TERM

4.1   This Agreement shall remain in force for three (3) years commencing on [*date*] [*from the date of signature*].

4.2   If the Company gives notice to the Personality not later than [*insert date*] the Company may extend the Term on the same terms contained in this Agreement except as to this clause for an additional twelve [*12*] months from the date of expiry of the Term.

5   EXCLUSIVITY

5.1   Subject to clause 5.2 the Personality shall not during the Term grant to any third party which manufactures, distributes or sells any Competing Products the right to use the Licensing Rights or the Promotional Services (or any Rights the same as or similar to the Rights granted to the Company under this Agreement).

5.2 Notwithstanding the provisions of clause 5.1 and clause 6.2 the Company recognises that representative national and club teams are sometimes required to wear apparel in connection with their representation of their national or club team which may conflict with the terms of this Agreement. The Company and the Personality agree that if the Personality is obliged to wear such apparel then in those circumstances only the Personality is excepted from the provisions of clause 5.1 and 6.2.

6 PERSONALITY'S OBLIGATIONS

6.1 During the Term the Personality shall:

6.1.1 render the Promotional Services to the best of his ability at such time and place as the Company requires;

6.1.2 in performing the Promotional Services follow all reasonable instructions made by the Company, co-operate with any third parties acting on the Company's behalf, conduct himself in a proper manner and maintain a tidy appearance;

6.1.3 comply with all relevant rules and regulations of the Governing Body;

6.1.4 use his best endeavours to maintain his physical and mental fitness so as to be fit for competition;

6.1.5 wear the Company Products whilst engaged in any sporting activities or competition and whilst performing the Promotional Services;

6.1.6 wherever possible wear the Company Products when promoting products of other non-competing manufacturers.

6.2 The Personality shall not:

6.2.1 exercise the Licensing Rights himself or permit any third party to exercise the Licensing Rights;

6.2.2 wear, carry or display any Products with a visible brand or logo other than the Company Products;

6.2.3 when performing the Promotional Services, make any remarks or take any actions that are defamatory of any person, obscene or in breach of any third party rights.

7 WARRANTIES

7.1 Each party warrants to the other that:

7.1.1 it is free to enter into this Agreement and grant the rights and perform the obligations undertaken by it;

7.1.2 it has not entered into and shall not enter any agreements which may conflict with this Agreement;

7.1.3 it will not incur any liability on behalf of the other party or represent that it has the authority to do so.

7.1.4 it will keep the terms of this Agreement confidential and still not disclose any financial information relating to the affairs of the others except to their respective professional advisers, or as required by law.

8 COMPANY'S OBLIGATIONS

8.1   The Company shall during the Term:

8.1.1   provide adequate free supplies of Company Products for the Personality's use at Personality's written request;

8.1.2   pay the Fee;

8.1.3   ensure that all Company Products comply with all relevant safety laws and regulations or such other relevant standards;

8.1.4   ensure that in exercising the Licensing Rights the Company complies with all relevant laws and regulations;

8.1.5   comply with the rules and regulations of the Governing Body;

8.1.6   comply with clause 9 (Approvals);

8.1.7   pay all reasonable out of pocket expenses, accommodation and travel costs incurred by the Personality in performing the Promotional Services.

8.2   The Company shall not:

8.1.2   exercise the Promotional Services at any time which would unreasonably conflict with the Personality's schedule of training or competition;

8.2.2   timetable any single appearance of the Personality in performing the Promotional Services for more than eight (8) hours duration, [exclusive of travel time].

9 APPROVALS

9.1   The Company must send the Personality all material used in exploiting the Licensing Rights for the Personality's approval not less than one (1) month before the Company intends to publish the material.

9.2   The Personality must give his written approval of the materials no later than ten (10) days after receiving any such material from the Company.

9.3   If the Personality does not give his written approval of the materials the Personality may indicate any suggested modifications to the materials which the Personality reasonably requires. If the Company and the Personality cannot agree on any suggested modifications the final decision on publication may be taken by the [Company].

9.4   If the Personality does not respond within ten (10) days after receiving the material then approval is deemed to be given.

10 LIMITATIONS

10.1   The Company has no liability under this Agreement for any claim the Personality may have for loss of publicity or chance to enhance reputation.

10.2   The Company is not liable to the Personality for any injury or damage suffered by the Personality from wearing or using the Company Products unless such injury or damage arises from the negligence of the Company.

10.3   The Company may enter a similar promotion and endorsement agreement for the Company Products with any other personality.

11   SUSPENSION

11.1   If the Personality is unable to perform the Promotional Services through reasons of ill health the Company may suspend the Term.

11.2   During any period of suspension of the Term the Company is not obliged to pay the Fee but in all other respects both parties continue to be bound by the terms of this Agreement.

11.3   The aggregate period of any suspension of the Term shall not exceed six (6) months.

12   TERMINATION

12.1   The Company may terminate this Agreement by giving notice to the Personality if the Personality:

12.1.1   fails to perform the Promotional Services; or

12.1.2   commits any act which affects the Company's reputation in an adverse manner; or

12.1.3   publicly admits to the use of any so called controlled substance or tests positive in any drug testing organised by the Governing Body; or

12.1.4   is convicted of any offence involving dishonesty or violence; or

12.1.5   dies, retires or is permanently disabled; or

12.1.6   endorses Competing Products; or

12.1.7   unless the provisions of clause 11 apply, is in breach of any term of this Agreement.

12.2   The Personality may terminate this Agreement by giving notice to the Company if the Company:

12.2.1   is in material breach of any terms of this Agreement and has not remedied that breach within fifteen (15) days of service of notice specifying such breach; or

12.2.2   if the Company goes into liquidation (except for the purposes of amalgamation or reconstruction), receivership (including administrative receivership), has an administrator appointed or makes any arrangement or composition with its creditors.

13   EFFECTS OF TERMINATION

13.1   Upon termination under clause 12 or expiry of this Agreement due to effluxion of time the rights and obligations of the parties to this Agreement cease.

13.2   Subject to clause 13.3 on termination the Company must immediately pay the Personality any money due under clause 3 and clause 8.1.7 up to the date of termination.

13.3   If this Agreement is terminated by the Company pursuant to clause 12.1 the Company may reclaim from the Personality any money in excess of the amount to which the Personality is entitled under a pro rata basis within the contract year. If requested by the Company the Personality must pay the amount due within thirty (30) days of the termination of this Agreement.

13.4   Termination of this Agreement is without prejudice to any rights or obligations of either party which may have accrued at the date of termination.

14 NOTICES

Any notice to be served under this Agreement must be in writing and served upon the other party at its address set out in this Agreement (or such other address as may be notified for this purpose) either by hand or by first class post. Notices are deemed served on delivery if delivered by hand or seventy two (72) hours after posting if sent by first class post.

15 MISCELLANEOUS

15.1   This Agreement does not constitute a partnership, joint venture or employment relationship between the parties.

15.2   The Personality shall be responsible for his own tax and national insurance and shall indemnify the Company against any liability for payment of such sums.

15.3   Neither party may assign any other rights or obligations under the Agreement without the prior written consent of the other party.

15.4   This Agreement is governed by laws of England and Wales where courts are the courts of competent jurisdiction.

6.4   MERCHANDISING

6.4.1   Introduction

Merchandising is an integral part of the sports marketing mix. It is commonplace throughout the entertainment business to manufacture and sell merchandise. This helps rights owners to do something that they cannot easily do themselves, which is to fully exploit the rights in various 'properties' such as films, television programmes, books and pop groups. This leaves the rights owner to get on with its business, which may be the running of events or, in the case of individual sportsmen, training and competing. The trend of merchandising has even spread to universities, museums and recently even hospitals. At the top end of the market, successful films, television programmes and popular combinations spin off merchandising campaigns of enormous proportions.

The business of sport is as much concerned with exploiting its rights as the rest of the entertainment business and lends itself conveniently to merchandising activities. The sale of merchandise is extensive in all major sports and around all major sporting events. The sale of merchandise in sport may be by governing bodies, clubs and participating individuals although it is more usual for a rights owner to appoint a third party to exploit its rights. This may be by using a separate company of its own which makes all the arrangements for the manufacture, distribution and sale of product. Alternatively, it may exploit its rights by appointing a third party manufacturer to do the same and pass on fees or royalties for the right to do so. The rights owner may appoint an agent to market the rights for it or find the merchandiser itself. In this respect a merchandising agreement is very similar to a traditional distribution agreement. It is also quite common for a rights owner to grant merchandising rights to a sponsor as part of a grant of sponsorship or endorsement rights.

The categories of merchandise that a company may wish to manufacture vary enormously. In sport, there are the traditional sporting goods categories, which mainly consist of playing shirts, shorts and socks. These categories are by no means closed, as all forms of clothing and apparently unrelated memorabilia are packaged up and sold around sport. Team strips, posters and other memorabilia are perennially popular with fans. In football, sales of merchandise represent significant additional revenue for club owners ever keen to maximise investor returns. It is reported that at Manchester United FC, sales of merchandise exceed gate revenue. Major events such as the Olympics sell merchandise as diverse as branded underwear and postcards. Sales of merchandise are not limited to clubs and major events, as many individuals in sport successfully launch their own ranges of merchandise. These tend to be ranges of sports and casual wear and are, very often, developed by leading individuals in golf and tennis. Merchandising deals for individuals are very often part of a wider endorsement agreement. This tends to make the financial aspects of the agreement more complicated, as elements of a fixed and variable income then come into play.

Merchandising in sport will generally involve one or both of the following situations:

(1) The sale of merchandise by reference to a particular event or team property. This usually involves the reproduction by a manufacturer of a particular logo or emblem on various categories of product.

(2) The sale of product by reference to an individual's name and image. This is known as character merchandising and in sport involves the marketing of products by reference to a real character.

Whatever category of merchandising is involved (character or otherwise) the product ranges are built around otherwise unconnected objects using the distinctive marks of the rights owner. Successful merchandising centres on the control by the rights owner of protectable rights that it can grant to the merchandiser.

6.4.2 Background law

The heart of a merchandising agreement usually takes the form of a licence of intellectual property rights. The licence is usually directly between the owner of the rights and the licensee. This ensures greater control over the use of the rights as well as direct contractual accountability to the rights owner from the merchandiser.

Although most of the terms of a merchandising agreement are common contractual provisions the area is not without its problems. Merchandising campaigns have traditionally encountered problems in protecting their 'rights' from third parties who produce merchandise without the sanction of the rights owner. These third parties are not always counterfeiters in the usual sense of the word because, in the UK at least, they may not be infringing any intellectual property rights.

The law in this country has not, until recently, provided anything more than patchy legal protection for rights owners against unauthorised production of merchandise. The position now is stronger for rights owners than it has ever been. A well-managed and well-policed portfolio of intellectual property rights should see off the most determined counterfeiter.

(a) Trade marks

The relaxation of the trade marks regime with the Trade Marks Act 1994[1] (TMA 1994) created a number of opportunities for rights owners who had previously faced considerable problems in registering a trade mark, because of the general prohibition imposed by the previous legislation forbidding a rights owner from registering a trade mark that it did not intend to use itself, but to licence for use on a range of products. Wherever possible a rights owner should now seek trade mark registration because of the extensive protection it grants rights owners.

A rights owner may seek to register an event or league competition logo, a team or individual name or nickname. Shapes and objects can be registered as well as the more traditional names and marks. Trade mark registration provides the strongest protection from infringement providing extensive civil remedies and criminal offences for infringers. Where counterfeit goods are concerned the provisions of TMA 1994, s 92 create offences related to the unauthorised use of

---

1   See Chapter 4.

trade marks. Section 93 requires local trading standards departments to enforce the rights. Under s 97, there is a power for such counterfeit goods to be destroyed.

Before TMA 1994, the rights owner and would-be merchandiser had to overcome the problem of 'trafficking' in trade marks. The legislation did not permit trade marks to be registered if they were not going to be used by the proprietor of the mark and only licensed to other people to produce goods. The 1994 Act places no restriction on such 'trafficking' in trade marks. A trade mark application may now be made by a person whose primary purpose is to license the mark to other people to produce goods. However, even now due regard must be had to such matters as quality control and the provisions of TMA 1994, s 6 regarding revocation of trade marks.

The provisions for licensing marks are contained in ss 28 to 31 and must be complied with in a merchandise licence. A trade mark licence must be in writing. It may be an exclusive licence.[1] The licence may relate to some but not all of the goods or services for which it is registered and may be limited to use in a particular manner and a particular location.[2] Trade mark owners should also note that unless the licence says otherwise they have to take action for infringement if the licensee requires them to do so.

(b) Passing off

Because of the historical problems merchandisers have faced in enforcing their rights, the traditional remedy for rights owners has involved the passing off action. Even now the tort of passing off is of more than residual importance because trends in sport are (or can often be) so ephemeral in nature that by the time a trade mark is obtained the popularity of the merchandise has waned. Rights owners looking for an effective remedy often turned to passing off to protect their rights. Problems were compounded under the old legislation because difficulties with the registration of marks meant an alternative remedy had to be found.

Unfortunately for rights owners, the use of passing off was not a solution. Passing off relies on trading goodwill, a misrepresentation which causes confusion between the infringing goods and the original ones and damage. Unless the rights owner is actually involved in licensing and exploiting their rights it is difficult to use the passing off remedy with any degree of certainty or reliability. There are a number of well-known cases that illustrate the problems with the passing off remedy. For example, the owners of rights in the Wombles were unable to stop a skip hire company from using their name because the Wombles were not in the business of hiring skips, they were fictional characters who despite the fact that they sold bins with the Wombles name and characters on, were in a different business to the defendants. As such, it was difficult to establish any confusion on the part of the skip hiring public as to the origin of the hire service. The tide seemed to turn with the Ninja Turtles case[3] but that tide may well be retreating again with recent cases involving the Spice Girls and the Estate of Elvis Presley.[4]

---

1   TMA 1994, s 29.
2   Ibid, s 28.
3   *Mirage Studios v Counter Feat Clothing* [1991] FSR 145.
4   *In re Elvis Presley* (1999) *The Times*, 22 March.

Although passing off is clearly available as a remedy against infringers it remains very difficult for aggrieved rights owners to enforce their rights unless they can show a managed campaign of merchandising exploitation and an expectation on the part of the buying public that goods emanate from that official source. The rights owner will always wish to stop the problem in its course by seeking an injunction prohibiting the sale of product until trial resolves the issues. The rights owner will argue that an injunction should be granted because damages are not an adequate remedy for the losses it will suffer.

(c) Copyright

A rights owner may have various copyright properties that are infringed if unauthorised use is made of them. This usually involves an infringement of copyright in photographs and other pictures or artistic works such as cartoon characters. A copyright infringement action is no use where the alleged infringement is of a name, as copyright does not protect a name, although it may protect quotations (as literary works) where these are used on merchandise or in general promotion of merchandise. The use of copyright material on merchandise is not limited to copying (by whatever means) of the exact same works: it can, in the right circumstances, also be used to protect an artist's own 'version' or copy of another artistic work. Although there is some latitude in the legislation to protect copyright owners from unauthorised reproduction of their work, it is still possible for any number of photographs to be taken by different photographers of the same event. Each photograph will probably have a different owner who may choose to licence its use to the unauthorised merchandise outfit. In such circumstances the copyright action could not be pursued and the rights owner should consider another remedy, such as passing off or trade mark infringement.

The unauthorised use of copyright material by an illicit merchandising operation is unlikely to take advantage of the fair dealing provisions of the copyright legislation, although other defences may be available. An important point for all sports rights owners to bear in mind is that if they are going to enforce or attempt to enforce a copyright that they actually own that copyright and that they can prove it.

(d) Other protection

There may be relevant trade descriptions offences similar to those available for unauthorised endorsements.[1]

6.4.3 The merchandising agreement

The heart of the merchandising agreement is the contractual licence between the rights owner and the merchandiser. The essential deal points of a merchandising agreement are similar to most other intellectual property deals with elements of a distribution contract thrown in for good measure.

(a) Parties

The parties to the agreement will usually be the rights owner (whether this is a governing body, league, club or individual) and the party wishing to exploit the

---

1   See **6.3.2**.

rights (commonly known as the licensee). Occasionally the rights owner may appoint an agent to exploit the rights on its behalf, in which case the agent may be a party to the contract and may even grant the rights. In any case the licensee should make some enquiries of the rights owner to ensure that there are some rights to grant. These will usually be a combination of intellectual property rights. If the only rights granted relate to the use of the name of the event or individual in question, and those rights are not registered trade marks, there may not actually be any protectable rights to grant. The rights owner is effectively relying on a passing off action to enforce its rights. Recent case-law makes it difficult to predict with any degree of certainty how such cases will be decided.[1] The merchandiser will be well aware of the vicissitudes of those actions and will be well advised to seek contractual assurances regarding the status of the rights and the rights owner's obligations to protect and enforce them diligently. Although the name itself may not be protectable, there may be other rights to grant such as copyrights in a logo or photographs. In the case of an individual there is also the right to call upon that individual's services. These rights will be similar to those granted in an endorsement agreement.

(b) Grant of rights

The contract should specify the exact rights that the rights owner wishes to grant. This may be a combination of copyright (words and pictures), registered Trade Marks and unregistered marks. There may also in appropriate cases be a grant of registered and unregistered design rights. The rights are usually defined as the 'Marks' or something similar and set out in a schedule to the agreement.

These rights are usually only granted for a particular specified category of products ('Products') which can be manufactured by the licensee. The definition of the products is central to both parties' intentions and should be carefully considered. The product category may be drawn very widely. If this is the case, the parties should both take care to ensure that they are receiving the rights to a category of products that they expect. The exact rights licensed must be defined in the agreement so the rights owner can, if it wants to, reserve other product categories for other merchandisers. This reservation of rights, coupled with a carefully, drafted product definition should enable the rights owner to maximise its revenue from different products, and also enable the merchandiser to maximise its own licensed exploitation of the rights.

The merchandising agreement then permits the licensee to combine the Marks with the Products to produce the 'Licensed Products'. These are the products which can be manufactured and are the subject matter of the agreement.

(c) Exclusivity

The next important issue for the parties is the issue of exclusivity. The rights owner must decide whether the licensee's grant of rights is exclusive or non-exclusive. There are a number of elements to this which need to be considered. An exclusive grant of rights can lock everyone else out of the market, including the rights owner. If this is the intention it may be limited in other ways such as to territory, or duration, or may even be conditional on certain sales and income targets.

---

1   See, for example, *Panini* case (1996) unreported.

The agreement will usually combine elements of exclusivity and non-exclusivity. The actual right to manufacture the licensed products may have to be non-exclusive. This is because many licensees will not actually manufacture the licensed products in the territory in which they go on to sell them. Many licensees appoint the cheapest manufacturers they can get away with, whilst also meeting the appropriate quality control standards set in the agreement. This tends to mean that the licensed products are manufactured abroad. This often means that they are manufactured in south east Asia, where it is cheaper to manufacture the merchandise. This allows other licensees to manufacture abroad or in the same territory without impinging on anyone's exclusivity.

The actual right to use the marks, and other intellectual property that is often licensed along with the marks, will also be non-exclusive since there will inevitably be other users of the same marks. Other users will include the rights owner who may use the marks in other contexts which will include its promotion and exploitation of the event itself. If there is any exclusivity in the agreement it usually only relates to the right of this particular licensee to use the marks on the licensed products. This means no other licensee can apply the marks to the same category of products. An exclusive licence is granted for the sale of the licensed products in the agreed territory for the duration of the agreement. No other licensee will be able to put the marks on those products. Accordingly, despite an exclusive licence the rights owner may still be able to reserve itself the right to conclude agreements in categories of product other than the licensed products within the same territory.

A non-exclusive grant of rights for the licensed products will allow the owner to appoint other merchandisers in the same and other product categories.

Another factor to consider with the exclusivity provisions of merchandising agreements are relevant provisions of EC and national laws which can threaten the grant of rights because of competition law problems and free movement of goods issues.

The exclusivity provisions may operate in respect of other agreements that the licensee may enter. The rights owner may try to limit the licensee's involvement with other sports or other teams.

(d) Territory
The agreement will usually specify a precise territory for its operation. The effect of this is twofold as it gives the licensee added exclusivity (within the limits of competition law) whilst allowing the rights owner to conclude identical arrangements with other licensees in other territories. The parties must draft these agreements carefully to comply with relevant competition and free movement of goods laws. In the EC, the ability of a rights owner to restrict its licensees to make sales outside their exclusive territories must not be unduly fettered. An absolute restriction on such sales offends EC law. The solution adopted in the Exclusive Distribution Agreement Block Exemption[1] allows passive unsolicited sales outside a licensee's exclusive territory. Active sales, or the establishment of a sales base in other territories, can be restricted by the rights owner in such distribution agreements. Although there is no similar exemption

---

1   Regulation 1983/83.

for merchandising agreements, drafting an agreement to comply with the terms of a relevant block exemption should help as should compliance with the relevant cases.[1] The agreement may also be de minimis in effect falling within the Notice of Agreements of Minor Importance.[2]

(e) Term

The agreement should set out how long it lasts. This may be a fixed period during which the licensee can manufacture the licensed products. The fixed period may be referable to the event in question and may end so many days after that event.

Equally, the duration of the agreement may be related to the recoupment of advances or guaranteed income under the agreement. If the licensee insists upon such a term (as it may be well advised to do where large recoupable but non-returnable advances and guarantees are concerned), the rights owner may wish to buy itself out of the agreement after a certain period of time has elapsed. This avoids the risk of the agreement continuing beyond the stage the rights owner wishes, perhaps into the next event staged.

The licensee may also wish to extend the term of a successful relationship. It may seek various options to extend the term. These options should, from the rights owner's point of view, be tied in to compliance with the terms of the agreement as well as the achievement of specified levels of financial performance by the licensee. The extended term can then include further advances and increased royalty payment and guarantee terms during the extended term. A well-advised licensee will wish to cap the level of any such advances just as the rights owner will want to place a minimum figure on them.

Alternatively the licensee may request a right of first negotiation or a matching rights clause to extend the term. The rights owner may wish to avoid such terms as it may be tied in to a company and relationship that is not, for any number of reasons, entirely satisfactory and does not leave it free to take its rights elsewhere.

The overwhelming objective of the licensee in its negotiations is to retain those rights which are profitable and to recoup any advance or fees it has paid the rights owner. The objective of the rights owner is to maximise its profits from exploitation of its rights and develop its rights as a 'brand' in a long term strategic manner. It may not wish to be tied into long-term deals and should retain some flexibility in its contracts to allow for this.

(f) Payment

It is usual for rights owners to receive a royalty on sales of licensed products. This royalty will be paid as a percentage of the sales price on total sales of products. The royalty may be a fixed percentage of the company's published retail price. An acceptable royalty rate for retail sales of merchandise is around 10–15% of the retail price. Alternatively, this may be a percentage of wholesale price, in which case the rights owner should receive an increased royalty. This price should not be subject to any deductions or discounts other than the deduction of VAT, if included in the sale price, and any other similar sales taxes.

---

1   *Re The Agreement of Davide Campari-Milano Spa* [1973] 2 CMLR 397.
2   OJ 1986 C–231/2.

The complex royalty calculations and reams of allowable deductions from sales figures and sales prices, adopted and raised to an art form in the music business, should be avoided in merchandising contracts.

Where royalties are concerned the company should not be allowed to sell products other than on an arms' length commercial basis. Discounts and sales to associated companies should not be reflected in a reduced royalty.

The rights owner may insist on an advance on signature of the agreement as well as guaranteed or minimum payment terms. These should operate as an additional incentive for the licensee to actively market the licensed products and exploit its rights. Alternatively, there may be a sliding scale royalty which may either increase or decrease as sales increase. The contractual advance and any guarantees payable are non-returnable but recoupable from sales of licensed product under the agreement. If the licensee pays the rights owner a fee on signing the agreement, this is not normally recoupable. It is a one-off payment in addition to any other payments under the agreement. This is not returnable or recoupable from royalty income. If the rights owner insists on a guarantee, it ensures that a minimum amount is paid by the licensee during the term of the agreement.

A licensee may require the term of the agreement to be tied to the recoupment provisions. For example, if at the time the agreement would normally come to an end the advance is not fully recouped from royalty income under the agreement, then the agreement does not end but continues until the advance is recouped. In such circumstances the rights owner should insist on a right to determine the agreement and buy the licensee out.

The licensee may seek to insert some additional warranties which require repayment of some elements of the advance or fee involved, if they are not met:

(1) if an event is not held or certain competitors do not compete in an event;
(2) if the anticipated audience does not appear;
(3) if there is no television coverage or a minimum number of hours of coverage is not reached.

If the rights owner is prepared to give any such warranties, they should be as limited as possible. Any sums the rights owner has to repay should also be limited and in no circumstances should the rights owner have to repay anything if payments are recouped.

The agreement must include some appropriate accounting provisions. These ensure the rights owner is accounted to by the licensee regularly and correctly. The company should account regularly to the rights owner by paying royalties due as well as maintaining detailed accounts of sales. The rights owner will also want the right to inspect or audit the company's relevant accounts should it wish to do so.

(g) Company's obligations

Manufacturing obligations

There are a number of terms the rights owner should impose on the licensee company: these are all aimed at securing matters such as the quality of the products as well as limiting the rights owner's liability for any defects in the products. These terms will also reflect various legislative requirements.

The licensee should be obliged to maintain product liability insurance for a minimum amount in respect of any one claim. The rights owner may want its interest noted on any such policy. The potential liability arises from particular legislation (such as the Sale of Goods Act 1979 and the Consumer Protection Act 1987) as well as common law rights and remedies which most consumers of the licensed products enjoy. The rights owner will normally require (in addition to the insurance) an additional full contractual indemnity from the licensee in respect of this liability. The risk to the rights owner being that due to the prominence of their marks on the licensed products they may be sued and will incur costs in defending any claim even if liability is ultimately established against the license or the licensee's manufacturer.

The rights owner should ask for an assurance that the licensee will not offer goods on sale or return and that there will be no financial reserves held against such goods.

The rights owner will insist that the licensee manufactures, promotes, distributes and sells the licensed products. Although the actual sale of products is something that the licensee cannot guarantee it takes the risk of there being no sales by offering non-recoupable advances and even guaranteed levels of income against its estimate of sales. If the licensee has to offer such financial terms to the rights owner to obtain the licence then it has plenty of incentive even without the sales obligations. The licensee will tend to make sure that it enters no more than a 'reasonable endeavours' obligation on some of these points.

As part of the rights package the rights owner may require a minimum advertising spend. This is similar to the obligation in a traditional distribution agreement and provides some further assurance for the rights owner that the merchandise actually reaches the market place.

The rights owner may insert a very general stipulation that the licensee exploits the rights and the licensed products to the best of its ability. Although such a clause is open to very wide interpretation, it may be particularised with other details.

The rights owner may forbid the distribution of any premium goods. These are usually free goods given out as part of a marketing campaign to the general public.

In addition to the obligation to actually manufacture the goods the rights owner should ensure that the licensee manufactures the licensed products to the highest standard and in accordance with all applicable rules and regulations. This wording covers product safety legislation as well as labelling requirements of local and national laws. If there are particular pieces of legislation that the rights owner is concerned about then it is best that these are specified in the agreement along with the general wording.

If the licensee appoints a third party to manufacture the licensed products, they will be required to promise that the licensee complies with all the restrictions in the terms of the agreement. The licensee may indemnify the rights owner against any defaults in the manufacturing process so must ensure they do so on approved terms.

Quality obligations

The rights owner should retain the right to approve all merchandise at each point in its design and manufacture. The licensee will usually have to submit the licensed products to the rights owner for specific approval. Although the agreement may contain terms stating that approval may be deemed to be given in certain circumstances or must not be withheld in certain circumstances the licensee must comply with the basic obligation. The rights owner will retain the right to alter or amend the licensed products up to manufacture as it sees fit. The rights owner may require an absolute discretion to do this or there may be provisions enabling the approval to be witheld on reasonable grounds.

The rights owner not only retains the right to approve the lay out and use of the mark but also the quality of the goods and products themselves. These must be of a minimum standard not only to comply with any relevant safety standards but also to protect the rights themselves. A loss of goodwill due to defective or substandard products could be serious for the long term exploitation of rights. Where a registered trade mark is concerned it is also very important for the rights owner to maintain quality control.

The licensee should submit the products for approval before manufacture. The rights owner should respond within a certain time. All new designs must be submitted for approval. A rights owner may want to inspect samples of products after manufacture, although it is always free to buy merchandise from retailers at its discretion.

The rights owners' right of approval should extend to all advertising and promotional material as well as the licensed products themselves.

The agreement will contain a number of terms dealing with these matters, for example the licensee may have to:

- manufacture the licensed products in accordance with a set of guidelines produced by the rights owner, these guidelines will set out in enormous detail exactly how the rights owners' marks can be reproduced;
- conform with the approved standard and the design of samples it has submitted;
- obtain written approval from the rights owner at each stage of design of licensed products and prior to manufacture;
- send samples of the licensed products to the rights owner at its own expense;
- label all licensed products with specified trade mark and copyright notices and some wording to specify that the licensed products are manufactured under licence of the rights owner;
- labelling in accordance with any other applicable rules and regulations;
- permit owner to inspect at any stage of manufacture and distribution.

Intellectual property rights

The agreement is essentially a licence of intellectual property rights, as such various intellectual property matters should be covered in the agreement. If the rights are infringed by unauthorised third-party use the rights owner and the licensee will want to ensure that action is taken. An exclusive licensee may be able to sue for infringements of certain intellectual property rights. For example, in the UK under both copyright and trade mark law an exclusive licensee, as well as the rights owner, has title to sue for infringement of the rights.[1]

An exclusive licensee may be obliged to sue infringers under the terms of its agreement with the rights owner although the licensee may retain the costs of the action and the sums recovered from any damages recovered. The protection of the rights is almost certainly central to the agreement as it prevents unauthorised products being sold.

Typically, the agreement is likely to include terms dealing with the following:

- the notification of any potential infringements and cooperation in any litigation;
- co-operation in securing any IP protection required;
- a term stating that if the merchandiser challenges any of the registered marks the agreement fails;
- the merchandiser cannot manufacture any products using similar marks for other people;
- the rights revert at the end of the agreement;
- enhancements and improvements to the rights are assigned to the rights owner.

There will also be general terms ensuring that the merchandiser does its utmost to protect the rights and does not denigrate them in any way.

Promotion and advertising obligations
The agreement may include various terms dealing with:

- the promotion of the licensed products (at its own cost);
- a prohibition on the active promotion outside the territory, set up outside the territory or advertise outside the territory although may meet unsolicited orders;
- a minimum level of advertising spending;
- rights owner must approve all promotional materials;
- rights owner has the right to use the promotional materials.

General warranties
The agreement may contain a number of general warranties which the rights owner and the licensee will promise each other. These mutual warranties are generally that:

- both parties are free to enter the agreement and have all the necessary rights and title to enter it;
- neither party has entered into any conflicting agreements;
- neither party shall hold itself out as representing the other or binding the other;
- neither party will do or omit to do or allow anything to be done to impair the rights.

---

1   CDPA 1988, ss 90, 91; TMA 1994, s 30.

Rights owner's obligations

Although the licensee has to do its part, it will expect some assurances from the rights owner that it will do its bit. There are a number of terms the company may seek.

In relation to the licensed intellectual property rights the rights owner will be required to maintain the rights and their registrations. These provisions will be similar to the provisions in the agreement dealing with intellectual property.

The licensee may require the rights owner to sue infringers of its marks. The rights owner may not want the licensee to sue infringers and may insist on retaining that right for itself. If it does so, the licensee will want some assurance that the rights owner will actually take action if infringers come to light. The rights owner will avoid an absolute obligation to take action and may only choose to do so in its absolute discretion, or if it receives a favourable legal opinion on the merits of a case. If the rights owner's action or inaction threatens the licensee's exclusivity, then it may have a separate contractual claim against the rights owner. The problem for the licensee, though, is that its sales may suffer as a result of the lack of action. This is a matter for negotiation.

The rights owner will have to approve the design of licensed products. These approvals and other steps should be done diligently and within time-limits set out.

If the licensee is to exercise the rights on the terms of the agreement, it will require full details of the licensed rights. The rights owner usually has to supply a set of delivery materials along with guidelines for their use. These guidelines are a type of style bible on the use of the marks. These will be used in the design of the licensed products.

(h) Termination

The agreement should specify the circumstances (other than through the passing of time) under which the agreement will end. These may be the termination provisions which are considered 'usual' in commercial agreements. These deal with, for example, insolvency and breach of the terms of the agreement, as well as the parties' opportunities to remedy such breaches and sometimes, further provisions depending on whether the breaches of agreement are of a serious or a minor nature.

A merchandising agreement may include additional terms include items dealing with:

–   failure to manufacture at all or a given number within a certain period of time;
–   abandonment of merchandising activities by the company.

(i) Effect of termination

Although the duration of the agreement may be referable to any number of factors the agreement must contain provisions stating exactly what will happen once the agreement does in fact come to an end.

The agreement is likely to end in two particular circumstances: it may end due to a breach of contract by either party, or it may end with the passing of time. The rights owner is likely to insist upon a number of provisions, as it needs to ensure that it can take its rights away 'clean' to offer elsewhere without any conflicting existing arrangements.

The agreement should specify exactly what happens with the manufacture and sale of licensed products immediately after termination. This is likely to vary depending upon the reason for termination.

If the agreement ends due to a breach of contract by the licensee then all its rights will immediately cease and it will have no right to sell off its products. All materials relating to the licensed rights should be paid immediately and there should be a final accounting to the rights owner.

If the agreement ends in the normal course, there will be provisions allowing the licensee to sell off the licensed products. In addition, during the last two or three accounting periods before the end of the agreement, the licensee should not be allowed to manufacture more than the average amount of licensed product it has manufactured previously during the agreement, to sell off after the agreement ends. This should solve the problem that can occur if the licensee over-manufactures and stockpiles licensed product for use during the sell-off period. Whilst the rights owner will not suffer financially, it may find that the products on the market are being discounted or dumped for short-term gains to the licensee. The rights owner may also face difficulties in appointing another licensee.

The licensee can sell off licensed products if the agreement ends simply due to the passage of time. During this period, the licensee is granted a non-exclusive licence allowing it to sell off its stock of licensed product. This period will usually last for the equivalent of one accounting period. Once this period has ended the sell-off right ends and the licensee usually has to destroy any remaining licensed products in its possession or control. The rights owner may require additional safeguards ensuring the licensee cannot (without the rights owner's permission) sell the products at a discount just to get rid of them. Some rights owners like the option to buy products at the end of the term, although they are unlikely to exercise this unless they know they can sell them on. It is also common for licensed products to be sent abroad for charities to use.

At the end of the contract period, the rights owner may want to licence another company to perform the same functions. The rights owner will want to be free to do so without breaching any terms of the previous agreement. Once the agreement has ended the company should return all materials supplied by the rights owner and agree that it can no longer manufacture the products. Any post-termination restrictions on the ability of the company to sell products will generally be unenforceable.

As a general rule, the owner may want to include terms dealing with the following:

- the delivery of accounting statements and payment of monies due at end of agreement;
- carry on accounting and paying dues for sell-off period;
- no excess manufacture prior to termination, then dumping goods on the market;

- where the agreement ends due to effluxion of time the merchandiser can sell off products for (eg) 90 days;
- if the agreement terminates for other reason the rights owner is entitled to immediate inventory, audit, full account and consider immediate delivery up of goods.

In any event, termination is likely to be without prejudice to the parties' rights. The merchandiser will also generally need to return any of the 'delivery materials' once the agreement terminates.

6.4.4   Merchandising licence agreement

DATE: [   ]

PARTIES:

(1)   [   ] of   ('Company')

(2)   [   ] of   ('Licensee')

IT IS AGREED as follows:

I   DEFINITIONS AND INTERPRETATION

     1.1   The following definitions apply in this Agreement:

'the Advance'	means [ ];
'the Agent'	means [ ] or such other agent as the Company appoints from time to time;
'the Contract Year'	means a 12 month period within the Term commencing with the first day of the Term or its anniversary date;
'the Delivery Date'	means [ ];
'the Delivery Materials'	means material relating to the Property short particulars of which are set out in Schedule 1;
'the Minimum Advertising Expenditure'	means [£];
'the Minimum Royalty'	means [£];
'the Term'	means [*two*] years commencing [*date*];
'the Licensed Product'	means any Product manufactured produced packaged sold or marketed by the Licensee its permitted assigns and sub-licensees derived from or incorporating any part of the Property and all activities of the Licensee which are advertised or promoted in connection with the Property;
'the Net Sales Revenue'	means 100% of all income derived from the sale of the Licensed Product in the Territory during the Term excluding sales taxes and value added taxes;
'the Product'	means [*define*];
'the Property'	means the fictional character known as [ ] and any associated characters featured in television cartoons and published works;
'Premiums'	means any item of Product offered to the public in connection with the sale or promotion of another product or service in such a way as to promote publicise and/or sell such other products services or their manufacturer or advertiser;
'Quarter'	means three calendar months expiring on a Quarter Date or such shorter period which shall run (a) from the commencement of this Agreement to the next Quarter Date or (b) from the last Quarter Date within the Term to the date of the expiry of the Term;

'Quarter Date'	means 31st March 30th June 30th September 31st December in any year;
'the Royalty'	means of Net Sales Revenue in respect of each item of Licensed Product sold during the Term and in no event less than the Minimum Royalty in each Contract Year during the Term;
'Territory'	means the UK.

1.2   Unless the context otherwise requires words denoting the singular shall include the plural and vice versa and words denoting any one gender shall include all genders and words denoting persons shall include bodies corporate unincorporated associations and partnerships.

1.3   In this Agreement where any provision refers to an obligation on the part of the Licensee to submit items for approval or make payment to the Agent on Company's behalf the obligation shall be to submit such items or make such payments directly to The Company if and with effect from the time when The Company shall notify the Licensee to this effect.

2   LICENSEE'S RIGHTS

2.1   In consideration of the Royalty and other payments to be made by the Licensee to the Agent on behalf of Company and subject to and conditional upon the full and timely performance and observance by the Licensee of all of the obligations warranties and undertakings of the Licensee contained in this Agreement Company grants to the Licensee a [non]-exclusive licence to manufacture the Licensed Product and the exclusive right to package market and sell the Licensed Product within the Territory during the Term.

2.2   The Licensee acknowledges that the Company is the owner of valuable goodwill which is attached to the reputation connected with the Property and its use in television cartoon programmes in literary works and in the promotion of a wide range of goods of high quality; and further acknowledges that the use of the Property which is permitted by this Agreement but for the rights granted hereby would or would be likely to constitute a misrepresentation by the Licensee to consumers which would inevitably cause substantial damage to the Company's aforementioned goodwill and business.

2.3   The Company undertakes to effect delivery of the Delivery Materials by no later than the Delivery Date.

3   QUALITY AND DESIGN OF LICENSED PRODUCT

The Licensee undertakes and agrees with the Company that:

3.1   The Licensee acknowledges that the reputation and goodwill of the Company is likely to suffer damage if any part of the Property is reproduced published or used otherwise than in connection with goods of high quality.

3.2   The Company shall make available to the Licensee such basic reference drawings photographs and models which are available to it and necessary to enable the Licensee to exercise its rights and fulfil its obligations under the Agreement.

3.3   It shall submit the Licensed Product, its packaging presentation and all matters relating thereto (including but not limited to all artwork and design) to the Agent who shall in turn submit the same to the Company for approval at all stages of development and production in accordance as far as reasonably practicable with the procedure set out in Schedule 2.

3.4 It shall not offer the Licensed Product for sale distributed to wholesale or retail outlets or otherwise marketed unless and until a reasonable number of production samples thereof together with all packaging and labels shall have been submitted pursuant to sub-clause 3.3 and final approval thereof given in writing. If final approval is withheld the Licensee shall be advised of the specific reasons in each case.

3.5 It shall carry out all artwork and design relating to the Licensed Product at its own cost.

3.6 The Licensed Product shall be of a high standard and of such style appearance and quality as to be adequate and suited to exploitation to the best advantage of the Property and to protect and enhance the value of the Property and the goodwill relating to it.

3.7 The Licensed Product shall be manufactured sold and distributed in accordance with all applicable laws in the Territory and the policy of sale distribution and exploitation by the Licensee shall be consistent with earning the highest possible royalties and making available Licensed Products at the highest possible standard so as not to reflect in any adverse manner on the good name of the Company or the Property.

3.8 Following approval of any sample or item pursuant to this Clause the Licensee shall not depart in any material respect from the quality of such sample or item in manufacturing the same or the Licensed Product without the prior written consent of the Company.

3.9 The Licensee shall from time to time as requested by the Company provide the Agent at the expense of the Licensee with samples of the Licensed Product to enable the Company to inspect and test the same.

3.10 It shall permit the Company (through its authorised representative) upon giving the Licensee reasonable notice and at its own expense to visit the premises of the Licensee during normal business hours to inspect the method of manufacture of the Licensed Product and the materials used and the packaging and storing of the Licensed Product.

3.11 The Licensee shall not alter the design or constitution of the Licensed Product without the prior written consent of the Company.

4   APPROVAL OF ADVERTISING

4.1 The Licensee acknowledges and agrees that the Company must maintain control over the manner in which the Property is used in advertising and that the Company must always be satisfied with the appearance of the Property and that the manufacturing or advertising concepts always remain within the range of good taste as reflected by the Property which includes the following:

4.1.1 the way the Property is drawn or appears; and

4.1.2 the use of the Property within a manufacturing or an advertising concept.

4.2 Accordingly the Licensee shall submit to the Agent on behalf of the Company for prior approval by the Agents on behalf of the Company in writing all marketing plans and all promotional and advertising materials relating to Licensed Products as to contents appearance and presentation. Before producing publishing or distributing any advertising materials hereunder the

Licensee shall submit to the Agent on behalf of the Company for approval by the Agent on behalf of the Company a sample thereof together with text colouring and any associated labels or packaging. If approval is withheld the Licensees will be advised of the specific reasons in each case.

4.3   If during the Licence Period any significantly unfavourable publicity or claim should arise or be made in relation to any particular item of advertising material the Company shall have the right to withdraw approval of such item of material and thereafter the Licensee shall discontinue the use or publication of that disapproved item of advertising material.

5   PRODUCT LIABILITY

5.1   The Licensee warrants that Licensed Products will be free from defects in workmanship and materials and safe and non-injurious to all persons who may use or have contact with them and shall indemnify the Company its officers employees and agents from and against all expenses damages claims actions judgments and costs whatsoever arising out of or in any way connected with any claim or action for personal injury death or other cause of action involving alleged defects in Licensed Products provided that the Licensee shall be given prompt notice of any such action or claim.

5.2   The Licensee shall at its own expense on behalf of itself and the Company in all parts of the Territory where the same is permitted carry product liability insurance in an amount which is not less than £500,000 and upon such other terms as the Company shall reasonably require and approve and shall upon request supply the Company with a copy of the relevant policy duly endorsed and with evidence that all premiums due have been paid. The Licensee shall do nothing which may in any way vitiate such policy.

5.3   The Licensee further warrants that the Licensed Products their packaging and getup and all promotional and advertising material will comply with all relevant laws regulations and codes of practice in the Territory and shall indemnify the Company in respect of any liability costs and expenses arising from any failure so to comply and in respect of any act or omission of the Licensee other than an act or omission which is expressly required of the Licensee by the terms of this Agreement.

6   MARKETING OF LICENSED PRODUCTS

The Licensee warrants undertakes and agrees with the Company that:

6.1   It shall use its best endeavours to ensure that the Licensed Products are well known and readily available to the public through retail outlets throughout the Territory by no later than the Target Date and thence throughout the Licence Period if the Licensee fails (in the reasonable opinion of the Company) to terminate this Agreement forthwith by notice to the Licensee to fulfil such obligation.

6.2   It shall use its best endeavours to exploit the Property and promote sales of the Licensed Products in all parts of the Territory and shall expend sums which shall at all times be sufficient to carry out its duties under this Agreement.

6.3   The Licensee shall refrain outside the Territory from seeking customers for the Licensed Products and from establishing any branch or maintaining any distribution depot in connection with the Licensed Products.

6.4   It shall maintain in the Territory such sales facilities as should ensure the most effective marketing of the Licensed Products and shall maintain a sufficiently representative and adequate stock of the Licensed Products to ensure a prompt and satisfactory response to customer demands.

6.5   The Licensee shall keep the Company informed of market conditions, competitive products and other factors material to the exploitation of the Property and marketing of the Licensed Products in the Territory.

6.6   The Licensee shall not without the consent of the Company in writing sell the Licensed Products as Premiums and shall not dispose of the Licensed Products otherwise than by wholesale or retail sale through normal wholesale and retail outlets and in particular shall not dispose of any Licensed Products by way of gift or as second-class or remaindered goods.

6.7   It is free to enter into and fully perform this Agreement.

6.8   It shall not do or omit to do or permit there to be done any act which may denigrate the value of or render invalid any right of copyright or other rights licensed under this Agreement or in any way detract from the value of the Property.

6.9   It shall at its own expense take all steps necessary to secure and protect the copyright and all other rights in the Property and the Licensed Product in the Territory and during the Licence Period in accordance with the directions (if any) of the Company.

6.10   It shall give full particulars to the Company on becoming aware of any actual or threatened claim by any third party in connection with the Licensed Product.

6.11   It shall advertise the Licensed Product throughout the Territory during the Term and shall expend in each year not less than the Annual Minimum Advertising Expenditure.

6.12   The Licensee shall ensure that the Licensed Product is given fair and equitable treatment and not discriminate in favour of any other property which the Licensee may have for distribution in the Territory.

6.13   No costs incurred in the manufacture sale distribution or exploitation of the Licensed Product shall be deductible from any sums payable by the Licensee.

6.14   Nothing in this Agreement shall or shall be deemed to prevent Company from granting licences in respect of the Property for products other than the Product.

6.15   The Company reserves to itself absolutely the right to use and/or manufacture Premiums.

6.16   The Licensee shall not harm misuse or bring into disrepute the Property the Licensed Product or any part of them.

6.17   The Licensee shall not knowingly manufacture or distribute any defective or sub-standard items of Licensed Product and shall ensure that all items of Licensed Product are of the highest attainable quality.

6.18   The Licensee shall punctually pay to the Agent on behalf of the Company all sums owing to the Company under this Agreement and in the event of any late payment all sums due shall bear interest in accordance with Clause 8.4.

6.19   The Licensee shall not assign charge license sub-license or otherwise part with possession of the benefit or burden of this Agreement without the prior written consent of the Company.

6.20   The Licensee shall indemnify and keep fully indemnified the Company from and against all actions proceedings claims demands costs (including without prejudice to the generality of this provision the legal costs of the Company or a solicitor and own client basis) awards and damages arising directly or indirectly as a result of any breach or non-performance by the Licensee of any of the Licensee's undertakings warranties or obligations under this Agreement.

7   ROYALTIES

7.1   The Licensee shall pay to the Agent on behalf of the Company:

7.1.1   the Advance on signature of the Agreement;

7.1.2   the Royalty within 30 days of each Quarter Date in accordance with the provisions of this Agreement.

7.2   The Advance is not refundable but may be recouped from the Royalty payable under Clause 7.1 in as far as these are sufficient.

7.3   The Licensee shall pay the Agent on behalf of the Company the Minimum Royalty in each Contract Year. If the Royalty payable in any Contract Year is less than the Minimum Royalty then (subject to the prior recoupment of the Advance) the Licensee shall pay the balance to the Agent on behalf of the Company within thirty days of the end of the Contract Year in question.

7.4   Any sales or disposals of Licensed Products by the Licensee to its associates or by way of promotional or other use shall be deemed to be sales at full value and shall be taken into account for the purpose of calculation of the Royalty payable to the Agent on behalf of the Company.

7.5   The Licensee may not withhold any sums due to the Agent on behalf of the Company as a reserve against returns and/or credits. If the Licensee is required by law to make any withholding from sums to be remitted to the Agent on behalf of the Company the Licensee shall prior to withholding such payment furnish the Company with evidence satisfactory to the Company as to the Licensee's obligation to make such withholding of payment.

7.6   If exchange control or other restrictions prevent or threaten to prevent the remittance to the Agent on behalf of the Company of any money payable under this Agreement the Licensee shall immediately advise the Company in writing and follow the Company's instructions in respect of the money to be remitted including if required depositing the same with any bank or other person designated by the Company at such location as may be designated by the Company.

7.7   If any withholding or other taxes are required to be deducted from any monies provided to be remitted to the Agent on behalf of the Company pursuant to this Agreement the Licensee must ensure that no improper deductions are made and that the Company is provided with all necessary receipts certificates and other documents and all information required in order to avail the Company of any tax credit or other fiscal advantage.

7.8   The Licensee shall keep confidential and shall not disclose to any third parties (other than professional advisers where necessary) any of the terms of this Agreement or any matters incidental thereto or relating to the business of the Company.

8   PAYMENT

8.1   The Licensee shall pay the Royalty due in respect of the Quarter ending on the Quarter Date within thirty days of the end of each Quarter Date calculated in accordance with the royalty report required under Clause 9.1 and accompanied by such report in all cases.

8.2   All payments shall be made and royalty reports sent to the Agent for and on behalf of the Company.

8.3   All payments shall be made in the relevant currency which shall be UK Pound Sterling unless otherwise stated.

8.4   Interest at 4 % above the base lending rate of [   ] Bank plc shall accrue from day to day before as well as after judgment on all payments from time to time outstanding under this Agreement and the Licensee shall pay such interest to the Agent on behalf of the Company at the same time as the payment in respect of which it has accrued.

8.5   All payments due hereunder are exclusive of Value Added Tax (VAT). All payments shall be accompanied by the appropriate VAT payment when made.

8.6   The Licensee shall in no circumstances be entitled to make any deduction from the payments due hereunder by way of set-off or otherwise in respect of any claim or counterclaim which it may have against the Company or the Agent.

9   ROYALTY REPORTS AND ACCOUNTING RECORDS

9.1   The Licensee shall send to the Agent on behalf of a royalty report in the form set out in Schedule 3 within thirty days of the end of each Quarter Date.

9.2   The Licensee shall keep full proper and up-to-date records relating to sales of the Licensed Products and shall allow the Company on no more than once in each Contract Year to carry out a full audit of the Licensee's accounts and records and a stock-take of Licensed Products on reasonable notice. Such audit and stock-take shall be carried out at the cost of the Company unless it discloses under-reporting by the Licensee resulting in underpayment in excess of 3% in any Contract Year and in such event the costs shall be paid by the Licensee.

9.3   The Licensee shall co-operate fully in any inspections audits and stock-takes carried out under sub-clause 9.2.

9.4   The Licensee shall inform the Company forthwith of any event or circumstances which may materially affect its ability to perform its obligations under this Agreement.

10   COPYRIGHT AND TRADEMARKS PROTECTION

10.1   The Licensee shall cause to be imprinted irremovably and legibly on each Licensed Product manufactured distributed or sold under this Agreement (included but not limited to advertising promotional packaging and wrapping material and any other such material wherein the Property shall appear) the following copyright notice: [insert] together with any additional notices which may be required by law within the Territory in order to protect the Licensed Product and the Property and in particular but without limitation all rights of copyright and trade mark in the Licensed Product and the Property. The Company may stipulate from time to time any other notices or credits which are to be so affixed incorporated or represented and the Licensee shall comply with all such stipulations reasonably made.

10.2   The Licensee shall promptly bring to the attention of the Company any unauthorised representation or imitation of any part of the Property or any improper or wrongful use or other infringement in the Territory of the copyright or other rights connected with the Property (including but not limited to the goodwill attached to the reputation connected with the Property) or any threat to do any of those things which may come to its notice and shall assist the Company in taking all steps (if any) which the Company may consider necessary to protect and defend such rights. The Licensee shall not take any action in respect of the same unless it shall have first sought and obtained the written consent of the Company.

10.3   The Licensee agrees to co-operate fully and in good faith with the Company for the purpose of securing or preserving the rights of the Company and to the Licensed Product and the Property.

10.4   At the termination or expiry of this Agreement the ownership of all rights licensed pursuant to this Agreement shall automatically revert to the Company and the Licensee shall execute any instruments required by the Company to confirm the foregoing.

11   INTELLECTUAL PROPERTY RIGHTS

11.1   No trade mark commercial description manufacturing symbol copyright slogan design or other property authorised hereby to be used in connection with the Licensed Product or goodwill connected therewith shall be or become the Licensee's property. The Licensee shall not be entitled to claim any rights or ownership in any of the above during or at any time after the Licence Period and will not register or arrange or seek to have registered in the Territory or elsewhere any trade mark trade description manufacturing symbol copyright slogan or design which is similar to or the same as or an imitation thereof.

11.2   The Licensee agrees that on termination or expiry of this Agreement the Licensee shall be deemed to have assigned transferred and conveyed to the Company any and all rights of copyright trade mark trade rights equity goodwill title or other right in and to the Property and the Licensed Product which may have been obtained by the Licensee or vested in the Licensee and the Licensee undertakes to execute any instruments requested by the Company to accomplish or confirm the foregoing.

11.3   The Licensee transfers to the Company by way of future assignment all such copyright and other rights referred to in Clause 11.2 together with any rights of the Company of whatever nature which may for whatever reason become vested in the Licensee so that and the Company has the right to licence such rights for gain or otherwise and the Licensee agrees to do all things which may become necessary to perfect such assignment.

11.4   The cost of all artwork to be used by the Licensee in connection with the Licensed Product shall be borne by the Licensee.

11.5   Without prejudice to the generality of this Clause all artwork developed by the Licensee in connection with the Property shall be assigned to the Company absolutely.

11.6   The Company shall have the non-exclusive and irrevocable licence in respect of all artwork produced by the Licensee to use such artwork in any Territory reserved by the Company or to licence the use of such artwork to other third party licensees of the Company and the Licensee acknowledges that it shall have no right in respect of the use of such artwork in any territories other than the Territory and the Company shall not be required to make any payments to the Licensee in respect of its use or the use by any third party of such artwork.

11.7   The Company shall have the right but not the obligation to use the name of the Licensee in any publicity or advertising relating to the Property or the Licensed Product.

11.8   The Licensee undertakes that it shall not during the Licence Period market manufacture sell or distribute any item or product of the description of the Licensed Product or any other product which may be similar to the Licensed Product.

11.9   The Licensee acknowledges that all existing and/or future goodwill in and to the Property the Licensed Product and any artwork associated with the same belongs or shall belong to the Company absolutely and that the Licensee has not now nor shall at any time in the future have any right title or interest in or to such goodwill.

12   DURATION AND TERMINATION BY NOTICE

12.1   Without prejudice to any other remedy for the breach or non-performance or observance of any of the Licensee's obligations hereunder the Company may terminate this Agreement forthwith by notice to the Licensee if:

12.1.1   the Licensee fails to make any payment hereunder in full on the date when it shall become due;

12.1.2   the Licensee commits a breach of any other of its obligations hereunder and shall not remedy such breach (if the same is capable of remedy) within 7 days of being required by notice to do so;

12.1.3   the Licensee is found on any inspection or audit materially to have under-reported sales on three or more occasions;

12.1.4   the Licensee is guilty of fraud or misconduct (whether or not in connection with this Agreement);

12.1.5   any indebtedness guarantee or similar obligation of the Agent or of any guarantor of the Licensee becomes due or capable of being declared due before its stated maturity or is not discharged at maturity or the Licensee or any guarantor of the Licensee defaults under or commits a breach of the provisions of any guarantee or other obligation (whether actual or contingent) of any agreement pursuant to which any such indebtedness guarantee or other obligation was incurred all or any of which in the reasonable opinion of the Company materially affects its rights and entitlements under this Agreement;

12.1.6   the Licensee is unable to pay its debts within the meaning of Section 123 of the Insolvency Act 1986;

12.1.7   the Licensee convenes a meeting of its creditors or progress or makes any arrangements or composition with or any assignment for the benefit of its creditors or a petition is presented or a meeting is convened for the purpose of considering a resolution or other steps are taken for the winding up of the Licensee or its estate (save for the purpose of a voluntary reconstruction or amalgamation previously approved in writing by the Company or if an encumbrancer takes possession of or a trustee receiver liquidator adminis-trator or similar officer is appointed in respect of all or any part of its business or assets or any distress execution or other legal process is levied threatened enforced upon or sued out against any of such assets;

12.1.8   the Licensee disposes of all or a substantial part of its business involving the sale of Licensed Products or abandons or announces that it intends to abandon the business of exploiting merchandising rights.

13   CONSEQUENCES OF TERMINATION

13.1   With effect from the termination of the Licence Period all rights of the Licensee to use the Property shall cease forthwith except as hereinafter expressly provided.

13.2   Licensed Products manufactured by or for the Licensee prior to the termination of the Licence Period may be sold by the Licensee the three calendar months following the date of termination provided that the Licensee shall have no such rights unless:

13.2.1   at least sixty days before the date of termination the Licensee sends a written statement of the number and description of Licensed Products which the Licensee reasonably believes will be in stock on the date of termination; and

13.2.2   the Licensee is not in default of any of its obligations hereunder on the date of termination; and

13.2.3   within fifteen days after the date of termination the Licensee sends the Company a written statement of the number and description of Licensed Products actually in stock on the date of termination and all tools moulds designs artwork and other materials then in the Licensee's possession or under its control; and

13.2.4   the quantity of Licensed Products in stock on the date of termination is not in excess of a reasonable quantity based upon the number of Licensed Products sold during the Term; and

13.2.5   the Licensee continues to pay to the Company; and

13.2.6   the Royalty is paid within fifteen days following the end of each calendar month with respect to sales made during such month.

13.3   At the end of any period applying under Clause 13.2 or otherwise at termination the Company may require the Licensee to redeliver to the Company or destroy all Licensed Products then existing and unsold and all tools moulds design artwork and other materials used in the manufacture of Licensed Products.

13.4   The Company may inspect the Licensee's premises in order to assess the accuracy of any statement supplied under Clause 13.2.1 or 13.2.3 above and/or to witness any destruction required under Clause 13.3.

13.35   The Company may within three months before expiry of this Agreement appoint the Licensee's successor or successors so that such successor(s) will be able to do business from the day after such expiry.

14   ADDITIONAL PROVISIONS

14.1   This Agreement contains all the terms agreed by the parties and no further or different terms shall have effect unless evidenced by a further agreement in writing signed by all the parties to be charged thereby.

14.2   This Agreement is personal to the Licensee which shall not assign or delegate all or any of its rights or obligations hereunder.

14.3   All notices given hereunder shall be in writing served on the relevant party at its usual trading or registered office address given in this Agreement or such new permanent address as shall have been notified to the other parties. Notices shall be deemed served on the next following working day (excluding Saturdays Sundays and Bank Holidays) if delivered by hand sent by telex or telecopier or handed in to a Post Office properly addressed and prepaid for transmission by first class post. In all other cases notices shall be deemed served when actually received. Any period of notice specified in this Agreement shall commence on the day of presumed service and shall be inclusive of Saturdays Sundays and Public Holidays.

14.4   Nothing in this Agreement shall imply a partnership [*or joint venture*] between the Company and the Licensee and the Licensee shall not hold itself out as the agent of the Company.

14.5   No failure or forbearance of either party to exercise any right conferred or to enforce any obligation imposed by this Agreement shall be deemed to be a waiver of any such right or obligation nor operate so as to bar or limit the exercise or enforcement thereof at any time thereafter.

14.6   The subject headings to the Clauses of this Agreement are for guidance only and are not intended to limit or restrict the wording of any clause.

14.7   This Agreement shall be subject to the law of England and Wales. The parties shall submit to the exclusive jurisdiction of the Courts of England and Wales.

SCHEDULE I

DELIVERY MATERIALS

SCHEDULE 2

ROYALTY REPORT – Quarter Ended

FROM:

TO: The Company

SECTION A: SALES OF LICENSED PRODUCTS DURING THE QUARTER

Product	Units Produced to date	Units sold to date	Units sold this Quarter	Unit price (excluding VAT)	Value of Sales this Quarter
I.					
2.					
3.					
4.					
5.					

SECTION B: ROYALTIES PAYABLE IN RESPECT OF THE QUARTER

(i)   TOTAL VALUE OF SALES THIS QUARTER (from Section A)   £.........

(ii)   ROYALTY RATE (Per Licence Agreement)   £.........

(iii)   GROSS ROYALTIES on Sales this Quarter (i $\times$ ii)   £.........

(iv)   less ADVANCE OUTSTANDING – brought forward from last Quarter   £.........

(v)   NET ROYALTIES on Sales this Quarter (iii – iv)   £.........

        VAT @ 17.5%   £.........

        TOTAL – PAYMENT ENCLOSED/TO FOLLOW   £.........

SECTION C: ADVANCE OF ROYALTIES OUTSTANDING

Original Advance paid (excluding VAT)   £.........
Total Gross Royalties – all Quarters to date   £.........
Advance outstanding – carried forward to next Quarter   £.........

I Certify on behalf of the Licensee that this Report is true and correct

SIGNED   DATE:

NAME: STATUS:

Signed for and on behalf of
the **Company** by

Signed for and on behalf of the
Licensee by

6.5   COMMERCIAL CONFLICTS AND AMBUSH MARKETING

6.5.1   Introduction

It is right to say that competition in sport is not restricted to the field of play. Each participant in the commercial business of sport wishes to maximise its own commercial advantages from its association with the sport in question. Although one level of balance needs to be struck between the various competing interests there are also very real issues which create tensions between the organisers of sports, its commercial partners, participants and other interested parties with their own commercial imperatives.

The tension in sports between governing bodies, event organisers and participants is simply explained. For example, if one considers an event such as a league competition (whether it is in football, rugby or another popular sport) there will be a whole number of contracts in commercial relationships which deal with the day-to-day running of the event as well as the sophisticated relationships between the sport and its commercial partners. The governing body or organiser of the competition is likely to appoint, with the authority of its members, a number of commercial partners who will include sponsors, merchandisers, broadcasters and may include official publications and an official photographic agency. The participating clubs will also pursue their own commercial interests and this will involve them appointing their own shirt sponsors, their own merchandising company and, in certain circumstances, they may also deal with the creation and distribution of videos of their matches and also establish their own web sites.

It is up to all the interested parties in the competitive and the commercial side of sport to reach an accommodation that suits and reflects their respective commercial interests. Such an accommodation must be carefully managed so that it is also legally effective and does not contravene any intellectual property, restraint of trade or competition laws.

It is these latter factors that can cause insurmountable problems to governing bodies that wish to tightly regulate the competitive and commercial activities of their members, and also to pursue their own commercial interests which ensure continued viability of the governing body, the events that it sanctions and produces sufficient surplus to reinvest in the sport at every level.

It is a situation which everyone involved in the commercial side of sport is all too aware of: the prospect of a sponsored event's participating clubs, themselves sponsored, taking part in a live broadcast which itself is a broadcast sponsor. It is also possible that the stadium in which the event takes place is sponsored and it may even have its own 'pourage' agreement with a brewer or soft drinks company who may itself be a competitor of the sponsors of one of the participating teams. It is of course also extremely likely that the individual players will have their own appointed sponsors and commercial programmes which may, in certain sports, rival the commercial activities of their clubs. The likelihood of all these competing interests being regulated and subject to a single arbiter who will decide whose commercial interests come first and who may undertake what commercial activities on and off the field of play, is unrealistic and within the European Community, is almost certainly unlikely to be enforced on the basis that it is anti-competitive. However, attempts by rights holders (meaning anyone with the ability to grant rights to the commercial partner) and their commercial partners to protect their own interests by ensuring a certain level of exclusivity is quite proper and may usually be regarded as legitimate even if it is scrutinised by competition authorities.

Regulating these intricacies is exceptionally difficult and mainly impractical. Certain events, such as the Olympics, ensure that within the stadium or in competition no sponsors or commercial partners are permitted any exposure. All their branding and promotional activity must take place outside the arena. The Olympics is virtually unique in this regard, although other major competitions will seek to impose a certain amount of uniformity on their participants whilst they are actually in competition, by means of a participation agreement, or else by ensuring that the rules and regulations of membership set out appropriate, enforceable restrictions.

Whether these restrictions are put in place in a participation agreement or in rules and regulations they should cover some or all of the following points:

- the use to which intellectual property owned by the event organiser may be put;
- any relevant restrictions on the participants' ability to bear their sponsors names or logos on their clothing or footwear which they wear in competition;
- an obligation to co-operate with the event owners' own commercial programme (to use certain specified products during and after the event);
- an obligation not to compete with the event's commercial programme or its individual sponsors;
- an obligation to appear at press conferences and post-match and post-event interviews and other hospitality functions;
- the grant of permission from the competitors to appear in broadcast footage of the event and (where appropriate) their permission to use their performances in any video or other exploitation of such broadcast footage;
- permission to use their name and likeness for inclusion in event literature, programmes and (possibly) promotional items solely associated with the event although not usually with the endorsement of or so as to imply an endorsement of the event's commercial partners;
- the participant's ticket entitlement and any restrictions on the resale or other use (for example in competitions) to which such tickets may be put;
- any fee, participation monies, expenses or a share of profits which its participants are entitled to receive;
- what commercial activities the participants may undertake of their own, the extent to which they can use intellectual property rights owned by the event owner and the extent to which they or their own commercial partners can claim any association with the event.

There may be other matters which could be included in such agreements but some or all of those would, if used in a sensible and limited way, provide a degree of comfort for commercial partners of major events.

Such an integrated approach is not practical for all but the top level international sporting events such as the football World Cup or the Rugby World Cup. Instead, most of the day-to-day business of sport such as league and cup competitions operates more or less as a commercial free-for-all. The degree to which any individual sponsor receives exclusivity to the extent that it can completely prohibit its competitors from being associated in any official capacity with the event organiser or any of its participants is extremely limited. Any game of the FA Premier League illustrates the tremendous tension between these competing interests. Indeed the extent to which an agreement reached between the clubs which control that league and the League's ability to grant broadcast rights and rights to other commercial partners has been challenged in the Restrictive Practices Court and illustrates the tremendous difficulties that sport faces in regulating its commercial activities even where it has a will to do so. It is not only the internal conflicts which can cause problems but also external forces such as competition law can lead to a legal challenge to the whole basis upon which commercial rights are owned and exploited.

6.5.2   Ambush marketing

Ambush marketing tends to contrast with the general run of commercial conflicts in sport in that it consists of the unauthorised association by businesses of one of more elements of their business (usually their name, trade mark or a particular product or service which they supply) with an event, team or individual. At its most blatant, ambush marketing (also known as parasitic marketing) takes the form of an actionable legal wrong such as trade mark infringement or passing off. There may also be trade descriptions offences which can be dealt with by Trading Standards offices and rights owners acting in unison. Ambush marketing operates by claiming or inferring a false relationship between a rights owner (whether it is a governing body or another participant in sport) without that rights owner's permission. The rights owner's permission usually takes the form of a contractual relationship which will be individually negotiated in return for rights fees. These activities are invariably undertaken by competitors of an event's 'official' commercial partner and tend to take place before, during and to a limited extent after a particular event. Obviously, where events are ongoing such as with league and cup competitions such strategies tend to be focused on particularly important parts of the season. Ambush marketing may take any number of forms but essentially it is an attack on the exclusivity which most commercial partners of a sport seek and will to a limited extent obtain.

6.5.3 Examples of ambush marketing

(a) Unauthorised use of intellectual property rights

This may involve the manufacture and sale of merchandise products bearing the name and logo of the event or of some or all of the participants in the event. Typically, an event organiser and some of its participants will appoint an official kit supplier who will be authorised to use identified intellectual property rights (typically registered or unregistered trade mark). The unauthorised supplier will effectively infringe these rights by illegally selling their own infringing merchandise. The remedies for such action tend to be an application for an injunction in the civil courts or else search and seizure using the various criminal remedies contained in trade mark and copyright legislation in the UK and abroad.

(b) Advertising

Advertising is a useful medium in which to 'ambush' an event. The bulk purchase of advertising in selected media in and around an event by an 'unofficial' supplier seeking to take advantage of the name and reputation of the event is relatively straightforward. Indeed, such advertising need not even make specific reference to the event, but just to the sport or activity involved. Such reference is unlikely to infringe any intellectual property right but, if well managed by the ambusher, can result in a high identification on the part of the public with that advertiser and the sport or event in question.

Many important events will attempt to tie up advertising at a stadium, advertising on the route to and in the vicinity of the stadium as well as, to the extent permissible and possible, broadcast advertising. It is broadcast advertising which, if bought up by an unofficial supplier can saturate the official sponsor's exposure. In such a situation, there is unlikely to be any legal remedy unless the advertiser oversteps the mark. The best action tends to be preventative. That is to say, appropriate contractual obligations should be obtained by the rights holders to limit the sale of advertising space to competitors in and around events and, wherever possible, to offer a first option to official partners to broadcast advertising. Although great care must be taken by all the parties involved to avoid any competition or problems intrinsic in such extensive and exclusive arrangements it should be possible and is certainly desirable to do so.

(c) Broadcast sponsorship

Although broadcast sponsorship is increasingly coming within the control of rights owners who tend to deal with such rights when negotiating broadcast contracts, it remains a very effective way of ambushing the event without actually being an official partner of the event itself. Broadcast sponsorship can diminish and in the right circumstances even negate the value of event sponsorship. The most obvious solution to avoid this is to ensure that all the rights in broadcast events are dealt with together, at least giving an events sponsor the opportunity to cover the transmission and be its broadcast sponsor if it wants. If it chooses not to do that then a simple restriction ensuring that no competitor of the event sponsor can be the broadcast sponsor should provide the degree of comfort required.

(d) Joint promotions

Another more subtle form of ambush marketing can involve joint promotions between official sponsors and other businesses who have not paid to be a commercial partner. For example, the joint promotion between the official airline of an event and an insurance company of its choice could also give the impression that the insurer is an official supplier to the event. Joint promotions between official partners and any third parties are usually dealt with in the sponsorship agreement.

(e) Competitions and promotions

Although competitions and promotions between rights owners or official partners and other commercial partners are quite common, unauthorised competitions and prize promotions represent a useful and valuable method of exploiting the goodwill of an event or a sport. It is quite difficult to control many competitions and prize promotions as they may be little more than generic in their scope; ie, they are simply football competitions or rugby prize promotions and bear no relation to a particular event, except for the fact that they share a sport in common. Again, these situations are unlikely to give rise to an actionable legal wrong.

(f) Pourage agreement

The sale of products at events is a useful and high profile way for certain types of potential sponsors (usually soft drinks and fast food suppliers) to both raise their profile in association with a sport and also to sell products. A 'popular' form of ambush marketing (although it is perhaps not properly viewed as such) involves a commercial tie up between such a supplier and the owners of a venue. It is often the case that a rights owner will not own the venue where its competition takes place, so it must ensure that its agreement with the venue owner provides a 'clean' venue. The one category where this is likely to be very difficult to achieve is in the category of pourage agreement, where venues tend to conclude longer term agreements which provide certain commercial advantages to them. These are often in the nature of franchise or concession stands which are expensive to set up and maintain, and very often venue owners are not equipped or willing to manage such premises other than by such arrangement.

The important point for rights owners and their official partners is to ensure that the grant of such franchise or concessions does not go hand-in-hand with a grant of other commercial rights over the venue such as the right to re-name or the right to place a large number of advertising hoardings at the venue.

(g) Corporate hospitality and ticketing

A seemingly innocuous method of ambushing an event is to buy up tickets for the event and offer hospitality packages which are not being sanctioned or approved by the rights owners, who usually keep a tight control over such activities. The ability to control tickets and corporate hospitality is often an integral part of the attractiveness of an event to its official partners, who regard it as an important part of their package of rights and, effectively, an important competitive tool and method of 'oneupmanship' over their business rivals. Fortunately for rights owners and commercial partners, such unofficial activities do not tend to involve a significant misappropriation of the goodwill of an event.

Effectively ambush marketing takes two forms. The first is the ambush which arises from genuine 'commercial' conflicts of rights, such as those which arise between the competitors in an event and the rights holder to the event itself. As has been noted above, there is an inherent tension in these arrangements which can be effectively managed with appropriate contractual terms. The second type of ambush marketing is the unauthorised marketing that attempts, as outlined above, to associate itself with and appropriate the goodwill of the event – this usually occurs where none of the 'rights holders' in the event has sanctioned or approved the activities in question.

6.5.4   Combating ambush marketing

The types of contractual controls which have already been mentioned can regulate the commercial conflicts between rights holders, participants, venue owners, broadcasters and all commercial partners.

It is also very important that all rights holders have an active policy of the registration and protection of all intellectual property rights associated with an event. These rights will typically be trade marks (whether registered or unregistered); appropriate copyrights (such as in broadcast footage and photo-graphs of an event) and, increasingly, the registration of an Internet site with the domain name of the event. Coupled with such intellectual property rights, all relevant contracts should contain obligations to use such intellectual property rights only in an agreed manner. It is usually the case that all intellectual property rights can be used only with the prior approval of the relevant rights owner. There should also be mechanisms in place to police the intellectual property rights and for all parties concerned to notify each other whenever any infringement of the relevant intellectual property rights comes to their attention. Although it is unlikely that the intellectual property rights owner will require anyone that notices an infringement to actually take action, the rights owners almost invariably require some notification of any such infringement.

It is the development of a strategy relating to intellectual property and all other aspects of the event which should ensure utmost value to the official commercial partners and hinder the attempts of a sport's illegitimate partners to take advantage of its good name and reputation. Essentially, rights owners need to control everything from the car park through to the broadcast. In this context the remainder of this section considers the common terms and provisions of a number of sports marketing agreements.

6.6   CHARITABLE FUND RAISING

6.6.1   Introduction

The relationship between charitable giving, sponsorship and sports events is a developing area. Charitable fund raising is as competitive an environment as sport and sports sponsorship itself. The opportunity for a charity to involve itself with a sports event can be as sought after as the rights to sponsor the event itself.

There are a number of events within Great Britain that actively encourage charitable participation. This participation has developed in two main ways, through place pledge schemes for charities and by means of direct agreements between an event, its sponsors and a particular charity to raise monies and make donations to the charity concerned.

6.6.2   Place pledges

The place pledge scheme involves very few formalities. A place pledge involves a charity buying a certain number of places in an event for its fundraising competitors. These schemes are typically used in mass participation events such as the London Marathon, where charities can buy up places in advance of the event guaranteeing their chosen participants a place in the event. The charity pays the organiser, who guarantees the place. The charity finds the competitor, who then agrees to compete in the event and to raise a minimum level of sponsorship donations from friends, colleagues, local businesses and any other source it can find. These schemes work well, although the event organiser should build some safeguards into the place pledge agreement.

The place pledge agreement should set out some of the following terms:

- the amount of money;
- the number of guaranteed places;
- the position if the charity cannot find enough 'volunteers' to participate;
- the position if the event is cancelled;
- permission and any obligations on the charity to use the event name and logo to publicise the charity's place pledges;
- any limitations on the charity's use of the event name and logo;
- the extent to which the charity can grant any commercial rights of sponsorship over its place pledges; and
- whether the place pledges can be assigned to other charities.

6.6.3   Charitable fund raising from events

The other aspect of charitable involvement in sports events is the fund raising element. An event organiser may wish to appoint particular charities to receive charitable donations received by the event and to conduct fund raising of its own.

The control of fund raising and giving to 'charitable institutions' is governed by Part II of the Charities Act 1992. A 'charitable institution' is:

> 'a charity or an institution (other than a charity) which is established for charitable, benevolent or philanthropic purposes.'[1]

The Act prohibits professional fundraisers from soliciting monies for charity and commercial participators from representing that contributions will be given to or applied for the benefit of charitable institutions unless there is an agreement in place with the charity concerned. This agreement must be on the prescribed terms. An organisation that fails to comply with the Act is committing an offence and liable on summary conviction to a fine not exceeding level five on the standard scale.[2] There is a due diligence defence to such charges.[3]

---

1   Charities Act 1992, s 58.
2   Ibid, s 60(7).
3   Ibid, s 60(8).

Where event organisation and fundraising is concerned, the provisions relating to 'commercial participators' are most likely to be relevant. A 'commercial participator' is:

> 'in relation to any charitable institution ... any person who – (a) carries on for gain a business other than a fund raising business, but (b) in the course of that business, engages in any promotional venture in the course of which it is represented that charitable contributions are to be given to or applied for the benefit of the institution.'[1]

A 'promotional venture' is any form of advertising or sales campaign or any other venture undertaken for promotional purposes. A 'charitable contribution' is defined in s 58 and means:

(a) the whole or part of consideration for goods or services sold or supplied by or any proceeds [other than such consideration] of a promotional venture undertaken by [a commercial participator]; or

(b) sums given by [a commercial participator] by way of donation in connection with the sale or supply of any such goods or services [whether the value of the donation is calculated by reference to the value of the goods or otherwise].

The Scheme of the Act is of very broad application and may apply whenever a business advertises the fact that it is involved with a charity. It does not just apply to event organisers (who are clearly caught by the Act) but also to their sponsors, if the sponsors are promoting the fact that they are making charitable contributions. This may cover the packaging of goods as well as advertising campaigns for the event itself. Accordingly, the sponsors, as well as the event organiser, may have to be party to an agreement in the prescribed form if they are to avoid committing an offence.

There are additional requirements for commercial participators representing that charitable contributions are to be given or applied for the benefit of charitable institutions. The representation must state the name of the institution concerned and in relation to consideration for the goods or services concerned the following:

– (if there is more than one institution) the proportion each will receive;
– the proportion of the consideration or proceeds of the promotional venture that is to be applied for the benefit of the institution concerned or the amount of the donation given.[2]

The Charitable Institutions (Fund-Raising) Regulations 1994 were made under the Charities Act 1992 and came into force on 1 March 1995. An agreement made between a charitable institution and a commercial participator must be in writing and signed by or on behalf of both parties[3] and must state:

– the name and address of the parties;
– the date of the agreement;
– the duration of the agreement;
– any early termination provisions;
– any terms relating to variation of the agreement;

---

1   Charities Act 1992, s 58.
2   Ibid, s 60(3).
3   Ibid, s 3(2).

- the principal objectives of the agreement;
- the amount the institution will receive; and
- provisions relating to any remuneration or expenses for the commercial participator.[1]

If there is more than one charitable institution involved, the amount or proportion of donations each will receive must be set out; as must the proportion of the price for goods and services sold or supplied or the amount of the donation.

It is possible that an event organiser or sponsor could be caught by the provisions of the Act relating to 'professional fund raisers'. Such a person is someone (other than a charitable institution) who: (a) carries on a fund raising business; or (b) any other person who for reward solicits money or other property for the benefit of a charitable institution.[2] The term 'solicits' is defined very widely by s 58(6) and covers direct communication as well as published statements in newspapers and broadcasts or otherwise. Whilst most sponsors and event organisers will not be carrying on a 'fund raising business' within the meaning of the Act, they may be caught by the Act on the basis that some of the proceeds of the event are going to good causes and that they solicit such contributions. A 'whiter than white' approach is recommended.

The form of the agreement between the charitable institution and the professional fundraiser is similar in form to the agreement with the commercial participator.

---

1   Charities Act 1992, s 3(3) and s 3(4).
2   Ibid, s 58.

6.6.4   Form of agreement

DATE: [   ]

PARTIES:

(1)   [   ] whose registered office is at [   ] ('the Organiser'); and

(2)   [   ] of [   ] ('the Charity')

RECITALS:

A.   The Organiser is the owner organiser and promoter of the Event in respect of which members of the public may through sponsorship and other means raise funds for charitable purposes.

B.   The Charity wishes to be and have been selected by the Organiser as the principal beneficiary of the Event upon the terms of this Agreement.

C.   The Organiser will receive donations from participants, members of the public and other sources some of which will be donated specifically to the Charity and some of which will not specify a recipient and be unallocated donations.

OPERATIVE PROVISIONS:

I   **INTERPRETATION**

   1.1   In this Agreement the following terms have the following meanings:

   'Costs'   all costs and expenses incurred by the Organiser in the administration management co-ordination and promotion of the Event.

   'Event'   [   ].

   'Funds'   the monies raised by Participants and members of the public generally for the Charity and received by the Company for distribution to the Charity (which for the avoidance of doubt does not include the entry fees to the Event paid by the Participants or any income arising from the exploitation of commercial rights relating to the Events) including interest (if any) arising thereon but less bank charges relating to the running of the Trust Account.

   'Participants'   members of the public who complete the entry requirements for and participate in the Event.

   'Payment Period'   the period from date of signature of this Agreement.

   'Payment Date'   the seventh working day of each month during the Payment Period.

   'Receipt Period'   the period ending on the last day of the month immediately preceding the month in which the Payment Date occurs.

   'Statement of Account'   a statement of account prepared by the Organiser setting out the amount of the Funds and the entitlement of the Charity as the end of the Term.

   'Term'   the period of this Agreement as set out in Clause 2.

   'Trust Account'   a separate nominated joint deposit account with a first class clearing bank in the name of the Organiser in which the Funds shall be held on trust for the Charity and from which distributions to the Charity shall be made in accordance with the terms of this Agreement.

2   TERM

With the exception of the continuing obligations contained in Clause this Agreement shall remain in force for a period commencing on the date of signature of this Agreement and ending on [   ].

3   OBJECTIVES

3.1   The Organiser shall organise the event on a fully commercial basis and make every reasonable effort to maximise the benefit for the commercial exploitation of rights to the Event.

3.2   The Organiser selects the Charity as beneficiary of the Event upon the terms set out in this Agreement. The Organiser undertakes (1) that no part of the Funds shall be applied in payment of the Costs and (2) that the Funds shall be paid exclusively to the Charity.

3.3   The Organiser will encourage the Participants to make charitable donations either directly to the Charity or by sending donations to the Organiser specifying the Charity as the recipient of the donations.

4   FUNDS

4.1   The Organiser irrevocably undertakes to pay the Funds into the Trust Account.

4.2   The Organiser shall pay the Charity all donations received by it which specifically nominate the Charity as the recipient of the donation.

4.3   The Organiser shall immediately forward to the Charity cheques it receives which are specifically made payable to the Charity.

4.4   The Organiser undertakes to pay the Charity all unallocated charitable donations received by the Organiser from Participants and from any other source.

4.5   On each Payment Date the Organiser shall:

4.5.1   submit a separate statement to the Charity setting out in respect of the Receipt Period (1) the Funds received by the Organiser and paid in the Trust Account and (2) the net amount of Funds payable to the Charity.

4.5.2   pay to the Charity its unpaid share of the Fund in respect of the Receipt Period.

4.6   Within twenty-eight days of the end of the Term the Organiser shall submit to the Charity the Statement of Account and pay the remainder of the income due during the Term.

4.7   The Organiser shall pay the Charity share of any Funds received after the end of the Term to the Charity at the end of each consecutive twenty-eight day period following the end of the Term.

5   RECORDS AND ACCOUNTING

The Company shall at its own expense keep full records and accounts of the Funds and shall prepare the Statement of Account.

6   THE CHARITY'S OBLIGATIONS

The Charity shall comply with all laws and regulations directly applicable to its support of the Event and in particular all the requirements of the Charities Acts 1992 and 1993 and all regulations made thereunder.

7   THE ORGANISER'S OBLIGATIONS

The Organiser shall undertake the organisation and management of the Event in an efficient manner and in accordance with good business practice and comply with the requirements of the Charitable Institutions (Fund Raising) Regulations 1994.

8   FORCE MAJEURE

Neither party shall be liable to the other for any loss or damage costs expenses or other claims for compensation arising as a direct or indirect result of breach or non-performance of its obligations under this Agreement due to any cause beyond either party's reasonable control including without limitation to any act of God war military operations riot accident failure or shortage of power supplies abnormally inclement weather fire flood hurricane drought explosion lightning strike lock out trade dispute or labour disturbance the act or other competent authority.

9   NOTICES

Any notice to be served under this Agreement shall be in writing and served upon the recipient at its address set out herein either by hand or by first class post or telex or facsimile and shall be deemed served forty-eight hours after posting if sent by post on delivery if delivered by hand on receipt of correct answer back if sent by telex and on completion of transmission if sent by facsimile.

10   CONFIDENTIALITY

It is mutually agreed that the content of this Agreement will not be disclosed to any third party other than to either party's professional advisers or as may be required by law or as may be agreed between the parties.

11   JURISDICTION AND LAW

This Agreement is made in England and the cnstruction validity and performance of this Agreement shall be governed in all respects by English Law and each party hereby submits to the non-exclusive jurisdiction of the Courts of England.

SIGNED by   )
for and on behalf of   )
in the presence of:)

SIGNED by   )
for and on behalf of   )
in the presence of:)

CHAPTER 7

SPORTS AGENTS

7.1 INTRODUCTION TO SPORTS AGENTS

Managers, agents and consultants of various types are closely involved in the day-to-day running and marketing of sport. The services provided cover the full range of sports management, sports marketing, media and press relations as well as general sports business consultancy. This chapter will consider two particularly important relationships: the sports personality manager and the commercial rights agent. These are both important roles within the sports industry, based on a contract to provide certain services to individuals, rights holders and investors, such as sponsors, in sport.

The first part of the chapter considers the role and contractual terms offered by managers to individuals within sport. Sports personality managers are often also referred to as sports agents and, to most intents and purposes, fulfil the same role. They are the 'fixers' for their clients and the first port of call for anyone wanting to deal with their client. They may handle the day-to-day affairs of their clients and negotiate all their contracts.

The role of the commercial rights agent is similar in concept. The agent is appointed to represent the commercial interests of its clients. The clients may be actual or potential sponsors, the rights holders in an event, a team, a governing body or a stadium owner. An agent is appointed to help this person maximise an investment, either by way of the return to their investors, or in terms of income for the rights holder.

SPORTS PERSONALITY MANAGEMENT

7.2 INTRODUCTION

This section considers the need for and role of a manager in the development and representation of a sportsman. In particular, some of the more common terms of management agreements will be considered, together with the more usual pitfalls.

7.3 CHOICE OF BUSINESS MEDIUM

It is important that the business side of a sportsman's career is managed professionally. All individuals involved in the sports business must manage their affairs as well as possible, and, in particular, to the satisfaction of the Inland Revenue, to avoid any problems. All income should be accounted for, as should all items of expenditure.

One of the initial considerations relates to the choice of business medium. An individual could consider running his affairs as a sole trader or a company. This aspect of a sportsman's affairs is usually tax driven. It is quite common for individuals to set up service companies which are wholly owned by them. In many cases the individuals may only use the company for promotional activities, especially where they are full time employees of a club and the sports governing body (as in football) prohibits the use of service companies by players contracted to play for clubs. Where an individual does use a service company, it is quite common for sponsors and other third parties to insist on a side letter from the individual confirming that he agrees to be bound by the terms of the agreement. Alternatively, the individual may need to be party to the agreement, although the tax position must be carefully examined in all such cases.

7.4 APPOINTMENT OF A MANAGER

7.4.1 Why appoint a manager?

A good manager has experience of management, good contacts within the sports business, will promote the sportsman and take active control and supervision of the sportsman's business affairs. Depending upon the terms of appointment, the manager will be responsible for all aspects of the sportsman's career. This commonly involves negotiating and agreeing terms for all the sportsman's contracts and business affairs.

7.4.2 Role of a manager

The manager may act as an agent for the sportsman. The relationship is one based on mutual trust and confidence and fidelity. A manager performs a personal service for a sportsman and acts on his behalf in dealings with third parties.

A manager's main concern is to find work for the sportsman. Ideally, this will be lucrative work entailing the negotiation and signing of employment, sponsorship, merchandising and television contracts, followed by the successful promotion and exploitation of the sportsman.

Prior to the appointment of a manager, both parties should be separately represented. There have been a number of cases where management contracts have been successfully challenged on the basis of undue influence being exercised by the manager over the artist or because arrangements have been in restraint of trade. If the sportsman obtains independent legal advice at this stage before signing an agreement with a manager, it should ensure both that the agreement is less open to challenge at a later stage and also that the terms negotiated on the sportsman's behalf are not unduly restrictive or financially onerous.

If a sportsman is keen to sign an agreement contrary to advice, the legal adviser should record his advice in writing and, if necessary, particularly onerous clauses should be drawn to the attention of the sportsman to avoid any liability at a later stage. If a management agreement is subject to analysis by a court, the availability and experience of the advice may be a major factor in the court's decision. A well-advised sportsman warned against an onerous contract would find it difficult to set the contract aside.

Despite the foregoing, it remains a fact that many managers and agents never sign any form of agreement with their clients. The relationship is based entirely on a handshake and the continued goodwill of both parties. None the less, a written agreement can clarify a number of matters.

The manager should be responsible for a number of matters.

- He should plan the sportsman's career (in consultation with the sportsman).
- He should deal with all necessary administration for the sportsman. This may include the arranging of insurance, work permits and visas, as well as arranging meetings with third parties involved in the sportsman's career.
- He should agree to negotiate contracts on behalf of the sportsman although the sportsman must approve and sign such contracts.
- Whilst the provision of the manager's service is usually non-exclusive to the sportsman, it is important that the manager does not take on too much other work thus disabling him from carrying out his duties under this agreement effectively. An obligation should be included in an agreement ensuring that the manager does not create a conflict of interest between one managed sportsman and another.
- There should be an all-inclusive obligation requiring the manager to provide any necessary advice and services which are customarily required or expected of a manager.

7.4.3 Manager's authority

The basis of the contract between sportsman and manager is usually an agency agreement. The sportsman gives the manager authority to act on his behalf. The usual agency rule applies in that the agent is not liable in any way under any contract negotiated with a third party, and cannot, in the normal course of business, be sued by a third party for the principal's default. It is important that most, if not all, obligations incurred by the manager on the sportsman's behalf are first approved and signed by the sportsman.

The sportsman should define carefully the nature and extent of the manager's authority, his duties and obligations. A valid contract will not arise between a principal, in this case the sportsman and a third party, unless the manager has authority to bind the principal.

In the absence of actual or apparent authority, the sportsman, as principal, is not bound or liable to a third party for the acts of his manager acting as agent. It will be appropriate to consider whether the manager was acting in accordance with accepted practices of the business, and also whether or not it is known or there has been any form of representation that a manager acts for a particular sportsman. A prudent third party would usually require some evidence that the sportsman is interested in the engagement or obligation before signing an agreement. If there is any dispute as to an agent's authority (whether actual or apparent), it is open to the principal to rectify an unauthorised act and thereby legitimise the contract with the third party. It is not uncommon in certain sports for any number of individuals to claim they act for or represent a sportsman in one capacity or another.

7.4.4   Implied obligations of the manager

The management agreement should set out the specific obligations of the manager to the sportsman. In the absence of any express prohibitions to the contrary in the contract, there are a number of implied obligations which arise because in law the relationship is that of principal and agent. The most important of these implied duties are as follows.

– Where the manager agrees to act for the sportsman he must carry out the terms of the agreement as agreed and, unless the agreement states otherwise, carry out the sportsman's lawful instructions.
– The manager must exercise due care and skill in acting on behalf of the sportsman. A straightforward example of this is to negotiate and contract on the best terms available for the sportsman.
– Unless otherwise agreed, the manager must also act personally for his principal. Whether or not a manager is obliged to act personally or is permitted to delegate will depend upon the arrangements with the sportsman. Where the management services are provided by a company, then the sportsman should specify or agree who is responsible for management.
– The manager has a duty to act in good faith towards the principal. The relationship between manager and sportsman has a fiduciary nature. Accordingly, the manager should not permit a conflict of interest between himself and the sportsman and, if any does arise, he must disclose that conflict to the sportsman. The manager must not make any secret profit or take a bribe from a third party. Any benefit that accrues to the manager for himself as a result of his agency will be a breach of this duty of good faith. If this trust breaks down, the sportsman may be able to terminate the management agreement.[1]
– The manager must not misuse confidential information for his own or a third party's benefit. This applies even after an agency ceases. 'What the butler saw' revelations by managers and employees of famous people are

---

1   See *Denmark Production v Boscobel* [1968] 3 All ER 513.

not uncommon and, in an appropriate case, the courts may prohibit such disclosure.
– The manager is under a duty to account to the sportsman. This involves a duty on the manager, as agent, to keep proper accounts of all transactions, and, in principle, the manager should keep the sportsman's money separate from his own. A sportsman should avoid the risk of trying to recover money from an insolvent manager. Any money the manager keeps on the sportsman's behalf should be placed in a separate trust account.

A number of implied terms affect the manager:
– The manager has the right to be indemnified by the sportsman for any expenses incurred acting on the sportsman's behalf. Once again, it is usual to include express terms in a management agreement detailing the amount and type of expenses that a manager can incur without having to seek express authorisation from the sportsman.
– Unless otherwise agreed, there is no right for an agent or manager to claim any remuneration from the sportsman as principal. Such a right must be expressly or impliedly agreed between the parties and, accordingly, extensive clauses are contained in management agreements which deal with payment of the manager by way of commission on a sportsman's gross or net earnings.
– Once a manager's contract is terminated, no further commission will be payable by the sportsman to the manager. It is very important that any continuing obligation to pay commission to a manager is carefully worded so that if one management agreement is terminated and replaced by another, there is no element of double payment. It is conceivable that the terms of the original management agreement provide for ongoing commission and that the new management agreement also provides for commission or remuneration on similar categories of earnings.

Whenever an agency relationship is created with the European Community the terms of the Agency Directive as implemented into national law must be considered.[1]

7.5 TERMS OF AGREEMENT

7.5.1 General

There are a number of areas which need to be covered in the terms of any management agreement. There is no industry standard, and there is inevitably a great difference in the terms that a manager would like to see in a finished agreement and the terms that the sportsman is well advised to insist upon. Although a good manager is important to a sportsman and may be able to influence his career path, terms should not be discussed on a 'take it or leave it' basis. The sportsman is using the manager's services and should retain some influence and control over his affairs.

The relationship between sportsman and manager is a business arrangement and, accordingly, the terms of the agreement should be reflected in writing. This is to

---

1   Notice of 24 December 1962 on Exclusive Dealing Contracts with Commercial Agents, OJ 1962/2921.

ensure certainty as much as to avoid any later dispute as to the actual terms of the agreement. Whilst subsequent disputes may arise as to what those terms on their natural construction cover, the use of a written agreement is preferable to an oral arrangement. Before entering into a written agreement, both manager and sportsman need to consider the following questions:

- Are there any previous agreements which may affect the terms of this new agreement?
- Is the manager to provide an individual or corporate service? The distinction is that with the latter, someone other than the person the sportsman has been dealing with may be responsible for the day-to-day management of his affairs. If this is to be the case, it should be ascertained at an early stage.
- For what territory and what activities is the manager appointed?
- Are there any problems with the solvency of either the manager or the sportsman?
- Is there a relationship of sufficient trust and confidence between the parties to the agreement to enable them to work together in a suitable way?
- Are there any external regulations to be complied with, such as the FIFA regulations, governing the role the manager may take in certain negotiations?

7.5.2   Appointment and exclusivity

The sportsman will appoint the manager to represent him in an agreed territory for an agreed period. In return, the manager receives a commission or percentage of the sportsman's receipts and provides the expertise to manage and administer his business affairs and career generally. The extent to which the manager has control over the sportsman and directs and advises him is very much a matter for negotiation. An inexperienced sportsman requires more guidance. An experienced manager with good contacts and business skills will be able to help the sportsman enormously. An inexperienced manager with few contacts may find it difficult to advance the sportsman. Of course, in sport, the sportsman must do his bit by training and playing.

It is unusual for a manager to agree to manage only one sportsman. If the manager is free to manage other sportsmen then it is important that the manager is able to fulfil his obligations under the agreement. A manager who fails to provide the necessary time and commitment may breach the terms of the agreement and, accordingly, entitle the sportsman to terminate the agreement. It is important that both parties consider this before signing the agreement. The sportsman wants to maximise the benefit from representation, and, equally, the manager wants to maximise his return by way of commission or royalties on the sportsman's earnings. A clause requiring the manager to use his best endeavours to further the sportsman's career is important.

7.5.3   Activities

The agreement should deal with the particular fields of business in which the manager is appointed to represent the sportsman. This may depend upon the skill and experience of the manager, although consideration should be given to the future aspirations of the sportsman as well as any current activities. A catch-all agreement which deals with any activity or performance by the artist in the 'sports and entertainment industry' should be avoided. Quite apart from the fact that a catch-all clause may be too wide and void for uncertainty, the activities of a manager should be directed at particular sectors of the industry. This representation should include all aspects of his sporting career but also include the entertainment industry and the making of sound and promotional video recordings, live performances whether in concerts, on radio, on TV or other broadcasts, as well as writing books and newspaper columns. Commercial promotions such as merchandising and product endorsement are normally included. The income from such activities may also be included in the scope of the manager's representation.

The manager's role is a matter for negotiation and agreement. A manager will not accept a role which is so narrow and well defined that his earning potential from the sportsman is severely limited and, likewise, a sportsman should not grant a manager rights over every aspect or potential aspect of his career at a stage when he does not know in what way his career may develop or where there are areas of his income which he can quite legitimately exclude.

7.5.4 Territory

As well as the exclusivity of the appointment, it must also be ascertained to what extent the manager can effectively represent the sportsman throughout the world. It may be more practical for the manager's appointment to be limited to, say, Great Britain and Northern Ireland and the European Community. Separate representation might be obtained for the USA, Japan, etc. Again, this is a matter for consideration in the light of the manager's experience and expertise. A well-connected manager with representation abroad may well be able to fulfil the obligations in a very wide territory and, accordingly, all countries throughout the world might be appropriate territory. Most managers insist upon exclusive world-wide representation.

7.5.5 Duration of the agreement

The management agreement may be for a fixed term with options to renew or it may be indefinite, terminable upon notice by one or other party. There should be termination provisions in the agreement which deal with breaches of contract by the parties. There are two periods in the agreement to consider: the term of the agreement itself; and the term after the agreement has ended during which the manager is still entitled to receive some commission from the sportsman. This latter period is discussed at 7.5.7.

The period of an agreement is open to negotiation. A manager will require a reasonable period of time – three years is acceptable – both to give him time to plan the affairs of the sportsman and to give him a substantial period over which to gain a return.

A management agreement may contain an option to renew the term for further periods exercisable by the manager. Ideally, the notice should be served some time before the end of the agreement enabling the sportsman to plan ahead and find another manager if he wishes. If the manager fails to exercise the option on time, the sportsman is not obliged to extend the agreement. A sportsman should avoid being tied to a manager indefinitely.

The agreement should also impose some performance obligations on the manager. If the manager does not secure a certain amount of earnings or an acceptable major deal to the sportsman's satisfaction within, say, one year, the sportsman may terminate the agreement.

7.5.6 Manager's commission

The manager provides his services in return for a commission which is usually based upon the sportsman's gross income from specified activities. This is usually at a rate of between 15 and 25%. The usual sources of income are those which cover the representation of the manager. Thus, a manager appointed only in respect of certain types of work can only claim a commission on receipts from those activities. It is possible to exclude certain categories of income from the manager's commission. During the agreement, commission should only be paid on income arising from contracts agreed or negotiated during the term of the agreement.

The first issue between the parties must be the agreed percentage of commission for the manager. This varies, although 20% is quite common, and depends upon the experience of the manager as well as the extent of his representation. This high percentage is unlikely to apply to a sportsman's income from an employment contract. The commission from this is likely to be around 3% of the player's salary, or else a fixed-fee lump sum. These payments are frequently payable in instalments. Many sportsmen, particularly in the early stages of their careers, are an unknown quantity and, accordingly, a manager will demand, and usually receive, a higher commission than for an established sportsman signing a new management agreement. Some agreements allow for an escalation of the commission percentage as income grows. The converse is also possible.

Net deals

A sportsman's expenses are not deductible from income before the calculation of commission unless it is a 'net' deal. In a net deal, if the sportsman makes a loss, the manager makes no money. The manager will want to control closely the categories of deductible expenditure for a net agreement.

The management agreement should set out the income and deductions for commission purposes.

Income

A sportsman's income for commission purposes is all the money he receives from the defined management activities. This includes all income, gifts and payments in kind. It is usual for gifts to be excluded from the category of income on which commission can be charged. However, a payment in kind which is clearly meant as consideration for services would be included in the income of the sportsman and thus subject to commission. As mentioned, salary from an employer is likely to be treated differently for commission purposes.

Manager's business expenses

The manager should be primarily responsible for his own business expenses, just as the sportsman is responsible for his own business expenses. There is certain expenditure the manager might seek to recover, namely expenditure which is directly referable to the management of the artist. This might include transport, travel and accommodation, as well as associated office and professional fees.

If any such deductions are to be allowed, they should be within specified limits, and all such expenses incurred by the manager must relate directly to the management of the sportsman. The deduction or recovery of such expenses is something that a sportsman may normally seek to resist. Some expenditure will clearly be in a sportsman's best interests and not expenditure which a manager would otherwise be expected to incur on his own account. The agreement should provide that expenses incurred necessarily and wholly on behalf of a sportsman are recoverable by the manager from the sportsman.

Manager's authority

Wherever the manager has authority to incur expenses on the sportsman's behalf, there must be an upper limit on expenditure on any particular item. The manager should seek the prior approval of the sportsman for expenses exceeding this limit. It is important, however, that the agreement is workable. No manager will want to be continually answerable to a sportsman for every single item of expenditure. Essentially, any expenditure that the manager incurs should be directly attributable to the promotion of the sportsman. If that is the case, and the expenses are reasonable, then there is no reason why a sportsman should complain at a later stage that the manager has exceeded his authority or incurred unnecessary or excessive expenditure.

Actual receipts

It is important that commission is only payable to the manager on the basis of moneys actually received. A sportsman should be concerned to ensure that the manager is only entitled to commission on moneys received and not moneys which are simply due to the sportsman, otherwise the manager may be entitled to his commission before income has finally been received from various sources.

Collection

If litigation is required to recover money, those costs should be deducted from income before commission.

7.5.7 Commission and termination of the agreement

Ideally, a sportsman will cease paying commission to a manager as soon as an agreement is terminated. In practice, the manager is entitled to commission on income from all contracts in existence at the end of the agreements.

Many agreements contain provisions which entitle the manager to commission on income on deals negotiated by him during the term of the agreement even though the management agreement has ended.

An indefinite obligation to pay commission once the agreement has ended, even on deals negotiated by the manager, should be avoided.

Commission can be limited as to amount (a reduced commission after the term) and time (commission for a specified number of years). Limitations should ensure that deals which did not exist at the end of the agreement are not commissionable. Attention must be paid to this subject so that a new manager can be appointed after the term with the prospect of some earnings for his commission.

7.6   MANAGER'S WARRANTIES AND OBLIGATIONS

7.6.1   Management of the sportsman

The purpose of a management agreement is that the manager agrees to the best of his ability to promote the sportsman. Failure by a manager to promote the sportsman using his best skill and endeavours may give the sportsman cause to terminate the agreement. Whilst the obligation to promote the sportsman underpins the manager's obligations, it is impossible for management to guarantee success. It is clearly in everyone's best interests for a sportsman to play and generate income.

7.6.2   Receipt of income

A prudent sportsman will ensure that specified income is paid directly into a bank account controlled by himself or his accountant. Mainstream employment income should be treated this way. Commission is then paid with the sportsman's authority to the manager by an accountant or other third party.

The manager is then left to deal directly with all other income for which he should open a separate designated trust account. This includes performance and merchandise income from which the manager is authorised to deduct his commission. The manager must take appropriate steps to ensure that the sportsman receives all moneys due to him. If this involves legal action, the sportsman should be consulted prior to proceedings being issued.

Both the manager and the sportsman must be obliged to pay each other their dues. The manager must receive his commission promptly, and the manager must not retain that part of the sportsman's income within his control.

7.6.3   Accounting

In respect of the income which he controls, the manager must provide full, accurate and regular statements of account to the sportsman. These statements must deal with all income received by the manager on behalf of the sportsman. Whilst it would not be usual to require the manager to provide audited accounts, the keeping of up-to-date accurate books is important. Without such information, the sportsman's accountant is unable to prepare tax returns. The manager should prepare cash-flow forecasts as well as estimates of expenditure. The manager must then provide brief but regular accounts and other financial information to keep the sportsman up to date with his financial situation. This may involve monthly accounting. The manager should also provide more detailed accounts on a half-yearly basis.

If the sportsman has appointed an accountant to receive some income, the accountant pays the manager's commission.

7.6.4 Compliance with regulations

Where appropriate, the manager must comply with any relevant regulation of a sports governing body. This is particularly important in football where the FIFA agent regulations apply.

7.6.5 Miscellaneous

The manager must confirm that he has not entered into any conflicting agreements or arrangements which would in any way limit or hinder his ability to provide services as agreed under the terms of the agreement.

The manager should also usually undertake not to assign or attempt to assign the benefit of the agreement to any third party. A sportsman may consider agreeing to such an assignment; however, any assignment must be made with his prior written consent. Ideally, a sportsman should take independent advice in such a situation to avoid the prospect of the manager effectively selling the benefit of the agreement.

It is also customary for an acknowledgement to be placed in the agreement on the part of the manager stating that no rights in the name or likenesses of the sportsman will vest in the manager. Accordingly, all intellectual property rights should, unless specifically assigned elsewhere, remain in the ownership of the sportsman. It is not usual for a sportsman to assign such rights to a manager, and he should resist such a requirement.

7.7 SPORTSMAN'S OBLIGATIONS

The fundamental obligation for the sportsman is to provide his services as and when directed by the manager. A refusal to do so will prevent the manager from performing his obligations and, accordingly, there may be a breach of the terms of the agreement. That is not to say that a sportsman should do everything that a manager requests. However, to give efficacy to the agreement, the sportsman must provide services as reasonably required. The types of services the sportsman should perform relate only to the scope of the manager's appointment.

The sportsman must disclose any prior or existing agreements which may hinder his ability to render his services. In particular, previous management agreements may hinder the manager in effectively performing his tasks. Any such agreements should be disclosed. A diligent manager will usually seek to perform a full review of a sportsman's existing obligations before agreeing to represent him.

7.8   OTHER PROVISIONS

There are a number of provisions relating to termination which should be included in the agreement.

A force majeure clause will deal with unforeseen circumstances beyond the control of the parties which would otherwise frustrate the contract by preventing one or both of the parties to the agreement from fulfilling their obligations.

Failure by the manager to perform any of his obligations could also give a right to terminate the agreement, for example where:

(1) an allegation is made that the manager is not using best endeavours to promote the sportsman and, accordingly, is not performing his side of the bargain;

(2) there is a failure to account or render accounts as required by the agreement. This should be a specific breach of obligation on the part of the manager which could result in termination;

(3) automatic termination of the agreement if the manager becomes insolvent or is in any way unable to meet his debts as they fall due. In such a situation, the right to commission under the terms of the agreement should also cease.

A time-limit should be set within which the sportsman must complain or serve notice on the manager terminating the agreement. A distinction will usually be drawn between a breach of contract which brings or gives a right to terminate and minor breaches of contract which are more easily remedied. In any event, a sportsman may, by conduct, affirm the contract despite a breach by a manager. In such a case, a sportsman would not subsequently be entitled to terminate an agreement unless there was a new breach of agreement giving the right to termination.

Other boiler-plate clauses dealing with assignment of rights, confidentiality, choice of law and jurisdiction, service of notices and other relevant matters, for example arbitration, should be included as appropriate.

7.9   MANAGEMENT AGREEMENT

This Management Agreement is made the   day of   [   ]

BETWEEN:

of

of

of

(Professionally known as   **); and**

('I', 'me' 'my')

('you', 'your')

This letter sets out the terms of your appointment as my manager.

I   TERRITORY

The world.

2   TERM

2.1   This Agreement shall last for three years from the date of signature ('the Term').

3   APPOINTMENT

I appoint you (and you accept this appointment) to be my exclusive manager for all my services in the *sports* business ('the Services'). The Services include by way of illustration:

3.1   any performance in competition, training and 'on the field of play' (whether as a full-time employee or otherwise) on a [professional] sportsman;

3.2   making/exploiting audio and audio-visual recordings of my works and of my performances;

3.3   all my performances and appearances whether they are live before an audience or not, or recorded for sale, exploitation or broadcast;

3.4   exploiting my name and image by merchandising, sponsorship, endorsement or other advertising or promotional means.

4   SPORTSMAN'S WARRANTIES

4.1   I warrant and agree that I:

4.1.1   have no outstanding agreements and that free to enter into this Agreement and to grant you the rights contained in this Agreement;

4.1.2   shall perform and carry out the Services to the best of my ability;

4.1.3   shall consult with you before performing and carry out the Services, sign any contracts with third parties, or communicate with the media or undertake any activity that could reasonably be considered as falling within the scope of this Agreement;

4.1.4   shall not engage any other person to manage me but I acknowledge that you may act as manager for any other sportsmen;

4.1.5   shall keep you informed of my whereabouts, availability, and current activities at all material times;

4.1.6   am over eighteen years of age;

4.2   If, during the Term, I receive any monies relating to my Services directly then we must immediately notify you and pay all such monies into the Account in accordance with Clause 7.

5   MANAGER'S OBLIGATIONS

5.1   You warrant and agree that you shall:

5.1.1   use your best endeavours to advance my career in the Activities;

5.1.2   render all services customarily rendered by a manager in the sports industries;

5.1.3   consult me on a regular basis;

5.1.4   inform me of all substantial negotiations being conducted by you on my behalf.

6   COMMISSION

6.1   Subject to Clause 6.2 I agree to pay you commission of fifteen per cent (15%) of all the monies and other consideration for my Services, less VAT or similar taxes ('Income') which arises from the exploitation of my Services.

6.2   In respect of full- or part-time contracts of employment, the commission payable is 3% of total salary entitlement (excluding any bonuses or performance-related payments) payable in [   ] equal instalments over the term of such agreements;

6.3   I shall pay you this commission only on Income that is received by you or me during the Term in respect of any contract relating to my Services carried out during the Term.

6.4   The following are excluded from Income:

6.4.1   all monies paid or credited after the Term which are paid in respect of my Services wholly rendered after the Term; and

6.4.2   any royalties, advances or fees paid or credited on my behalf to independent third parties; and

6.4.3   you may not receive commission on royalties credited against advances in respect of which you have already received commission.

7   ACCOUNTING AND BANKING

7.1   You must pay all Income from the Services directly into a separate account to be operated and maintained in my name by my nominated accountant at [Bank] ('the Account').

7.2   I exclusively authorise you to collect all monies payable to me during the Term in respect of the Services.

7.3   My nominated accountant shall prepare, in conjunction with you, a statement of account within 60 (sixty) days after 31 March, 30 June, 30 September and 31 December ('Quarter Days') showing all transactions in relation to the Account, following which I shall pay you all commission and expenses properly due to you under this Agreement. Any credit balance on the Account shall also be paid to us at such time.

7.4   I shall agree with you a reasonable sum out of Income as a reserve against future expenditure and liabilities.

7.5   At the end of the Term I shall instruct my nominated accountant to maintain accurate records of all Income received by us upon which you are entitled to commission.

8   EXPENSES

8.1   Subject to 8.2 you are responsible for your own general office overheads.

8.2   Any expenses reasonably incurred by you in connection with the performance of your obligations and the enhancement of your career are my responsibility and shall be paid from the Account. Any travel or accommodation expenses you incur must not be at a more expensive rate than I incur.

8.3   I shall pay the cost of any non-secretarial staff or third parties engaged by you (with my prior approval) to help you perform your obligations in this Agreement in relation to the Services. Such engagements may include the (without limitation) booking agents, promotional or marketing personnel, as well as professional legal and accounting advice.

8.4   You must not incur any item of expense on my behalf in excess of £750 (seven hundred and fifty pounds) without my prior approval.

8.5   I shall pay you the costs of any equipment, transport, goods or clothing of any nature ('Goods') purchased by you on my behalf in connection with the Services. Until I have paid you such expenses for the Goods they shall remain your property and shall be returnable by me to you upon demand.

9   PROVISIONS RELATING TO THIS AGREEMENT

9.1   If either party to this Agreement is in breach of any material provisions hereof then that person will indemnify the other against any loss, damage, cost or fees (including reasonable legal fees) arising out of such breach.

9.2   Either party may terminate this Agreement by written notice served upon the other if the other:

9.2.1   is adjudicated bankrupt; or

9.2.2   is convicted of a criminal offence involving dishonesty; or

9.2.3   is in material breach of this Agreement and shall not have remedied that breach within thirty (30) days of written notice requiring him so to do.

9.3   Termination of the term for any reason shall be without prejudice to the rights of either of us accrued at the date of termination and to any rights or obligations which are expressed or by implication intended to continue in force thereafter.

9.4   You may invoice me for Value Added Tax on your commission and expenses for your management under this Agreement.

9.5   This Agreement constitutes the whole Agreement between the parties relating to its subject matter and supersedes and extinguishes any prior drafts, agreements, undertakings, representations, warranties and arrangements whether written or oral relating to its subject matter.

9.6   Wherever the approval or consent of either of us is required it must not be unreasonably withheld or delayed.

9.7 The warranties, obligations and terms contained in this Agreement shall continue in force after the date of signature of this Agreement and continue in full force and effect for the duration of the terms of this Agreement.

9.8 At any time after the date of this Agreement each of the parties shall at the request and cost of the other party acknowledge, execute and deliver such documents and do all acts as the other party may request for the purpose of giving to the other party the full benefit of the terms of this Agreement.

9.9 If any provision of this Agreement is held to be illegal, void, invalid or unenforceable the legality, validity and enforceability of the remaining terms of this Agreement shall not be affected.

9.10 Any notice required to be given under this Agreement shall be in writing and may be:

9.10.1 personally delivered or sent by facsimile in which case it shall be deemed to have been given on delivery at the relevant address or in the case of facsimile on transmission subject to confirmation of uninterrupted transmission by a transmission report, if it is delivered not later than 16.30 hours on any business day, or, if it is delivered later than 16.30 hours on a business day or at any time on a day which is not a business day at 09.00 hours on the next business day; or

9.10.2 sent by first-class pre-paid post, in which case it is deemed given two business days after posting;

9.10.3 in this clause 'business day' means a day other than Saturday or Sunday or a bank holiday and all notices shall be addressed to the respective addresses of the parties set out at the head of this Agreement.

9.11 Nothing in this Agreement constitutes a partnership between the parties.

9.12 This Agreement shall be governed by and construed in accordance with English law.

9.13 In relation to any legal action arising out of this Agreement both parties submit to the exclusive jurisdiction of the English courts and waive any objection to legal action in such court.

9.14 I confirm that I have taken independent advice on the terms of this Agreement from a commercial lawyer specialising in the sports industry.

Yours faithfully

COMMERCIAL RIGHTS AGENTS

7.10   LEGAL BACKGROUND

A commercial rights agency contract is one under which a rights holder appoints an agency to represent its commercial interests. The relationship between a principal and its agent has already been discussed and brings with it a whole raft of implied rights and obligations. The written agreement between the principal and the agent defines the roles of each party and the role in terms of duties and authority of the agent. An important distinction in agency contracts exists between the duties and authority of the sales agent contrasted with those of the marketing agent. The sales agent has authority to conclude contracts on behalf of its principal. In contrast, a marketing agent has no authority to conclude agreements on behalf of its principal: it merely introduces 'customers' to the rights holder. The usual relationship in sport between agent and principal is that of the marketing agent.

The majority of principals decide to appoint a sports agent to identify and negotiate deals for them. The main considerations in the relationship are the application of European and domestic competition law[1] and the Commercial Agents Regulations.[2]

7.11   PARTIES

The parties to an agency contract and the problems typically encountered are discussed elsewhere[3] and are common to most agreements within sport. The agent needs to ensure that the principal has authority to enter the agreement. The agent should also consider, where it is advising a rights holder, whether there are any other rights holders that could affect the value of the rights, or may even be able to limit its principal's ability to negotiate and conclude agreements. This may be the case where the principal is a team in a league or a local federation not a national or international one. The various layers of administrative regulation imposed in some circumstances can also fetter the commercial rights on offer in any situation. This is something agents are generally well aware of in any particular sport and which they will accordingly take into account when negotiating their own agency deal. Although this is unlikely to be a significant problem there may be instances where the actual status of the principal can affect other terms of the agreement and any financial or other guarantees that the agent may offer.

There will be extensive warranties dealing with the principal's authority to grant the rights in question. In a situation where the principal is the organiser of an event, there will be a warranty stating that the event will be held with the approval of and in accordance with the regulations of the relevant governing bodies. Where the principal is staging an event at a location or stadium that it does not own, then the agent may require a further warranty that the owner or (in

---

1   See **3.9**.
2   Commercial Agents (Council Directive) Regulations 1993, SI 1993/3053.
3   See **3.2.1**.

the case of events held on public property such as road races) the body controlling the location will cooperate with the rights owner in granting any commercial rights to the event.

7.12 RIGHTS AND EXCLUSIVITY

An agent is usually appointed on an exclusive basis to perform a specified role or function. The danger of appointing more than one agent or appointing an agent on a non-exclusive basis is that there will be a duplication of effort by each agent or agent and rights holder and that some sponsors will be discouraged by approaches from more than one agent dealing with the same set of rights. It is quite possible to divide the role and functions of agents and grant them exclusivity within particular activities in relation to the principal. A common and easily achieved split is to take the ability to grant broadcast rights away from the agent. This is not without its problems as the close association between the delivery of sponsorship rights packages and the interests of commercial broadcasters in appointing broadcast sponsors is not without its tension and must be closely coordinated. A common split is to take any public relations function away from a commercial rights agent as well as appointing separate specialist agencies to exploit rights on an 'above-the-line' and a 'below-the-line' basis. Whatever the solution, clarity is the important issue in all the contractual relationships.

The agent and the principal will also define the extent of the agent's function. The appointment is generally to supply a set of specified purposes and the development of a marketing strategy for the rights holder or investor in question. Assuming the agent is being appointed by a rights holder, the appointment should set out what commercial or sponsorship rights the agent is negotiating. There are usually two aspects to this arrangement. First, the general scope of the rights the agent represents and secondly, the precise requirements that the principal and agent have agreed as to level and categories of sponsorship. The agreement may set out certain agreed levels of sponsorship and the minimum price that the principal and agent anticipate for each category of rights.

7.12.1 Commercial rights

The agent will usually seek as wide a representation as possible, as this represents its best ability to earn a higher commission and meet any financial guarantees it offers the principal. If the agent is not active in particular areas, or the principal wishes to reserve certain rights, then the agreement should make it clear what rights are granted and what rights are reserved. In broad terms the principal may appoint the agent to deal with some or all of the rights to:

– appoint a title sponsor;
– appoint secondary sponsors in various categories, perhaps as Official Partners and Official Sponsors;
– authorise the use of the principal's trade marks and intellectual property rights;
– sell advertising on boards and other media at the event;

- sell admission tickets to the event;
- (if available) grant pouring rights and concessions at the event;
- sell broadcast rights to an event;[1]
- market and sell or appoint someone to deal with tours and hospitality at the event;
- sell merchandise and exploit merchandising rights;[2]
- produce official publications and exploit publishing rights;
- allow access to news companies to the event;
- set up a web site or promote the event and the principal using other new technology or on line means;
- appoint an official photographer or photographic agency;
- operate premium rate telephone lines.

The principal must carefully consider whether the agent can usefully exploit these rights, or whether it should either exploit them itself by finding and appointing the third parties directly, or by appointing other agents to exploit these rights. This is a commercial decision for the principal, based upon the ability of the agent to deal with such rights and to convince the principal of that fact. The principal must also be alive to the fact that some of the categories of rights set out above contain very lucrative and specialist areas of business. For example, broadcast rights are an increasingly complex and potentially lucrative area of exploitation for rights holders and an area of major concern for most sponsors. The grant of rights to a commercial broadcaster can create significant commercial opportunities, as well as pose significant problems for principal, agent and everyone involved with the event. The agent and principal should ensure the rights package offered to a broadcaster reflects the wishes of their sponsors and is carefully coordinated with all aspects of the commercial rights.

Merchandising and publishing rights are also areas where there is scope for tremendous overlap and the need for careful definition as to exactly what is a merchandise right and what is a publishing right. Merchandising and publishing are undergoing significant change as methods of electronic storage and delivery of the rights expand and develop new markets. The significance of the market for videos, as well as video game spin-offs from events, is considerable. These may be rights that the principal is well placed to exploit itself, without the potential reduction in income resulting from an agent exploiting the rights and deducting its commission from income.

7.12.2 The rights packages

The principal and the agent should agree an outline of the rights packages the agent will offer in relation to the property in question. The principal may wish to standardise the main commercial elements of each package offered to sponsors at particular levels. This also means the principal and agent must agree the various levels of sponsorship packages that the agent can offer. For example, if it is being offered, there will only be one title sponsor package. There may also be a number of secondary sponsors whose sponsorship packages will include the right to use an agreed designation for their category of product or service. The title and secondary sponsors will provide a combination of cash and benefits in kind for

---

1   See **7.19**.
2   See **7.5.7**.

the rights owner. There may be an additional category of sponsor that only provides benefits in kind for the rights owner. This type of sponsorship may involve free clothes and products for competitors and officials which, the sponsor hopes, will be featured in press coverage. Alternatively, this may involve the provision of important and valuable services and equipment for the rights holder. In each category, the agent and the principal will agree a minimum fee or equivalent benefit for the rights package in question. When a sponsor is found, it will be granted an agreed package of rights and expected to sign a sponsorship contract in a relatively standard form.

7.13   RIGHTS DELIVERY

The agent may also be involved in the actual delivery of the rights to the sponsors. There are two aspects to this role. The first usually involves the agent in a role at the event or competition itself. This is a role that needs to be fulfilled on site at the event or competition itself. The rights holder will have to grant the agent some authority to deal with the event organisers and the other third parties appointed by the rights owner to ensure the running of the event or competition and the delivery of the rights. The second aspect is the delivery of the rights in the broader market. This involves active involvement in policing the rights to ensure sponsors are not over-stepping the mark and going outside their rights. It also involves policing third party 'infringers'. This may involve anti-counterfeiting activity or more subtle 'ambush marketing' activities.

7.14   DURATION

There are two aspects to the duration of the agreement which are similar to the issues that arise in personality management. The first is the actual length of time during which the agent actively represents the rights holder. The second period is the time after the agreement during which the agent continues to be entitled to commission and is dealt with later in this part and in the earlier section dealing with personality management.

The first period is a simple practical matter for negotiation between the parties. An agent is unlikely to feel that anything useful can be achieved in less than one year and would normally prefer a period of exclusive representation that lasts for up to three years with either an option to renew or a right of first negotiation coupled with a matching rights clause. The rights holder is unlikely to want to be tied into an agent for a long period of time for the simple reason that it will want to retain flexibility in its external marketing arrangements and a long-term appointment may not suit this goal. It will also wish to control any renegotiation process so a definite right to renew in the agent's favour will not suit this objective.

7.15 PAYMENT TERMS

7.15.1 Fee and commission

The agent will be paid on the basis of a fee or a commission or a mixture of both. A fee paying basis can be structured in a number of ways. It may be a flat fee agreed between agent and principal. It may be a fee based on the principal's projected income for the rights. There may also be various payments which are only paid if the agent achieves certain stated levels of performance. The agent may suggest a flat fee which is payable in any event, whether it is successful or not in its search for sponsors and in exploiting the rights generally. An arrangement such as this, where the agent is paid its fee whatever happens, is best used when the agent is providing services which the principal needs anyway such as consultancy, research, general public relations and marketing advice. In these circumstances the basis upon which the fee is calculated should be clearly set out and agreed.

The principal may want a financial arrangement with the agent that only reflects the agent's success in exploiting the commercial rights and achieving certain stated levels of income for the rights. This is likely to be a commission paying basis. There may be a relatively standard flat 15–20% commission on all income and benefits in kind. Alternatively, there may be a sliding scale of commission based on increasing levels of income for the commercial rights. This may mean that if the agent does not achieve a minimum level of income it receives no commission at all. For example, between £0 and £100,000 the agent may receive no commission, but on income over that amount it may receive its agreed percentage. Commission rates may increase or decrease at certain levels of income.

Commission should be paid only on money or benefits in kind that are actually received. The agent may argue it should be paid its commission as soon as an agreement is entered into and whether or not the monies due are paid in full. The principal may not actually have the money to pay the agent until it has received its money from the sponsor or third party in question, in which case the agent may agree to receive commission on money actually received. If the money is not received because of the principal's breach of contract with a sponsor then the agent will still want to be paid. Similarly, if the event is cancelled for a reason beyond the agent's control the agent may require the principal to pay its commission. The principal should take out insurance to cover this risk whether the agent insists upon it or not.

The other aspect that often arises is how long (if at all) after the end of the term the agent can receive commission from exploitation of the commercial rights. The agent will argue that for agreements negotiated during its term of appointment but signed once its agreement is over it should receive its commission. The agent may also argue that it should receive commission on agreements that it negotiated which are subsequently renewed once its appointment is over. This may occur where a sponsor exercises an option or a matching right to renew a sponsorship. The important point from a drafting point of view is the definition of 'income' under the agreement. This may state that commission is due on all income received from contracts signed during the term of the agreement. This wording is wide enough to catch income arising after the term from contracts signed during the term. If this is not the principal's intention, the wording should be amended to make it clear that the agent only receives commission on income received during the term.

Once the term ends, there is no further entitlement to commission except perhaps for a sweeping up accounting to catch final amounts of income. This is an amendment the agent may strenuously resist, on the basis that it will want to carry on receiving commission for the hard work it put into finding the contract in the first place. Since the agent will no longer provide the support services after the term that it provided during the term, much of its commission may be reduced to reflect this reduced function. The principal, however, may wish to appoint a new agent and may need income to pay this agent a fee and/or a commission for its services. The principal will wish to avoid an element of double deduction on its income. A compromise may be a 'sunset' clause reducing the agent's commission and then ending it after a suitable period of time.

7.15.2   Benefits in kind

The contract should set out how benefits in kind are valued and what level of commission they attract. This is usually a lower rate of commission than with cash payments and is often based on the wholesale price of the benefits in case. Alternatively, it may be based upon the best price that the rights owner could achieve in the open market for the goods in question or the price it has previously paid for the benefits in question.

7.15.3   Accounting

The principal and the agent must agree who will actually receive the payments due under any contract signed. This is normally the principal and not the agent although there may be circumstances where the agent does receive money under these contracts.

If the principal receives the money, the agent will want regular statements of account along with payments when the statements are delivered. The statement will set out the gross income and the value of benefits in kind received in the accounting period as well as the amount of commission due to the agent. The agreement will specify a method of payment. VAT should be dealt with in the agreement. Commission payments are usually exclusive of any VAT payable and the agent should invoice the principal separately for VAT. If there is any withholding tax, the statement should also indicate the amount retained and provide an appropriate certificate of deduction for the agent to reclaim the tax.

If the agent is receiving and holding cash from exploitation of the commercial rights, it should account to the principal in a similar way. The principal should require the agent to bank the money separately, although it will usually authorise it to deduct commission either from the account or before paying it into the account. The various agreements between the principal and its sponsors may specify where payments should be made and, if possible, even where the agent is holding the monies they should be paid directly into the separate account, with the agent mandated to withdraw its commission. The agent will be obliged to draw up statements for the principal in much the same way as the principal does for the agent, except that the principal may be the only one mandated to withdraw money from the account.

The agreement may also contain 'standard' provisions relating to inspection of accounts and may also contain provisions for interest on late or overdue payments.

7.16 AGENT'S OBLIGATIONS

7.16.1 Agent's services

The basic obligation of the agent is to provide the agreed services to its principal. This is an obligation to maximise income from the exploitation of the commercial rights. The agent's general responsibility may be to coordinate the overall sale and delivery of the commercial rights on the principal's behalf and provide such assistance as the principal reasonably requires to do this. As part and parcel of this obligation the agent may agree to do some or all of the following:

- find third parties to exploit the commercial rights;
- negotiate contracts with these third parties to exploit the commercial rights;
- attend meetings with the potential sponsors and other third parties to exploit the commercial rights;
- attend meetings with the principal at reasonable times;
- prepare appropriate sales and promotional materials including presentations for potential sponsors and conduct sales presentations to the best of its ability;
- allocate sufficient staff to the principal's commercial rights;
- liaise with the venue owner and/or the event organiser as appropriate; and
- liaise with and conduct 'workshops' for sponsors.

7.16.2 Agent's guarantees

The principal is largely dependent upon the ability of the agent to deliver on its obligations and to maximise income and the exploitation of the commercial rights. As part of this, the principal may ask the agent for a guarantee that certain levels of income will be achieved. Although there may be financial incentives for the agent if it does achieve minimum income levels in the form of increased commission and fees, a guarantee that a minimum level will be achieved is quite different. If the agent fails to achieve the guarantee, it usually leaves the principal open to terminate the agreement. The wise agent may try to insert a watered down obligation such as a 'reasonable endeavours' term that gives it further leeway in achieving its stated target and would not automatically allow the principal to terminate the agreement. The subject of guarantees is a matter for negotiation. Whatever form of obligation or guarantee the agent does give, the agent will want it backing up with suitable obligations on the principal as to the maintenance of the rights themselves.

7.16.3   Contractual procedures

The contract must deal with the procedures for negotiating and finalising contracts for the exploitation of the commercial rights. The agent will require a reasonably wide discretion to approach, negotiate and conclude contracts with sponsors. There will be certain assurances that the principal will seek relating to the rights. In particular, the agent may have to negotiate within parameters set and agreed with the principal and perhaps on the basis of a standard form of contract. The agent must also ensure that there are no potential conflicts between the rights granted to sponsors and other third parties. Detailed and agreed rights packages are important here.

The principal will require assurances that the agent will not pledge its credit or make any misrepresentations relating to it or to the commercial rights themselves. The principal may also retain the right to approve and sign all contracts, although where the agent is giving any form of guarantee or receives any bonus payments it will want to limit the principal's right to refuse to sign a particular contract. If the agent has kept the principal fully informed throughout all negotiations, this problem should not arise.

7.16.4   Miscellaneous agent's obligations

The agent and the principal may give each other relatively 'standard' mutual warranties and indemnities relating to their ability to perform their respective obligations under the agreement and to grant the rights granted. They may also indemnify each other for any breach of their respective warranties and obligations although such an indemnity may be limited.

There are a number of additional general obligations the agent may undertake. It should agree to comply with the rules and regulations of the principal, the event or competition itself, as well as the rules of the appropriate governing body. It should also agree to comply with the general rules of law that apply to the contract, although the principal may wish to incorporate specific reference to the terms implied between and agent and principal by the general law. There will be general obligations relating to intellectual property as well as an obligation not to bring the principal, the event or the governing bodies into disrepute or make any comments that are defamatory. The agent may also be precluded from making any press comments or releasing any press releases relating to any aspect of the agreement. There may also be procedures in place relating to the approval of materials using the name and logo of the event. If these are materials created and used by the agent then the principal will want to approve them. If the agent is approving material produced by sponsors and third parties exploiting the commercial rights as part of its service to the principal then it should undertake to do so within agreed time limits.

7.17   PRINCIPAL'S OBLIGATIONS

The precise nature of the principal's obligations will depend upon the nature of the commercial rights the subject of the agreement. An important aspect will be that the sports event in question is sanctioned by the appropriate governing body (which may be the principal) and that it will be run in accordance with any applicable regulations. If this is not the case the agent may find the commercial rights are worth a lot less or, worse still, that the event cannot be run.

If the principal does not own the venue for its event or there are a number of venues in question then the agent may want some reassurance that the venue will be 'clean' of advertising and that it has a free run to exploit the commercial rights. If there are any consents or licences required to run the event then the responsibility for obtaining these usually falls upon the principal.

There may also be other obligations relating to the delivery of the commercial rights to sponsors and third parties which the agent will insist upon as a failure to deliver on these points can seriously damage the agent's reputation.

7.18   INTELLECTUAL PROPERTY

The principal must ensure that its intellectual property rights are adequately protected and policed. The agent will need assurances that the principal owns or has the right to use any intellectual property it needs. The provisions inserted to reflect this should be relatively standard.

7.19   TERMINATION

Although there may be a number of typical termination provisions in the agreement there may be one or two additional terms that are specific to agency agreements. The right to commission (if any) after the agreement ends is important and may be dealt with in this part of the agreement if it has not been picked up elsewhere. If the principal terminates the agreement because of the agent's default then all right to payment should end.

There may also be a termination right if the agent does not meet its guarantees or if the principal is, for whatever reason, no longer in a position to grant the rights or run the event. This may arise if there is a split in the relevant governing body or the governing body becomes insolvent or has a receiver or administrator appointed.

7.20   CHECKLIST: AGENCY AGREEMENT

–   PARTIES
     rights holder's status
     check constitution for authority
     consider other rights holders
     agent's ability
–   RIGHTS AND EXCLUSIVITY
     what commercial rights and in what territory is the rights holder granting the agent?
     Can the agent grant: title rights?
     official supplier or sponsor status?
     product/service category exclusivity?
     advertising hoardings?
     distribution of premiums?
     ticket allocation?
     corporate hospitality?
     press conferences?

post-event interviews and branding?
joint promotion rights?
broadcast advertising and sponsorship?
– DURATION
fixed term referable to length of the event or competition
number of events
postponement and extension of the term
rights of renewal: options or
first negotiation/matching rights
– PAYMENT
commission on cash income from exploitation of the commercial rights
includes in kind consideration
minimum performance or organisational bonuses/instalments
guarantees
stepped commission
VAT
– AGENT'S OBLIGATIONS
payment
use of rights on terms of the agreement
not to exercise the rights in a derogatory manner
comply with rules and regulations of the sport
supply samples of materials using event name or logo for prior approval
– RIGHTS HOLDER'S OBLIGATIONS
to hold the event
limitations on other sponsorship packages, eg agreed number of sponsors
and no competitors
authority to grant the rights
not grant the rights to a third party
no conflicting contracts
to deliver the rights
– BROADCASTING
amount and quality
identity of host and overseas broadcasters
virtual billboard technology
broadcast sponsorship
broadcast advertising
– MUTUAL WARRANTIES
authority to enter the agreement and perform its terms
no conflicting agreements
confidentiality of terms
mutual indemnity for breaches of contract
– INTELLECTUAL PROPERTY
ownership of IPR created by agent
ownership of other IPR
use of IPR
sub-licensing of IPR
protection of IPR
notification of infringements
action for infringements
– TERMINATION
list breaches
effect of breaches

7.20.1   Agency agreement

THIS AGREEMENT is made the   day of   [   ]

BETWEEN:

of   ('Organiser') and
of   ('Agent')

WHEREAS:

(1)   Organiser has the rights to and is responsible for promoting staging and controlling the Event

(2)   Agent is a company engaged in the business of procuring sponsorship and as a consultant on marketing and television for such events

(3)   Organiser has agreed to appoint Agent to provide certain services on the terms of this Agreement for the Event

IT IS AGREED as follows:

1   **DEFINITIONS AND INTERPRETATIONS**

   1.1   In this Agreement the following words or phrases shall unless the context otherwise requires have the following meanings:

   'Benefits in Kind'   means benefits products or services (other than cash) provided by any person (individual or corporate) by way of sponsorship of the Event;

   'Broadcaster'   means a person that transmits by wireless telegraph or by means of a telecommunication system visual images sounds or other information which is capable of being lawfully received by members of the public or is transmitted for presentation to members of the public;

   'Commercial Rights'   means the following rights in relation to the Event:
   (i)   advertising media of any kind along the route and in any venues or areas in relation to the Event;
   (ii)   developing marketing of and advertising on all official printed matters including but not limited to tickets posters guides programmes bulletins calendars books magazines in relation to the Event;
   (iii)   appointing Sponsors and Broadcasters;
   (iv)   franchising concessions and other sales facilities at any Events;
   (v)   distribution of premiums or giveaways at the Event;
   (vi)   corporate hospitality at the Event;
   (vii)   to develop and market ancillary events to the Event;

   ['Commission'   *means*   ];

   'Event'   means the [   ];

   'Fee'   means [£   ];

   'Governing Bodies'   means [   ];

'Gross Sums'   means all sums (excluding VAT thereon) payable under all contracts licenses and arrangements negotiated and/or supervised by the Agent pursuant to this Agreement;

'Intellectual Property'   means patents trade marks (whether registered or unregistered) rights in any designs (whether registered or unregistered) and applications for any of the foregoing trade or business names copyright and rights in performances;

'Official Sponsor' or
'Official Supplier'   means any person who sponsors the Event by the provision of money or Benefit in Kind;

'Event Marks'   means all trade marks service marks logos trade names symbols or other identification used or owned by the Organiser;

'Representatives'   means all third parties engaged by the Organiser to carry out services in relation to the Event;

'Sponsor'   means any person granted Sponsorship Rights under a Sponsorship Agreement;

'Sponsorship Agreements'   means those Agreements entered into with Sponsors pursuant to this Agreement;

'the Sponsorship Rights'   means the right to sponsor the Event and to be called an Official Sponsor or an Official Supplier of the Event;

'Term'   means the period in Clause 5;

'Territory'   means [*the world*];

'Venues'   means the venues used for the Event in any year including the immediately surrounding areas from which any material for broadcasting rights could be obtained or which could be used for advertising which would be visible to television cameras within the venue including areas used for official functions press centres media areas information centres and other areas necessary for the proper organisation of the Event.

1.2   In this Agreement where the context admits:

1.2.1   references to statutory provisions shall be construed as references to those provisions as amended or re-enacted or as their application is modified by other provisions from time to time and shall include references to any provisions of which they are re-enactments (whether with or without modification);

1.2.2   references to 'this Agreement' or to any other agreement or document referred to in this Agreement mean this Agreement or such other agreement or document as amended varied supplemented modified or novated from time to time and include the schedules;

1.2.3   references to clause(s) and schedule(s) are references to clause(s) and schedule(s) of and to this Agreement and references to sub-clause(s) or paragraph(s) are unless otherwise stated references to sub-clause(s) of the clause or paragraph(s) of the schedule in which the reference appears;

1.2.4   references to a 'person' include any individual company body corporate corporation sole or aggregate government state or agency of a state firm partnership joint venture association organisation or trust (in each case whether or not having separate legal personality and irrespective of the jurisdiction in or under the law of which it was incorporated or exists) and a reference to any of them shall include a reference to the others;

1.2.5   reference to the singular include the plural and to the masculine includes the feminine;

1.2.6   any reference to writing shall include typewriting printing lithography photography and other modes of representing or reproducing words in a legible form other than writing on an electronic display screen or similar device.

1.3   The headings and sub-headings are inserted for convenience only and shall not affect the construction of this Agreement.

1.4   Each of the schedules has effect as if set out in this Agreement.

2   SPONSORSHIP AGENCY

Organiser appoints Agent as its agent on the terms of the Agreement in the Territory for the Term for the Event and Agent agrees to act in that capacity as set out in this Agreement.

3   AGENT SPONSORSHIP DUTIES

3.1   Agent shall use its best endeavours to:

3.1.1   procure Sponsors for the Event; and

3.1.2   provide marketing and sponsorship consultancy for Organiser and the Event; and

3.1.3   procure Broadcasters for the Event; and

3.1.4   provide advice and create, implement and exploit all aspects of the Commercial Rights to the Event.

3.2   Agent may not appoint or conclude any contracts for the sponsorship of the Event on behalf of Organiser or bind Organiser in any way.

3.3   Agent shall seek Sponsors and Broadcasters for the Event with all due care and diligence and shall cultivate and maintain good relations with Sponsors and Broadcasters and potential Sponsors and potential Broadcasters in accordance with sound commercial principles.

3.4   Subject as provided in this Agreement and to any directions which Organiser may give Agent may perform its duties in such manner as it thinks fit.

3.5   Agent shall procure that its representatives:

3.5.1   make themselves available at all reasonable times and upon reasonable notice to Organiser for the purposes of consultation and advice relating to this Agreement and the Event;

3.5.2   at the expense of Agent attend meetings in London with representatives of Organiser and such Sponsors and Broadcasters or prospective Sponsors and prospective Broadcasters as may be necessary for the performance of its duties under this Agreement;

3.5.3   at the expense of Organiser attend meetings outside London with representatives of Organiser and such Sponsors and Broadcasters or prospective Sponsors and prospective Broadcasters as may be necessary for the performance of its duties under this Agreement;

3.5.4   at the expense of Organiser (such expenses to be agreed in advance for travel accommodation and subsistence) make themselves available during the Event for such purposes as Organiser may reasonably require under the terms of this Agreement.

3.6   Agent shall promptly notify Organiser of all enquiries and negotiations regarding the Event generally and concerning the Commercial Rights which it receives.

3.7   Agent shall in relation to its appointment under this clause:

3.7.1   describe itself as 'Commercial Rights Marketing Agent' for Organiser;

3.7.2   not hold itself out or permit any person to hold it out as being authorised (otherwise than in accordance with the Agreement) to bind Organiser in any way; and

3.7.3   not do any act which might reasonably create the impression that it is so authorised.

3.8   Agent shall not without the prior written consent of Organiser offer its services and enter into any agreement with any other organisation concerned in the management or promotion of any other professional cycling tour or event of more than three (3) consecutive days duration in the UK whether in respect of sponsorship or otherwise which in the reasonable opinion of Organiser competes with the Event.

3.9   Organiser shall provide Agent with an adequate statement confirming Agent's appointment under this Agreement.

3.10   Agent shall comply with the terms and perform its obligations set out in Schedule 1.

4 APPOINTMENT OF SPONSORS AND REPRESENTATIVES

4.1   The appointment of Sponsors, Broadcasters and third parties in relation to the Event shall be made on such terms and conditions as the Organiser may from time to time determine and:

4.1.1   Organiser shall provide Agent with an outline of the main terms it is seeking for such appointments to the Event;

4.1.2   Agent shall not (unless previously agreed in writing with Organiser) make or give any promises warranties guarantees or representations concerning the Commercial Rights or the Event other than those contained in such outline.

4.2   Organiser may:

4.2.1   for any reason reject any proposed sponsor's broadcaster or third party;

4.2.2   from time to time vary the outline terms or discontinue any of the outline terms for the sponsors of the Event.

5 TERM OF AGREEMENT

This Agreement shall be deemed to have come into force on [   ] and shall remain in force until thirty days after the Event unless previously determined as provided for in this Agreement.

6   OBLIGATIONS OF AGENT

Agent undertakes during the Term that it shall:

6.1   help create a marketing programme for the exploitation of the Commercial Rights to maximise revenue;

6.2   advise Organiser upon all material aspects of constructing or devising the Event and/or television programmes to enable Agent to commercially exploit and promote the Event generally;

6.3   use its best endeavours to procure and supervise on behalf of Organiser Sponsorship Agreements for the sponsorship of the Event;

6.4   (subject to the terms of this Agreement) use its best endeavours to procure and supervise agreements with other parties for the marketing exploitation and use of the Commercial Rights subject only to any limitation thereon due to prior rights having been granted to sponsors under Sponsorship Agreements;

6.5   use its best endeavours to procure on behalf of Organiser the appointment of a Broadcaster for the Event;

6.6   use its best endeavours to encourage Sponsors to promote the Event;

6.7   use its best endeavours to supervise the due performance of all Sponsorship Agreements by the respective other parties thereto;

6.8   use its best endeavours to control and supervise all commercial activities at all sites relating to the Event;

6.9   keep full and proper records and accounts of all dealings and transactions relating to this Agreement;

6.10   make available all such records and accounts at all reasonable times for inspection by Organiser or its duly authorised agents which or who shall be entitled to take copies and extracts thereof or therefrom;

6.11   keep Organiser informed at all times of any breach or non-performance by the other party thereto of which it becomes aware of any agreement the supervision of which is being conducted by Agent under this Agreement;

6.12   immediately notify Organiser if any claim is notified to Agent by a third party against Organiser or Agent in respect of any agreement supervised by Agent pursuant to this Agreement. Agent may not settle and/or compromise any such claim without the prior written approval of Organiser;

6.13   not issue any press releases relating to the Event or Organiser;

6.14   not do anything which in the reasonable opinion of Organiser is or might be prejudicial or defamatory to the name and image of Organiser the Governing Bodies the Event or the sport of cycling;

6.15   use its best endeavours to comply with and observe all provisions in the Governing Bodies rules and regulations from time to time in force;

6.16   comply with all applicable laws and regulations in the exploitation of the Commercial Rights and the organisation of the Event;

6.17   liaise and cooperate with the Representatives when performing the terms of this Agreement to the best of its ability.

7 PAYMENT TERMS

7.1 The Organiser shall pay the Agent the Fee as follows:

7.1.1 [ ] or [ ]

7.1.2 [ ] or [ ]

7.1.3 [ ] or [ ]

7.2 All payments are exclusive of VAT. Organiser shall pay any VAT payable upon receipt of a VAT invoice from the Agent.

8 INTELLECTUAL PROPERTY

8.1 All Intellectual Property which arises from the exploitation of the Commercial Rights shall vest in Organiser as owner absolutely.

8.2 Agent shall promptly and fully notify Organiser of any actual threatened or suspected infringement in the Territory of any Intellectual Property of Organiser which comes to Agent's notice and of any claim by any third party so coming to its notice and Agent shall at the request and expense of Organiser do all such things as may be reasonably required to assist Organiser in taking or resisting any proceedings in relation to any such infringement or claim.

8.3 Nothing in this Agreement shall give Agent any rights in respect of the Event Marks or any Intellectual Property used by Organiser in relation to the Event or of the goodwill associated therewith and Agent acknowledges that except as expressly provided in this Agreement it shall not acquire any rights in respect thereof and that all such rights and goodwill are and shall remain vested in Organiser.

8.4 Agent shall not use any trade marks or trade names resembling the Event Marks or any trade marks or trade names of the Event or of the Governing Bodies as to be likely to cause confusion or deception.

8.5 Agent shall not authorise any third party to use the Event Marks or any Intellectual Property of Organiser or of the Event or of the Governing Bodies. If any third party requires the use of the Event Marks or any Intellectual Property of Organiser or of the Event then Agent shall inform Organiser of such requirement. Organiser may (in its absolute discretion) grant such third party the right or licence required.

8.6 Agent shall at the expense of Organiser take all such steps as Organiser may reasonably require to assist Organiser in maintaining the validity and enforce-ability of the Intellectual Property of Organiser during the Term.

8.7 Without prejudice to the right of Agent or any third party to challenge the validity of the Event Marks or of any Intellectual Property of Organiser and Agent shall not do or authorise any third party to do any act which would or might invalidate or be inconsistent with the Event Marks or the Intellectual Property of Organiser and shall not omit or authorise any third party to omit to do any act which by its omission would have that effect or character.

9 CONFIDENTIALITY

9.1 Confidentiality

Subject to sub-clauses 9.2 and 9.3 each party:

9.1.1   shall treat as strictly confidential and use solely for the purposes contemplated by this Agreement all documents materials and other information whether technical or commercial obtained or received by it as a result of entering into or performing its obligations under this Agreement and relating to the negotiations relating to or the provisions or subject matter of this Agreement ('confidential information'); and

9.1.2   shall not except with the prior written consent of the party from whom the confidential information was obtained publish or otherwise disclose to any person any confidential information.

9.2   Permitted disclosures

Each party may disclose confidential information which would otherwise be subject to sub-clause 9.1 if but only to the extent that it can demonstrate that:

9.2.1   such disclosure is required by law or by any securities exchange or regulatory or governmental body having jurisdiction over it wherever situated (and including without limitation the London Stock Exchange the Panel on Takeovers and Mergers and the Serious Fraud Office) and whether or not the requirement has the force of law;

9.2.2   the confidential information was lawfully in its possession prior to its disclosure by the other party (as evidenced by written records) and had not been obtained from the other party;

9.2.3   the confidential information has come into the public domain other than through its fault or the fault of any person to whom the confidential information has been disclosed in accordance with sub-clause 13.3;

provided that any such disclosure shall not be made without prior notice to the party from whom the confidential information was obtained.

10   TERMINATION

Either party may terminate this Agreement forthwith upon notice if the other:

10.1   commits a material breach of any obligation under this Agreement which breach is incapable of remedy or cannot be remedied in time for the Event;

10.2   commits a material breach of any obligation under this Agreement and if such breach is capable of remedy fails to so remedy such breach within twenty-eight days of receiving notice from the other requiring remedy;

10.3   enters into a composition or arrangement with its creditors has a receiver or administrator or administrative receiver appointed or becomes insolvent or unable to pay its debts when they fall due.

10.4   Consequences of termination

Upon termination in accordance with Clause 10:

10.4.1   the rights and obligations of the parties under this Agreement shall terminate and be of no future effect except that Clause 8 and 9 shall remain in full force and effect;

10.4.2   any rights or obligations to which any of the parties to this Agreement may be entitled or be subject before such termination shall remain in full force and effect;

10.4.3   termination shall not affect or prejudice any right to damages or other remedy which the terminating party may have in respect of the circumstances which gave rise to the termination or any other right to damages or other remedy which any party may have in respect of any breach of this Agreement which existed at or before the date of termination.

10.5 Upon termination in accordance with Clause 10 and upon expiry of the Term Agent shall (at the request of Organiser) return all items (including but not limited to) signage, materials, premises, promotional publication, advertising material relating to Organiser and/or the Event to Organiser.

11 FORCE MAJEURE

11.1 Effect of force majeure

Neither party to this Agreement shall be deemed to be in breach of this Agreement or otherwise liable to the other as a result of any delay or failure in the performance of its obligations under this Agreement if and to the extent that such delay or failure is caused by force majeure (as defined in sub-clause 11.2) and the time for performance of the relevant obligation(s) shall be extended accordingly.

11.2 Definition of force majeure

For the purpose of this clause 'force majeure' means any circumstances not foreseeable at the date of this Agreement and not within the reasonable control of the party in question including without limitation:

11.2.1 any strike lockout or other industrial action or any shortage of or difficulty in obtaining labour or raw materials;

11.2.2 any destruction temporary or permanent breakdown malfunction or damage of or to any premises plant equipment (including computer systems) or materials;

11.2.3 any breach of contract default or insolvency by or of any third party (including an agent or sub-contractor) other than a company in the same group as the party affected by the force majeure or an employee or officer of that party or company;

11.2.4 any action taken by a governmental or public authority of any kind including not granting a consent exemption approval or clearance;

11.2.5 any civil commotion or disorder riot invasion war threat of or preparation for war;

11.2.6 any fire explosion storm flood earthquake subsidence epidemic or other natural physical disaster.

11.3 Obligations of affected party

A party whose performance of its obligations under this Agreement is delayed or prevented by force majeure:

11.3.1 shall forthwith notify the other party of the nature extent effect and likely duration of the circumstances constituting the force majeure;

11.3.2 shall use all reasonable endeavours to minimise the effect of the force majeure on its performance of its obligations under this Agreement; and

11.3.3 shall subject to sub-clause 11.4 forthwith after the cessation of the force majeure notify the other party thereof and resume full performance of its obligations under this Agreement.

11.4 Termination for force majeure

If any force majeure delays or prevents the performance of the obligations of either party for a continuous period in excess of [one] month the party not so affected may give notice to the affected party to terminate this Agreement specifying the date (which shall not be less than seven days after the date on which the notice is given) on which termination takes effect. Such a termination notice is irrevocable except with the consent of both parties and upon termination the provisions of Clauses 13.4 and 13.5 apply.

12 INDEMNITY

Each party (a 'defaulting party') agrees to indemnify and keep indemnified the other party (a 'non-defaulting party') from and against any cost loss liability claim or damage which any non-defaulting party incurs or suffers as a result of any default by the defaulting party in the due and punctual performance of any of its obligations or breach of its warranties under this Agreement.

13 NATURE OF AGREEMENT

13.1   Organiser shall be entitled to perform any of the obligations undertaken by it and to exercise any of the rights granted to it under this Agreement through any other person and any act or omission of any such company shall for the purposes of this Agreement be deemed to be the act or omission of Organiser.

13.2   Agent shall ensure that all dealings with sponsors Representatives and third parties it introduces to Organiser in performing its duties under this Agreement for the Event are on the best arms length commercial terms available and where dealing with any associated company of Agent (as defined by The Income and Corporation Taxes Act ss 416–417) shall procure at least two other quotations for the provision of the services in quotation which it shall send to Organiser.

13.3   Organiser may assign this Agreement and the rights and obligations hereunder.

13.4   This Agreement is personal to Agent which may not without the written consent of Organiser assign mortgage charge (otherwise than by floating charge) dispose of or declare a trust over any of its rights hereunder or sub-contract or otherwise delegate any of its obligations hereunder.

13.5   Agent shall not without the prior written consent of Organiser employ sub-agents if with such consent it does so every act or omission of the sub-agent shall for the purposes of this Agreement be deemed to be the act or omission of Agent.

13.6   Nothing in this Agreement shall create or be deemed to create a partnership or the relationship of employer and employee between the parties.

13.7   This Agreement contains the entire agreement between the parties with respect to the subject matter hereof and supersedes all previous agreements and understandings between the parties with respect thereto and may not be modified except by an instrument in writing signed by the duly authorised representatives of the parties.

13.8   Each party acknowledges that in entering into this Agreement it does not do so on the basis of and does not rely on any representation warranty or other provision except as expressly provided herein and all conditions warranties or other terms implied by statute or common law are hereby excluded to the fullest extent permitted by law.

13.9   If any provision of this Agreement is held by any court or other competent authority to be void or unenforceable in whole or part this Agreement shall continue to be valid as to the other provisions thereof and the remainder of the affected provisions.

13.10 At any time after the date hereof each of the parties shall at the request and cost of the other party execute or procure the execution of such documents and do or procure the doing of such acts and things as the party so requiring may reasonably require for the purpose of giving to the party so requiring the full benefit of all the provisions of this Agreement.

13.11 Each party to this Agreement shall pay its own costs of and incidental to the negotiation preparation execution and carrying into effect of this Agreement.

14 PROPER LAW

This Agreement shall be governed by and construed in all respects in accordance with the Laws of England and each party hereby submits to the exclusive jurisdiction of the English Courts.

15 NOTICES AND SERVICE

15.1 Any notice or other information required or authorised by this Agreement to be given by either party to the other may be given by hand or sent (by first class pre-paid post telex cable facsimile transmission or comparable means of communication) to the other party at the address referred to in Clause 15.4.

15.2 Any notice or other information given by post pursuant to Clause 15.1 which is not returned to the sender as undelivered shall be deemed to have been given on the second day after the envelope containing the same was so posted and proof that the envelope containing any such notice or information was properly addressed pre-paid registered and posted and that it has not been so returned to the sender shall be sufficient evidence that such notice or information has been duly given.

15.3 Any notice or other information sent by telex cable facsimile transmission or comparable means of communication shall be deemed to have been duly sent on the date of transmission provided that a confirming copy thereof is sent by first class pre-paid post to the other party at the address referred to in Clause 15.4 within twenty-four hours after transmission.

15.4 Service of any legal proceedings concerning or arising out of this Agreement shall be effected by causing the same to be delivered to the Company Secretary of the party to be served at its principal place of business (in the case of Organiser) or its registered office (in the case of SFT) or to such other address as may from time to time be notified in writing by the party concerned.

SIGNED by ....
For and on behalf of
Organiser
A duly authorised signatory

SIGNED by ....
For and on behalf of
Agent
A duly authorised signatory

CHAPTER 8

VENUE CONSIDERATIONS

8.1 Introduction – 8.2 Terms of occupation – 8.3 Commercial exploitation of the venue – 8.4 Ticketing – 8.5 Protecting commercial interests at the venue – 8.6 Pourage agreement with concessionaire – 8.7 Concession agreement – 8.8 Ground regulations – 8.9 Executive box licence agreement – 8.10 Events management agreement

8.1 INTRODUCTION

It is clearly trite to point out that the focal point of any sports business's effort is the home venue for its matches. That is the place where it will concentrate all its sponsorship effort and where it will sell tickets. The main income streams to any sports business are derived from broadcasting, sponsorship and ticketing and each of these comes under the control of that business when the event which is being broadcast, sponsored or for which tickets are sold takes place at that venue. It is therefore crucial that the business thinks very carefully about the full exploitation of its venue.

Many sports businesses of course have had traditional venues with which they have been associated for time out of mind. Indeed, for many of the older sports businesses, such as long-established football or rugby league clubs, that venue, often a large patch of city centre real estate, becomes an unexpected asset. The business may, therefore, as one or two football clubs have done, look to sell up that asset in order to realise a rapid injection of funds for the other purposes of the club and either move to purpose-built other premises 'out of town', or even seek a more radical solution, such as that of sharing a ground with another sports club. Others may rent or share their space by definition. For instance, an ice hockey or basketball team in the UK will very probably simply have agreements entitling it to play at a venue at given times and not be effectively in control of that venue as the sole full time occupant. That temporary occupation, however, must be exploited to the full for the club to realise its potential.

The considerations, therefore, which must inform the way the venue is exploited by the sport business (referred to for the sake of brevity here as the club) split into the following main areas:

(1) terms of occupation;
(2) commercial exploitation and sponsorship;
(3) ticketing;
(4) protecting commercial interests at the Venue.

These are discussed in turn. In dealing with them, certain shorthand expressions will be used deriving from specific instances (such as 'club' for the event promoter) but the majority of these concerns will cover the whole grant of venue exploitation by all sports businesses for all manner of sporting events.

8.2 TERMS OF OCCUPATION

Terms of occupation are comparatively straightforward if the club is in the fortunate position of being the freeholder and sole occupant of the venue. Here the club need only concern itself with those issues which apply to everybody and which are effectively matters of general public venue management: for instance, it should ensure that there are full and effective fire certificates in place; it should ensure that its insurance in respect of the venue is in order and that all possible safety precautions are in place, in order to provide a safe environment for spectators; it needs to ensure that it has all requisite planning consents for all uses which take place at the venue. These are factors that are applicable to anybody operating any public space and therefore need no detailed explanation here.

8.2.1 Occupier's Liability Act 1957

However, to a certain extent, sports venues are specific cases. There are certain specific pieces of legislation that deal with the duties of operators of sports grounds. Before dealing with that, however, the starting point should be the Occupier's Liability Act 1957, which provides that an occupier having control associated with and arising from its presence in and use of or activity in premises owes a duty of care to all visitors. That duty is that the operator should take such care as is reasonable to ensure that the visitor will be reasonably safe in using the premises for the purposes for which he is invited or permitted by the occupier to be present. The standard of care expected of the occupier is largely the same as that in an ordinary action in negligence. The duty is not so much to make the premises safe, but rather the visitor reasonably safe in visiting those premises and, therefore, the precautions required to discharge the duty incumbent upon the occupier vary from case to case and from visitor to visitor. For instance, disabled visitors must be provided with facilities which are safe for them to use, which may entail different standards from the general standards for the able-bodied visitor.

Breach of the occupier's duty under the Act where the occupier is using the premises for his business will give rise to liability. An occupier may seek to limit his potential liability by giving warnings of potential dangers, but mere warnings are not enough to absolve the occupier from liability unless in all circumstances the warning in itself was enough to enable the visitor to be reasonably safe. The occupier also cannot limit or exclude liability for death or personal injury when the premises occupied are occupied for the business purposes of the occupier.[1] In most cases, the granting of access to premises for recreational or educational purposes is not considered to be business use, but the Occupier's Liability Act 1984 makes it clear that where granting such access falls within the business purposes of the occupier, as it would for the club, that is business occupation and, therefore, it is reasonable to say that liability cannot be restricted for death or personal injury to spectators by any sports club.

---

1   Unfair Contract Terms Act 1977.

8.2.2 Safety of Sports Grounds Act 1975 and later enactments

In addition to this general legislation, there is the Safety of Sports Grounds Act 1975 which was introduced (as most Acts in this area) following tragic events at sports grounds. The Act has been amended by other legislation, including the Fire Safety and Safety of Places of Sport Act 1987, and effectively provides for a regime of licensing and control. Large sports stadia (being those having a capacity of more than 10,000 for any sport or 5,000 for certain grounds at which Association Football is played – an amendment introduced by the Safety of Sports Grounds (Accommodation of Spectators) Order 1996 – can be designated by the Secretary of State as grounds in respect of which a current Safety Certificate issued by the local authority must be held. Section 17 of the 1975 Act defines a sports ground as a place where sports or other competitive activities take place in the open air and where accommodation is provided for spectators which consists either of artificial structures or adapted natural structures.

The local authority has broad powers. The Safety Certificate may specify the maximum number of spectators allowed into the stadium, the number, size and situation of entrances, exits and any crush barriers and, in addition, the local authority has wide powers to require that measures are taken by the club as pre-conditions of the Safety Certificate being issued. Other conditions may also be attached to the Safety Certificate. In appropriate cases, the local authority even has the power to issue what is termed a 'prohibition notice' where it considers that a serious risk attaches to the admission of spectators: that notice may stipulate that the club restricts numbers of spectators allowed into the venue, or into any part of the venue, or may even prohibit admission until such time as any remedial measures specified have been carried out.

A number of designating orders have taken place so that almost all major sports grounds in the country have now been brought within the compass of the Act.

The Safety Certificate issued by the local authority may be either general or special. A Special Certificate relates solely to a designated class of events and a multi-use stadium may have a Safety Certificate only for certain events. Very great care needs to be taken as regards these aspects of management of the stadium and constant liaison with the local authority is strongly recommended.

The regime was extended somewhat by the Fire Safety and Safety of Places of Sport Act 1987 which was largely the result of the Popplewell Report into various tragedies including the Valley Parade fire in Bradford and the Heysel Stadium disaster in Brussels. Under Part III of the 1987 Act, even where a ground is not designated under the terms of the 1975 Act, where a stand provides accommodation for 500 or more spectators which is covered accommodation there must be a Safety Certificate in force covering that stand, issued by the local authority whose powers and duties are largely similar to those provided under the 1975 Act.

8.2.3 Football Spectators' Act 1989

Finally, where the Club is an Association Football Club, the Football Spectators' Act 1989 is relevant. This Act provides a statutory framework both for a national football membership scheme for spectators at designated football matches in England and Wales and also for the licensing of football grounds in relation to that scheme. Under s 11 of the Football Spectators Act 1989, the Secretary of State may require conditions relating to seating to be included in licences (ie tickets) to admit spectators to venues for designated football matches. The exercise of that power to date has meant that all the clubs within the FA Premier League and the Football League are required to have all seater stadia by the following route.

The Football Licensing Authority

The 1989 Act creates a new authority, the Football Licensing Authority, which has the task of issuing licences to the operators of venues and regulating the conditions of ticketing for all grounds designated under the Act. It also supervises the local authorities' duties under the 1975 Act in relation to those sports grounds at which designated football matches are played. As part of that supervision of local authorities the Football Licensing Authority has the power to require that local authorities impose certain conditions on the Safety Certificates they issue. Under the Football Spectators (Seating) Order 1994, a local authority is directed to include a condition imposing the requirements that only seated accommodation shall be provided for spectators at designated football matches and that spectators shall only be admitted to watch a designated football match where seated accommodation is provided.

8.2.4   Ground-sharing

However, in addition to its duties as operator of the venue any freeholder of a venue also needs to be aware of the comparatively new practice of ground-sharing and the commercial potential of such arrangements. Certain rugby union clubs have taken to sharing premises with football clubs. One famous example of ground-sharing is Selhurst Park in London which was used as the home venue for both Crystal Palace Football Club and Wimbledon Football Club while they both played in the FA Premier League. It is likely that this ground-sharing arrangement will become more and more common, both between clubs in different sports and between clubs in the same competition. Not the least significant factor is, it is understood, a new type of genetically engineered grass which is more hard wearing and will grow for longer periods. That may sound trivial, but it is not. Past experiments in ground-sharing have frequently foundered on the demands made on the playing surface, such as rugby league occupants leaving the ground unsuitable for the needs of a football team.

One of the points that has repeatedly been made throughout the course of this book is that, whenever advising any sports professional or sports club, regard must be had in every respect to the rules of the governing body of that sport on all potentially relevant aspects. In relation to any proposals of ground-sharing, this is once again crucial. There have been a number of occasions where sports clubs have satisfied all the criteria for entrance to a new level of the game, except that their ground does not comply. A number of non-league football teams have been denied entry to the Football League proper on account of the condition of or facilities provided in their ground. Consent must be obtained from the league by both parties to the proposal before making any attempt to share premises, not least because, of course, that league will have to schedule matches in accordance with the other calls on that stadium. The league may simply object on other bases, such as those of considerations of the lack of comfort to be supplied for spectators. If an objection is made by a governing body, subject to litigation against that body, that is the end of the matter and so the enquiry should be made before negotiations become advanced. Before framing any agreement to share a ground, the consent of the governing body of both sharing parties is necessary, together with full knowledge of any conditions each governing body sees fit to impose. Further, the criteria laid down in the playing conditions for the sport for the pitch, both in terms of its standard dimensions, technical specifications, markings and so forth, and also in terms of the sanctions that are handed out in the event of a substandard pitch or substandard ground amenities should be considered. It is not unknown for points to be deducted from a team because its playing surface is not of a good enough quality. Clear guidance, therefore, should be obtained and each of those aspects will lead to fundamental and non-negotiable terms in any negotiations for the right to occupy the venue.

The terms of any agreement providing for ground-sharing, or for the occupation by the club of a venue at which it is effectively the visitor, will usually take the form of a licence. The reason for this is clear: it is the fundamental characteristic of a lease that it confers rights of exclusive occupation over the demised premises which can be defended even against the freehold owner of the premises. In order effectively to split the occupation of premises in terms of intermittent time periods rather than area, a licence is the appropriate format.

The comments below are specifically directed at ground-sharing but the majority would have equal relevance for any temporary occupation, whether regular arrangements, or occupation entirely isolated in its nature, such as the hire of a venue for a one-off event.

The club should be vigilant to ensure that the licence has certain fundamental terms of compliance with official requirements as outlined above in relation to the playing areas and spectator facilities. Once it is happy that the venue has the capability of satisfying its requirements, it should seek to ensure that it has access to all the areas it will need allocated to it, such as the pitch, the changing rooms and any office space, on all occasions it requires. That can be tied to the publication of fixture lists if need be, or to specific days of the week, but it may be that it would require exclusive possession at all times of certain areas such as store rooms and office space. It may, therefore, take a lease over some areas and a licence over others, or all areas may be the subject of a licence but with differing terms relating to different areas.

The permitted user of the premises must be in all ways consistent with the club's activities. Those activities extend beyond the purely playing side into the commercial and sponsorship side of the club's operations. The other consider-ations relating to commercial exploitation[1] should be considered when for-mulating the licence. It should be made clear in the licence that, for instance, not only is the club allowed to do all its own ticketing (and to have access to any ticketing computers at all times either directly or by modem link to enable it to make ticket sales) and to have a licence which encompasses all seats and all executive areas and viewing areas for its events, but also, it is to have the sole right

---

1   See **8.3**.

when it is in occupation to operate and sub-licence all concessions such as souvenir stands, fast food stands, bars and restaurants. It should have the right to set up its own sponsorship arrangements, such as the selling of perimeter boards around the pitch and the use of all scoreboards, giant screens and public address systems at all times it is in occupation. The club might also fruitfully seek access to databases of people who might attend other events at the venue and the right (if such can be granted under data protection legislation) to approach those people and businesses both as potential spectators and sponsors of the events they will be promoting at the venue.

The licence must provide clear provisions as to who maintains the playing surface and, if it is the venue owner as opposed to the club, strict parameters and specifications for such maintenance must be laid down. There should be regular consultation between the owner and the club on the quality of the playing surface and the final decision on all questions in that regard must rest with the club. Insurance of the premises and the consequent application of insurance proceeds to the reinstatement of the premises, together with any compensation payable to the club for interruption of its business, should be provided for and the cost of that insurance allocated. Payment for electricity and other fuels should be provided for. Any employees of the owner who are to attend the premises, for instance, the stadium manager and any licensees of the bars and any ground staff, must be clearly identified and the venue owner obliged to provide personnel of proper quality to fulfil these roles in accordance with the club's detailed instructions. The owner must pay business rates and other outgoings and ensure that the premises at all times comply with fire certificates, safety legislation and all other statutory requirements as set out above. There should be full access to the premises for the purposes of training as and when that is required. Access should be unrestricted at appropriate times to enable the venue to be set up with all requisite sponsorship and concession insignia and equipment, signs and messages in preparation for any club event taking place. In order to enable this, it would be advisable to stipulate that the venue owner remove, or stipulate its other licensees to remove, from the stadium all such items not belonging to the club in good time prior to the commencement of the club's own access to give it sufficient time to set up the venue.

Crucially, it must be made absolutely clear that all broadcasting rights relating to the events both by television (terrestrial, satellite and inclusion in any cable programme service) and by radio are exclusively vested in the club and the club has access to and the right to grant to third parties access to all areas (such as press boxes) and technical facilities (such as power facilities and on-site transmitters) required to facilitate such broadcasts. If any community programmes or training schemes are to be undertaken by the club, there should be access to the venue for those to take place.

The club may wish to grant certain concessions such as pouring rights,[1] food concessions or exclusive arrangements with breweries and so forth to third parties. Those considerations should be factored into the agreement. Such facilities need only be granted when the club is at the venue. It may, however, wish to retain, for instance, a permanent ticketing outlet or a retail unit and those also should be provided for.

---

1   See **8.3.3**.

The club should have, if it can be negotiated, a right to veto any other activities which are to take place at the venue. Some parameters in the agreement, at the very least, would no doubt be of assistance. For instance, the club may not want a rival club to be granted rights to the venue, or it may not want the venue to be used for any sport or activity which is clearly going to damage the venue from the point of view of the club. For instance, if the venue is a cricket ground, the ground must not be used for vintage car rallies or so forth which will obviously entirely ruin the playing surface. It is difficult to be exhaustive on the negative side and so it may be prudent to lay down only a list of permitted alternate uses by the venue owner, with an overriding veto being in the hands of the club.

The club may wish the licence to be for a long period of time and it may wish to have certain development rights. For instance, as will be seen below,[1] there are potentially lucrative spin-offs from the operation of a sports venue such as the conference trade, civil weddings and other events. If the facilities are already in place, the club should negotiate at least its fair share of access to those facilities outside the times at which sporting events are taking place at the venue. It may further require the right, or an option, to develop certain areas and to take leases or licences over those areas when developed. Indeed, it may be appropriate in the circumstances for an option to purchase the venue or at least a right of first refusal to be negotiated, lest the venue fall into the ownership of a party with whom the club may find it impossible to do business. The club must have the capacity to move with the times and any stipulation of its governing body: if the governing body lays down criteria for venues the club must have rights which will enable it to comply.

8.2.5 Venue sponsorship

The club may also seek the right to sell sponsorship in the form of naming the venue. That will usually be available only where the club is the dominant occupier. Stadium naming can appear be very lucrative as it is one way a sponsor can ensure a very high profile. The acid test on such arrangements may be, however, that at the time of writing not many have been concluded. They are dealt with in further detail below.[2]

8.2.6 Licence fee

The licence fee to be paid will be a matter of commercial negotiation. It may be some percentage of the total income of the club related to all its activities at the venue, or it may be a fixed amount, or a combination of the two. The 'percentage of income' route, however, does appear to be more appropriate, given the vagaries of professional sport, for both parties to the transaction.

The venue owner will require comparatively straightforward obligations. It will require payment of its licence fee and there will be stringent obligations about the use of the premises. That which is permitted should be clearly permitted and that which is not permitted should be clearly prohibited. There should be no ambiguities. Everything should be laid down in fine detail, as the alternative is chaos. There should be an indemnity from the club to the owner against any

---

1   See **8.3**.
2   See **8.3.1**.

claims arising against the owner as a result of the club's occupation of or operation of the premises, and that indemnity must be backed up with suitable insurance. The club should have an obligation to reinstate any damage to the premises caused whilst the premises are under its control. Insurance on this point is again an issue on both sides and therefore those provisions will need to be exhaustively set out. The question of repairing the venue to reinstate the effect of ordinary wear and tear and dilapidations will be crucial: the best advice for both sides is to try to oblige the other to do it!

The owner will want to ensure also that the premises are not brought into disrepute by the club's operation. For instance, the owner cannot allow the venue to have the reputation of being a place where violence occurs. The owner should therefore stipulate very clearly that public order issues must be treated as matters of paramount importance and that all proper stewarding and liaison with police is maintained. It would be a good idea for the owner to ensure that it has the power of veto over any commercial deals performed by the club while it is in situ. For instance, the club must not sub-licence its right to use the stadium as a sporting venue to other sports clubs. Where it sub-licenses concessions for alcohol, fast food and so forth, the owner should not only have the power to veto the appointment if it requires on reasonable grounds, but also the power to stipulate the terms on which the appointment is made. The owner would be well advised to stipulate the terms on which tickets, executive packages, season tickets and so forth are issued. In this regard, it should look to protect not only its own interests but also those of its other licensees and potential licensees: there must be harmony between licensees and what one demands, the other must give, or at least not prevent.

The owner must stipulate that full insurance is held by the club against any claims by its own licensees, namely spectators attending the venue with the consent of the club. The club must ensure that all staff required to carry out its functions properly at the venue and not supplied by the venue owner are supplied by the club and that full financial books and records are kept, particularly in the event that the licensing is tied to a percentage of the club's income. There should also be the right for the owner to inspect the club's books and to receive a certificate of all income on the basis of which licence fees are paid from the club's auditors. The club must not do anything which interrupts or impairs the enjoyment of the venue of any other licensee and, therefore, there should be clear obligations for the club to take down its signage and remove its rubbish and so forth within a short period of any event thus allowing the next event to take place unimpaired.

The above can only be a sample of the main terms of such an agreement and the negotiations leading toward an agreement will be hard and complex. Other considerations beyond those of the club's playing activities must be considered by those advising the club as well, such as the suitability for security purposes to the club's bankers and financiers of the club's rights over the venue.

8.3   COMMERCIAL EXPLOITATION OF THE VENUE

As is touched upon above, there are many opportunities for a club to exploit its venue for other purposes than those of simply participating in the sport and providing tickets to spectators. Anyone who has attended a first-class sport venue will be aware of the hive of commercial activity which takes place there. There are vendors of souvenirs and programmes; there are food and drink concessions; there are bars and restaurants; there may even be shops or shopping areas both for the club's own benefit and those which are comparatively unconnected with the club. There may be executive meeting and entertaining facilities and possibly even full time leisure facilities such as gymnasia and sports facilities open to the public. There will be sponsorship signs, publicity materials, events and promotions; there will be pre-match entertainment and sponsored competitions: the list is extensive even when confined just to the things that can be done at the venue at the time of the sporting event. In addition, however, there is also the possibility of using the venue outside the times when sporting events are taking place. A sports venue is an immediately impressive place for a number of purposes. There is a very healthy conference and training industry which is looking for venues. The same can be said of formal dinners, weddings and other celebrations. Often a football club will have highly developed facilities which are the equal, if not superior, to those of all but the largest hotels, often constructed and marketed on considerations only of their capacity for sporting events. Outside those sporting events those facilities can and should, wherever possible, be made available to the public. Sports stadia can also be used for other sports, for instance boxing matches at football grounds, or other events such as rock concerts.

8.3.1 Stadium naming

The fundamental thread which draws everyone to the sports ground is the club in occupation and all those attracted will want to associate themselves with the club in some way. The most valuable right that can potentially be granted to a sponsor relating to the venue is the naming of the venue itself. This has been touched on above with the caveat that not many of these deals seem to have been concluded. The Oval Cricket Ground has been named the 'Fosters Oval', for instance, and there have been one or two other instances but these deals have not as yet made any real impact on the commercialisation of sport. There is no reason why that necessarily should be, except that, in all likelihood, the sort of fees demanded for such a high profile right have been rather more than sponsors have been willing to pay. There is also another major problem. Because of the very strength of identification between the sponsor and the club given by stadium naming, it is likely that other sponsorship agreements would be compromised. A stadium name sponsor will have its name associated at all times with the club whose stadium bears its name. All broadcasting will include an acknowledgement of that sponsorship simply by naming the stadium and the sponsor's name is on all tickets and all publicity associated with the club by definition. On balance, it may be that the net effect would be to detract from the club's other sponsorship income and that should be the subject of some fairly considerable research. For instance, the main club sponsor may object to sharing the headline billing, as it were, with another party and therefore pay less; the income from ground perimeter boards and other signage and concessions within the stadium may be reduced by the gravitational force of the stadium sponsor. Finally, a governing body may object particularly if the venue is used for matches of an official nature such as Cup semi-finals and international matches.

It is likely that stadium naming will become most prevalent where a club has actually built its own stadium. It may be possible to raise a sizeable contribution towards building costs if one can grant the name of the stadium to a sponsor, and the kind of identification sponsorship around the stadium that can be given when the stadium is all available to be customised at the outset of its use. This would be a good way of realising a fairly large capital contribution at the outset; the downside would be a potentially damaging effect on the long term income of the club. If a club is considering granting stadium naming rights, it should ensure that it does so only for a limited period of time. The time period would probably be a period of approximately 10 years, which would allow the club to find another sponsor in due course (subject to potential misgivings over wishing to be seen as the successor to the first and wanting to pay for a long period, when there is an effective hangover in public perception from the first stadium sponsor) but perhaps more importantly so that if the sponsorship pays off there can be a renegotiation in due course.

The nature of the sponsorship for a stadium name sponsor would take the form of very noticeable branding at all points where the stadium is named and perhaps very large signage on the exterior of the stadium, visible from road and major railways, together with a raft of measures effectively putting the stadium sponsor in the same sort of position as regards the extensive nature of the package as the main club sponsor. The main club sponsor may, however, wish in its sponsorship agreement to take some action to prevent, or at least to forestall, a stadium sponsor from ambushing it. It would be well advised to include in any sponsorship contract at least a right of first refusal over any proposal for stadium naming, together with provisions prohibiting the granting of stadium naming rights to its main competitors.

8.3.2 Signage sponsorship

At a lesser level, an important facet of stadium exploitation is the grant of rights to sponsors over signage. Once again, we would emphasise the need to consult as a first step the appropriate rules of the governing body. For instance, the FA Premier League stipulates that certain parts of the ground level perimeter signage which are visible on television coverage of Premier League matches must display the signage of the main Premier League sponsors. On top of that, the club will have certain fundamental sponsorship obligations: for instance, those to a kit sponsor and a main club sponsor will almost invariably include rights to display their signage in certain key areas of the ground, with a particular eye on likely television coverage. Further, those main sponsors and in all likelihood, any main sponsor of the governing body, will have stipulated in their sponsorship agreements that there must be no 'ambush marketing'. This is a topic covered extensively elsewhere, but one form is for competitors to buy prominent signage where events sponsored by the competition are taking place. The ingenuity of the devices used will put those advising the sponsors to considerable efforts to protect them – and the concern is justified. The main sponsorship agreement will therefore preclude the club from offering sponsorship to direct competitors of those main sponsors, and the more broadly the excluded categories are drawn the greater the potential restriction upon the club's potential earnings. The club must be vigilant that when offering its sponsorship benefits to other parties on an open market basis, it is clear that it is offering those benefits to parties who will not cause it damage by compromising its other sponsorship arrangements. The word 'exclusive' crops up time and time again in sponsorship issues: clubs must be wary of giving any form of exclusivity and, frankly, only give it when the price is right.

It is often most economical and most beneficial to the club to grant a licence to a sponsorship consultant or agent (of which there are an ever-proliferating number) to sell certain categories of sponsorship. The club may grant to a sponsorship consultant all available advertising hoardings and perimeter boards subject to certain criteria, such as the anti-ambush marketing criteria discussed above. In return, therefore, for a guaranteed percentage of the income such as 70–80% of all income over and above the costs of the sponsorship consultant, backed always by the comfort of a guaranteed minimum amount payable by the consultant, the club may grant to the sponsorship consultant the right to sell all signage available after the club has fulfilled its obligations to the governing body and its main sponsors. The sponsorship consultant would be obliged to design the signage (subject to the club's veto over content and undertakings that it will not be obscene, defamatory or infringe third party intellectual property rights), put the signage in place and to collect all revenues. The club should then receive a bonus for every time that signage appears on television, either in a full broadcast of the entirety of an event or in highlights form and depending upon the potential audience; so in other words, 20 minutes on a minor cable channel would lead to a low bonus but a full match or event on BBC or network ITV should yield a large bonus.

8.3.3 Concessions

Further, the club might have a lucrative income stream in granting either exclusive or non-exclusive concessions for the sale of certain goods. For instance, it might sell the right to operate all fast food concessions at the ground to a fast food chain. In return for that, it may generate far more than it would do in terms of profit generated by the operation of that concession itself. Quite apart from the goods they sell, the concessionaires will consider the identification of their product with the sporting event and club to be of a distinct value and to have a captive public every week is a very good advertisement for the product. As a sample of such an arrangement, a specimen 'pourage' agreement and a specimen concession agreement are included at **8.6** and **8.7**. These deal with exclusive pourage rights for a certain soft drink and the operation of a food concession but can be extrapolated into any form of concession for goods or even for services at the venue.

Proper management and orchestration of these rights is crucial. One cannot tread on the toes of the soft drinks concessionaire by granting advertising space elsewhere in the stadium to its major competitors. Also, whilst it may appear that, for example, there is not a single blade of grass at a premiership football club which is not sponsored by somebody or other, it is crucial that the value of sponsorship is not diluted by over-kill. New technologies do, however, add further opportunities. Electronic scoreboards give the opportunity to flash sponsor messages. Giant screens might show reels of pre-match entertainment such as memorable tries from the last season or old footage of successful campaigns and these programmes can also be used to provide sponsorship benefits by the interpolation of advertising materials. Public address systems can acknowledge sponsorship. Match balls, mascots, individual players, man of the match awards, half-time competitions and all manner of other incidentals can be sponsored. However, the value of cohesion and good taste cannot be stressed too much. The sponsorship of sport is a lucrative business at present but if sold too hard will lose its value: a small number of high value 'exclusive' deals may net far more both for the club and the sponsor in terms of income than a series of fragmented non-exclusive deals. This has led to a common practice of granting effective parity to a raft of main sponsors numbering about a dozen, particularly for events such as World Cups and Olympic Games.

When any agreements are formulated granting any sponsorship rights care should be had to identify exactly what events those rights cover. For instance the venue may be a venue for a number of different purposes. A cricket ground may be a county cricket ground and also a test match venue. A football ground might be used for semi-finals of cup competitions in which the club which operates that venue ordinarily does not participate. In circumstances therefore where the event is promoted by a party which is not the club normally operating that venue, that party will usually require what is known as a 'clean venue'. That means, therefore, that when the venue is used for those events there must not be any sponsors' signage belonging to the club usually operating the venue of any nature present in and around the venue but that all signage and other sponsors' material must be removed to enable those sponsorship rights to be granted by the promoter of the event to its own sponsors. The club naturally should ensure that it gets a healthy cut of the takings of the promoter of the event in turn, but it must ensure when formulating its sponsorship agreements that in giving the promoters of other events the clean stadium they require, it is not placing itself in breach of those sponsorship agreements.

Even when the club is dealing with a venue where its own events are the only events in question, it is quite in order to grant certain rights for certain categories of events only and this indeed is a potential way of maximising revenue. Certain rights may be granted to one sponsor in one competition and to another in another competition. In any event, it should be absolutely clear in any agreement exactly what events are covered.

8.3.4 Broadcasting

It would be appropriate to say a word here about broadcasting. The broadcasting rights for a sporting event are juridically somewhat questionable: one could mount an interesting learned debate over who owned the right to broadcast the performance of the event. This is dealt with in more detail in Chapter 9. For the purposes of this discussion, however, it is enough to point out that the club must ensure (with a very large caveat that at all times it must be acting within the rules of the governing body under whose auspices the event takes place) that it has the opportunity to make the broadcasting deals for the event. It must ensure that it has in place contractual agreements with all participants in the event clearly enabling it alone to sell broadcasting rights world-wide in the event. Even if there is a television deal put in place by the governing body, there is always the possibility that radio broadcasting rights might be available. Radio broadcasts obviously are commentaries on the event rather than broadcasts of the event itself and therefore the complexities of the situation regarding broadcasting rights are largely eliminated: what is broadcast is effectively the vocal perform-ance of the commentator.

8.3.5 Audio-visual recording

Even if broadcasting is not an option, the club should ensure that it has in place an agreement with a video production company for audio-visual recording of the event. This sort of arrangement is becoming more important all the time and the range of services that are being required from video producers is increasing. Historically, often clubs have engaged video producers on a fairly ad hoc basis and on a fairly low technological level to take video recordings of events which mainly might be used for coaching purposes but also, on occasion, for compilation into videos which are then sold to the general public in the form of a review of the season or a recording of a memorable individual event. However, with the advent of new technologies such as giant screens, the use for video pictures at the venue has increased. The club may, therefore, commission a video production company to take video and sound recordings of the event to a fairly high technological level, for instance with six to eight cameras; and further, use that footage to provide instantaneous action replay footage to giant screens around the ground using two or three recorders. In doing that, it should be aware that there are often regulations of the governing body as to what can be replayed: a memorable shot or kick at goal may be acceptable, but a more negative image or controversial incident may not. Any operators of such facilities must be contractually obliged to follow all such guidelines. The club may further stipulate that edited highlights are made available within a certain short period (often of a matter of one or two hours) of the conclusion of the event, to enable the event to be reflected upon on closed circuit televisions or around the hospitality facilities at the venue. Videos of the whole match or event may be required to be made available within a certain time period, both to the club and possibly also the other participants in the event for broadcast or other exploitation.

These services do not come cheap. However, they are in many ways part and parcel of the experience offered to the spectator of top-level sporting events and a proper archive of video footage can be very valuable, both from the point of view of the club's own exploitation through videos and other products such as CD-ROM products, or computer games which might capitalise upon that video footage, and also from the point of view of the prospect of broadcasting. The approach of multi-channel digital television means that in the very near future many sports clubs and promoters of events may choose to broadcast these events themselves. Many of the principles are still to be worked out as the current status quo in most sports is that an overall broadcasting deal is formulated by the governing body, the corollary to which is that broadcasting by the club by terrestrial or satellite broadcasting or inclusion in a cable programme service is absolutely prohibited. One of the things which will need to be worked out is an acceptable format for outsourcing the technical aspect of the broadcasts – it is likely that such an agreement will be a crucial component of venue operation in the future. However, even on the basis of current restrictions the historic archive may be free from broadcasting prohibitions and may therefore be available for broadcast exploitation by the club. Clubs should now think of getting an archive together and getting arrangements in place to take advantage of the new technologies and the new opportunities that may arise. There has been some considerable interest in live broadcasting over the Internet, perhaps offering a loophole in the current prohibitions on broadcasting that exist in many places: it is arguable that such a broadcast would be the inclusion of footage of a cable programme service according to the definitions in the broadcasting legislation and therefore would be subject to the standard prohibitions on individual broadcasting agreements, but clubs need to be ready to exploit whatever opportunities come their way. The current and possible future challenges under competition law, both domestic and European, to the current status quo described above may also bring forward many of these considerations considerably and clubs must not get caught out.

For that reason, a good contract with a video producer will be a fairly crucial element of the club's commercial arrangements. It should provide clearly at the outset that any and all copyright in the footage taken (both sound and video) throughout the world should be assigned absolutely for the duration of copyright to the club: as the agreement will be put in place at the outset of the relationship that would be an assignment of future copyright pursuant to the CDPA 1988, s 91. The club should then licence back to the video producer the copyright it has had assigned to it, for the strictly confined purpose of producing programmes for exploitation in video format, which can then be badged with the club's trade marks and distributed to the general public and supplied at a cheaper rate to the club's own retail outlets. There should be a licence to enable the video producer to perform all acts necessary to produce the specific video products and the other products such as highlights packages, action replays and so forth required as outlined above. The agreement should further provide for the usual trade mark licensing and merchandising provisions dealt with in Chapter 6 and should provide for the delivery to the club, in the formats requested by the club, all pictures taken by the video producer within a very short time of their being taken.

There is of course the possibility for there to be free exchange between clubs of their video footage. This has historically taken place on a fairly informal basis. For instance, it is standard for football clubs to produce a video reviewing their season. Naturally, the video footage to which they have best access is that of matches which took place at their own stadium because that is the footage which has been taken by their own video contractor. However, it is helpful of course to have footage of away games as well and therefore good liaison with other clubs is of assistance in compiling those products which the club requires.

The cost of the facilities brought to the ground by the video producer can in some part be set off against the guaranteed minimum royalty which the producer should be paying in relation to its rights in respect of the distribution of the club's videos.

Regard needs to be had when formulating such an agreement to the rules of the governing body, as always: in particular, it must be recognised that the governing body may require its own appointed broadcaster to attend the venue to take pictures, and that broadcaster does not want to be impeded by having a rival team of cameramen and editors present at the venue. In those circumstances, it is always useful for the club to have access to the footage from the broadcaster in the same way as it has access to footage from its own contractor, but that is not always possible. Liaison and negotiation is therefore necessary.

8.4   TICKETING

Almost all discussions of the increasing commercialisation of sport turn upon income streams to sports organisations which are non-traditional. Sponsorship is one and broadcasting another. It is often easy to forget that the most crucial income stream to all sport arises through ticketing.

It is frequently pointed out that, for the big Premier League football clubs, the ticketing income to the club has reduced in corporate value as an income stream and does not even cover the wage bill for the club's players. That is a fairly unique case at the current time and for other sports, such as both rugby codes, ticketing remains a crucial income stream. Further, the importance of proper ticketing to the other income streams available through sponsorship and broadcasting cannot be underestimated. Any sponsor's primary public, whether it is a shirt sponsor or whether it commissions a sign or a scoreboard flash or sponsors a player, is the paying public at the match. Sponsors need also to be associated with good quality events to which the public have access in a comparatively easy, affordable and most of all safe way. For broadcasters (to put it at its most blunt) the paying public provide atmosphere for the broadcast and to broadcast an event which is not healthily attended live is distinctly unattractive.

Consequently, a sports organisation must have regard to the commercial and public order aspects of ticketing. In a commercial sense, the issues are comparatively straightforward when one is just dealing with the one-ticket-per-person paying public. It becomes more difficult commercially where there is seen to be a conflict between the requirements of sponsors and requirements of the individual supporters of that club or event. The 1998 World Cup Finals were under heavy criticism even before they began on account of a perceived imbalance in ticketing allocation between the sponsors of the tournament and the general public. Moreover, ticket allocation between nations was also controversial.

8.4.1   Corporate entertaining

There is always an overlap between ticketing and sponsorship. Put in one way, one could say that someone who pays £20 per ticket is a supporter and therefore falls under the ticketing heading and someone who pays £150 for their ticket is a sponsor and falls into that discussion. However flippant that formulation may sound, it does help to bring out how much breadth of range there is available to a club in organising its ticketing arrangements. The old days of 70,000 people shivering together in identical squalor on the terraces are long gone. The legislation relating to the safety of large stadia touched upon above, a watershed for which perhaps was the Taylor Report into the Hillsborough disaster, necessarily drove much of the concentration of many of the major spectator sports away from the popular market and the result has been a drive towards the provision of high quality facilities and services at comparatively high prices for which the main customers will be businesses, rather than private individuals. Corporate entertaining is a fact of life and one of the most lucrative income streams available to any sports club. Most major sports clubs now will retain staff of a level which would not disgrace a major hotel in number and expertise in catering, hospitality and bar areas. Those venues will have a number of bars and private rooms available for hire and will offer a range of packages beginning with the one-off ticket for entry to the ground passing through season tickets, family enclosure season tickets, to packages which offer lunch before the event and culminating with the hire of executive boxes and even entry into the inner sanctum of the club, such as suites or bar areas which are shared with the club's directors and sporting personnel.

Liquor licensing

Liquor licensing is a crucial issue in all catering matters and particularly at sporting events, where there may be not only legislation and directives of the governing body regulating the sale and supply of alcohol within the ground, but also tight agreements with breweries and other concessionaires. Any modern sports business which has ambitions in this regard and does not employ highly trained specialists in all areas of catering is frankly being foolish. The delegation of these functions to concessionaires should be seriously considered at least in the early stages of development, not only for the guaranteed income stream they can offer by the concessionaire taking the financial risk, but also for the expertise they can bring to the exercise.

Executive boxes

Executive boxes will be sold usually by the season, mostly to businesses. This is a good opportunity for business to entertain clients and employees and to attach that business to the brand represented by the club. Usually the rental of the executive box will be accompanied with a sponsorship package offering signage relating to that business as part of the package. However, the licence of an executive box must be quite clear in certain respects. First, it should strictly specify those events which are covered. The licence will usually be for a period beginning an hour or so before the commencement of each event in the specified class and terminating a little afterwards. The club should be vigilant not to grant any more extensive rights in terms of time, unless it is intended that the box or area is to be available for use by the business as an office or meeting room outside the time of sporting events: if it is so intended, there should be a major element of charge for that privilege as the club should remember that it might have a fairly lucrative trade in renting out the same boxes at different times of the week or year specifically as meeting rooms or training suites. If the venue is to be used for other events than those in which the club participates, the sale of those executive boxes for the duration of those other events will usually be demanded by their promoters. For instance, a county cricket club might grant a licence for use of an executive box for all county matches for a certain fee, but charge a further fee for one day matches. The business may choose to take only a certain class of matches or all matches, depending on its budget. For test matches, it will usually be the case that the box is no longer under the control of the county cricket club.

The box licence should set out certain other crucial issues. It will usually be prudent to set down codes of behaviour and dress. There should be a maximum number of persons who can be invited by the licensee into the box at any one event to avoid overcrowding and over-exploitation of the facility. It should be clear that the licensee of the box is responsible for all their invitees' behaviour, dress and expenses and for any and all damage caused by them or their invitees. It should also make quite clear that use of the box is subject at all times to the ground regulations and conditions of issue of tickets which will be dealt with below. A specimen executive box licence appears at **8.9**.

8.4.2   Sponsor's allocation of tickets

Any sponsorship agreement will include an allocation of tickets to the sponsor. A club's main sponsor may be entitled to between 50 and 100 tickets in a designated area of the ground for each home match. On top of that, it will demand executive facilities for its employees and guests. The lesser forms of sponsorship dealt with above, such as sponsorship of signs, match balls, mascots and so forth will also bring with them ticketing allocations.

The club must be extremely vigilant to ensure that the allocation of tickets to sponsors is very carefully structured so that mechanisms are in place which prevent an errant sponsor from distributing tickets in a manner which places the reputation of the club or the event in jeopardy and which, perhaps most importantly, may compromise the safety of spectators. For instance, in an ideal world spectators could be unsegregated but that is not the case. Segregation of spectators is a crucial issue and will often be insisted upon by police authorities as a condition of the policing, both of the stadium, and of the area surrounding the stadium. If sponsors or the purchasers of corporate hospitality packages do not adhere to the segregation regulations imposed upon the tickets, the results can be catastrophic.

The conditions of issue of the ticket will always stipulate that the club reserves the right at all times to refuse entry to the venue as it sees fit. However, the refusal of entry to a sports ground is a sanction which needs to be considered with great care. First, it can be inflammatory and lead to major problems of public order. Secondly, as was tragically seen in the Hillsborough disaster, bottle necks at crucial points around the ground can lead to severe problems of crowd flow. It should not, therefore, be the responsibility of the man on the turnstile to police supporters. The club, therefore, when providing tickets to sponsors, must stipulate very strongly indeed what persons those tickets can be allocated to and must provide for a strict code of behaviour in line with the code of behaviour enshrined in ground regulations[1] for all the guests of that sponsor. In the event that those conditions are breached by the sponsor, the club should ensure that it is in a position to terminate the sponsorship contract. Any lesser sanction fails to reflect the importance of the issue.

Quite apart from the public order issues, the sponsorship contract should contain provisions requiring any sponsor in receipt of tickets only to allocate those tickets to bona fide contacts and trading partners of that company or along specific channels. It must ensure that the tickets do not seep through the sponsor

---

1   See **8.4.3** and **8.8**.

out into the black market to ticket touts. The ticket tout problem not only leads to severe difficulties in relation to public order, as indicated above, in relation to segregation of the fans but also leads to a general lowering of the reputation of the event, where tickets have been touted around at prohibitive prices and the ordinary fan cannot obtain the allocation he considers himself entitled to at the ordinary price.

Mentioned above was the possibility of alternative regimes for distribution of sponsor's tickets beyond the trading partners of the sponsors. A common practice by sponsors is to offer tickets to the public by way of competitions, which they use to enhance the sponsor's product prior to the event. In that case, the specific terms or parameters of the competition and publicity relating to it must be laid down in the sponsorship contract and the conditions on which those tickets are issued to the competition winners must be stipulated. The sponsor must vet all competition entrants. It is not uncommon, therefore, to stipulate that a sponsor must require entrants to submit their passport details for scrutiny. They should be asked before being permitted to pass to the next phase of the competition to confirm that they have no convictions for offences in relation to public order, or that they have not been arrested at a sports stadium, or been excluded from any sports stadium. When any competition winners are brought to the event, they must be accompanied at all times by a representative of the official sponsor who is responsible for their conduct.

The same restrictions should apply to any staff of the sponsor permitted to attend the event. Any sale by the staff of tickets allocated to them must be strictly prohibited and treated as a serious disciplinary matter by the sponsor, and a serious breach by the sponsor of the sponsorship contract.

8.4.3   Terms and conditions of issue

Whether dealing with sponsors or members of the wider paying public, however, it is crucial that the club always ensures that its terms and conditions of issue in respect of ticketing are very durable and are strictly enforced. All ticketing must be sold subject to those stringent terms and conditions and each ticket must explicitly incorporate the code of conduct which is enshrined in the ground regulations. When tickets are allocated to any ticketing agency or other team or body participating in the event, it must be on the basis that they are all sold subject to those conditions. Notices at each entrance to the ground should be displayed showing those ground regulations as express terms of the licence granted to the holder of the ticket to enter the ground. Those terms must have been agreed with the police who will be policing the ground and the surrounding area, the local authority which has powers and duties in relation to the stadium, and any governing body of the sport, to ensure uniformity between all venues and compliance with all applicable legislation and regulations of the sport. Stewarding by the club's employees must be firm but sensitive and proper training of such personnel is essential.

Often sponsors concerned about ambush marketing will wish the conditions of issue of tickets to incorporate provisions such as no persons being allowed into the stadium wearing garments or hats or carrying signs or products of or bearing the logos of any competing business. Such terms should be resisted by the club at the negotiation stage. Any attempt by coercion to remove articles of clothing or banners from fans as they enter into the stadium is inadvisable from the point of view of public order and such attempts, on the rare occasions that they are made, should be made out of such public order considerations, not commercial considerations. The proper and sensible policing of mass events involves sensitivity and a commitment to treating members of the public with a modicum of respect. Issues which must, however, be dealt with in the conditions of issue of tickets and ground regulations are set out in the specimen form at **8.8**. The terms summarised in that form should be made very eye-catching and should be accompanied by clear and unequivocal statements made both on the ticket issued to the public and in appropriate areas around the venue, that entry is strictly on the basis of acceptance of those regulations and that entry constitutes unqualified acceptance of those terms as terms of the licence to enter the ground. It should be clearly stated that failure to comply in any way, shape or form with any or all of these regulations, by any person entering the ground, shall entitle the organiser without further warning to eject that individual from the ground, and that the organiser reserves the right to eject any individual from the ground whose presence may constitute any form of annoyance, nuisance or danger to any person, or whose own safety is in any way compromised in the opinion of any steward, officer of the club or police officer.

If appropriate, it is a good idea to place a full print of these statements and the full ground regulations either on the ticket itself or on any documentation accompanying the ticket. Certainly in the case of season tickets of any nature and any sponsorship arrangements which include the provision of tickets, such a document should be enclosed without fail. It should be very clearly specified with those season or extended tickets that breach of the conditions of issue and/or ground regulations will lead to the forfeiture of all rights conferred by the season or extended ticket as a whole, not just the rights in respect of the specific event at which the breach took place. Season tickets should remain the property of the club at all times and the club must be entitled to recover possession of the season ticket at any time if it believes there to have been any breach of conditions of issue or ground regulations.

8.5 PROTECTING COMMERCIAL INTERESTS AT THE VENUE

8.5.1 Ambush marketing

Mention has been made above of the concept of ambush marketing.[1] This is becoming both more common and more ingenious. The main sponsor of an inner city marathon was severely disconcerted to find that its main competitor had bought up all the main advertising hoardings on the marathon route resulting in the television cameras tracking the runners from one advertisement to the next for its competitor. Airships have been flown across the skyline of major events by those wanting to hi-jack the profile of the sporting event and not wanting to pay the event organiser for the privilege. Sponsors who pay for sponsorship benefits at the venue will also want the negative benefits of ensuring that they cannot simply be hi-jacked or made to look foolish by their competitors.

---

1   See **6.5**.

When negotiating sponsorship agreements, therefore, the club should be sensitive to this issue and should understand the crucial nature of it to its sponsors. However, it should not give undertakings it cannot deliver. The club can never guarantee 100% that it can beat the ingenuity of the commercial organisations who engage in such tactics – and it is often the biggest and best resourced organisations who do so – and the club should restrict any obligations therefore to those of the nature of using reasonable endeavours to ensure that ambush marketing does not take place or taking certain specified steps which it knows it is in a position to take to avoid ambush marketing taking place. It should never be complacent enough to give an absolute guarantee that this will not happen.

8.5.2 Unauthorised merchandise

In addition to policing the stadium for its sponsors, the club will want to keep the stadium free of unauthorised traders for itself. A lucrative business exists in counterfeit replicas of club strip. Unauthorised souvenirs using club trade marks and club copyright items enjoy a healthy market particularly in the peripheral area around the venue.

The first thing for the club to do is to ensure that the personnel are available on match days to check products being carried by supporters on entry to the ground and all products that are on sale outside the venue. The club should never be so naïve as to think that the police will be the least bit interested in this sort of activity, unless and until it causes problems with crowd dynamics. The approach of the police to major sporting events is one–quite understandably–concentrated almost entirely on public safety and public order. Commercial matters are matters for the club and it should ensure that it has in place properly trained personnel with full instructions on what they are to do. Liaison should be made at a very early stage with the local Trading Standards Departments. They should be notified of all the club's trade marks and copies of registration certificates should be supplied. Trading Standards should be actively encouraged to operate their statutory powers under TMA 1994 and to make seizures and take out prosecutions in relation to infringing goods. As dealt with in Chapter 4, TMA 1994, s 92 sets out a range of criminal offences punishable potentially with up to 10 years imprisonment on indictment where a registered trade mark or mark likely to be mistaken for a registered trade mark is applied to goods or their packaging, or some person is in possession of such goods with intent to sell the same.

The use of the criminal law is crucial. There are obviously civil causes of action available to the club in relation to infringement of its intellectual property rights and these should be used whenever appropriate, but the club should also recognise that many unauthorised traders are not particularly intimidated by civil actions. It will be difficult to trace them, difficult to litigate against them and difficult to execute any judgment. The criminal law is the front line issue in the policing of the stadium and Trading Standards officers should therefore be actively encouraged to assist. The club can also take out private prosecutions rather than rely on any statutory agency and that should be actively considered. Enquiry agents should be used to assist Trading Standards officers in locating the infringers, making test purchases as proof of infringement and proof that criminal offences have been committed, obtaining witness statements and effectively taking whatever steps are needed to back up the Trading Standards Department. Where major operations are identified, Trading Standards might even raid warehouses containing counterfeit items and any information relating to such operations that comes into the club's hands should be notified immediately to them.

As infringing goods are frequently imported, Customs & Excise should be notified of any registered trade marks held by the club and again, registration certificates supplied. Customs are able to monitor imported goods and can inspect and even seize goods which have originated outside the European Union or Turkey.

In addition to TMA 1994, CDPA 1988 gives the power under s 100 for the copyright owner to seize infringing materials. There are a range of criminal offences in CDPA 1988 as dealt with in Chapter 4. Once again prosecutions should be considered both by statutory agencies or even on a private basis by the club.

Where orthodox intellectual property law cannot be of direct assistance, for instance, in the cases of ambush marketing where tactics concentrate on competing rather than counterfeit products, or when articles for sale do not directly infringe trade marks or copyright, the club needs to be more creative. The constant liaison it should have as a venue operator with the local police and local authorities should also take into account any stalls set up by vendors which obstruct the public highway. It should encourage the policing, where that falls within the police remit, of those stalls and particularly seek to prevent the grant of any street trading licences by the local authority. The local authority should be encouraged not to grant such licences not only from the point of view of the commercial probity of the operations to which they are likely to be granted, but also from the point of view of the safety of the public who should not be impeded in their access to and from the stadium. It may be possible to arrange a police operation based on the laws against obstructing the public highway or under any local bye-laws dealing with similar matters. Such an operation would probably take place, if at all, some time prior to the start of the event because, as indicated above, by the time the event is imminent the attention of the police will be concentrated firmly on public order.

Where fixed stalls are not used, the Peddlars' Acts 1871 and 1881 can provide a useful, if indirect, weapon. Where persons travel from one place to another in order to sell goods they need to have a licence issued under the 1871 Act. To sell goods without such a licence is a criminal offence. Often the people employed to sell these goods will not wish to have a criminal conviction, however petty the likely penalty, and the issue of criminal summonses will often seriously damage the trade that takes place. Such prosecutions will almost inevitably need to be private prosecutions, for perhaps obvious reasons.

The use of ticketing conditions to prevent ambush marketing by the entry into the stadium of any person holding counterfeit or competing goods has been dealt with above: these conditions can be used against unauthorised traders but should not be turned upon members of the public who have bought or been given such goods, not least out of considerations of public order as outlined above.

The club should ensure that it has a unified and comprehensive policy involving the coordination of a number of club personnel, independent contractors and statutory agencies. Planning is crucial. There are a number of specialised companies which have trained personnel used to policing events for counterfeit goods and ambush marketing, particularly in the music industry, who can provide specialist services in this area.

The club should also be creative in its approach. Inland Revenue, Customs & Excise and the Benefits Agency may also be interested in the activities of unauthorised traders. Someone selling counterfeit goods on a stall outside a sports ground is often also claiming unemployment benefit and may be trading at a level of turnover where he or she should be registered for VAT. It is no great leap of faith to assume that they are not so registered. The interest in such persons to those agencies is clear and if those agencies wish to perform a sweep of the area at a specific time in order to take names, addresses and details, that is an extremely effective way of clearing the area, to say the least.

Finally, where the club does find itself up against substantial and determined concerns it should consider proceedings based around the so-called 'industrial torts' of inducing breach of contract, conspiracy and interference with a trade or business. These torts are complex and somewhat nebulous in their nature and this is not the proper place for a detailed discussion of that nature or the likelihood of success, but injunctions have been granted on an interlocutory basis to prevent cases of industrial espionage and obstruction: the possibility should be considered in hard cases.

8.6 POURAGE AGREEMENT WITH CONCESSIONAIRE

(1)   Name and address of the Club (the 'Club')
(2)   Name and address of the Advertiser (the 'Advertiser')

DEFINITIONS

'Advertiser's Products' [the products being promoted eg 'Fizzy, Diet Fizzy, caffeine free Fizzy etc']

'Events'   [the Events in respect of which sponsorship rights are granted]

'Products'   [the generic products eg 'soft drinks whether in canned or bottled form or in the form of syrups or powders etc']

'Venue'   means the sports stadium known as [   ] at [   ]

In consideration of each party entering into its obligations hereunder

It is agreed as follows:

1. Payments

1   In consideration of the rights and benefits granted to the Advertiser by the Club as set out in this Agreement the Advertiser shall pay to the Club the sum of £[   ] plus VAT per annum for the duration of this agreement payable upon presentation of an appropriate VAT invoice by the Club as follows:

1.1   £[   ] plus VAT on the date hereof; and

1.2   £[   ] plus VAT on the date one calendar year following the date hereof; and

1.3   £[   ] plus VAT on the date two calendar years following the date hereof.

2. Club's obligations

2   The Club:

2.1   will purchase solely from the Advertiser such of the Advertiser's Products as the Club sees fit such that the Advertiser's Products are served (on a non-exclusive basis) in any and all food and beverage locations from time to time situated by the Club at its absolute discretion in and around the Venue where Events are held;

2.2   grants to the Advertiser those pourage rights product marketing (excluding sales) advertising and promotional rights at all Events set out in and upon the terms of this Agreement.

3. Exclusions

3   Nothing in this Agreement shall prevent or restrict the Club from:

3.1   observing and complying with the rules and regulations of any of [   ] and any other governing body of [the sport] having power to issue regulations or directives with which the Club must comply for any reason and/or abiding by the terms of entry and/or sponsorship of any tournament, league or competition in which the Club at any time may participate whilst this Agreement is in force (a 'Club Competition') and/or any contractual arrangements pursuant to which the Venue is used by any person, firm or company for any purpose not being that of a Club Competition AND FOR THE AVOIDANCE OF DOUBT in the event that any such condition or term of entry and/or sponsorship and/or any such regulation or directive of any governing body and/or any such contractual arrangements shall conflict with any obligation arising hereunder then that condition or term of sponsorship and/or regulation or directive and/or contractual arrangements shall prevail over the conflicting obligation arising hereunder and no failure by the Club to comply with such an obligation arising hereunder shall be construed as or have the effect of being any breach of this Agreement, but rather the effect of the conflicting obligation arising pursuant to this Agreement shall be deemed to be suspended throughout any period for which such conflict exists;

3.2   from serving or offering for sale [*any potentially rival product having sponsorship rights granted by the Club or incumbent upon the Club*]; or

3.3   from continuing the operation of any vending machines or other equipment belonging to or operated by or on behalf of any other Product manufacturer PROVIDED ALWAYS that advertising for any other Product shall be displayed at the site of such vending machine only.

4. Signage

4.1   The Advertiser shall be entitled to erect signage of a nature and quality acceptable to the Club at its own expense (both of construction and erection) such signs to be of a number to be mutually agreed from time to time between the parties and to be displayed at each and all of those outlets at which the Advertiser's Products are exposed for sale from time to time at the Venue.

4.2   The Advertiser's said signage shall not be physically or electronically removed replaced or covered up by any means save where the Venue is being used for functions or purposes other than the Events.

4.3   In the event that the Club reasonably objects to the nature of any signage erected by the Advertiser pursuant to its rights granted in this Agreement the Advertiser shall forthwith at its own expense remove the said signage and (if it so wishes) replace the same with such signage as is reasonably acceptable to the Club.

5. Display of products

5   The Advertiser's Products shall be prominently displayed at each and all of those outlets of the Venue at which the Advertiser's Products are exposed for sale from time to time in a manner and to an extent to be mutually agreed from time to time between the parties.

6. Maintenance

6   Those signs and panels advertising or promoting the Advertiser's Products at the Venue which are constructed in a manner enabling them to be illuminated shall be illuminated at all Events. The Advertiser shall have the right of access to the Venue at reasonable times by prior arrangement with the Club to its permanent signage for the purpose of such replacement modification or removal of such signage as may be mutually agreed from time to time between the parties. The Advertiser will be solely responsible for the insurance and general maintenance (in each case to the reasonable satisfaction of the Club and in relation to insurance, such insurance to include insurance against all reasonable third party risks and consequential damages as may prudently be insured against by any reasonable business) of the said signs and panels throughout the duration of this Agreement. The Club shall pay all electrical and

other normal operation costs of the said signs and panels throughout the duration of this Agreement save where expressly agreed otherwise.

7. Containers

7   All cups and containers dispensed at any outlets in the Venue at which the Advertiser's Products are exposed for sale from time to time which are to be used to hold the Advertiser's Products shall be trade mark cups and containers approved by the Advertiser and which prominently bear the exclusive trade marks of the Advertiser (the 'Advertiser's Containers'). The price paid for the Advertiser's Containers shall be mutually agreed from time to time between the Advertiser and the Club.

8. Promotion rights

8   Subject to the Club's reasonable prior written approval, the Advertiser shall have the right throughout the duration of this Agreement to conduct consumer promotions related to the Products at the Venue during not more than ten (10) Events. All fees and expenses related to such promotions shall be paid by the Advertiser. The nature of such promotions their duration content and scheduled dates and times for commencement and conclusion shall be consistent with usual promotions permitted by the Club and shall be agreed in advance of any such promotion in writing between the Advertiser and the Club. The Club shall extend its reasonable and agreed cooperation to the Advertiser in the conduct and staging of such promotions.

9. Duration

9   This Agreement shall commence upon the date hereof and shall terminate on the date [   ] calendar years thereafter unless otherwise terminated pursuant to Clause 10 hereof.

10. Termination

10   Either party may terminate this Agreement upon [   ] business days' notice by service upon the other at the other's principal place of business of notice in writing either by facsimile or by first class post in the event that:

10.1.1 the other party has committed any persistent material or fundamental breach of any of its obligations hereunder, provided that if the breach is capable of remedy such notice shall only be given if the party in breach shall not have remedied the said breach within two weeks of receipt of notice in writing specifying the breach and requiring it to be remedied, or

10.1.2 the other ceases to carry on business has a receiver or administrator appointed over all or any part of its assets or undertaking enters into any composition or arrangement with its creditors or enters into liquidation (other than for the purposes of amalgamation or reconstruction).

10.2   No failure to terminate this Agreement or to exercise any rights hereunder shall operate or be construed as a waiver of such rights and any such termination shall be entirely without prejudice to any and all rights having accrued to either party hereunder.

11. Advertiser's warranty

11.1   The Advertiser hereby warrants that any and all signage erected by the Advertiser pursuant to its rights granted by this Agreement shall not be obscene blasphemous or defamatory of any person firm or company and shall not infringe any rights of intellectual property of any nature belonging to any person firm or company.

11.2   The Advertiser hereby covenants that it will fully and effectively indemnify and keep indemnified the Club against any claims damage or loss howsoever arising (including but not limited to any indirect or consequential damage) howsoever arising to the Club as a result of breach by the Advertiser of the warranties set out at Clause 11.1.

12. Force majeure

12.1   If by reason of any event of force majeure either of the parties to this Agreement shall be delayed in or prevented from performing any of the provisions of this Agreement (save only any obligation to pay money) then such delay or non-performance shall not be deemed to be a breach of this Agreement and no loss or damage shall be claimed by either of the parties hereto from the other by reason thereof;

12.2   Should the exercise of the rights and obligations under this Agreement be materially hampered interrupted or interfered with by reason of any event of force majeure then the obligations of the parties shall be suspended during the period of such hampering interference or interruption consequent upon such event or events of force majeure and shall be postponed for a period of time equivalent to the period or periods of suspension and the parties hereto will use their best endeavours to minimise and reduce any period of suspension occasioned by any of the events aforesaid.

12.3   The expression 'an event of force majeure' shall mean and include fire flood casualty lockout strike labour disputes industrial action of any kind unavoidable accident breakdown of equipment national calamity or riot Act of God the enactment of any Act of Parliament or the act of any other legally constituted authority any cause or event arising out of or attributable to war or any other cause or event (whether of a similar or dissimilar nature) outside the control of the parties hereto other than a shortage or lack of money including (without prejudice to the generality of the foregoing) any instruction or order of any competent police, sporting authority or governing body of [the sport] having the power to issue regulations and/or directives with which the Club must comply for any reason.

13. General

13.1   This Agreement shall not be construed as constituting any form of partnership or joint venture between the parties hereto.

13.2   Each party undertakes to keep confidential all information of a confidential nature relating to this Agreement (including but not limited to any information relating to the other parties' business finances, business methods, business opportunities, financial projections, customers, contracts or research and development).

13.3   No announcement in connection with this Agreement shall be made by or on behalf of either party without the prior written consent of the other save that a press release in a form agreed in writing by both parties shall be issued within 48 hours of the execution of this Agreement by both parties.

13.4   For a period of [   ] weeks prior to the expiration of this Agreement, the Advertiser will have the exclusive right to enter into negotiation with the Club for an option to renew this Agreement for a further three year period always provided that nothing in this clause shall be construed as or have the effect of obliging the parties so to renew this Agreement.

As witness the hands of the duly authorised representatives of the parties

This   day of [   ]

8.7   CONCESSION AGREEMENT

THIS AGREEMENT is made the   day of

BETWEEN

(1)   [   ] of [   ] [the 'Club'] and

(2)   [   ] of [   ] [the 'Licensee']

I   DEFINITIONS

In this Agreement the following expressions shall have the following meanings:

'**Access Ways**'   means the entrance hall corridors lobbies staircases access ways passages lifts and escalators of the Venue or over which the Venue enjoys rights of access the use of which is necessary for obtaining access to and egress from the Licensed Area or such of them as afford reasonable access and egress both for goods and for personnel as above as the Club may from time to time in its absolute discretion designate by the service of not less than 28 days' written notice to the Licensee;

'**Designated Hours**'   means [am] to [pm] on Mondays to Fridays, [am] to [pm] on Saturdays inclusive (Bank or other Public Holidays excepted) or such other hours including time on Sundays as the Club may from time to time in its absolute discretion determine by service of not less than 28 days' written notice to the Licensee together with that period (if not included in the above) commencing 2 hours before the commencement of and ending 2 hours following the end of any and all Events;

'**Equipment**'   means those items of equipment set out at the Schedule annexed hereto;

'**Events**'   means any and all competitive first team matches taking place at the Venue (in any competition of whatever nature) in which the Club participates throughout the duration of this Agreement;

'**Licensed Area**'   means the area shown for the purposes of identification only edged and hatched yellow on the plan annexed or such other single continuous area of appropriate space for the Licensee's Business of the same or greater total area within the Venue as the Club may from time to time in its absolute discretion designate by the service of not less than 28 days' written notice to the Licensee;

'**Licence Fee**'   means One pound per annum payable on the date hereof and thereafter annually upon each anniversary of the date hereof;

'**Office**'   means that office area with secure locking door and cupboard space for the purpose of identification only edged blue on the plan annexed hereto;

'Venue'   means the sports stadium known as [   ] at
                 [   ].

2 LICENCE

2.1   Subject to clauses 3 and 5 and in consideration of the Licence Fee the Club
         hereby grants to the Licensee the right (in common with the Club and all others
         authorised by the Club so far as is not inconsistent with the rights granted
         hereunder to the Licensee) to use for the duration of this Agreement during the
         Designated Hours:

2.1.1   for the purpose of the sale to all invitees to the Venue of the Licensee's hot
         takeaway foods the Licensed Area;

2.1.2   for the purpose of ordinary clerical and accounts work solely connected with
         the Licensee's business at the Venue the Office;

2.1.3   for the purposes of access to and egress from the Licensed Area the Access
         Ways;

2.1.4   reasonable access in common with the employees of the Club to such of the
         amenity and toilet areas provided at the Venue for the employees of the Club as
         the Club may from time to time reasonably designate by the service of not less
         than 28 days' written notice to the Licensee.

2.2   The Licensee shall be entitled to erect signage of a nature and quality acceptable
         to the Club at its own expense (both of construction and erection) such signs to
         be of a number to be mutually agreed from time to time between the parties and
         to be displayed at those places in the Licensed Area as the parties may from time
         to time agree.

2.3   Subject to the Club's reasonable prior written approval, the Licensee shall have
         the right throughout the duration of this Agreement to conduct consumer
         promotions related to the Licensee's Goods at the Venue during not more than
         ten (10) Events. All fees and expenses related to such promotions shall be paid
         by the Licensee. The nature of such promotions their duration content and
         scheduled dates and times for commencement and conclusion shall be
         consistent with usual promotions permitted by the Club and shall be agreed
         between the Licensee and the Club. The Club shall extend its reasonable
         cooperation to the Licensee in the conduct and staging of such promotions.

3 LICENSEE'S UNDERTAKINGS

The Licensee agrees and undertakes:

3.1   to pay to the Club:

3.1.1   the Licence Fee (together with any VAT) in advance at the date provided
         therefor;

3.1.2   a sum equal to [   ]% of the gross turnover in the Licensee's trading in the
         Licensed Area such payments to be made in respect of each calendar month's
         trading in the Licensed Area within [   ] days of the end of the said calendar
         month together with any VAT payable thereon;

3.1.3   those sums required to be paid by the Licensee pursuant to the provisions of
         clause 4;

3.2   not to bring any furniture equipment goods or chattels into the Venue without
         the consent of the Club save as may be strictly necessary for the proper
         exercise of the rights given in clause 2 or in order to carry out the Licensee's
         obligations hereunder;

3.3   to keep the Licensed Area and the Office clean and tidy and clear of rubbish at all times and to leave the same in a clean and tidy condition and in good serviceable and decorative repair and free of the Licensee's furniture equipment goods and chattels upon termination of this Agreement for any reason;

3.4   to maintain at the Licensed Area an attractive display of goods in keeping with the standards maintained elsewhere in the Venue;

3.5   not to obstruct the Access Ways or cause the same to become dirty or untidy nor to leave any rubbish on them;

3.6   not to display any signs notices or promotional materials at the Licensed Area save those specifically authorised in this Agreement without the prior consent of a properly authorised employee of the Club and for the purposes of this clause the Catering Manager from time to time of the Venue employed by the Club shall be deemed properly authorised;

3.7   not to use the Licensed Area, the Office or Access Ways in such a way as to cause a nuisance damage disturbance annoyance inconvenience or interference of any nature (including but not limited to noise and smell) to the Club or Venue or any other Licensee or occupant or user of the Venue or adjoining or neighbouring property or to the owners occupiers or users of such adjoining or neighbouring property;

3.8   to comply with any and all instructions given by the Club in relation to hygiene and food safety and in any event to operate the highest standards of cleanliness and hygiene at all times in the Licensed Area;

3.9   not to commit any act omission matter or thing which would or might constitute a breach of any statutory requirement affecting the Licensed Area and/or the Office and/or the Venue or which would or might vitiate in whole or in part any insurance effected in respect of the Venue from time to time;

3.10   to observe any and all reasonable rules and regulations as the Club may make and of which the Club shall notify the Licensee from time to time in writing governing the Licensee's use of the Licensed Area and/or the Office and/or the Access Ways;

3.11   not to impede in any way the Club or its officers servants or agents in the exercise of the Club's rights of possession and control of the Venue and every part of the Venue;

3.12   to keep the Licensed Area fully and properly staffed during the Designated Hours;

3.13   to keep full and adequate records of all business conducted within the Licensed Area and upon reasonable notice to afford the Club suitable facilities and information (including but not limited to the right to inspect the said records on reasonable notice) to assess the Licensee's turnover for the purpose of calculating the payment referred to in clause 3.1.2 of this Agreement;

3.14   to indemnify the Club and keep the Club fully and effectively indemnified against any and all losses claims demands actions proceedings damages costs or expenses or other liability arising in any way from this Licence any breach of the Licensee's undertakings contained in this clause or the exercise or purported exercise of any of the rights given in clause 2 by the Licensee and or invitee or customer of the Licensee.

3.15   to use the Equipment only for the purpose for which it is designed and in accordance with any instructions issued by the Club from time to time and to indemnify the Club against any loss or damage to the Equipment.

4   CLUB'S UNDERTAKINGS

The Club agrees and undertakes:

4.1   to provide reasonable space at the Club's discretion:

4.1.1   within the storeroom which forms part of the Venue for storage of the Licensee's goods; and

4.1.2   at the entrance to the Venue for such of the Licensee's advertisements and signage as the Club may from time to time agree with the Licensee;

4.2   to provide all services of power reasonably required for the Licensee's business at the Licensed Area and fax and telephone lines for use by the Licensee only at the Licensed Area always provided that the Licensee shall be responsible for any and all charges in relation to the use of any facilities provided pursuant to this sub-clause 4.2;

4.3   not to permit any of the Licensee's goods to be sold within the Venue save by the Licensee's personnel at the Licensee's cash register at the Licensed Area;

4.4   to instruct the Club's cleaners to clean the Licensed Area to the same standard as the remainder of the Venue as part of the Club's cleaning schedule and at no cost to the Licensee;

4.5   to provide and maintain in full and effective working order in the Licensed Area the Equipment for the Licensee's exclusive use always provided that the Licensee shall pay the Club's reasonable charges in connection with all such maintenance and the full costs of any repair or replacements (fair wear and tear excepted) to the said Equipment required as a result of the Licensee's use thereof;

4.6   not to grant any rights of a similar nature to those granted to the Licensee hereunder to any person firm or company which in the reasonable opinion of the Licensee operates any business directly competing with the business of the Licensee to be operated from the Licensed Area.

5   GENERAL

5.1   The rights granted in clause 2 shall determine (without prejudice to the Club's other rights in respect of any breach of the undertakings contained in clause 3):

5.1.1   immediately on written notice given by the Club at any time following any breach by the Licensee of its undertakings contained in clause 3 provided that if the breach is capable of remedy such notice shall only be given if the Licensee shall not have remedied the said breach within two weeks of receipt of notice in writing specifying the breach and requiring it to be remedied;

5.1.2   on not less than six months written notice given either by the Club or the Licensee to the other to expire at any time.

5.2   Forthwith upon termination of this Agreement for any reason the Licensee shall vacate the Licensed Area the Office and the Venue and shall remove any and all signage advertising and promotional materials furniture equipment goods and chattels belonging to the Licensee from the Licensed Area the Office and the Venue.

5.3   The benefit of this License is personal to the Licensee and not assignable and the rights given in clause 2 may only be exercised by the Licensee and its employees duly authorised independent contractors and customers.

5.4 The Club gives no warranty that the Venue is legally or physically fit for the purposes specified in clause 2.

5.5 The Club shall not be liable for the death of or injury to any employees independant contractors or customers of the Licensee save only such as may be caused solely by the Club's negligence or for damage to any property of the Licensee or for any losses claims demands actions proceedings damages costs or expenses or other liability howsoever incurred by the Licensee or any person referred to in clause 5.3 in the exercise or purported exercise of the rights granted by clause 2.

5.6 Any notice given by either party pursuant to the provisions of this Agreement shall be in writing and shall be sufficiently served if delivered by hand or sent by recorded delivery to the other at its registered office.

SIGNED for and on behalf of the)

Club)

Signed for and on behalf of the)

Licensee)

SCHEDULE

Equipment: [list]

8.8   GROUND REGULATIONS

Notice: entry to the Ground is expressly subject to each and all of these Ground Regulations

1.   Permission for any person to enter or to remain within the Ground notwithstanding possession of any ticket by that person is at the absolute discretion of the stewards and officers of the Club and/or any police officer.

2.   No guarantees can be given by the Club that the Event will take place at any particular time or on any particular date and the Club reserves the right to reschedule the Event without notice and without any liability for so doing.

3.   In the event of the postponement or abandonment of the Event refunds of ticket prices if any will be made at the absolute discretion of the Club. The Club will have no legal liability to make a refund or to pay any form of consequential or indirect damage such as loss of enjoyment or travel costs.

4.   The Club reserves the right to search any person entering the Ground and to refuse entry to any person refusing to submit to such a search.

5.   The following are articles which must not be brought within the Ground (*eg knives, glasses, fireworks, smoke canisters, air-horns, flares, bottles, weapons of any sort or banners and signs exceeding certain dimensions*). Any person in possession of such items will be refused entry at the absolute discretion of any steward or officer of the Club and/or any police officer.

6.   All persons entering the Ground may only occupy the seat allocated to them by their ticket and must not move from any one part of the Ground to another without the express permission or instructions of any steward or officer of the Club and/or any police officer.

7.   No object may be thrown within the Ground.

8.   No foul or abusive language, singing, chanting or other offensive words such as racial or sexual abuse may be used within the Ground.

9.   Nobody entering the Ground shall be permitted to climb any structures within the Ground.

10.   Nobody may stand in any seating area whilst play is in progress.

11.   No alcohol may be consumed within the Ground except in those areas specifically designated for such purposes and in accordance with any terms displayed in those areas.

12.   No person may take photographs or use any video recording equipment inside the Ground without the express written permission of the Club.

13.   No articles, periodicals, publications, flyers or goods of any nature may be offered either free or for sale by any person save only the Club within the Ground without the express written permission of the Club.

14.   Any person entering the Ground must at all times comply with any and all instructions of any steward or officer of the Club and/or any police officer. Failure to comply within a reasonable time with any such instruction will lead to immediate ejection from the Ground.

15.   Any individual who has entered any area of the Ground designated for the use of any group of supporters to which he does not belong may be ejected from the Ground either for the purposes of his own safety or for any other reason.

16. No tickets may be offered for resale within the Ground. Any such tickets offered for sale may be confiscated by any steward or officer of the Club or any police officer.

The Club reserves absolutely the right to eject from the Ground any person failing to comply with each and all of the Ground Regulations

8.9 EXECUTIVE BOX LICENCE AGREEMENT

THIS LICENCE AGREEMENT is made the   day of   [   ]

BETWEEN

(1)   [   ] whose registered office is situate at
       [   ] ('the Club'); and

(2)   [   ] whose address/registered office is situate at
       [   ] ('the Licensee)

I DEFINITIONS

In this Agreement the following expressions shall have the following meanings:

'Access Ways'	means the entrance hall corridors lobbies staircase access ways passages lifts and escalators of the Premises or over which the Premises enjoys rights of access the use of which is necessary for obtaining access to and egress from the Box and the Designated Areas or such of them as afford reasonable access and egress as above as the Club may from time to time in its absolute discretion designate on thirty days notice to the Licensee;
'Advertising Fees'	means the sum of [£] plus VAT payable on the date hereof in respect of the Advertising Benefits set out at clause 3 hereof;
'Box'	means Executive Box No in the [ ] Stand at the Premises or such other Executive Box at the Premises its the Club may from time to time in its absolute discretion designate on thirty days notice to the Licensee;
'Designated Areas'	means those areas set out in Schedule I hereof or such other areas as the Club may from time to time in its absoute discretion designate on thirty days notice to the Licensee;
'Designated Times'	means those periods commencing two hours before the commencement and terminating one hour following the conclusion of each of the Relevant Events;
'Licence Fee'	means the sum of [£] plus VAT payable on the date hereof in respect of the Licence set out at clause 2 hereof;
'Licence Period'	means the period from the date of this Agreement until the date on which the Licensee's rights under clauses 2 and 3 are determined in accordance with clause 7 hereof;
'Premises'	means parts of the [ ] Stand of the Stadium;
'Relevant Events'	means all and any home [ ] matches played at the Stadium;
'Stadium'	means the [ ] stadium at [ ].

2 LICENCE

2.1   Subject to the provisions of this Agreement and in consideration of the Licence Fee the Club hereby grants to the Licensee the right (in common with the Club and all others authorised by the Club so far as is not inconsistent with the rights given to the Licensee) to use upon the terms set out in this Agreement and subject always to any and all Ground Regulations and Conditions of Issue of tickets promulgated by the Club at its absolute discretion from time to time by not more than [   ] representatives and invitees of the Licensee at any of the Relevant Events for the Licence Period during the Designated Times:

2.2   For the purposes of viewing the Relevant Events in the company only of the Licencee's representatives and invitees the Box;

2.3   For the purpose of activities ancillary to the viewing of the Relevant Events the Designated Areas;

2.4   For the purposes of access to and egress from the Box and the Designated Areas the Access Ways.

3   ADVERTISING BENEFITS

3.1   In consideration of the Advertising Fees and subject to the proviso set out at clause 3.2 the Club shall provide the following Advertising Benefits for the Licence Period to the Licensee:

3.1.1   an advertising board the artwork and dimensions of which shall be agreed between the parties displayed adjacent to the Box during all Relevent Events;

3.1.2   a half page advertisement in the Club's 'Match Day Programme' in respect of [No] of the Relevant Events during the course of the complete [   ] Season [year] such advertisements to be in a form agreed between the parties and placed in the Club's 'Match Day Programme' at intervals and dates determined by the Club in its absolute discretion ALWAYS PROVIDED THAT in the event of the termination of this Agreement for whatever reason prior to the expiry of the said [   ] Season nothing in this clause shall entitle the Licensee to any such advertisement following the date of such termination irrespective of the number of such advertisements having appeared prior to the date of such termination;

3.1.3   the name of the Licensee displayed on the door of the Box during all Relevant Events in a form which shall be agreed between the parties;

3.1.4   the name of the Licensee displayed during all Relevant Events on a Board displayed the names of all the Executive Box Holders in the reception area to the Designated Areas in a form which shall be agreed between the parties;

3.1.5   the 'flashing' of the Licensee's name and/or trading style on the electronic scoreboard at the Stadium on not less than [   ] occasions during the Designated Times in respect of each Relevant Event provided that the said electronic scoreboard is in operation.

3.2   Each and all of the obligations of the Club pursuant to clause 3.1 shall be subject to the express proviso that the Licensee and the Club hereby acknowledge that the Club shall not be in breach of any obligation to the Licensee where the Club is prevented from providing any of the advertising benefits set out at this clause 3 on account of any obligations of the Club howsoever arising:

3.2.1   to any relevant governing body of [the sport] (including but not limited to [   ]); and/or

3.2.2   to any sponsor of any competition or tournament in which the Club is engaged or for which the Stadium is a designated venue; and/or

3.2.3   to any broadcasting organisation having rights to broadcast in respect of any of the Relevant Events or in respect of any event of whatever nature taking place at the Stadium; and/or

3.2.4   any promoter of any event of whatsoever nature taking place at the Stadium.

3.3   The cost of the preparation of any artwork and/or signage to be displayed by the Club in accordance with this clause 3 shall be borne by the Club save where the parties are unable reasonably to agree the form and/or content thereof in which event the Licensee may at its own expense produce such signage and/or artwork as it requires and the Club may at its absolute discretion agree to display the same in accordance with the provisions of this clause 3 or reject the same and display artwork and/or signage on behalf of the Licensee as the Club in its absolute discretion sees fit.

4   LICENSEE'S UNDERTAKINGS

The Licensee agrees and undertakes:

4.1   to pay to the Club:

4.1.1   the Licence Fee within twenty-eight days of the date hereof; and

4.1.2   the Advertising Fee within twenty-eight days of the date hereof;

4.2   to use the Box only for the purposes of viewing the Relevant Events and not to use the Box for the purpose of any trade or business of the Licensee or of any other person;

4.3   not to permit any more than [   ] persons to enter the Box for the purpose of viewing the Relevant Events;

4.4   to ensure that all persons entering the Box and/or Designated Areas as its representatives and/or invitees shall be smartly dressed in accordance with any dress code laid down by the Club from time to time and in any event not to permit any person wearing jeans and/or training shoes to enter the Box and/or Designated Areas;

4.5   to ensure that no persons entering the Box and/or Designated Areas as its representatives and/or invitees shall consume alcohol save during those times within the Designated Times as are stipulated by the Club from time to time by notices posted within the Box in accordance with the terms set out in the said notices;

4.6   to ensure at all times that all persons entering the Box and/or Designated Areas as its representatives and/or invitees observe and conform in all respects with any and all ground regulations and conditions of issue of tickets promulgated by the Club at its absolute discretion from time to time and with any and all other rules and regulations from time to time stipulated by the Club and/or any governing body of [the sport] (including but not limited to [   ]);

4.7   not to bring any furniture equipment goods or chattels onto the Premises or the Designated Areas or the Box save as may be necessary for the exercise of the rights granted in clause 2 hereof;

4.8   not to obstruct the Access Ways or cause the same to become dirty or untidy not to leave any rubbish on them;

4.9   not to display any sign or notice at the Premises the Designated Areas the Access Ways and/or the Box save those provided by the Club pursuant to clause 3 hereof;

4.10   not to use the Premises the Designated Areas the Access Ways or the Box in such a way as to cause a nuisance damage disturbance annoyance interference or inconvenience to the Club to the said areas or to any adjoining or neighbouring areas or to any person using the said areas or adjoining or neighbouring areas;

4.11   not to do any act matter or thing which would or might constitute a breach of any statutory requirement affecting the Premises or which would or might vitiate in whole or in part any insurance effected in respect of the Premises from time to time;

4.12   to indemnify the Club and keep the Club indemnified against all losses claims demands actions proceedings damages costs or expenses or other liability arising in any way from this Agreement any breach of the Licensee's undertakings contained in clause 4 hereof or the exercise or purported exercise of any of the rights granted pursuant to clause 2 hereof and/or clause 3 hereof;

4.13   without prejudice to any and all of the Club's rights in respect of any breach of this Agreement to make good at the Licensee's expense any damage to the Premises the Designated Areas the Access Ways and/or the Box and/or to the furniture and appointments thereof attributable to any act or omission of the Licensee and/or its representatives and/or its invitees other than fair wear and tear and in the event that the Licensee shall not have made good such damage within seven days of the said damage having occurred to indemnify the Club against any costs damages and expenses incurred by the Club in making good the said damage on behalf of the Licensee (which the Club shall be entitled absolutely at its own discretion to do);

4.14   not to impede in any way the Club or its officers servants or agents in the exercise of the Club's rights of possession and control of the premises and every part of the Premises.

5   CLUB'S UNDERTAKINGS

The Club agrees and undertakes:

5.1   to provide suitable and reasonably priced catering services at such areas forming part of the Designated Areas as the Club shall in its absolute discretion see fit;

5.2   to provide by prior arrangement and upon reasonable notice of the Licensee's requirements having been given to the Club suitable and reasonably priced catering services at the Box ALWAYS PROVIDED THAT any and all costs in respect of such catering services shall be borne by the Licensee and the terms on which the said catering services are supplied shall have been agreed between the parties in advance of the date of the Relevant Event at which the said services are to be supplied;

5.3   to use its reasonable endeavours to maintain a satisfactory standard of service at all times in connection with its performance of its obligations pursuant to this Agreement;

5.4   to maintain at all times in force a policy of insurance issued by a reputable insurer pursuant to which the Box may be repaired or replaced at no cost to the Licensee in the event of damage or destruction (without prejudice to the Club's rights pursuant to clause 4.13 hereof).

6 RENEWAL AND FURTHER EVENTS

6.1 Upon the termination of this Agreement pursuant to clause 7.2 the Club shall offer upon such terms as the Club shall in its absolute discretion designate by notice in writing to the Licensee a further Agreement in respect of a licence of the Box or such other alternative executive box at the Stadium as the Club shall designate and in respect of advertising benefits. The facilities offered in such notice to the Licensee in respect of licensing of the Box or alternative executive box shall not be offered to any other person for a period of twenty-one days following the date of such notice. In the event that the Licensee shall not have accepted the said offer upon the expiry of the said twenty-one day period the Club shall be entitled to offer any and all such facilities to any person at its absolute discretion upon such terms as the Club sees fit.

6.2 In respect of any event taking place at the Stadium which is not a Relevant Event but in respect of which the Club is able to offer such a facility the Club shall offer upon such terms as to payment and otherwise as the Club shall in its absolute discretion designate by notice in writing to the Licensee the right to occupy the Box for the purpose of viewing the said event and shall not offer the said right to any other person for a period of seven days following the date of such notice. In the event that the Licensee shall not have accepted the said offer upon the expiry of the said seven day period the Club shall be entitled to offer the said right to any person at its absolute discretion upon such terms as the Club sees fit.

7 TERMINATION

The rights granted in clause 2 and clause 3 hereof shall determine (without prejudice to the Club's other rights in respect of any breach of the undertakings of the Licensee set out in clause 4 hereof):

7.1 immediately on notice given by the Club at any time following any breach by the Licensee of its undertakings set out at clause 4 hereof provided that if the breach is capable of remedy such notice shall only be given if the Licensee shall not have remedied the said breach within fourteen days of receipt of notice in writing specifying the breach and requiring the same to be remedied;

7.2 immediately upon the final day of the [   ] [   ] Season the precise date of which will be notified by the Club to the Licensee in writing not less than one month before the said date;

7.3 immediately in the event that the Licensee (being an individual or firm) shall become bankrupt and/or enter into an Individual Voluntary Arrangement with its creditors and/or make any arrangement or compensation with its creditors generally and/or have an Interim Receiver or Receiver appointed in respect of its assets;

7.4 immediately in the event that the Licensee (being a company) becomes insolvent and/or has a Receiver or Administrative Receiver or Administrator appointed over the whole or any part of its undertaking and/or assets and/or makes any arrangement or compound with its creditors and/or has an order made or resolution passed for it to be wound up (otherwise than in furtherance of a scheme for amalgamation or reconstruction on a solvent basis).

8 FORCE MAJEURE

8.1 In the event that the Club shall be prevented or delayed in the performance of any of its obligations under this Agreement by Force Majeure and the Club gives written notice thereof to the Licensee specifying the matters constituting Force Majeure and specifying the period for which it is estimated that such prevention or delay will continue then the Club shall be excused the performance and/or punctual performance as the case may be of any and all of its obligations hereunder from the date of such notice for so long as such cause of prevention or delay shall continue.

8.2   For the purpose of this Agreement 'Force Majeure' shall be deemed to be any cause affecting the performance of this Agreement arising from or attributable to acts events omissions or accidents beyond the reasonable control of the Club and without limitation to the generality thereof shall include the following:

8.2.1   strikes, lock outs or other industrial action;

8.2.2   civil commotion riot invasion war threat or preparation for war;

8.2.3   fire explosion storm flood earthquake subsidence epidemic or other physical disaster;

8.2.4   instructions and/or orders of any Police Force, Local Authority, organ of Local Government or organ of Central Government;

8.2.5   directives and/or regulations and/or instructions and/or orders of any governing body of [the sport] (including but not limited to [   ]).

9   GENERAL

9.1   The Benefit of this Agreement is personal to the Licensee and not assignable and the rights given in clause 2 hereof may only be exercised by the Licensee by way of a maximum at any one Relevant Event of [   ] of its representatives and invitees.

9.2   The Club shall not be liable for any injury or damage to or loss of property of the Licensee or of any other person or for any losses claims demands actions proceedings damages costs or expenses or other liability incurred by the Licensee in relation to the Advertising Benefits granted by clause 3 and/or by the Licensee or any person referred to in clause 9.1 in the exercise or purported exercise of the rights granted in clause 2 ALWAYS PROVIDED THAT nothing in this clause shall have the effect of excluding or restricting any liability for the death of or personal injury to any person save as permitted by law.

9.3   All notices given by either party pursuant to the provisions of this Agreement shall be in writing and shall be sufficiently served if delivered by hand or sent by first class post to the other at the address shown at the head of this Agreement.

SCHEDULE I

Designated Areas

8.10   EVENTS MANAGEMENT AGREEMENT

THIS AGREEMENT is made the   day of   [   ]

BETWEEN:

(1)   **THE RIGHTS HOLDER** of [   ] ('the
Rights Holder')

(2)   [   ] of [   ] ('the
Event Manager')

WHEREAS:

(A)   The Rights Holder controls all rights relating to the Event (as defined below) and

(B)   The Rights Holder wishes to appoint the Event Manager to organise and stage the Event

NOW IT IS HEREBY AGREED as follows:—

1.1   DEFINITIONS

'Budget'	means the budget for the Event set by the Rights Holder and agreed with the Event Manager or as varied in accordance with this Agreement;
'Consideration'	means the sums set out in Clause 9;
'Event'	means [ ] due to take place in years [ ] and any associated or ancillary event or competition taking place at the same time;
'Governing Body'	means [ ];
'Intellectual Property'	means patents, trade marks (whether registered or unregistered) rights in any designs (whether registered or unregistered) and applications for any of the foregoing, trade or business names, copyright and rights in performances;
'Representatives'	means those third parties engaged by the Rights Holder to carry out services in relation to the Event including without being limited to television production and broadcasting, public relations and promotions and all commercial partners, sponsors and advertisers appointed by the Rights Holder in relation to the Event;
'Services'	means those services in relation to the Even which are described in Schedule 1;
'Term'	means the period from the date of this Agreement until thirty days after the end of the Event unless terminated earlier in accordance with this Agreement;
'Territory'	means the United Kingdom;
'Trade Marks'	means the marks set out in Schedule 2;
'Venues'	means the venues used for the Event in any year including the immediately surrounding areas from which any material for broadcasting rights could be obtained or

which could be used for advertising which would be visible to television cameras within the venue including the city centre areas roads used in the Event areas used for official functions press centres media area information centres and all other areas necessary for the proper organisation of the Event;

1.2 **IN** this Agreement where the context admits:—

1.2.1   references to statutory provisions shall be construed as references to those provisions as amended or re-enacted or as their application is modified by other provisions from time to time and shall include references to any provisions of which they are re-enactments (whether with or without modification);

1.2.2   references to 'this Agreement' or to any other agreement or document referred to in this Agreement mean this Agreement or such other agreement or document as amended varied supplemented modified or novated from time to time and include the schedules;

1.2.3   references to clause(s) and schedule(s) are references to clause(s) and schedule(s) of and to this Agreement and references to sub-clause(s) or paragraph(s) are unless otherwise stated references to sub-clause(s) of the clause or paragraph(s) in which the reference appears;

1.2.4   references to a 'person' include any individual company body corporate corporation sole or aggregate government state or agency of a state firm partnership joint venture association organisation or trust (in each case whether or not having separate legal personality and irrespective of the jurisdiction in or under the law of which it was incorporated or exists) and a reference to any of them shall include a reference to the others;

1.2.5   any reference to writing includes typewriting printing lithography photography and other modes of representing or reproducing words in a legible form other than writing on an electronic display screen or similar device.

1.3 HEADINGS

The headings and sub-headings are inserted for convenience only and shall not affect the construction of this Agreement.

1.4 SCHEDULES

Each of the schedules shall have effect as if set out in this Agreememt.

2. APPOINTMENT

2.1   The Rights Holder appoints the Event Manager to provide the Services for the Event throughout the Term in the Territory upon the terms and conditions set out in this Agreement and its Schedules.

2.2   The Event Manager agrees to perform the Services in the Territory for the Event throughout the Term.

3. EXCLUSIVITY

3.1   The Rights Holder shall not appoint any third party to provide the Services in the Territory during the Term.

3.2   The Event Manager shall provide the Services for the Rights Holder in the Territory during the Term on the following basis:—

3.2.1   (subject to Clause 3.2.2) on a non-exclusive basis during year year of the Term; and

3.2.2   on an exclusive basis for the period of time commencing at least [   ] days prior to the start of the Event, during the Event and for not less than [   ] days after the Event.

4.   FINANCES

4.1   In consideration of the Event Manager performing the Services and subject to the terms of this Agreement the Rights Holder shall pay to the Event Manager the Consideration in the amounts and on the dates set out in Clause 9.

4.2   The Event Manager shall perform the Services in accordance with the Budget.

4.3   Subject to Clause 11 the Rights Holder shall provide such monies and pay all invoices and bills and enter into such contracts as are necessary for the Event Manager to provide the Services as soon as practicable after receipt of such invoices bills and contracts from the Event Manager.

4.4   The Event Manager shall forward immediately after receipt all invoices, bills and contracts entered in accordance with the Budget relating to the provisions of the Services directly to the Rights Holder for payment.

4.5   Subject to Clause 4.7 and unless otherwise agreed in writing by the Rights Holder the Event Manager is not entitled to receive or hold any income monies arising or refunds of expenditure ('monies') in providing the Services for the Event. If the Event Manager does receive or hold such monies it must immediately inform the Rights Holder, hold such monies to the Rights Holder's order as bare trustee for the benefit of the Rights Holder and immediately forward such monies to the Rights Holder in accordance with the Rights Holder's instructions.

4.6   The Event Manager shall not contract with or invoice for the services of any associated company of the Event Manager (within the meaning of the Income and Corporation Taxes Act 1988 Sections 416 and 417) except as expressly provided in the Budget or otherwise in this Agreement.

4.7   The parties shall agree the most practicable method of payment for expenses and costs incurred during the Event.

5.   BUDGET AND ACCOUNTING

5.1   the Rights Holder may (in consultation with the Event Manager) vary: the Budget, the allocation of funds from the categories specified within the Budget and vary the Budget for items of expenditure not anticipated by the Budget. Any such variation may be made by the Rights Holder and may also be made at the reasonable request of and in consultation with the Event Manager but is subject to the final decision of the Rights Holder.

5.2   The Event Manager shall remain responsible for the Budget and shall not incur any expenditure in excess of the itemised amount anticipated in the Budget unless the Budget is varied in accordance with Clause 5.1.

5.3   If the Budget exceeds the total costs actually incurred for the Event then the amount of underspend on any item of the Budget may (in the absolute discretion of the Rights Holder) be utilised for other items in the Budget in accordance with Clause 5.1.

5.4   The Event Manager shall during the Term submit to the Rights Holder such information regarding the progress of Event organisation, an analysis of expenditure to date, estimates of any likely variation to the Budget, as well as copies of contracts, correspondence, invoices, receipts and any other documentation relating to the Services and/or the Event as the Rights Holder may reasonably request.

5.5   The Event Manager shall maintain full accurate and proper records and books of account relating to the Event with all invoices, vouchers and other records evidencing all receipts expenses charges and taxes incurred in providing the Services for the Event.

5.6   The Rights Holder may inspect audit and take copies of all books and records relating to the Event the Event Manager shall produce all such material to the Rights Holder with reasonable notice of such request provided that the Rights Holder is not entitled to computer programmes and materials relating to systems and controls independently created and wholly owned by the Event Manager.

6. THE EVENT MANAGER'S OBLIGATIONS

The Event Manager shall:—

6.1   provide the Services and organise the Event to the best of its ability in accordance with best commercial practice;

6.2   at all times comply with the Rights Holder's instructions and provide the Services in a timely and professional manner;

6.3   not do anything which in the reasonable opinion of the Rights Holder is or might be prejudicial or defamatory to the name and image of the Rights Holder, the Governing Bodies, the Event or the sport of [   ];

6.4   shall not issue any press releases on or relating to the Event or make any comment on the Rights Holder other than as permitted under this Agreement;

6.5   endeavour to comply with and observe all provisions in the Governing Bodies' rules and regulations from time to time in force;

6.6   use its reasonable endeavours to comply with all applicable laws and regulations in the provision of the Services and the organisation of the Event;

6.7   ensure that the sufficient personnel of a suitably senior or junior level are available at all reasonable times to carry out the Services along with such other personnel as the Event Manager may decide (in consultation with the Rights Holder) to use in providing the Services;

6.8   liaise and co-operate with the Representatives when providing the Services to the best of its ability;

6.9   The Event Manager shall procure that its representatives:—

6.9.1   make themselves available at all reasonable times and upon reasonable notice to the Rights Holder for the purposes of consultation and advice relating to this Agreement and the Event;

6.9.2   at the event of the Event Manager attend meetings with representatives of the Rights Holder and such Representatives, sponsors or prospective sponsors as may be necessary for the performance of its duties under this Agrement;

6.10   The Events Manager shall in relation to its appointment under this Agreement:—

6.10.1 describe itself as 'Events Manager' for the Rights Holder;

6.10.2 not hold itself out or permit any person to hold it out as being authorised to bind the Rights Holder in any way; and

6.10.3 not do any act which might reasonably create the impression that it is so authorised.

7. THE EVENT MANAGER WARRANTIES

The Event Manager warrants and represents that:—

7.1 it has the full rights and title to enter this Agreement and to perform the obligations undertaken by it and that it has not entered into any agreement with any third party which might conflcit with the terms of this Agrement;

7.2 neither the signature nor the execution nor the performance by the Event Manager of this Agreement contravenes any law regulation or similar enactment or any judgment injunction or award of any court or authority or any provision of any existing agreement or contract or the Event Manager Memorandum and Articles of Association or any limitation on the powers of the directors or other officers of the Event Manager;

7.3 as of the date of this Agreement there is no litigation arbitration or administrative proceedings before any court arbitrator or authority presently pending or threatened against the Event Manager.

8. THE RIGHTS HOLDER'S WARRANTIES AND OBLIGATIONS

The Rights Holder warrants and agrees that it:—

8.1 has full authority to enter into this Agreement and to undertake all of the obligations on its part contained in this Agreement;

8.2 shall keep the Event Manager fully informed of all relevant matters relating to the Event;

8.3 shall provide the Event Manager with an adequate statement confirming its appointment under this Agreement;

8.4 shall take any action which (in its reasonable opinion) is necessary to ensure that the Event Manager can provide its services under this Agreement.

9. THE CONSIDERATION

9.1 The Rights Holder shall pay the Event Manager [   ] ('the fee') in [   ] equal monthly instalments of [   ].

9.2 All payments due are exclusive of VAT which may be or become payable. The Rights Holder shall pay any such VAT to the Event Manager upon receipt of an appropriate VAT invoice from the Event Manager.

10. APPOINTMENT OF REPRESENTATIVES

The appointment of Representatives in relation to the Event shall be made on such terms and conditions as the Rights Holder in its absolute discretion may from time to time determine. The Event Manager shall not (unless previously agreed in writing with the Rights Holder) make or give any promises warranties guarantees or representations concerning the Event and shall use all reasonable endeavours to ensure full delivery of the Rights Holder's commitments and obligations to the Representatives and shall inform the Rights Holder of an act, omission or breach of contract by any Representative of which it becomes aware during the Term. The

Event Manager shall render all reasonable assistance to the Rights Holder at the Rights Holder's expense and request in dealing with any such act, omission or breach of contract.

11. INTELLECTUAL PROPERTY

11.1   The Event Manager shall promptly and fully notify the Rights Holder of any actual threatened or suspected infringement in the Territory of any Intellectual Property of the Rights Holder which comes to the Event Manager's notice and of any claim by any third party so coming to its notice and the Event Manager shall at the request and expense of the Rights Holder do all such things as may be reasonably required to assist the Rights Holder in taking or resisting any proceedings in relation to any such infringement or claim.

11.2   Nothing in this Agreement shall give the Event Manager any rights in respect of any Intellectual Property or Trade Marks used by the Rights Holder in relation to the Event or of the goodwill associated therewith and the Event Manager hereby acknowledges that except as expressly provided in this Agreement it shall not acquire any rights in respect thereof and that all such rights and goodwill are and shall remain vested in the Rights Holder.

11.3   The Event Manager shall not use any trade marks or trade names so resembling the Trade Marks or trade names of the Rights Holder or of the Event or of the Governing Body as to be likely to cause confusion or deception.

11.4   The Event Manager shall not authorise any third party to use the Trade Mark or any Intellectual Property of the Rights Holder or of the Event or of the Governing Body. If any third party requires the use of the Trade Marks or any Intellectual Property of the Rights Holder or of the Event then the Event Manager shall inform the Rights Holder of such requirement. The Rights Holder may (in its absolute discretion) grant such third party the right or licence required.

11.5   The Event Manager shall at the expense of the Rights Holder take all such steps as the Rights Holder may reasonably require to assist the Rights Holder in maintaining the validity and enforceability of the Intellectual Property of the Rights Holder durign the continuance of this Agreement.

11.6   Without prejudice to the right of the Event Manager or any third party to challenge the validity of any Intellectual Property of the Rights Holder the Event Manager shall not do or authorise any third party to do any act which would or might invalidate or be inconsistent with the Intellectual Property of the Rights Holder and shall not omit or authorise any third party to omit to do any act which by its omission would have that effect or character.

12. CONFIDENTIALITY

12.1 Confidentiality

Subject to sub-clauses 12.2 and 12.3 each party:—

12.1.1   shall treat as strictly confidential and use solely for the purposes contemplated by this Agreement all documents materials and other information whether technical or commercial obtained or received by it as a result of entering into or performing its obligations under this Agreement and relating to the negotiations relating to or the provisions or subject matter of this Agreement ('confidential information'); and

12.1.2   shall not except with the prior written consent of the party from whom the confidential information was obtained publish or otherwise disclose to any person any confidential information.

12.2.Permitted Disclosures

Each party may disclose confidential information which would otherwise be subject to sub-clause 12.1 if but only to the extent that it can demonstrate that:—

12.2.1   such disclosure is required by law or by any securities exchange or regulatory or governmental body having jurisdiction over it wherever situated (and including without limitation the London Stock Exchange, the Panel on Takeovers and Mergers and the Serious Fraud Office) and whether or not the requirement has the force of law;

12.2.2   the confidential information was lawfully in its possession prior to its disclosure by the other party (as evidenced by written records) and had not been obtained from the other party;

12.2.3   the confidential information has come into the public domain other than through its fault or the fault of any person to whom the confidential information has been disclosed in accordance with sub-clause 12.3;

12.2.4   information required by the Governing Body;

provided that any such disclosure shall not be made without prior notice to the party from whom the confidential information was obtained.

12.3 Persistence of restrictions

The restrictions contained in this Clause shall survive the termination of this Agreement.

13. TERMINATION

13.1   The Rights Holder may terminate this Agreement in any year during the Term by giving [   ] days notice of such termination to the Event Manager. Upon termination the Event Manager shall send the Rights Holder a final account of all commitments of whatever nature up to the date of receipt of such notice along with all papers relating to the Event and the Rights Holder in its possession, custody or power and the provisions of Clauses 13.3 and 13.4 shall apply. The Rights Holder shall not be liable to the Event Manager for any further payments or any claims whatsoever.

13.2   Either party may terminate this Agreement forthwith upon notice in the event that the other:

13.2.1   commits a material breach of any obligation under this Agreement which breach is incapable of remedy or cannot be remedied in time for the Event;

13.2.2   commits a material breach of any obligation under this Agreement and if such breach is capable of remedy fails to so remedy such breach within twenty-eight days of receiving notice from the other requiring remedy;

13.2.3   enters into a composition or arrangement with its creditors has a receiver or administrator or administrative receiver appointed or becomes insolvent or unable to pay its debts when they fall due.

13.3 Consequences of termination

Upon termination in accordance with Clause 13:

13.3.1   the rights and obligations of the parties under this Agreement shall terminate and be of no future effect except that Clause 11 and 12 shall remain in full force and effect;

13.3.2   any rights or obligations to which any of the parties to this Agreement may be entitled or be subject before such termination shall remain in full force and effect;

13.3.3   termination shall not affect or prejudice any right to damages or other remedy which the terminating party may have in respect of the circumstances which gave rise to the termination or any other right to damages or other remedy which any party may have in respect of any breach of this Agreement which existed at or before the date of termination.

13.4   Upon termination in accordance with Clause 14 and upon expiry of the Term the Event Manager shall (at the request of the Rights Holder) return all items (including but not limited to) signage, materials, premises, promotional publication, advertising material relating to the Rights Holder and/or the Event to the Rights Holder or such third party as the Rights Holder nominates.

14. INSURANCE

Subject to any exclusions excesses condition and limitations imposed by the insurers and provided insurance can be obtained at reasonable rates the Rights Holder agrees to take out and maintain an insurance policy to cover usual damages claims actions judgments costs and expenses arising out of with the staging of the Event.

15. CO-OPERATION AND COMMUNICATION

Both Parties agree to work in close co-operation to the benefit of the Event.

16. FORCE MAJEURE

16.1 Effect of force majeure

Neither party to this Agreement shall be deemed to be in breach of this Agreement or otherwise liable to the other as a result of any delay or failure in the performance of its obligations under this Agreement if and to the extent that such delay or failure is caused by force majeure (as defined in sub-clause 16.2) and the time for performance of the relevant obligation(s) shall be extended accordingly.

16.2 Definition of force majeure

For the purpose of this clause 'force majeure' means any circumstances not foreseeable at the date of this Agreement and not within the reasonable control of the party in question including without limitation:

16.2.1   any strike lockout or other industrial action or any shortage of or difficulty in obtaining labour or raw materials;

16.2.2   any destruction temporary or permanent breakdown malfunction or damage of or to any premises plant equipment (including computer systems) or materials;

16.2.3   any breach of contract default or insolvency by or of any third party (including an agent or sub-contractor) other than a company in the same group as the party affected by the force majeure or an employee or officer of that party or company;

16.2.4   any action taken by a governmental or public authority of any kind including not granting a consent exemption approval or clearance;

16.2.5   any civil commotion or disorder riot invasion war threat of or preparation for war;

16.2.6   any fire explosion storm flood earthquake subsidence epidemic or other natural physical disaster.

16.3 Obligations of affected party

A party whose performance of its obligations under this Agreement is delayed or prevented by force majeure:

16.3.1   shall forthwith notify the other party of the nature extent effect and likely duration of the circumstances constituting the force majeure;

16.3.2   shall use all reasonable endeavours to minimise the effect of the force majeure on its performance of its obligations under this Agreement and

16.3.2   shall subject to sub-clause 16.4 forthwith after the cessation of the force majeure notify the other party thereof and resume full performance of its obligations under this Agreement.

16.4 Termination for force majeure

If any force majeure delays or prevents the performance of the obligations of either party for a continuous period in excess of one month the party not so affected shall then be entitled to give notice to the affected party to terminate this Agreement specifying the date (which shall not be less than seven days after the date on which the notice is given) on which termination will take effect. Such a termination notice shall be irrevocable except with the consent of both parties and upon termination the provisions of Clauses 14.4 and 14.5 apply.

17. INDEMNITY

Each party (a 'defaulting party') agrees to indemnify and keep indemnified the other party (a 'non-defaulting party') from and against any cost loss liability claim or damage which any non-defaulting party incurs or suffers as a result of any default by the defaulting party in the due and punctual performance of any of its obligations or breach of its warranties under this Agreement.

18. NATURE OF AGREEMENT

18.1   The Rights Holder may perform any of the obligations undertaken by it and exercise any of the rights granted to it under this Agreement through any other company which at the relevant time is its holding company or subsidiary (as defined by s 736 of the Companies Act 1985) or the subsidiary of any such holding company and any act or omission of any such company shall for the purposes of this Agreement be deemed to be the act or omission of the Rights Holder.

18.2   The Event Manager shall ensure that all dealings with sponsors Representatives and third parties it introduces to the Rights Holder in providing the Services for the Event are on the best arms length commercial terms available and where dealing with any associated company of the Event Manager (as defined by the Income and Corporation Taxes Act, s 416–417) shall where practicable procure at least two other quotations for the provision of the Services in quotation which it shall send to the Rights Holder.

18.3   The Rights Holder may assign this Agreement and the rights and obligations hereunder.

18.4   This Agreement is personal to the Event Manager which may not without the written consent of the Rights Holder assign mortgage charge (otherwise than by floating charge) or dispose of any of its rights hereunder or sub-contract or otherwise delegate any of its obligations hereunder.

18.5   The Event Manager shall not without the prior written consent of the Rights Holder employ sub-agents. If with such consent it does so every act or omission of the sub-agent shall for the purposes of this Agreement be deemed to be the act or omission of the Event Manager.

18.6   Nothing in this Agreement shall create or be deemed to create a partnership or the relationship of employer and employee between the parties.

18.7   This Agreement contains the entire agreement between parties with respect to the subject matter hereof and supersedes all previous agreements and understandings between the parties with respect thereto and may not be modified except by an instrument in writing signed by the duly authorised representatives of the parties.

18.8   Each party acknowledges that in entering into this Agreement it does not do so on the basis of and does not rely on any representation warranty or other provision except as expressly provided herein and all conditions warranties or other terms implied by statute or common law are hereby excluded to the fullest extent permitted by law.

18.9   If any provision of this Agreement is held by any court or other competent authority to be void or unenforceable in whole or part this Agreement shall continue to be valid as to the other provisions thereof and the remainder of the affected provisions.

18.10   At any time after the date hereof each of the parties shall at the request and cost of the other party execute or procure the execution of such documents and do or procure the doing of such acts and things as the party so requiring may reasonably require for the purpose of giving to the party so requiring the full benefit of all the provisions of this Agreement.

18.11   Each party to this Agreement shall pay its own costs of and incidental to the negotiation preparation execution and carrying into effect of this Agreement.

19. PROPER LAW

This Agreement shall be governed by and construed in all respects in accordance with the Laws of England and each party hereby submits to the exclusive jurisdiction of the English Courts.

20. NOTICES AND SERVICE

20.1   Any notice or other information required or authorised by this Agreement to be given by either party to the other may be given by hand or sent (by first class pre-paid post telex cable facsimile transmission or comparable means of communication) to the other party at the address referred to in Clause 21.4.

20.2   Any notice or other information given by post pursuant to Clause 21.1 which is not returned to the sender as undelivered shall be deemed to have been given on the second day after the envelope containing the same was so posted and proof that the envelope containing any such notice or information was properly addressed pre-paid registered and posted and that it has not been so returned to the sender shall be sufficient evidence that such notice or information has been duly given.

20.3   Any notice or other information sent by telex cable facsimile transmission or comparable means of communication shall be deemed to have been duly sent on the date of transmission provided that a confirming copy thereof is sent by first class pre-paid post to the other party at the address referred to in Clause 20.4 within twenty-four hours after transmission.

20.4   Service of any legal proceedings concerning or arising out of this Agreement shall be effected by causing the same to be delivered to the Company Secretary of the party to be served at its principal place of business (in the case of the Rights Holder) or its registered office (in the case of the Event Manager) or to such other address as may from time to time be notified in writing by the party concerned.

SCHEDULE I

The Services

1.   The Event Manager will have regard at all times to the Rights Holder's objectives and instructions in relation to the smooth running and organisation of the Event and shall provide the Rights Holder with the following services during the Term including (without limitation) the following:

1.1.1   all matters relating to Event personnel including without being limited to accommodation and travel arrangements;

1.1.2   organisation of prize money;

1.1.3   assisting in the development of all organisational printed materials;

1.1.4   production of signage and advertising boards;

1.1.5   liaison with city authorities and police;

1.1.6   organisation of the transport fleet;

1.1.7   Event infrastructure and all matters connected with equipment;

1.1.8   core press centre and facilities;

1.1.9   liaison with media specialist writers/broadcasters and dealing with enquiries relating to the Event;

1.1.10 radio broadcasting and communications;

1.1.11 Event preparation and planning;

1.1.12 liaison with all necessary local authorities;

1.1.13 liaison with and provision of rights to Representatives

1.1.14 ticketing arrangements;

1.1.15 assistance for broadcasters, outside broadcast units and other Representatives;

1.1.16 liaison with the Governing Bodies.

1.2   Close liaision with the Rights Holder and the Representatives to co-ordinate their respective roles in connection with the Event.

2.   The parties may agree that the Event Manager shall be responsible for further services which are similar to the Services and shall negotiate an appropriate increase in the Consideration.

SCHEDULE 2

The Trade Marks

SIGNED BY ....
For and on behalf of
The Rights Holder
A duly authorised signatory

SIGNED BY ....
For and on behalf of
The Event Manager
A duly authorised signatory

CHAPTER 9

BROADCASTING AND TELEVISION

Broadcast contracts
9.1 Introduction – 9.2 Regulatory aspects of broadcasting – 9.3 Legal basis of sports broadcasting rights – 9.4 Ownership/control of sports broadcasting rights – 9.5 Intellectual property rights and sports broadcasting – 9.6 Other intellectual property aspects – 9.7 Production and broadcasting – 9.8 Broadcast contracts: common terms – 9.9 Licensing of broadcast footage

Broadcast sponsorship
9.10 Introduction – 9.11 Programme sponsorship defined – 9.12 General provisions – 9.13 Branding and credits generally – 9.14 Event coverage – 9.15 Electronic imaging systems – 9.16 Broadcast sponsorship agreement

BROADCAST CONTRACTS

9.1 INTRODUCTION

The business of television and the legal and regulatory aspects which govern the way that business is run is worthy of a full book of its own.[1] This chapter concentrates on the relevant regulatory restraints in the regime within which sports broadcasting operates, the legal basis for the grant of broadcasting rights in sport and the common terms in documentation for sports broadcasting agreements. It then goes on to briefly consider the terms of a video distribution agreement, another lucrative way of exploiting sports footage. The sports broadcasting contract is commonly and probably correctly regarded as being the greatest prize to both sports rights holders, commercial partners and broad-casters alike. At the top end of the popularity scale (which in practice means broadcasting rights to major football competitions), sports broadcasting rights are regarded as the jewel in the crown for broadcasters. Contracts for the televising of sports events represent enormous potential revenue for the sports rights holders and a hard fought prize in the ratings wars between broadcasters. Sports news, magazine and highlights programmes are equally attractive to sports rights holders, broadcasters and the viewing public alike.

Recent years have seen the escalation in rights fees for sports broadcasting and this has been very much led by the increasing influence of satellite and cable channels and the advent of pay-per-view and digital television. Increased competition between broadcasters together with the advent of these new technologies means the price paid by broadcasters to rights holders for a few top-quality sports rights is higher than it has ever been. Equally, the amount and the variety of coverage of sport from top class high quality popular events right down to grass roots sports is greater than it has ever been. There are a number of

---

1   See, for example, Rhonda Baker, *Media Law* (Routledge, 1994).

dedicated sports channels in the UK and throughout Europe with cable, satellite and terrestrial television which makes sports broadcasting an integral part of programme schedules across the board.

Sports broadcasting is not the sole reserve of the BBC, ITV or even the major satellite broadcasters such as BSkyB. It is also now the preserve of the major entrepreneurs and sports clubs who, driven by the significant investments made in sport and the demands for returns on those investments, are increasingly finding ways to exploit their own rights. This has led to the establishment of dedicated sports channels (the obvious example being the Manchester United channel which is a joint venture between BSkyB, Granada and Manchester United Plc) in an effort to increase total revenue from sports rights. At the other end of the scale many rights owners find it impossible to obtain significant television coverage without funding the actual production costs themselves. The broadcaster then effectively obtains a broadcasted feed of the event (which may or may not include commentary) which it broadcasts. The rights owner gains its coverage which in turn helps to raise the profile and (hopefully) commercial viability of the sport.

Sports broadcasting is important not only to broadcasters and rights holders but also to the sports marketing industry, where the availability of programme sponsorship and advertising around commercial programming is an important part of the sports marketing mix. The exploitation of current and back catalogue sports events footage and programming through re-broadcasts and sales of videos is another important income stream for rights holders and their business partners alike.

Sports broadcasting should not be thought of as being limited to audio-visual broadcast and programming. There is an important and lucrative market of audio only radio broadcasting which can represent significant additional rights revenues for sports rights holders (the FA Premier League reportedly sold radio broadcasting rights to Radio 5 Live for £8 million). Although this section concentrates on broadcasting on television, many of the legal principles discussed are equally relevant to radio broadcasting agreements.

9.2   REGULATORY ASPECTS OF BROADCASTING

Sports broadcasting is subject to a number of regulatory controls laid down in the Broadcasting Act 1990 and the Broadcasting Act 1996. In addition to these, there are various issues which arise from the application of general legal principles which apply to sports broadcasting. In particular, these include intellectual property issues as well as the increasing relevance of local and international competition law.

9.3 LEGAL BASIS OF SPORTS BROADCASTING RIGHTS

It is well established that there is no 'property' right in a sports event. Although the leading authority dates from just after the turn of the century,[1] the principle is sound and has not changed with the passing of the years. In this case, a broadcasting company erected scaffolding outside a race track. It used the scaffolding to film the racing on the track itself. In the subsequent action, the broadcasting company was held not to have infringed any proprietary rights in the race. Accordingly, there is no distinct legal property right in an event itself. Rights owners and, indeed, broadcasters must look elsewhere for legal protection for the rights.

Indeed, it was said in the Victoria Park racing case that: 'a "spectacle" cannot be "owned" in any ordinary sense of the word'.

Notwithstanding this judicial pronouncement, the ability to grant broadcasting rights in an event is a valuable 'property' regulated by sophisticated contractual rights, the price of which has escalated rapidly in recent years. In this sense then, a broadcasting contract does not (initially at least) rely upon a proprietary right. Rather, the rights that arise are created and governed by the contract between the rights owner and the relevant broadcaster. Because of the tenuous legal basis upon which these rights can be protected, distinct problems can arise for the broadcasters and the rights holders alike.

In the case of sports events which are held at a venue where entry can be controlled and, as often as not, entrance will only be granted when a ticket is bought, a broadcaster will insist that the rights holder imposes contractual conditions on spectators (and indeed any other persons entering the stadium) rights. For example, it will be a condition of entry to watch an event in the stadium that no filming or photography takes place for any commercial usage and even photography and filming for private usage may be strictly prohibited. Further, the broadcaster will also ensure that no other broadcasters or television production crews are granted entry to the venue for the purpose of filming the event.

The risk of imposing no conditions on spectators is highlighted by the case of *Sports and General Press Agency Ltd v 'Our Dogs' Publishing Co Ltd*.[2] In this case the exclusive photography rights, were required for a dog show. However, the organiser of the show failed to impose a contractual condition on all spectators prohibiting them from taking any photographs. One spectator was a journalist who took photographs which were subsequently published with his permission in a rival journal.

Frequently, the first clause in a 'live' sports broadcasting contract will set out the rights of a broadcaster to attend live matches to set up cameras to film the event in question. The contract will then go on to stipulate that no other person may exercise such a right within the stadium or venue in the control of the rights holder.

---

1   *Victoria Park Racing and Recreation Ground Company v Taylor* (1938) 58 CLR 479.
2   [1917] KB 125.

The other problem that can arise relates to events held in public spaces. In this situation, it is much more difficult for the rights owner or events organiser to control the environment from which the broadcaster will seek to exercise its rights. The rights holder may well be able to reserve prime positions for the broadcaster and these positions will frequently be at a key point in which the race or the event takes place. This may involve enclosing areas in which the event takes place and ensuring that otherwise 'public' parts of the event cannot be used by broadcasters. This may involve erecting scaffolding and gantries at other important positions to ensure that any rival broadcaster cannot occupy such favourable positions if it attempts to film or broadcast the 'public' spectacle. Equally the rights owner may try to control the air space of the event and buildings that overlook it to prevent rival broadcasters positioning their cameras and broadcasting their own pictures.

In the case of venue events, there will be a contract between the rights holder/events organiser and the owner of the stadium in which the event is held. Assuming the rights holder/event organiser is not the owner of the stadium this contract must set out precisely what rights the rights holder has to allow entry to the broadcaster and his equipment to the venue. Equally, the agreement should stipulate that the venue owner may not grant anyone the right to enter the venue and set up their own equipment for the purposes of broadcasting or filming for any commercial purpose which would cause problems for the rights owner and its commercial partners.

It is possible in the case of public events that the rights holder/event organiser may be able to obtain a degree of exclusivity if any form of licence or permission is required from, for example, the local authority or a department of government to actually stage the event. If the rights holder/event organiser does obtain such permission from their local authority or department of government then that body should be able to grant some comfort and some degree of control over the public venue. This comfort can then be passed on to the broadcaster which should be assured its exclusivity.

Although to all legal intents and purposes the rights holder has no property rights in its event it can acquire this right through a chain of contracts which create important and valuable exclusive rights which it can pass on to broadcasters.

9.4 OWNERSHIP/CONTROL OF SPORTS BROADCASTING RIGHTS

There is some debate over who actually owns or controls what legal rights there are to broadcast an event. The candidates for ownership are (in no particular order):

- sports governing bodies;
- the event organiser/local organising committee;
- stadium owner or the controller of the place or the environment where the event is to be held;
- the participants in the event (ie the clubs or individuals concerned);
- any entrepreneur involved with or creating the event;

– the sponsors and other commercial partners to the event.

In practice, although each of these 'candidates' may have (or be able to manufacture) a legitimate claim to exercise the sports broadcasting rights, it is typically the governing body or event organiser who will claim ownership of the rights because that is usually the body that manages to put the whole event together. The governing body may claim the rights on the basis of its contract or other agreement with the event organiser and/or its members. Any stadium owner is clearly important in the rights debate because without its permission no one can actually enter the stadium to set up their equipment, to film and broadcast the event. Participants in an event may claim to exercise the rights because without their participation there would be no spectacle or event at all. Entrepreneur and sponsor may claim ownership through contractual terms.

Despite these competing claims the issue is usually resolved in a very practical way by a chain of agreements between the various parties mentioned above. If there are any issues of copyright ownership and protection these arise for the actual broadcast of an event and the question of access to the event to film it is fundamental. On the basis that it is the stadium owner that controls the right to access to the stadium, it is the stadium owner that (initially at least) controls the rights to broadcast from the stadium. However, the governing body or event organiser will choose a venue for the event and by its contract with the venue owner it will ensure that all necessary rights to broadcast from the venue are passed to the governing body/event organiser who can in turn pass them on to the broadcaster. In the case of a league or other competition where there are a number of different venues involved, each venue concerned will need to cede the right to the governing body/event organiser to permit the broadcaster entry to the stadium to exercise the broadcasting rights.

Where the governing body/event organiser has members who are effectively the competitors in the event in question the agreement between the governing body/events organiser and these competitors will deal with the broadcast rights to the event. These competitors usually effectively sign away any rights to control broadcasting directly and receive a share of income, prize money or appearance fees accruing from the governing body/events organiser. Very often this share will include all monies from whatever source and will include the broadcasting, sponsorship, merchandising and ticket income and possibly other revenue created by or attributable to the event which they are participating in.

The position of individuals in the broadcast scheme of things is slightly different. Although there is legislation in place to protect performers,[1] sports players are not performers within this definition. Accordingly, any rights that sports players have to broadcasting income deriving from the broadcast of an event are based on their willingness to participate in the event in question and the fact that if they all do not turn up to compete there will be no such spectacle. Although players strikes are not unknown within professional sport, the fact is that most professional sports people will effectively relinquish any possible controls they may have over the broadcasting (or indeed many of the other commercial rights in a sports event) in their own professional sports employment or participation contracts or by agreeing to the rules of their governing body. An exception to

---

1 See the Copyright Designs and Patents Act 1988, s 131.

this is boxing, where it is quite common for the participants to control broadcasting rights to their bouts. Notwithstanding the lack of intellectual property protection available to individual sportsman within the UK an event organiser or governing body will usually be sensitive to the fact that other intellectual property rights may be relevant if the broadcaster exercises its broadcast rights in a particular way. For example, if an individual player or team is represented in such a way that it is seen to endorse the broadcaster itself then there may be a trade mark infringement or action for passing off. Individuals (especially high profile and extremely successful sporting individuals) can as a matter of commercial practice exercise some control over the activities of the governing bodies and broadcasters simply by the fact that their presence in the events and at pre- and post-match interviews can be an important asset and part of the general spectacle of the broadcast itself. In other jurisdictions, players may have more defined personality rights which protect them.

Event organisers, governing bodies, broadcasters and individual competitors alike should be aware that intellectual property rights differ throughout the world and so an individual may find that although he has no or very little legal protection in one jurisdiction he may have quite extensive protection against the misuse or appropriation of his 'personality rights' in other jurisdictions. This means that any rights to use players' or any competitor's name, image and reputation beyond what is strictly necessary to relay the actual event itself may amount to an actionable legal wrong. Such rights are a valuable property right for sports individuals and often the subject of separately negotiated endorsement or merchandising agreements.[1] If the governing body/events organiser wishes to use or grant the right to use an individual's name, image or goodwill in such a manner then it should ensure that it has a properly negotiated agreement in place to do so. This may mean that the governing body/event organiser in question has a form of contract with the individual participants. For example, many professional international sportsmen will have agreements with their particular national governing body which will carefully delineate such rights.

9.5 INTELLECTUAL PROPERTY RIGHTS AND SPORTS BROADCASTING

Although a sports event is not a separately protected legal property right, it is also not a protected work within any of the relevant intellectual property legislation. In particular, a sports event is not a protected copyright work within any of the definitions in CDPA 1988. The first right granted by a 'live' sports broadcasting agreement is the right to attend and film the event. It is only at this stage when the event is filmed (ie recorded) and/or broadcast or put on cable that any copyright arises. Copyright will arise in the film or sound recording of the event as well as in the broadcast and/or cable transmission of it.[2] Until that stage is reached, there are no copyright issues other than the issue of prospective ownership of the relevant copyright.[3] It is this matter with which the sports broadcasting agreement goes on to deal.

---

1   See Chapter 6.
2   CDPA 1988, ss 5–7.
3   Ibid, s 91.

The contract to film and/or broadcast a live event will contain provisions dealing with ownership and exploitation of the copyright that arises. It is quite possible to deal with or assign future copyright[1] and this is done by way of a future assignment or licence of the copyright work.

It is important that the rights holder and the broadcaster establish precisely what rights exist and precisely the use to which each of them needs to be able to put those rights. Assuming the main right that arises is copyright the rights owner and the broadcaster will be concerned with the ownership of copyright[2] and permission to broadcast the copyright work and all the other restricted rights in the film or sound recording of the event. For example, the broadcaster may retain all rights to actually broadcast the film or sound recording of the event whilst all other rights to actually copy and distribute that recording (eg by way of video sales) may be retained or assigned to the rights holder.

The copyright legislation expressly envisages dealings with copyright which differentiate between different methods of exploitation and which may last for the whole period or only part of the period of copyright protection.[3] However, it is also common for the section of the broadcasting agreement that deals with copyright to impose express territorial limitations on the broadcaster. This may mean that the broadcaster cannot broadcast the event outside of the specific agreed area or with commentary and titles in anything other than an agreed language. Strictly speaking, dealing with copyright on a territorial basis is a licence of copyright.[4]

The initial ownership of copyright in the recording and/or broadcast of the event requires an examination of the basic copyright principles concerned.[5] The first owner will be the broadcaster and/or the production company that has actually created the recording.[6] The broadcasting agreement will then set out by way of an assignment or license of those copyrights who gets precisely what rights to do what with such footage. This is a matter for negotiation between the parties and will depend not only on bargaining power but the commercial attractiveness of the event. The simple fact that such rights can be apportioned and dealt with in this way gives the rights holder the opportunity and the ability to exploit rights which it retains either itself or through its members (usually clubs or individuals) or through other appointed commercial partners (such as sponsors and merchandisers). Such exploitation usually involves a grant of rights to other broadcasters in different territories and by way of the grant of video rights and even new media rights such as the right to exploit the copyright work by way of the Internet or pay-per-view television.

---

1   CDPA 1988, s 91.
2   Ibid, s 11.
3   Ibid, s 90.
4   Ibid, s 91.
5   Ibid, ss 9, 11
6   Ibid, s 11.

9.6　OTHER INTELLECTUAL PROPERTY ASPECTS

It is important that both the rights owner and broadcaster do not neglect the other protectable elements of the event. For example, there may be trade marks (whether registered or unregistered) which are used in the event. Both parties must take care to ensure that no third party rights are infringed by the broadcast and reference should be made to the relevant legislation and common law principles for guidance on these matters.[1]

It is also important to appreciate that there may be other copyright elements in the recording and/or broadcast of the event. If a commentary is added then there will be copyright and performers' rights issues in relation to that commentary.[2] In addition, it is quite common for sports events to feature live music and/or other entertainment either during the event itself or in breaks and intervals. Where the copyright work such as songs and/or recordings of songs are featured in the recording or the broadcast of the event then these may incorporate third party copyrights. If this is the case then the permission of such third parties is usually required[3] or certain defences within the copyright legislation may be relied upon.[4]

9.7　PRODUCTION AND BROADCASTING

The actual mechanics of creating a broadcast deserve some further consideration. Although as has already been seen there is no specific proprietary right in an event itself, the copyright issues that arise once a film and/or sound recording and/or broadcast have been made or created represent important rights for both broadcaster and rights owner alike. Before the copyright work can be created the machinery must be put in place to create it. This involves the positioning of cameras and all the associated paraphernalia and technical equipment involved in creating an outside broadcast. This also usually means there will be outside broadcast units which are very often lorries or vans which take a feed created by the cameras and the commentators and then record and relay it on to relevant broadcasters.

The primary audio and/or visual elements of the broadcast are commonly referred to as the 'event feed' and are created by an outside broadcast unit. It is still relatively expensive to create a technically acceptable event feed as the costs of either owning or hiring the necessary equipment to create it are quite substantial.

If the event itself is the starting point prior to the creation of the event feed the rights owner must consider who will be responsible for the actual production of the event feed itself. There are a number of alternatives, as follows.

(1)　The rights owner itself may commission a production company to create an event feed. This event feed will then be fed on to the various appointed broadcasters who will exercise the rights they are granted within their

---

1　See Chapter 4.
2　See Chapter 4.
3　For example, from PRS/PPL or MCPS.
4　For example in the defence of fair dealing or incidental inclusion see, CDPA 1988, ss 30, 31.

respective territories. If the rights owner has appointed the host producer itself, it is likely that the rights owner will licence broadcast rights to the various broadcasters within their various territories. It is also the rights owner that will exploit other rights (such as broadcast highlights packages and video rights) by licensing them to its other appointed commercial partners.

(2) The rights owner may appoint a host broadcaster who will be responsible for creating the event feed itself. The rights owner will regulate its relationship with the host broadcaster in an agreement. The host broadcaster will either use its own equipment or else appoint a producer of its own to create the event feed. This agreement will specify precisely what copyrights the host broadcaster retains in the event feed and which rights are transferred to the rights owner. Although it is possible that the rights owner may permit the host broadcaster to broadcast in its own territory, to sub-licence other broadcasters and exploit all the other commercial rights in the event feed itself, the rights owner is better advised to limit the host broadcaster's rights in relation to the event feed.

Once the mechanics are in place to actually produce the event feed then, depending on the status of the event and the needs of other broadcasters, access may be required to the venue or area of the event for commentary teams from territories throughout the world and not just the territory in which the event is being held.

If the rights owner is not in a position to exploit further rights in the event feed itself, it is quite common for it to appoint a sales agent or commercial rights marketing agent to exploit those rights on its behalf. The terms of such agreements are discussed elsewhere[1] and the rights owner may require certain guarantees in relation to the level of income which the agent will achieve, as well as assurances that the rights owners' other commercial partners (and in particular sponsors) receive the rights and credits that they are entitled to under their agreements with the rights owner.[2]

Whatever route the rights owner chooses they will also need to consider the possibility that the host broadcaster and other broadcasters may appoint broadcast sponsors who will be given appropriate credits around the broadcast coverage of the event. This is a matter which is considered further in comments on the form of the broadcast agreement.[3]

Finally, whatever happens, the quality of the event feed must be assured so that it is the correct technical specification for broadcasters and other third parties to use.

---

1   See Chapter 7.
2   See Chapter 7.
3   See **9.8**.

9.8 BROADCAST CONTRACTS: COMMON TERMS

9.8.1 The parties

A small amount of preliminary due diligence should be undertaken by both parties to the broadcasting contract. The rights owner should be able to establish some clear authority or chain of title to grant the rights to the broadcaster. He must also be able to establish and (if necessary) to demonstrate that it can deliver exactly what it contracts to deliver to the broadcaster. This may involve undertakings to ensure that stadium owners and competitors will assist it in delivering or, at least, not prohibit it from delivering rights under the broadcasting agreements. These undertakings will manifest themselves particularly in the warranties that the rights owner is required to give. The broadcaster will usually require a warranty that the rights holder has the full authority to grant the rights on behalf of itself and its members and that it shall ensure (or at least use its best or reasonable endeavours to ensure) that its members give effect to the rights that are granted to the broadcaster under the agreement. There are other warranties which may be important and which will also relate to its ability to grant the rights and these may relate to the constitution of the event itself. If, for example, the event is a league or a cup competition, the broadcaster will want the rights holder to warrant that it will not sanction or promote any other similar competition, thereby depriving the broadcaster of its rights. It may also be important that if clubs are relegated and other clubs promoted into a particular competition that the newly promoted clubs will comply with the terms of the broadcasting agreement.

The broadcaster will also be required to satisfy the rights owner that it has the authority to enter into the agreement. In the case of substantial broadcasting contracts where the rights fees may run into many millions of pounds, the rights owner will want a clear indication that the transaction has Board approval before detailed negotiations are undertaken. Although the broadcaster will be required to give certain other warranties and undertakings, it is unlikely that they will relate specifically to its capacity or its authority to enter into the transaction.

9.8.2 The event

It is important that the subject matter of the contract is carefully defined. A sporting event can be a very flexible beast which may encompass any number of different types of competitions or events all run by one governing body with the same or very similar competitors in each event. For this reason, it is important that the precise ambit of the event in question is covered and defined well enough to ensure that it does not include competitions or events other than the ones specifically intended by the parties. It is also important that both the broadcaster and the rights owner consider exactly how much of the event will be broadcast. In the case of league and cup competitions, there may be a number of rounds leading to quarter-finals, semi-finals and an ultimate final, with possible replays along the route. In the case of a league competition, it is likely that the broadcaster's obligations will relate to league matches which will need to be carefully defined within the agreement. In the case of certain events, there may be opening and closing ceremonies which the rights owner will also require the broadcaster to cover and broadcast live. There may also be presentation ceremonies for prize winners, all of which may be taken as part of the event if questioned.

It is also useful if both the rights owner and the broadcaster consider matters such as the timing of the events as well as, in some cases, the location of the events. There may be important technical as well as commercial issues raised by such matters. For example, the broadcaster may want to ensure that there is a minimum amount of time during the half time interval in a competition or between events for it to include broadcast sponsorship credits as well as advertising sales space. The broadcaster will almost certainly want to be consulted and possibly even to control or be consulted over the timing of games and individual events when it is acquiring rights.

9.8.3 Facilities and access

Even if the rights owner is providing a full event feed for the broadcaster to utilise, the broadcaster is likely to have some requirements for facilities and access to the event itself. In the case of a straightforward licensing deal of an existing broadcast where full commentary and audio sound track are provided, the broadcaster will probably only be concerned to establish that it can acquire the rights in question. In the case of events where the broadcaster is being provided with a live feed, it may still need the right to access to the event for its commentators as well as its camera crew and other staff so that it can suitably embellish the event feed for its own style of broadcasting.

Where the broadcaster will be producing the event feed itself then it will need full access to the event and all sites. The broadcaster will need to specify exactly what its requirements are in relation to access at the event. Essentially the broadcaster will want to introduce its own outside broadcast units and equipment to the event. Access will need to be free of charge to the broadcaster. There will also need to be sufficient parking for all its broadcast vans and equipment. There needs to be a power supply for the broadcaster and access to the ground before, during and after the game for all its staff. In addition, either the rights owner or the broadcaster will need to get access to gantries, cameras and a room or other facilities for commentators.

The rights holder may need to supply team sheets and photographs to the broadcaster for its commentary team. The broadcaster may also wish to interview players and managers before and after matches. Access for cameramen with hand-held cameras to the players tunnel and even dressing rooms may be sought and agreed. If evening games are going to be broadcast, the broadcaster will want to be satisfied that there is adequate flood lighting capability at the ground to ensure that it can film the event and broadcast it on.

It is quite common for rights owners to insist that the broadcaster also provides a direct feed of the event including its commentary to the various boxes, dining rooms and bars at the venues or the event itself. In certain events, there may also be a jumbo television screen which relays live coverage (including replays and sometimes even advertising) of coverage of the event to the spectators at the live event.

9.8.4   The broadcaster's rights

The grant of rights to the broadcaster will need to be clear as to the precise delivery system or medium of the broadcast as well as the exact type of coverage that the broadcaster will provide.

(a)   Broadcast medium

The establishment of new delivery systems reflects the increasing advance and sophistication of broadcast technology. Traditionally broadcasting rights would be for terrestrial free-to-air television. The advent of cable, satellite, pay-per-view and increasingly new on-line delivery systems means that contracts will generally specify exactly what broadcast medium is anticipated. In part, this relates to the exclusivity provisions of the agreement which may stipulate that only one particular medium of delivery is anticipated in the agreement.

(b)   Types of coverage

The rights sold or licensed to the broadcaster will then be defined by reference to the particular type of coverage that the broadcaster will use. These may be as follows:

- live coverage;
- 'as live' coverage (ie full coverage but not simultaneous with the playing of the match or event itself, often known as a replay right);
- highlights packages;
- magazine packages;
- news footage.

Broadcasters are typically interested in either live, as live (ie replays) or highlights packages. Although most broadcasters will have news access to footage of important events through the new access agreement between UK-based broadcasters[1] the commercial value tends to be in these other types of rights. These particular rights will then attach to a particular medium of delivery.

The rights may be mixed up so that there is live satellite and cable coverage of an event and highlights packages appear on standard terrestrial free-to-air television. It is quite possible that the rights will be live rights but it will only attach to pay-per-view or on demand systems. Although pay-per-view is still very much in its early days it is likely that it will become increasingly important as a revenue stream for rights owners and as an alternative for viewers who will pick and choose the events they prefer. This means it is possible for a rights package to incorporate elements of live and pay-per-view broadcasts in which case the agreement must be appropriately drafted to reflect this.

Each of the other rights may also be further subdivided not only by reference to exclusivity[2] but also by reference to the duration[3] and the territory[4] of the rights which are being granted.

Given the pace of change in methods of delivery of broadcasting it is important that the agreement deals carefully with any new or developing delivery systems

---

1   New Sports Access Code.
2   See **9.8.4**(d).
3   See **9.8.4**(f).
4   See **9.8.4**(e).

and that the agreement does not contain a clause stating that it covers any and all delivery systems, whether they are known at the time of the agreement or created after its date. This should avoid problems for rights owners who find that advances in technology create additional commercial opportunities for them where none previously existed.

(c) Secondary rights

Although the basic rights package in the agreement will relate to the method of delivery and the type of coverage being granted and there are also important secondary rights in most broadcast footage. These rights may follow copyright ownership but a broadcaster may seek to acquire something more than the right to simply broadcast the event in question. It may want the right to exploit videos using its footage and then manufacture and distribute them for retail sale within its territory. This is a commercial matter for agreement between the rights holder and the broadcaster. In many cases, it may be appropriate for the broadcaster to create suitable videos for sale, in return for which it will pay the broadcaster an advance in royalty on sales for the right to do so. It is also likely that the rights owner will want to retain this right itself in which case this must be set out in the agreement. Similar considerations will apply to use of footage and video compilations, magazine programming, highlights, best-of videos, multi-media and any form of Internet or on-line exploitation. These are all rights which are commercially significant which the broadcaster may acquire through overly inclusive drafting because the rights holder and its advisers have not properly considered the points.[1]

(d) Exclusivity

The extent to which the rights owner grants the broadcaster complete or partial exclusivity over the rights will vary. A broadcaster may be granted complete or partial exclusivity in relation to some or all of the rights granted by the rights owner. For example, a broadcaster may have complete exclusivity for live and replay broadcasts within all possible methods of delivery. None the less, the rights owner may reserve the right to grant another broadcaster highlights rights for the same footage. The live broadcaster will be concerned to ensure that any highlights broadcast packages which are sold do not impinge upon its own rights. Practically speaking, this means that highlights will be shown later in the day and the match will be in an abbreviated form.

Exclusivity may attach to a type of rights as well as a method of delivery. There may also be issues of exclusivity which relate to the territory and the duration of the agreement.[2]

Most but not all broadcasting agreements provide complete exclusivity within a particular territory for all types of broadcasts and all methods of delivery. Although broadcasters do not always insist on such exclusivity as a practical matter, exclusive rights tend to be more highly valued both by rights owners, broadcasters and other commercial partners (such as broadcasts sponsors and advertisers) alike.

---

1   See precedent document at **9.9.9**.
2   See **9.8.4**(e) and **9.8.4**(f).

Depending on what has been agreed the agreement should set out whether any other party has the right to enter and set up their equipment at the event or matches forming part of the event for the purpose of broadcasting. It should also set out what rights other parties have to broadcast the footage of the event. In particular, most broadcasters will allow access to a small amount of footage of the event for the purpose of news reporting. The essential copyright position was set out in the case of the *BBC v BSB*[1] which established that fair dealing provisions of the CDPA 1988 apply to the use of recorded material from live transmissions for news purposes. Recording the goals and incidents from games can often be broadcast by other broadcasters in their news coverage. There is an agreed code of practice between the broadcasters within the UK which permits the use of items of broadcast footage in return for an appropriate screen credit.

The broadcaster may require the rights owner to promise that it will not grant the rights to attend matches to anyone else; nor will it grant the right to transmit matches to anyone else. Usually these rights will be limited to broadcasts within the territory. It is also the case that the rights owner may reserve the right for access for the purposes of news reporting and documentary filming. It is often the case that other broadcasters will wish to create behind the scenes programmes about sports clubs, individual participants as well as the sport and the event in which they compete.

Where another broadcaster is exercising any rights within the territory (such as highlights rights) then the contract will need to stipulate that the broadcasters' rights are non-exclusive against that other broadcaster but exclusive against all other parties and broadcasters.

(e) Territory
Broadcast rights are frequently granted on a territorial basis. Although this can cause problems with satellite broadcasting it is a generally accepted method of exploiting rights to best advantage. Where a broadcaster is granted rights within a specific territory the rights owner needs to make it clear in the agreement that its rights do not extend beyond that territory and the rights owner must ensure that the contract is drafted carefully to grant itself any necessary copyrights in the broadcaster's footage of the event, or else reserve itself all the rights necessary so that it can grant rights on to broadcasters in other territories for them to broadcast and exploit the rights.

Where satellite is concerned there is an inherent problem known as 'overspill' in that programmes transmitted by a satellite broadcaster (and, indeed, some terrestrial broadcasters) may be capable of reception outside the territorial bounds of their agreement. It is often the case that the rights owner will acknowledge that such overspill by the broadcaster will not constitute a breach of the territorial restrictions contained in the agreement.

(f) Duration
The agreement may be tied into a one-off match or event or it may be for a number of years and tied to a particular competition. This is a matter for commercial agreement. Long-term exclusive arrangements may be subject to

---

1   [1991] 3 WLR 174.

examination by relevant competition authorities and as such should be carefully scrutinised by the parties and the legal advisers before they are agreed.

Otherwise, the rights may simply be for an agreed number of transmissions within a certain period of time after which the rights revert to the rights owner.

9.8.5 Rights fees

The amount of money which the broadcaster will pay the rights owner is purely a reflection of the popularity and perceived value of the event. In some cases, a broadcaster will not do anything other than meet the production costs of the event, although it is not unknown for a rights owner to appoint its own production company and grant rights to a broadcaster for purely nominal consideration.

Whatever agreement is reached, the documentation should properly reflect the financial terms and it should set out when and by what method payments are to be made. A broadcaster will generally prefer to make payments in instalments, although a rights owner will inevitably prefer a lump sum advance payment. Where VAT is payable this should be additional to the basic rights fees and the agreement should reflect this fact.

If a payment is made late then the broadcaster may have to pay interest at one or two points above the base rate. The parties may also wish to consider the position on early termination of the agreement where unpaid instalments of the rights fees are due. In certain circumstances, the rights owner will require the broadcaster to pay any unpaid instalments (normally if the broadcaster is in breach of the terms of the agreement) and likewise the broadcaster will require the rights owner to pay any instalments where termination of the agreement takes place due to the rights owner's breach of contract.

9.8.6 The broadcaster's obligations

The agreement will contain a number of terms relating to the broadcaster's central obligations under the agreement. All but the dedicated sports channels are reluctant to specify that a broadcast will be made at any particular time or for any minimum number of hours. However, for a dedicated sports channel, it is more usual for the rights owner and the broadcaster to agree some minimum broadcast commitments. This may relate to the minimum number of hours of live coverage but will also relate to magazine programming as well as replays and highlights of the games which are being broadcast. The rights owner may also want the broadcast to provide it with audience statistics which may relate to the size, location and profile of the audience in question. It may also require the broadcaster to provide copies of all broadcast footage for its own purposes or to provide such footage to specific commercial parties, typically sponsors and publishers.

There will usually be a general requirement on the broadcaster to comply with all statutory and regulatory obligations. There may also be general obligations on the broadcaster not to do anything which may be prejudicial or defamatory to the name and image of the event or the rights owner and not to interfere with the running of the sport in question otherwise than as agreed between the rights owner and the broadcaster. On this later point, the broadcaster may have certain requirements relating to the timing of events and in particular kick-off, half-time breaks and end-times. The rights owner may also require the broadcaster to retain all necessary clearances and permissions incurred or required in connection with production and broadcast of the event. Obviously to some extent this will depend on the precise deal which has been struck between the parties but it may include appropriate copyright clearances, the payment of production costs as well as salaries to employees and any other relevant expenses.

9.8.7   The rights owner's obligations

The essential obligation of the rights owner is to grant the rights required by the agreement to the broadcaster. However, as part and parcel of this obligation a broadcaster may seek assurance on some or all of the following points.

(1) Attendance at matches for the broadcaster and its production unit. This may include access to power supply and parking as well as all areas of the grounds and venues at which the event being broadcast are held.
(2) Access to team sheets and information for the broadcaster. In addition, the broadcaster may want access to individual players, managers and coaches before and after matches for interview and comment. This may be extended to include access team photo calls, training, dressing rooms and pre-match talks, as well as exclusive interviews with individual players, managers and coaches at key times during the course of the agreement.

The broadcaster may also require additional rights which will be similar to the rights a sponsor will require such as the right to advertising in match programmes, perimeter advertising boards and even a certain number of free tickets or hospitality facilities for its own use.

The broadcaster will be most concerned to ensure that the access and technical facilities available enable it to fulfil its own obligations to produce and broadcast the event. Unless the rights owner is able to provide the appropriate facilities and rights of access then the broadcaster will be unable to comply with its own undertakings and commitments in the agreement.

9.8.8   Sponsorship and advertising

There tend to be two specific issues which arise. The first relates to the rights owner's ability to protect its own commercial partners and the second relates to the commercial freedom which the broadcaster has to exploit its own commercial rights in relation to its coverage of the event. This latter point tends to only apply to commercial broadcasters.

The rights owner will very often find that its own commercial partners impose obligations on it in their sponsorship and advertising contract ensuring that their rights are protected in any broadcast and that they are given some assurance that their competitors will not achieve any commercial opportunities over the broadcast of the event. The rights owner will seek to pass these obligations on to the broadcaster by requiring it to give the event or title sponsor of the event a broadcasting credit. This may mean that the broadcaster is required to refer to the event using its title sponsorship credit and that the other commercial partners and sponsors that the rights owner has appointed also receive their dues.

Typically this will mean references are made to the sponsors in trailers and credits produced around the broadcast as well as in any references made during the broadcast by commentators or in post-match interviews. The rights owner may also insist that the broadcast coverage of the event does not obscure, exclude or restrict on-screen coverage of any advertising boards or signage or even other promotional material which is placed at the perimeter, for instance by the cameras at the event. The rights owners will also seek an undertaking that the broadcaster complies with all the applicable obligations of the rights owner to its sponsors which are consistent with the grant of rights and which have been notified to the broadcaster by the rights owner.

The broadcaster will need to ensure that both it and the rights owner comply with all the relevant restrictions on advertising and signage at the event to ensure that the broadcaster applies with the relevant codes of practice and legislation. In particular, this means the Broadcasting Acts 1990 and 1996 as well as the various ITC codes of practice which apply.

The second point relates to the broadcaster's ability to appoint its own commercial partners, in particular, to appoint a broadcast sponsor. There are a number of variables here:

(1) the broadcaster may retain for the company the freedom to appoint any broadcast sponsor as it sees fit;

(2) the broadcaster may appoint any broadcaster it sees fit other than competitors to the rights owner's commercial partners;

(3) the broadcaster may not appoint any broadcast sponsor without the prior written approval of the rights owner;

(4) the broadcaster must notify the rights owner of its intention to appoint a broadcast sponsor. It may, having announced its intention, appoint any broadcast sponsor it wishes, or appoint any broadcast sponsor other than a competitor of the rights owner's sponsors; the rights owner must approve the broadcast sponsor; or the rights owner may prohibit the appointment of the sponsor with or without reason;

(5) the broadcaster may appoint its own broadcast sponsors but the rights owner has the right to nominate a potential broadcast sponsor as it sees fit. This nominee will then conclude its own terms with the broadcaster.

The possibilities here all depend on the relevant bargaining power of the parties and the willingness of the broadcaster to comply with the rights owner and its commercial partners by ensuring that they receive the exclusivity and the prominence which they require. There may be any combination of options[1] and matching rights clauses[2] or general rights of first negotiation in relation to broadcast sponsorship rights.

It is also common in certain sports and higher profile events for the rights owner to insist upon complete control of the appointment of a broadcast sponsor. Effectively the rights owner may acquire broadcast sponsorship rights from the broadcaster either by way of payment or a reduction in the rights fee and can then offer integrated packages of sponsorship rights to its own sponsors. These sponsors will then gain event sponsorship status as well as broadcast sponsorship

---

1   See Chapter 3.
2   See Chapter 3.

rights in the same package. This integrated approach tends to operate only for sponsors who have sufficient cash and who are particularly concerned about the possibility of ambush marketing taking place by broadcast sponsorship.

The rights owner may wish to impose similar obligations and restrictions on the sale of broadcast advertising time, although it is extremely unlikely that the broadcaster will be willing to accept such further restrictions. It should also be borne in mind that all restrictions may be further subject to the scrutiny of the competition authorities as they go well beyond restrictions necessary for a broadcast agreement.

9.8.9   Miscellaneous

There may be other provisions in the agreement relating to the protection of intellectual property rights, force majeure and termination provisions. In addition, there will be various boiler-plate clauses dealing with any number of matters. The termination provisions in the agreement may be particularly important. The parties will need to set out precisely what events trigger termination of the agreement and what effect termination has on the rights granted and payments made under the agreement to date. There may be a number of particular concerns in relation to broadcast agreements as follows:

(1) the effectiveness of an adverse competition law ruling which rules that the grant of rights under the broadcasting contract is unlawful or otherwise in contravention of relevant legislation;

(2) if it breaches any of its obligations particularly as they relate to the minimum level of broadcast coverage or other terms which the parties deem important. Very often the right to termination will arise whenever there is a material breach of the terms of the agreement which is not remedied within a given number of days.

The agreement may also contain restrictions on the use of new and developed technology by the broadcaster, in particular, so-called 'broadcasts substitution technology' which potentially allows broadcasters to superimpose imagery upon the broadcast of an event. Such post-production technology may have the ability to alter advertising and other branding and signage at an event as well as insert logos on the field of play. At the date of writing such technology remains unproven although given the rate of change and development it is likely that such technology will create significant opportunities for broadcasters and rights owners alike. Such opportunities will need to be dealt with and regulated within the context of the broadcast agreement if both parties are to find that their own expectations are realised.[1]

---

1   The ITC has issued a guidance note on the use of such technology.

9.9 LICENSING OF BROADCAST FOOTAGE

9.9.1 Introduction

This part briefly considers the additional terms which are relevant when licensing footage of an event. Such footage may be licensed for broadcast or any number of other uses.

9.9.2 Parties

The first important point is that the party granting the rights in the footage has the ability to do so. Since the footage will be protected by copyright, it is important that the rights owner is able to prove title to the rights in question. If there are other broadcasters already in place then reference should be made to those documents to make sure that the rights that are being granted have not already been granted to another party for the same purposes and/or within the same territories. Where a commercial rights agent is involved in the negotiation and sale of footage, it must be clear precisely what authority the agent has to contract on behalf of its principal. Usually the rights agent will negotiate the terms of the agreement but may not actually sign or conclude the deal.

9.9.3 Rights and exclusivity

The terms of the agreement must specify precisely what rights are being granted in the footage. If the grant of rights is being made to a broadcaster then the rights will usually be to broadcast the material or programme concerned (and these must be carefully defined). The broadcaster may also require the right to copy, edit, cut and alter the footage in question. The broadcaster may also want to insert advertising and appoint broadcast sponsors and the considerations already mentioned in this regard[1] are equally relevant here. In addition, the broadcaster may want to, or even be required to, licence news clips and excerpts from the footage to third parties and produce its own trailers and still photographs for other promotional purposes.

The broadcaster will also require the rights owner to warrant that all underlying rights in the material being acquired have been suitably cleared. This may mean any underlying copyrights in material such as featured music and graphics used in the material are cleared for use by the broadcaster. If a broadcast features any performers or performances within the meaning of the CDPA 1988, Part II, the rights owner must have acquired appropriate consents to ensure that the performances in question can be exploited by the broadcaster when it exercises its rights.

Such clearances will also relate to the use of any other intellectual property rights and in particular trade marks, names and logos of sponsors and advertisers who are featured in the material.

As a general rule, the broadcaster will need to obtain all necessary rights and clearances from the rights owner, although there may be certain rights and clearances or consents which it will obtain itself. For example, although the

---

1   See **9.8.8.**

rights owner may be required to warrant that it has the permission of the copyright owner in any music feature to actually copy that music and to copy the recording concerned in relation to the actual performance of that music and that recording, it will be up to the broadcaster to obtain appropriate permission (usually under some form of blanket licence arrangement) for itself.

The rights owner will also wish to ensure that the broadcaster grants it suitable credits and that its copyright ownership is reflected in those credits.

9.9.4 Territory and duration

The territorial extent of the rights that have been granted must be carefully defined in the agreement. If this is a broadcast licence then it is typical for the broadcaster's right to exploit the copyright to be restricted to a particular territory. Any exploitation outside of that territory will constitute an infringement of the copyright as well as a breach of contract. It is a matter for agreement and negotiation between the parties.

As far as the duration of the rights is concerned, this again relates to the specific needs of the broadcaster. It may be limited to a certain amount of time and/or to a certain number of transmissions within that time. Again this is a matter for agreement between the parties.

9.9.5 Fees

Where the rights are being exploited by a broadcaster on a straightforward broadcast basis there will usually be a licence fee payable. This may be payable, as a one-off payment or in a number of instalments. If the footage or material in question is not actually being created at the time the agreement is signed (and this is quite common when an event has not yet taken place) then the broadcaster will not usually agree to make any substantial payment until the material has been created and delivered in acceptable technical and possibly commercial form.

If the material is being exploited in some other form (for example by way of pay-per-view) then the financial terms of the agreement may vary. There may be an initial advance payment which will then be recouped from income attributable to pay-per-view receipts. If this is the case then the agreement will contain appropriate accounting and auditing provisions.

In the case of video distribution, the financial terms are likely to include advance payments, royalty payments and accounting provisions.[1]

9.9.6 Production obligations

In the case of existing material, the broadcaster will be able to view that material and decide whether or not it wishes to acquire it. If it does wish to acquire it then the terms of that acquisition will be negotiated and agreed.

Where the material in question does not yet exist because the event is being held in the future or the broadcaster is effectively commissioning the rights owner or producer to create a work, then the agreement may start to look more like a

---

1   See Chapter 3.

traditional production contract. If this is the case then the agreement is likely to contain a number of terms dealing with some or all of the following:

(1) the agreement may specify delivery date for the material. If the delivery date is not met then the broadcaster may not be required to accept delivery of the material in question. Delivery will usually be by a due date. If the date is not met then the broadcaster may well be able to refuse to accept the material;

(2) the material may also need to be of acceptable quality. There will usually be two aspects to this. First of all the material must be technically acceptable. The broadcaster will specify precisely what the specifications are in this regard. The second aspect is that the material may need to be commercially acceptable. If the rights owner is simply providing an event feed of a live match then commercial equality should not come into it. The broadcaster should simply be accepting the material produced to suitable technical standards. If the rights owner is also providing commentary and opening and closing credits then the broadcaster may wish to ensure that such credits and commentary are of an appropriate standard and commercially suitable for its market. If the material does not tend to be commercially satisfactory then the rights owner should be given the opportunity to amend the material in line with the broadcaster's requirements. The material should then be redelivered to the broadcaster. If the material is satisfactory then it should be accepted. If the broadcaster still feels that the material is not of an acceptable commercial standard then the broadcaster may retain the right to terminate the agreement. If this is the case then it may require repayment of any rights fees which have already been paid. Alternatively, the broadcaster may attempt to take over the production of the material in which case it would be able to deduct the costs of putting it into a commercially satisfactory form for many further fees payable to the rights owner under the agreement.

9.9.7 Miscellaneous provisions

The agreement should contain standard clauses[1] which tend to be similar from contract to contract.

1　See Chapter 3.

9.9.8   Broadcast licence agreement

AGREEMENT dated the   day of   [   ]

BETWEEN:

(1)   [   ] of [   ] ('the Organiser')

(2)   **[BROADCASTER]** of [   ] ('the Broadcaster')

RECITAL

(1)   The Organiser is the organiser of the Event (as defined in this Agreement)

(2)   The Organiser wishes to grant Broadcaster certain rights in connection with the [live and delayed broadcast] of the Event

I   DEFINITIONS AND INTERPRETATION

    1.1   In this Agreement the following terms have the following meanings:

'the Governing Body'	means [ ];
'Broadcast Substitution'	means the ability to superimpose an electronic image onto any surface whether real or imaginary or the ability to alter any image by any means whether electronic or otherwise;
'the Commercial Partners'	means [ ];
'the Event'	means the event which is planned to be run on the dates and at the time set out in Schedule 1;
'Intellectual Property'	means patents trade marks (whether registered or unregistered) rights in any designs (whether registered or unregistered) and applications for any of the foregoing trade or business names copyright and rights in performances;
'the Rights'	means the Broadcaster's right at its own cost to:

        (i)   produce the Programme and broadcast it by means of live or delayed recorded encrypted or unencrypted transmission to persons by [*a satellite direct to domestic reception equipment*];

        (ii)   advertise promote or publicise the Programme by transmission to its audience;

        (iii)   include instant replays as part of the Programme;

        (iv)   insert commercial and promotional announcements during the Programme;

        (v)   insert on-screen graphics and information;

        (vi)   add commentary and sound to the Event Feed in producing the Programme;

'the Programme'	means the audio-visual programme produced by the Broadcaster based on and including the Event using the Event Feed;

'the Event Feed'	means the live signal of the Event produced by the Producer with [*1*] audio track of natural sound;
'the Producer'	means [*insert name*] or such other person as the Broadcaster appoints to produce the Event Feed;
'the Term'	means the period from date of signature of this Agreement up to and including the date of the Event;
'the Territory'	[*insert details*];
'the Event Marks'	means [*insert details*].

1.2   In this Agreement where the context admits:

1.2.1   references to statutory provisions shall be construed as references to those provisions as amended or re-enacted or as their application is modified by other provisions from time to time and shall include references to any provisions of which they are re-enactments (whether with or without modification);

1.2.2   references to 'this Agreement' or to any other agreement or document referred to in this Agreement mean this Agreement or such other agreement or document as amended varied supplemented modified or novated from time to time and include the schedules;

1.2.3   references to clause(s) and schedule(s) are references to clause(s) and schedule(s) of and to this Agreement and references to sub-clause(s) or paragraph(s) are unless otherwise stated references to sub-clauses(s) of the clause or paragraph(s) in which the reference appear;

1.2.4   references to a *'person'* include any individual company body corporate corporation sole or aggregate government state or agency of a state firm partnership joint venture association organisation or trust (in each case whether or not having separate legal personality and irrespective of the jurisdiction in or under the law of which it was incorporated or exists) and a reference to any of them shall include a reference to the others;

1.2.5   any reference to writing shall include typewriting printing lithography photography and other modes of representing or reproducing words in a legible form other than writing on an electronic display screen or similar device.

1.3   **Headings**

The headings and sub-headings are inserted for convenience only and shall not affect the construction of this Agreement.

1.4   **Schedules**

Each of the schedules shall have effect as if set out in this Agreement.

2   LICENSED RIGHTS

2.1   Subject to and in consideration of the terms of this Agreement the Organiser grants to the Broadcaster the Rights in the Territory during the Term.

2.2   The Organiser reserves to itself all rights in the Event other than the Rights.

3   EXPENSES

Each party shall bear its own costs of complying with the terms of and undertaking its obligations under this Agreement.

4 OBLIGATIONS OF THE BROADCASTER

4.1 The Broadcaster shall produce the Programme to a standard of at least the same quality and have the same production standards as other sports programming currently being produced by the Broadcaster.

4.2 The Broadcaster shall pay its own costs of production of the Programme.

4.3 The Broadcaster shall use its best endeavours to exploit the Rights licensed to it under this Agreement by procuring the transmission of the Programme in the Territory simultaneously with the Event or at the times dates and from the locations set out in Schedule 2.

4.4 If the Broadcaster is for any reason unable to transmit the Programme as required by this clause it shall do so as soon as reasonably practicable afterwards.

4.5 The Broadcaster shall:

4.5.1 not appoint a broadcast sponsor or grant any sponsorship rights over the Rights the Event or the Programme;

4.5.2 not accept any advertising intended for transmission during, immediately before or after the Programme that is in the reasonable opinion of the Organiser in direct competition with the Organiser or any Commercial Partners;

4.5.3 not do anything which in the reasonable opinion of the Organiser is or might be prejudicial or defamatory to the name and image of the Organiser the Governing Body the Event or the sport of [   ];

4.5.4 comply with and observe all provisions in the Governing Bodies' rules and regulations from time to time in force;

4.5.5 comply with all particular laws and regulations applicable to the exploitation of the Rights and the organisation of the Event;

4.5.6 not effect any Broadcast Substitution on any signal transmitting the Programme unless specifically requested in writing by the Organiser;

4.5.7 at its expense select and provide announcers commentators technical and other personnel sufficient to produce the Programme;

4.5.8 not interfere with the running of the Event;

4.5.9 use its best endeavours to provide two (2) hours broadcast coverage (whether live or delayed) during each day of the Event;

4.5.10 arrange for and be responsible for all necessary licences clearances permissions and fees required in connection with the production and distribution of the Programme and the exercise of the Rights;

4.5.11 provide access to footage for the Programme for use by other broadcasters in accordance with the new Code of Practice from time to time.

4.6 The Broadcaster shall procure that its personnel agents and independent contractors comply with all reasonable directions given by the Organiser its employees agents and representatives in relation to the positioning of its personnel and equipment at the Event.

5 OBLIGATIONS OF THE ORGANISER

5.1 The Organiser shall use its reasonable endeavours to ensure that the Event is properly and professionally organised.

5.2 The Organiser shall procure that the Broadcaster has access for its personnel and equipment at the Event at the times reasonably required by the Broadcaster and at no charge to the Broadcaster. In addition the Organiser shall ensure that the Broadcaster has access to a power supply, car parking sufficient for its equipment and personnel at the event and such other reasonable facilities as the Broadcaster notifies to the Organiser from time to time as long as the provision of such facilities involves no expense to the Organiser and the Broadcaster agrees to bear the reasonable agreed costs of such facilities.

5.3 The Organiser shall provide or shall procure that the Broadcaster is provided with such information as the Broadcaster may reasonably request in relation to the Event.

5.4 Subject to the terms of this Agreement the Organiser grants to the Broadcaster the non-exclusive right to incorporate the Event Marks in the Programme and in exploiting the Rights.

5.5 The Organiser will endeavour to make participants in the Event available to the Broadcaster for the purposes of interviews and commentary for the Programme and reasonable promotional and cross-promotional activities relating to the Programme.

6 OWNERSHIP OF THE RIGHTS

6.1 The Broadcaster shall be the first owner of the copyright in the Programme.

6.2 The Broadcaster shall not exploit its copyright in the Programme other than in the exploitation of the Rights on the terms of this Agreement.

6.3 At the end of the Term and in consideration of the sum of £1 (receipt of which is acknowledged) the Broadcaster shall assign to the Organiser all of its copyright in the Programme for the remaining unexpired period of copyright and all rights of the Broadcaster shall cease.

7 WARRANTIES AND INDEMNITIES

7.1 Each party warrants to the other that it has the full right power and authority to enter into and perform its obligations under this Agreement.

7.2 The Broadcaster shall indemnify the Organiser against any loss, cost, charge, liability or expense the Organiser (or any employee of the Organiser or any Commercial Partner) may sustain or incur as a direct or indirect consequence of the breach by the Broadcaster of any of its obligations under this Agreement.

8 INTELLECTUAL PROPERTY

8.1 The Broadcaster shall promptly and fully notify the Organiser of any actual threatened or suspected infringement in the Territory of any Intellectual Property of the Organiser which comes to the Broadcaster's notice and of any claim by any third party so coming to its notice and the Broadcaster shall at the request and expense of the Organiser do all such things as may be reasonably required to assist the Organiser in taking or resisting any proceedings in relation to any such infringement or claim.

8.2 Nothing in this Agreement shall give the Broadcaster any rights in respect of any Intellectual Property or the Event Marks used by the Organiser in relation to the Event or of the goodwill associated therewith and the Broadcaster acknowledges that except as expressly provided in this Agreement it shall not acquire any rights in respect thereof and that all such rights and goodwill are and shall remain vested in the Organiser.

8.3   The Broadcaster shall not use any trade marks or trade names so resembling the Event Marks or trade names of the Organiser or of the Governing Bodies as to be likely to cause confusion or deception.

8.4   The Broadcaster shall not authorise any third party to use the Event Marks or any Intellectual Property of the Organiser or of the Governing Bodies. If any third party requires the use of the Event Marks or any Intellectual Property of the Organiser or of the Event then the Broadcaster shall inform the Organiser of such requirement. The Organiser may (in its absolute discretion and where it is able to) grant such third party the right or licence required.

8.5   The Broadcaster shall at the expense of the Organiser take all such steps as the Organiser may reasonably require to assist the Organiser in mainlining the validity and enforceability of the Intellectual Property of the Organiser during the continuance of this Agreement.

8.6   Without prejudice to the right of the Broadcaster or any third party to challenge the validity of any Intellectual Property of the Organiser the Broadcaster shall not do or authorise any third party to do any act which would or might invalidate or be inconsistent with the Intellectual Property of the Organiser and shall not omit or authorise any third party to omit to do any act which by its omission would have that effect or character.

8.7   The Broadcaster shall take such reasonable action and steps in relation to any potential or actual infringement of its Intellectual Property in the Rights which comes to its notice as the Organiser shall at the request and expense of the Broadcaster do all such things as may be reasonably required to take or remit any proceedings in relation to such infringement of the Rights.

9   CONFIDENTIALITY

9.1   Confidentiality

Subject to sub-clauses 9.2 and 9.3 each party:

9.1.1   shall treat as strictly confidential and use solely for the purposes contemplated by this Agreement all documents materials and other information whether technical or commercial obtained or received by it as a result of entering into or performing its obligation under this Agreement and relating to the negotiations relating to or the provisions or subject matter of this Agreement ('confidential information'); and

9.1.2   shall not accept with the prior written consent of the party from whom the confidential information was obtained publish or otherwise disclose to any person any confidential information.

9.2   Permitted disclosures

Each party may disclose confidential information which would otherwise be subject to sub-clause 9.1 if but only to the extent that it can demonstrate that:

9.2.1   such disclosure is required by law or by any securities exchange or regulatory or governmental body having jurisdiction over it wherever situated (and including without limitation the London Stock Exchange the Panel on Takeovers and Mergers and the Serious Fraud Office) and whether or not the requirement has the force of law;

9.2.2   the confidential information has come into the public domain other than through its fault or the fault of any person to whom the confidential information has been disclosed in accordance with sub-clause 9.3.

Provided that any such disclosure shall not be made without prior notice to the party from whom the confidential information was obtained.

9.3   Persistence of restrictions

The restrictions contained in this clause shall survive the termination of this Agreement.

10   TERMINATION

Either party may terminate this Agreement forthwith upon notice in the event that the other:

10.1   commits a material breach of any obligation under this Agreement which breach is incapable of remedy or cannot be remedied in time for the Event;

10.2   commits a material breach of any obligation under this Agreement and if such breach is capable of remedy fails to so remedy such breach within twenty-eight days of receiving notice from the other requiring remedy;

10.3   enters into a composition or arrangement with its creditors has a receiver or administrator or administrative receiver appointed or becomes insolvent or unable to pay its debts when they fall due.

10.4   Consequences of termination

Upon termination in accordance with Clause 10:

10.4.1   the rights and obligations of the parties under this Agreement shall terminate and be of no future effect except that Clauses 8 and 9 shall remain in full force and effect;

10.4.2   any rights or obligations to which any of the parties to this Agreement may be entitled or be subject before such termination shall remain in full force and effect;

10.4.3   termination shall not affect or prejudice any right to damages or other remedy which the terminating party may have in respect of the circumstances which gave rise to the termination or any other right to damages or other remedy which any party may have in respect of any breach of this Agreement which existed at or before the date of termination.

10.5   Effect on the rights

10.5.1   If the Organiser terminates this Agreement under Clause 10 then it will be taken to have received the assignment from the Broadcaster of all rights including any unexpired copyright in the Programme under Clause 6.3. The termination of this Agreement by the Organiser will terminate the Organiser's right to exploit the Rights.

10.5.2   If the Broadcaster terminates this Agreement under Clause 10 during or immediately after the Event has been held that termination will not affect the assignment of all rights in the Programme to the Organiser at the expiration of the Term under Clause 6.3.

11   FORCE MAJEURE

Neither party to this Agreement shall be deemed to be in breach of this Agreement or otherwise liable to the other as a result of any delay or failure in the performance of its obligations under this Agreement if and to the extent that such delay or failure is caused by force majeure (as defined in sub-clause 11.2) and the time for performance of the relevant obligation(s) shall be extended accordingly.

11.2   **Definition of force majeure**

For the purpose of this clause 'force majeure' means any circumstances not foreseeable at the date of this Agreement and not within the reasonable control of the party in question including without limitation:

11.2.1   any strike lockout or other industrial action or any shortage of or difficulty in obtaining labour or raw materials;

11.2.2   any destruction temporary or permanent breakdown malfunction or damage of or to any premises plant equipment (including computer systems) or materials;

11.2.3   any breach of contract default or insolvency by or of any third party (including an agent or sub-contractor) other than a company in the same group as the party affected by the force majeure or an employee or officer of that party or company;

11.2.4   any action taken by government or public authority of any kind including not granting a consent exemption approval or clearance;

11.2.5   any civil commotion or disorder riot invasion war threat of or preparation of war;

11.2.6   any fire explosion storm flood earthquake subsidence epidemic or other natural physical disaster.

11.3   **Obligations of affected party**

A party whose performance of its obligations under this Agreement is delayed or prevented by force majeure:

11.3.1   shall forthwith notify the other party of the nature extent effect and likely duration of the circumstances constituting the force majeure;

11.3.2   shall use all reasonable endeavours to minimise the effect of the force majeure on its performance of its obligations under this Agreement; and

11.3.3   shall subject to sub-clause 17.4 forthwith after the cessation of the force majeure notify the other party thereof and resume full performance of its obligations under this Agreement.

11.4   **Termination for force majeure**

If any force majeure delays or prevents the performance of the obligations of either party for a continuous period in excess of one month the party not so affected shall then be entitled to give notice to the affected party to terminate this Agreement specifying the date (which shall not be less than seven days after the date on which the notice is given) on which termination will take effect. Such a termination notice shall be irrevocable except with the consent of both parties and upon termination the provisions of Clauses 10.4 and 10.5 apply.

12   LIMITATION OF LIABILITY

The Organiser shall not be liable to the Broadcaster for breach of any of the terms of this Agreement for an amount of money that is greater than the direct costs to the Broadcaster of producing the Programme.

13   NATURE OF AGREEMENT

13.1   The Organiser may perform any of its obligations and exercise any of the rights granted to it under this Agreement through any other person and any act or omission of any such person shall for the purposes of this Agreement be deemed to be the act or omission of the Organiser.

13.2 The Organiser may assign this Agreement and the rights and obligations hereunder.

13.3 This Agreement is personal to the Broadcaster which may not without the written consent of the Organiser assign mortgage charge (otherwise than by floating charge) or dispose of any of its rights hereunder or sub-contract or otherwise delegate any of its obligations hereunder.

13.4 Nothing in this Agreement shall create or be deemed to create a partnership or the relationship of employer and employee between the parties.

13.5 This Agreement contains the entire agreement between the parties with respect to the subject matter hereof and supersedes all previous agreements and understandings between the parties with respect thereto and may not be modified except by an instrument in writing signed by the duly authorised representatives of the parties.

13.6 Each party acknowledges that in entering into this Agreement it does not do so on the basis of and does not rely on any representation warranty or other provision except as expressly provided herein and all conditions warranties or other terms implied by statute or common law are hereby excluded to the fullest extent permitted by law.

13.7 If any provision of this Agreement is held by any court or other competent authority to be void or unenforceable in whole or part this Agreement shall continue to be valid as to the other provisions thereof and the remainder of the affected provisions.

13.8 At any time after the date hereof each of the parties shall at the request and cost of the other party execute or procure the execution of such documents and do or procure the doing of such acts and things as the party so requiring may reasonably require for the purpose of giving to the party so requiring the full benefit of all the provisions of this Agreement.

13.9 Each party to this Agreement shall pay its own costs of and incidental to the negotiation preparation execution and carrying into effect of this Agreement.

14 PROPER LAW

This Agreement shall be governed by and construed in all respects in accordance with the Laws of England and each party hereby submits to the exclusive jurisdiction of the English Courts.

15 NOTICES AND SERVICE

15.1 Any notice or other information required or authorised by this Agreement to be given by either party to the other may be given by hand or sent (by first class pre-paid post telex cable facsimile transmission or comparable means of communication) to the other party at the address referred to in Clause 15.4.

15.2 Any notice or other information given by post pursuant to Clause 15.1 which is not returned to the sender as undelivered shall be deemed to have been given on the second day after the envelope containing the same was so posted and proof that the envelope containing any such notice or information was properly addressed pre-paid registered and posted and that it has not been so returned to the sender shall be sufficient evidence that such notice or information has been duly given.

15.3   Any notice or other information sent by telex cable facsimile transmission or comparable means of communication shall be deemed to have been duly sent on the date of transmission provided that a confirming copy thereof is sent by first class pre-paid post to the other party at the address referred to in Clause 15.4 within twenty-four hours after transmission.

15.4   Service of any legal proceedings concerning or arising out of this Agreement shall be effected by causing the same to be delivered to the Company Secretary of the party to be served at its principal place of business (in the case of the Organiser) or its registered office (in the case of the Broadcaster) or to such other address as may from time to time be notified in writing by the party concerned.

SIGNED on behalf of **THE ORGANISER**   )
in the presence of:)

SIGNED on behalf of **THE BROADCASTER**   )
in the presence of:)

9.9.9 Video distribution agreement

THIS AGREEMENT is made the   day of   [   ]

BETWEEN

(1) [   ] whose registered office is at
     [   ] ('the Company');

(2) [   ] whose registered office is at
     [   ] ('the Club');

BACKGROUND

A. The business of the Company is the production manufacture marketing distribution and sale of television and video Programmes and Videograms.

B. The Club wishes to engage the Company to film the Club's games and to produce market distribute and sell Videograms about the Club and its games in accordance with the terms of this Agreement.

C. The parties recognise the rules and directions of the Governing Bodies which bind the Club and both limit its rights and in certain circumstances oblige it to licence the recording and broadcast of Matches played at the Club's Home Ground and accordingly limits the Company's rights to exploit the Pictures.

OPERATIVE PROVISIONS

1   **Interpretation**

     1.1   The following expressions shall have the following meanings unless inconsistent with the context:

'The Accounting Dates'	means during the Term, 1st April and 1st October; for the subsequent 10 years 1st October;
'Associate Company'	means any company which is a holding or subsidiary company of the Club as defined in s 736 of the Companies Act 1985 or any company which is a subsidiary of any holding company of the Club;
'The Club Shops'	means any retail outlet owned or managed by the Club or [ ] or any other subsidiary of [ ] as defined by s 736 of the Companies Act 1985 to sell official Club merchandise;
'Discount Price'	means the price from time to time agreed by the Company with the Club at which the Company will sell Videograms to the Club and Club Shops which price shall not exceed [ ]% of the Published Dealer Price;
'Governing Bodies'	means [ ] and any other body having the power to issue regulations to which the Club is or may at any time be subject in respect of the game of [ ] and/or any aspect thereof together with any bodies which shall at any time succeed to the rights and/or obligations or come into being by way of replacement of the said bodies (and the phrase 'Governing Body' shall be construed accordingly);
'Home Ground'	means the [ ] ground pitch or stadium used by

the Club from time to time for the playing of fixtures at which it is deemed to be the home Club by any Governing Body responsible for organising the league in which the Club is playing from time to time;

'Licence'   means the licence granted by the Club to the Company pursuant to clause 2 of this Agreement;

'Matches'   means those games played at the Home Ground during the Term by the Club's team in the [   ] League the [   ] Cup or any competitions which reasonably may be deemed to be successors to the said competitions and such competitions such as the Club and the Company may from time to time agree between them shall be subject to this Agreement;

'Net Receipts'   means all sums actually received by the Company from exploitation and/or sale of the Videograms and the Pictures and the Programmes less taxes and duties thereon only;

'Outside Broadcast Unit'   means a unit of television production facilities where the output is mixed or cut together to form a single television picture or Programme in accordance with generally accepted standards of broadcast television production;

'Broadcasters'   means any company holding rights by virtue of any agreement with or derived from any agreement with any Governing Body to broadcast or include in a cable programme service for reception in [Territory] any footage of Matches from time to time;

'Pictures'   means any and all unedited or edited motion pictures films or video recording (including (but not limited to) the Programmes and any edited version of the said motion pictures films or video recordings and/or any compilations made thereof) together with any and all associated sound track and/or commentary made by the Company pursuant to its rights granted in this Agreement and/or its obligations hereunder of and in relation to the Matches;

'Programmes'   means any video recording made by the Company directly derived from the Pictures and mixed edited and titled with all music effects and dialogue synchronised which can be exhibited with or without the sound as a television Programme or Videogram;

'Published Dealer Price'   means the standard price at which the distributor of the Videograms supplies the Videograms to trade customers in the absence of any discount agreement;

'Royalty'   means the Royalty payable by the Company to the Club pursuant to the terms of this Agreement;

'Royalty Advance'   means a non-refundable advance payable by the Company to the Club on account of the Royalty;

'Television Rights'   means the right to transmit or diffuse sound and visual images for direct reception by domestic television receivers or comparable devices by means of a terrestrial

	cable or fibre optic head or wireless telegraphy;
'Term'	means the period commencing on the first day of the [ ] season for the year [ ] and ending on the date before the first day of the season for the year [ ] unless earlier terminated in accordance with the terms of clause 15 of this Agreement;
'Territory'	means the World;
'Total Sales'	means the total number of Videograms sold by the Company excluding any Videograms sold to the Club or the Club Shops and any Videograms sold but subsequently returned to the Company for a refund;
'Trade Marks'	means those Trade Marks listed in Part 1 of Schedule 4 registered in the territories set out therein and the unregistered Trade Marks listed in Part 2 of Schedule 4 and any reference to 'Trade Marks' shall include a reference to any one of them;
'Videograms'	means any video cassette videodisk compact videocassette or any electronic magnetic or other physical storage device whatsoever existing now or later invented on which the Programs are reproduced for retail to the general public under this Agreement (excluding CD-Rom CD-i and other interactive media).

1.2   The headings to the clauses shall not affect the construction of this agreement.

2   Licence

2.1   Subject to clause 2.2 the Club grants to the Company the exclusive right for the Term to attend the Home Ground for the purpose of filming and recording Pictures ('the Licence').

2.2   The grant of the Licence is without prejudice to the regulations of any Governing Body to which the Club may be subject to permit the attendance and filming of Matches by Outside Broadcast Units on behalf of companies which are the owners or licensees of Television Rights in the Matches.

2.3   The Company may waive the exclusivity of the Licence granted in clause 2.1 at the request of the Club but any such waiver shall not be deemed to vary the terms of this clause to prevent the Company from enforcing its rights under this clause at a later stage.

3   Copyright

3.1   In consideration of the Club's undertakings set out in this Agreement the Company HEREBY ASSIGNS to The Club with full title guarantee (by way where appropriate of a present assignment of future copyright pursuant to Section 91 of Copyright, Designs & Patents Act 1988) any and all copyrights throughout the world in the Pictures for all purposes TO HOLD the same unto the Club absolutely until the expiry of copyright in the Pictures.

3.2   In consideration of the assignment in clause 3.1 the Club hereby grants to the Company for the duration of copyright therein (by way where appropriate of a present assignment of future copyright pursuant to section 91 of Copyright, Designs and Patents Act 1988) a non-exclusive licence to use the copyright in the Pictures for the sole purpose of producing Programs which shall be incorporated in and exploited as Videograms only to be manufactured and distributed in the Territory upon the terms of this Agreement.

4   Obligations of the Company

4.1   The Company shall attend all Matches taking place during the Term and further in respect of each Match the Company shall film and record Pictures as specified by the Club with not less than [   ] video cameras and cameramen and all requisite technical facilities and arrangements in order to provide the Pictures to a commercially accepted high quality standard for use both by the Club as it sees fit and by the Company in the production of the Videograms.

4.2   The Company shall use the Pictures to produce such Programmes as the Club may agree in writing (including but not limited to those Programmes listed in Schedule 1) which the Company shall exploit as Videograms only upon the terms of this Agreement.

4.3   During the Royalty Period the Company shall use its reasonable endeavours to produce promote market and distribute the Videograms in a manner which in its reasonable opinion will result in the greatest possible financial return. The Company may at its discretion license the manufacture or distribution of any or all of the Videograms to a reputable third party distribution company ALWAYS PROVIDED THAT the terms of such appointment are those set out at Schedule 6 hereof or such terms as the Club has approved in writing and further that by so doing the Company shall not be excused from the performance of any of its obligations pursuant to this Agreement and in the event of any act or omission by such a third party manufacturer or distribution company which would if committed by the Company be a breach of any terms of this Agreement the Company shall be liable to the Club as if it had itself committed such act or omission and shall indemnify the Club against any and all claims loss damages costs expenses of whatsoever nature and howsoever arising directly or indirectly to the Club as a result of any such act or omission including but not limited to all indirect or consequential damages and the Club's legal costs on an indemnity basis.

4.4   The Company undertakes to sell the Videograms to the Club and the Club Shops at the Discounted Price during the Royalty Period.

4.5   Without prejudice to the generality of clause 3.1 the Company agrees that it will do all things and execute all documents reasonably necessary to ensure that any and all Pictures Programmes and Videograms and other material in relation to the Club or the Club's Matches (including but not limited to the Matches) at any time held by the Company in any form or format whatsoever ('Footage') shall be made available to the Club for exploitation in whatever manner the Club in its absolute discretion sees fit ALWAYS PROVIDED THAT the Company shall be entitled to make reasonable technical and research charges in respect of the provision of the said Footage which shall be borne by the Club.

5   Obligations of the Club

5.1   The Club undertakes that it has as at the date of this Agreement the rights necessary to grant the Company the Licence and rights granted in this Agreement.

5.2   The Club will use its reasonable endeavours to procure where necessary the reasonable cooperation with the Company in the production of the Pro-grammes of its managers players and other employees upon the basis that the

Company shall not be required to pay to such person any fee or indulgence in respect of an appearance in the Programmes. Nothing in this clause shall entitle the Company to demand the detailed cooperation of any person employed by the Club in the production of the Programmes.

5.3   The Club shall afford the Company and its manufacturers and distributors appointed in accordance with clause 4.3 every reasonable assistance and cooperation in the marketing and distribution of the Programmes and Videograms including but not by way of limitation:

5.3.1   the use of any still photograph of the Matches or any of the Club's players managers or employees provided always that the cost of providing a copy of any photograph including obtaining the licence of the copyright owner of such photograph shall be the Company's;

5.3.2   subject to the Club's normal commercial charges the use of advertising and other media in the control of the Club including but not limited to the use of hospitality facilities at the Home Ground and other premises of the Club;

5.3.3   the Club shall use reasonable endeavours to secure on favourable terms the services of such of its players managers and employees as the Company may reasonably request for personal appearances and endorsement to promote the Programmes. The reasonable cost of such appearances and endorsements shall be the Company's.

5.4   The Club undertakes not to permit encourage or endorse the production of any video or Videogram similar in nature to the Videograms produced by any third party save only such Videograms produced by or on behalf of other member clubs of [the League] pursuant to arrangements made by [the League's Governing Body] or with its consent.

6   Content of the Programmes

6.1   Subject to clauses 6.2 and 6.3 the Company shall have full editorial discretion in the production of the Programmes.

6.2   The Company and the Club shall decide jointly the subject matter technological and storage medium format title and script shooting schedule release schedule and featured persons in respect of the Programmes and the Videograms more particularly described in Schedule 1.

6.3   The Company warrants that nothing appearing in any of the Programmes and/or the Videograms or any packaging used therefor and/or promotional materials used therewith ('Materials') shall infringe the copyright or other intellectual property rights or moral rights of any person and nothing appearing therein shall be obscene blasphemous or defamatory of any person or bring the Club or any officer employee or Associate Company of the Club into disrepute and the Company shall submit for prior written approval to the Club samples of any Programmes and/or Videograms and Materials intended to be distributed. In the event that within seven (7) days of receipt thereof the Club objects to any of the content of the said samples the Company shall ensure the content to which objection has been raised shall be deleted before any such Programme and/or Videogram and Materials are distributed pursuant to the terms of this Agreement. In the event that no such objection is raised within seven (7) days of receipt by the Club of the said samples then the content of the said samples shall be deemed to have been approved. The Company shall indemnify and keep indemnified the Club against any loss claims damages expenses or liability howsoever arising whether directly or indirectly to the Club as a result of breach by the Company of this clause 6 including but not limited to all indirect and/or consequential damages and the Club's legal costs on an indemnity basis

6.4   If required by the Club the Company shall include in the Programmes and/or Videograms referred to in Schedule 1 not more than 30 seconds of advertising material promoting such of the Club's sponsors as the Club may direct and to ensure the inclusion on the packaging of the Videograms of such acknowledgement of the Club's sponsors as the Club may require. The reasonable costs of production of such advertising material shall be borne by the Company

7   Intellectual Property

7.1   Subject to the grant of the Licence all recording rights in the Matches shall remain vested exclusively in the Club.

7.2   Nothing in this contract shall be construed as a grant of Television Rights in the Matches Pictures Programmes or Videograms and the Company shall have no rights whatsoever save those expressly set out in this Agreement.

8   Further Grant of Rights

8.1   The Club hereby grants to the Company the non-exclusive revocable right to use for the Term the Trade Marks in relation solely to the production of the Programmes and/or Videograms upon the following basis:

8.1.1   all use of the Trade Marks by the Company shall be for the benefit of the Club and the goodwill accrued to the Company arising from its use of the Trade Marks (but no greater or other goodwill) shall accrue to and be held in trust by the Company for the Club which goodwill the Company agrees to assign to the Club at its request at any time whether during or after the Term of this Agreement;

8.1.2   whenever the Trade Marks are used by the Company they shall be accompanied by wording to show that they are registered Trade Marks (or as the case may be, Trade Marks) used by the Company with the permission of the Club. The terms of such wording and its placing shall be as reasonably requested by the Club;

8.1.3   the Company shall use the Trade Marks in the form stipulated by the Club and shall observe any reasonable directions given by the Club as to colours and size of the representations of the Trade Marks;

8.1.4   the use of the Trade Marks by the Company shall be at all times in keeping with and seek to maintain their distinctiveness and reputation as determined by the Club, and the Company shall cease forthwith any use not consistent therewith as the Club may reasonably require;

8.1.5   the Company shall not use any mark or name confusingly similar to the Trade Marks in respect of any product similar to the Programmes and/or Videograms and shall not use the Trade Marks on any goods or services other than the Programmes and/or Videograms;

8.1.6   the Company shall not use the Trade Marks as part of any corporate business or trading name or style of the Company;

8.1.7   the Company undertakes not to do or permit to be done any act which would or might jeopardise or invalidate any registration of the registered Trade Marks or application therefor nor to do any act which might assist or give rise to an application to remove any of the registered Trade Marks from the Register or which might prejudice the right or title of the Club to any of the Trade Marks;

8.1.8   the Company will on request give to the Club or its authorised representative any information as to its use of the Trade Marks which the Club may require and will render any assistance reasonably required by the Club in maintaining the registrations of the registered Trade Marks or in prosecuting any application therefor;

8.1.9   the Company will not make or permit any representation or do any act which may be taken to indicate that it has any right title or interest in or to the ownership or use of any of the Trade Marks except under the terms of this Agreement, and acknowledges that nothing contained in this Agreement shall give the Company any right title or interest in or to the Trade Marks save as granted hereby;

8.1.10   the Company shall assist the Club (in the event that the Club so requests) as may be reasonably necessary (including by executing any necessary documents) in recording the Company as a user of the registered Trade Marks on the Register (including such of the applications as mature into registrations during the Term), and the Company hereby agrees that such entry may be cancelled by the Club on expiry or termination of this Agreement, for whatever reason, and that it will assist the Club so far as may be necessary to achieve such cancellation including by executing at the request of the Club any documents necessary for that purpose;

8.1.11   the Company as soon as it becomes aware thereof shall give the Club in writing full particulars of any use or proposed use by any other person, firm or company of a trade name, trade mark or get-up of goods or mode of promotion or advertising which amounts or might amount either to infringement of the Club's rights in relation to the Trade Marks or to passing-off;

8.1.12   the Club shall have the conduct of all proceedings relating to the Trade Marks and shall in its sole discretion decide what action if any to take in respect of any infringement or alleged infringement of the Trade Marks or passing-off or any other claim or counterclaim brought or threatened in respect of the use or registration of the Trade Marks. The Company shall not be entitled to bring any action for infringement under Sections 30 or 31 of the Trade Marks Act 1994, and the Club shall not be obliged to bring or defend any proceedings in relation to the Trade Marks if it decides in its sole discretion not to do so;

8.1.13   the Company will at the request of the Club give full cooperation to the Club in any action, claim or proceedings brought or threatened in relation to the Trade Marks;

8.1.14   upon the expiry or termination of this Agreement for whatever reason the Company shall cease to make any use of the Trade Marks save only that in the event of expiry of this Agreement by effluxion of time if the Company has a stock of Videograms existing or in the course of manufacture or unfulfilled orders on hand at the date of such expiry of this Agreement the Company may sell such stock on the terms hereof for a period of ten (10) years following the date of such expiry. In the event of expiry or termination of this Agreement for any other reason the Company upon such expiry or termination either shall deliver up to the Club or shall destroy (in either case at its own expense) forthwith upon receipt of written instructions from the Club so to do any and all Videograms and/or materials bearing the Trade Marks within its possession power custody and control or in the event that the Club gives specific written permission for the Company so to do the Company may sell such stock on the terms hereof or such other terms as the Club may stipulate in the said written permission or otherwise agree in writing;

8.1.15   all Videograms sold by the Company to which the Trade Marks are affixed shall conform to the highest standards of merchantable quality and shall be manufactured packaged and stored to the highest standards and the Company shall maintain at all times in force public liability insurance with a reputable insurer to a minimum extent of three million pounds (£3,000,000) per claim and shall supply to the Club a copy of the said policy upon request at any time;

8.1.16   the Company agrees to permit the Club or its authorised representative at all reasonable times to enter the Company's premises for the purpose of inspecting the Videograms and the methods of manufacturing packaging and storing them and if and when called upon by the Club to do so the Company agrees to submit samples of the Videograms for inspection by the Club. In the event that in the reasonable opinion of the Club the said inspections reveal any aspect of the Videograms the manufacture packaging and storage of the Videograms and/or of the samples submitted to the Club which does not comply with the highest standards of quality the Company agrees to conform with any instructions in respect of such non-compliance or non-complying Videograms the Club reasonably shall give without prejudice to any other rights the Club may have in respect thereof.

9 Royalty

9.1   The Company undertakes to pay to the Club:

9.1.1   the Royalty Advance for the Term of £[   ] ([   ] pounds) in accordance with Schedule 2;

9.1.2   the balance of the Royalty calculated pursuant to the terms of Schedule 3 for the Royalty Period in accordance with the provisions of clause 11;

9.1.3   all payments are exclusive of any VAT which shall be paid as required by law;

9.1.4   interest upon any sum payable to the Club and not paid on the due date provided therefor in this Agreement at a rate of 4% above the base interest rate of Lloyds Bank plc from time to time in force from the date on which payment of the said sum fell due to the date of actual payment to the Club.

10 Supply of Videograms

10.1   The Company shall supply to the Club and/or shall procure that there shall be supplied to the Club by a reputable distributor Videograms in accordance with the provisions of Schedule 5 hereto.

11 Accounting

11.1   The Company shall account to the Club within thirty (30) days of the Accounting Dates for all Royalties payable under clause 9.1.2 by the issue to the Club of detailed statements showing on a territory by territory and product by product basis the Total Sales of all Programmes and Videograms the average price charged for the same the Net Receipts and the Royalty payable as at the said Accounting Date together with any other information the Club reasonably may require from time to time.

11.2   If the Royalty payable at any Accounting Date exceeds the amount of the Royalty Advance paid by that Accounting Date the Company shall pay to the Club the difference between the Royalty due and the amount of the Royalty Advance paid by that Accounting Date.

11.3   The Company undertakes to keep and to procure that any third party manufacturer or distributor appointed in accordance with clause 4.5 shall keep true and accurate records and books of account containing all data necessary for the determination of the Royalty.

11.4   The Company undertakes to make and to procure that any third party manufacturer or distributor appointed in accordance with clause 4.5 shall make the records and books of account kept pursuant to clause 11.3 available upon reasonable notice for inspection at any reasonable time either before or after any Accounting Date by the Club or any person appointed by the Club and in the event that the said inspection reveals that there has been an underpayment to the Club the Company shall pay forthwith to the Club the amount of any such underpayment together with interest payable thereon calculated pursuant to clause 9.1.4. In the event that the said inspection shows that statements rendered pursuant to clause 11.1 are inaccurate by more than 5% the costs of the said inspection shall be paid by the Company.

11.5   If requested by the Club the Company undertakes to provide no more than once in each year (within three (3) months of the end of the Company's financial year) a Chartered Accountants' Certificate that the statement of Royalties issued to the Club by the Company are in accordance with the records and books of account kept by the Company under clause 11.4.

12   Copyright Infringements

12.1   The Company shall ensure at all times that any Videograms and/or Pictures and/or Programmes together with any and all promotional and packaging materials used in connection therewith produced by the Company pursuant to this Agreement shall bear a copyright notice in a place agreed by the Club identifying the Club as the proprietor of the relevant copyright therein such notice to be in such form as the Club reasonably may stipulate.

12.2   If the Company becomes aware of any use or proposed use by any other person firm or company of the Pictures or the Programmes without licence or authority from the Club the Company shall give promptly to the Club full particulars in writing and at the request of the Club give full cooperation to the Club in any action or proceedings brought or threatened in respect of the Pictures or the Programmes.

12.3   The Club shall have the conduct of all proceedings relating to the Pictures and shall in its sole discretion decide what action if any to take in respect of any infringements or alleged infringements of copyright in the Pictures or the Programmes PROVIDED ALWAYS THAT in the event that the Club decides that it does not wish to take any action in respect of any such infringement or alleged infringement it shall notify the Company in writing of that decision. Thereafter the Company may at its own expense and risk take proceedings in its own name only in relation to any rights granted to it in this Agreement having first given the Club five [5] working days' notice in writing of its intention so to do. In the event that the Company is successful in the said proceedings the Company shall account to the Club for a sum equal to [   ]% of the damages recovered over and above the Company's total costs in relation to the said proceedings.

13   Force Majeure

13.1   If either party is prevented or delayed in the due performance of its obligations hereunder or placed in breach of this Agreement by any cause beyond its reasonable control (including but not limited to fire Act of God strike lock-out or other industrial dispute act or omission of Government war military operations riot direction or resolution of any Governing Body ('An Event of Force Majeure') it shall immediately notify the other of the nature and extend thereof.

13.2   The party directly affected by the Event of Force Majeure shall not be deemed to be in breach of this Agreement or otherwise be liable to the other by reason of any delay or prevention in the due performance of its obligations or breach of this Agreement to the extent that such delay non-performance or breach is due to any Event of Force Majeure of which it has notified the other and the time for performance of that obligation shall be extended accordingly.

13.3   If any Event of Force Majeure continues for a period of ninety (90) days the party not directly affected hereby shall be entitled to terminate this Agreement by serving written notice on the other party such notice to take immediate effect.

14   Confidentiality

14.1   Subject to clause 14.2 each party shall treat as strictly confidential all information received or obtained as a result of entering into or performing this Agreement which relates to:

14.1.1 the provisions or subject matter of this Agreement;

14.1.2 the other party or its affairs.

14.2   Either party may disclose information which would otherwise be confidential if and to the extent:

14.2.1 required by law; and/or

14.2.2 disclosed to the professional advisors auditors bankers of each party under terms of confidentiality; and/or

14.2.3 the other party has given prior consent to the disclosure; and/or

14.2.4 such disclosure is requested by any Governing Body to whose rules the Club may be subject from time to time.

14.3   The restrictions contained in this clause 14 shall continue to apply after the termination of this Agreement without limit in time.

15   Duration and Termination

15.1   This Agreement shall commence on the date of this Agreement and shall terminate automatically (subject to earlier termination pursuant to 15.2) without notice at the end of the Term.

15.2   Either party may terminate this Agreement forthwith by notice in writing to the other if:

15.2.1 the other party commits a material breach of any of the terms or conditions of this Agreement provided that in the case of a breach which is capable of remedy no such notice of termination should be given unless the party in breach has failed to remedy the breach within thirty (30) days of the receipt of a request in writing from the party not in breach to remedy the breach such request setting out the breach and indicating that failure to remedy the breach may result in termination of this Agreement;

15.2.2   the other party becomes insolvent or compounds with its creditors or has a receiver appointed over all or any part of its assets or if a petition is presented or resolution passed to wind it up whether compulsory or voluntarily (other than winding up as a solvent company for the purpose of reconstruction or amalgamation).

15.3   The termination of this Agreement is without prejudice to the rights duties and liabilities of either party accrued prior to termination. The clauses in this Agreement which expressly or impliedly have effect after termination will continue to be enforceable notwithstanding termination.

15.4   On termination the parties will return to each other all documents and other things on loan or free issue in their possession power custody and control owned by the other party.

15.5   In the event that this Agreement is terminated under clause 15.2 the Company shall account at the next Accounting Date after termination to the Club for all Royalties outstanding at the date of termination (without prejudice to any obligation of the Company to account further to the Club pursuant to any terms agreed by the Club whereby the Company may continue to sell Videograms).

16   Indemnity

16.1   The Company shall be liable for and will indemnify the Club (together with its officers servants and agents) against any and all liability loss damages costs legal costs professional and other expenses of any nature whatsoever incurred or suffered by the Club whether direct or consequential (including but without limitation any economic loss or other loss of profits business or goodwill) arising out of any dispute or contractual tortious or other claims or proceedings brought against the Club by a third party claiming relief against the Club by reason of the manufacture use or sale of any Programmes and/or Videograms by the Company or the use of the Company of the Trade Marks except insofar as any such claims may arise from:

16.1.1   any breach of this Agreement by the Club;

16.1.2   any invalidity or defect in the title of the Club to the Trade Marks not caused by any act or default of the Company; or

16.1.3   from the instructions given to the Company by the Club provided such instructions have been properly carried out by the Company.

17   Assignment

17.1   Subject only to the Company's rights pursuant to clause 4.5 and the express provisions of this clause 17 neither party shall assign transfer sub-contract or in any other manner make over to any third party the benefit and/or burden of this Agreement without the prior written consent of the other save that the Club shall be entitled to assign the benefit and burden of this Agreement to any party to which it may assign the Trade Marks and shall use its best endeavours to procure that such assignee if the Company so requires shall grant a licence direct to the Company on the same terms mutatis mutandis as those contained in this Agreement.

17.2   In the event of an assignment this Agreement shall be binding upon such successor or assignee and the name of a party appearing herein shall be deemed to include the names of any successor or assignee.

18 Illegality

18.1   If any provision or term of this Agreement shall become or be declared illegal invalid or unenforceable for any reason whatsoever such term or provision shall be divisible from this Agreement and shall be deemed to be deleted from this Agreement provided always that if such deletion substantially affects or alters the commercial basis of this Agreement the parties shall negotiate in good faith to amend and modify the provisions and terms of this Agreement so as to achieve so far as possible the same economic effect without rendering the Agreement so amended or modified illegal invalid or unenforceable.

19 Entire Agreement/Amendment/Press Releases/Costs

19.1   This Agreement constitutes the entire agreement and understanding of the parties and supersedes all prior oral or written agreements understandings or arrangements between them relating to the subject matter of this Agreement. Neither party shall be entitled to rely on any agreement understanding or arrangement which is not expressly contained in this Agreement and no change may be made to it except in writing signed by duly authorised representatives of both parties.

19.2   Nothing in this Agreement shall create or be deemed to create any form of partnership or joint venture or agency between the parties.

19.3   No failure or delay on the part of either of the parties to exercise any right or remedy under this Agreement shall be construed or operate as a waiver thereof nor shall any single or partial exercise of any right or remedy preclude the further exercise of such right or remedy as the case may be. The rights and remedies provided in this Agreement are cumulative and are not exclusive of any rights or remedies provided by law.

19.4   The text of any press release or other communication to be published by or in the media concerning the subject matter of this Agreement shall require the written approval of each of the parties.

19.5   Each of the parties shall be responsible for its respective legal and other costs incurred in relation to the preparation of this Agreement.

20 Notice

20.1   Any notice or other document to be given under this Agreement shall be in writing and shall be deemed to have been duly given if left at or sent by hand or by registered post; or by facsimile or other electronic media to a party at the address or facsimile number out below for such party or such other address as one party may from time to time designate by written notice to the other.

20.2   Any such notice or other document shall be deemed to have been received by the addressee two working days following the date of dispatch if the notice or other document is sent by registered post or simultaneously with the delivery or transmission if sent by hand or if given by facsimile or other electronic means provided that confirmation of sending (in the case of notice given by facsimile) or electronic acknowledgement of delivery (in the case of notice given by electronic means) is received by the sender in respect of the said notice and a confirmatory copy of the said notice is despatched by registered post not less than 2 days following despatch of the said notice by facsimile or electronic means.

20.3   The Club's address for service is:

Address:

Fax:

20.4 The Company's address for service is:

Address:

Fax:

21 Interpretation

21.1 The headings in this Agreement are inserted only for convenience and shall not affect its construction.

21.2 Where appropriate words denoting a singular number only shall include the plural and vice versa.

21.3 Reference to any statute or statutory provision includes a reference to the statute or statutory provision as from time to time amended extended or re-enacted.

22 Governing Law and Jurisdiction

22.1 The validity construction and performance of this Agreement shall be governed by English law and shall be subject to the exclusive jurisdiction of the High Court of Justice in England.

SCHEDULE 1

The Programmes

1. A season review program for each [   ] season ending during the Term.

2. At least one further program for each season that the agreement is in force.

SCHEDULE 2

Royalty Advance Payments

Date   **Amount**

SCHEDULE 3

1.	For sales of first edition copies of Videograms at the full retail price	[ ]% of the Company's Net Receipts in respect of such sales
2.	For all Videograms sold in a re-issued edition at a reduced price or through a mail order or other concessionary or promotional scheme	[ ]% of the Company's Net Receipts in respect of such sales
3.	For all Videograms sold to the Club or Club Shops	Nil

4.	On all sales of Videograms not covered by the above	[ ]% of the Company's Net Receipts from such sales

SCHEDULE 4

Part 1 : Registered Trade Marks

The Mark	No	Class	Territory	Date of reg	Goods

Part 2 : Unregistered Trade Marks

Mark or Representation or Get-Up	Goods Description of

SCHEDULE 5

(Standard Commercial Supply Terms)

IN WITNESS whereof this Agreement has been executed by the parties as a deed on the day and year written above

SIGNED as a **DEED** by   )

for and on behalf of [ ]   )

   in the presence of:)

SIGNED as a **DEED** by   )

for and on behalf of [ ]   )

   in the presence of:)

BROADCAST SPONSORSHIP

9.10   INTRODUCTION

The Broadcasting Act 1990 established the Independent Television Commission (ITC). It is the duty of the ITC to regulate commercial broadcasting within the UK. As part of its role it is the duty of the ITC to draw up a code governing the content of programmes, commercial advertising and sponsoring of programmes.

The ITC sponsorship code was adopted as part of the ITC statutory duty and is separate from, but complementary to the ITC code of advertising standards and practice and the ITC rules on advertising breaks.

The code applies to all television programs licensed by the ITC under the Broadcasting Act 1990. These include Channel 3, Channel 4, Channel 5 and non-domestic satellite services (principally BskyB) which operate from the UK but do not use broadcasting frequencies allocated to the UK. The code also applies to the Cable Channels and to the Welsh 4 Channel. Bringing the code into existence was not only a requirement of the Broadcasting Act 1990 but also one of the requirements of the EC Directive on Television Broadcasting.[1] Compliance with the ITC sponsorship code as well as the various other ITC codes is a condition of an ITC licence and it is the duty of the licensee to ensure that relevant employees, programme makers as well as independent producers understand and comply with the contents of the sponsorship code.

Although guidance is available from the ITC on the contents and application of various codes of practice as a matter of principle and advice may be sought from the ITC, the ITC does not accept liability for loss or damage arising from any reliance placed on advice given by the ITC in connection with its codes.

The full text of the ITC code of programmes sponsorship is available from the ITC[2] and this part just outlines relevant matters contained in the code. Reference to the full text should be made for detailed coverage.

9.11   PROGRAMME SPONSORSHIP DEFINED

Rule 1 of the code states that a program is deemed to be sponsored if any part of its costs of production or transmission is met by an advertiser with a view to promoting its own or another's name, trade mark, image, activities, products or other direct or indirect commercial interests. The code defines an advertiser as any organisation or person other than the broadcaster or television producer.

Effectively this means that programme makers who seek production funding from an advertiser (as defined in the code) must ensure compliance with the code of programme sponsorship. Funding by advertisers is not prohibited but it is regulated.

---

1   89/552/EC.
2   The Independent Television Commission, 33 Foley Street, London W1P 7LB.

9.12   GENERAL PROVISIONS

The sponsorship code contains a number of more detailed provisions governing the types of credit the sponsors may receive and further attempts to establish acceptable parameters within which licensees and programme makers may operate. The code's general stated aim is to maintain the distinction between advertising and sponsor's credits in order to ensure that credits are not used as a means to extend allowable advertising time (Rule 2.1).

The code sets out various categories of prohibited and restricted sponsors (Rule 4.1) and lists the usual suspects of political, tobacco and pharmaceutical products. The code goes on to specify (Rule 5) the types of programme for which sponsorship is permitted. It also goes on to set out certain programmes which are deemed to be unsponsorable programmes (Rule 6) and these include the news, business and financial reports and current affairs programmes. Essentially sponsorship is allowed for whole programmes or substantive programme strands (Rule 5) as long as they do not fall within one of the categories of unsponsorable programmes or restricted programmes (Rules 6 and 7).

9.13   BRANDING AND CREDITS GENERALLY

The code provides very generally that sponsorship must be clearly identified at the beginning and/or end of a programme and there may also be bumper credits (these are the credits which one sees entering or leaving a commercial break during programming). A sponsor's credits may be oral and/or visual (Rule 8.1).

Although sponsor credits are not permitted within programmes (Rule 8.2) there are detailed Rules governing precisely what a sponsor may do and where it may place its credits (Rule 8.2), the length of credits (Rule 8.3) as well as the clear identification of the sponsor (Rule 8.4).

Importantly in the context of sport and other events a sponsor's name may be used in a programme title where the title is that of a sponsored event covered by a programme. An obvious example is the Worthington League Cup Final (Rule 11). This same Rule also goes on to state that where a sponsored event is covered in a programme which is itself sponsored and titled with a programme sponsor's name this must not be done in such a way as to imply that the programme sponsor is the event sponsor if this is not in fact the case (Rule 8.11(ii)). This represents important protection for the event sponsor and although it does not protect them from the sale of broadcast sponsorship rights it imposes certain restrictions on the manner in which those rights may be exploited. However, protection is effectively limited to title sponsorship of events, so events where there is no title sponsor will not benefit greatly from these provisions.

There are also detailed provisions governing and dealing with programme integrity (Rule 9) and the core principle of the code is that programme integrity must not be distorted for commercial purposes. In this respect the sponsor is not permitted any influence on either the content or the scheduling of a programme in such way as to affect the editorial independence and responsibility of the broadcaster (Rule 9.1).

Any undue prominence for commercial goods and services in the programme is forbidden (Rule 10.1 of the sponsorship code and Section 10.6 of the ITC programme code). This applies whether or not a programme is sponsored. The code suggests that it is unlikely that any reference at all in a programme to the programme sponsor will be editorially justified (Rule 10.2).

Product placement, ie the inclusion of, or reference to, a product or service within a programme in return for payment or of a valuable consideration to the programme maker or ITC licensee is prohibited (Rule 12). Although where the use of particular goods and services is clearly justified editorially they may be acquired for nothing or at less than their full cost (Rule 12.2). However, it must be left to the programme makers to precisely how the goods or services appear within the programme.

The provisions relating to product placement are unlikely to affect an event sponsor that supplies products or services to the event, as the event sponsor will not generally be paying the programme maker or ITC licensee to include reference to their product or service within the programme. Although such goods and services must not be given undue prominence (Rule 10.1 of the code) their inclusion is not completely prohibited. This leaves rights owners and their commercial partners sufficient commercial flexibility to conclude arrangements which are not purely reliant on cash, but also the provision of in-kind consideration.

9.14 EVENT COVERAGE

Rule 13 of the code provides detailed rules governing the coverage of events. Programme coverage of events and locations which are sponsored or at which advertising or branding is present may also be sponsored and an event or location sponsor may also be the programme sponsor (Rule 13.1).

Any references to advertising or branding at an event must be limited to the justifiable editorial needs of the programme (Rule 13.2) and such advertising or branding is acceptable as long as the event has a bona fide non-television status. There are three conditions for an event to satisfy that status which are that

(i)   the development and running of the event must be done by a body whose existence is independent of television, advertising and promotional interests;
(ii) television coverage must not be the principal purpose of the event;
(iii) the event must be open to members of the public irrespective of whether or not it is televised.

The sale of advertising and other branding arrangements on site are then a matter for the relevant rights owner which will often be a sports governing body (Rule 13.2).

An event sponsor is allowed appropriate recognition within the programme coverage of an event (Rule 13.3) although such coverage must be justified by the editorial needs of the programme itself. It is also interesting to note that if an event sponsor's identity is not otherwise apparent an end credit not lasting more than five seconds identifying the event sponsor may be included within the end credits of the programme (Rule 13.3).

Coverage of tobacco sponsored events must be consistent with relevant voluntary agreements and other applicable regulations (Rule 13.4).

9.15   ELECTRONIC IMAGING SYSTEMS

Rule 13.5 of the code refers to the ITC Sponsorship Guidance Note on Virtual Advertising. The use of virtual advertising will undoubtedly become an important tool for rights owners, sponsors and broadcasters alike as they seek to extract the maximum revenue and brand exposure from the events in which they are involved. Although many rights owners and their sponsors will seek to limit the rights of a broadcaster to utilise such virtual advertising technology, as that technology improves it is quite clear that more people will seek to take advantage of it.

The Guidance Notes on the use of electronic imaging systems or virtual advertising states that special precautions must be taken to ensure that the broadcasters do not lose editorial control of the television signal. Virtual advertising works by altering the broadcast signal itself. In particular, the guidelines state that:

(i)   The use of electronic imaging systems must be made transparent to viewers. In general this means there should be a credit at some point in the programme explaining that such systems have been used in the broadcast.

(ii) Such electronic systems may only be used to replace existing advertising signage at an event and such an event must qualify under Rule 13.2 of the code and the three criteria set out there. Additional advertising must not be placed at an event, nor must advertisements be placed on unused billboards or other sites.

The guidance note also states that the use of electronic systems should not result in a discernible degradation in picture quality and the broadcast must comply at all times with the requirements of the ITC technical performance code.

Perhaps most importantly for rights owners and sponsors the guidance note states that the ITC licensee must retain the contractual right to refuse to carry an electronically altered signal and it may exercise that right in its reasonable discretion. Furthermore, an ITC licensee must not be involved in selling virtual advertising to advertisers or the agents.

Although this developing technology presents an important commercial opportunity for rights owners and sponsors alike, if it is to be utilised in broadcasts involving an ITC licensee great care must be taken to ensure that it complies with ITC sponsorship code and the guidance note on the use of such systems. Presumably, where a rights owner or advertiser wishes to use such electronic systems to replace or augment advertising or signage at an event for use in videos or other media which do not fall under the regulatory auspices of the ITC then there are no barriers and greater if not unlimited freedom to exploit these opportunities. This, presumably, will be a matter for sponsors to consider when they are negotiating appropriate restrictions or options in their agreements with rights owners and broadcasters as they (or indeed any other third party) obtain the right to use recorded footage of the broadcast of an event for their own use then they may use such electronic systems in the post-production stage for their own commercial ends. Rights owners may wish to ensure that opportunities are limited or cannot be exercised without their prior approval.

9.16 BROADCAST SPONSORSHIP AGREEMENT

A sample agreement for terrestrial sponsorship of a television programme is set out below.[1]

The format of this agreement reflects the general approach of this work: it must clearly identify the parties, the rights being granted and the degree of exclusivity acquired, the duration, territory and the fee involved. In addition, both parties must ensure that they comply with the relevant regulatory regime and in particular this means the provisions of the Broadcasting Act 1990 as well as the various ITC codes.

If the programme sponsor is creating or commissioning visual and/or oral credits for its programme sponsorship then the question of ownership of the intellectual property rights in such credit should also be addressed in such agreement. In general, the programme sponsor will wish to retain or acquire the copyrights and the associated intellectual property rights in such credits but grant the broadcaster the appropriate licence of rights to undertake its obligation to broadcast the relevant credits.

Programme sponsorship agreements are, in line with sponsorship itself, becoming increasingly sophisticated in the use of imagery and in putting the promotional message across to the viewing public. The rights fees involved are also quite considerable and, in the case of the broadcast sponsorship of sports events or with most producers of programming that airs on commercial television, payable to the broadcaster and not to the rights owner of the event or the producer. Broadcasters argue that as they are the ITC licensees, they retain the discretion to exercise their right to appoint a programme sponsor. It is they who ultimately bear the responsibility of complying with the ITC sponsorship code as they stand to lose their licence or face heavy fines and censure if they do not. Rights owners are taking an increasingly integrated approach to sponsorship at every level and often seek to prohibit the appointment of a programme sponsor, or restrict the categories of the programme sponsor that may be appointed (no competitors of the events sponsor may sponsor the broadcast coverage) or else to acquire the programme sponsorship rights themselves from the broadcasters. This final option tends to be the most expensive as a broadcaster will require the rights owner to pay an equivalent rights fee to the ultimate broadcast sponsors. The broadcaster will also nevertheless require the rights owner and its ultimate appointed broadcast sponsor to comply with the provisions of the ITC sponsorship code and will always note that its editorial independence remains intact.

---

1   See **9.16.1**.

9.16.1   Agreement for terrestrial television programme sponsorship

AN AGREEMENT made this   day of   [   ]

BETWEEN

(1)   of   **('the Sponsor')**
(2)   of   (to be known as **'the Broadcaster'**

WHEREAS:

(1)   The Sponsor is a company engaged in the business of [   ] who wish to sponsor programmes through the Broadcaster
(2)   The Broadcaster is the broadcaster of the programmes the Sponsor wishes to sponsor and is licensed to broadcast in the United Kingdom under a licence awarded by the Independent Television Commission under the Broadcasting Act 1990

OPERATIVE PROVISIONS:

It is Agreed as follows:

I   DEFINITIONS

In this Agreement the following terms have the meanings ascribed to them:

'Broadcast'	has the meanings ascribed to it in the Copyright, Design and Patents Act 1988 (as amended from time to time);
'Fee'	means £[ ] plus VAT;
'Programme'	means the terrestrial broadcast television programmes and any associated sound recordings titled [' '] being [ ] minutes long;
'Programme Schedules'	means the provisional broadcast transmission details of the Programmes set out in Schedule 2;
'Rights'	(i) means the exclusive right for the Sponsor to sponsor the programme using the Sponsors Credit;
	(ii) the additional rights set out in Clause [ ] of this Agreement;
'Sponsor's Credits'	means the agreed visual and/or audio-visual recorded sequence incorporating the logo and trade mark of the Sponsor together with associated words to be agreed between the parties;
'Term'	means the period commencing on the date of signature of this Agreement and expiring on [*date*];
'Territory'	means the United Kingdom the Channel Islands and the Isle of Man.

1.2   References in this Agreement to Schedules are to Schedules in this Agreement.

1.3   Words importing the singular include the plural and vice versa and words importing one gender include all other genders.

1.4   The clause headings in this Agreement are for convenience only and shall not affect the construction of the Agreement or any part of it.

2   GRANT OF RIGHTS

2.1   In consideration of the Fee and subject to the terms of this Agreement the Broadcaster grants to the Sponsor the Rights for the Term throughout the Territory.

2.2   The Broadcaster undertakes that it shall not grant any third party the right to sponsor the Programme during the Term.

2.3   The Broadcaster undertakes to use its reasonable endeavours to broadcast or transmit or procure the broadcast or transmission of the Programme in accordance with the Programme Schedules throughout the Territory during the Term.

2.4   The Sponsor acknowledges and agrees that all copyright and all other rights of whatever nature in the Programme are the property of the Broadcaster and that this Agreement grants the Sponsor rights in the Programme.

2.5   The Broadcaster acknowledges and agrees that any copyright and any other rights in the Sponsor's Credits shall remain the sole and exclusive property of The Sponsor together with any goodwill and that the Broadcaster shall not acquire any rights in the Sponsor's Credits.

2.6   The Sponsor hereby grants to the Broadcaster an exclusive licence to broadcast the Sponsor's Credits on the terms of this Agreement for the Term in the Territory.

[2.7   *The Sponsor acknowledges the common custom and practice as with all sponsored sporting events that whilst the Sponsor remains at all times the exclusive and official sponsor of the Programme it may well be the case that the official timing and computer companies will be visible on-screen from time to time*].

3   EDITORIAL CONTROL AND PROGRAMME SCHEDULING

3.1   The Sponsor acknowledges and agrees that all final editorial and creative decisions concerning the development production content and scheduling of the Programme shall be the sole responsibility of the Broadcaster.

3.2   The Broadcaster shall consult the Sponsor with a view to agreeing jointly the design of the opening title sequence of the Programme incorporating The Sponsor's Credits.

3.3   Without prejudice to the generality of Clause 3.2 above the Broadcaster may at its sole discretion and cost make such changes deletions alterations interruptions or additions to the Programme as may be required by the scheduling requirements of the Broadcaster in line with the terms of its licence or any generally applicable relevant rule of law or by the Independent Broadcaster or any other statutory body and agrees to ensure that as far as reasonably practicable the Sponsor shall be informed in advance of any significant alterations to the Programme.

3.4   Both parties acknowledge that the transmission dates and scheduling are still to be confirmed. The Broadcaster shall use its reasonable endeavours to ensure that broadcast of the Programme will be the same as or reasonably similar to Schedule 2. The Broadcaster shall supply a more detailed and accurate Programme Schedule to the Sponsor prior to broadcast.

4   CONSIDERATION

4.1   The Sponsor shall pay to the Broadcaster the Fee as follows:

In respect of the Programme:

4.1.1   £   plus VAT upon signature of this Agreement;

4.1.2   £   plus VAT on delivery by the Sponsor of the Sponsor's Credit to the TV Company;

4.1.3   £   plus VAT on the day after the first broadcast referred to in the Programme Schedule.

5   OBLIGATIONS OF THE SPONSOR

5.1   The Sponsor warrants that it is the sole owner of or controls all the intellectual property in the Sponsor's Credits. The Sponsor confirms that any use by the Broadcaster of the Sponsor's Credits in accordance with this Agreement will not infringe the intellectual property of any third party.

5.2   The Sponsor warrants that the Sponsor's Credits do not contain any obscene offensive or defamatory material and will not expose the Broadcaster to any civil or criminal proceedings.

5.3   The Sponsor confirms that it will obtain comprehensive public liability insurance cover which will be in force during the Sponsorship Period covering any writs claims actions or damages which may arise as a direct or indirect result of the use by the public of the specific products or services being credited under this Agreement together with all other products or services owned or controlled by The Sponsor which the public would reasonably associate with the Sponsor's Credits. The Sponsor undertakes to provide the Broadcaster with a copy of all relevant insurance policies upon request.

5.4   The Sponsor confirms that it has and will retain good title and authority to enter into this Agreement.

5.5   The Sponsor acknowledges that the Broadcaster may use its sole discretion as to the manner and method to be used in the marketing promoting and advertising of the Programme irrespective of any rights granted under this Agreement and that the Broadcaster shall retain all proceeds from the exploitation of the Programme in any manner or media at any time.

5.6   The Sponsor shall bear all costs of creating producing designing and the Sponsor's Credits and of supplying the Sponsor's Credit to the Broadcaster for incorporation in the Programme.

5.7   The Sponsor agrees to be bound by the requirements of the Broadcaster in respect of any sponsorship or advertising rules directives or statutes which apply to the Broadcaster or have been issued by the Independent Television Commission concerning the broadcast or transmission of the Sponsor's Credits including but not limited to its size, shape, colour, wording and on-screen position and general nature.

6   OBLIGATIONS OF THE BROADCASTER

6.1   The Broadcaster agrees to use its reasonable endeavours to broadcast, transmit or procure such broadcast or transmission of the Programme as per the Programme Schedules incorporating the Sponsor's Credits as follows:

15 seconds (maximum) opening titles – voice and visual credits;

10 seconds (maximum) break-bumpers – visual credits only;

10 seconds (maximum) closing titles-voice and visual credits.

6.2   The Broadcaster undertakes to give the Sponsor a visual credit of five seconds maximum on all trailers for the Programme.

6.3   The Broadcaster agrees to give the Sponsor access to all the recorded footage of the Programme for its own promotional purposes only. The Sponsor may edit the footage at its own cost for such purposes as are agreed between the Broadcaster and the Sponsor.

6.4   The Broadcaster undertakes to use all reasonable endeavours to ensure that the Programme will not contain any material which infringes the copyright or any other rights of any third party throughout the Territory during the Term.

6.5   The Broadcaster shall ensure that the broadcast or transmission of the Sponsor's Credits does not infringe any sponsorship or advertising rules directives or statutes which apply to the Broadcaster or have been issued by the Independent Television Commission concerning the Sponsor's Credits.

6.6   The Broadcaster confirms that it is the sole owner of or controls all copyright and any other rights in the Programme.

6.7   The Broadcaster confirms that it shall be solely responsible for all costs incurred (except those involved in the Sponsor's Credits) in the production broadcast transmission distribution and exploitation of the Programme and that the Sponsor shall not be liable for any such sums except as provided in clause 6.3 above and further if agreed in writing.

7   MUTUAL INDEMNITY

7.1   The Sponsor and the Broadcaster each undertakes to indemnify the others against all liabilities claims demands actions costs damages or loss arising out of any breach by each of them respectively of any of the terms of this Agreement.

7.2   In the event of any claim dispute action writ or summons in connection with Clause 7.1 above the Sponsor and the Broadcaster agree to provide full details to the other party at the earliest opportunity and shall not settle any such matter without first consulting the other party.

8   CONFIDENTIALITY

The Sponsor and the Broadcaster shall not disclose to any third party any confidential business or future plans of the other party at any time acquired during the existence of this Agreement and no reference is to be made to the terms of this Agreement by either party in any advertising publicity or promotional material without the prior written consent of the other party.

9   AMENDMENTS AND ALTERATIONS

This Agreement supersedes all previous agreements representations or promises and sets out all the terms agreed between the parties. Any amendment or alteration to this Agreement must be in writing and signed by an authorised signatory of each party.

10   NO PARTNERSHIP OR EMPLOYMENT

This Agreement shall not be deemed to create any partnership agency or employment relationship between parties.

11 NOTICES

Without prejudice to the right to serve notices by any other means any notice served under this Agreement shall be in writing. Any notice which has been sent by first class pre-paid post shall be deemed to be received forty-eight hours thereafter (excluding Saturdays Sundays and public holidays). For the purpose of this Agreement all notices shall be sent to the following addresses:

12 VAT

All sums payable under this Agreement are exclusive of any value added tax that may be payable by either party.

13 ASSIGNMENT

Neither party shall assign transfer charge or make over this Agreement or any of its rights or obligations hereunder without the prior written consent of the other party.

14 FORCE MAJEURE

In any term of this Agreement cannot be performed or its obligations fulfilled for any reason beyond the reasonable control of either party including war industrial action floods acts of God unforeseen technical failure then such non-performance or failure to fulfil its obligations shall be deemed not to be a breach of this Agreement.

In the event that this Agreement cannot be performed or its obligations fulfilled for any reason beyond the reasonable control of the defaulting party for a continuous period of one month then the other party may at its discretion terminate this Agreement by notice in writing at the end of that period provided that both parties agree to negotiate in good faith an equitable settlement in respect of work already performed to the date of termination.

15 TERMINATION AND EXPIRY OF THE AGREEMENT

15.1   In addition to any other rights and remedies at law this Agreement may be terminated by a party giving written notice of at least four weeks to the other party which has breached this Agreement or had defaulted on any of the following grounds:

15.1.1   where the Sponsor has failed to account or make payments as required under this Agreement;

15.1.2   where the Sponsor or the Broadcaster has committed a serious breach of its obligations under this Agreement unless such party rectifies the position as far as reasonably possible within thirty days;

15.1.3   where the Sponsor or the Broadcaster goes into voluntary or involuntary liquidation;

15.1.4   where the Sponsor or the Broadcaster is declared insolvent either in bankruptcy proceedings or other legal proceedings;

15.1.5   where an agreement with creditors has been reached by the Sponsor or the Broadcaster due to its failure or inability to pay its debts as they fall due;

15.1.6   where a receiver is appointed over the whole or part of the Sponsor's or the Broadcaster's business.

16 GOVERNING LAW

This Agreement shall be subject to the laws of England and Wales and the jurisdiction of the English Courts.

Signed by...

For and on behalf of the Sponsor

Witnessed by ....

Signed by...

For and on behalf of the Broadcaster

Witnessed by ....

THE FIRST SCHEDULE

THE SECOND SCHEDULE

INDEX

References are to paragraph numbers.